For Reference

Not to be taken from this room

Researching the Song ❧

RESEARCHING THE SONG

A LEXICON

Shirlee Emmons and Wilbur Watkin Lewis

OXFORD

UNIVERSITY PRESS

2006

OXFORD
UNIVERSITY PRESS

Oxford University Press, Inc., publishes works that further
Oxford University's objective of excellence
in research, scholarship, and education.

Oxford   New York
Auckland   Cape Town   Dar es Salaam   Hong Kong   Karachi
Kuala Lumpur   Madrid   Melbourne   Mexico City   Nairobi
New Delhi   Shanghai   Taipei   Toronto

With offices in
Argentina   Austria   Brazil   Chile   Czech Republic   France   Greece
Guatemala   Hungary   Italy   Japan   Poland   Portugal   Singapore
South Korea   Switzerland   Thailand   Turkey   Ukraine   Vietnam

Copyright © 2006 by Oxford University Press, Inc.

Published by Oxford University Press, Inc.
198 Madison Avenue, New York, New York 10016

www.oup.com

Oxford is a registered trademark of Oxford University Press

Library of Congress Cataloging-in-Publication Data
Emmons, Shirlee.
Researching the song : a lexicon / by Shirlee Emmons
& Wilbur Watkin Lewis
p. cm.
Includes bibliographical references.
ISBN-13 978-0-19-515202-9
ISBN 0-19-515202-6
1. Songs—Dictionaries. I. Lewis, Wilbur Watkin.
II. Title.
ML102.S6E46   2005
782'.003—dc22   2005001658

9 8 7 6 5 4 3 2 1

Printed in the United States of America
on acid-free paper

To the late Stanley Sonntag,

a supremely knowledgeable and passionate

lover of song literature,

whose creative idea this book was

Acknowledgments ⌀

We extend sincere gratitude to members of our families for their cheerful acceptance of our absences from family activities, which were caused by the heavy work schedule the completion of this lexicon mandated: Annette Mulholland-Lewis, Rollin Baldwin, Samuel and Danielle Lewis, Hilary Baldwin, and Joseph Guagliardo (whose input saved the project more than once).

Our appreciation to Kim Robinson and Eve Bachrach for their never ending patience and the stream of helpful suggestions, and to Maribeth Anderson Payne, who oversaw the very beginning of this project that started so many years ago.

To Lewis Daniels of the Westbrook, Connecticut, Public Library, ever staunch in his helpful attitude and computer expertise, never less than enthusiastic about spending his time to find the answers to our difficult issues—many thanks.

To Natasha Lutov, who provided much expertise on Russian song literature and pointed the way to Prince Mirsky's invaluable volume, containing first-hand information about the poets—our appreciation.

Thanks to the excellent libraries of Rutgers, the State University of New Jersey, where much of the research for this book was done.

Last, thanks to the students who kept their eyes and ears open and faithfully reported delicious tidbits of information gleaned from their experiences in the immense landscape of song composers and poets.

Contents ✐

Introduction ⮂

Singing, whatever the level of vocal and artistic development, is about communication. Singers have been blessed not only with the music of those remarkable composers who write for the voice but also by the words of the world's greatest as well as the not-quite-great poets, both of whom inspire them to communicate. The greatest help in probing the meaning of poetry, even bad poetry, is supplied by the music, which offers a lyric subtext. Sometimes the composer rises above a mediocre lyric and transforms a sow's ear into a silk purse. Other times the composer rises to the sublime, hand in hand with a poet of equal genius, as Schubert did with Goethe. Nevertheless, singers need always to deal with the meaning of the lyrics, frequently in a language not their own and of a culture unfamiliar to them. Our aim is that this book shall, to a large extent, supply singers, teachers, collaborative artists, fans, and all interested parties with information that will help them better understand the poetry of great art songs and through that, the song itself. We are committed to this premise: the more performers know and understand about the literary elements of a song, the more they will understand the work and the richer their communication will be.

Principles of Selection

A lexicon is a technical dictionary devoted to a specific discipline. *Researching the Song* is just such a lexicon. Every entry is related to at least one art song. Basic information about composers is not included in this text, since research on particular composers has never been easier nor available information more prolific. That information is easily and comprehensively available in numerous music histories, dictionaries, encyclopedias, and biographies. A single volume devoted to the poets who wrote the texts and literary allusions contained in art song, however, has not existed until *Researching the Song*.

There is a great deal of truth in Mark Twain's pithy remark: a classic is a book everybody knows about and no one has read. Many celebrated works, like Goethe's *Faust* or *Wilhelm Meister*, are not known to the general public. The Bible is not as familiar today as it was only a generation ago. Reading lists for some schools abound in contemporary works that simply are not the sources for art song.

Within *Researching the Song* readers will encounter explanations of most of the mythological, historical, geographical, and literary references contained in western art song, gods and goddesses of ancient Greece and Rome making up a large portion of the entries. As an aid to their performances of song literature, readers will find here entries that are referenced to specific art songs of the German, French, Italian, Russian, Spanish, South American, Greek, Finnish, Scandinavian, and both American and British English repertoires. Also included are brief biographies of poets, lists of composers who set each poet's work, and frequently the specific poems that were set. Both definitions of mythological names and unusual terminology and the background of historical names are included, since these references abound. Pertinent geographical information will supply context. Sources, narratives, and explanations of major song cycles are given. Brief synopses of major works from which song texts were taken are given.

Although definitions of poetry types and song genres that have proved attractive to composers are included, this book is not intended to be a history of song. Even as composers' biographies are excluded, so is any attempt at harmonic analysis or stylistic criticism. Words and terminology easily found in dictionaries and encyclopedias are also excluded, unless we have found pertinent information of unusual interest. It was not possible to include details of really obscure songs or curiosity pieces seldom performed, however appealing or interesting they might be. When a song has been written by a lower echelon composer and set to the words of an equally unrecognized poet, we have not included allusions that might pertain. The omission of certain poets was caused largely by the fact that composers frequently set the poetic works of their non-professional friends. Unless the composer is heavily researched, like Schubert, the friends generally remain unknown.

How to Use *Researching the Song*

In a perfect world, in a world where time is plentiful, in a world where the singer has a deep interest in thorough preparation of his or her repertoire, the following would be an optimal way to use this book. First select a song that touches you. Read the text. If it is in a foreign language, obtain a dictionary and make your own translation. Note the poet's name and copy down any dates the considerate publisher offers you. If the text is taken from a larger work, make a note of that work's title. Read that work. (This last point probably happens *only* in a perfect world, but ought to be standard practice.) Compile a list of any names, words, or terms unfamiliar to you. If you use a free English translation or one intended to be sung, compare difficult words to the original text in order to make sure that you are not the victim of bad (or excessively creative) translation. Try to find your list in a good dictionary or an encyclopedia. Finally, enlarge your knowledge by checking your list against entries in *Researching the Song*.

When necessary, look in this book's synopses of major works so as to place songs in the narrative context. Asterisks will be found at the first mention of each entry from the lexicon when it pops up in the text of another entry, for example, a reference to Jupiter in an entry about Hera will appear like this: ★Jupiter.

Assessed in terms of the degree of assistance the knowledge might give singers, some single songs from larger works appear as individual entries and also within the entry that describes that larger work. The source entries will offer some history, plot, and placement of the songs. As an example, it is often difficult to know from which Restoration drama or comedy Purcell's songs were drawn and how they figured in the plot. Therefore the theater songs of Henry Purcell appear as (1) an entry named for the song itself and (2) within the plot description of the theatrical work. For example, there is this entry for a Purcell song:

"Seek Not to Know": a song from the tragic extravaganza *The Indian Queen*, written by John ★Dryden and Sir Robert Howard, first produced in 1677, then altered in 1695 to include music by Henry Purcell. *See* ★*Indian Queen, The* for plot details and placement of songs.

The words in Scottish songs are frequently incomprehensible to the non-Scottish. You will find some fifty entries of such words in *Researching the Song*. In the cases where it was possible to decipher the pronunciation, that has been included. We had envisioned an entry that told how to pronounce the words, but it happens that there are three methods of Scottish pronunciation based on historical periods. Even the Scottish dictionary cannot offer certainty. Since finding out which period each word represents was beyond the scope of this volume, that idea was abandoned.

Russian names often have more than one transliteration of the surname, due to the difference between the Russian and English alphabets.

A Last Word

Some twenty years ago our friend and colleague the late Stanley Sonntag originally conceived the idea for this book. We have made use of thousands of pages of notes for this book left to us by him. Essentially, we rewrote or re-researched the entire book over the last ten years. During decades of work and friendship Stanley generously shared his encyclopedic knowledge with us and with countless other singers and pianists. We miss him still.

Researching the Song ❧

A

AAWHERE: (Scot.) (pr. aw–where), *everywhere.*

ABBICCÌ: (It.), *the alphabet, the ABCs.*

SONG	COMPOSER	POET
"San Basilio"	Ildebrando Pizzetti	Greek Traditional, tr. Tommaseo

ABLOW: (Scot.) (pr. uh–blo), *below, under, beneath.*

ABOON, ABÜNE: (Scot.), *above; in good cheer.*

SONG	COMPOSER	POET
"A Laddie's Sang"	Benjamin Britten	William Soutar

ABRAHAM AND ISAAC: biblical characters, father and son. The son of Terah, Abraham was called Abram at the time. His two brothers, Nahor and Haran, were born in Ur of the Chaldeans when their father was seventy years old. Terah moved his entire family, including Abram and his childless wife Sarai, to the town of Haran in Canaan. When Abram was seventy-five years old, his god, Yahweh, instructed him to leave home and go to a new land, which Yahweh would show him. If he obeyed, Yahweh would give him a great nation and bless him—"in you all the families of the earth shall be blessed" (Genesis 12.3). Abram wandered from place to place, amassing ever more wealth. When he was ninety-nine years old, Yahweh spoke to him again, repeating his promise that Abram and his descendants would possess the entire land of Canaan if Abram would obey him and follow his commandments. Yahweh changed Abram's name to Abraham and Sarai's to Sarah, reiterating his promise that they would have numerous descendants. As Yahweh promised that Sarah, who was then ninety years old, would give birth to Abraham's son, Abraham was reduced to laughter. Sarah, who was well past the age of childbearing, also laughed hearing the prediction (Genesis 18). Yahweh commanded Abraham to name his son Isaac, which in Hebrew means "he who laughs." To seal the agreement, Yahweh declared that Abraham and all the males in his household were to be circumcised, each on the eighth day of his life (Genesis 17). One year after this last promise, when Abraham was one hundred years old, Sarah gave birth to Abraham's second son, Isaac (the first had been born to his slave concubine). Speaking to Abraham again to test him, Yahweh instructed him to take Isaac to Moriah and sacrifice his son as an offering to Yahweh. Abraham traveled to Moriah with Isaac and two young men. After Yahweh showed Abraham the site of the sacrifice, Abraham loaded some wood on Isaac's back, while he himself carried the knife and fire. Father and son set off to finish the journey alone. Isaac said to his father that he saw nothing to be the sacrifice, only wood, the knife, and the fire. "Yahweh will supply the sacrifice," responded Abraham. After they arrived at the designated spot, Abraham built an altar and arranged the wood on top of it. He then tied Isaac up and placed him on the wood. Just as he raised the knife to kill his son, an angel called out and Abraham was instructed not to harm the child. A ram caught in a nearby thicket was quickly substituted for Isaac, to the relief of all. The promises were renewed (Genesis 22). Britten's "Canticle II, Abraham and Isaac," written as an epilogue to *Billy Budd,* tells the story. (SOURCE: Salter, 1968)

SONG	COMPOSER	POET
1. "Canticle II, Abraham and Isaac"	Benjamin Britten	Chester miracle plays
2. "A Tale of Abraham and Isaac"	Judith Zaimont	Wilfred Owen and religious texts
3. "Abraham and Isaac"	Igor Stravinsky	Masoretic texts of Genesis 22

ABRUZZI: the mountainous section of Italy just east of Rome. It includes some seashore on the Adriatic. The native Abruzzesi are commonly described as "forte e gentile," *strong and kind.*

SONG	COMPOSER	POET
"I Pastori"	Ildebrando Pizzetti	Gabriele d'Annunzio

ABSALOM, ABSOLOM: son of Maacah and ★David, king of Israel. In addition to Absalom, David had other children: a daughter Tamar, a son Amnon by another mother, and others, including ★Solomon. Very angry that David would not punish Amnon for having raped his stepsister Tamar, Absalom had Amnon murdered two years after the incident. After enduring a three-year exile for his crime, Absalom was forgiven and brought home to Jerusalem. By various underhanded means Absalom won over the populace, forced David to flee in fear for his life, and, to punish him further, had relations with David's concubines. Absalom, a very handsome man, was admired for his luxuriant hair, which he cut only once each year. In the final battle between him and his father, Absalom was caught in the trees by his long hair, pulled from his mount, and left hanging in such a way that David's men found him and killed him, although against David's orders. David's reaction to the news is his famous lament, "O, my son Absalom! Would that I had died instead of you, O Absalom, my son!" (SOURCE: Metzger, Murphy, 1994)

SONG	COMPOSER	POET
1. "David Weeps for Absalom"	David Diamond	2 Samuel 19.1
2. "Triste estaba el Rey David"	Alonso Mudarra	anonymous
3. "Absalom"	Ned Rorem	Paul Goodman

ABUELA: (Sp.), *grandmother.* A proper euphemism for a braggart in the Spanish language is the phrase *"no tiene abuela."* This phrase refers to the fact that, while alive, the grandmother would give praise, but, after her death, the individual would be forced to praise him- or herself. (SOURCE: Cockburn, Stokes, 1992)

SONG	COMPOSER	POET
"Las currutacas modestas"	Enrique Granados	Fernando Periquet

ACADIA: the Canadian province of Nova Scotia, which the French ceded to Great Britain in 1713.

ACHATES: a *fidus Achates* is a faithful companion, a bosom friend. In Virgil's *Aeneid*, Achates was the chosen comrade of Aeneas. (SOURCE: Cooper, 1992)

ACHELOÜS: an ancient Greek river deity, the eldest son of Oceanus and Tethys. Assuming the form of a bull, Acheloüs fought with Heracles (Latin form, Hercules) for Deianira, but was vanquished by Heracles, who broke off one of his horns, which, according to one tradition, became the cornucopia or Horn of Plenty. (SOURCE: Kaster, 1964)

ACIS: the legendary Sicilian shepherd, son of Faunus and a nymph. Acis was beloved of the nymph ★Galatea, but was slain by his rival, the ★Cyclops, Polyphemus. (SOURCE: Kaster, 1964)

ACMEISM: a school of Russian poetry, whose leaders were Nikolai Gumilyov and Sergei Gorodetsky. Other members included Anna ★Akhmatova and Osip Mandelstam. Their group was called the Poets' Guild, organized in 1911. Although born of ★symbolism, acmeism was opposed to Symbolist vagueness. Its two important convictions were that the everyday world should be depicted with brevity and clarity and that poetic words should be used precisely and logically. The acmeists had a historical consciousness and thought that their poetry had an ethical dimension. (SOURCES: Drabble, 2000; Terras, 1991)

ACROSTIC: (Gk.), akros, *outermost*; stichlos, *line of verse*; verse in which initial letters of each line read downward to form a word. If the final letters also form a word, it is a double acrostic; if the middle letters also form a word, it is a triple acrostic. The term was first applied to obscure prophecies made by the Erythraean ★Sibyl and written on loose leaves, which made a word when sorted in order. (SOURCE: Cooper, 1992)

ACTEON: a legendary Greek huntsman, son of Aristaeus and Autonoë, the daughter of ★Cadmus. Acteon was turned into a stag by Artemis and torn to pieces by the hounds, either because he came upon the naked goddess while she was bathing or because he boasted of excelling her as a hunter. (SOURCE: Kaster, 1964)

ADAM: the first man, also Hebrew for *man*. In Genesis 1, after God separates night from day; creates a dome called Sky; gathers the waters into seas; creates dry land, fruit trees, and plants; and creates the Sun, Moon, and Stars, fish and birds, animals and humans (both male and female at the same time and in his image), on the seventh day he rests. In Genesis 2.7–25, a more detailed telling, man is made first from the dust of creation and becomes a living being as God breathes into his nostrils. God plants a garden in Eden, and in it he places Adam, who is free to eat from all trees except the tree of good and evil knowledge. God then creates animals and birds, but they are not suitable to be man's companion. God, having put Adam into a deep sleep, removes one of his ribs and from this creates woman. Both live in the garden, naked, and without shame. In Genesis 3.1–24, The Fall, the serpent tempts the woman and persuades her to eat from the forbidden tree. As both Adam and the woman eat the fruit, they discover the shame of their nakedness. They confess their transgression to God, Adam blaming woman, woman blaming the serpent. God condemns the serpent to be forever considered an enemy by mankind. God increases the woman's birth pains and condemns Adam to labor all his days to earn the daily bread. Adam is credited with bringing sin and death into the world and passing on original sin to his descendants. (SOURCE: Metzger, Murphy, 1994)

SONG	COMPOSER	POET
1. "Adam was my Grandfather"	Douglas Moore	Stephen Vincent Benét
2. "As Adam Early in the Morning"	Ned Rorem	Walt Whitman
3. "Remember Adam's Fall"	Virgil Thomson	anonymous
4. "Fussreise"	Hugo Wolf	Eduard Mörike

ADONAI: one of the names given to the Deity; when reading, Jews substitute Adonai for Yahweh or ★Jehovah, the Supreme Being.

SONG	COMPOSER	POET
Psalm CXXX	Arthur Honegger	Bible

ADONIS: in Greek mythology, a youth beloved by ★Aphrodite. His ecstatic spring feast became a rite of spring. Adonis died because of a wound inflicted by a boar in the hunt. Aphrodite made the anemone grow from his blood. According to Bion, the Adonis flower is the rose; Pliny says it is the anemone; others say it is the field poppy. In ★Hades ★Persephone fell in love with ★Apollo but, in pity for the great grief of Aphrodite, ★Zeus decreed that Adonis should spend six months of the year in the underworld with Persephone and the other six with Aphrodite in the upper world. The myth and ritual of Adonis, with the weeping for the slain youth and the joy at his resurrection, was imported from Syria, where he was identified with Tammuz (an ancient fertility god). His name is also Syrian, from the Semitic ★Adonai (*lord, master*) and has the same meaning as Baal. (SOURCE: Cooper, 1992)

SONG	COMPOSER	POET
"Frühlingsfeier"	Richard Strauss	Heinrich Heine

ADY, ENDRE (1877–1919): Hungarian poet. Ady's lyrical poems, which are his chief claim to fame, were influenced by the French ★Symbolists. His poetry was set by Béla Bartók in *Five Songs*, op. 16.

AEGEUS, AEGAEUS: legendary king of early Athens and father of ★Theseus. When Theseus returned to Athens, he had restored Aegaeus to his throne. After sailing to Crete to deliver Athens from the Minoan tribute, Theseus had promised his father that he would hoist white sails to replace the original black ones during the return voyage to signal a successful mission. However, he forgot. When he saw the black sails, Aegaeus, thinking his son had perished, threw himself into the sea, which was then named the Aegean. (SOURCE: Kaster, 1964)

SONG	COMPOSER	POET
"When My Acmelia Smiles"	Henry Purcell	unknown

AEOLIAN HARP: a wind harp with a set of strings that vibrate in response to air currents, named after ★Aeolus, the classical god of the winds, invoked by German and English romantic writers such as Samuel Taylor ★Coleridge. With a friend, Hugo Wolf once made a walking tour of Upper Styria, Austria, in the course of which they visited the castle of Hoch-Osterwitz. When Wolf heard strange sounds in the distance as if someone were playing a piano, he walked toward the last room of the castle, where he found an Aeolian harp set in the window. After listening, enchanted, he ran back to his friend, saying, "Never had I heard an Aeolian before this moment, and yet it is in my song exactly as this one is." (SOURCE: *OED*, 1989)

SONG	COMPOSER	POET
"An eine Äolsharfe"	J. Brahms, H. Wolf	Eduard Mörike

AEOLUS: according to some traditions, a son of ★Poseidon and ruler of the Aeolian Islands. ★Zeus appointed him keeper of the winds, which were held in vast caves. Aeolus gave ★Odysseus a bag of winds to help him on his voyage homeward, but Odysseus's men opened the bag and the winds escaped. (SOURCE: Kaster, 1964)

AESCHYLUS, AISCHYLUS (Ger.) (?524–456 B.C.E.**):** Greek dramatist, first of the three great ancient Athenian writers of tragedies. Best known for his trilogy dealing with the story of ★Orestes, Aeschylus is considered to be the creator of the Greek tragedy, since ★Sophocles and ★Euripides were younger. Aeschylus introduced a second actor into the tragedies. Before this each play had only one actor, who assumed more than one role by changing mask and costume, but communicated only by way of the chorus. Often allusions to Aeschylus refer to his baldness and the legend of an eagle, who, mistaking his bald head for a rock, dropped a tortoise on it to break the shell and killed Aeschylus. Aeschylus made several trips to Sicily and died there. Among the Romans he won admiration and respect, but not popularity or affection. The twentieth century appreciated Aeschylus for the depth of his religious thought, for the great scope of his dramatic structure, and for the mastery of his poetic imagery in more than ninety plays. The text of the Schubert song listed here is extracted from Aeschylus's play *Eumenides*, the lines being from the chorus "Of Justice we are ministers." (SOURCE: *Americana*, 2001)

SONG	COMPOSER	POET
1. "Aeschylus and Sophocles"	Charles Ives	Walter Landor
2. "Fragment aus dem Aischylus"	Franz Schubert	Johann Mayrhofer

AFTON WATER: the River Afton, a Scottish river that flows from the Nith near New Cumnock. Robert ★Burns wrote his poem and song "Sweet Afton" as a compliment to this river and the "charming, wild, romantic scenery on its banks." (SOURCE: McIntyre, 1995)

SONG	COMPOSER	POET
"Afton Water"	Benjamin Britten	Robert Burns

AGANOOR POMPILJ, VICTORIA (1855–1910): Italian poet of Armenian descent. Her grandparents were from a rich and noble family that left Armenia in the twelfth century for Persia, eventually moving to Paris, locating finally in Venice. Aganoor's father married a descendant of a noble Milanese family and settled in Padova, where Victoria was born. Educated by outstanding tutors, including poet/translator Andrea Maffei, she read the classics and contemporary Italian authors and poets, and also European authors like ★Baudelaire, ★Heine, ★Lessing, ★Runeberg, and ★Byron. After the death of her parents, she published a small volume of poems, *Eternal Legend*, which established her as a major poet. When she died in 1910, her husband fatally shot himself in grief. The poetry of Aganoor Pompilj was set by Ottorino Respighi. PRINCIPAL WORKS: *La leggenda eterna*; *Intermezzo*; *Risveglio*, 1900, 1903; *Nuove liriche*, 1908; *Poesia completa*, 1912, 1927.

AGEE, JAMES (1909–1955): American poet, critic, novelist, reporter, screen writer. Born in Knoxville, Tennessee, Agee attained his greatest fame posthumously when, two years after his death, he was awarded the Pulitzer Prize for his novel *A Death in the Family*, and when his movie reviews were gathered and published during the following three years. In 1960 *Let Us Now Praise Famous Men* was published, after which came collections of his poetry, his shorter prose, and letters written to his teacher and lifelong friend James H. Flye. Although conflicted about his aspirations, Agee found his major literary themes in the death of his father, the life of his Knoxville family, the intellectual issues that he shared with Flye, and the social and religious attitudes of his community at St. Andrew's School. In his later years he suffered from many heart attacks, probably resulting from habitually neglecting his health. The collection of his poems show Agee's abiding conviction that poetry (and even prose) is essentially music, as can be seen from various titles such as "Theme and Variations" and "Two Songs on the Economy of Abundance." He also wrote some of the lyrics (unused) for Bernstein's *Candide*. Two of the well-known movies that he wrote were *The African Queen* and *Night of the Hunter*. An essential part of Agee's style is the use of a narrator's eye as a camera that pans back and forth and in and out. James Agee's writings were set in song by many American composers, including Samuel Barber, David Diamond, John Alden Carpenter, and Thomas Pasatieri. PRINCIPAL WORKS: *Permit Me Voyage*, 1934; *The Morning Watch*, 1951; *A Death in the Family*, 1957; *Let Us Now Praise Famous Men*, 1960; *Collected Poems of James Agee*, 1984. SELECTED READING: Laurence Bergreen, *James Agee: A Life*, 1984. (SOURCES: Unger, 1, 1974; Kunitz, Colby, 1955)

A-GLEY: (Scot.), *astray*.

AGNES, SAINT: a Christian saint (d. ca. 305). There are several Saint Agneses: Agnes, feast day, January 21; Agnes of Assisi, feast day, November 16; Agnes of Bohemia, feast day, March 2; and Agnes of Montepulciano, feast day, April 16. It is likely that the St. Agnes in ★Tennyson's poem "St. Agnes' Eve" was none of these, but plain Agnes, a virgin martyr in Rome. According to one legend, Agnes was a fifteen-year-old virgin who was determined to remain so. The infuriated Roman officials had her stabbed in the throat with a sword. Other legends were popular, including one in which she was said to have been imprisoned in a brothel, where a man was struck blind when he saw her naked. Both ★Keats and ★Tennyson wrote poems based on this legend, on which Schubert's "Die junge Nonne" is also based. (SOURCES: Farmer, 1997; Walsh, 1991)

SONG	COMPOSER	POET
1. "St. Agnes Morning"	Henry Cowell	Maxwell Anderson
2. "Die junge Nonne"	Franz Schubert	J. N. Craigher de Jachelutta

AGNES'S EVE, SAINT: a poem by Alfred, Lord ★Tennyson (1809–1892), set by several composers, including Sir Arthur Sullivan. The fictional Saint Agnes's Eve would fall upon January 20, the evening before the feast day of St. Agnes, January 21. The woman in Tennyson's poem is pondering her entry into a convent to become a nun, to become a "bride of Christ." St. Agnes herself refused marriage to keep her virginity as a bride of Christ. Since the feast day of a saint is frequently the day of his or her death or martyrdom, it is appropriate that Tennyson depicted the future nun in the poem as contemplating her role, the bride of Christ, on the eve of the feast day of one of the famous virgin martyrs, also appropriate that she would finally enter the convent on St. Agnes's Day. Today, a maiden who observes the ritual of St. Agnes's Eve believes that she will see a vision of her husband-to-be. Note the similarity of the Tennyson poem to J. N. ★Craigher de Jachelutta's poem, "Die junge Nonne," set by Schubert.

AGNI: in Hindu mythology, the god of the divine fire and the spirit of the Soma. Agni forms one of the divine triads with ★Indra and Surya. (SOURCE: Kaster, 1964)

AGUE: a fever of malarial character, marked by paroxysms of chills, fever, and sweating at regular intervals.

SONG	COMPOSER	POET
1. "O, to Vex Me"	Benjamin Britten	John Donne
2. "At the Round Earth's Imagined Corners"	Benjamin Britten	John Donne

"AH" AND "OH": In the Restoration theater the words *oh* and *ah* had specific contrasting meanings. *Ah*, often expressed in a quick, rising musical figure, is meant to represent sexual release or resignation. *Oh*, often set in descending melismas, is meant to represent desire rather than consummation and is more overtly sensual. (SOURCE: Price, 1984)

"Ah, Cruel Bloody Fate": a song composed by Henry Purcell to the words of Nathaniel ★Lee, from his heroic play *Theodosius*, produced in 1680. *See* ★*Theodosius* for plot details and position of the song within the plot.

"Ah, How Happy We Are": a duet from the tragic extravaganza *The Indian Queen*, written by John *Dryden and Sir Robert Howard, first produced in 1677, then altered in 1695 to include music by Henry Purcell. *See *Indian Queen, The,* for plot details and song placement.

"Ah, Me! To Many Deaths Decreed": a song written by Henry Purcell to words of John Crowne from his play *Regulus*. For plot details and position of the song within the play, *see *Regulus*.

AHNUNG UND GEGENWART: a novella by Joseph von *Eichendorff. In this work Eichendorff evokes the romantic atmosphere stemming from his concepts of nature in order to show religious thought and moral concepts. The story begins when young Graf Friedrich is attracted to Rosa at their first meeting. She later appears at different points in Friedrich's travels, first as the sister of Graf Leontine, at whose home Friedrich recovers from a fight. Then she is swept into the midst of shallow, meaningless Vienna society, where Friedrich visits her. Still later she is disguised as a hunter. Finally she is seen as a veiled lady at the chapel of a monastery that Friedrich has joined. Other adventures of Graf Friedrich involve a beautiful boy, Erwin, who later turns out to be a highly sensual woman, the Gräfin Romana, who commits suicide after being repelled by Friedrich. The story teems with scattered episodes, confused identities, and various characters who appear and disappear. Robert Schumann's Opus 39 contains three songs, 4, 9, and 10 ("Die Stille," "Wehmuth," "Zwielicht"), from the novel. Their content is mostly atmospheric.

AICARD, JEAN (1848–1921): French poet, novelist, short story writer, and scholar. Aicard's love for his home region of Provence is evident in his prose and verse. Like his Provençal compatriot, the poet Frédéric Mistral, his poetry was sunny, strong, contented, and steady. Jean Aicard was both studious and inventive, broad in taste, and prolific. His interests ranged from great works of antiquity to the moral problems of French education. The verse of Jean Aicard was set by Camille Saint-Saëns. PRINCIPAL WORKS: *Poèmes de Provence*; *Maurin des Maures*, trans. Alfred A. Maurin, 1905; *The Illustrious*, 1910; *L'été à l'ombre* [The Summer in the Shade], 1895; *Pygmalion*, 1872 (1-act dramatic poem); *Smilis*, 1884 (prose play); *La Prose de Jean Aicard* (essays), 1910. (SOURCE: Beum, 2000)

AIKEN, CONRAD (1889–1973): American poet, writer of varied fiction, criticism, and journalism. Conrad Aiken's work encompassed fifty years of writing. Allen Tate called him "one of the few genuine men of letters left" (Unger, 1, 1974). Aiken was the first of three sons born to Northeast-bred parents of Scottish descent living in Savannah, Georgia. Like his father, a Harvard-trained doctor, Aiken also went to Harvard (1907). There he joined one of the most influential groups of writers of the twentieth century: T. S. *Eliot, John Reed, Walter Lippman, E. E. *Cummings, and Robert Benchley among them. Aiken and the fellow writers of his generation avidly studied the *Symbolist movement. His musical interests centered upon the capacity of music to present simultaneously several different levels of awareness and unawareness, because he saw man as a creature existing in both sound and feeling. His solution for the writing process has now become conventional: he makes these voices carry a symbolic content in which tradition and psychology are blended. He used the word "chorus" in connection with his method: the familiar Greek chorus commenting and meditating, these themes treated as the themes in a symphony. Indeed, his long narrative poems were called "symphonies," but his solution might be described as more an oratorio than a chorus. Conrad Aiken's poetry has been set by composers Paul Nordoff, Bainbridge Crist, Herbert Elwell, Richard Hageman, and John Duke among others. PRINCIPAL WORKS: Poetry: *The Jig of Forslin: A Symphony*, 1916, 1921; *Preludes for Memnon*, 1931; *And in the Hanging Gardens*, 1933; *Brownstone Eclogues and Other Poems*, 1942; *The Kid*, 1947; *Collected Poems*, 1950. Novel: *A Heart for the Gods of Mexico*, 1939. Other prose: *Ushant: An Essay*, 1952; *A Reviewer's ABC*, 1968; *Collected Criticism*, ed. Rufus A. Blanshard, 1958 (reprinted as *Collected Criticism*, 1968). SELECTED READING: Edward Butscher, *Conrad Aiken, Poet of White Horse Vale*, 1988. (SOURCE: Unger, 1, 1974)

AIN: (Scot.), *own*.

AIR BACHIQUE: a form of seventeenth-century French solo song. As a reaction to the somewhat mannered *air de cour*, there was the *air bachique*, a trivial and burlesque form, gay and dancelike, celebrating the pleasures of wine and the flesh, and enjoyed by refined society. Molière used *airs bachiques* in his plays, and Louis XIV enjoyed hearing them sung by young girls.

AIR DE COUR: a courtly, refined, and amorous solo song of the seventeenth century in France. The lute, guitar, or harpsichord accompaniments were carefully written out, and the poetry of the songs echoed the over-precious tastes of the society.

AJAX: a hero of the Trojan War, son of the king of Salamis and Telamon. Ajax the Greater was a man of giant stature, daring but slow-witted. In the *Odyssey*, when Achilles' armor was awarded to ★Odysseus (★Ulysses) as champion, Ajax killed himself. In Homer, Ajax the Lesser, son of Oileus, the king of Locris, was a man of small stature. Because he attacked ★Priam's daughter ★Cassandra, Ajax was drowned by ★Poseidon after being shipwrecked. (SOURCE: Cooper, 1992)

SONG	COMPOSER	POET
"Dieu vous gard'"	Darius Milhaud	Pierre de Ronsard

AKHMATOVA (GORENKO), ANNA (1889–1966): Russian poet. Akhmatova is one of the two greatest women poets in the history of Russian poetry, and one of three great ★Acmeists. Daughter of a merchant marine engineer, she spent her childhood in ★Tsarskoye Selo, the village near St. Petersburg where the Tsar's summer palace was located, its royal environment perhaps reflected in her poetry. Akhmatova's husband founded the Acmeist literary movement, to which she committed herself. Her first books of poetry (1912–13) brought her success. Akhmatova is a purely lyric poet, whose visions are feminine but not modernist, and she is distinguished for her religious, mystical sentiments as well as her economy of words and unusual rhythms. Each of her poems is a dramatic moment frozen in time. A contemporary critic, Valerian Chudovsky, pointed out that her poems, as in Japanese art, have the ability to create a total picture by presenting a few fragments of impressions.

After the Revolution, Akhmatova brought out two books, but was not thereafter allowed to publish her poetry until 1940. During Stalin's purges (1937–39) her son was arrested and persecuted; yet she bore her trouble with dignity. Akhmatova was one of the poets who were criticized in the widespread repression of the arts of 1946. In 1964 she was awarded an Italian prize, and in 1965 she was given an honorary doctorate by Oxford University. Only then was she fully rehabilitated, highly acclaimed at home and abroad. The verse of Anna Akhmatova was set by Sergei Prokofiev. WORKS: *Vecher* [Evening], 1912; *Chotki* [Rosary], 1914; *Belaya staya* [The White Flock], 1917; *Anno Domini MCMXXI* [C.E. 1921], 1921; *Second Birth*, 1932; *Iva* [The Willow], 1940; *Rekviem*, 1963; Requiem, 1964. SELECTED READING: R. Reider, *Anna Akhmatova: Poet and Prophet*, 1995. (SOURCES: Todd, Hayward, 1994; Terras, 1991)

ALADDIN, ALADIN (Fr.): a character in *Arabian Nights*. He obtains a magic lamp and has the genie of the lamp build a splendid palace for him and his wife. Her father, the Sultan of China, disposes of the lamp and transports the palace to Africa. Aladdin eventually recovers the lamp and returns to China and his palace with his wife to live happily for many years. (SOURCE: Cooper, 1992)

SONG	COMPOSER	POET
"Zaïde"	Hector Berlioz	Roger de Beauvoir

"Alas! My Dear, You're Cold as Stone": a song written by Henry Purcell to lyrics of William ★Shakespeare in his play, *The Tempest*, adapted for a revival by ★D'Avenant and ★Dryden. For the position of the song within the plot, *see* ★*Tempest, The.*

ALBA: the kingdom of King Numitor. Mars, the god of war, had surprised the vestal virgin, Rhea Silvia, daughter of Numitor, while she was asleep. Their sons were Romulus and Remus. (SOURCE: *OED*, 1989)

ALBEE, EDWARD (b. 1928): American absurdist and minimalist playwright. Born in Virginia, Albee was taken to Washington, D.C. before he was two weeks old and given up for adoption to the Albee family of Larchmont, New York. Because his adoptive father was a wealthy theater owner, Edward was raised in privilege and surrounded by an artistic atmosphere. He attended Broadway plays and came into contact with theater people at an early age. An indifferent student, Albee left college before the end of his second year. During his subsequent life, doing menial jobs in Greenwich Village, he met W. H. ★Auden, who encouraged his writing. At thirty, his first play, *The Zoo Story*, had a great impact on the public, as did *Who's Afraid of Virginia* ★*Woolf*, a minimalist drama. Albee's works took their place in the classic repertoire of the twentieth century, winning for him two Pulitzer Prizes. He was a master of language and absurd humor. Albee's work was set to music by William Flanagan. PRINCIPAL WORKS: *The Zoo Story*, 1959; *The Sandbox*, 1960; *Bartleby*, libretto with James Hinton, Jr., set by William Flanagan; *A Delicate Balance*, 1966; *Seascape*, 1975; *Three Tall Women,* 1991. SELECTED READING: C. W. E. Bigeby, ed., *Edward Albee: Twentieth Century Views*, 1975; *Conversations with Edward Albee*, ed. Philip C. Colin, 1988. (SOURCE: Magill, 1, 1997)

ALBERTI, RAFAEL (1902–1999): Spanish poet. Rafael Alberti was born in Cádiz, Spain and was given a Jesuit education before settling in Madrid in 1917. His early poetry was refined and scholarly, based on folk themes. After his 1924 collection of verse about the sea and sailors won the national prize for literature, he soon adopted a style in which he imitated with great virtuosity the elaborate verse forms of sixteenth- and seventeenth-century Spanish poetry, similar to the poetry of his friend ★García Lorca. Alberti then moved toward his own modern idiom of intense self-analysis. In 1934 he traveled and observed the political movements of the Left, and during the Spanish Civil War he fought on the Loyalist side. After their defeat, Alberti moved to Buenos Aires, where he published poetry, dramas, essays, and a collection of Spanish fables. Both Alberti and García Lorca tried to free pure emotion from the control of logic, believing that free association of words, images, and ideas were an important part of the poetic process. Alberti's verse has been set by Oscar Esplà, Jesús Bal y Gay, and Xavier Montsalvatge. ENGLISH TRANSLATIONS: *A Spectre is Haunting Europe*, 1936; *Selected Poems*, 1944, 1966; *The Owl's Insomnia*, 1973; *The Other Shore*, 1981; *90 Poems*, 1992. SELECTED READING: Robert Havard, *The Crucified Mind: Rafael Alberti and the Surrealist Ethos in Spain*, 2001. (SOURCE: Kunitz, Colby, 1955)

ALCADE: a Spanish or Portuguese magistrate, stemming from the Arabic *al cadi*, the judge.

SONG	COMPOSER	POET
"Le Bachelier de Salamanque"	Albert Roussel	René Chalupt

ALCESTIS AND ADMETUS: In Greek legend Alcestis was the youngest daughter of Pelias, loved by Admetus, king of Pherae, whom ★Apollo helped to win her. The couple lived very happily, but the king was doomed to an early death, which could only be avoided if another died instead of him. Alcestis gave herself as a substitute and died accordingly. ★Heracles arrived and fought Death successfully in order to bring Alcestis back to her husband. This story was used by ★Sophocles, ★Euripides, ★Chaucer, ★Milton, ★Goethe, ★Browning, and ★Rilke. ★Hofmannsthal created an opera libretto from it, set to music by Egon Wellesz. (SOURCE: Steinberg, 1, 1973)

ALCIBIADES (ca. 450–404 B.C.E.): an Athenian aristocrat, general, and politician. Alcibiades was reared in the home of Pericles, his cousin and guardian, and was a frequent companion of ★Socrates. Alcibiades shared Socrates' individualistic outlook but was not influenced by his moral and ethical teachings. Alcibiades served in the army with distinction in the early years of the Peloponnesian War, during which time he saved Socrates' life. An egoist and an opportunist, he was radically pro-war and would stop at nothing to further his own interests. He was a good general but an unprincipled demagogue. (SOURCE: *Americana*, 2001)

SONG	COMPOSER	POET
"Socrates and Alcibiades"	Benjamin Britten	Friedrich Hölderlin

ALCIDES: *see* ★HERCULES.

ALCINA: the ★Circe of fable, the personification of carnal pleasure in ★Ariosto's *Orlando Furioso* (1516). Alcina also appears in Handel's opera *Alcina*. (SOURCE: Cooper, 1992)

ALDRICH, THOMAS BAILEY (1836–1907): American poet, novelist, editor. Aldrich was born in New Hampshire. His father being a wanderer, much of Charles's childhood was spent in New York and New Orleans. When his father died (1849), Aldrich had to give up Harvard and go to work as a junior literary critic of a newspaper. During the Civil War, Aldrich was sent to the front as a war correspondent for the *Tribune*. After the war, he was made a managing editor of another newspaper, later returning to Boston to be editor of *Every Saturday*, which position he held until the newspaper folded in 1874. In 1881 he was selected to take William Dean ★Howells's place as editor of the *Atlantic Monthly*, where he stayed until 1890, when he retired to do his own writing, from which he derived recognition and prosperity. Aldrich was witty, urbane, popular, and youthful looking to the end. He believed that reformers were cranks and Bohemians were cheats. His poetry, better than his prose, was perhaps nearest to the urbanity and grace of ★Horace, its workmanship superb. America produced few poets capable of Aldrich's craftsmanship at its best. The verses of Thomas Bailey Aldrich were set by G. W. Chadwick, John Alden Carpenter, and Charles Ives. PRINCIPAL WORKS: Poetry: *Cloth of Gold*, 1874; *Flower and Thorn*, 1877; *Mercedes and Later Lyrics*, 1884; *Wyndham Towers*, 1890; *Judith and Holofernes*, 1896. Prose: *Story of a Bad Boy*, 1870; *Marjorie Daw and Other People*, 1873. SELECTED READING: F. Greenslet, *Life of Thomas Bailey Aldrich*, 1936. (SOURCES: Kunitz, Haycraft, 1938; Drabble, 1985)

ALECTO, ALEKTO: (lit., *one who never rests*) in Greek mythology one of the three ★Erinnyes (lit., *angry ones*), who are the goddesses of vengeance (in Roman mythology, the ★Furies). Alecto was sent by Juno to stir up discord among the Trojans. The Furies' heads were horrifyingly wreathed with serpents. (SOURCE: Cooper, 1992)

SONG	COMPOSER	POET
"Music for a While"	Henry Purcell	John Dryden, Nathaniel Lee

ALEXANDER the GREAT: Alexander III of Macedon (356–323 B.C.E.). The territorial conquests won by Alexander encompassed Greece, Persia, western Asia, Egypt, and North India. In addition to historical reports, a large amount of legendary material surrounds him. There are many versions of his battles and conquests, adapted to fit nationalistic points of view: European, Coptic, Syrian, Hebrew, Korean, Arabic, Persian, and Islamic. (SOURCE: Steinberg, 1, 1973)

ALEXANDRINE: the most famous of French poetic meters, widely used from 1800 to the twentieth century. A line has twelve syllables, divided into two equal six-syllable sections around a caesura (a pause in the middle of a metrical line). Stresses are obligatory, on the sixth and twelfth syllables—at the caesura and at the end of the line. Two additional secondary stresses can fall on any syllable not already accented.

ALFONSO UND ESTRELLA: an opera written by Franz von *Schober with some music by Franz Schubert. Set in Spain, the work tells a tale of kingdoms lost and found, love at first sight between a prince and a princess, with a true villain to push the plot along and fill the stage with his revolutionary forces. The opera is rich in trios, ensembles, and twelve duets, two set by Schubert: "Tief im Getümmel der Schlacht" and "Cavatine."

ALFRED, KING: *see* *RULE, BRITANNIA.

ALGUAZILS: Spanish policemen.

SONG	COMPOSER	POET
1. "Guitare"	Jules Massenet	Victor Hugo
2. "Comment disaient-ils"	Franz Liszt	Victor Hugo

ALHAMA: a Spanish town perched on the cliff above *Granada, whose capture in 1482 was of great importance in the fight against the Moors. (SOURCE: Cockburn, Stokes, 1992)

SONG	COMPOSER	POET
"Pase ábase el rey moro"	Luiz de Narváez	unknown

ALHAMBRA: palace of the Moorish kings at *Granada, built mostly in the thirteenth century. In the Arabic *al-hamra* meant "the Red," the color of the stone from which the palace was built. (SOURCE: Cockburn, Stokes, 1992)

SONG	COMPOSER	POET
"Pase ábase el rey moro"	Luiz de Narváez	unknown

ALISSA: a song cycle by Darius Milhaud derived from a novel by André *Gide, *La Porte étroite* (Narrow Is the Gate). The novel is a powerful psychological study of a sensitive young woman, Alissa Bucolin, who renounces her passion, although deeply in love, and seeks religious virtue built on martyrdom. The man who loves her, Jerome, patiently waits for her to accept his proposal of marriage. Alissa repels any happiness that is easily attained. The final section of the book is a journal written just before her death, explaining: God teaches a narrow way, so narrow that two cannot walk in it abreast.

ALLAH: lit., *the god* in Arabic; the designation of the exclusively monotheistic deity in Islam.

SONG	COMPOSER	POET
1. "Allah's Good Laws"	Robert Baksa	Ambrose Bierce
2. "Allah"	George Chadwick	H. W. Longfellow
3. "Songs of the Infatuated Muezzin"	Karol Szymanowski	Jarislav Iwaszkiewicz

ALLEGORY: a story or a description in which the characters and/or events symbolize some deeper underlying meaning, conveying a veiled moral meaning; an extended metaphor. In the medieval ages people tended to think allegorically, but

the device was also used by more modern writers, such as Hawthorne and Virginia
★Woolf.

ALLMERS, HERMAN (1821–1902): German poet and dramatist. Allmers was born
in Bremen and died there. He was a well-to-do farmer who became the mayor of his
city of birth, Rechtenflet. In his youth he traveled widely, but was devoted to the Frie-
sian region and its culture. His best work involved environmental descriptions. Mahler
admired his poetry, and Brahms set his poem "Feldeinsamkeit" in a famous song.
PRINCIPAL WORKS: *Marschenbuch,* 1858; *Die Pflege des Volksgesangs im deutscher Nor-
dwesten,* 1878; *Sämtliche Werke,* 6 vols., 1891–96. (SOURCE: Garland, 1976)

ALL SAINTS' DAY: a special religious feast day, November 1. All Saints' Day celebrates all the redeemed souls in heaven. Originally, All Saints' Day was an Eastern
Orthodox feast celebrating the lives of the martyrs. In France, people visit the cemetery on All Saints' Day. (SOURCES: Farmer, 1997; Walsh, 1991)

SONG	COMPOSER	POET
"Cimitière"	Francis Poulenc	Max Jacob

ALL SOULS' DAY: a Christian feast day, November 2, following All Saints' Day.
On All Souls' Day prayers and masses are dedicated to the souls of all the departed,
the purpose being to reduce the time required to be spent by the soul in Purgatory
before passing to heaven. In modern times, this day, first instituted at the Monastery
of Cluny in 998, supports a custom of placing lighted candles on the graves of friends
and family on the previous evening. Tradition has it that a pilgrim, returning from
the Holy Land, was compelled by a storm to land on a rocky island, where he found
a hermit who told him that among the cliffs of the island there was an opening leading to the infernal regions. Huge flames ascended through it, and the groans of the
tormented were audible. When the Abbot of Cluny was told of this, he appointed
the following day, November 2, to be set apart for the benefit of the souls in purgatory. (SOURCE: Farmer, 1997)

SONG	COMPOSER	POET
"Allerselen"	Richard Strauss	Hermann von Gilm

ALPUJARRAS: a mountain range, the southern face of the Sierra Nevada in the
south of Spain. The Alpujarras is a wild and little-traveled part of Andalusia. Here the
Moors fled after the final Christian conquest of ★Granada in 1492. They were not
expelled from this remote area until Philip III did so in 1609. The roads are tortur-
ous; the mountains are steep and snowcapped until June; the valleys are deep, green,
and dark and become sluices for rushing water in the spring.

SONG	COMPOSER	POET
"La Buenaventura"	Amadeo Vives	unknown

ALTAR: the table or block on which the mass is celebrated. In the primitive church,
the mass was celebrated on a table with no particular form prevailing. Later, when
the church was forced into the catacombs, mass was offered on the tomb of a martyr.
In ancient days the altar was situated so that the priest could face the people. Later
altars were built in the apse so that the people were behind the priest. Still later, the

altars were placed as an island so that the priests could be either behind or before it. (SOURCE: Nevins, 1964)

SONG	COMPOSER	POET
"Les Cloches"	Claude Debussy	Paul Bourget

ALTE WEISEN: a cycle of poems by Gottfried ★Keller, published in 1851, 1854, and 1883, from which publication Hugo Wolf chose to set six poems: "Tretet ein, hoher Krieger," "Singt mein Schatz wie ein Fink," "Du milch junge Knabe," "Wandle ich in dem Morgentau," "Das Köhlerweib ist trunken," and "Wie glänzt der heller Mond." For his settings, Brahms used the 1851 edition of these poems, called *Von Weibern*. In this version, each poem had a woman's name as the title. Thus, "Du milch junge Knabe" was called "Therese"; "Singt mein Schatz" was "Salome"; "Wie glänzt der heller Mond" was "Creszenz."

ALVÁREZ QUINTERO, SERAFÍN AND JOAQUÍN (1871–1938), (1873–1944): Spanish poet and playwright brothers who wrote together. The Alvárez Quintero brothers were born in Utrera and educated in Seville. They began writing in school, and, by the time they were seventeen and fifteen, they had dozens of plays to their credit. Recognition came in the late 1890s. In 1896 their first book of verse was published. The brothers saw material for plays all around themselves and dramatized every incident. At the beginning of the twentieth century their best poetical qualities came to the fore. With inspiration they pictured their native Andalusia in all its radiance. Their sole purpose being to entertain, their work was clear, bright, light, and gay with the keen wit and delicate touch that was typical of Seville. The city erected a monument to the brothers Quintero, who were in favor with Franco, but imprisoned nonetheless. In 1938 Serafín died in prison, but Joaquín wrote under both names until his own death in 1944. Since his death, the *Obras Completas of Serafín and Joaquín Alvárez Quintero* have been published in six volumes: 8,503 pages, 228 dramatic works. The verses of the Quintero brothers have been set by Joaquín Turina. ENGLISH TRANSLATIONS: *A Sunny Morning*, 1914; *Malvaloca*, 1916; *Fortunato*, 1918; *The Fountain of Youth*, 1922; *The Widow's Eyes,* 1929; *Grief*, 1930; *By the Light of the Moon*, 1943. READING: A. F. G. Bell, *Contemporary Spanish Literature*, 1932. (SOURCE: Kunitz, Haycraft, 1942)

AMADIS: the love-child of Perion, king of Wales, and Elizena, princess of Brittany. At birth Amadis was cast away in a box on a river, rescued, and then raised in Scotland. He became known as the Child of the Sea. After many adventures Amadis secured the hand of Oriana, daughter of Lisuarte, king of Great Britain. Amadis was renowned as poet and musician, knight-errant, and king, the very model of chivalry. The arrival of the emperor was followed closely by his defeat, but Amadis was reconciled with the king and permitted to marry Oriana. (SOURCE: Cooper, 1992)

SONG	COMPOSER	POET
"Der neue Amadis"	Armin Knab, Ernst Krenek, H. Wolf	Johann Wolfgang von Goethe

AMADIS OF GAUL: a fourteenth century Spanish romance of chivalry, of which only fragments remain: Amadis's birth, how he overcame his enemies, enchanters, and Oriana's suspicions, only to die by mischance at the hands of his son. Many of the details are derived from the Arthurian and Trojan legends. This fictional romance had a long popularity and exerted a wide influence on literature, inspiring other works (Lully: *Amadis*; Handel: *Amadigi*; Krenek: *Der neue Amadis*). The Portuguese originals were written in the fourteenth and fifteenth centuries, and the next version (1508) was written by a Spaniard. (SOURCE: Steinberg, 1, 1973)

AMALFI: originally a Byzantine settlement, now an Italian town in Salerno Province in the region of Campania. Amalfi is located 24 miles southeast of ★Naples on the Gulf of Salerno. The beautiful Amalfi Drive is cut from the rugged cliffs along the gulf, extending as far west as Sorrento and east to Salerno.

SONG	COMPOSER	POET
"Night Song at Amalfi"	Wintter Watts	Sara Teasdale

AMALIA: a character in Friedrich von ★Schiller's 1782 five-act play *Die Räuber* (The Robbers). Karl, one of a Franconian nobleman's two sons, has been disinherited through a trick perpetrated by the other son. Consequently, Karl joins a robber band that terrorizes the Bohemian Forest region. Karl is in love with his cousin Amalia, who returns his love despite his activities. In her garden during act 3, scene 4 of the play, she sings of that love in a song set by Franz Schubert, "Amalie."

AMALTHEIA: a goat, given as a wet nurse to the baby ★Zeus as he grew up in the forests of Mount Ida. Amaltheia was a wondrous animal whose aspect terrified even the immortals. In gratitude Zeus later placed her among the constellations. To the ★nymphs he gave one of her horns and made it unemptiable, thus a horn of plenty. From her hide, which no arrow could pierce, Zeus made the aegis, a sort of skin covered with scales and fringed about with serpents, an awesome protective device. (SOURCE: Kaster, 1964)

AMARYLLIS, AMARILLI (It.): a sweetheart in pastoral poetry, the name borrowed from the pastoral writing of Virgil and ★Theocritus. ★Milton mentions Amaryllis in his *Lycidas*.

AMBROSIA: the food of the Greek and Roman gods, extremely pleasing to the taste and smell.

SONG	COMPOSER	POET
1. "Bess o'Bedlam"	Henry Purcell	anonymous
2. "Der neue Amadis"	A. Knab, E. Krenek, H. Wolf	Johann Wolfgang von Goethe

AMEN: (Heb.), *certainly, truly*; an expression indicating assent or agreement. The original Hebrew use was carried over into the New Testament. The Amen now said when receiving Holy Communion is a profession of faith in the Eucharist, dating back to earliest Christianity. When speaking, it is properly pronounced aye-men; when singing, ah-men. (SOURCE: Nevins, 1964)

SONG	COMPOSER	POET
"A Clymène"	Gabriel Fauré	Paul Verlaine

AMINTA (It.), AMINTE: a faithful shepherd. The character Aminta first appeared in 1573 in Tasso's *Aminta*, translated into English by John *Fletcher (1610), also in Molière's *Les Prècieuses ridicules*, wherein Cathos assumed the name Aminte because it seemed more aristocratic. In the Middle Ages changing one's name had been the prevailing fashion. (SOURCE: Preminger, 1986)

SONG	COMPOSER	POET
1. "Rondeley"	Ned Rorem	John Dryden
2. "Clair de lune"	Gabriel Fauré	Paul Verlaine
3. "Mandoline"	Claude Debussy, Gabriel Fauré	Paul Verlaine

AMOR, AMOUR, AMORE: *see* *CUPID.

AMORET: a love song, love-knot, love affair, or love personified; also a character in *Spenser's *The Faerie-Queene*, daughter of nymph Chrysogone, twin sister of Belphoebe. Amoret has been married to Sir Scudamour but is carried off immediately after the wedding by the enchanter Busirane and imprisoned by him. Timias loves her but, being reproved by Belphoebe, leaves her. This refers to the displeasure of Queen Elizabeth at the relationship of Raleigh to Elizabeth Throckmorton.

SONG	COMPOSER	POET
"As Amoret and Thyrsis Lay"	Henry Purcell	William Congreve

AMPHION: the son of *Zeus (Jupiter) and *Antiope, queen of *Thebes. Exposed at birth on Mt. Cithaeron by the usurping King Lycus and his wife Dirce, Amphion and his twin brother Zethus, when grown up, marched against *Thebes and conquered it, exacting a terrible revenge upon Lycus, the king, and Dirce, his wife, who had mistreated their mother Antiope. In another legend, Amphion rebuilt the city of Thebes with the aid of his golden lyre, given him by Hermes, whose tone was so melodious that stones were said to have danced into the walls and houses of their own accord. Later, Amphion married Niobe, whose boasting about their children caused the tragic vengeance of *Apollo and Artemis. (SOURCE: Kaster, 1964)

AMPHION ANGELICUS: the collection of John Blow's works.

AMPHITRYON: a play by John *Dryden, containing one song by Henry Purcell, produced in 1690, the plot of which Dryden adapted from comedies by Plautus and Molière that use the story of *Jupiter's seduction of Alcmena in the disguise of her husband, Amphitryon. Jupiter forces Alcmena to tell which one is the real Amphitryon. When she chooses Jupiter, her husband, the real Amphitryon, is almost destroyed. At the end of act 3, after Jupiter in Amphitryon's form leaves Alcmena's bed, her real husband arrives. When Alcmena describes their night of passion, jealous Amphitryon leaves. Jupiter returns for a conjugal visit but is intercepted by Phaedra, Alcmena's money-mad friend, who warns Jupiter of Alcmena's bad disposition. Jupiter bribes Phaedra and organizes a serenade, which he hopes will win Alcmena's forgiveness. Phaedra leads Alcmena to the balcony, and Jupiter signals the musicians to begin. Purcell's song, "Celia, That I Once was Blest," is sung by an unspecified Theban. (SOURCE: Price, 1984)

ANACREON, ANAKREON (Ger.): Greek lyric poet, born circa 570 B.C.E., in Teos in Asia Minor. The date and place of Anacreon's death are unknown. Murray states that he lived to the age of eighty-five, having resided in Thrace, Samos, Athens, and Thessaly. Of Anacreon's five books of poetry dealing with love and the good life, only a few survive as quotations in other books. Franz von ★Bruchmann's "An die Leier" (Schubert D 737) was a free translation of a poem by Anacreon. *Anacrontea* is a collection of sixty some short poems on love, wine, and song written in the style of Anacreon between 200 B.C.E. and 300 C.E. and known to be by Seneca and Boethius. This work exercised influence on Renaissance and later European poets like ★Ronsard, Tasso, ★Gleim, ★Uz, and ★Goethe. Anacreon's style was also imitated by many eighteenth- and nineteenth-century English and European poets. Lord ★Byron and Thomas ★Moore made English translations of Anacreon and *Anacrontea*. (SOURCES: Howatson, 1989; Murray, 1966; Preminger, 1986; Reed, 1997)

SONG	COMPOSER	POET
1. "Anakreons Grab"	F. Schubert; H. Wolf	J. W. von Goethe
2. "I Wish to Tune My Quivering Lyre"	Arthur Sullivan	J. W. von Goethe, Lord Byron
3. "La Rose, Ode Anacréontique"	Gabriel Fauré	Charles Leconte de L'Isle
4. "Air d'Anaïs"	André Grétry	Jean Henri Guy

ANACREONTIC VERSE: a movement of French, German, and English poets who competed in imitating poetry from a collection of late Greek Anacreontic poetry published in 1554, believing it to be the work of the poet ★Anacreon himself. In this poetry, there abound gentle breezes, myrtle and laurel, caves and dragons, silvery flowers, wild animals, doves, lambs, nightingales; a muse replaces the poet's ego; the names are from mythology; tears, smiles, eyes are personified. These poets virtually exhausted themselves in repetitions of the same themes. Inspired by Anacreontic verse were ★Jonson, ★Herrick, ★Lovelace, and ★Cowley. In 1800 Thomas ★Moore published his translation of the *Odes* of Anacreon into English verse. (SOURCE: Drabble, 1985)

ANAÏS: the daughter of ★Polycrates. (*See* ★Anacréon.) Grétry's opera is named *Anacréon chez Polycrate*. Anaïs is a leading role. Another of her arias is "Eprise d'un feu têmêraire."

SONG	COMPOSER	POET
"Air d'Anaïs"	André Grétry	Jean Henri Guy

ANCONA: an east-coast Italian port on the Adriatic Sea in the province of Marches, south of Ravenna and Rimini.

SONG	COMPOSER	POET
"Ich hab in Penna"	Hugo Wolf	Paul Heyse, from the Italian

ANDERSEN, HANS CHRISTIAN (1805–1875): Danish poet, novelist, playwright, and writer of fairy tales. Hans Christian Andersen was born in Odense, Denmark, where he was educated to the age of fourteen. After completing his grammar school education in 1827, he was tutored in Copenhagen in order to complete his examination successfully (1828). From that time on he was a freelance writer. He was given royal grants for travel in 1833 and 1844, and a pension from King Frederick VI in 1838, who also awarded him the Order of the Dannebrog (1846). Andersen was a very Danish author, but he was not in the least parochial. He was well read, well traveled, and well informed about the scientific developments of his time. Yet he was more at home in the free form of a novel than in the disciplined forms of drama and poetry. All of Andersen's work was based on his own experience and his own childhood, and it was in the short form of fairy tales that he found his voice. As he gained confidence he developed the folk tale form into an original art by creating a new literary language that was deceptively simple. His best stories show an accurate observation of human behavior and an understanding of the problems of human existence. Andersen's work was admired by Charles Dickens and Elizabeth Barrett ★Browning, who wrote her last poem to him. The work of Hans Christian Andersen has been set to music by Honegger, Schumann, Grieg, Prokofiev, and Niels Gade. WORKS: *Fairy Tales for Children*, 6 vols., 1835–42; *New Fairy Tales*, 4 vols., 1843–47, ed. Erik Dal and Erling Nielsen, 1963; *Complete Fairy Tales and Stories*, trans. Erik Haugaard, 1974. READING: Reginald Spink, *Andersen and His World*, 1972; Elias Bredsdorff, *Andersen: The Story of His Life and Work*, 1975. (SOURCE: Vinson, Kirkpatrick (1), 1984)

SONG	COMPOSER	POET
"Sonatina to Hans Christian Andersen"	Vincent Persichetti	Wallace Stevens

ANDERSON, MAXWELL (1888–1959): American dramatist born in Pennsylvania. Anderson was a pacifist in World War I but rejected the contemporary naturalistic manner of dramatizing social injustice. His first successful play, *What Price Glory* (1926), satirizes war while at the same time acknowledging its romantic appeal. Anderson experimented with verse drama in his *Elizabeth the Queen* (1930), and used the ★Sacco and Vanzetti case in his *Winterset* (1935), blending tough realism and poetic technique. A literary but stoic tone characterized his best work. Among his other works are the plays *High Tor*, 1937; *Key Largo*, 1939; *Joan of Lorraine*, 1947; *Anne of the Thousand Days*, 1947, and two librettos, *Knickerbocker Holiday*, 1938 and *Lost in the Stars*, 1949. Charles Ives and Henry Cowell have set the work of Maxwell Anderson. SELECTED READING: J. Gould, *Modern American Playwrights*, 1966. (SOURCE: Steinberg, 2, 1973)

ANDERSON, SHERWOOD (1876–1941): American writer of naturalistic novels and short stories. Anderson wrote about the life in Midwestern small towns, being most renowned for his novel *Winesburg, Ohio* (1919). Anderson was born in Ohio and enlisted in the Army, serving in Cuba during the Spanish-American War. The so-called "Chicago Group," which listed among its members Theodore Dreiser and Carl ★Sandburg, encouraged Anderson in his desire to write. *Winesburg, Ohio* revealed the conflict between the instinctive forces of human nature and the stultifying effect of the narrow, conventional industrial society of small town America. (SOURCE: *Americana*, 2001)

SONG	COMPOSER	POET
"Valentine to Sherwood Anderson"	William Flanagan	Gertrude Stein

ANDRÉE EXPEDITION: an expedition that was the first attempt to reach the North Pole by air, made by Salomon August Andrée (1854–97), a Swedish explorer-engineer, and two other colleagues, all three of whom perished in this try. On July 11, 1897, Andrée and his two companions took off from Dane Island in a balloon. No one knew for thirty-three years what had happened to them. In 1930 a scientific expedition found bodies on White Island, north of Russia. Diaries and films found there helped to piece the story together. After sixty-five hours in the air the explorers had come down on the ice 300 miles northeast of Dane Island. Three months later they had reached White Island, which was 200 miles south of where the balloon came down. The 1930 expedition found their loaded sledges and boat together with plentiful food and fuel. This indicated that Andrée and his colleagues may have died of illness or from being poisoned by gas from their kerosene stoves. (SOURCE: *Americana*, 2003)

SONG	COMPOSER	POET
"The Andrée Expedition"	Dominick Argento	Journals of Salomon August Andrée

ANDROMACHE: in Greek legend the wife of ★Hector who is given to Pyrrhus (Neoptolemus) on Hector's death. Pyrrhus is killed by ★Orestes and Andromache becomes the wife of Helenus, Hector's brother. *Andromache* is also the name of a play by ★Euripides. (SOURCE: Cooper, 1992)

SONG	COMPOSER	POET
"Andromache's Farewell"	Samuel Barber	Euripides, trans. J. P. Creagh

ANDROMEDA: daughter of Cepheus, king of Ethiopia, and his queen Cassiopeia. Because Cassiopeia had boasted that she was more beautiful than the ★Nereids, ★Poseidon sent a sea-dragon to destroy the country. The oracle of Ammon (Amen) predicted that the land would be saved only if Andromeda were given to the dragon. Cepheus chained her to a rock by the sea, but ★Perseus saved her by slaying the monster. Perseus was given Andromeda as his wife as a reward. (SOURCE: Kaster, 1964)

SONG	COMPOSER	POET
"Ah, lo previdi"	Wolfgang Amadeus Mozart	V. A. Cigna-Santi

ANGEL: from the Greek *angelos*, a messenger. Judaism, Christianity, and Islam consider angels to be spirits without bodies, having understanding and free will, inferior to God, superior to men. According to the Bible, they are endowed with great power and intellect and are of such majesty that those who see visions of them are usually overwhelmed with awe. In the Old Testament angels play crucial roles, such as visiting ★Abraham and Lot before the destruction of ★Sodom and ★Gomorrah and saving Daniel when he is thrown into the lions' den. In the New Testament angels announce the Resurrection on Easter morning. St. ★Paul lists the hierarchy of angels in the following descending order: Seraphim, Cherubim, Thrones, Dominions, Virtues, Principalities, Archangels, Angels. Guardian angels watch over countries or over people; in Protestantism the cult of angels is less important than in Catholicism. After rebelling against God, Lucifer and his angels were expelled from Heaven and condemned to Hell. (SOURCE: Bridgwater, Kurtz, 1968)

SONG	COMPOSER	POET
1. "La Mort des amants"	Claude Debussy	Charles Baudelaire
2. "Chanson d'amour"	Gabriel Fauré	Armand Silvestre
3. "La Rançon"	Gabriel Fauré	Charles Baudelaire
4. "Hymne"	Gabriel Fauré	Charles Baudelaire
5. "A Clymène"	Gabriel Fauré	Paul Verlaine
6. "Montparnasse"	Francis Poulenc	Louise de Vilmorin

ANGELUS: a prayer said three times daily (6 A.M., Noon, 6:00 P.M.) in the Catholic tradition, the name taken from the Latin text of the prayer that celebrates the doctrine of the Incarnation: *Angelus Domini nuntiavil Mariae* (An angel of the Lord announced to Mary). As the church bell rings in a specific pattern of three strokes three times and then nine strokes in succession, the angelus is said. It consists of the Hail Mary (★Ave Maria), the announcement of the Incarnation to Mary, and several Bible verses. (SOURCE: Bridgwater, Kurtz, 1968)

SONG	COMPOSER	POET
1. "Les Cigales"	Emmanuel Chabrier	Rosemonde Gérard
2. "Les Angélus"	Claude Debussy	Guy le Roy
3. "De Grève"	Claude Debussy	Claude Debussy

ANNA MAGDALENA BACH, LIEDER AUS DEM NOTENBUCH DER: professional singer and second wife to Johann Sebastian Bach. Anna Magdalen Wilcken married the widowed Bach in 1721. Well known as a singer, she continued to hold her position at the court of Anholt-Zerbst when she married. Her salary amounted to half that of her husband's, with whom she studied both the clavichord and the harpsichord. The original notebook that Bach wrote for her contained musical exercises and piano pieces in addition to eight songs.

ANNIE LAURIE: eldest of the three daughters of Sir Robert Laurie of Maxwellton, of Scotland. Annie, born December 16, 1682, married James Fergusson of Craigdarroch in 1709. She was also the mother of Alexander Fergusson, the hero of Robert Burns's song, "The Whistle."

ANN STREET: a New York street, exactly three blocks long, down at the tip of Manhattan Island. It is situated at the south end of City Hall Park, east of Broadway, two blocks from the approach to the Brooklyn Bridge, in the vicinity of Maiden Lane, Beekman, and Fulton Streets.

SONG	COMPOSER	POET
"Ann Street"	Charles Ives	Maurice Morris

ANOUILH, JEAN (1910–1987): French playwright. Son of a violinist mother and a father who was a tailor's cutter, Jean Anouilh started writing plays imitative of *Rostand at the age of ten. After eighteen months as a law student at the University of Paris, he took a position as an advertising copywriter. At nineteen he wrote his first play with a coauthor. Anouilh tells the old stories from the Bible, from classical Greek, and from Shakespeare. His work is philosophically existentialist, close to Pirandello. In the United States some of his plays were failures, some ran for sixty performances. There are English translations of *Antigone*, 1946; *Ring Around the Moon*, 1950; *Eurydice*, 1951; *Colombe*, 1952; *Legend of Lovers*, 1952; *Thieves' Carnival*, 1952. The work of Jean Anouilh has been set by Francis Poulenc. SELECTED READING: E. O. Marsh, *Jean Anouilh: Poet of Pierrot and Pantaloon*, 1968. (SOURCE: Brown, 1985)

ANTEQUERA: a Spanish town 30 miles north of Málaga, which is on the Costa del Sol (the Sun Coast) on the Mediterranean Sea.

SONG	COMPOSER	POET
"De Antequera salió el Moro"	Miguel de Fuenllana	unknown

ANTIGONE: in Greek and Roman mythology there are no fewer than four stories featuring Antigone with various fathers. 1. (*Rom.*) Antigone was the daughter of *Oedipus and Jocasta. After Oedipus learned that he had married and cohabited with his mother, he put out his eyes, later going into exile accompanied by his faithful daughter Antigone. 2. (*Rom.*) Peleus, one of the most famous heroes of Thessaly, went to Phthia, where he visited Eurytion, who welcomed Peleus and gave him one-third of his estates and the hand of his daughter Antigone. Peleus accidentally killed Eurytion when they were on a boar hunt. Peleus fled and took refuge in Iolcus with Acastus, whose wife took a passion for Peleus, who repulsed her. In revenge she told Antigone that Peleus had been unfaithful. Antigone hanged herself. 3. (*Gk.*) Antigone, the daughter of Laomedon, boasted of having hair more beautiful than Hera (Juno, *Rom.*). Hera then turned her locks into serpents. 4. (*Rom.*) Antigone killed herself to avoid being buried alive for disobeying an edict of Creon's. Schubert's song takes place on a road to Colonos. The blind king sleeps. Antigone prays that the gods will shift their fury from him to her. Oedipus wakes and bids a farewell to his tragic life. (SOURCE: Guirand, 1968)

SONG	COMPOSER	POET
"Antigone und Oedip"	Franz Schubert	Johann Mayrhofer

ANTIOCHUS, ANTIOCO (Sp.): an inter-testamental figure. Five different kings of Syria were named Antiochus, all descendants of Seleucus I. When Alexander the Great died, his empire had been divided between his generals. One Antiochus fell passionately in love with Stratonice, his stepmother. In order to save his son's life, Seleucus gave Stratonice to him. King Antiochus Epiphanes, who died in 163 B.C.E., was known for continuing Alexander's policy of Hellenization, to bring all things Greek to conquered nations. Antiochus brought this policy to *Judea, trying to replace the religion of the area with Greek culture and the Greek religion. These efforts to Hellenize the Jews led to the Maccabean revolt, which briefly freed Judea from foreign rule. (SOURCE: Metzger, Murphy, 1994; Bridgwater, Kurtz, 1968)

SONG	COMPOSER	POET
"Enferma estaba Antioco"	Esteban Daza	folk poetry

ANTIOPE: the Amazon queen *see* ★ANTIOPES.

ANTIOPES: the French title of a painting by the Italian painter Correggio, Corrèges (Fr.). Correggio made three paintings titled with the name of Antiope with a descriptive phrase attached, for example, *Antiope's Dream*, thus the plural reference in Koechlin's "L'Hiver" to more than one Antiope—*Antiopes de Corrèges*. The classical figure Antiope had several identities, but the most widely agreed-upon is in Roman mythology. ★Theseus's last exploit was to attack the Amazons and abduct Antiope, the Amazon queen, sometimes known as Hippolyta. Thereupon Amazon warriors invaded the islands of Lesbos and Samothrace to avenge the abduction of Antiope by Theseus. (SOURCES: Guirand, 1968; Cooper, 1992; Bulfinch, 1979)

SONG	COMPOSER	POET
"L'Hiver"	Charles Koechlin	Théodore de Banville

ANTONY, SAINT, ST. ANTONY OF PADUA (1193–1231): monk, priest, saint, and doctor of the Catholic Church. (Note that in the correct spelling of this name the *h* is omitted.) At sixteen St. Antony, christened Ferdinand, became a monk in the regular canons of St. Augustine. His early training was strongly based on knowledge of the Bible and the refuting of Muslim claims. Later, he joined a group of Franciscans bound for Morocco, intending to follow them to Morocco, but fell ill, which forced his return to Europe where he participated in the last gathering of all members of the Franciscan order. St. ★Francis, founder of the order and still alive, attended the 1221 meeting. Some time after St. Antony had been assigned to a lonely hermitage in San Paolo, his considerable skills as a learned and devout preacher were made known. After a public display of his attributes, St. Francis himself, it is said, appointed St. Antony—the first Franciscan to hold this position—as lector in theology to the monks of the order in Bologna and Padua. During the time he was the elected Provincial of northern Italy (1227), he wrote *Sermons for Sundays*. Being highly regarded in Rome, he was asked to produce another book of sermons entitled *Sermons for Feast Days*. St. Antony spent his last days preaching in and around Padua, where he died. In Padua a basilica was constructed around his tomb. He was canonized one year after his death, and his feast day was proclaimed to be June 13. He is the patron saint of Brazil and of the poor and starving, and is frequently invoked to help find lost items. Just as St. Francis is known to have preached to birds, St. Antony is often represented preaching to fish. Some stories suggest that the animals to whom St.

Antony preached were smarter than the people, who sometimes resisted his eloquence. (SOURCES: Farmer, 1997; Walsh, 1991)

SONG	COMPOSER	POET
1. "Der Antonius von Padua Fischpredigt"	Gustav Mahler	Des Knaben Wunderhorn
2. "A Prayer to St. Antony of Padua"	Peter Warlock	Arthur Symons

APHRODITE: the Greek ★Venus (from the word Aphros, *foam*) so called because she sprang from the foam of the sea, goddess of fertility and sexual love. Aphrodite was sometimes worshiped as Cytherea, since she was born on the shores of the island of ★Cythera. (SOURCE: Cooper, 1992)

SONG	COMPOSER	POET
1. "La Rose, Ode Anacréontique"	Gabriel Fauré	Charles Leconte de L'Isle
2. "Four Ladies"	David Diamond	Ezra Pound
3. "Invito all'Erano"	Goffredo Petrassi	Sappho

APOCRYPHA: from the Greek *hidden*, hence of unknown authorship, spurious; those books included in the Septuagint and Vulgate versions of the Old Testament that were not originally written in Hebrew and not counted as genuine by Jews, and which, at the Reformation, were excluded from the Sacred Canon by the Protestants as having no good claim to inspired authorship. (SOURCE: *OED*, 1989)

SONG	COMPOSER	POET
"Four Serious Songs"	Johannes Brahms	The Bible

APOLLINAIRE, GUILLAUME (1880–1918): French poet, novelist, playwright, editor, essayist. Born Guillaume Apollinaris de Kostrowitzky in Rome, Apollinaire was educated in Monte Carlo, Nice, and Cannes, served in World War I for the French despite being a foreigner, and was invalided out. His poetry would reflect his life as a soldier and the mentality of war. He worked as a tutor in Germany and as a freelance writer and critic in Paris, later as an editor of periodicals. At the first showing of the celebrated Salon des Indépendants painters (1911), he helped organize the Cubist room, after which he wrote a manifesto of ★Futurism. Apollinaire was "an innocent hero, part braggart, part simpleton, who discovered in war the brotherhood of man and revealed to his many friends one of the truly noble, truly good souls of his age" (Vinson, Kirkpatrick (1), 1984). Although he wished his public and his friends to love his character, he did not want them to know him too intimately. He disguised the sadness of his life with his stories and his mischievous tricks. The fantasy of his poetry remaining always close to the ★surrealists, he broke with the poetic clichés of the ★Parnassians and the ★Symbolists and eventually returned to the most basic source of realism. His articles and essays on painting make him second only to ★Baudelaire among the critics of modern French art. The verse of Apollinaire has been set in songs by Lennox Berkeley, Jean Rivier, Louis Durey, Daniel Ruyneman, and by Francis Poulenc in both song and opera. PRINCIPAL WORKS: Poetry: *Le*

Bestiaire, 1911; *Alcools*, 1913, English trans., 1964, 1965; *Calligrammes*, tr. Anne Greet, 1980; *Selected Writings*, tr. Roger Shattuck, 1948, 1971; *Selected Poems*, 1956, ed. Olivier Bernard. Plays: *Les Mamelles de Tirésias*, produced 1917, published 1918, later, as a libretto for an opera by Francis Poulenc. Essays: *The Cubist Painters: Aesthetic Meditations*, 1913, 1949; *L'Esprit nouveau et les poètes*, 1946; *Selected Writings*, ed. Roger Shattuck, 1950. SELECTED READING: Timothy Matthews Reading, *Apollinaire: Theories of Poetic Language*, 1987; David Berry, *The Creative Vision of Apollinaire*, 1982. (SOURCE: Vinson, Kirkpatrick (1), 1984)

APOLLO, APOLLON (Fr.): son of ★Zeus and Leto, primarily the god of prophecy, whose shrine and oracle at Delphi were famous throughout the ancient world. Apollo was the patron of poetry and music, leader of the ★Muses. As prophet, he was the patron of medicine and the healing arts. He is represented as an archer, who slays with his arrows. He came to be associated with the sun and was sometimes given the epithet ★Phoebus ("the bright one"). Representing order, reason, and self-discipline, Apollo is often compared to ★Dionysus, who represents creativity, sensuality, and lack of inhibition. In art Apollo is represented as a beautiful young male. He had numerous affairs with nymphs, mortal women, and young men. Apollo's son was ★Asclepius, his mother Koronis, a lake nymph. The world-renowned Apollo type of American spacecraft was named in honor of its superhuman abilities. (SOURCES: Kaster, 1964; Delahunty et al., 2001)

SONG	COMPOSER	POET
1. "La Cigale"	Ernest Chausson	Charles Leconte de L'Isle
2. "Je n'ai plus que les os"	Francis Poulenc	Pierre de Ronsard
3. "Apollo Circling"	Ronald Perera	James Dickey
4. "Canticle to Apollo"	Anthony Strilko	Robert Herrick
5. "Archaic Torso of Apollo"	Stephen Paulus	Rainer Maria Rilke

APUKHTIN, ALEXEI N. (1841–1893): Russian poet. Apukhtin, descended from ancient nobility, was the most popular art-for-art's-sake poet of the time, a popular figure in St. Petersburg society, where he was noted for his abnormal stoutness. Brilliantly gifted, he graduated from the Petersburg School of Jurisprudence, where Tchaikovsky was his friend and classmate, remaining so for life. Apukhtin's verse was acclaimed by aristocrats and the official classes. He was regarded as a sort of aristocratic counterpart of ★Nadson, whose poetry was admired by the radical intelligentsia. A great success with the public in the 1880s, the imagery and emotions of his verses fluent but hardly new, Apukhtin wrote of regret for the days of youth when he could better enjoy women and wine. It was the poetry of a man who had indulged himself to the ruin of his health. Yet his verses included realism and concrete detail, unlike Nadson. Apukhtin's themes were the familiar elegiac themes of the Russian golden age just slightly modernized. The verse of Alexei Apukhtin was set by Tchaikovsky and Rachmaninoff. PRINCIPAL WORK: *Poems*, 1886. (SOURCE: Mirsky, 1958; Terras, 1991)

AQUARELLES: a set of poems by Paul ★Verlaine from which Debussy chose to set two. The English title was Verlaine's, since Debussy knew little English. The *Aquarelles* were designed to give the feeling of watercolors in verse. For example, "Green" is a love song, not a picture of nature—the love song of a ★Symbolist whose ardor has the freshness of the color green and who seeks its coolness in the arms of his beloved.

ARAGON, DEUX POÈMES DE LOUIS: two songs composed by Francis Poulenc to the verse of Louis ★Aragon. One of the poems, "C," was so titled because all the lines end in the syllable *c'è*. The poem evokes the tragic days of May 1940 when a great portion of the French population fled before the Nazi armies. Amidst the confusion of France invaded, Aragon himself had crossed the ★Loire River at the Bridge of Cè, which was crowded with the abandoned vehicles and discarded weapons that he describes in his poem. (SOURCE: Bernac, 1977)

ARAGON, LOUIS (LOUIS ANDRIEUX) (1897–1982): French writer, essayist, novelist, and propagandist. Louis Aragon was born in Paris, where he helped launch the ★Surrealist movement after World War I. Little is known of his early or personal life, but, following his becoming a member of the Communist Party around 1931, his work had a political cast. After his surrealist period, Aragon wrote in a traditional manner for a short time, but he was never primarily a poet, rather a journalist. He was a member of the editorial staff of the Communist paper and the managing editor of the evening Communist paper, *Ce Soir*, which was suppressed by the government before World War II. As a soldier, Aragon was evacuated from Dunkirk to England, but returned to France in June of 1940 and faced hand-to-hand fighting with German troops, after which he was awarded two Croix de Guerre medals for his wartime services. Personally, Aragon was abstemious, proud, a mix of quick, cruel wit and literary erudition, but with an ingratiating smile. The poetry of Louis Aragon was set by Georges Auric and Francis Poulenc. PRINCIPAL WORKS: Surrealist poetry: *Feu de joie*, 1920, trans. as *Bonfire*; *Mouvement perpétuel*, 1925, trans. as *Perpetual Motion*; *Red Front*, trans. e. e. cummings, 1933; *The Bells of Basel*, 1936; *Residential Quarter*, 1938; *The Century was Young*, 1941. Poetry of the French resistance: *Le Crève-coeur*, 1941, trans. as *Heartbreak*; *La Diane française*, 1945, trans. as *The French Diana*. SELECTED READING: M. Adareth, *Aragon, the Resistance Poems*, 1985. (SOURCE: Vinson, Kirkpatrick (1), 1984)

ARBUTUS: a group of evergreen plants of the heath family, usually shrubs or trees. In the eastern and central Canada and the United States, the best known variety is the trailing arbutus, a creeping plant with shining green leaves, with fragrant white or pink flowers. In New England it is called a mayflower. (SOURCE: *Americana*, 2003)

SONG	COMPOSER	POET
"En sourdine"	Claude Debussy, Reynaldo Hahn	Paul Verlaine

ARCADIA, ARCADY, ARKADY: the traditional symbols of the perfect pastoral landscape in southern Greece, or any place of rural peace and simplicity.

ARDERIU, CLEMENTINE (1893–?): a Spanish poet. Arderiu was the wife of Carlos Riba. She wrote deceptively simple lyrics that seemed to come directly from her own spontaneous sense of life without dilutions from literary models. The verse of Clementine Arderiu was set by Joaquín Turina. READING: Arthur Terry, *A Literary History of Spain: Catalan Literature*, 1972.

ARES: the Greek god of war to whom Mars (Roman) corresponded. Ares was the son of ★Zeus and Hera. According to Homer, he had inherited his mother's fierce temper, hence his delight in battles and bloodshed. Ares was attended by his sister ★Eris (goddess of strife and discord), his sons Deimos and Phobos (gods of fear and fright), and Enyo, an old war goddess. Ares personifies blind, bloodthirsty rage and is often outwitted by his rival war deity, Athena, who combines wisdom and cunning with warlike qualities. Ares is most famous for his love affair with ★Aphrodite. The story of her husband Hephaestus catching the guilty pair in flagrante delicto is told by Homer. (SOURCE: Kaster, 1964)

ARGIRI: *see* ★ARGIVES.

ARGIVES (Fr.), ARGIRI (Gk.): adj., pertaining to Argos, of or pertaining to the ancient city of Argos or the territory of Argolis, hence used in Homer and later classical writers as meaning Grecian or Greek; a native of Argos, generally a Greek. (SOURCE: *OED*, 1989)

SONG	COMPOSER	POET
1. "La Naiade"	Ottorino Respighi	Gabriele d'Annunzio
2. "Arianna à Naxos"	Franz Josef Haydn	unknown

ARGUS: a hundred-eyed giant sent by Hera (Roman, Juno) to guard Io after she had been turned into a young cow. Commanded by ★Zeus, Hermes killed Argus. Hera took the eyes of Argus and placed them on the tail of her favorite bird, the peacock. (SOURCE: Kaster, 1964)

SONG	COMPOSER	POET
"Misera, dove son?"	Wolfgang Amadeus Mozart	Pietro Metastasio

ARIADNE, ARIANNA (It.): a Cretan princess, daughter of King Minos. Ariadne gave ★Theseus a skein of thread that allowed him to escape from Daedalus's labyrinth after he had killed the Minotaur (a monster, half man and half bull). Ariadne went with Theseus to ★Naxos, where he deserted her. There ★Dionysus found her and married her. It is possible that this myth is a version of older tales of sacred bullfights from the pre-Greek era of Cretan history. (SOURCE: Cotterell, 1986)

SONG	COMPOSER	POET
1. "Arianna à Naxos"	Franz Josef Haydn	unknown
2. "Lamento di Arianna"	Goffredo Petrassi	Libero di Libero
3. "Lasciatemi morire"	Claudio Monteverdi	Ottavio Rinuccini

ARIEL: a name given to many different characters in early English Restoration and Elizabethan drama, and applied variously in the Bible, astronomy, demonology, and literature. Ariel is a Hebrew name that signifies the *lion of God*. In Isaiah 29.1–7, it is applied to Jerusalem; in astronomy it refers to a satellite of Uranus; in demonology and literature it is the name of a spirit. Thus, it is the name given to one of the seven angelic princes in Heywood's *Hierarchie of the Blessed Angels* (1635), to one of the rebel angels in ★Milton's *Paradise Lost* (1667), to a sylph, the guardian of Belinda, in Pope's *Rape of the Lock* (1712), but best known as "an ayrie spirit" in ★Shakespeare's *The ★Tempest*. All light and spirit in the play, Ariel is able to make himself invisible and symbolizes man's imagination. In the play (act 1, scene 2), Ariel was enslaved to the witch Sycorax, who gave him tasks beyond his abilities, and, as punishment for not doing what was impossible for him to do, shut him up in a pine-rift for twelve years. On the death of Sycorax, Ariel became the slave of ★Caliban, who tortured him cruelly. Prospero liberated him and was gratefully served by Ariel until he was set free. The horse that poet Sylvia Plath often rode she named Ariel. (SOURCE: Cooper, 1992)

SONG	COMPOSER	POET
1. "Ariel's Song"	Henry Purcell	W. Shakespeare, J. Dryden, T. Shadwell
2. "Ariel"	Ned Rorem	Sylvia Plath

ARIETTES OUBLIÉES (*Forgotten Ariettas*): nine poems that open French poet Paul ★Verlaine's *Romances sans paroles* (1874), the compositions *Aquarelles*, and *Paysages belges*, set to music by Claude Debussy. The nine poems of *Ariettes oubliées* were written by Verlaine during his *Wanderjahre* (wandering years) with Rimbaud. They are considered his first great original works. (SOURCE: Borel, 1962)

ARION: a wild horse endowed with the power of speech, whose right feet were those of a man. ★Poseidon took the form of a stallion because Demeter had changed herself into a mare to escape him. From their inevitable union came the wild horse Arion. (SOURCE: Cotterell, 1986)

ARIOSTO, LUDOVICO (1474–1533): Italian poet and playwright. Ariosto was born in Reggio Emilio and studied at the University of Ferrara (1489–94). During the unrest of the 1490s, he took a court post, becoming the captain of the garrison at Canossa in 1502, then was given a position in the service of Cardinal Ippolito d'Este as a courtier, diplomat, and writer until 1517, when he began to work in the service of Alfonso d'Este, the Duke of Ferrara (1518–33). Ariosto's masterpiece, *Orlando Furioso*, was the culmination of a long tradition that began in the eleventh century with the Old French *La Chanson de Roland*. It continued in Italy and other countries as a series of extravagant romances. In the fifteenth century Luigi Pulci wrote his elaborate version of Roland's (Orlando's) adventures. Following Pulci came Matteo Boiardo, who added some Oriental elements in his *Orlando Innamorato*, but stopped writing when the French invaded Italy (1494). Some twenty years later Ariosto completed Boiardo's poem as a romantic epic by adding history, poeticizing the facts, but still keeping themes of beauty, chivalry, war, and nobility. His writing was not simply solemn; it had humor and suspense. Ariosto's other works include *capitoli* (burlesques), satires, and five comedies. His poetry was set by Charles Ives. PRINCIPAL WORKS:

Orlando Furioso, 1515, trans. as *Orlando Furioso*, 1591, as *Frenzy of Orlando*, trans. Barbara Reynolds, 2 vols., 1975. SELECTED READING: E. G. Gardner, *The King of the Court Poets, Ariosto*, 1906; Albert R. Ascoli, *Ariosto's Bitter Harmony: Crisis and Evasion in the Italian Renaissance*, 1987. (SOURCE: Vinson, Kirkpatrick (1) 1984)

ARKADY: *see* ★ARCADIA.

ARLECCHINO: *see* ★HARLEQUIN.

ARMAGEDDON: a biblical term, literally: *the hill of Megiddo*. The term "Armageddon" occurs in the Bible only once: in the last book of the New Testament, the Revelation of St. ★John 16.16. Revelation is an example of Apocalyptic literature, wherein the author claims to reveal in colorful and sometimes repugnant detail the events that will lead up to the final judgment of God upon humanity. John relates (Revelation 16.16–21) that it is at Armageddon that the conclusion of the final conflict between good and evil will begin:

> And he gathered them together into a place called in the Hebrew tongue Armageddon. And the seventh angel poured out his vial into the air, and there came a great voice out of the temple of heaven, from the throne, saying, It is done. And there were voices, and thunders, and lightnings; and there was a great earthquake, such as was not since men were upon the earth, so mighty an earthquake, and so great. And the great city was divided into three parts, and the cities of the nations fell; and great Babylon came in remembrance before God, to give unto her the cup of the wine of the fierceness of his wrath. And every island fled away, and the mountains were not found. And there fell upon men a great hail out of heaven, every stone about the weight of a talent and men blasphemed God because of the plague of the hail; for the plague thereof was exceeding great.

(SOURCE: Young, no date)

ARMIDA: a beautiful sorceress in Tasso's *Jerusalem Delivered*. Rinaldo fell in love with Armida and wasted his time in voluptuous pleasures. After Rinaldo escaped from her, Armida followed him, but, unable to lure him back, set fire to her palace, rushed into combat, and was slain. (SOURCE: Cooper, 1992)

ARNIM, ACHIM VON (1781–1831): German novelist. Arnim was born in Berlin, his family descended from ancient Prussian nobility. His father had served Frederick the Great as a diplomat and as the director of the royal opera. His mother died two weeks after the boy's birth, so Arnim was raised by his maternal grandmother. In 1798 he entered the University of Halle, where his interests were mathematics and natural science, his first publication being in physics. In 1800 he attended the University of Göttingen, where he met Clemens ★Brentano, with whom he would put together a renowned collection of folk lyrics, ★*Des Knaben Wunderhorn*. After *Des Knaben Wunderhorn* was published, Arnim lived in Heidelberg as a leader of the young ★Romantics. In 1809 he returned to Prussia and spent the rest of his life between his estate and Berlin, then the center of resistance to Napoleon. A number of dramas and poems were produced by Arnim, but his reputation rests on a few prose narratives, some historical novels, and short novels, which blended bizarre fantasies with realistic detail. The poems of Brentano and Arnim have been set by Mahler, Schumann, Strauss, and Louise Reichardt. SELECTED READING: H. R. Liedke, *Literary Criticism and Romantic Theory in the Work of Achim von Arnim*, 1937. (SOURCE: Kunitz, Colby, 1967)

ARNO: a famous river in northwest Italy. The Arno rises in the Apennine Mountains, winds to the Ligurian Sea for 150 miles, the cities of Florence and Pisa on its banks. The fertile Arno Valley is covered with vineyards and olive groves.

SONG	COMPOSER	POET
"Lass sie nur gehn"	Hugo Wolf	Paul Heyse, from the Italian

ARNOLD, MATTHEW (1822–1888): English poet, critic, educator. After being educated at Oxford, Matthew Arnold became an inspector of schools, traveling throughout England and observing social conditions that motivated his later work. Poetry was the writing he did in the early part of his life, part of "Dover Beach" having been written on his honeymoon. The problems of writing his subtle and varied poetry made him fear that his would be "wanting in moral grandeur" (Drabble, 2000). In his mature years he turned to prose, topics like education, literature, and the ills of society, becoming a leading critic of his day. His thesis was that England needed more intellectual curiosity, more ideas, a more European point of view, and that "a critic should be able to see the object as it itself really is" (Drabble, 2000). In his lifetime Arnold had little popularity compared to ★Tennyson and the ★Brownings. It was said that his range was narrow, but his "Dover Beach" was one of the finest poems of the Victorian era. After years of trying to prompt an improvement of English education, his fame was international and he delivered a series of lectures in the United States. His literary criticism was some of the most influential of the second half of the twentieth century. The poetry of Matthew Arnold has been set by Charles Ives and Samuel Barber. PRINCIPAL WORKS: *The Strayed Reveller and Other Poems*, 1849; *Poems*, Second Series, 1855; *Dover Beach*, 1867; *Poems*, ed. and annotated, K. Allott, 1965. (SOURCE: Drabble, 2000)

ARTHUR, KING: a romantic figure that probably has some historical basis as a general or chieftain in the fifth or sixth century. The battle of Mt. Badon, in which Arthur carried the cross on his shoulders, is placed in 518, and the battle of Camlon, in which Arthur fell, in 539. There is mention of Arthur in some ancient poems and in an ancient Welsh romance. He was said to die in 542 after a reign of twenty-two years. Guinivere was the daughter of his ally, Leodegan. Geoffrey of Monmouth (*Historia Regum Britanniae*) has him become king at the age of fifteen, defeat the heathens with his sword Excalibur, and conquer Scotland, Ireland, Iceland, and Orkney. Arthur resists paying tribute to the Roman emperor Lucius and declares war, leaving his nephew Modred in charge of the kingdom. About to enter Rome, Arthur is told that Modred has seized his wife and the kingdom. In the final battle Modred is killed and Arthur is mortally wounded. The Round Table was first mentioned by a

Norman writer, Wace. In his version Arthur is borne off to Avalon in a magic boat. Chrétien de Troyes and Marie de France developed the story in France, gradually introducing other characters—Merlin, Lancelot, and Tristram. In the later versions Arthur is superseded by the adventures of the various knights. Malory's version gives prominence to the exploits of the knights of the Round Table, the quest of the Holy Grail, the love of Lancelot and Guinevere, and the love of Tristram and Isoud (Tristan and Isolde). (SOURCE: Drabble, 2000)

"As ★Amoret and ★Thyrsis Lay": a song composed by Henry Purcell, set to the words of William ★Congreve for his first comedy, *The Old Batchelour*, produced in 1693. *See ★Old Batchelour, The* for details of the plot and placement of the songs.

ASCLEPIUS: the patron of medicine and son of ★Apollo. Not only did he cure the sick, but he recalled the dead to life. His authority over ★Hades is probably due to the circumstances of his birth. A lake ★nymph, Koronis, was impregnated by Apollo, but dared to take a second lover in the person of a human being. Apollo, furious at the infidelity, sent his sister Artemis to slay Koronis with a pestilence. As the fire was blazing around the nymph, Apollo, feeling compassion for his unborn son, removed him from the corpse. So did Asclepius come into this world. He was taught the art of healing by Chiron, the wisest of the Centaurs, beastlike monsters who dwelt in the woodlands. ★Zeus, fearing that humans might manage to escape death altogether, killed Asclepius, but, at Apollo's request, placed the medicine god among the stars. (SOURCE: Cotterell, 1986)

SONG	COMPOSER	POET
"Je n'ai plus que les os"	Francis Poulenc	Pierre de Ronsard

ASHBERY, JOHN (1927–): American poet, playwright, translator, editor. Ashbery grew up on a farm in upstate New York and was educated at Harvard, where he concentrated on English literature; Columbia University, where he received his M.A. in 1951; and New York University (1957–58), after which he spent a decade in Paris working and writing. His awards include Guggenheim Fellowships in 1967 and 1973, and, during 1976 when *Self-Portrait in a Convex Mirror* was published, the Pulitzer Prize, the National Book Award, and the National Book Critics Circle Award. One word that describes the poetry of John Ashbery is *difficult*: difficult to read, difficult to understand, perhaps even difficult to like. It is not that Ashbery uses complex structure or involved imagery or ★symbolism or obscure allusions. His work is difficult because it lacks these things. "The mystery in Ashbery's poetry is irreducible to any stylistic trick, and it will be exorcized by no amount of critical explanation or footnoting" (Greiner, 5, 1980). Critics, it has been said, are often annoyed by the randomness of Ashbery's verses. During Ashbery's years in Paris, he worked as a critic of modern art for various journals. He was interested in the music of Webern, Cage, and Busoni. Far from trying for a personal poetic voice, he maintains an almost anonymous voice. Yet he tries to avoid a romantic mode and rejects metaphorical complexity. Indeed, there is often no predictable shape to his poems. Ashbery was the first of the New York School (Frank ★O'Hara, Kenneth ★Koch, James Schuyler) to achieve recognition. The poetry of John Ashbery has been set by Ned Rorem.

PRINCIPAL WORKS: Poetry: *Song Trees*, 1956; *The Tennis Court Oath*, 1962; *Self-Portrait in a Convex Mirror*, 1975. Plays: *The Heroes*, 1952; *The Compromise*, 1955; *The Philosopher*, 1964. SELECTED READING: Susan M. Schultz, ed., *The Tribe of John: Ashbery and Contemporary Poetry*, 1995. (SOURCE: Greiner, 5, 1980)

ASTAROTH: the goddess of fertility and reproduction among Canaanites and Phoenicians. The Babylonians called her Ishtar (★Venus), the Greeks, ★Astarte, and John ★Milton referred to her as Ashtaroth. *See also* ★Astarte. (SOURCE: Guirand, 1968)

SONG	COMPOSER	POET
"Theodora"	Jan Sibelius	Bertel Grippenberg

ASTARTE: the ancient Syrian/Palestinian mother and fertility goddess, the consort and sister of Baal, the most active Canaanite god; also called Anat, Athirat, Athtart. The New Kingdom of Egypt imported this goddess as well as Ishtar of Mesopotamia and often confused the two. She was called "the queen of heaven" by the Hebrews, who worshiped her although she was the goddess of the Sidonians. Astarte was dangerous as well as beautiful. She wore the horns of the bull as mistress of horses and chariots, and the dove was an attribute of hers, according to the Phoenicians. In Milton's *Paradise Lost* Astarte's epithet is "queen of heaven, with crescent horns." Astarte is closely connected with the sea, as is the Greek ★Aphrodite. In the Old Testament her name was spelled as Ashtoreth, but the later Greek writers in Syria called her Astarte. As the Phoenician goddess of love, she was used by ★Byron in his "Manfred" and appears in Koechlin's "Songs of Bilitis." (SOURCE: Cotterell, 1986)

SONG	COMPOSER	POET
"Madrigal"	Gabriel Fauré	Edmond Haraucourt

ASTOLAT: the place where Lancelot meets Elaine. Astolat is a town mentioned in Arthurian romances, generally identified as Guilford in Surrey, England. Elaine is generally known as the Lily Maid of Astolat; Mallory (author of *Le Morte d'Arthur*) calls her the Fair Maid of Astolat, and ★Tennyson refers to her as the Lady of Shalott. (SOURCE: Cooper, 1992)

SONG	COMPOSER	POET
"Elaine"	John Duke	Edna St. Vincent Millay

ASTREA: the goddess of justice and innocence. During the Golden Age, this goddess dwelled on earth, but when sin began to prevail, she reluctantly left earth and was changed into the constellation Virgo. (SOURCE: Cooper, 1992)

SONG	COMPOSER	POET
1. "Ev'ry Dame Affects Good Fame"	Thomas Campion	Thomas Campion
2. "Since from My Dear"	Henry Purcell	P. Massinger, J. Fletcher

ASTYANAX: the young son of ★Hector and ★Andromache of Troy.

SONG	COMPOSER	POET
"Andromache's Farewell"	Samuel Barber	Euripides, *The Trojan Women*

ATLANTIS: according to an ancient myth, a large island in the Atlantic Ocean, said to have been a powerful kingdom before it was overwhelmed by the sea. Archeologists and scientists have more recently placed it in the Mediterranean Sea, at the center of the island of Santorini, which collapsed after drastic volcanic action and was submerged ca.1500 B.C.E. (SOURCE: Cooper, 1992)

"At Dawning": a song by Charles Wakefield Cadman, words by Cadman's friend and neighbor Mrs. Nelli Richmond Eberhart. Mrs. Eberhart had written the poem, put it away, and forgotten it for seventeen years. Resurrected one day to supply words for one of Cadman's melodies, the lyric and air were sold to a publisher for a flat sum of fifteen dollars. Opera singer Alessandro Boncé discovered it in a music store four years later. After Boncé sang it, John McCormack took it up and sang it everywhere. With its growing fame, "At Dawning" became a favorite as a wedding song, which it remains.

ATLAS: brother of ★Prometheus and father of the ★Pleiades, one of the ★Titans (according to ★Graves, 1960) or a king and a giant, but not a Titan (*Bulfinch*, 1978). The Titans ruled the world before ★Zeus rebelled against his father ★Chronos. Atlas led the resistance against Zeus with the result that he was condemned to carry the heavens on his shoulders until the end of time. Two stories from classical mythology involve Atlas. After killing Medusa, ★Perseus carried her head with him. On his journeys he met Atlas, who refused Perseus hospitality. In retaliation, Perseus showed Medusa's head to Atlas, which act transformed him into a mountain. In a second story, Prometheus advised ★Hercules, in one of his final labors, to send Atlas to gather the Golden Apples of ★Hesperides instead of going himself. Atlas agreed on the condition that Hercules take his place and bear the heavens on his shoulders. Hercules did so and Atlas gathered the apples but refused to resume his position. Hercules tricked the Titan into taking the heavens back on his shoulders for a short moment and then left with the Golden Apples. A book of maps is called an *atlas* because it holds the world. (SOURCES: Graves (1), 1960; Mayerson, 1971; *Bulfinch*, 1978)

SONG	COMPOSER	POET
"Der Atlas"	Franz Schubert	Heinrich Heine

ATREUS: son of Pelops, grandson of ★Tantalus, father of Agamemnon and ★Menaleus. Atreus's grandfather, Tantalus, had invited the gods to his home for dinner. He served them his son Pelops, who had been slaughtered. Atreus's wife, Aërope, was seduced by his brother Thyestes, who used her to steal the golden fleece that made him king of Mycenae. Learning of this, Atreus invited his brother to dinner and served him Thyestes's own son for the meal. Atreus then showed his brother the bones of his son. Looking for vengeance, Thyestes married Atreus's daughter Pelopia, who bore him a son, Aegisthus. Pelopia set Aegisthus out to die of exposure, but shepherds rescued and raised the boy. Atreus found Aegisthus, brought him home, and raised him as a son. When he learned that he was Thyestes's son, Aegisthus killed Atreus and made his real father king. Because the whole family was involved in mutual murder and betrayal for several generations, Atreus's name is linked in literature with the idea of being cursed. (SOURCES: Mayerson, 1971; Graves (2), 1960; Guirand, 1963; Murray, 1988)

SONG	COMPOSER	POET
1. "An die Leier"	Franz Schubert	tr. Franz von Bruchmann
2. "Misera, dove son?"	Wolfgang Amadeus Mozart	Pietro Metastasio

"At the River": a song from Aaron Copland's two collections, *Old American Songs*, composed of indigenous American folk material. The words and music of "At the River" are by the Reverend Robert Lowry, a Baptist minister. In 1864, on a very hot summer day, during an epidemic that swept through the city, Lowry contemplated two questions: "Shall we meet again? We are parting at the river of death. Shall we meet at the river of life?"

ATTIC: the Attic boy, Cephalos, beloved by ★Aurora (Morn), passionately fond of hunting; or generally used when referring to the country of Greece in early times; also, a form of Greek spoken in Athens during its period of literary eminence. Attic later became the common speech of the Greek-speaking East. Attic as a speech-style was a reaction against the formal and exaggerated diction fashionable in the first century B.C.E., originated by the great Athenian orators who aimed at dry, grammatically correct lucidity. (SOURCES: Cooper, 1992; Drabble, 2000)

SONG	COMPOSER	POET
"La Cigale"	Ernest Chausson	Charles Leconte de L'Isle

ATTIS: *see* ★ATYS.

ATYS, ATTIS: a young Phrygian fertility deity beloved by the great earth goddess ★Cybele, the wife of ★Chronos and mother of the gods of Olympus. Atys belongs to a general category with ★Adonis, Tammuz, Baal, and ★Osiris. When he fell in love with a mortal princess, Cybele drove him mad. In his frenzy he castrated himself. Violets sprang from his blood as he died. Three days later, Cybele caused his body to be resurrected. His followers mourned for three days while they sought for him. When they found him on the third day, there came a period of wild rejoicing. During his orgiastic rites, novitiates of his priesthood imitated his deeds by castrating themselves. (SOURCE: Kaster, 1964)

SONG	COMPOSER	POET
"Atys"	Franz Schubert	Johann Mayrhofer

AUBADE: a dawn song, from Provençal, *alba*; Ger., *Tagelied*. An *aubade* usually describes the regret of two lovers at the imminent separation that daybreak brings. The form flourished with the conventions of courtly love. (SOURCE: Drabble, 2000)

SONG	COMPOSER	POET
"Aubade"	Gabriel Fauré	Louis Pommez

AUDEN, W(YSTEN) H(UGH) (1907–1973): American poet, librettist, editor, translator, playwright. Auden, although born in York, England, became a naturalized American citizen in 1946, having immigrated to the United States in 1939 shortly beforeWorld War II after being educated at Oxford University. Married in 1935, he became a schoolmaster, also worked in film, and traveled extensively during the 1930s in Europe, Iceland, and China. In the United States he taught at the University of Michigan and at Swarthmore, Bryn Mawr, Bennington, Barnard, and Smith Colleges. Recipient of many awards including the Guggenheim Fellowship, he was Professor of Poetry at Oxford from 1956 to 1961. Underlying all Auden's poetry is a conflict between aristocratic disdain and a humble love for the things of this world, which accounts for the deliberate artificiality he employs. Auden, first studying geology and mining and thinking of becoming an engineer, held always to his belief that we locate ourselves in space, in a specific landscape to which we alter and adapt. W. H. Auden's poetry has been set by Daniel Pinkham, Benjamin Britten, Peter Dickinson, Lennox Berkeley, as well as many other composers both British and American. He wrote opera librettos for Britten, Stravinsky, Henze, and others; he collaborated with Chester Kallman as co-author and translator of opera librettos into English (*The Rake's Progress*, music by Stravinsky; *Elegy for Young Lovers*, music by Henze; *Die Basariden*, music by Henze; *Love's Labor Lost*, music by Nabokov; *The Magic Flute*, music by Mozart; *The Seven Deadly Sins of the Lower Middle Class*, music by Kurt Weill; *Don Giovanni*, music by Mozart; *Arcifanfarlo, King of Fools; or It's Always Too Late to Learn*, music by Dittersdorf; *The Rise and Fall of the City of Mahagonny* (Brecht), music by Weill). PRINCIPAL WORKS: Poetry: *Collected Shorter Poems, 1927–1957*, 1966; *Another Time*, 1940; *The Collected Poetry*, 1945; *Nones*, 1951, 1952; *The Shield of Achilles*, 1955; *Auden: A Selection by the Author*, 1958, as *Selected Poetry*, 1959; *Homage to Clio*, 1960; *About the House*, 1965; *Collected Poems*, ed. Edward Mendelson, 1991. Plays: *The Dog Beneath the Skin; or, Where is Francis?* with Christopher Isherwood, 1935; *The Ascent of F6*, with Christopher Isherwood, 1937. Opera Librettos: *Paul Bunyan*, music by Britten, 1941; *The Duchess of Malfi*, music by Britten, 1946; *The Play of Daniel* (narration only), edited with Noah Greenberg; *Moralities: Three Scenic Plays from Fables by Aesop*, music by Henze, 1966. SELECTED READING: *A Tribute*, ed. Stephen Spender, 1975; Frederick Buell, *Auden as a Social Poet*, 1973; S. Hynes, *The Auden Generation*, 1976; Harold Bloom, ed., *W. H. Auden: Modern Critical Views*, 1989. (SOURCES: Unger, 1, 1974; Scott-Kilvert, 1, 1997; Vinson, 1979)

AUGENZELT: (Ger.), literally, *eye on the canopy of heaven*. In the song "Du bist die Ruh," composed by Franz Schubert to a poem by ★Rückert. *Augenzelt* is one of Rückert's orientalisms, a word he invented from *Augen* (eye) and *zelt* (pavilion, vault, or canopy of heaven). In the music it is set as a slow climbing of the scale up to the highest note, A♭, in the high key.

AURAY: an ancient French town in ★Brittany, located some seventy kilometers off the Atlantic Coast on the banks of the Loch River.

SONG	COMPOSER	POET
"Berceuse"	Francis Poulenc	Max Jacob

AURENG-ZEBE: a tragedy written by John ★Dryden containing one song by Henry Purcell. This rhymed play is based on true events in seventeenth-century India, in which Mogul Aureng-Zebe wrested the empire of India from his father and brothers. He is a figure of rationality, virtue, and patience. "I See She Flies Me," composed in Purcell's design that he adopted for lyrics that have few interior contrasts, is said to have been sung, but a place in the plot has not been found where it would not disturb the dramatic flow. Perhaps it was sung during the interval after act 1. It was intended for a soprano, but the words express the sentiments of a man refused. It might have been intended for Indamora to sing to Aureng-Zebe at the end of act 1. There it reflects Aureng-Zebe's feelings at Indamora's cool dismissal. Act 1 ends with his being rejected by his father, the emperor, in the battle of the other sons to gain the throne by force. The reason for the king's rejection is his desire for Indamora, the promised bride of Aureng-Zebe. (SOURCE: Price, 1984)

AURORA (Lat.), AURORE (Fr.): Latin name for Eos, the Greek goddess of the dawn. Aurora, called "rosy-fingered" by Homer, sets out before the sun to proclaim the coming of day. Her tears are the morning dew. (SOURCE: Cooper, 1992)

SONG	COMPOSER	POET
1. "When lo! By Breake of Morning"	Thomas Morley	anonymous
2. "When Laura Smiles"	Phillip Rosseter	Thomas Campion
3. "Aurore"	Gabriel Fauré	Armand Silvestre
4. "Memnon"	Franz Schubert	Johann Mayrhofer

AVALON: in Celtic legend an idyllic place, the island paradise to which King ★Arthur and other heroes were taken after death. In Medieval romantic poetry, Avalon is the region where the fairy, Fata Morgana (Morgan le Fay) held court.

SONG	COMPOSER	POET
"Avalon"	Mary Howe	Nancy Byrd Turner

AVE MARIA: *Hail, Mary,* a Catholic prayer written in Latin, addressed to the ★Virgin Mary, the first two words of the angel's salutation to Mary (Luke 1.28). As the practice of venerating the saints developed in the Catholic Church, the adoration of the Virgin Mary as the "Mother of God" (in Greek, *Theo Teknon,* Θεου Τεκνον) and the prayer "Ave Maria" became extremely popular. The text of the "Ave Maria" prayer, borrowing from Luke, begins: "Hail Mary, full of grace, the Lord is with you. Blessed are you among women and the fruit of your womb, Jesus. Pray for us sinners now and at the hour of our death." Only the Gospel according to Luke contains the story of the conversation between Mary and the angel ★Gabriel, who announced the coming event to the young girl (Luke 1.26–38). According to the Revised Standard Version of the Bible, the angel said: "Hail, O favored one, the Lord is with you! . . . Do not be afraid, Mary, for you have found favor with God. And behold, you will conceive in your womb and bear a son, and you shall call his name Jesus." The text of the "Ave Maria" has been set too many times to enumerate all, but best known are these settings: an aria by Verdi in *Otello,* a song by Gounod, using the first prelude from Bach's *Well Tempered Clavier* as a basis, and, most well known of all, the Schubert song. Singers will have noticed that the traditional Latin text does not scan in the Schubert. Schubert's setting is actually not the prayer, but lines from the end of canto

3 of Sir Walter Scott's *The Lady of the Lake* as translated by Adam Storck. The song with German text is also known as "Ellens Gesang III" (D839).

SONG	COMPOSER	POET
1. "Ave Maria"	Franz Schubert	Sir Walter Scott
2. "Ave Maria"	Franz Abt	St. Luke
3. "Ave Maria"	Charles Gounod/J. S. Bach	St. Luke

AVENARIUS, FERDINAND (1856–1923): German poet. Avenarius was an undistinguished but prolific poet. He acted as editor of an important anthology of poetry, *Handbuch der deutscher Lyrik*, 1903, and founded a journal devoted to educating the public's literary taste, *Der Kunstwart*, 1887. Avenarius wrote a substitute to part 2 of Goethe's *Faust,* titled *Faust, Ein Spiel*, 1919. The poetry of Ferdinand Avenarius was set by Anton Webern. (SOURCE: Garland, 1976)

AVIGNON: a city in southeastern France, the capital of the department of Vaucluse, situated on the left bank of the Rhône River. When the Romans occupied Southern Gaul, Avignon became a thriving city, but under its German invaders it declined in the fifth and sixth centuries. In 1226 Louis VIII destroyed the city as punishment for having supported a heretical tribe. Pope Clement V made Avignon his residence in 1309. From then to 1337 every pope resided there, the center of western Christendom. In 1348 Pope Clement VI purchased Avignon for the church. During the Great Schism (1378–1417), it was the residence of two popes. In 1791 the city was annexed to France once again. On a high rocky plateau called Rocher des Doms stands a twelfth-century Romanesque cathedral, essentially a stone fortress designed for the protection of the popes.

ÁVILA: a Spanish medieval city 68 miles northwest of Madrid along the Adaja River on the road to ★Salamanca. The city has a medieval appearance, and its buildings date to the twelfth century. The city walls, the ramparts of Ávila, the oldest and best preserved in Spain, ten feet thick and thirty-three feet high on average, were built during the last years of the eleventh century and are still intact, as are the eighty-eight cylindrical towers and bastions and the nine gateways to the town. Ávila remained a Christian stronghold and kept the Moors at bay. The apse of the cathedral was incorporated into the walls during the twelfth century, and its sculptures date from the thirteenth century to the Renaissance. St. ★Teresa of Ávila is the most important figure of their history.

SONG	COMPOSER	POET
1. "Donde estan estas serranas"	Enriquez de Valderrábano	unknown
2. "Let Nothing Disturb Thee"	David Diamond	Saint Teresa of Ávila

AVRILLÉ: a French city located near the Atlantic Ocean, south of Nantes and northwest of La Rochelle.

SONG	COMPOSER	POET
"The Road to Avrillé"	Sven Lekberg	Edna St. Vincent Millay

"Away, My Elves": an air composed by Henry Purcell to a text written by Elkanah ★Settle for his work *The Fairie-Queene*, produced in 1692 and 1693. For plot details and song placement, *see* ★*Fairie-Queene, The*.

AYIO CONSTANNDINA: *see* ★CONSTANTINE, SAINT.

AYRE: a type of song popular in England during the late sixteenth and early seventeenth centuries, a solo song accompanied by lute, bass lute (theorbo), or other instrument.

B ✍

BABYLON: a famous city of the ancient world, the capital of ancient Babylonia, located 60 miles south of modern Baghdad. Babylon means *gate of God*, and the biblical word for Babylon was *Babel*. The temples and palaces of Babylon were among the most splendid buildings of the ancient world. The ★Euphrates River flowed through the city, which was built in a square with two sets of walls that were ten and twelve feet thick, respectively. A moat and fields for growing, good in the case of a siege, were situated between the walls. The ★hanging gardens comprised part of one of Nebuchadnezzar's palaces. Babylon was destroyed by the Assyrians in 689 B.C.E. ★Belshazzar was the ruler when the city was rebuilt. ★Alexander the Great entered Babylon in 331 B.C.E. (SOURCE: *Americana*, 2002)

SONG	COMPOSER	POET
1. "Belsazar"	Robert Schumann	Heinrich Heine
2. "By the Waters of Babylon"	Antonín Dvořák	Bible text
3. "The City in the Sea"	Richard Faith	Edgar Allen Poe
4. "As by the Streams of Babylon"	Thomas Campion	anonymous

BAÇA, BAZA: a city of the Sierra Nevada in the southeast corner of the Andalusia province of Spain, north of the Gulf of Almería, 50 miles northeast of ★Granada.

SONG	COMPOSER	POET
"Sobre Baça estaba el Rey"	Joaquín Rodrigo	unknown

BACCHELLI, RICCARDO (1891–1985): Italian novelist and poet. Bacchelli is one of the few Italian writers with a varied and large output. Born to a liberal and wealthy Bologna family, he studied literature at the University of Bologna with ★Pascoli but took no degree. At the start of World War I, during which he served as an artillery officer, he had already published his first novel (1911) and was regularly writing for journals. Bacchelli was among the founders of *La Ronda*, a Roman literary magazine. Having written and published during the Fascist period, he became recognized as a major literary personage and was inducted into the Accademia d'Italia (1941). Probably most admired for his historical novels, Bacchelli mixed facts and inventive details. In his other writing he combined the popular with the literary and the erudite. Bacchelli's most famous work was a three-volume best-seller, *Il molino del Po.* He wrote many novelle, fables, poems, and plays, as well as travel books, and critical essays on nineteenth-century Italian literature and operas. The verse of Riccardo Bacchelli was set by G. F. Ghedini. PRINCIPAL WORKS: *Il filo meraviglioso di Lodovico Clò*, 1911; *Lo sa il tonno*, 1923; *Il diavolo al Pontelungo*, 1927; *Il molino del Po*, 3 vols., 1938–40. (SOURCE: Hainsworth, Robbey, 2002)

BACCHUS: *see* ★DIONYSUS.

BACHELIER DE SALAMANQUE, LE: the final novel of Alain René Lesage. It tells of the adventures of a young Spanish bachelor of arts, Don Chérubin de la Ronda. The novel is a cynical satire of the ruling classes, but although the locale of the story is Spanish, the plot is an attack against the intrigues of French society. The story prompted poet René Chalupt to write a poem of the same title on the subject.

SONG	COMPOSER	POET
"Le Bachelier de Salamanque"	Albert Roussel	René Chalupt

BAÏF, JEAN ANTOINE DE (1532–1589): French poet. Jean de Baïf was born in Venice of an Italian mother and a French father who was a humanist, translator of ★Euripides and ★Sophocles, and a diplomat, the ambassador of Francis I to Venice. Baïf received an excellent education, and at school met ★Ronsard, who taught versification to him. When his father died, Baïf inherited an income sufficient to allow him to study and write. Little is known of his personal life, but, living in Paris, Baïf became an active member of ★Pléiade, to which he contributed a reform of metrics and prosody. After his first poems appeared (1551), he published a series of ★sonnet cycles imitative of ★Petrarch. Because his talents were inventive but not creative, Baïf is best remembered as a scholar and reformer of French verse, a champion of classical meters, and the inventor of a system of phonetic spelling. Baïf's aim was to fuse the arts of music and poetry in the Greek manner, and to that end he founded the Academy of Poetry and of Music. The great amount of poetry written in his lifetime is not considered to be of merit today. One explanation for the sharp decline of Baïf's reputation in the seventeenth century is the belief of some that the faults of that particular school of writing were his: a dependence upon models, pretension, and artificiality. The verse of Jean de Baïf was set by Charles Gounod. PRINCIPAL WORKS: *Poésies choisies*, ed. L. Becq de Fouquières, 1874; *Chanticleer: A Study of the French Muse*, trans. J. G. Legge, 1936. SELECTED READING: George Wyndham, *Ronsard and the Pléiade*, 1906. (SOURCE: Kunitz, Colby, 1967)

"Bailey Beareth the Bell Away": a song by Peter Warlock set to an anonymous text, printed in *Early English Lyrics*. At the time of making the setting, Warlock later confessed, he did not have the faintest idea of what it was all about. He was bewitched by the sound of the words.

BAIRNS: (Scot.), *children.*

BALLAD (Eng.), BALLADE (Fr.): originally a song intended to be an accompaniment to a dance, now a light, simple song of any kind, frequently including a refrain, stock descriptive phrases, and simple, economical dialogue. The French poetic form called *ballade* refers to a poem consisting of one or more triplets or, later, eight-line stanzas, each ending with the same line as a refrain, usually addressed to a prince or his substitute. This form was dominant in fourteenth- and fifteenth-century French poetry, of which one of the great masters was François ★Villon. The form was revived in late nineteenth-century England in the work of Algernon Swinburne, William ★Henley, and Henry Dobson.

SONG	COMPOSER	POET
1. "Trois ballades de François Villon"	Claude Debussy	François Villon
2. "Le Presents"	Gabriel Fauré	Jean Villiers de l'Isle-Adam
3. "Ballade"	Frederick Jacobi	Geoffrey Chaucer

BALMONT, KONSTANTIN (1867–1942): Russian poet, writer, and translator. Balmont came from a provincial family in a class just below the nobility. Having been expelled from Moscow University for leading student demonstrations, he decided early to become a professional writer. He had traveled on five continents, seldom living in Russia before 1920, when he left Russia forever to live in Brittany. The exotic themes of his poetry were owed to his knowledge of some forty languages, including Spanish and Mexican, Indian, Egyptian, and Scandinavian. Yet English poetry was his favorite, ★Shelley above all. He masterfully translated ★Blake, ★Byron, ★Tennyson, ★Wilde, ★Whitman, and ★Poe as well. Balmont was basically an improviser, believing in inspiration, refusing to polish his work. He was at his best in poems that dealt with the elements—fire, wind, and water, and solar, lunar, and stellar events. In his religious poetry is a theme of an earthbound soul yearning for heaven. Without neglecting the somber and menacing, he leaned toward the merry more than the melancholy, taking inspiration and creative cues from the European ★Symbolist movement. He wrote poetry until the end of his life, without a decline in his skills, and challenged the concepts and techniques of an earlier period. Balmont was known as the "★Orpheus of the ★Symbolist movement" because of his highly musical verses. The poetry of Konstantin Balmont was set by Gretchaninoff, Rachmaninoff, Stravinsky, Prokofiev, and Rimsky-Korsakov. WORKS: *Pod severnym nebom* [Under Northern Skies], 1894; *Goryashchiye zdaniya* [Flaming Buildings], 1900; *Budim kak solntse* [Let us be like the Sun], 1903; *Tolko lyubov* [Love Alone], 1903; *Liturgis krasoty* [The Liturgy of Beauty], 1905. SELECTED READING: S. Althaus-Schönbucher, *Konstantin Dmitrievich Balmont*, 1975. (SOURCE: Terras, 1991)

BALOU: (Scot.), *a lullaby.*

SONG	COMPOSER	POET
"The Highland Balou"	Benjamin Britten	Robert Burns

BANALITÉS: a song cycle (1940) by Francis Poulenc to *surrealistic poems by *Apollinaire. The cycle is a cryptic expression of Apollinaire's and Poulenc's anguish at the fate suffered by France in the year of the Nazis' invasion and conquest.

BANDERILLA: a small dart that picadors plunge into the neck and shoulders of the bull before the *toreador begins his tournée.

SONG	COMPOSER	POET
"El toro"	Roberto Gerhard	anonymous

BANVILLE, THÉODORE DE (1823–1891): French poet, critic, and playwright. A handsome child, son of a naval officer, Théodore de Banville had a happy childhood, adored both his parents, and was to lead a serene life. He was still a law student when his first volume of poetry, *Les Cariatides*, appearing in 1842, drew immediate approval. His second book of verse, *Les Stalactites* (1846), was also a product of nineteenth-century *Romanticism, reflecting *Gautier, *Musset, and *Hugo. In 1857, however, he published *Odes Funambulesque* under a penname. These whimsical satires, named for the *funambule* or rope dancer, marked the beginning of his original verse, which was without much intellectual content but spoke of joy, beauty, and love. Socially popular, admired and respected as a poet, and influential in the literary movements of his day, Banville was made a Chevalier of the Legion of Honor in 1858. In *d'Orléans, *Villon, and *Marot he found the precise metrical and rhyming effects in which he delighted. Together with *Baudelaire and *Leconte de L'Isle, Banville was a founder of the *Parnassian movement. His plays were in the repertory of the Comédie Française, and he worked at reviving the poetry of the French Renaissance, which work influenced English as well as French poets. Banville died one day after his sixty-eighth birthday, neglected by the public but respected by many poets and men of letters, including Englishmen such as Algernon Swinburne, William Morris, and Dante Gabriel *Rossetti. Banville's poetry was set by Camille Saint-Saëns, Claude Debussy, and Charles Koechlin. PRINCIPAL WORKS: *Les Cariatides*, 1842; *Les Stalactites*, 1846; *Odes Funambulesque*, 1857. SELECTED READING: Anatole France, *Life and Letters*, 4th Series, 1925. (SOURCE: Kunitz, Colby, 1967)

BARBIER, JULES (1822–1901): French poet and librettist. Barbier is generally associated with Michel Carré, the pair being the talented writers who supplied Gounod with most of his opera libretti. Barbier's poetry was set in songs by Bizet, Gounod, and Massenet, and the poet was one of the eulogists for Georges Bizet's funeral.

BARBUSSE, HENRI (1873–1935): French poet, novelist, essayist. Barbusse was born in Paris, his father a journalist and man of letters. As a youth Barbusse was first influenced by Zola, then took Catulle *Mendès as his poetic model. His attachment to *Symbolist circles waned eventually, but he did contribute poetry to literary periodicals. Anatole France, *Maeterlinck, and *Mendès admired his novel *L'Enfer* (1908). Working as a literary editor in a large publishing house, he undertook a pacifist role when it was believed that World War I could be avoided. Although he was exempted because of tuberculosis, he insisted on being drafted, served as a private, and was awarded many military citations. His novel *Le Feu: Journal d'une esconade*, a strong indictment of war, won many prizes and was translated into fifty languages. After the war Barbusse became a leader in international pacifist circles, joined the Communist Party, glorified Stalin in his later books, and died on a trip to the Soviet Union. The eloquence of his writing is derived from its basic simplicity. The poetry of Henri Barbusse was set by Louis Aubert. PRINCIPAL WORKS: Novels: *L'Enfer*, 1908, translated as Hell, 1995; *Le Feu: Journal d'une esconade*, 1916. (SOURCE: Serafin, 1999)

BARCAROLE, BARKAROLE (Ger.): a gondolier's song or a song of that type.

SONG	COMPOSER	POET
1. "A Clymène"	Gabriel Fauré	Paul Verlaine
2. "Barkarole"	Joseph Marx, Richard Strauss	Adolf von Schack

BARD: among the ancient Celtic peoples, a poet, whose function it was to celebrate the heroes, victories, or laws of the nation. In modern usage, by extension, the term came to mean any poet, although it has been applied to specific poets, notably *Shakespeare and *Milton.

BARTAS, SALUSTE DU (1544–1590): a Gascon gentleman, who, after a studious youth, took up arms in the service of Henri of Navarre in 1558. Du Bartas was not only a country squire but also an important Protestant poet whose religious verse is still remembered. Arthur Honegger set some *villanelles of Pierre Bédat de Moniaur in which du Bartas is mentioned.

BASALT: any dark, non-porphyritic rock without luster, as Ethiopian black marble.

SONG	COMPOSER	POET
"La Vie antérieure"	Henri Duparc	Charles Baudelaire

BASIL, SAINT, SAN BASILIO (It.) (ca.330–379): Greek saint. St. Basil the Great was the bishop of *Caesarea in Cappadocia, a doctor of the church, and one of the Four Fathers of the Greek Church, whose revision of the liturgy the Byzantine rite sometimes used. In the Greek verse of this song, St. Basil's appearance clearly awes the child observing, who does not understand St. Basil's use of the word *maestro* to indicate *God*, but believes it to mean *teacher*, its literal meaning. Hence the mention of the *abbiccì*, the alphabet.

SONG	COMPOSER	POET
"San Basilio"	Ildebrando Pizzetti	Greek folk verse, trans. Tommaseo

BATHSHEBA: wife of *David, the king of Israel, mother of *Solomon. One day David happened to see Bathsheba, at that time the wife of Uriah, one of his soldiers, bathing on the roof of her house. They began an illicit relationship that resulted in Bathsheba's pregnancy. David attempted to hide his guilt by urging Uriah to go home and sleep with his wife. When Uriah refused, David sent him to the front to be killed. After a mourning period, David and Bathsheba were married and she delivered a son. The prophet Nathan confronted David with his misdeeds and told him he would be punished by the death of his son. David and Bathsheba continued as man and wife, and their next son *Solomon was favored by God. (SOURCE: Metzger, Murphy, 1994)

SONG	COMPOSER	POET
"Bethsabe Bathing (Bathsheba)"	William Bergsma	George Peele

BAUDELAIRE, CHARLES (PIERRE) (1821–1867): French poet, critic, essayist, translator. Charles Baudelaire was born in Paris and educated at boarding schools in Lyons and Paris, finally studying law at the University of Paris. After graduating, he was able to live on the inheritance from his father. The publication of his major work, *Les Fleurs du mal*, led to a trial for indecency, after which the six poems were suppressed. Virtually ignored in his own time, he is today considered one of the greats of the nineteenth century. He championed the work of Edgar Allen *Poe with a five-volume translation of the American's works. Baudelaire's essays on art and literature and his famous article on Wagner make him one of the most important critics of his time. Baudelaire believed that the goal of art was beauty and that beauty could be purified by art. "'You have given me your mud and I have turned it into gold,' he said to Paris" (Vinson, Kirkpatrick, 1984). In his use of dreams, myths, and fantasies, Baudelaire's work foreshadowed *surrealism. Yet he was able to treat reality with poetic enhancement and preferred his beauty combined with melancholy. His poetry never lost its musical sonorities: "subtle and suggestive rhythms, frequent use of monologue or dialogue to achieve a dramatic effect, and a mingling of the grand manner with a quiet, subdued and conversational tone" (Vinson, Kirkpatrick, 1984). The verse of Charles Baudelaire has been set by Debussy, Fauré, Berg, Duparc, Gretchaninoff, Henri Sauguet, Gustave Charpentier, Déodat de Séverac, and Charles Loeffler. PRINCIPAL WORKS: Poetry: *Les Fleurs du mal*, revised ed. 1868, trans. Richard Howard, 1982; *Petits poèmes en prose*, 1869. Essays: *Richard Wagner et Tannhäuser à Paris*, 1861; *The Painter of Modern Life and Other Essays*, ed. J. Mayne, 1964. SELECTED READING: Lois Boe Hyslop, *Baudelaire, Man of His Time*, 1980; F. W. J. Hemmings, *Baudelaire the Damned: A Biography*, 1982; Susan Blood, *Baudelaire and the Aesthetics of Bad Faith*, 1997. (SOURCE: Vinson, Kirkpatrick (1), 1984)

BAUERNFELD, EDUARD VON (1802–1890): Austrian poet, critic, and playwright, translator of *Shakespeare and Dickens. Bauernfeld was born out of wedlock, but his father, a doctor, took a special interest in his child's training in philosophy and law at Vienna University. By 1825 he had become one of the editors of the *Shakespeare-Ausgabe* in Vienna, for which he translated and co-translated eight Shakespeare plays. He entered the civil service, albeit reluctantly, working as an official in the Lottery Office (1826–48), living on his pension and the proceeds from his plays when he retired. In his old age he was celebrated as the "symbol of an earlier Vienna," probably because of his lightness and wit in the Viennese tradition. His published reminiscences are a valuable resource, and he was one of the editors of the 1825 German edition of Shakespeare. Bauernfeld and Schubert had met in

1822, but it was not until they were introduced in 1825 by the artist Moritz von Schwind that they became close friends. Schwind, Bauernfeld, and Schubert were constant companions, often staying out late in the pubs and coffeehouses of Vienna. Two years before his death Schubert worked on an opera libretto by Bauernfeld, only to have the libretto banned by the censor. Bauernfeld persuaded Schubert to produce the first and only concert comprising solely his own music. The concert, held on March 26, 1828, the first anniversary of Beethoven's death, was ignored by the "musical world." Before Schubert's death, Bauernfeld was among the last of his friends to visit him on November 17, 1828. Franz Schubert set four poems by Bauernfeld, including "An Silvia." PRINCIPAL WORKS: *Gesammelte Schriften*, 12 vols., 1871–73. SELECTED READING: A. Dressler, *Eduard von Bauernfeld*, 1927. (SOURCES: Garland, 1976; Clive, 1997; Fischer-Dieskau, 1987)

BAUMBERG, GABRIELE VON (1766–1839): Austrian poet. Baumberg is one of Schubert's more obscure poets, whose poetry was praised by ★Goethe. The Viennese called her "Sappho." The daughter of a high government official, Baumberg was born in Vienna. Her father, a well-educated man with interests in the arts, was her first teacher. He introduced his daughter to the works of Virgil, ★Goethe, and ★Schiller and encouraged her literary efforts, resulting in her first poetry publication in 1800. In 1805 the Hungarian poet Johann Batsányi became her husband in a marriage whose effects on Baumberg were disastrous. While pretending to admire and support her, Batsányi was in fact jealous and highly critical of her work. He forced her to rewrite much of her earlier work and tried to make her write in a style foreign to her nature. In addition, Batsányi was a radical. He was the translator of the plea that Napoleon made to the Hungarians when he stormed Vienna: to revolt against Austrian rule. Batsányi fled Vienna and eventually settled in Paris with a pension given him by Napoleon. In 1809 Baumberg followed her husband to Paris. However, after Napoleon's defeat Batsányi was imprisoned as an enemy of the state. In the end he and his wife were exiled to Linz, where they spent the rest of their lives. After trying unsuccessfully to set a Baumberg poem in 1809 or 1810, Schubert returned to her poetry in 1815 and set five additional songs. Mozart set her "Als Luise die Briefe." (SOURCES: Fischer-Dieskau, 1987; Reed, 1997; Youens, 1996)

BAWBEE: (Scot.), *half-penny.*

BAWK: (Scot.), *a strip of untilled land; a bat.*

SONG	COMPOSER	POET
"My Early Walk"	Benjamin Britten	Robert Burns

BAY: several species of small trees and shrubs with stiff leaves and small fragrant, cherrylike, purple, edible seeds, widely cultivated in the United States and Europe. The sweet bay is the laurel referred to by poets and the tree used in crowning heroes in ancient times. (SOURCE: *Americana*, 2003)

SONG	COMPOSER	POET
"L'Échelonnement des Haies"	Claude Debussy	Paul Verlaine

BAYADERE: an Indian professional dancing girl, employed for religious dances or private amusement. The word is a corruption of the Portuguese *bailadeira*, a female dancer. An Indian legend is part of the Schubert song, "Du Gott und die Bayadere," in which the god, Mahadiva, bestows himself on an outcast girl in one of his incarnations.

BAYARD: a horse of incredible swiftness given by Charlemagne to the four sons of Aymon. If only one son mounted, the horse was of ordinary size. If all four mounted, the horse's body became elongated to the required length. Thus, the name is used to describe any valuable or wonderful horse. (SOURCE: Cooper, 1992)

BAZA: *see* ★BAÇA.

BEADLE: the messenger or announcer for a court of law; a parish official whose job is to keep order in church, to punish minor offenses, and to announce vestry meetings; a university official who carries a mace as he or she leads the public processions of the university. (SOURCE: *OED*, 1989)

SONG	COMPOSER	POET
"Chanson du clair tamis"	Francis Poulenc	Maurice Fombeure

BEAUMONT, FRANCIS (1584–1616): English poet and dramatist, buried in Westminster Abbey. Born in Leicestershire and educated at Oxford, Beaumont is best known for his theatrical collaborations with John ★Fletcher (1606–1613). ★Dryden said of them, "Both had natural gifts improved by study" (Drabble, 2000). Ben ★Jonson often submitted his plays to Beaumont for criticism. By the late seventeenth century informed opinion attributed the tragic scenes of their collaborative efforts to Beaumont and the comic scenes to Fletcher. There is some confusion as to whether some texts that Purcell set were by Fletcher or Beaumont. (SOURCE: Drabble, 2000)

BEAUTY AND THE BEAST: the heroine and hero of a fairy tale by Mme. Villeneuve. Beauty saves the life of her father by consenting to live with the Beast. Beauty's love breaks the spell that binds the Beast. He becomes again a handsome prince, and they marry.

BECQUER, GUSTAVO ADOLFO (1836–1870): Spanish poet. Born in Seville, Becquer was the son of a local painter, orphaned from childhood. His godmother took charge of his education after he failed as a student in his uncle's painting studio. At eighteen Becquer went to Madrid in search of literary glory. After working as a translator and a journalist, he held some official posts before he died, which happened just as his name began to be known as a poet. Most of his works were published posthumously in two volumes (1871). Becquer's seventy-nine short lyrics are still among Spain's greatest lyric poems. Writing with an extraordinary economy of medium and a "natural," unadorned style, Becquer used assonance, not rhyme, words of everyday use, and metaphors of seeming simplicity. Concerned with the nature of poetry, he saw it as a feeble expression of an ideal existing outside ordinary life. His work on the problems of communication made him an important influence on Spanish poets of the twentieth century. The verses of Becquer were set by Isaac

Albéniz, Manuel de Falla, Joaquín Turina, and Federico Mompou. PRINCIPAL WORKS: *Rimas*, ed. J. P. Díaz, 1963; *Poems*, tr. H. M. Carnes, 1891; *Tales and Poems of Gustavo Adolfo Becquer*, tr. H. F. W. Olmstead, 1907; *Twenty Poems*, tr. R. Croft-Cooke, 1927. SELECTED READING: E. L. King, *Gustavo Adolfo Becquer: From Painter to Poet*, 1953. (SOURCE: Kunitz, Colby, 1967)

BEDDOES, THOMAS LOVELL (1803–1849): English poet. Son of Dr. Thomas Beddoes, a friend and doctor to ★Coleridge and ★Wordsworth, the young Beddoes was educated at Oxford and settled in Zurich, Switzerland in 1835. Beddoes, obsessed with the macabre, the supernatural, and body decay, committed suicide in Basel. Poet Arthur ★Symons compared Beddoes to ★Baudelaire and ★Poe. Best known now for his shorter pieces, his verse has been set by Gordon Binkerd, Robert Fairfax Birch, John Ireland, Lennox Berkeley, and Bainbridge Crist. PRINCIPAL WORK: *Death's Jest Book*, 1850. SELECTED READING: James R. Thompson, *Thomas Lovell Beddoes*, 1985. (SOURCE: Drabble, 2000)

BEDEAU: *see* ★BEADLE.

BEDLAM: a corruption of the word Bethlehem, the Hospital of St. Mary of Bethlehem in London. St. Mary's was founded as a priory in 1247 and became a hospital in 1330. By 1402 it was called a hospital for lunatics. From Bedlam came expressions such as *Tom o' Bedlam* and *Bess o' Bedlam*, terms for wandering lunatics or beggars posing as lunatics. Elizabeth Bishop's poem was based on a visit to Ezra Pound when he was incarcerated there. Later her mother had to be confined there also. (SOURCE: Drabble, 2000)

SONG	COMPOSER	POET
1. "Bess o' Bedlam"	Henry Purcell	anonymous
2. "Visits to St. Elizabeth's"	Ned Rorem	Elizabeth Bishop

BEELZEBUB: a biblical character, one of the rebellious angels, next to Satan in importance, lit., *the Lord of the Flies*. The name was spelled Baalzebub in the Old Testament, where he is the god of the enemies of Israel, the Philistines. In the Gospels of Matthew, Mark, and Luke, he is promoted to the "prince of demons" (Matt. 12.24). In all three synoptic Gospels, the Pharisees credit Jesus' power over evil spirits and demons to an agreement between him and Beelzebub (Matthew 12, Mark 3, and Luke 11). In book 1 of *Paradise Lost*, while describing Satan's first thoughts after being ejected from Heaven by God, ★Milton says that Beelzebub was "next in power and next in crime" to Satan. In book 2 of *Paradise Lost* we read that none of the rebellious angels but Satan ranked above Beelzebub, that his aspect was grave, that deliberation marked his face, and that he was majestic though in ruin, with Atlantean shoulders. Beelzebub suggests to the other fallen angels that, since they have been cast into Hell and cannot return to conquer Heaven, perhaps they should try to conquer a new creation, Earth, which is inhabited by "some new Race call'd Men." (SOURCES: King James Version of the Holy Bible, 1611; Kerrigan, 1983)

BEENY SISTERS: two rocks off the coast of Cornwall in England, associated with the poet Thomas ★Hardy's courtship of Emma Gifford.

"Behold the Man": a dialogue composed by Henry Purcell, set to words written by Thomas ★D'Urfey for his play *The Richmond Heiress*, produced in 1693. For plot details and placement of the songs, *see ★Richmond Heiress, The.*

BELIAL: the Hebrew personification of lawlessness, thus one of the names for the devil.

BELLAGIO: a beautiful Italian town on the east shore of Lake Como.

SONG	COMPOSER	POET
"Villa Serbelloni, Bellagio"	Wintter Watts	Sara Teasdale

BELLE DAME SANS MERCI, LA: a beautiful woman celebrated in ★Keats's poem, in which she enthralls a knight-at-arms as she has enthralled kings and princes before him, but cruelly leaves him in the end.

SONG	COMPOSER	POET
"La Belle Dame sans merci"	Paul Hindemith	John Keats

BELLOC, (JOSEPH) HILAIRE (PIERRE) (1870–1953): British poet, journalist, editor, columnist, literary critic, historian, travel writer, biographer, member of Parliament. Hilaire Belloc was born near Paris and became a naturalized British subject in 1902. Educated at Oxford, he served in the French army before teaching at the University of Glasgow. Belloc was a crusader who wrote polemical works of historical biography, essays, and tracts laden with anti-modern opinions. A militant Catholic, he was an anti-Protestant, anti-socialist, radical, republican revolutionary, whose years as a liberal in Parliament gave him a distaste for British political life. His great ally in journalism and radicalism, Catholicism, and even light verse, was G. K. Chesterton. Belloc's charm and distinct personality exhibit themselves in his travel writing, and he is best remembered for his light verse. Hilaire Belloc's poetry has been set by Peter Warlock, Benjamin Britten, Donald Martino, Vincent Persichetti, Anthony Milner, and Richard Hageman. PRINCIPAL WORKS: Poetry: *The Bad Child's Book of Verse*, 1896; *Cautionary Tales for Children*, 1907; *Sonnets and Verse*, 1923; revised edition 1938; as *Collected Verse*, 1958; *Cautionary Verses: The Collected Humorous Poems*, 1907. Fiction: *Mr. Clutterbuck's Election*, 1908; *The Girondin*, 1911; *The Green Overcoat*, 1912. Travel: *The Path to Rome*, 1902; *The Pyrenees*, 1909. Biography: *Marie Antoinette*, 1909; *Oliver Cromwell*, 1927; *The Last Rally: A Story of Charles II*, 1940. History: *The French Revolution*, 1911; *The History of England from the First Invasion by the Romans to the Accession of King George V*, 1915. SELECTED READING: Robert Speaight, *The Life of Belloc*, 1957; A. N. Wilson, *Hilaire Belloc*, 1984. (SOURCE: Vinson, 1979)

BELPHEGOR: the Assyrian form of Baal-Peor, the Moabite god to whom the Israelites became attached in Skittim (Numbers 25.3). The god was associated with licentious orgies. In medieval Latin legend, the name was given to a demon sent into the world by his fellows to test rumors concerning the happiness of married life on earth. After a thorough trial, he fled to happier regions where there were no females. Thus the name is applied to misanthropes and to nasty, obscene, licentious fellows. (SOURCE: Cooper, 1992)

BELSHAZZAR, BELSAZAR (Ger.): an Old Testament figure, the last king of ★Babylon, son of Nebuchadnezzar. According to the Old Testament Book of Daniel, chapter 5, upon the death of his father, Nebuchadnezzar, Belshazzar became the new king. One night Belshazzar gave a large feast for a thousand of his noblemen. After imbibing a great deal of wine, he ordered that the gold and silver vessels that were taken by his father to Babylon from the Temple in Jerusalem be brought to the hall so that he, his wives, concubines, and noblemen could drink wine from them. As they drank, they praised the gods of gold, silver, wood, iron, and stone. Suddenly the fingers of a hand appeared and began to write on the plaster walls. Belshazzar was terrified; "the joints of his loins were loosed, and his knees smote one against another" (Daniel 5.6). The king called for wise men and astrologers to come and interpret the writing on the wall. He proclaimed that "whosoever shall read this writing, and shew me the interpretation thereof, shall be clothed with scarlet, and have a chain of gold about his neck, and shall be the third ruler in the kingdom" (Daniel 5.7). None of the established wise men was able to help the king, but someone remembered a wonder worker named Daniel, who had served Belshazzar's father. This Daniel had been so wise that Nebuchadnezzar had made him his "master of the magicians, astrologers, Chaldeans, and soothsayers." Daniel was sent for and brought into the presence of the king. Belshazzar offered Daniel the magnificent rewards he had promised. Daniel refused them but agreed to interpret the king's vision. Daniel retold the story of Nebuchadnezzar's rule: how he became proud, how God took away his senses and his kingdom. Once Nebuchadnezzar had humbled himself, God gave the king back his senses and his kingdom and allowed him to prosper and to rule a long time. However, said Daniel, Belshazzar had not only failed to humble himself but had desecrated the gold vessels from the Temple. Therefore God had sent him a message: "MENE, MENE, TEKEL, UPHARSIN" (Daniel 5.25). Daniel's interpretation was this: MENE: God hath numbered thy kingdom and finished it; TEKEL: Thou art weighed in the balances, and art found wanting; PERES: Thy kingdom is divided and given to the Medes and the Persians. That night, Belshazzar was killed, and Darius the Mede took over the kingdom. This name is often used to allude to great feasts. Belshazzar is the subject of a poem by ★Byron and an oratorio by William Walton. (SOURCE: King James Version of the Holy Bible, 1611)

SONG	COMPOSER	POET
"Belsazar"	Robert Schumann	Heinrich Heine

BELY, ANDREI (pseudonym for Boris Bugaev) (1880–1934): Russian poet, editor, lecturer. Bely studied science first, then philology, then philosophy at the University of Moscow (1899–1934). He married three times, traveled abroad, studied with Rudolf Steiner (1910–16), and lectured in Moscow, St. Petersburg, and Berlin. Bely was considered Russia's greatest ★modernist writer and leading poet of the Silver Age; he was the theorist of Russian ★Symbolism and a pioneer in the structural method of literary analysis. Before he changed his name, Bely thought of himself as a philosopher, scientist, and composer because he searched for new forms of art, wanting to fuse art with music and religion. Symbolism was his way of thinking, writing, and living. His chosen name, Bely, means white, significant as a recurring symbol in his poetry. The phonetic structure of his poetry was more important than its meaning, as he repeated images without development of thought. "Bely's poetry is uneven: strong and original lines and stanzas may be followed by banal and uninspired ones" (Terras, 1991). He upheld the October Revolution as the birth of a new world, but, after an attack by Trotsky, he appealed to Stalin and became a Marxist, compromising his conscience. When he tried hard to destroy the simplicity of poetic forms, these experiments discouraged foreign readers. Andrei Bely's verses were set by Sergei Rachmaninoff and Nikolai Medtner. PRINCIPAL WORKS: *Zoloto v lazuri* [Gold in Azure], 1904; *Pepel* [Ashes], 1909; *Urna* [The Urn], 1909; 4 "Symphonies," 1902, 1904, 1905, 1908. SELECTED READING: S. Cioran, *The Apocalyptic Symbolism of Andrei Bely*, 1973; Anton Kovač, *Bely: The "Symphonies,"* 1976. (SOURCES: Vinson, 1984; Terras, 1991)

BENÉT, STEPHEN VINCENT (1898–1943): American poet, novelist, storyteller, lecturer, radio propagandist for liberal causes. Stephen Vincent Benét, brother of the poet William Rose Benét, was born in Pennsylvania in 1898 and educated at Yale University and the Sorbonne. Among his many awards were the Guggenheim Scholarship (1926), the Pulitzer Prize (1929), and a second Pulitzer Prize awarded posthumously in 1944. Benét died in 1943, one of America's best-known poets and storytellers, but virtually ignored by the academics. Compared to his friends and fellow students at Yale—among them Thornton Wilder and Archibald ★MacLeish—his reputation was slender, despite the fact that his work included several minor classics that were widely read and admired. Early light and ironic verse like "The Ballad of William Sycamore" (set by Douglas Moore) were highly regarded; his long narrative poem about the Civil War, "John Brown's Body," won him his first Pulitzer Prize in 1929; his best known short story, "The Devil and Daniel Webster," also set by Moore as an opera, shows his flare for folktale traditions. He had a nineteenth-century faith in the promises of American democracy and a love that he shared with ★Whitman for the special attributes of America: diversity, self-sufficiency, frankness, and innocence. These elements were in every poem, story, and novel he wrote. Benét's poetry has also been set by William Ames, John Duke, Katherine Davis, Sam Raphling, and Gene Bone. PRINCIPAL WORKS: *Tiger Joy*, 1925; *John Brown's Body*, 1928, reprinted 1982; *Ballads and Poems*, 1931; *A Book of Americans*, 1933; *The Burning City*, 1936; *The Devil and Daniel Webster*, 1939 (libretto). SELECTED READING: Charles A. Fenton, *Stephen Vincent Benét: The Life and Times of an American Man of Letters, 1898–1943*, 1958; Parry Stroud, *Stephen Vincent Benét*, 1962. (SOURCES: Vinson, 1979; Hamilton, 1994)

BENN, GOTTFRIED (1886–1956): German poet and critic. Son of a Lutheran pastor and a French mother, Benn studied medicine and became a specialist in venereal diseases. His early poetic technique was that of ★Expressionism, but the subject matter was his own, drawn from his medical experience. Although he had welcomed National Socialism and the Nazi Party, his works were banned in 1937. After the war, his fame increased steadily. Benn's view of poetic form was existential: "the form is the poem." His poetry was stirring and engaging to young people, and he was a powerful and inspired critic, altogether a leading twentieth-century poet. The verses of Gottfried Benn were set by Paul Hindemith. PRINCIPAL WORKS: *Das Unaufhörliche* (an oratorio, music by Hindemith), 1931. SELECTED READING: Reinhard Alter, *Gottfried Benn: The Artist and Politics, 1910–34*, 1976. (SOURCE: Steinberg, 2, 1973)

BERGAMASQUE (Fr.), BERGAMASK (Eng.): *a clown*, also *a rustic dance*, named from Bergamo, a Venetian province whose inhabitants were noted for their clownishness (Shakespeare's *Midsummer Night's Dream*). (SOURCE: Cooper, 1992)

SONG	COMPOSER	POET
1. "Clair de lune"	Gabriel Fauré	Paul Verlaine
2. "Mandoline"	Claude Debussy, Gabriel Dupont	Paul Verlaine

BERGERETTES: one of several French song forms of the seventeenth and eighteenth centuries, composed and sung for the most part for and by the upper strata of French pre-revolutionary society as they played at imitating the simpler pastoral life. Some of them were shepherds' songs intended to accompany dances or songs relating to pastoral matters. They could be defined as old popular songs that have survived because of the essential charm and grace of their tunes and words. A collection of such folk songs, titled *Bergerettes*, edited by J. B. Weckerlin, is in publication.

BERGMAN, BO HJALMAR (1869–1967): Swedish poet, novelist, short story writer, and critic. Bergman is particularly known for the lyrics from his first collection, *Marionetterna* (1903) and his last, *Aventyret* (1969). The pessimism that marked his early works gave way in his later love poetry to a more positive attitude and acceptance of life's realities. Bergman's poetry was set by Ture Rangström and Wilhelm Stenhammar.

BERNARD, KARL JOSEF (1786–1850): Austrian poet, journalist, and critic, well-known figure in literary Vienna during Schubert's lifetime. Bernard was born in Saaz, Austria and died in Vienna. From 1819 to 1848 he was the editor of *Wiener Zeitschrift für Kunst, Literatur, Theater und Mode*. His text "Ihr weissen Gründer" was used by Beethoven in his "Chor auf die verbündeten Fürsten" (1814). Bernard wrote an oratorio libretto, "Der Sieg des Kreuzes" for Beethoven, but it was never set. He was the librettist for Louis Spohr's *Faust* in 1816, and for Conradin Krutzer's *Libussa*. His poetry briefly attracted Schubert early in his career as a song composer when he set Bernard's poem "Vergebliches Liebe." (SOURCES: Clive, 1997; Reed, 1997)

BERNERS STREET: a dismal, murky, but respectable residential part of London. (SOURCE: Friedberg, 1984)

SONG	COMPOSER	POET
"When I Died in Berners St."	Mary Howe	Elinor Wylie

BERTELLI, LUIGI: *see* ★VAMBA.

BERTRAND, FRIEDRICH ANTON FRANZ (1787–1830): poet and essayist, one of the more obscure poets whose poems were set by Schubert. Unfortunately, little information about Bertrand is available. Reed believes that he may have been a member of the Schubert circle. Schubert set two of Bertrand's ballad-style poems, among his longest songs, "Adlewold und Emma" being over twenty pages in length. The bare facts of his life are these: after studying law at Halle, he then worked for several years in the tax office of Calbe an der Saale. He settled in Köthen in 1806. After moving to Dessau in 1829, it is presumed that he ended his life there. Bertrand was a contributor to W. G. Becker's *Taschenbuch zum geselligen Vergnügen* (Leipzig), and published his *Gedichte und Prosaische Aufsätze* in 1813 in Zerbst, near Magdeburg. His poetry was also set by John Corigliano. (SOURCES: Capell, 1957; Clive, 1997; Reed, 1997)

BESTIAIRE (Fr.), BESTIARY, BESTIALS: medieval treatises that were in great favor between the eleventh and fourteenth centuries, describing the supposed habits and peculiarities of real and fabled animals with legendary lore and moral symbolism. These books were derived from the Greek *Physiologus* (a collection of fifty anecdotes mostly from animal history, followed by a Christian moral); those in English were translations of continental originals. The most popular were those of Phillippe de Taun, Guillaume le Clerc, and Richard de Fournival's satirical *Bestiaire d'Amour*, written about 1250. (SOURCES: Cooper, 1992; Drabble, 2000)

SONG	COMPOSER	POET
"Le Bestiaire"	Francis Poulenc, Louis Durey	Guillaume Apollinaire

BETHSABE: *see* ★BATHSHEBA

BETJEMAN, JOHN (1906–1984): English poet, architecture and topography writer, editor, film critic. John Betjeman was born in London, the only child of a prosperous father of Dutch origin, from whom his son's fierce determination to become a poet estranged him. Betjeman was educated at Oxford (1925–28), which university, despite the fact that he had left without a degree, gave him an honorary degree years later. He was awarded the Queen's Gold Medal in 1960, was made a Knight Commander of the British Empire in 1969, and named poet laureate in 1972. Betjeman was a unique figure in twentieth-century poetry. No poet had reaped such fame and success since ★Byron. He was read by people who are not commonly believed to read or understand poetry. A pillar of the establishment, he was a friend to an admiring Princess Margaret of the royal family. The amount of publicity that Betjeman enjoyed evoked a certain amount of distrust in the purists. Others believed that he was properly included in the tradition of ★Tennyson, ★Hardy, and ★Kipling. Yet there was no dispute about the great contribution his architecture writings had made, although he claimed that those works were only the means of gaining the financial freedom that allowed him to pursue poetry. Betjeman had an early talent for comic verse and gentle satire, but suffered from their popularity because of his desire to be taken seriously. He preferred to create within the limits of piety and sentimentality. He strived for simple, direct expression; he struggled to accept modernity; he never ceased his spiritual questioning. Most critics conclude that he is a poet of considerable importance who narrowly failed to reach the front rank of modern English poetry. The verse of John Betjeman has been set by Jack Beeson. PRINCIPAL WORKS: *Old Lights for New Chancels*, 1940; *A Few Late Chrysanthemums*, 1954; *Collected Poems*, 1958, 1962; *A Nip in the Air*, 1972; *John Betjeman: A Bibliography of Writings by and about Him*, 1974; *High and Low*, 1976; *Ghastly Good Taste*, 1972 (architecture criticism). SELECTED READING: John Press, *John Betjeman*, 1974; Frank Delany, *Betjeman Country*, 1983. (SOURCE: Stanford, 20, 1983)

BEUCH: (Scot.) (pr. byooch, ch as in Ger. *Buch*), *bough*.

BEULAH, LAND OF: in Bunyan's *Pilgrim's Progress*, the land of heavenly joy where pilgrims tarry until they are summoned to enter the Celestial City, the paradise before the resurrection; in the Old Testament, the name given to Israel when the Lord restores it to his favor after an initial period of punishment (Isaiah 62.4). (SOURCE: Cooper, 1992)

BEYLIÉ, LAURENCE DE (1893–1968): French poet. Beylié, whose maiden name was Laurence de Ferry, lived in Marseilles. *Lueurs*, a booklet of her verses, was published after her death, from which Francis Poulenc set the song "Nuage." (SOURCE: Bernac, 1977)

BIBLICAL SONGS: a set of ten songs with texts from the Psalms, written by Antonín Dvořák while he was in New York. These excerpts were originally set by the composer in the seventeenth-century Czech version of the so-called ★Kralice Bible. Realizing the impossibility of fitting a tolerable German translation to his music, Dvořák completely rewrote the voice parts and thus destroyed much of their rhythmic life. Also, the English texts are poorly adapted on to the German vocal line. At the time, Czechoslovakia was bilingual, and many patriotic Czechs, including Dvořák and Smetana, felt more at home in German than in their mother tongue.

BIEDERMEIER: a period in Germany (1830–48), an age of graceful resignation, of confronting the adversities of life with sentimental lament. Hugo Wolf's song "Gebet," set to verses by Eduard ★Mörike, contains a reference to the Biedermeier period. From 1815, when hope died that revolutionary enterprises might redeem suffering Europe, the German spirit was humbled and intimidated. This era was capable only of *holden Bescheiden*—graceful resignation—as Mörike expresses it. A stanza of "Gebet" appears in ★*Maler Nolten*.

SONG	COMPOSER	POET
"Gebet"	Hugo Wolf	Eduard Mörike

BIERBAUM, OTTO JULIUS (1865–1910): German poet, editor, novelist, playwright, and singspiel author. Bierbaum studied at the universities of Zürich, Leipzig, Munich, and Berlin. He served as editor of important artistic periodicals from 1891 to 1894, was the founder of *Pan*, 1895, and co-editor of *Die Insel* from 1899 to 1902. His poetry was set by Richard Strauss, Max Reger, Henry Hadley, and Ernst Toch. PRINCIPAL WORKS: Poetry: *Erlebte Gedichte*, 1892; *Nehmt, Frouwe, diesen Kranz,*

1894; *Der Ingaarten die Liebe*, 1901; *Maultrommel und Flöte*, 1907. Singspiel: *Die Hirten und der Schomsteinfeger*. (SOURCE: Garland, 1976)

BIERCE, AMBROSE (1842–1914?): American writer. Bierce was born in Ohio and fought in the Civil War (1861–65). He became a prominent journalist, living and working for a time in England (1872–76). Upon return to Washington, he worked as a correspondent. Influenced by Edgar Allen ★Poe, Bierce is best known for his short stories, which reveal a realistic, yet sardonic style. In 1913 he traveled to Mexico, where he mysteriously disappeared. Robert Baksa has set Ambrose Bierce's work. (SOURCE: Drabble, 2000)

BIG: (Scot.), *build.*

BILLIES: (Scot.), *peddlers.*

BIRKEN: (Scot.) (pr. beerkin), *birch tree.*

SONG	COMPOSER	POET
"A Laddie's Sang"	Benjamin Britten	William Soutar

BIRKIE: (Scot.) (pr. beerkee), *a lively, smart, assertive person; a man with a mind of his own; a fellow; a boy.*

BISHOP, ELIZABETH (1911–1979): American poet and prose writer. Elizabeth Bishop was born in Worcester, Massachusetts, but it was her mother's birthplace, Great Village on the Bay of Fundy in Nova Scotia, that she called "home." Her mother's mental health deteriorated severely after her husband died some eight months following her daughter's birth. From the age of seven until college, Elizabeth lived with an aunt in the Boston suburbs, often ill, taking piano lessons and reading voraciously. At Vassar, Bishop and her friend Mary McCarthy started a literary magazine. After graduating, she lived in Paris, traveled in Italy, returned to Great Village, and then settled down for a time in Key West, Florida, where she wrote a great deal and published little. Following the publication of her first book, *North and South*, in 1946, she accumulated many honors—a Guggenheim in 1947 (another in 1978), the National Book Award in 1969 among others—but she did not boast a wide readership, although Robert ★Lowell, Marianne ★Moore, and Pablo Neruda were early admirers. In 1966 she began a teaching career; Harvard and New York University were the last of her positions. Much of Bishop's writing art was the shaping of "almost-lost" things into works of extraordinary power. She struggled to understand the past and shaped the "almost-lost" memories into satisfying forms. Bishop was a formal poet but realized that form was most interesting when pulled almost out of shape. Her early work is cool and witty, reticent and spare, yet colloquial; strong personal feelings are masked. In her later poetry she uncovered those feelings. The poetry of Elizabeth Bishop has been set in songs by Ned Rorem and William Bolcom. PRINCIPAL WORKS: Poetry: *Poems: North and South—A Cold Spring*, 1955; *Poems*, 1956; *Geography III*, 1976; *The Complete Poems*, 1983. Prose: *Brazil*, 1962 (In Life World Library); *Questions of Travel*, 1965; *An Anthology of Twentieth-Century Brazilian Poetry*, Elizabeth Bishop and Emanuel Brasil, eds.,

1972. SELECTED READING: Bonnie Costello, *Elizabeth Bishop: Questions of Mastery*, 1991. (SOURCE: Unger, 1992)

BISMILLAH: (Arab.), *in the name of God!* a common Mohammedan exclamation.

SONG	COMPOSER	POET
"Songs of the Infatuated Muezzin"	Karol Szymanowski	Jaroslav Iwaszkewicz

BITEROLF: a twelfth-century Crusader; an epic poet of whose work no trace remains today; also a character in the Wagner opera, *Tannhäuser*. Biterolf is the subject of a cycle of five poems by J.V. von *Scheffel. In one of these poems, which is set by Hugo Wolf, the crusader stands in the sun-drenched sands of Acre (Akkon), a seaport of modern Israel that was prominent during the Crusades.

SONG	COMPOSER	POET
"Im Lager von Akkon"	Hugo Wolf	J.V. von Scheffel

BJELBOG: (Slav.), bjel, *white*; bog, *God*; the white god of the Slavs.

BJØRNSON, BJØRNSTJERNE (1832–1910): Norwegian poet, novelist, playwright. Born in his father's vicarage in a mountainous inland region southeast of Trondheim, Bjørnson was uninterested in school work, but he did study native and foreign literature. This led to writing poetry, plays, and newspaper articles as well as passing his matriculation exam in 1854. His peasant novels with their concise style, excellent character descriptions, and sympathy for old Norse *sagas made him a popular author. In 1857 Bjørnson succeeded *Ibsen as stage manager at the National Theater in Bergen, where he founded a new school of drama, whose goal was to make the people aware of their heritage in the ancient sagas. He continued to write poetry, including that of Norway's national anthem, becoming known as the national poet of his country. The ten years 1863–73 were given over to writing his successful verse novel, *Arnljot Gelline*, but his written attacks on the church brought criticism. After receiving his 1903 Nobel Prize in literature, he still remained prolific in prose, poetry, and the theater. Bjørnson's verse was set by Edvard Grieg, Frederick Delius, and Halfdan Kjerulf. WORKS: *Poems and Songs*, 1870; *Arnljot Gelline*, trans. W. M. Payne, 1917. SELECTED READING: H. A. Beyer, *A History of Norwegian Literature*. (SOURCE: Kunitz, Colby, 1967)

"Black Is the Color of My True Love's Hair": a traditional love song of the southern mountains in the United States, sung to several different melodies, characterized by the farewell-fidelity theme. The original was arranged by John Jacob Niles in the style of a typical Elizabethan love song. No English original is known, except for the title line found in an old sea song, which appears to be unrelated to the American mountain song. (SOURCE: Preminger, 1986)

BLAKE, WILLIAM (1757–1827): British artist, poet, engraver, illustrator, graphic designer. Blake was born in London, where he studied drawing, engraving, and art at the Royal Academy of Arts. There he worked as an illustrator and graphic designer, and also gave drawing lessons. After an unsuccessful one-man show in London in 1809, he retreated into obscurity, but in the 1820s attracted a group of young painter disciples. When he died, general opinion held that he had been, if gifted, quite insane. ★Wordsworth thought his madness more interesting that others' sanity; Ruskin declared his manner diseased but his mind wise. Blake achieved greatness in several different fields, being one of the best lyrical poets England had seen in five hundred years. As a painter, the quality of his work is still a matter of controversy. His visionary work, a violent reaction against the fashionable portraits of Sir Joshua Reynolds, was regarded as crazy. Blake was actually a prophet, convinced that he had rediscovered the truth of Christianity, perverted as it was by the churches. He supported the French Revolution, was horrified by the results of the industrial revolution, and stood almost alone in descrying the age he lived in. It is impossible to consider Blake's poetry in isolation from his work as an artist and from his political ideas. All his verses were printed by himself from engraved copper plates with hand-colored illustrations that give clues to his meaning. "Songs of Innocence," his first illustrated poems whose subject is childhood, were simple without being naive. "Songs of Experience" were written five years later and in deliberate contrast. "Herein Love is treated as a crime, religion as mere hypocrisy, and society in the grip of a tyrannical class system. Instead of the Lamb, there is the Tyger" (Vinson, 1979). Many interpretative studies exist, relating his work to traditional Christianity, to Neoplatonic and ★Swedenborgian traditions, to Jungian, Freudian, and Marxist theory. His influence upon the "beat generation" and the English poets of the underground movement was particularly strong. William Blake's poetry has been set by many composers, including Ernst Bacon, Gardner Read, Theodore Chanler, Henry Cowell, John Alden Carpenter, Celius Dougherty, John Duke, Paul Nordoff, Ralph Vaughan Williams, Daron Hagen, Virgil Thomson, Richard Cumming, Arthur Farwell, Nicholas Flagello, Otto Luening, Benjamin Lees, Sidney Homer, Charles Griffes, Sergius Kagen, John Ireland, Gordon Jacobs, William Walton, Benjamin Britten, and Paul Hindemith. PRINCIPAL WORKS: *Poetical Sketches*, 1783; *The Book of Thel*, 1789; *Songs of Innocence and of Experience, Shewing the Two Contrary States of the Human Soul*, 1794; *The Book of Ahania*, 1795; *The Book of Los*, 1795; *The Song of Los*, 1795. SELECTED READING: Stanley Gardner, *Infinity on the Anvil: A Critical Study of Blake's Poetry*, 1954; S. Foster Damon, *A Blake Dictionary: The Ideas and Symbols of Blake*, 1973. (SOURCES: Drabble, 1985; Vinson, 1979)

BLAKE SONGS FOR VOICE AND OBOE: a collection of ten William ★Blake poems set by Ralph Vaughan Williams with piano accompaniment. Written at Christmas 1957 for a short film, *The Vision of William Blake*, produced by Guy Brenton, they marked the bicentenary of Blake's birth. Ursula Vaughan Williams tells us that her husband was not initially very enthusiastic about the project, his preference being for Blake the artist over Blake the poet. Yet he agreed to consider the poems, with the proviso that he not be compelled to set "that horrible little lamb poem that I hate." After writing nine songs in four days, he announced one day that he had awoken in the night "with a tune for that beastly little lamb, and it's rather a good tune."

BLANCAFORT, MANUEL (1897–1987): a Catalan composer and sometimes poet. His oeuvre includes symphonic compositions, string quartets, several art songs, and a very successful opera, *Parc d'attraccions* (Amusement Park). His verse has been set by Federico Mompou. (SOURCE: Cockburn, Stokes, 1992)

BLESSED VIRGIN'S *EXPOSTULATION, THE: an extended song by Henry Purcell set to Nahum *Tate's narration of *Mary's feelings when she discovered that the boy *Jesus was missing. The family had gone to Jerusalem to observe the feast of Passover. As they returned, the child Jesus "tarried behind in Jerusalem; and *Joseph and his mother knew not of it." Three days passed before his parents found the boy in the Temple, sitting in the midst of learned men. (Luke 2.40–52)

BLEU, BLEUET: lit., *cornflower;* a colloquialism for *a young soldier.* Apollinaire wrote this poem in 1917, when returning to Paris after having been wounded in the head by a shell splinter.

SONG	COMPOSER	POET
"Bleuet"	Francis Poulenc	Guillaume Apollinaire

BLITTER: (Scot.), *bitter;* also, an Old World common bird, a *snipe.*

SONG	COMPOSER	POET
"My Hoggie"	Benjamin Britten	Robert Burns

BLOK, ALEKSANDR (1880–1921): Russian poet, playwright, critic. Blok's father was a professor of law in Warsaw; his maternal grandfather a famous scientist and rector of St. Petersburg University, from which Aleksandr graduated with a degree in the humanities. Many Russians believe Blok to be the last romantic poet and the greatest after *Pushkin. Not only his art but his poetic appearance mesmerized his contemporaries. A totally intuitive poet, he considered any intellectual analysis of poetry to be philistinism. Yet he was a master of technique—rhythm his great forte—and in control of all kinds of language, from slang to scholarly Russian. Of the Russian *Symbolists, Blok was the easiest to understand. The book that made him famous was *Verses about the Beautiful Lady* (1904). Since his relationship with his native land was divided between hatred and adoration, most of his poems were based on the medieval past. *The Twelve* was his masterpiece. There are English translations of *Song of Fate* and *Spirit of Music,* 1946, and some poems translated by A. Yarmolinsky in his *A Treasury of Russian Verse.* M. Gorky's *Reminiscences* is of interest. The verse of Aleksandr Blok was set by Prokofiev, Rachmaninoff, Yuri Shaporin, Vasily Nechaev, and himself. SELECTED READING: David A. Sloane, *Aleksandr Blok and the Dynamics of the Lyric Cycles,* 1987. (SOURCE: Brown, 1985)

BLONDEL: a minstrel who is said to have found and released Richard I, the Lion-hearted, who was being held for ransom by Leopold of Austria.

SONG	COMPOSER	POET
"Blondel, zu Marien"	Franz Schubert	Ascribed to Grillparzer

BLOOMSBURY: an area of London near the British Museum, with pleasant late eighteenth-century houses, a literary district during the nineteenth and twentieth centuries. (SOURCE: Friedberg, 1984)

SONG	COMPOSER	POET
"When I Died in Berners St."	Mary Howe	Elinor Wylie

"Blow, ★Boreas, Blow": a song composed by Henry Purcell, set to words by Thomas ★D'Urfey in his comedy, *Sir Barnaby Whigg*, produced in 1681. *See* ★*Sir Barnaby Whigg* for plot details and placement of songs.

BLOWS HIS NAIL: an expression used in Elizabethan lyrics, meaning *rubs his hands together to keep them warm.*

SONG	COMPOSER	POET
"Winter (6 Elizabethan Songs)"	Dominick Argento	William Shakespeare

BLUE MOUNTAIN: an imaginary town in Mississippi that represents Camden on Clarksdale, where the poet/playwright Tennessee Williams lived happily as a boy with his grandparents.

SONG	COMPOSER	POET
"Blue Mountain Ballads"	Paul Bowles	Tennessee Williams

BLUMAUER, ALOIS (1755–1798): Austrian poet from Steyr. Blumauer was a Jesuit until Austria banned the Jesuits in 1781. In that year Blumauer was the Censor of Books; by 1793 he had become a bookseller. An author of elegant poetry, influenced by ★Bürger, he was best known for his *Virgils Aenis oder Abenteur des frommen helden Aeneas*, 1783, a parody of Virgil's *Aeneid*. Mozart set poetry by Alois Blumauer. (SOURCE: Garland, 1976)

BOBRIK, JOHANN FRIEDRICH (1781–1844): Prussian lawyer, poet, and translator, who published under the pseudonym B-b-k. In 1815 Franz Schubert set his poem "Die drei Sänger," which had been published earlier. (SOURCE: Reed, 1997)

BOCCACCIO, GIOVANNI (Giovanni di Boccaccio da Chellino) (1313–1375): Italian poet and prose writer, scholar, lecturer, biographer. Born in Florence, Boccaccio was apprenticed in his father's banking business in Naples, interrupting this to study canon law from 1331 to 1336. He worked in banking until 1341, when he returned to Florence, where he was during the plague, the Black Death (1348). In 1350 he met ★Petrarch, becoming his friend, thereafter devoting himself to humanistic studies. Boccaccio took minor clerical orders in 1357, became active in the public life of Florence, and took part in many diplomatic missions in the 1350s and 1360s. He was a writer of unusual versatility, using a variety of genres in his work, many of which were pioneer endeavors. His early works reflected feudal Neapolitan taste, but that changed when he returned to Tuscany. *The Decameron* was his masterpiece, a collection of a hundred short stories told by a company of seven young ladies and three young men, ten stories each day, during a retreat to the hills of ★Fiesole above Florence, organized in an effort to escape the plague. Boccaccio wrote it in the vernacular and used no more allegory but added realism without didacticism. His vernacular fiction revolves around the motive of love, its illusions and delusions of faithfulness and treachery, happiness and tragedy. *The Decameron* was democratic, feminist, and optimistic, and is as entertaining now as it was when written. The poetry of Giovanni Boccaccio was set by Ottorino Respighi. PRINCIPAL WORKS: *Il ninfale fiesolano*, trans. Daniel J. Donno, as *The Nymph of Fiesole*, 1960, trans. Joseph Tusiani, as *Nymphs of Fiesole*, 1971; *Rime*, ed. Vittore Branca, 1958; *The Decameron*, trans. Harry McWilliam, 1972, trans. John Payne, 1984. SELECTED READING: M. Cottino-Jones, *An Anatomy of Boccaccio's Style*, 1968. (SOURCE: Vinson, Kirkpatrick (1), 1984)

BODENSTEDT, FRIEDRICH VON (1819–1892): German poet and journalist. Bodenstedt was born and grew up in Hanover. Although his father insisted that he go to a commercial school, the youthful Friedrich wrote poetry and translated ★Shakespeare into German. Even when apprenticed to a business firm, he wrote on the side. Attending lectures at the University of Göttingen he became interested in Russia. When he subsequently traveled to Russia, he studied the language assiduously and became the tutor of Prince Gallitzyn's two sons. ★Lermontov, who became Bodenstedt's friend, introduced him to the leading Russian writers. Bodenstedt obtained a teaching position in the Ukraine. The poetry, art, and customs were so interesting to him that he decided to learn Tatar. After studying with the renowned Mirza (a title meaning "man of letters") Schaffy, Bodenstedt appropriated the name for his own collection of poetry, *Die Lieder des Mirza-Schaffy*, which enjoyed 142 printings. From Schaffy and the Shiite Muslims (among whose numbers were ★Khayyam and ★Hafiz) Bodenstedt learned about Sufism, the search for a mystical union of the soul with Allah. His travel stories and poems from the Ukraine were published in Germany, followed by the story of his Russian adventures, *Tausend und ein Tag im Orient*. It was Bodenstedt who, in Lermontov's will, was given the privilege of translating the posthumous poems of Lermontov and ★Pushkin. King Maximilian made Bodenstedt professor of Slavic Studies at the University of Munich. When Maximilian died, his son Ludwig venerated Wagner more than he admired Bodenstedt, whose human qualities had endeared him to the reading public. His sensitive translations of Russian, Middle Eastern, and Elizabethan literature are still admired. Friedrich von Bodenstedt's poetry was set by Brahms, Liszt, Robert Franz, and Anton Rubenstein. PRINCIPAL WORKS: *Die Poetische Ukraine* [The Poetry of the Ukraine], 1845; *Tausend und Ein Tag im Orient* [A Thousand and One Nights in the Orient], 2 vols., 1849, 1850; *Die Lieder des Mirza-Schaffy*, 1851. (SOURCE: Hardin, Mews, 1993)

BOGAN, LOUISE (1897–1970): American poet, critic, novelist. She was born in Maine, where her paternal grandfather was a sea captain out of Portland Harbor. After four years of marriage, she was left a widow with a daughter. Her second marriage to a poet (1925) ended in divorce in 1937. Bogan lived in New York and Santa Fe and spent 1933 and 1937 abroad on a Guggenheim fellowship in Vienna. From the beginning of her career she received the acclaim of critics such as Ford Maddox ★Ford, who placed her on a par with George ★Herbert and John ★Donne. In 1931 she started as the regular poetry reviewer for *The New Yorker* magazine. These reviews were said to be the only sustained criticism of modern poetry that the general reader could follow. Bogan held the Chair of Poetry at the Library of Congress (1945–46). In 1951 she wrote a formidable book on the history of American poetry from 1900 to 1950. Bogan's best work is described as displaying an intricacy of feeling and style, as well as brilliant craftsmanship. "The feeling is of somber strength, of a strong nature controlling powerful emotions by highly conscious art" (Kunitz, Colby, 1955). The poetry of Louise Bogan was set by John Musto and William Bolcom. PRINCIPAL WORKS: *Body of This Death*, 1923; *Dark Summer*, 1929; *The Sleeping Fury*, 1937; *Poems and New Poems*, 1941; *Achievement in American Poetry 1900–1950*, 1951; *Collected Poems*, 1954. SELECTED READING: Elizabeth Frank, *Louise Bogan: A Portrait*, 1985. (SOURCE: Kunitz, Haycraft, 1942)

BOHEMIAN: the French have applied this term to gypsies, since their first appearance during the fifteenth century, believing that they came from Bohemia in the south of Germany. In modern times the term is applied by the French to vagabonds, adventurers, persons of irregular life or habits, who despise conventions. (SOURCE: *OED*, 1989)

BOIARDO, MATTEO, COUNT OF SCANDIANO (1441–1494): Italian poet, translator, and scholar. Born near Reggio, Boiardo was a favorite of the Este family at the Court of Ferrara and eventually became the governor of Reggio and Modena. Boiardo's lyrics, strong and sincere, are imitative of ★Petrarch, and deal mainly with his unhappy love affair (1469). Boiardo's poetic fame rests on his *Orlando Innamorato*, which story ★Ariosto continued in his ★*Orlando Furioso*, merging the ★Carolingian and Breton cycles of the story. Boiardo did many translations from the Greek. His lyrics were set by G. F. Ghedini. WORKS: *Orlando Innamorato*; *Amorum liber*; *Capitoli sopra el timore*; *Eclogues*. (SOURCE: De Lucchi, 1967)

BOLINGBROKE, HENRY ST. JAMES: King Henry IV of England (1366–1413), so called from the town of Bolingbroke in Lincolnshire, where he was born; also an English political author (1678–1751), whose philosophical writings and extreme criticisms were responsible for his dismissal from several important positions during his lifetime.

BONNE CHANSON, LA (The Good Song): A series of twenty-one poems (1869) by Paul Verlaine. In 1869 Paul Verlaine was introduced to Mathilde Mauté, half sister of his friend Charles de Sivry. The two fell in love and, as a part of their courtship, Verlaine began writing the poems that make up *La Bonne Chanson*, dedicated to Mathilde. They were married on August 11, 1870; their son Georges was born in 1871. In July 1870 the Franco-Prussian War began, and Verlaine enlisted in the national guard by November. As his drinking began to increase, the relationship with his wife slowly deteriorated. The death knell to the marriage was sounded in September 1871, when Arthur Rimbaud arrived in Paris at Verlaine's invitation. By the early part of 1872 Verlaine and Mathilde had quarreled over his relationship with Rimbaud. Mathilde left Paris, refusing to return until Rimbaud had departed. In July 1872, Rimbaud and Verlaine left for Brussels. Mathilde followed them, making an unsuccessful attempt to persuade her husband to return with her to Paris. A legal separation was officially granted in March 1874, the permission expedited by

Verlaine's imprisonment for the shooting of Rimbaud. The idyll that had produced *La Bonne Chanson*, a brief period when Verlaine's demons were more or less under control, was short-lived. Gabriel Fauré set eight of the twenty-one poems from *La Bonne Chanson*. (SOURCE: Borel, 1962)

BONNIE: (Scot.), *pretty.*

BONNIÈRES, ROBERT DE (1850–1905): French poet. Bonnières was educated for a diplomatic career and fought in the wars of 1870. He wrote political articles for the French newspaper *Figaro* as well as a novel on Jewish society and its relationship to the aristocracy. The poetry of Robert de Bonnières, deeply affected by his travels in India, was set by Henri Duparc. (SOURCE: France, 1995)

BONTEMPS, ARNA (1902–1973): American poet, novelist, playwright, juvenile fiction writer, editor, essayist, historian, biographer, short story writer, anthologist. Arna Bontemps was born Arnaud Bontemps in Alexandria, Louisiana. His father was a strong-willed brick mason who became a lay minister in the Seventh Day Adventist Church. After a racial incident in Louisiana, he moved his family to Los Angeles. Following the death of his mother, young Bontemps lived with his grandmother and his uncle, who was a strong repository of black culture. His father, however, wishing his son to be accepted by the white community, sent him to a predominantly white school. The opposing racial attitudes of his father and uncle made Bontemps aware of the conflict most black Americans must face. Bontemps vowed to devote his life to rectifying the glaring omissions concerning black history that appeared in the usual American textbooks. In 1923 he earned a B.A. from the Pacific Union College and then taught in New York City private schools while beginning his writing career. In 1924 Bontemps's poetry began to appear in literary magazines. He resigned from a teaching post at a southern Seventh Day Adventist school over "racial awareness," which attitude (central to Bontemps's life endeavors) was forbidden. He took a masters degree in library science from the University of Chicago in 1943 and was thereafter appointed head librarian at Fisk University in Nashville (1943–65). In 1949 he was awarded a Guggenheim Fellowship (another in 1954) for creative writing. He then moved on to a position as curator of the James Weldon Johnson Memorial Collection at Yale, holder of the Harlem Renaissance material. In 1971 Bontemps moved back to Fisk University, where he remained until his death. He was a friend in New York of Countée ★Cullen, Langston ★Hughes, and others of the Harlem Renaissance writers; his publication *Personals* was a significant reflection of the growth of black American literature during the 1920s. On the whole, Bontemps's poems speak more about the persistent will of black Americans to endure until a better day. Bontemps wrote extensively on the history of the black experience, biographies of notable black Americans, and anthologies of the works by black writers, although poetry remained the center of his experience. His poetry has been set by William Grant Still and Hermann Reutter. PRINCIPAL WORKS: *Personals* (poems of the 1920s), 1963; *Black Thunder* (novel), 1936; *The Story of George Washington Carver* (juvenile), 1954; *St. Louis Woman* (musical comedy) with Countée Cullen, produced 1946; *American Negro Poetry* (editor), 1963; *The Harlem Renaissance*

Remembered: Essays, 1972. SELECTED READING: Roger Whitlow, *Black American Literature: A Critical History*, 1974. (SOURCE: Stanford, Quartermain, 1986)

BOREAS: in Greek mythology, the god of north wind and the north wind itself. Boreas was the son of Astraeus (a ★Titan) and Eos (the morning); he lived in a cave on Mt. Haemus in Thrace. (SOURCE: Cooper, 1992)

SONG	COMPOSER	POET
"Blow, Boreas, Blow"	Henry Purcell	Thomas D'Urfey

BOUCHOR, MAURICE (1855–1929): French poet, sculptor, puppeteer. Bouchor is now almost completely forgotten, his books are difficult to find, and little is written about him. During his lifetime he was independent of literary circles, living quietly and attracting no disciples. He collected folk songs, *Chants populaires pour les Écoles*, 1897, and adapted a medieval mystery play, *Sainte Cécile*, 1892. His most original work was *Les Symboles*, published in 1888. The poetry of Maurice Bouchor was set by Ernest Chausson. PRINCIPAL WORKS: *Chansons joyeuses*, 1874; *Poèmes de l'amour et de la mer*, 1875; *Le Faust moderne*, 1878; *Les Contes parisiens*, 1880; *Les Symboles*, 1888. (SOURCE: Beum, 2000)

BOUILHET, LOUIS (1822–1869): French poet and playwright. Bouilhet's father, a medical doctor, had been the chief director of military hospitals in Napoleon Bonaparte's campaign against Russia. Being born near Rouen and educated there at the university in medicine and the sciences gave young Bouilhet the subject and formative notions for his most well-known poems. One of them, "Fossiles," was in his collection *Festons et astragales*, which described geological epochs. Most of his plays were successful and reached a wide audience. Bouilhet acquired the habit of writing about modern scientific subjects in old-fashioned poetry, "the forward-looking attitudes expressed in the verse coexist with the backward-looking historical dramas" (Beum, 2000). Yet his most admired single poem, "Vers à une femme," has nothing to do with science or history. The verses of Bouilhet were set by Georges Bizet. PRINCIPAL WORKS: *Mme. de Montarci*; *Hélène Peyron*, 1858; *Festons et astragales*, 1859; *L'Oncle Million*, 1860. (SOURCE: Beum, 2000)

BOULEVARD DE GRENELLE: a "rare and poetic" street in Montmartre in Paris, which leads to the banks of the Seine River. (SOURCE: Bernac, 1977)

SONG	COMPOSER	POET
"Allons plus vite"	Francis Poulenc	Guillaume Apollinaire

BOURGET, PAUL (1852–1935): French novelist, critic, and essayist. Son of a mathematics instructor and born in Amiens, Bourget began a career bent on science, but, when he decided to emulate Balzac and be a writer, his family allowance was cut off, and he was forced to work as a tutor. His friends were the poets, ★Coppée and ★Richepin, and he worshiped ★Musset, ★Hugo, and ★Sully Prudhomme. For twenty-seven years he contributed regularly to periodicals as a drama critic. By 1880 he had arrived as a poet, but he then turned gradually from poetry to criticism. In 1895 Bourget was made a member of the French Academy and an Officer of the Legion of Honor. The same year he visited the United States, where Mark Twain lampooned him. In 1903, Bourget threw off the last vestiges of his science-heavy childhood and converted to the Roman Catholic religion. The ills of his time, Bourget believed, could be remedied by a return to religion and the monarchy, and this moralistic attitude was evident in his writings. His poetry was set to music by Claude Debussy and Ernest Chausson. PRINCIPAL WORKS: *La Vie inquiète,* 1875; *Essais de psychologie contemporaine,* 2 vols., 1883–85; *Outre mer: Impressions of America,* 1895. SELECTED READING: W. T. Secor, *Paul Bourget and the Novel,* 1948; E. Dimnet, *Paul Bourget,* 1913. (SOURCES: Steinberg, 2, 1973; Kunitz, Haycraft, 1942)

BOWLES, PAUL (1910–1999): American poet, novelist, and composer. Born in New York City, the son of a dentist father and a schoolteacher mother, Bowles was multi-talented. By seventeen he was writing seriously. In 1928 his ★surrealist poetry was published in a Paris literary magazine, but seventeen years passed before he published his first fiction. After one semester at the University of Virginia, Bowles left for Paris to spend six months, but returned to the United States to study composition with Aaron Copland, who nurtured Bowles's musical ability. Back in Paris again, Gertrude ★Stein and her companion, Alice B. Toklas, encouraged him in his writing and recommended that he try living in Morocco, since he needed a mild climate. Settled in Tangier, he devoted himself at first to his music, writing theater scores and chamber music. His enjoyment of the city was not limited to its climate. He found that the two cultures, Arab and western, gave him a context for expressing his growing nihilism, which derived from his exposure to Camus, ★Gide, and Sartre. His translation of Sartre's 1944 play, *Huis-clos* (No Exit), brought him renown. His short stories and novels explored the question of bridging opposing cultures. In 1960 he began collecting and translating Moghrebi literature, in particular much of Mohammed Mrabet's fiction, in order to preserve the native literature of his adopted Moroccan home. Paul Bowles often set his own poems, and his verse was also set by Peggy Glanville-Hicks. PRINCIPAL WORKS: *Next to Nothing: Collected Poems 1926–1977,* 1981; *The Spider's House,* 1955. SELECTED READING: Gena Dagel Caponi, *Paul Bowles: Romantic Savage,* 1994. (SOURCE: Magill, 1, 1997)

BRADSTREET, ANNE (1612–1672): American poet. Anne Bradstreet was born in Northampton, England, where her father, Thomas Dudley, was steward to the Earl of Lincoln. Owing to the efforts of her father and the earl, Anne was given an unusually good education for a woman. She may even have had access to the earl's library. In 1621 Simon Bradstreet joined the earl's household. After he and Anne fell in love (1630) and were married, both families left for America. Bradstreet rose from judge to governor of the Massachusetts colony. Although the Bradstreets had eight children, their socioeconomic status was conducive to Anne Bradstreet's writing. Her first collection of poems was published in London in 1650, the poetry having a public tone and content. The second collection, published posthumously in 1678, was more private and personal, feminine but straightforward. Bradstreet wrote with much variety: epics, ★dialogues, love lyrics, public and private ★elegies, meditative poems, and religious verse. The love poems written to her husband were admired for their wit, intricate construction, and emotional force. They reveal the human side of puritanism from a woman's vantage point. Anne Bradstreet died in Andover, Massachusetts. Her verses have been set by composers Leslie Bassett and Ned Rorem. PRINCIPAL WORKS: *The Tenth Muse Lately Sprung up in America*, 1650; *Several Poems Compiled with a Great Variety of Wit and Learning*, 1678. SELECTED READING: Ann Stanford, *Anne Bradstreet: The Worldly Puritan*, 1974; *Critical Essays on Anne Bradsteet*, ed. Pattie Cowell and Ann Stanford, 1983. (SOURCE: Magill, 1, 1992)

BRAE: (Scot.) (pr. bray), *a hillside along a river, a mountain or hill district.*

SONG	COMPOSER	POET
1. "A Laddie's Sang"	Benjamin Britten	William Soutar
2. "Ye Banks and Braes of Bonnie Doon"	Amy Beach	Robert Burns

BRAHMA: a Hindu god. In Hinduism, Brahma is the Absolute, or God conceived as entirely impersonal. Eventually this theological abstraction was given personality and became Creator of the Universe, the first in the divine Triad, of which other partners were Vishnu, the maintainer, and Siva, the destroyer. As such, the Brahmans claim Brahma as the founder of their religion. (SOURCE: Cotterell, 1986)

SONG	COMPOSER	POET
"Die ihr des unermesslichen Weltalls"	Wolfgang Mozart	Franz Ziegenhagen

BRAHMAN, BRAHMIN: a member of the highest or priestly caste among Hindus (of the two spellings, *Brahman* is the more correct); also, a member of the upper class of Boston, Massachusetts. *See* ★BRAHMA. (SOURCE: *OED*, 1989)

BRAND: (Scot.), *sword.*

BRAQUE, GEORGES (1882–1963): a French painter, born in Argenteuil. Braque was influenced by Cézanne and took Cézanne's simple forms as a basis of his work, while simplifying them further. Together with ★Picasso, he founded Cubism around 1909, his keen sense of structure useful in this form of art. By 1910 Braque was showing the objects in his paintings from several points of view. His still lifes used the arbitrary planes and close-knit designs of Cubism. Braque also used paper to create designs, works that he called *collages*. Bits of newspaper, playing cards, tobacco packages, and other material were glued to canvas as parts of the paintings. His work was characterized by restraint and subtlety in both design and color. After World War I he began to avoid the angular Cubist style and adopted a more curvilinear approach. Carol Kimball reminds us (Kimball, 1987) that Braque's recurring image of a bird: "was the universal figure of space, the embodiment of movement, and . . . is the most vivid image in the poem and in the music." (SOURCE: Benét, 1965)

SONG	COMPOSER	POET
"Georges Braque (Le Travail du peintre)"	Francis Poulenc	Paul Éluard

BRAW: (Scot.), *brave, worthy, fine, handsome, pretty.*

SONG	COMPOSER	POET
"Black Day"	Benjamin Britten	William Soutar

BRECHT, BERTHOLD (1898–1956): German playwright, poet, innovator of theatrical techniques. When the Nazis ascended to power, Brecht immediately took himself into exile. It is characteristic of his vision and dedication that Brecht, at this time driven from one country to another and deprived of a German-speaking public, created the five plays that established his international reputation, among which were: *Mother Courage* and *The Caucasian Chalk Circle*. Gifted, original, controversial, he owed his fame, however, to the success of the *Three Penny Opera*, music by Kurt Weill. At the end of World War II, Brecht made his way back to Europe, still a Marxist, and settled in East Berlin (1949), where he was treated royally as the most prized figure of the German Democratic Republic's cultural world. With his actress wife, he founded the Berliner Ensemble. It gave him control of unlimited theatrical resources with which to try out and refine his ideas on writing, acting, and production. One of the most important elements in Brecht's theories was what he called the "alienation effect." His aim was to foster insight into the workings of society, setting men's thinking free from the rigidities of tradition by distancing his audience from the play. Brecht was a most controversial figure. The constant battles centered on his allegiance to Marxist doctrine, his merit as an artist, and his relevance as an entirely new kind of director for theater. His answer was ever: Man cannot be good in an evil society. As a poet, Brecht excelled in the sauciness of his ballads, although his humor was not far from despair. Berthold Brecht's poetry was set by Gottfried von Einem and Kurt Weill. PRINCIPAL POETIC WORKS: *Hauspostille*, 1927, trans. as *Manual of Piety*, 1966; *Selected Poems*, trans. H. R. Hays, 1947, 1959. SELECTED READING: Eric Bentley, *Bentley on Brecht*, 1998. (SOURCES: Steinberg, 2, 1973; Vinson, Kirkpatrick (1), 1984)

BREDON HILL: a hill 991 feet in height in the town of Bredon, a large picturesque village on the Avon River in Worcestershire, England. From the crest of Bredon Hill are many fine views; at the foot are Romano-British earthworks and a 200-year-old tower.

SONG	COMPOSER	POET
1. "On Wenlock Edge"	Ralph Vaughn Williams	A. E. Housman
2. "Bredon Hill"	George Butterworth, John Duke	A. E. Housman

BREIR: (Scot.) (pr. bray-er), *brim, margin, top surface; briar.*

SONG	COMPOSER	POET
"Wee Willie"	Benjamin Britten	Robert Burns

BRENTANO, CLEMENS (1778–1842): German poet. Brentano was the brilliant and unstable son of an Italian merchant of Frankfurt. In school and at home his dreamy nature collided with discipline, to which he reacted with pranks and refusal to learn. Brentano's father finally sent him to the University of Halle, where he was an unsuccessful student of mines (1797). The next year at Jena he flourished due to the intellectual atmosphere. The collaboration with Achim von★Arnim on folk lyrics (1800) gave him a much needed stability. His unruly imagination focused best in lyric poetry, but he was altogether a typical romantic poet of the popular image. His two marriages ended in divorce partly because of his constant travel. In Berlin (1809) Brentano completed most of his fairy tales, but his creative work finished in 1818, when he turned to Catholicism and writing religious prose. Brentano's poetry was set by Strauss, Brahms, Ildebrando Pizzetti, and Johann and Louise Reichardt. PRINCIPAL WORKS: *Geschichte vom braven Kasperl*, 1817, Eng. trans. as *The Story of Just Caspar and the Fair Annie,* C. F. Schreiber, 1927; *Rheinmärchen*, 2 vols., 1846–47, Eng. trans. K. F. Kroecker, *Fairy Tales from Brentano*, 2 vols., 1885–88. SELECTED READING: S. S. Prawer, *German Lyric Poetry*, 1952. (SOURCE: Steinberg, 2, 1973)

BRETTL: a type of cabaret at the turn of the twentieth century. The poets of the period declaimed their verse to the accompaniment of music. This type of casual pop singing took place in a venue that was akin to a variety theater. (SOURCE: Kimball, 1996)

SONG	COMPOSER	POET
"Brettl-Lieder"	Arnold Schönberg	Hugo Salus

BREUGHEL: the family name of several Flemish painters: Pieter the Elder (1525?–1569) and Younger (1564?–1638), Jan the Elder (1568–1625) and Younger (1601–1678). Pieter the Elder was the greatest Flemish artist of the 1500s and the best landscape artist of his time. He was a moralist who saw man's folly in many disguises. One of his earliest works was a series of allegorical drawings of virtues and vices. A remarkably keen observer of human character, he used Hieronymus Bosch's manner of distributing many small figures over a large landscape, combined with a satirical view of folly, vice, and the sins of the flesh. Pieter the Younger imitated his father's style. Jan the Elder worked with Peter Paul Reubens and painted still lifes and landscapes; his son Jan the Younger painted flowers and landscapes.

SONG	COMPOSER	POET
"The Dance"	Ned Rorem	William Carlos Williams

BREVIARY: from the Latin, meaning a short summary, either the book containing psalms, prayers, hymns, etc. of the Liturgy of the Hours, or that Liturgy itself recited privately.

SONG	COMPOSER	POET
"Hymne"	Francis Poulenc	Jean Racine

BRIDE OF THE SEA: the city of Venice, so called from an ancient Venetian ceremony in which the *Doge threw a ring into the Adriatic Sea, saying, "We wed thee, O sea, in token of perpetual domination."

BRIDGES, ROBERT (1844–1930): English poet laureate 1913–30. Bridges was interested in languages, natural science, music, and prosody. He wrote elegant poems in a great variety of meters, and in old age surprised himself and others with a long poem, *The Testament of Beauty*, his concluding reflections about life and art. The verse of Robert Bridges was set by Sidney Homer. PRINCIPAL WORKS: *Poetical Works of Robert Bridges,* 5 vols., 1898–1905, enlarged ed. 1931; *Poetical Works*, 1912, 1926, 1953; *The Testament of Beauty*, 1929; *Poetry and Prose*, ed. J. Sparrow, 1955. SELECTED

READING: J. G. Ritz, *Bridges and Hopkins: A Literary Friendship*, 1960. (SOURCE: Steinberg, 2, 1973)

BRIG: (Scot.), *bridge*; also an abbreviation of *brigantine*, a vessel with two masts, square-rigged, carrying on the main mast a lower fore-and-aft sail with a gaff and a boom in order to obtain greater sail power. A brig o' dread, literally *a bridge of dread*, is a circle before purgatory. (SOURCE: *OED*, 1989)

SONG	COMPOSER	POET
"Serenade for Tenor and Horn"	Benjamin Britten	anon. fifteenth-century verses

BRIGHTON: one of the most popular seaside resorts in England. It lies in west Sussex on the coast of the English Channel, 50 miles south of London. Once a fishing village, now a bustling seaside town with a mild, pleasant climate, its success assured since George VI stayed there (1783) as Prince Regent.

SONG	COMPOSER	POET
"Tell Me the Truth about Love"	Benjamin Britten	W. H. Auden

BRINDISI: a toast to a particular person; also a town near the southern tip of the Italian peninsula, a principal port of the Adriatic Sea. In the Ibert song, it is the name of a steamer, indicating the name of its port and the probability of having a good time.

SONG	COMPOSER	POET
1. "Familière"	Jacques Ibert	Philippe Chabaneix
2. "Brindisi"	Giuseppe Verdi	Andrea Maffei

BRITTANY: the bulbous portion of western France that juts out into the Atlantic. Brittany has jagged rocky coastal cliffs, cobbled seaport streets, Celtic music, Stonehenge-like dolmens and menhirs (prehistorical standing stones). The Bretons have a cultural affinity with the Celts across the channel. The Celts that migrated to France had spent most of the Iron Age on the British Isles. For that reason the Celtic bloodlines maintain as part of Brittany the legends, the language, the types of flowers, the number of fishermen, even the pervasive use of bagpipes.

SONG	COMPOSER	POET
"Chanson bretonne"	Francis Poulenc	Max Jacob

BRONTË, EMILY (1818–1848): English poet, sister of writers Charlotte and Anne Brontë. Educated primarily at home, Emily created with sister Anne the imaginary world of Gondal, the setting for many of her best narrative and lyric poems. The moorlands, which often appeared in her writing, were even more beloved to Emily than they were to her sisters. After a brief period as a governess and nine months in Brussels with Charlotte, studying French, German, and music, she returned to her home and remained there for the rest of her life. In 1845 Charlotte "discovered" Emily's poems and arranged a joint publication (1846). *Wuthering Heights* was written in 1845–46 and published in 1847, but recognized as a masterpiece only after Emily's death (of consumption). She is now established as one of the most original poets of the century. Emily Brontë was a stoic and a mystic, had no close friends, and wrote few letters. Her poetry was set by Ernst Bacon and John Ireland. PRIN-CIPAL WORKS: *Wuthering Heights*, 1847; *Poems*, ed. D. Roper and E. Chitham, 1994. SELECTED READING: S. Davies, *Emily Brontë: Heretic*, 1994. (SOURCE: Drabble, 2000)

BROOKE, RUPERT (1887–1915): English poet, journalist, playwright. Rupert Brooke was educated at King's College, Cambridge University. Early on, he wrote travel letters from the United States and the South Seas for a London paper, then served his country in World War I, and died at the age of twenty-seven at the height of his fame and popularity. Brooke's fame was achieved and now rests on a legend of his physical beauty and the passionate and patriotic sonnets that he wrote on the outbreak of the war. His poems proclaim the value of sacrifice and suffering over the selfishness of everyday life. Their one-time appeal has been diminished by the slaughter that Brooke never actually witnessed. The poetry of Rupert Brooke was set by John Ireland, Charles Ives, Harry Burleigh, Bainbridge Crist, and Charles Griffes. PRINCIPAL WORKS: Verse: *Poems*, 1911; *1914, and Other Poems*, 1915; *Collected Poems*, 1915, as *Complete Poems*, 1932. Play: *Lithuania*, 1915. Other: *Letters from America*, 1916. SELECTED READING: Nigel H. Jones, *Rupert Brooke: Life, Death, and Myth*, 1999. (SOURCES: Vinson, 1979; Drabble, 1985)

BROWNING, ELIZABETH BARRETT (1806–1861): English poet, essayist, reviewer. Born at her father's estate where she was educated privately, an injury to her spine (1821) forced Elizabeth Barrett to live as a semi-invalid from then on. Settled in London in 1828, the drowning of her brother exacerbated her delicate condition, confining her to a sick room so that her time in London was spent writing verse, contributing literary articles, and helping friends with their writing projects. In 1846 Elizabeth Barrett and Robert ★Browning were married, afterward residing in Pisa and Florence until her death in 1861. The two Brownings were partners in one of the most famous romances of the nineteenth century, but Elizabeth Barrett was already a well-known poet when she met her future husband in 1846. Modern readers see in her poetry few of the innovations shown by her husband's best work; they often find her poetry full of conventional phraseology. Clearly, her public was far less cynical than today's. The *Sonnets from the Portuguese* probably succeed best in overcoming her limitations because the sonnet form imposes its own discipline. Elizabeth Barrett Browning's poetry has been set by Libby Larsen, Carlos Surinach, Ernst Bacon, Edward Elgar, Mario Castelnuovo-Tedesco, and Norman dello Joio. PRINCIPAL WORKS: *The Seraphim and Other Poems*, 1838; *Poems*, 1844; *Sonnets from the Portuguese*, 1850; *Aurora Leigh*, 1857; *Last Poems*, 1862. SELECTED READING: M. Forster, *Elizabeth Barrett Browning*, 1988; Julia Markus, *Dared and Done*, 1995. (SOURCE: Vinson, 1979)

BROWNING, ROBERT (1812–1889): an English poet of German-Scottish descent. Born in the southeast of London, Browning was educated mainly from his father's library of 6,000 volumes. Contrasting childhood influences were his mother's strong piety and his reading of ★Shelley, ★Byron, and ★Keats. In 1828 he enrolled at London University, but completed only one term, thereafter traveling to Russia

(1834) and Italy for the first time (1838). His first great critical success was *Paracelsus*, which led to important literary friendships with men who persuaded him to write for the stage. Browning's second play, *Sordello*, inspired such a hostile reception that it depressed his reputation for twenty years. After a correspondence with Elizabeth *Barrett, the two finally married and eloped to Italy (1846) to escape her father's disapproval of the match. They lived in Pisa, then Florence, until Elizabeth's death (1861). His reputation began to be corrected with the publication of *Men and Women*, a masterpiece of his middle period. *The Ring and the Book* (1868) solidified his new reputation, and Browning returned to England after his wife's death, to live there with his sister. Browning died in Venice and was buried in Westminster Abbey. He had grown to maturity during the decline of *Romanticism, when poetic vision had yielded to social and religious values. The late Victorians had idolized him and his experimental style, especially his development of the dramatic monologue, which, when set to music, became a *melodrama*. Browning was capable of introspective subtlety in his characterizations. He believed that art was rooted in human ethical nature; therefore his point of view is a moral one. Browning's verse was set by Alice Barnett, Ned Rorem, Amy Beach, Norman Dello Joio, Henry Hadley, Sidney Homer, and Charles Ives. PRINCIPAL WORKS: *Paracelsus*, 1835; *Men and Women*, 1855; *Dramatic Personae*, 1864; *The Ring and the Book*, 1868–69. SUGGESTED READING: Donald S. Hair, *Robert Browning's Language*, 1999. (SOURCE: Drabble, 2000)

BRUCHMANN, FRANZ VON (1798–1867): Austrian poet, later a Redemptorist priest. Son of a wealthy merchant, Bruchmann first studied law before changing to philosophy. The Schubertiads (1822–1825) took place in his father's home, and Bruchmann and his two sisters took an active part in them. It was probably Bruchmann who introduced Schubert to the poetry of Friedrich von *Schlegel, a regular visitor to the father's home. Although Bruchmann had left the church in his student days, he rejoined the Catholic Church and was ordained in 1833. His poetry was never published, surviving only in the five poems set in 1822–23 by Schubert: "An die Leier," "Im Haine," "Am See," "Schwestergruss," and "Der zürnende Barde." (SOURCE: Reed, 1997)

BRUDER LIEDERLICH: (Ger.), colloquialism for *black sheep of the family.*

SONG	COMPOSER	POET
"Bruder Liederlich"	Richard Strauss	Detlov von Liliencron

BRUNETTE: one of the many forms of French songs of the seventeenth and eighteenth centuries; a simple, unaffected, tender, lighthearted piece named after the dark-haired girl to whom it was often addressed.

BRYANT, WILLIAM CULLEN (1794–1878): American poet, travel writer, historian, biographer, editor, translator. William Cullen Bryant was born in Massachusetts, educated privately and at Williams College. After studying law, he was admitted to the Massachusetts bar and practiced law in Great Barrington, Massachusetts (1816–25). He became editor of the *New York Review* and *Athenaeum* magazine, and was a significant pioneer in American literature. As a poet, Bryant's strong points are not passion, delicacy, or soaring imagination, but dignity and power. Even his lighter poems have a lecturing tone, reminding us that his forebears were rock-ribbed New England Puritans. The classic dignity of Bryant's best work is nicely balanced by his *Romantic sense of the divinity of nature; thus he was America's first Romantic poet. His favorite form was a series of descriptive stanzas followed by one or two moral stanzas, which he blended into powerful works of art. "He proudly celebrated the American landscape, American nature, and American history and legend. . . . Limited in range, his poetry has simplicity and dignity, and some delicate observations of a natural world" (Vinson, 1979). Charles Ives set some poems of William Cullen Bryant. PRINCIPAL WORKS: *Thanatopsis,* 1817; *Poems,* 1821; *Poems,* 1832. SELECTED READING: Norbert Krapf, *Under Open Sky: Poets on William Cullen Bryant,* 1986. (SOURCE: Vinson, 1979)

BRYUSOV, VALERY (1873–1924): Russian poet, novelist, and critic. Bryusov was a central figure of Russian *Symbolism. Son of a Moscow merchant and grandson of a serf, Bryusov had developed an early interest in poetry, mostly French. He graduated from Moscow University with a degree in the humanities (1899). By 1900 he had become the managing editor of a publishing house that published works by Russian Symbolists. When the reaction against Symbolism set in, Bryusov was often made the main butt of the criticism. In 1910 he parted from the Symbolists and, accepting the Bolshevik Revolution without reservation, became a functionary in the education commissariat. He spent the rest of his life lecturing, writing essays on Russian poets, and translating Virgil and French poetry of the nineteenth century, as well as Armenian, Finnish, Latvian, and other poetry. His poetry was really nineteenth-century verse, often striving to capture the spirit of alien cultures and their mythologies. His rich language and imagery lack originality, but he believed in the worth of art for art's sake in poetry, devoting the better part of his oeuvre to western culture. The poetry of Valery Bryusov was set by Rachmaninoff and Gretchaninoff. WORKS: *Tertia Vigilia* [Third Vigil], 1900; *Urbi et Orbi* [To the City and the World], 1903; *Stephanos,* 1906; *Zerkalo teney* [Mirror of the Shades], 1912. SELECTED READING: M. P. Rice, *Bryusov and the Rise of Russian Symbolism,* 1975. (SOURCE: Terras, 1991)

BUDDHA: in Sanskrit, "the Enlightened One," the title given to Prince Siddhartha or Gautama, the founder of Buddhism, who lived in the sixth century B.C.E.

BUDMOUTH: in the poems and novels of Thomas *Hardy, a fictitious name for a place that resembles the real city of Weymouth.

BUNÍN, IVAN (1870–1953): Russian poet. Ivan Bunín died in Paris at the end of the classical period of Russian literature. His early volumes of poetry appeared in the 1890s, when the Russian *Symbolists were renewing the art of poetry. Yet Bunín continued serenely in the tradition of *Fet and was never tempted by modern styles, although Symbolism was an urban happening. Bunín had been born into a family of noblemen, poor but agrarian. Thus his best work used themes familiar to American Southern writers: the decay of the gentry and the degradation of the local community. His extensive travels gave him the material with which to write stories set in exotic Mediterranean and Oriental locales. For a time Bunín collaborated with

Gorky on his magazine, *Knowledge*. Opposed to the Bolshevik regime, he left Russia in 1920 and spent the rest of his life in exile, writing bitterly about the circumstances in his homeland. He was the first Russian writer to receive the Nobel Prize (1935), which annoyed the Soviet establishment. Another author, who, in 1937, stated that Bunín was the great classicist of Russian literature, was given for his trouble seventeen years at hard labor in Siberia. Bunín's prose was superior and more poetic than his rather conventional verse. Although he wrote nothing during the Nazi occupation of France, in 1951 he published a small volume of autobiography and literary reminiscences, *Memoirs and Portraits*, translated into English as *Dark Avenue and Other Stories*, 1951. The poetry of Ivan Bunín was set by Rachmaninoff and Gretchaninoff. WORKS: *Listopad* [Leaves Fall], 1900; *Zhizn Arsieneva* [The Well of Days], 1933; *The Gentleman from San Francisco and Other Stories*, 1964. SELECTED READING: S. Kryzytski, *The Works of Ivan Bunín*, 1971; M. Gorky, *Reminiscences*. (SOURCES: Brown, 1985; Kunitz, Colby, 1955)

BUNYAN, JOHN (1628–1688): English writer. Son of a tinker and one himself, Bunyan was born near Bedford. He was drafted into the parliamentary army and served from 1644 to 1646. Bunyan was introduced to religious works when he married his first wife (1649). In 1653 he joined a Nonconformist church and came into conflict with the Quakers, against whom he published his first writings. Living as an itinerant tinker, Bunyan was considered by the Restoration authorities a militant subversive because he placed the poor and simple above the mighty. Bunyan was arrested for preaching without a license (1660), after which he spent twelve years in the Bedford jail. During the first six years he wrote nine books, among them the beginning of *The Pilgrim's Progress*. Bunyan was released in 1672, appointed pastor at the same church, but imprisoned again for a short period (1677), during which time he finished *The Pilgrim's Progress*. In his widespread preaching, his style was down to earth, humorous, and impassioned. The work of John Bunyan was set by Ralph Vaughan Williams. PRINCIPAL WORKS: *The Pilgrim's Progress,* 1678, 1684; *The Life and Death of Mr. Badman,* 1680; *The Holy War,* 1682; *Works*, ed. R. Sharrock. (SOURCE: Drabble, 2000)

BUONAROTTI, MICHELANGELO (1475–1564): Florentine sculptor, painter, architect, poet. Michelangelo was born in Caprese to a father who was from a poor but proud family line, all of whose members were minor state officers under the patronage of the Medici family. As a baby, he was put out in a family of stone cutters to nurse, then was educated in Florence, where he showed early artistic promise. At thirteen he was apprenticed to the workshop of the Ghirlandaio brothers to learn painting. When his talent came to the attention of Lorenzo de Medici, Michelangelo was brought to live at Casa Medici, where he worked at sculpture. Here he met poets and other great artists and scholars and built a reputation as one of the great sculptors of the day, doing his great works, the Pietà and the David, between 1492 and 1505. In 1505 he was summoned to Rome to build a marble monument for Pope Julius II's tomb. The sculptor worked for four decades on this project, delayed by the pope's constant demands for changes. One of the interruptions was an order to decorate the ceiling of the Sistine Chapel with frescoes, which he began in 1508, spending three and one half years flat on his back on a scaffold, eyes on the ceiling, the experience later described in some of his three hundred poems. In 1534 Michelangelo returned to Rome for the last time, to design the dome of St. Peter's and to complete his life's work with The Last Judgment painting in the Sistine Chapel. He was made an honored citizen of Rome and died peacefully only a few weeks before his eighty-ninth birthday. That the greatest artist of the sixteenth century should also be the greatest poet of that era demonstrates the high level of creative artistry in that time. Michelangelo's finest poems, *sonnets and madrigals, were written in his last twenty years of life. "His poems are like his sculpture: lofty but rough-hewn" (Kunitz, Colby, 1967). The later poems, showing fears of sin and salvation, were acknowledged to be the finest poems written in Italian since *Dante and *Petrarch, and described as bringing to perfection an artistic tradition. Among his passionate admirers were *Goethe, *Blake, Delacroix, and Stendhal. The poems of Michelangelo have been set by Liszt, Pizzetti, Strauss, Wolf, Britten, Ezra Laderman, Nicholas Flagello, Goffredo Petrassi, and Ottmar Schoeck. PRINCIPAL WORKS: The standard English translations of Michelangelo's poetry are by J. A. Symonds; *The Sonnets of Michelangelo Buonarotti and Tommaso Campanella*, 1878; Joseph Tusiani, *The Complete Poems of Michelangelo*, 1960. SELECTED READING: J. A. Symonds, *Life of Michelangelo Buonarotti*, 1893; A. Condivi. *Life of Michelangelo Buonarotti*. (SOURCE: Kunitz, Colby, 1967)

BURCHIELLO, IL (pseudonym of Domenico di Giovanni) (1404–1449): Florentine poet, barber. Burchiello lived in the Calimala quarter of Florence and took his pseudonym from the poems he wrote *alla burchia*, meaning in casual style, some of which could be described as nonsense poetry. He was friendly with the artists and witty people of Florence. It is thought that his hostility to the Medici caused him to leave Florence for Siena, where his misdeeds resulted in a prison term. In 1443 he moved to Rome where he lived for the rest of his life. The verses of Burchiello were set by GianFranco Malipiero. (SOURCE: Hainsworth, Robbey, 2002)

BURDOCK: a cocklebur, a coarse, weedy plant with prickly flower heads.

SONG	COMPOSER	POET
"From a Very Little Sphinx"	Bernard Wagenaar	Edna St. Vincent Millay

BÜRGER, GOTTFRIED (1747–1794): German poet. Bürger spent a dissipated youth and lived a life of deprivation, professional crises, and emotional turmoil. All his life he had to earn his living by doing literary hackwork. After spending a small time as professor of literature at the University of Göttingen, other positions smothered his creative abilities. His three marriages were all disastrous. Bürger linked his poems to contemporary events and issues, striking a popular note by modeling them on folk songs and popular ballads that reached a wide audience. His political essays and poetry attacked the abuses of Germany's tyrannical leaders. Schiller savagely reviewed his collection of poems in 1791; that review together with the scandal of his third marriage contributed to his early death. The verse of Gottfried Bürger has been set by Beethoven, Haydn, Strauss, Václav Momášek, and Hans Pfitzner. PRIN-CIPAL WORKS: *Sämtliche Schriften (1796–1802)*, 4 vols., ed. W. von Wurzbach, 1904. SELECTED READING: E. S. Blenkinsop, *Bürger's Originality*, 1936. (SOURCES: Mathieu, Stern, 1987; Steinberg, 2, 1973)

BURNIES: (Scot.), n. *little streams*; v. *to burn*.

SONG	COMPOSER	POET
"A Laddie's Sang"	Benjamin Britten	William Soutar

BURNS, ROBERT (1759–1796): Scottish poet and travel writer. Robert Burns, a farmer, was born near Ayr, Scotland, educated at a local school and at home. He was the father of nine children in wedlock and three illegitimate children. In 1788 he was commissioned as tax inspector, which occupation he combined with farming. When the farm failed, he moved his family to Dumfries, remaining there until his death. Burns was not an innovator. He took the existing stanza forms and the Scots tongue as they were shaped by his poet predecessors and applied them to his own situations. The fact that he was born a farmer ensured that he would be brought into contact with rural Scotland where, before the industrial revolution, agriculture was still the greatest strength of the economy. Changed little since medieval times, both Scottish life and the physical environment were to change within Burns's lifetime. He made use of images and situations he found around him to fix in his poetry the essential qualities of that old way of life. He used a standard stanza form called *rime couée*, developed from an early form used by French troubadours and in English miracle plays. Robert Burns's main strength lay in his commitment to the Scots tongue at a time when any Scottish man who wanted to rise in the world was abandoning it in favor of English, and in his alignment with the common sense interests of the ordinary man at a time when the fairness of privilege was being questioned throughout Europe. It is not surprising that his "Kilmarnock Poems" and Mozart's *Marriage of Figaro* appeared in the same year. A highly sexed man, Burns celebrated in his love songs every aspect of the relationship between man and woman, inferring the physical realities of that relationship. His poetry was set by such varied composers as Britten, Schumann, Shostakovich, Ernst Bacon, John Koch, Amy Beach, George Walker, Miriam Gideon, Ernest Gold, and Gordon Binkerd. PRINCIPAL WORKS: Collections: *Poems and Songs*, 3 vols., ed. James Kingsley, 1968; *Select Collection of Original Scottish Airs*, 4 vols., ed. G. Thomson, 1793–99; *The Scots Musical Museum*, 6 vols., with others, ed. James Johnson, 1787–1803. Verse: *Poems, Chiefly in the Scottish Dialect*, 1786, revised edition, 1787, 2 vols., 1793, 1794, 1801. SELECTED READING: Ian A. Nimmo, *Burns: His Life and Tradition in Words and Sounds*, 1965; Robert T. Fitzhugh, *Robert Burns, the Man and Poet: A Round, Unvarnished Account*, 1970. (SOURCES: Vinson, 1979; Drabble, 1985)

BUSSE, CARL (1872–1918) (sometimes pen name Fritz Döhring): German poet, novelist, and short story writer. Busse studied German literature at the universities of Berlin and Rostock, and worked as a journalist in Augsburg before settling in Berlin, where he published several collections of poetry. Busse's poetry was written in the popular style, but his ★impressionistic poem "Rote Husaren" appeared in several anthologies. Busse's poetry was set by composers Hans Pfitzner, Richard Strauss, and Richard Trunk. PRINCIPAL WORKS: Poetry: *Gedichte*, 1892; *Neue Gedichte*, 1896; *Vagabunden*, 1901; *Heilige Not*, 1910. Novels: *Jadwiga*, 1899; *Lena Küppers*, 1910. (SOURCE: Garland, 1976)

BUSSINE, ROMAIN (1830–1899): French poet and teacher of singing. Bussine, along with his friends, Saint-Saëns, Franck, Fauré, and Lalo, organized the Société Nationale de Musique, whose motto was *"ars gallica,"* to encourage the performance of the works of young French composers. The verse of Romain Bussine was set by Gabriel Fauré, notably the celebrated song "Après un rêve." Brian Rees, in his book on Camille Saint-Saëns (1999), states, "I was delighted to discover. . . that Romain Bussine . . . was Professor of Singing at the Conservatoire (this explains why the poem is nowhere to be found in print, and why the song has the character of a *vocalise*)."

BYRON, BARON GEORGE GORDON (1788–1824): English poet. The son of Captain John Byron and his second wife, Lord Byron inherited his title of sixth baron at the age of ten. The club-foot with which he was born was said to influence not only his every action but also every line of poetry he wrote. At Cambridge (1805) he attended to his studies only intermittently, between his debaucheries. Although he took his seat in the House of Lords in 1809, he soon left to visit Portugal, Spain, Malta, Greece, and the Levant, where he swam the ★Hellespont and became obsessed with the idea that Greece must be freed from the Turks. The publication of the first two cantos of *Childe Harold's Pilgrimage* (1812) made Byron a celebrity in literary London. His half-sister Augusta, to whom he was a constant companion, gave birth to a daughter who was almost certainly his child. Yet, in 1815 he married another woman, while he sank further into debt and was publicly condemned for his incest. After a legal separation from his wife, Byron left England forever, living first in Geneva, where he fathered another child, then in Venice and Ravenna, where he formed a liaison with an Italian countess. When he managed to sell his English estate, he finally achieved freedom from financial worries. Moving to Greece, he gave large sums of money and much encouragement to the Greeks in order to foster their action against the Turks, but he himself died before seeing any military action. Greece mourned Byron's death, but St. Paul's deans and Westminster Abbey denied him burial. Byron's passionate poetry was much admired in Germany, France, and America, and very popular in England, although it was condemned for moral reasons. Lord Byron's poetry was set by Mendelssohn, Schumann, Rimsky-Korsakov, Mussorgsky, Wolf, Charles Ives, George Walker, Wintter Watts, David Diamond, and William Schumann. PRINCIPAL WORKS: *The Prisoner of Chillon*, a dramatic monologue, 1816; *Manfred*, a poetic drama, 1817; *Childe Harold*, 1812, 1816, 1818; *The Two Foscari*, a poetic drama, 1821, later an opera by Verdi; *Complete Poetical Works*, 3 vols., 1980, ed. J. J. McGann. SELECTED READING: Leslie A. Marchand, *Byron: A Portrait*, 1970; Phyllis Crosswith, *Byron: The Flawed Angel*, 1997. (SOURCE: Drabble, 2000)

"By the Croaking of the Toad": a song from the tragic extravaganza *The Indian Queen*, by John ★Dryden and Sir Robert Howard, first produced in 1677, altered in 1695 to include music by Henry Purcell. *See ★Indian Queen, The* for plot details and placement of songs.

C

CABANILLAS, RAMÓN (1873–1959): Spanish poet and playwright. Born in Cambados, the Province of Pontevedra, which is in Galicia, Cabanillas wrote in Galician and his poems speak of the Galician countryside. His output includes love lyrics, *A rose de cen follas*, sea poetry, *Vento mareiro*, and a collection of oral poetry, *Antifona da cantiga*. The verse of Ramón Cabanillas was set by Federico Mompou. (SOURCE: Cockburn, Stokes, 1992)

CABARET SONGS: songs in the style of theater and cabaret, compositions written by Benjamin Britten, Arnold Schönberg, William Bolcom, and Milton Babbitt. Britten originally wrote a song, "Funeral Blues" (originally called "Stop All the Clocks") for W. H. ★Auden's play, *The Ascent of F6*, produced in London in 1937. So taken was Britten with the performer's rendition of this song that he wrote a series of songs in that vein to Auden's verse, of which two have apparently been lost.

CACCIA: a fourteenth-century Italian musical/poetic form, which, together with the *ballata* and the *madrigal*, were the three most important secular forms of the time. The poems were usually on commonplace subjects and were set to lively music in the form of a two-part canon.

CÁDIZ, CADIX (Fr.): a city of Phoenician origins in southern Spain, the capital of Cádiz province. Cádiz occupies the tip of a narrow peninsula called the Island of León, which separates the Bay of Cádiz from the Atlantic Ocean. It has a mild climate and cooling breezes from the Mediterranean Sea. City walls, white buildings, and a thirteenth-century cathedral give the city character. Columns left from the time when Columbus sailed off on his second voyage still remain. The important and busy port city was attacked by Sir Francis Drake in 1587.

SONG	COMPOSER	POET
"Les Filles de Cadix"	Léo Délibes	Alfred de Musset

CADMUS, KADMOS (Ger.): founder of the ancient fortress at ★Thebes, son of Agenor, king of Phoenecia, and Telephassa, grandson of ★Poseidon, father of Leukothea, a marine deity, and protector of those who traveled by sea. Cadmus's daughter, Semele, was the mother of ★Bacchus (Dionysus), whose father was ★Zeus. Cadmus, husband of Harmonia, one of the ★Muses, gave the Greeks their alphabet. Cadmus and his brothers, Phoenix and Kilix, searched for their one sister, Europa, who was carried off by Zeus in the form of a white bull. The Delphic oracle told Cadmus to follow a cow and to found a city where the cow stopped and lay down. Cadmus sent his men for water at a nearby fountain, intending to sacrifice the cow, but his men were killed by a dragon that guarded the fountain. Cadmus killed the dragon and, at Athene's command, planted its teeth. These teeth grew into the gigantic Spartae warriors. Throwing a stone into their midst, Cadmus incited a fight from which only five Spartae survived. It was to these surviving Spartae that the leading families of Thebes traced their lineage. Because the dragon he slew was the son of ★Ares, Cadmus was punished by being made to serve as a slave for eight years. (SOURCES: *Bulfinch*, 1978; Graves, 1960 (2); Guirand, 1968; Mayerson, 1971; Murray, 1988)

SONG	COMPOSER	POET
1. "An die Leier"	Franz Schubert	tr. Franz von Bruchmann
2. "Misera, dove son!"	Wolfgang Amadeus Mozart	Pietro Metastasio

CAIN AND ABEL: biblical Old Testament brothers, the first two sons of ★Adam and Eve (Genesis 4). Cain, the first-born son, was a farmer, "a tiller of the ground," and Abel, the second son and a shepherd, "a keeper of sheep." Each brought an offering to God. Cain, the farmer, brought a selection of his crops, "the fruit of the ground"; Abel, the shepherd, brought "the firstlings of his flock and of the fat thereof." God had "regard" for Abel's offering, but not for Cain's. When this angered Cain, God warned him that sin was lying in wait for him, that he must master it or fall into its power (Genesis 7). In the course of talking with Abel in a field, Cain killed his brother. This is the first murder recorded in the Bible, a fratricide. Later, God asks Cain where his brother is. Cain's reply is one of the most famous quotes in the Bible: "Am I my brother's keeper?" When God tells Cain that he can hear Abel's blood crying out from the ground, the land is cursed for Cain. He will no longer be able to wrest his living from the soil. He will be a fugitive and a vagabond on the earth. He cries out that his punishment is too hard, that others will now hunt him down and kill him. In response, God places a mark on Cain, so that whoever sees it will not kill him. If someone did so, Cain would be avenged sevenfold. Driven from the presence of God, Cain lives in the land of Nod, east of the Garden of Eden. There he marries and has children. Among his descendants is ★Jubal, "the father of all such as handle the harp and organ" (Genesis 4.21). The rationale behind God's preference for Abel's offering over Cain's has perplexed biblical commentators for centuries. Many see it as a reflection of the conflict between nomadic and agrarian societies. It has been suggested that the rejection was based on quality: an offering of fruits and vegetables is not as much of a sacrifice as Abel's more meaningful offering, the sacrifice of a living creature. (SOURCE: King James Version of the Holy Bible, 1611)

SONG	COMPOSER	POET
"Still Falls the Rain"	Benjamin Britten	Edith Sitwell

CALAMUS: a group of poems, the "Calamus poems," in *Leaves of Grass* by Walt Whitman. A manuscript cluster of twelve poems marked by Roman numerals, intended originally for a commemorative notebook, the Calamus poems as they appeared in the final *Leaves of Grass* (1881), numbered thirty-nine. Whitman wrote, when asked for a definition of the term by his English publisher, "Calamus is a common word here. It is a very large and aromatic grass, or rush, growing about water-ponds in the valleys—spears about three feet high—often called 'sweet-flag'—grows all over the Northern and Middle States."Whitman also insisted that the significance of Calamus was not homoerotic, but mainly political, possessing a tragic and idealistic power.

SONG	COMPOSER	POET
"Three Calamus Poems"	Ned Rorem	Walt Whitman

CALATRAVA: a Spanish military order given papal sanction in 1164. The Spanish orders were similar to the monastic orders of the Holy Land. The Knights Templar had obtained extensive rights in Spain, but when their empire weakened, the Spanish orders took first place. The Order of Calatrava was created when the Templars abandoned the fortress of Calatrava near Ciudad Real. (SOURCE: Cockburn, Stokes, 1992)

SONG	COMPOSER	POET
"Al val de Fuente Ovejuna"	Joaquín Turina	Lope de Vega

CALDERÓN DE LA BARCA, PEDRO (1600–1681): Spanish poet and dramatist. Calderón was born to a wealthy Madrid family, his father an accountant in the royal treasury. As such, his life was spent either at court or in church. Jesuit educated, Calderón began to study for the priesthood in 1614. When his father died, Calderón went to Salamanca (1615), where for four years he studied canon law. During the Catalan revolt Calderón served as a soldier, and his bravery won for him a pension. Upon the deaths of his mistress and two brothers (1648), Calderón embraced the priesthood, turning his genius toward sacred dramas and writing eighty sacramental plays, 120 serious and comic dramas, twenty minor *entremeses* (interludes), *loas* (panegyrical prologues), and *jácaras* (witty ballads). The recurrent use of Honor, Duty, Loyalty, etc. in his writing reflects the aristocratic social codes of the times. Calderón's imagery was sensuous, revealing the beauty of religious grace and the awfulness of sin. In 1824 *Shelley translated some Calderón scenes and verses. The work of Calderón de la Barca was set by Richard Strauss. WORKS: *Psalle et sile,* ed. Leopaldo Trenor, 1936; *8 Dramas of Calderón,* 1853, trans. Edward Fitzgerald. READING: Gilbert Chase, *Music in Spain*; Charlene E. Calderón, *Calderón: The Imagery of Tragedy,* 1991. (SOURCE: Kunitz, Colby, 1967)

CALIBAN: a character in *Shakespeare's *The* *Tempest,* described as a deformed slave. His name may stem from *Carib* or *cannibal.* Sycorax, the witch, was his mother, and Caliban was the original owner of Prospero's island. Although he is only semi-human, his poetic speech has contributed to sympathetic portrayals of him. (SOURCE: Drabble, 2000)

SONG	COMPOSER	POET
"Caliban"	Ernst Bacon	William Shakespeare

CALLIGRAMME: a poem typeset to form a visual image. In *Apollinaire's poetic cycle, *Calligrammes,* some of which were set to music by Francis Poulenc, several of the poems are in the form of an ideogram: a graphic symbol representing an object or idea without expressing the sounds that form its name, or, a symbol representing an idea rather than a word. For example, one poem in honor of ★Bacchus is shaped in the form of a bottle.

CALLIMACHUS (ca.310–after 256 B.C.E.): Greek poet, scholar. Callimachus worked in the library at Alexandria and was admired by first century B.C.E. Roman poets such as ★Catullus, who imitated him, and also by the Byzantines. The upheavals of the thirteenth century resulted in only a few of his manuscripts being preserved: six hymns, sixty epigrams, and a number of fragments. Because of the difficulty of Callimachus's writing, he had few readers until the end of the seventeenth century, when a number of editions appeared. ★Tennyson and ★Bridges drew mythological material from his hymns. The writing of Callimachus was set by Peter Warlock. SELECTED READING: Richard Bentley contributed to an edition of his works in 1697; John Ferguson, *Callimachus*, 1980. (SOURCE: Drabble, 2000)

CALLIOPE: in Greek mythology, chief of the nine ★Muses, she herself the muse of epic or heroic poetry and of poetic inspiration and eloquence. Calliope possessed a beautiful voice. Her emblems are a stylus and a wax tablet. The name refers also to a steam organ that makes raucous music. (SOURCE: Cooper, 1992)

CALVARY: from the Latin, *skull*, the proper name of the place where Christ was crucified, near Jerusalem, so called from the fanciful resemblance it bore to a human skull (Luke 23.33; Matthew 27.33).

CALVINISTIC: characteristic of Calvinism, a theological system of the Christian reformer John Calvin and his followers, emphasizing sovereignty of God in the bestowal of grace and the doctrine of predestination—God has already determined who will go to Heaven or Hell.

SONG	COMPOSER	POET
"Calvinistic Evensong"	Jack Beeson	John Betjeman

CALVOCORESSI, MICHEL DIMITRI (1877–1944): poet and critic, born in Greece but educated in France. Calvocoressi, a skilled linguist, wrote in several languages, publishing books on Liszt, Mussorgsky, Glinka, Schumann, and many translations into English. In 1898 he and Ravel met. After a time of mutual suspicion, they became lifelong friends. Calvocoressi introduced Ravel to the folk texts that Ravel used for his *Cinq mélodies populaires grecques*. After World War I, the writer moved to England, where he died. In 1923 Oxford University Press published his *On Musical Criticism*. *Musician's Gallery* was published in 1933. Ravel dedicated his *Alborada del gracioso* to Calvocoressi. (SOURCE: Magill, 1, 1997)

CALYDON: in romances relating to King ★Arthur, a forest supposed to occupy the northern portion of England; the home of Meleager; the site of the Caledonian boar hunt.

CALYPSO: a sea-nymph, who was the queen of the island Ogygia, on which ★Ulysses (Odysseus) was wrecked; also a musical style of West Indian origin influenced by the offbeat syllabic stress and loose rhymes of jazz, the name of obscure origin, perhaps only copying the name of the sea-nymph. A sea-nymph was one of a heavily populated class of female divinities. They were of the lower rank, but shared many of the attributes of the gods. Calypso received Ulysses hospitably, entertained him magnificently, but became enamored of him. She kept him there for seven years, promising him perpetual youth and immortality if he would become her husband and remain with her forever. His desire to return to his country, wife, and son was too strong. Calypso at last was commanded by *Jove to dismiss Ulysses she thereby supplied him with the means of constructing a raft, provisioned it, and gave him a favoring gale. Calypso is an allusion used to portray a siren who is dangerously attractive to men. (SOURCE: *Bulfinch*, 1978)

SONG	COMPOSER	POET
"Calypso"	Benjamin Britten	W. H. Auden

CAMBRIA: a variant of Cumbria, the Latinized derivative of Cymry (Welshman or Wales), thus pertaining to Wales or the Welsh.

CAMELOT: In British fable, the legendary spot where King *Arthur held court, tentatively located at Caerleon in Somerset, in a hillfort known as Cadbury Castle. (SOURCE: Cooper, 1992)

SONG	COMPOSER	POET
"Miniver Cheevy"	John Duke	Edwin Arlington Robinson

CAMMAERTS, ÉMILE (1878–1953): Belgian poet, cartographer, journalist, playwright, historian, and essayist. Born in Brussels, Cammaerts was raised by his mother, a well-educated and intelligent woman. Often ill as a child, he was educated at home by tutors, then attended the University of Brussels. Here he discovered *Michelangelo and Rabelais, and studied English in order to read *Shakespeare. By the time he settled in England (1908), later to teach at the University of London, he was already well known in Belgium as a lyric poet who wrote verse, verse plays, and art criticism. He married a British actress and entered the Church of England. The development of his spirituality is revealed in *The Flower of Grass*, which *Auden compared favorably to the writings of St. Augustine. The sound scholarship of his political writing was rewarded with the CBE decoration. The verse of Émile Cammaerts was set by John Alden Carpenter and Edward Elgar. PRINCIPAL WORKS in English: *Belgian Poems*, 1915; *New Belgian Poems*, 1916; *Messines and Other Poems*, 1918; *The Poetry of Nonsense*, 1925; *Upon This Rock*, 1943; *The Flower of Grass*, 1944. (SOURCE: Kunitz, Colby, 1955)

CAMÕES, LUIZ DE (1524?–1580): Portugal's greatest poet. Camões was probably born in Lisbon, both parents from great Portuguese families. He was probably educated at the University of Coimbra, where a strong classical curriculum existed. His first poems were imitative of *Petrarch's models. When Camões settled in Lisbon about 1542, he had a secure place in the circle around King João III because of his family connections. A dashing figure as a court poet who had written three plays and many poems, he lost all his patronage when he pursued a romance with the queen's lady-in-waiting. Subsequently, on his first tour as a soldier in Africa, he lost his right eye. In 1553 he joined an expedition to India, after which he did not see Portugal for seventeen years, living the life of a warrior adventurer, while observing the lives and habits of the Hindus and primitive peoples of India, serving in Goa, sojourning with Buddhist monks in China—all the while pouring forth poetry. Camões turned these years away from Portugal into masterpieces, notably his *Os Lucíadas* (The Lusiads), Lusitania being the legendary name for Portugal. When he finally returned to Portugal in 1570, he enjoyed immediate fame and honor with the publication of *The Lusiads*, which related the voyages of the explorer Vasco da Gama that led to the discovery of a sea route to India in 1498. "He represented the adventures not of a single man, but of an entire civilization" (Kunitz, Colby, 1967). Camões was celebrated in poems by Lord ★Byron, Elizabeth Barrett ★Browning, and William ★Wordsworth. He wrote in all the Renaissance genres of poetry: epics, verse dramas, ★sonnets, odes, ★elegies, eclogues (some written in Castilian Spanish). When the Spanish occupied Lisbon and made Castilian the official language, it was the work of Camões that saved his native Portuguese tongue from extinction. His poetry was set by Jean Berger. PRINCIPAL WORKS: *The Lusiads*, most recent translation, Leonard Bacon, 1950. SELECTED READING: George Monteiro, *The Presence of Camoës: Influences on the Literature of England, America, and Southern Africa,* 1996. (SOURCE: Kunitz, Colby, 1967)

CAMPE, JOHANN HEINRICH (1746–1818): German poet. Campe worked as a school organizer and administrator. So sympathetic to the French Revolution was he that he visited Paris in 1789. Although he studied theology briefly and worked as a tutor, he persisted in writing educational books and children's literature, a dictionary, satires, and an epic. Mozart set Campe's poetry. PRINCIPAL WORKS: *Sämtliche Kinder- und Jugendschriften* (including a German adaptation of *Robinson Crusoe*), 37 vols. from 1807; *Wörterbuch der deutschen Sprache*, a dictionary, 5 vols., 1801–11. (SOURCE: Garland, 1976)

CAMPION, THOMAS (1567–1620): English poet, musician, and doctor. Educated first at Cambridge and Gray's Inn, Campion at middle age studied medicine and took his M.D. from the University of Caen (1605). Together with composer Philip Rosseter, he wrote *A Book of Ayres* (1601), then published four *Bookes of Ayres* himself between 1613 and 1617. In his *Observations in the Art of English Poesie* (1602) he stated that he was against "the vulgar and unarteficiall custome of riming" (Drabble, 2000). He wrote several court masques during the early reign of James I. Campion's poetry was set by himself and also by Philip Rosseter, John ★Dowland, Robert Jones, Virgil Thomson, Louis Gruenberg, Stephen Paulus, and Peter Warlock. An edition of Campion's poems and the *Observations*, was edited by W. R. Davis in 1967. SELECTED READING: David Lindley, *Thomas Campion*, 1986. (SOURCE: Drabble, 2000)

CAMPOAMOR Y CAMPOSORIO, RAMÓN DE (1817–1901): Spanish poet and epigrammist. Campoamor was born in the province of Asturias. First he dabbled in theology, then medicine, then law, but found his true vocation in writing. Although his temperament was jovial and good-natured, he had an interest in politics. The best poems of his youth can be found in *Cantares*. Later he claimed to have invented new poetic forms, among them the *dolora*, which was a concise poem dramatizing a universal truth, characterized by delicacy, pathos, and a moral message expressed in irony. Campoamor was one of the first writers to break with the romantic tradition. A ★Symbolist, Campoamor is best known for *Doloras*, *Humorades*, and *Pequeños Poemas*, which volumes he filled with poems in the style he favored: philosophic ★epigrams that expressed a humorous point of view. His poetry was set by Joaquín Turina and Julio Osma. PRINCIPAL WORKS: *Obras completas*, 8 vols., 1901–03. SELECTED READING: R. Hilton, *Campoamor, Spain and the World,* 1940. (SOURCE: Kunitz, Colby, 1967)

CANA, KANA (Ger.): a biblical village in Galilee that overlooks a marshy plain, the scene of the first two miracles performed by ★Jesus. It is identical with the ancient village of Khirbet Qana, 9 miles north of Nazareth, the name meaning the place of reeds. According to St. John, it is the place where Jesus turned water into wine at a wedding feast and where he healed the son of a nobleman from Capernaum.

SONG	COMPOSER	POET
"Von der Hochzeit zu Kana"	Paul Hindemith	Rainer Maria Rilke

CANCIONERO: a Spanish songbook; the name given in the fifteenth or sixteenth centuries to various anthologies of courtly lyrics and longer poems, such as the Spanish *Cancionero de Palaçio*; also a collection of a single poet, such as the songbooks of John ★Dowland. In northern Spain poems were written in the Galician-Portuguese dialect; the dialect of southern Spain eventually became the official Spanish language. For example, even the *Cantigas de Santa Maria*, a cancionero collected by Alfonso el Sabio (1221–1284), was written in Galician-Portuguese, although the king himself was a Castilian.

CANCIONERO DE PALACIO: the single largest Spanish manuscript collection of Medieval and Renaissance songs, discovered on a musty top shelf of the library in the Royal Palace of Madrid in 1870. The *Cancionero de Palacio* was first published in 1890 by Francisco Barbiere, Spain's first musicologist, under the title *Cancionero Musical Espagñol de los siglos XV y XVI*. A reprint appeared in Buenos Aires in 1945. Although well over sixty composers are represented in this anthology, the major share is that of Juan del Encina.

CANEVAS: a phrase in Viennese dialect, meaning in High German *kann er etwas* (can he do anything?). When Schubert's circle of friends and their ladies met in a friendly home to hear music, the evenings were called Schubertiads. They were also referred to as a *canevas*. This nickname grew from Schubert's habit of inquiring about a newcomer in their midst, "can e vas?"

CANNY: (Scot.), *pleasant.*

CANTE HONDO, or JONDO: a *"deep" song*; a type of sorrowful song of Andalusia, preserved by gypsy singers and dancers. The type includes tragic love songs, plaints, and prison songs sung in long undulating notes, possibly related to the music of Sephardic Jews, and accompanied by the guitar.

CANTERBURY GUESTS, THE; OR, A BARGAIN BROKEN: a play by Edward Ravenscroft, produced in 1694, containing one duet by Henry Purcell. Hastily put together from Ravenscroft's other works, this play is a variation on an old plot used in many opera librettos. A clever heiress, destined for marriage with a fool, tricks her guardian into letting her marry a thinly disguised rascal. There follow grotesque displays of gluttony and an obscene bedroom farce prepared by broken barriers of good taste. In act 3 two male characters and two prostitutes are entertained by a bickering dialogue between two hostile housewives, "Good neighbor, why do you look awry?" A series of jolly insults are exchanged in 6/4, which changes to duple meter and dotted rhythms as one of the women accuses the other of trying to seduce her husband, after which the argument escalates. The women heatedly sing different words at the same time, as Purcell sets the crude words faithfully. (SOURCE: Price, 1984)

CANTERBURY TALES, THE: a work by the English writer Geoffrey ★Chaucer (c.1343–1400), extending to 17,000 lines in prose and verse of various meters. The party assembles at the Tabard Inn. There the host, Bailly, proposes that the pilgrims should shorten the road to Canterbury (where they are traveling to pay their devotions at the Shrine of St. Thomas à Becket) by telling four stories each, two on the way to Canterbury and two on the way back. He who tells the best tale will be treated with supper on the homeward journey. The work is incomplete, since only twenty-four stories are told altogether, although there are thirty-one pilgrims. The best complete edition of Chaucer is *The Riverside Chaucer*, ed. L. D. Benson et al., 1988.

CANTICLE: a song; a hymn taken from the Scriptures, used in the public services of a church. Benjamin Britten developed the canticle into an extended song for solo voice or voices with piano, set to religious or quasi-religious text.

SONG	COMPOSER	POET
"Canticle I: My Beloved is Mine"	Benjamin Britten	Francis Quarles
"Canticle II: Abraham and Isaac"	Benjamin Britten	Chester Miracle Play
"Canticle III: Still Falls the Rain"	Benjamin Britten	Edith Sitwell
"Canticle IV: Journey of the Magi"	Benjamin Britten	T. S. Eliot
"Canticle V: The Death of St. Narcissus"	Benjamin Britten	T. S. Eliot

CANTO: one of the divisions of a long poem, used in Italian by ★Dante and in English by ★Spenser.

CANTY: (Scot.), *merry.*

CAPETANAKIS, DEMETRIOS (1912–1944): Greek poet and critic, who wrote mostly in English. Capetanakis moved to Athens in 1922 when the Greeks were driven out of Smyrna where he had been born. At the university he studied law, philosophy, and the political and social sciences, publishing four Greek poems and a drama while there. In 1935 Capetanakis went to Germany to study philosophy under an existentialist professor at Heidelberg, where he met the disciples of Stefan ★George. The great influence of George's work upon Capetanakis ultimately turned to distaste. In 1939 Capetanakis went to Cambridge in England. By 1941 he was working in the Greek Department of Information in exile, where he met important literary figures. As a result, he fell in love with the English language and began to write in English, which he used with authority, creativity, clarity, and grace. An admirer of Dostoyevsky, ★Rimbaud, and Emily ★Dickinson, Capetanakis was drawn to melancholy and passion. The poems published in English were largely written in the middle of the war. His practice was to produce cryptic poems containing hints of what to hope for and how to live, but the poems had undertones of tragedy. Ironically, eighteen months before his death Capetanakis had a crisis of despair over his own illness, the war, and doubts about his artistry, from which he emerged with new confidence that was reflected in his last poem "Lazarus." The poetry of Demetrios Capetanakis has been set by Ned Rorem. SELECTED READING: *A Greek Poet in English*, ed. John Lehmann, 1947. (SOURCE: Wakeman, 1980)

CAPOTE: a brightly colored cloak used by bullfighters.

SONG	COMPOSER	POET
"Llamale con el pañuelo"	Jesús Guridi	Castilian folk song

CAPRI: one of the Italian islands in the Gulf of Naples, south of the city of ★Naples.

SONG	COMPOSER	POET
1. "Capri"	Wintter Watts	Sara Teasdale
2. "In Heaven"	Edward Elgar	Elizabeth Barrett Browning

CAPTAIN, THE: a character from the ★*commedia dell'arte*. Captains are always in full uniform and are lady-killers. They are easily fooled or tricked by ★Harlequin or others and frequently physically beaten. All are bombastic and boring in their speech. Some captains in French farce are Boudouffe, Taille-bras, and Engoulevent. Many Italian captains have names that allude to big mouths. (SOURCE: Duchartre, 1966)

CARAMBA, LA: a nickname for an immensely popular Spanish singer, María Antonia Fernández. She habitually wore a hat of many, many highly colored ribbons that gave rise to the nickname. Hence the popular phrase, "Ay, Caramba!" A song of the late eighteenth century, "Alma sintamos," is a mock pathetic lament for her feigned death. In actuality, she ran off with a French lover, leaving her troupe without a leading singer. (SOURCE: Chase, 1959)

CARAVAN: a group traveling together for safety and mutual support, especially a group of merchants. The word refers especially to travel in Asia and through the desert of North Africa, where trips between cities and places of commerce were dangerous, and local governments were unable to guarantee travelers' safety. The word sometimes refers to a house on wheels used by gypsies and traveling showmen. (SOURCE: Bridgwater, Kurtz, 1968)

SONG	COMPOSER	POET
"Miel de Narbonne"	Francis Poulenc	Jean Cocteau

CARDENIO: in *Cervantes's story of *Don Quixote*, part 1, the Ragged Knight who, driven mad by the loss of his beloved Lucinda, haunts the Sierra Morena and is eventually reunited with her. He appears also in *D'Urfey's semi-opera *Don Quixote*, part 1, for which Henry Purcell wrote music.

SONG	COMPOSER	POET
"Let the Dreadful Engines"	Henry Purcell	Thomas D'Urfey

CARDUCCI, GIOSUÈ (1835–1907): Italian poet and classicist. Born in Tuscany and inspired by classical traditions, Carducci was the dominant figure of Italian poetry in the last quarter of the nineteenth century. His love for Italy was passionate, but his impatience with its ills in the period following unification inspired the early poetry. When Carducci's nationalism settled down, his poetry began to be energized by an interest in classical civilizations and by his sensitivity to nature. From 1860 he held the position as Professor of Literature at the University of Bologna, the city in which he died. Following years of bitter literary and political fighting, Carducci renounced republicanism and became the official poet of a unified Italy. He was named a senator of the Italian kingdom (1890) and in 1906 he was awarded the Nobel Prize for Literature. The verses of Giosuè Carducci were set by Sebastiano Caltabiano and Heitor Villa-Lobos. PRINCIPAL WORKS: *Rime nuove*, 1861–67; *Odi barbare*, 1873–89; *Rimi e Ritmi*, 1898. (SOURCES: De Lucchi, 1967; Drabble, 2000)

CARÈME, MAURICE (1899–1924): Belgian poet, novelist. Born in Brabant, Carème was a schoolteacher before he turned to writing as a profession. For most of his works he used the background of his native Brabant, its rural life and scenery. His exquisite fantasy and gentle emotion blend into a charming lyricism especially appropriate for children. Affectionate epithets that were applied to Carème included "the poet of joy," "the poet of peace," and "the poet of children." Darius Milhaud and Francis Poulenc set his verses. PRINCIPAL WORKS: *Mère*, 1935; *La Lanterne magique*, 1947; *La Bien-aimée*, 1965; *Brabant*; 1967; *Mer du Nord*, 1968; *Entre deux mondes*, 1970. SELECTED READING: P. Coran, *Maurice Carème*, 1967. (SOURCE: Steinberg, 2, 1973)

"Cares of Lovers, The": a song composed by Henry Purcell to the words of Thomas *Shadwell in his adaptation of William *Shakespeare's work. See *Timon of Athens for plot details and positioning of the song within the plot.

CARLOVINGIAN: referring to those French persons who are related to a Frank-ish family founded in C.E. 613, as in "of the Carlovingian dynasty." Among their members were the rulers of France from 751 to 987; of Germany from 753 to 911; of Italy from 774 to 961. In Gabriel Fauré's setting of ★Verlaine's song "Une Sainte en son auréole" (*La ★Bonne Chanson*), a "Carlovingian name" refers to Mathilde Mauté de Fleurville, whom Verlaine was about to marry. (SOURCE: Cooper, 1992)

CARMINA BURANA: a collection of Latin and German poems discovered in the monastery Benedictbeuern (1803). It was probably written around 1230, perhaps in Carinthia. The work of thirteen compilers, it contains two kinds of work in catego-ries similar to the poetry written by twelfth-century troubadours: (1) moral satirical poems, (2) love poems, camaraderie, drinking songs. It is the most important collec-tion of ★Goliardic Latin poetry, which is both satirical and profane. Carl Orff used a selection for his cantata, *Carmina Burana*. (SOURCE: Drabble, 1985)

CARNER, JOSEP (1884–1971): Catalan poet. Josep Carner attended the Uni-versity of Barcelona before going into the Spanish diplomatic service, in which he served as First Councillor at the Paris embassy during the Spanish Civil War. Later, exiled as a consequence of the war, he lived in France, Mexico, and Belgium. In an echo of ★Mallarmé, Carner's early poems were written in ambiguous language that related to the aural elements of verse. In contrast, the later style was elegant and ironically subtle. After his exile his poetry had a deeper tone filled with melancholy and nostalgia. Carner's long poem *Nabi*, on a biblical subject, written in Mexico, was one of the great mature works of Catalan literature. Although he lived for many years outside Catalonia, he still revered his part of Spain. The poetry of Josep Carner was set by Eduardo Toldrà and Federico Mompou. PRINCIPAL WORKS: *Obras completas: Poems*, trans. P. Hutchinson, 1962. (SOURCE: Steinberg, 2, 1973)

CARNIVAL: from Latin, *carnem levare*, putting away flesh, farewell to meat. In Roman Catholic countries Lent is characterized by the shunning of meat. In the week preceding Lent, many celebrations take place, featuring parades, masquerades, and pageants. Carnival's original roots were in pagan spring fertility festivals. In gen-eral, the meaning is any period of celebration.

SONG	COMPOSER	POET
1. "1904"	Francis Poulenc	Guillaume Apollinaire
2. "Le Carnaval"	Jacques Leguerney	Marc-Antoine Saint-Amant

CAROL: any light-hearted song of religious festive joy. In America, the carol is now almost invariably associated with Christmas. This is less true of England where Easter carols are also widely sung. The French counterpart is the *noël*.

CARROLL, LEWIS (Charles Lutwige Dodgson) (1832–1898): English poet, writer of fiction and children's classics. Son of a minister, Lewis Carroll was edu-cated at home until he was twelve. Under his real name, Dodgson, Carroll had a career as a Victorian mathematician and don at Christ Church College of Oxford. He matriculated there in 1850 and taught mathematics from 1855 to 1881. As Dodgson he was an academic, interested in photography, at which he was very skilled, the theater, preaching, and writing. As Carroll he wrote what he called "nonsense." A lifelong stammer perhaps contributed to his introversion as well as to his predilection for funny words, puns, and nonsense in general. As a child he invented games, wrote and staged marionette plays. As an adult he acquired his sure sense of what makes nonsense work from his "child friends," little girls whose friendship he cultivated until they reached puberty. The composer Lee Hoiby has set texts by Lewis Carroll. PRINCIPAL WORKS: Poetry: *Phantasmagoria and Other Poems*, 1869; *The Hunting of the Snark: Or, An Agony in Eight Fits*, 1876; *Rhyme? And Reason?* 1883; *The Collected Verse of Lewis Carroll*, 1932; *The Humorous Verse of Lewis Carroll*, 1960. Prose: *Alice's Adventures in Wonderland*, 1865; *Through the Looking Glass and What Alice Found There*, 1871; *The Lewis Carroll Handbook*, rev. Dennis Crutch, ed., 1979. SELECTED READING: Walter de la Mare, *Lewis Carroll*, 1932 (contains a bibliography). (SOURCE: Magill, 2, 1992)

CASSANDRA: a prophetess in Greek legend, daughter of Priam and Hecuba. ★Apollo gifted Cassandra with the power of prophecy because he loved her. When she refused Apollo's advances, he punished her by seeing to it that no one believed in her predictions, although they were invariably correct. She appears in *Troilus and Cressida* by ★Shakespeare. In the figurative sense her name is applied to a prophet of doom or anyone whose warnings are doubted but eventually prove to be correct. (SOURCE: Cooper, 1992)

SONG	COMPOSER	POET
1. "Tais-toi babillarde"	Darius Milhaud	Pierre de Ronsard
2. "Pantomime"	Claude Debussy	Paul Verlaine

CASTIGLIONE: an inland Italian town in the Abruzzi section of the country, east of Rome.

SONG	COMPOSER	POET
"Ich hab in Penna"	Hugo Wolf	Paul Heyse, after the Italian

CASTILLEJO, CRISTÓBAL DE (1492–1550): Spanish poet. First a page to Archduke Ferdinand, Castillejo became a Cistercian monk in 1515. Nevertheless, he abandoned his cloister to act as secretary to Archduke Ferdinand in 1525. Castillejo suffered a sickly and impecunious old age. Two long poems that he wrote, *Sermón de amores* and *Diálogo de mujeres*, were destroyed by the Inquisition. Imitating ★Catullus and Ovid, Castillejo wrote satires of court life and of the love poetry of the ★cancioneros. His own love poetry was in the traditional attractive style, and he also wrote religious lyrics. The verses of Cristóbal de Castillejo were set by Fernando Obradors. SELECTED READING: C. L. Nicolay, *The Life and Works of Cristóbal de Castillejo*, 1910. (SOURCE: Steinberg, 2, 1973)

CASTOR AND POLLUX: This heavenly pair were symbols of true love and constancy. In English poetry, references to "the twins" often referred to Castor and Pollux. (SOURCE: *Norton*, 1996)

CASTRO, CRISTÓBAL DE (1880–1953): Spanish novelist, playwright, poet, translator, and journalist. Born in Córdoba, Castro, like many poets, came to a literary life after studying law in Granada and medicine in Madrid. As a journalist, Castro edited such journals as *La Epoca* and *El Liberal*. His translations include works by Molière, ★Goldoni, ★Ibsen, ★Tolstoy, Wilde, and Luigi Pirandello. His verse has been set by Manuel de Falla. (SOURCE: Cockburn, Stokes, 1992)

CATALOGUE DES FLEURS: a cycle of seven songs composed by Darius Milhaud (1920) to words by Lucien ★Daudet. The poet had selected the words from a seedsman's advertisement, knowing that Milhaud found inspiration in trade catalogue descriptions, such as his *Machines agricoles* (1919). *Catalogue des fleurs* was arranged for voice with piano or chamber ensemble.

CATASÚS, TRINITAT (1887–1940): Catalan poet. Catasús was born in Sitges and, together with Miguel Utrillo, founded the journal *La Cantonada*. His several volumes of poetry include *De l'hort i de la costa* (1915), *Poemes del temps* (1919), and *Robins de magrana* (1930). His poems have a certain religious cast and betray a fondness for landscapes. The verse of Trinitat Catasús was set by Eduardo Toldrà. (SOURCE: Cockburn, Stokes, 1992)

CATCH: a short composition for three or more voices singing the same melody, the second singer singing the first line as the first singer goes on to the second, and so on; a round.

CATHERINE OF SIENNA, SAINT: Christian saint, born 1347. Catherine was the youngest of twenty-five children born to a wealthy dyer and his wife. At the age of six she had a mystical experience—★Christ seated in heaven with notable saints around him, all smiling down upon her—that made her determine to be a nun despite family objections. When the family relented, they allowed her to become a Dominican tertiary. On Shrove Tuesday, the day before Ash Wednesday 1366, Christ, the ★Virgin Mary, and the Hosts of Heaven appeared to Catherine. On her finger Christ placed a ring, invisible to all but Catherine. Shortly after this betrothal, she began to journey out into the public, where she did good works, gathered followers around her, and became skilled at settling disputes. Although she never learned to write, she dictated her famous four treatises known as the Dialogues of St. Catherine. She sided with Pope Gregory XI, calling for a crusade to liberate the Holy Sepulcher from Muslim control. In February 1375 at a church in Pisa she was meditating on the crucifix after communion when suddenly she saw five bright lights that pierced her, causing such pain that she fainted. Thereafter she bore stigmata, the wounds of Christ's crucifixion. During her lifetime, the stigmata were visible only to her, but at her death they appeared to everyone. When she helped Gregory XI in his decision to leave Avignon and return to Rome, it led to a schism with the two popes. Politically astute, Catherine was active as a mediator and advisor to the two popes, one in Italy and one in France, Gregory XI and Urban VI. Catherine died in 1380, was canonized in 1461, and declared a Doctor of the Church in 1970. Her Feast Day is now April 29. (SOURCES: Walsh, 1991; Farmer, 1997; Thurston, Attwater, 1963)

SONG	COMPOSER	POET
"A Prayer to Saint Catherine"	Virgil Thomson	Kenneth Koch

CATULLUS, GAIUS VALERIUS (ca.84—ca.54 B.C.E.): regarded as one of the greatest Latin poets. Catullus was from a prosperous Verona family; he came to Rome (ca.62), where he became infatuated with the *Lesbia* of his poems. His verse concentrates on love: joyous expressions, reproaches, rifts, reconciliations, showing the course of romantic liaisons. Poetry was essential to Catullus's life, and his love poems, ★elegies, and satirical ★epigrams were characterized by a deep sincerity. In simple language he expressed tenderness as well as fierce intensity of feeling. During the Middle Ages, Catullus was virtually unknown, but when the manuscript of his poems came to light at Verona in the fourteenth century, revealing 116 verses, he began to exercise extensive influence over poets like ★Campion, ★Jonson, ★Herrick, and ★Lovelace. He is ranked with ★Sappho and ★Shelley as a lyricist, managing a fusion of form and emotion that is the essence of poetry. The poetry of Gaius Catullus has been set by Ned Rorem and by Fernando Obradors in a translation by Cristóbal de ★Castillejo. PRINCIPAL WORKS: *Catulli Carmina*, many editions from 1958 to 1969. SELECTED READING: A. L. Wheeler, *Catullus and the Traditions of Ancient Poetry*, 1934, 1964; E. A. Havelock, *The Lyric Genius of Catullus*, 1939; Julia Haig Geisser, *Catullus and His Renaissance Readers*, 1993. (SOURCES: Steinberg, 2, 1973; Vinson, Kirkpatrick (1), 1984)

CAUNDES: (Scot.) (pr. cown-des), *candles*.

CAZALIS, HENRI: *see* ★LAHOR, JEAN.

CÉ: a bridge across the Seine in Paris, over which the fleeing French people crossed before the invading Germans.

SONG	COMPOSER	POET
"C"	Francis Poulenc	Louis Aragon

CECILIA, SAINT: a Catholic saint and martyr of the third century, patron saint of musicians. There is no factual information about St. Cecilia in any of the customary volumes. According to the legend, however, even as the organ played during her marriage to Valerian, a pagan, Cecilia was determined to remain a virgin, singing to God in her heart, asking Him to keep her chaste and unviolated. She converted her martyred husband and brother; she converted her judges when taken into custody. When a sentence of death by suffocation in her bath failed, a soldier was sent to behead her. Three sword strikes to the neck wounded her, but she did not die for three days. St. Cecilia was named patron saint of music and musicians because of her habit of singing to herself. In 1584 she was chosen patron saint of the Rome Music Academy. Her feast day is November 22, which was devoted to music in England. ★Dryden wrote "Song for St. Cecilia's Day" for her, and Pope wrote "Ode for Music on St. Cecilia's Day." "The Second Nun's Tale" from ★Chaucer's *Canterbury Tales* retells her legend. (SOURCES: Farmer, 1997; Walsh, 1991)

SONG	COMPOSER	POET
1. "Sainte"	Maurice Ravel	Stéphane Mallarmé
2. "Wond'rous Machine"	Henry Purcell	Nicholas Brady

"Celemene, Pray Tell Me": a duet composed by Henry Purcell for a production of *Oroonoko*, written by Thomas ★Southerne. *See* ★*Oroonoko* for plot details and placement of songs.

CELIA: conventional poetic name used in pastoral poetry.

"Celia Has a Thousand Charms": a song composed by Henry Purcell to the words of Robert Gould. *See* ★*Rival Sisters, The* for plot details and position of the song.

"Celia, That I Once was Blessed": a song composed by Henry Purcell, set to the words of John ★Dryden in his play *Amphitryon*, produced in 1690. *See* ★*Amphitryon* for plot details and placement of the songs.

CENSER: a container in which incense is burned in a religious ceremony, swung on chains to disperse its fragrance.

SONG	COMPOSER	POET
"Harmonie du soir"	Claude Debussy	Charles Baudelaire

CERBERUS: a dog with three heads, a mane of serpents' heads, and a serpent's tail. Cerberus, an offspring of Typhaon and Echidna, guarded the entrance to ★Hades. He could be appeased with cake (as Aeneas did) or lulled to sleep with lyre music (as ★Orpheus did). One of the twelve labors of ★Hercules was to bring Cerberus up from the underworld. Anyone who guards the entrance to a place can be called a Cerberus. (SOURCE: *Bulfinch*, 1978)

SONG	COMPOSER	POET
"A Charm"	Benjamin Britten	Thomas Randolph

CERES: the Roman name for Mother Earth, the corn goddess, the protectress of agriculture and of all the fruits of the earth, called Demeter in Greek mythology. (SOURCE: Cooper, 1992)

SONG	COMPOSER	POET
1. "A une fontaine"	Darius Milhaud	Pierre de Ronsard
2. "Attributs"	Francis Poulenc	Pierre de Ronsard
3. "Orest auf Tauris"	Franz Schubert	Johann Mayrhofer

CERVANTES, MIGUEL DE (1547–1616): Spanish poet and novelist. Cervantes studied in Valladolid, Seville, and Madrid. In 1569 he entered the service of an Italian cardinal, but by 1570 was a soldier. Wounded in the naval battle of Lepanto in 1571, Cervantes participated in further expeditions to Corfu, Navarino, and Tunis, later serving in southern Italian garrisons. In 1580 he was ransomed from his five-year imprisonment by the Turks, following which he earned a livelihood being a tax collector and purchasing agent in Spain. After 1606 he lived in Madrid a life as fascinating as his personality and equal to the quality of his literary work. Cervantes bore his bad luck and bad fortune with resignation and generosity of spirit. He accepted the burden of being imprisoned (during a period when he should have been building a foundation for his future life) as well as the surprising absence of favoritism shown him at court despite his wartime heroism. He was an untalented literary business-man, never able to make a living by his pen, always needing to continue as a tax col-lector. Two short prison terms for bookkeeping irregularities (1598, 1602) indicate his financial difficulties; he could not afford to stop writing. Cervantes's masterwork, *Don Quixote, begun as a parody of the popular books of chivalry, was commended for its author's ability to create characters and believable dialogue, for its tone of optimistic good humor, and for the moral clarity of his characterizations of the social mores of his time. Don Quixote is generally regarded as the first modern novel, conceived on a grand scale, engaging the reader with basic human questions and offering a worldview. Cervantes's genius can be found in his masterpieces: the *Exemplary Novels* and the two parts of *Don Quixote*. His poetry has been set by Fernando Obradors and Antonio Vives. PRINCIPAL WORKS IN ENGLISH: *The Portable Cervantes*, ed. and trans. Samuel Putnam, 1947; *Don Quixote*, trans. Samuel Putnam, 1949, J. M. Cohen, 1950; *Exemplary Novels*, trans. C. A. Jones, 1972; *Interludes* (play), trans. Edwin Honig, 1964. SELECTED READING: Francisco Navarro y Ledesma, *Cervantes: The Man and the Genius*, 1973. (SOURCE: Vinson, Kirkpatrick (1), 1984)

CESAREA (It.), CAESAREA (Eng.): ruins on the shore of the Mediterranean between Haifa and Netanya in Israel, once a prosperous seaport.

SONG	COMPOSER	POET
"San Basilio"	Ildebrando Pizzetti	Nicolò Tommasèo, trans. from Greek

CHACONA (Sp.), CHACONNE (Fr.): a stately dance in triple time presumed to have been imported into Spain from Mexico in the late eighteenth century. (SOURCE: Cockburn, Stokes, 1992)

SONG	COMPOSER	POET
"Oh qué bien que baila Gil"	anonymous	anonymous

CHAGALL, MARC (1887–1985): Russian-born artist who lived in France for many years. Chagall was born in the village of Vitebsk, studied in St. Petersburg with Bakst, and settled in Paris in 1910, where he came under the influence of the Cubists. Chagall's art is fanciful with brilliantly colored images he recalled from his childhood, objects he knew in Vitebsk, Jewish life and folklore, flower and animal symbolism. His ideas were presented in a topsy-turvy world of resonant color. His images have a lyrical quality unusual in the painters of his time. Chagall illustrated Nikolay Gogol's *Dead Souls* (1948), Jean *La Fontaine's *Fables* (1952) and an edition of the Bible (1956). (SOURCE: Benét, 1965)

SONG	COMPOSER	POET
"Marc Chagall"	Francis Poulenc	Paul Éluard

CHAMISSO, ADALBERT (Louis Charles Adelaide) (1781–1838): German poet, translator, and botanist. Chamisso was born at an ancestral castle in Champagne,

France. In 1790, during the Revolution, the castle was destroyed by fire, the family forced to flee, finally arriving in Germany when Chamisso was eight years old. He was to spend the rest of his life shuttling back and forth between Germany and France, between feeling a German citizen and a French-born patriot, between using French or German as his poetic medium. Ending a period of severe deprivation for him and his family, Chamisso was given a position as a page in the royal household of Berlin. By the time his family was allowed to return to France under the general amnesty given by Napoleon (1801), he had been commissioned a lieutenant in the Prussian army and had made himself at home in German letters. *Schiller was his favorite, and he modeled his poetry after *Klopstock, *Goethe, *Novalis, and *Tieck. In his literary groups, the members vied with each other to correct Chamisso's German. With the decision that Germany was his home, he resigned his commission, and enrolled in the new University of Berlin (1812) as a medical student. When the War of Liberation broke out, he escaped, but managed to write his popular fable *Peter Schlemihl* in exile. When he returned to Berlin once again, he was permanently employed in the Botanical Garden. Now he published his poems, in which he fused realistic portrayals with a keen sense of rhythm and his great empathy for the common people. Nevertheless, Chamisso was a transitional poet between romanticism and naturalism, a poet firm in a second place position. Chamisso's poetry was set most famously by Robert Schumann (*Frauenliebe und -leben*) also in translation and by Grieg, Strauss, and Carl Loewe. PRINCIPAL WORKS: *Peter Schlemihl,* 1814, trans. J. Bowring, 1957; *Woman's Love and Life*, trans. F.V. McDonald, 1881. SELECTED READING: selected poems in Francke and Howard's *German Classics*, 1913–14; T. Mann, *Essays of Three Decades*, 1947. (SOURCE: Vinson, Kirkpatrick (1), 1984; Steinberg, 2, 1973)

CHAMPÊTRE: a quick and lively dance, said to have been invented by *Pan. The open-air dancers wore wreaths of oak and garlands of flowers.

CHAMPS ELYSÉES (lit., *Elysian fields*): a Parisian avenue, the finest promenade in Paris that runs from the Place de la Concorde to the Arc de Triomphe.

SONG	COMPOSER	POET
"Cinq chansons de Lise Hirtz"	Georges Auric	Lise Hirtz

CHANSON D'EVE, LA: a collection of poems by the Belgian poet, Charles van *Lerberghe (1861–1907). The work is made up of five sections: "Prelude," "Premières paroles," "La Tentation," "La Faute," and "Crépuscule." We are put in the presence of God, who instructs Eve for the mission of soaking up life's secrets, and listening to the voices of nature and the elements. It is a symbolic paradise where Eve has just awakened to God, who converses with his creature. Gabriel Fauré set ten poems from the collection, the first six songs and the eighth song come from "Premières paroles," the seventh from "La Tentation." Fauré then took two extracts from "Crépuscule," avoiding "La Faute" altogether, and shortening or altering many of the poems. The length of the resulting cycle and its musical sophistication have discouraged frequent performance. Bernac (1977) suggests a shortened version.

CHANSONS DE BILITIS, LES: a collection of poems written by Pierre ★Louÿs in 1894 in imitation of Bilitis, the Greek poet, a contemporary of ★Sappho. Louÿs's dedication read, "This little book of ancient love is respectfully dedicated to the young ladies of the society of the future." Upon publication of the work, several scholars mistook the "little book of ancient love," written in a harmoniously classic style and giving the impression of sound research, for an authentic work by Bilitis. Louÿs's *Les Chansons de Bilities, traduites du Grec* is divided into four sections: 1. Bucolics in Pamphylia; 2. Elegies at Mytilene; 3. Epigrams in the Isle of ★Cyprus; 4. The Tomb of Bilitis. In an introduction titled "Life of Bilitis" Louÿs explains her birth, travels, loves, etc. She was born at the beginning of the sixth century in Melas. About part 1, "Bucolics in Pamphylia," Louÿs says, "The end of her pastoral life was saddened by a love affair about which we know little. Having become the mother of a child whom she abandoned, Bilitis left Pamphylia and never returned." It is suspected that Lykas, a young shepherd, was her lover, as he is mentioned in several poems of part 1. "La Chevelure," the first song of the three set by Debussy under the title *Les Chansons de Bilitis*, clearly refers to Lykas when using the pronoun *il*, since Bilitis's girl friends tease her about a young man in other poems. The last poem of part 1, "Le Tombeau des ★Naïades" and the third song of the Debussy cycle, represents Bilitis's passing from childhood and a certain disillusionment. In a winter landscape, Bilitis is told by "fate" that the traces of a ★satyr that she sees are part of her childhood fantasies; he says, "the satyrs are dead, also the ★nymphs" as he looks through a piece of ice that symbolizes the end of her protected childhood toward the beginning of a colder, lonelier life. In addition to Debussy's three settings, Georges Dadelot has set three volumes of Bilitis poems; Charles Koechlin has set three poems from part 3, "Epigrams," one from part 2, "Élégies," and one from part 4, "Le Tombeau"; Francesco Santoliquido set one poem, "Malinconia," in his own translation.

CHANSONS DE DON QUICHOTTE: *see* ★QUIXOTE, DON.

CHANSONS DE RONSARD: four songs by Darius Milhaud set to poems by Pierre de ★Ronsard, commissioned in 1941 by French coloratura soprano, Lily Pons, who was a regular performer at the Metropolitan Opera in New York.

CHANSONS GAILLARDS: lit., *ribald songs*; a cycle of eight songs on texts that Francis Poulenc found in an old edition of seventeenth-century songs. Pierre Bernac affirms that Poulenc detested smutty stories but liked obscenity. The texts of the *Chansons Gaillards* are very spicy, sometimes in *double entendre*.

CHANSONS MADÉCASSES: a set of three songs by Maurice Ravel, texts by Evariste Désiré de ★Parny, a poet of the eighteenth century. In his preface, Parny writes, "The isle of Madagascar is divided into an endless number of small territories which belong to as many princes. These princes are always battling one another, the purpose of these wars being to take prisoners in order to sell them to Europeans. Thus, without them, these people would be peaceful and happy. . . . The Madegascans are happy by nature. The men live in idleness and the women work. They are passionately fond of music and dance. . . . Their music is simple, gentle, always melancholy." Modern scholarship has established, however, that Parny never set foot in Madagascar, nor was he acquainted with the language. The poems were written in India in 1784–85, and it appears that the *hain-tenys*, popular Madagascan poems, served as Parny's model.

CHANSONS VILLAGEOISES: a set of six songs composed by Francis Poulenc to poems of Maurice ★Fombeure, originally written for voice with orchestra, later reduced for piano by Poulenc. The poems are taken from a small booklet of verse called *Chansons de la grand hune* (Songs of the Maintop). The original title of "Le Mendiant" was "Complainte de ★Jean Martin," and Bernac (1977) describes "Chanson du claire tamis" as total nonsense.

CHANTIES, SHANTIES: songs of the sailing days, sung by a "shanty man" to help the sailors keep rhythmical their actions, such as hauling on ropes, working the capstan, etc. The sailors joined in the choruses. The word is probably taken from the French *chanter*, to sing. (SOURCE: Cooper, 1992)

SONG	COMPOSER	POET
"Sea Chanties"	Celius Dougherty	traditional songs

CHANTS D'AUVERGNE: a collection of folk songs arranged by Joseph Canteloube (1879–1957), who traveled widely from 1900 to the end of his life, ever in search of folk songs. He prized them for their intrinsic merits—they were unconventional and charming; they revealed facets of national character; they brought new and revitalizing elements into contemporary French music. The mountainous area of Auvergne, with its chains of *puys*, wild volcanic peaks that lend the countryside a rugged prospect, is rich in folk material. The provinces of Touraine, Languedoc, Angoumois, and the Pays Basque generated four sets of songs for Canteloube.

CHAOS: the heavy mass mixed with air and sea that became earth. Originally *chaos* meant confusion, before the creation of the earth, when air and sea were mixed in a primordial soup called Chaos. Chaos, as referred to by the Greeks, was the most ancient of the gods. (SOURCE: *Bulfinch*, 1978)

SONG	COMPOSER	POET
1. "When a Cruel Long Winter"	Henry Purcell	Elkanah Settle
2. "An Laura"	Franz Schubert	Friedrich von Matthison

CHAPELIER, LE: Erik Satie's version of the Mad Hatter, a character in *Alice Through the Looking Glass* by Lewis ★Carroll, published in 1865. The melody, as part of Satie's spoof, is taken from a tenor aria from Charles Gounod's opera *Mireille*.

SONG	COMPOSER	POET
"Le Chapelier"	Erik Satie	René Chalupt

CHARITY: one of the three virtues, loving kindness toward others; unwillingness to think badly of others; generosity in giving to the needy. (SOURCE: Glazier, Hellwig, 1994)

SONG	COMPOSER	POET
1. "Ophelia Lieder #3"	Richard Strauss	William Shakespeare
2. "Charity"	Richard Hageman	Emily Dickinson

CHARM: the chanting of a verse supposed to have magic or occult powers.

SONG	COMPOSER	POET
"A Charm"	Benjamin Britten	Thomas Randolph

CHARON: in Greek and Roman mythology, the man who ferried the souls of the deceased across the river ★Styx to ★Hades. In order for the souls of deceased mortals to gain access to Hades, the realm of the dead, it was necessary for them to cross the foul river Styx. A coin placed under the tongues of the deceased persons served as payment to Charon for taking the soul across the river to its fate. Those buried without a coin and those not buried at all were condemned to roam the banks of the river Styx forever. King or shepherd, all must cross, and all must pay. In Handel's *Alexander's Feast*, Timotheus sings the aria "Revenge, Revenge, Timotheus cries," because there are bodies of Greek warriors lying unburied on the battlefield. Had the necessary coins been placed under the tongues of those poor souls, they would have been able to pay the frugal boatman and attain rest. Three living men succeeded in crossing the river Styx in Charon's boat: ★Orpheus, who charmed Charon with his music when he came in search of ★Eurydice; ★Hercules, who frightened Charon with his grimaces when he came to capture the many-headed dog that guards the gates of Hell; and Aeneas, who, carrying the Golden Bough as safe passage, tried to see his father and learn of his fate. (SOURCE: Graves, 1960 (2); Hamilton, 1969)

SONG	COMPOSER	POET
1. "Rich or Poor"	Arthur Bliss	W. H. Davies
2. "Bess o'Bedlam"	Henry Purcell	anonymous
3. "Charon, the Peaceful Shade Invites"	Henry Purcell	John Fletcher
4. "Canzone per Ballo"	Ildebrando Pizzetti	traditional Greek
5. "Tramontata è la luna"	Goffredo Petrassi	Sappho, trans. Quasimodo

"★Charon, the Peaceful Shade Invites": a song from the 1690 semi-opera *Dioclesian*, with music written solely by Henry Purcell to the text of Massinger and ★Fletcher's original play. *See* ★*Dioclesian* for plot details and placement of the songs.

CHAT BOTTÉ, LE: *see* ★PUSS IN BOOTS.

CHATTERTON, THOMAS (1752–1770): English poet. Chatterton was born to a Bristol family, and after the death of his father, became a schoolmaster. When he later lived in London, he turned out poems, burlettas, satires, and political tirades, which were rejected by many publishers. Desperate after one such refusal of a poem, he drank arsenic in his Holborn attic. He was buried in a pauper's grave. The verses of Thomas Chatterton were set by Seymour Barab. A volume of Chatterton's *Poetical Works* was edited by Walter Sheat in 1871. READING: E. H. W. Meyerstein, *A Life of Thomas Chatterton*, 1930. (SOURCE: Drabble, 1985)

CHAUCER, GEOFFREY (ca.1343–1400): writer of fiction, translator, and the greatest poet of medieval England. Probably born in London, Chaucer was the son of a wine merchant. He served with the English forces in France (1359), was captured and ransomed in 1360. After returning to England, he served the British

Crown all his life by undertaking diplomatic missions to the Continent, as controller of customs for the port of London (1374–86), and finally as deputy forester of the royal Somerset forest. Chaucer lived in a house within the garden of Westminster Abbey and was buried there. Consistently popular and admired by his fellow poets, critics, and the public, Chaucer was possessed of poetic talent, charm, wit, and deep understanding of human diversity. Nevertheless, he was not, as often surmised, the primary shaper of the English language, for there was a long tradition before him. In his work, some of which used experimental verse forms, what looks to be natural is his genius at exploiting convention. Chaucer is the best example of a Gothic artist: that is, he synthesized everyday subjects with the supernatural and philosophical. The verse of Geoffrey Chaucer was set by Frederick Jacobi and Arnold Bax. PRINCIPAL WORKS: *House of Fame*, 1372–80; *Legend of St. Cecilia*, 1372–80; *Tragedies of Fortune*, 1372–80; *Parlement of Foules*, 1380; *Legend of Good Women*, 1380–86; *Troilus and Criseyde*, 1382; *The Canterbury Tales*, 1387–1400. SELECTED READING: D. W. Robertson, Jr., *Preface to Chaucer: Studies in Medieval Perspective*, 1962. (SOURCE: Magill, 2, 1992)

CHEESE OF THE FABLE, ROUND: in the fable about the crow and the fox by Jean de ★La Fontaine, the fox is the thief of the crow's round cheese. (SOURCE: Bernac, 1977)

SONG	COMPOSER	POET
"Il vole"	Francis Poulenc	Louise de Vilmorin

CHEKHOV, ANTON (1860–1904): Russian dramatist and short story writer. Chekhov's grandfather had been a serf who bought his freedom and that of his father, the owner of a small grocery store. He was born in south Russia; Chekhov's family ties were strong all his life. In school, he was well read, popular with the other students who liked his humorous stories. Although students were supposedly forbidden entrance, Anton went to the theater often. He was a gifted mimic, skilled at improvisations, and performed for his family with his brothers. In 1879 he finished school and entered the medical faculty of Moscow University. During his studies, anxious to make money, he began writing for newspapers and small magazines. By the time he earned his diploma in 1884, he was already known as a contributor to humor magazines. The publication of his second book of short stories was an important literary event. In 1887 Chekhov's first play was produced, and a collection of his stories received the ★Pushkin award. Traveling was a great interest, and he wrote on such travels through Russia, Siberia, and Western Europe. Soon he bought a farm where he did some of his best writing. By 1885 tuberculosis began to limit his activities, but he continued to write and published much during the last years of his life. Suffering from melancholia, Chekhov took sojourns in Yalta, where he met Leo ★Tolstoy, by whose literal Christianity he was influenced for a time. When the Academy of Sciences excluded Gorky from membership, only two members, Chekhov one of them, resigned in protest. His four great dramatic masterpieces—*The Sea Gull, Uncle Vanya, The Three Sisters*, and *The Cherry Orchard*—were written in his last decade. A national period of mourning followed his death. The characters in his plays are moody, introspective, and self-centered; their lives are fraught with quiet desperation. The plays are somewhat static, but full of implications and lyricism that is both realistic and poetic. Chekhov's influence upon foreign writers such as Bernard Shaw, James ★Joyce, Virginia ★Woolf, and Ernest Hemingway was enormous. His works were translated into innumerable languages and set to music by Sergei Rachmaninoff. PRINCIPAL WORKS: *Complete Works*, trans. Constance Garnett, 1916–22; *The Portable Chekhov*, ed. A. Yarmolinsky, 1947. SELECTED READING: Walter H. Bruford, *Chekhov and His Russia*, 1948; Simon Karlinsky, *Anton Chekhov's Life and Thought*, trans. Michael H. Heim, 1975. (SOURCE: Kunitz, Colby, 1967)

CHESTERTON, G. K. (GILBERT KEITH) (1874–1901): British novelist and poet. Chesterton was a controversial writer on literature, religion, and society. A traditionalist, a romanticist, and a Catholic, he spoke and wrote with exuberant wit and was a public-speaking opponent of Bernard Shaw. Chesterton was known for championing simple and orthodox writing and for ridiculing pretentiousness. The poetry of G. K. Chesterton was set by Henry Cowell. WORKS: *Collected Poems*, 1933; *Autobiography*, 1936. SELECTED READING: C. Hollis, *The Mind of Chesterton*, 1970. (SOURCE: Colby, 1985)

CHÉVERE: a Spanish dandy.

SONG	COMPOSER	POET
"Chévere"	Xavier Montsalvatge	Nicolás Guillén

CHÉZY, WILHEMINE CHRISTIANE VON (1783–1856): German novelist, poet, and playwright. Chézy was born in Berlin but settled in Vienna. She was the librettist for Weber's opera *Euryanthe* and wrote the play *Rosamunde*, for which Schubert supplied the incidental music. Chézy also wrote the verse for the middle section of Schubert's "Der Hirt auf dem Felsen." The poetry of Wilhemine von Chézy was also set by Charles Ives. (SOURCE: Reed, 1997)

CHISPERO: a Madrid ruffian.

SONG	COMPOSER	POET
"El mirar de la maja"	Enrique Granados	Fernando Periquet

CHLOE: the shepherdess loved by ★Daphnis in the Greek pastoral romance of Longus, hence a generic name adopted in literature for a maiden who is rustic but not necessarily artless. (SOURCE: Cooper, 1992)

SONG	COMPOSER	POET
1. "Rondeley"	Ned Rorem	John Dryden
2. "An Chloë"	Wolfgang Amadeus Mozart	Johann Jacobi
3. "Die betrogene Welt"	Wolfgang Amadeus Mozart	Christian Weisse
4. "Der Kuss"	Ludwig van Beethoven	Christian Weisse
5. "Die Verschweigung"	Wolfgang Amadeus Mozart	Christian Weisse
6. "Sonst"	Hans Pfitzner	Joseph von Eichendorff

CHLORIS, CLORIS: in Greek mythology, a representation of the Roman goddess ★Flora, the personification of blossoming flowers of spring. When ★Zephyrus, the west wind, who was at first violent, became a sweet-scented wind that gently fanned the blessed regions of ★Elysium, he was given for a wife the gracious Chloris, who was worshiped in yearly festivals in which May blossoms were used. (SOURCE: Guirand, 1968)

SONG	COMPOSER	POET
1. "Canzonetta #6"	J. C. Bach	unknown
2. "Zefiro torna"	Claudio Monteverdi	Francesco Petrarca

CHRIST: from the Greek *Christos*, meaning *the anointed one*, from the ancient custom of anointing with oil the head of a future king. *Christos* is a Greek translation of the Hebrew word *messia (masiah)*; it was a title added to the name ★Jesus. Most references to Christ are to Jesus of Nazareth, a carpenter turned itinerant rabbi who was crucified by the Romans under Pontius Pilate and arose from the dead three days later. Christians believe that he is the son of God. (SOURCE: Nevins, 1964)

SONG	COMPOSER	POET
1. "Hymne"	Francis Poulenc	Jean Racine
2. "Noël"	Gabriel Fauré	Victor Wilder
3. "Herr, was trägt der Boden hier"	Hugo Wolf	Paul Heyse and Emanuel Geibel

CHRISTMAS ROSE: from Medieval legends; in German, *Christblume*.

SONG	COMPOSER	POET
"Auf eine Christblume"	Hugo Wolf	Eduard Mörike

CHRISTOPHER, SAINT: a Christian saint and martyr of the third century. Facts about St. Christopher are few, but legends abound. According to The ★*Golden Legend*, Christopher, a giant of a man, decided early on to follow the devil. When he discovered, however, that the devil was afraid of Christ, he determined to become a Christian. He was instructed in the faith by a hermit, who ordered him to sit by the riverside and help travelers to cross. One day, asked by a young boy for help, Christopher agreed to carry him across the river, but the boy was so heavy that Christopher had to bend over to carry him. The boy said, "I am ★Jesus. When you carry me, you carry the weight of the world and its creator on your shoulders. The truth of what I tell you will be proved if you plant your staff on the river bank. Tomorrow the staff will flower and yield fruit." The standard representation of St. Christopher is that of a large man carrying the young Jesus on his shoulders. Christopher preached with great success in Asia Minor until, refusing to sacrifice to pagan gods, he was persecuted, finally arrested, and sent to prison. Legend has it that two women were sent to his prison cell in an attempt to seduce him. Instead, Christopher's preaching converted them. In punishment for this, he was beaten with iron rods, shot with arrows, and, in the end, beheaded. Not only is St. Christopher the patron saint of travelers but he was also venerated for his protection against water, tempest, plague, and sudden death. In 1969 his feast day, July 25, was reduced by the Vatican to a local cult celebration. (SOURCES: Farmer, 1997; Walsh, 1991)

SONG	COMPOSER	POET
1. "Die alten bösen Lieder"	Robert Schumann	Heinrich Heine
2. "Im Rhein, im heiligen Strome"	Robert Schumann	Heinrich Heine

CHRONOS, KRONOS: the father of ★Zeus, Hera, ★Hades, and ★Poseidon; also, time, a certain time, a period, season, or space of time. Ophism, a religious movement dating from the sixth century B.C.E. and devoted to the worship of ★Dionysus, took its name from ★Orpheus, the great musician. In Ophic theology, Chronos existed from the beginning and never aged. Chronos produced Aether, ★Chaos, and ★Erebus. From Aether, Chronos produced an egg that made Phanes, who created everything and was the first ruler of the gods. Chronos was also a name for one of the winged horses that pulled ★Helios's chariot across the sky. (SOURCES: Liddell, Scott, 1966; Mayerson, 1971; Guirand, 1968)

SONG	COMPOSER	POET
"An schwager Kronos"	Franz Schubert	Johann Wolfgang von Goethe

CHURL: a man without rank or of the lowest rank of freemen, a ★yeoman, a rustic, a countryman, a peasant, a stingy, grasping, and morose, ungracious person.

SONG	COMPOSER	POET
"St. Ita's Vision"	Samuel Barber	Medieval Irish poem

CIBBER, COLLEY (1671–1757): English poet, dramatist, and actor. In his varied theatrical career, Cibber wrote many plays and adaptations, some of ★Shakespeare and Molière. He acquired many enemies by his rudeness, but made a contribution to eighteenth-century drama, especially in the genre of sentimental comedy. Cibber was poet laureate of England from 1730 to 1757. ★Craigher de Jachelutta translated Cibber's poem *The Blind Boy*, which Schubert set in 1825 as "Der blinde Knabe." A biography by R. H. Barker, *Mr. Cibber of Drury Lane*, was published and Helene Koon published *Colley Cibber: A Biography* in 1986. (SOURCES: Drabble, 2000; Reed, 1997)

CICADA: a large, grasshopper-like insect with transparent wings. The male makes a loud, shrill chirping sound by vibrating an organ on its undersurface.

SONG	COMPOSER	POET
"Keepsake"	Goffredo Petrassi	Eugenio Montale

CIRCE: a sorceress in Greek mythology. Circe lived in the island of Aeaea. When ★Ulysses landed there, Circe turned his companions into swine, but Ulysses resisted this with an herb called Moly, given to him by Mercury. This story is told by ★Milton in *Comus*. (SOURCE: Cooper, 1992)

CIVIC POET: *see* ★CIVIC ROMANTICISM.

CIVIC ROMANTICISM: a strain of Russian ★Romanticism practiced by poets such as Kondraty Ryleev (1795–1826), Nikolai Gnedich (1784–1833), and Aleksandr Bestuzhev (1797–1837). The civic-minded romantic poets, also known as the Decembrists, were opposed to the Germanic mysticism adopted by ★Zhukovsky as much as to the ironic outlook on life displayed by ★Pushkin. The rallying cry of the movement was made by Ryleev: "I am not a poet, but a citizen." The civic poets rejected the division of poetry into classical and romantic, insisting that poetry should serve the people by personifying the most exalted ideas and feelings of an era and identifying with the national past. (SOURCE: Terras, 1991)

CLÄRCHEN, KLÄRCHEN: *see* ★EGMONT.

CLARE, JOHN (1793–1864): English poet. Born in Helpston, England, Clare was an agricultural worker in his youth. His formal schooling was minimal, and Clare was actually malnourished for many years because his family was illiterate and desperately poor, although totally supportive of their son. His father was a singer of ballads and a teller of oral tales, and Clare himself played the violin and collected folk songs and ballads. Clare's intense dedication to poetry surmounted both the financial failure of three of his four books published during his lifetime and the insensitivity and heavy censorship of his editors. In confinement at a mental asylum during his middle years, he wrote his "animal" poems, which rose to a universality widely admired. Despite these problems, Clare wrote over 3,000 poems in his fifty-five-year career. Arthur Symons's commentary (1908) initiated a new appreciation for Clare's work, although it had been critically ignored during his lifetime. His poetry shows the influence of three forces: the culture and social class of villages, nature, and the pastoral poetry of the previous century. Clare was a master at creating multiple levels of significance through a world of sight and sounds that were seemingly random. This made him one of the great lyric poets of the English language. The poetry of John Clare was set by David Diamond. PRINCIPAL WORKS: *Poems Descriptive of Rural Life and Scenery*, 1820; *The Village Minstrel and Other Poems*, 1821; *The Shepherd's Calendar*, 1827; *The Rural Muse*, 1835; *Selected Poems and Prose of John Clare*, 1967; *The Midsummer Cushion*, 1979; *The Later Poems of John Clare: 1837–1864*, 1984; *The Early Poems of John Clare: 1804–1822*, 1988–89. SELECTED READING: Edward Storey, *A Right to Song: The Life of John Clare*, 1981. (SOURCE: Magill, 2, 1992)

CLATTER: (Scot.), *talk*.

CLAUDEL, PAUL (1868–1955): French playwright, poet, translator, writer of religious prose, and diplomat. Born in France, Claudel studied law and political science, which led him to a forty-year career in the French diplomatic service with posts in the United States, China, Japan, Brazil, and many European countries. He worked in the French Ministry of Propaganda during World War II, retiring after the war. His place in literature and Catholic thought is still disputed, partially as a result of his belligerence and violent temper. Admirers and critics both abound to this day.

His close association with ★Rimbaud helped him to discover that what he prized about poetry was its association with religion. He learned from Rimbaud, attending the Tuesday evening gatherings, to look at the universe "as if it were a text on the symbolism of the universe" (Vinson, Kirkpatrick, 1984). French writers tend to psychological preoccupations, but Claudel had a brusqueness and intensity that separated him from the traditional French style. He believed that the poet's mission is to point out man's relationship with the realities of the world, basing his original type of free verse on biblical poetry, which represented an innovation of great importance to French prosody. Paul Claudel's complete works comprise one hundred volumes, and his poetry has been set to music by Arthur Honegger and Hendrik Andriessen. PRINCIPAL WORKS: *Cinque grandes odes,* 1910, *Five Great Odes,* 1967; *Poèmes et paroles durant la guerre,* 1916; *The Satin Slipper,* 1928, music by Honegger; *Visages radieux,* 1946. SELECTED READING: John A. MacCombie, *The Prince and the Genie: A Study of Rimbaud's Influence on Claudel,* 1972; Lynne L. Gelber, *In/stability: The Shape and Space of Claudel's Art,* 1980. (SOURCE: Vinson, Kirkpatrick (1), 1984; Steinberg, 2, 1973)

CLAUDINE: the protagonist in ★Goethe's play *Claudine von Villa Bella.* According to Goethe's critics, the play was not one of his best efforts. The story concerns the lovers Claudine and Pedro. Pedro's lost brother, a dashing vagabond highwayman, turns out to be a "rather decent fellow," but not before he has flirted with Claudine and distressed her otherwise. The Schubert song, taken from the play and sung by Claudine, represents her philosophy of love and fidelity.

SONG	COMPOSER	POET
"Liebe schwärmt auf allen Wegen"	Franz Schubert	Johann Wolfgang von Goethe

CLAUDIUS, MATTHIAS (1740–1815): German poet and essayist. Son of a clergyman, full of humor, peasant simplicity, and delightful frankness, Claudius had planned to follow his father's calling, but instead, worked as an editor of various journals and country newspapers and became a poet. He wrote prolifically and easily both prose and poetry, expressing his religious feelings in words that resemble church hymns in their childlike piety. Living most of his life in villages and small towns, Claudius used rural scenes for color in his poetry. He believed that nature testified to God's goodness and that death was a friend, as exemplified in his poem "Der Tod und das Mädchen," set by Schubert, with its contrast between the frightened cry of the maiden and the soothing speech of Death. The simplicity of his poetry was sometimes inspired with great imaginative power and an ability to communicate atmosphere. The poetry of Matthias Claudius has been set by Schubert, Beethoven, Carl Loewe, Anton Webern, Johann Reichardt, Othmar Schoeck, Miriam Gideon, and Hermann Reutter. SELECTED READING: Eng. trans. in A. S. Baskerville, *The Poetry of Germany,* 1853; A. H. Goodwin, *Rhymes from the Rhineland,* 1913. (SOURCE: Mathieu, Stern, 1987; Steinberg, 2, 1973)

CLEFTA: an Italian translation of the Greek word *klepht*, brigand or bandit. (SOURCE: Lakeway, White, 1989)

SONG	COMPOSER	POET
"Il clefta prigione"	Ildebrando Pizzetti	Nicolò Tommasèo, trans. from Greek

CLEOMENES, THE SPARTAN HERO: a tragic drama written by John ★Dryden, produced in 1692, containing one song by Henry Purcell. Cleomenes, king of Sparta, has fled to Alexandria with his family to seek support from the Egyptians, because his battle with the Macedonians has gone against him. Since he now has no base of power, Cleomenes must resort to railing and vulgar bargaining in order to get an audience with lazy King Ptolomy, who keeps the Spartan waiting three months while he dotes on his mistress Cassandra and entertains himself with sex and music. Dryden delays the Cleomenes/Ptolomy meeting while showing us the singing and dancing entertainment in Cassandra's apartment. Purcell's music for "No, No, Poor Suff'ring Heart," the focal point of this scene, expresses Ptolomy's passion for Cassandra and underlines his decadence. It is "one of Purcell's few serious songs not to declare its message openly" (Price). (SOURCE: Price, 1984)

CLEOPATRA: the throne name of a number of Macedonian queens of ancient Egypt. The most renowned of these was Cleopatra VII Philopater (69–30 B.C.E.). The last of the Ptolemaic line, part Macedonian, part Greek and Iranian, she ruled in Alexandria (47–30 B.C.E.) but, as mistress and wife to Mark Antony, played a decisive role in the course of Roman/European history. Her goal being to rule Egypt alone, in order to consolidate her position, she originally secured Caesar's support and bore him a son. Caesar brought her to Rome where she stayed until his assassination. Back in Egypt, she put her son on the throne, made herself indispensable to Mark Antony, eventually marrying him and bearing his twins. Mark Antony enlarged Cleopatra's power by huge gifts of territory but was stripped of his own powers because of their relationship. When it was clear that her dreams of power were hopeless, Cleopatra killed herself by ordering an asp (cobra) to be smuggled in to her rooms and allowing it to bite her. Berlioz's lyric scene was his third attempt at trying to win the Prix de Rome.

SONG	COMPOSER	POET
1. "Cleopatra to the Asp"	Charles Griffes	John B. Tabb
2. "Cléopatre"	Hector Berlioz	P. A. Viellard

CLINTY: (Scot.), *rocky.*

CLITANDRE: *see* ★TIRCIS.

CLOISTERS, THE: a branch of the New York Metropolitan Museum of Art, built of parts of five monasteries, a Romanesque chapel, and a twelfth-century Spanish apse with extensive gardens and many examples of sculpture, painting and stained glass from the ninth to the fifteenth centuries. The Cloisters is located in Fort Tryon Park on the Hudson River at the northern end of Manhattan in a section called

Inwood. In the Corigliano cycle, each song represents a different season and a different aspect of love. "Fort Tryon Park" takes place in the fall, "Song to the Witch of the Cloisters" in summer, "Christmas at the Cloisters" in winter, and "The Unicorn" in spring.

SONG	COMPOSER	POET
"The Cloisters"	John Corigliano	William Hoffman

CLOOS, CONSUELO (1887–1985): American poet and painter. Cloos was born in New England and much of her painting celebrated the coast of that area. Her surrealistic impressionistic paintings numbered nearly one thousand works in oils, pastels, watercolors, and mixed media. Her major art works were produced during the 1940s and 1950s. In 1976 she and Salvador Dali met in New York, after which he invited her to exhibit some of her works in his gallery in Spain. Not known for promoting other artists, Dali described her work as "magnifique." Her verse was set to music by Alan Hovhaness.

CLORIS: *see* *CHLORIS.

CLOURIN: (Scot.), *battering, thumping something or someone.*

SONG	COMPOSER	POET
"Black Day"	Benjamin Britten	William Soutar

CLUN: a town situated just inside the Welsh/English border at the south end of *Wenlock Edge. On all sides are hills, barren on top, and showing scanty trees below, the houses half-timbered with wood from the Forest of Clun.

SONG	COMPOSER	POET
"On Wenlock Edge"	Ralph Vaughan Williams	A. E. Housman

CLYMÈNE: the daughter of Oceanus and Tethys. She bore the *Titan Iapetus three boys, *Atlas, *Prometheus, and Epimetheus. (SOURCE: Kaster, 1964)

SONG	COMPOSER	POET
"A Clymène"	Gabriel Fauré	Paul Verlaine

COCARDE (Fr.), COCKADE (Eng.): lit., a rosette or knot of ribbon worn on the hat as a badge. In France the tri-colored ribbons represented the country as a flag does. In Jean *Cocteau's poems set by Francis Poulenc in a cycle, *Cocardes*, the texts are word puzzles. One of the last syllables of each line is repeated to begin the following word, such as in the titles "Miel de Narbonnes" followed by "Bonne d'enfant."

COCKIT: (Scot.), v. *a fist raised threateningly;* adj. *stuck up; lively, merry.*

SONG	COMPOSER	POET
"The Larky Lad"	Benjamin Britten	William Soutar

COCTEAU, JEAN (MAURICE EUGENE CLÉMENT) (1889–1963): French poet, writer, artist, journalist, film writer, and director. Cocteau was born in Maisons-Lafitte, educated in Paris and privately. His first volume of verse was published at the age of nineteen, and a small public applauded his effortless brilliance. With three works that appeared between 1917 and 1919, he became a public figure: *Parade*

(1917), a ballet performed in Rome; *Le Coq et l'Arlequin* (1918), a public criticism of the principles of Debussy and Wagner; *Le Cap de Bonne-espérance* (1919), a volume of war poems that put him in the top rank of young poets. He was made the honorary president of the Cannes Film Festival, given an honorary degree from Oxford (1956), and became a member of the French Académie as well as a Commander of the Légion d'Honneur. The hallmark of his work is his ability to express complicated matters with perceptive simplicity. The poetry of Jean Cocteau has been set by Poulenc, Satie, Arthur Honegger, Georges Auric, and Lennox Berkeley. PRINCIPAL WORKS: Poetry: *Vocabulaire*, 1922; *Plain-Chant, Romans, Le Grand Ecart*. Plays: *Antigone*, produced 1922, revised version with music by Honegger produced 1927; *Orphée*, produced 1926; *Oedipus Rex*, music by Stravinsky, produced 1927; *La Voix humaine*, produced 1930, set by Poulenc in an opera. Fiction: *Les Enfants terribles*, 1929, trans. as *Children of the Game*, 1955. SELECTED READING: Wallace Fowlie, *Cocteau: The History of a Poet's Age*, 1966; Frederick Brown, *An Impersonation of Angels: A Biography of Jean Cocteau*, 1969. (SOURCE: Vinson, Kirkpatrick (1), 1984)

COCYTUS: one of the five rivers surrounding *Hades. The meanings assigned to these rivers speak death: *Styx, the Abhorrent or the Hated; Cocytus, the Wailing; Pyriphlegethon (or Phlegethon), the Burning; Acheron, the Sorrowful; and *Lethe, Forgetfulness. Those dead who were deprived of burial were forced to wander the banks of the Cocytus, which flowed underground for part of the journey into the Acheron, for one hundred years. *Dante, in the *Divine Comedy*, describes Cocytus as a frozen region that surrounds the lowest part of Hell, holding Lucifer and Judas. (SOURCES: Mayerson, 1971; *Bulfinch*, 1978; Benét, 1, 1965)

SONG	COMPOSER	POET
1. "Gruppe aus Tartarus"	Franz Schubert	Friedrich von Schiller
2. "An Laura"	Franz Schubert	Friedrich von Matthison

COLCHIS: an ancient city on the Black Sea, called the Sea of Colchis at that time. *Jason and the Argonauts met and survived a great storm in the Sea of Colchis during the search for the *Golden Fleece. (SOURCE: Guirand, 1968)

COLERIDGE, SAMUEL TAYLOR (1772–1834): English poet, playwright, philosopher, biographer, lecturer, essayist, critic, and translator. Coleridge was born in 1772, attended Cambridge University and the University of Göttingen. In 1797 he settled near his friends William Wordsworths and his sister, Dorothy, who settled an annuity upon him in 1798. Coleridge's opium use, which had already become an addiction by 1799, successfully tempted him to the abstractions of philosophy and precipitated the breakdown of his marriage and a quarrel with Wordsworth. He lived in Malta (1804–6) in an effort to restore his health. Having lectured extensively in London (1808–11), Coleridge returned to a final residence near London in 1816. His reconciliation with Wordsworth made it possible for them to tour the Rhineland together in 1828. The two poets enjoyed a fourteen-year friendship and one of the most creative partnerships in English Romanticism. Their plans were to write a book of verses called *Lyrical Ballads*, in which Coleridge's contributions were to be concerned with persons and characters supernatural and romantic, while the objective of Wordsworth's writing was the show the charm of everyday things and the wonders of the world. When published in 1798, "The Rime of the Ancient Mariner" realized Coleridge's intention and assured his reputation. "Kubla Khan," another of his poems, was the forerunner of the later ★Symbolist and ★Surrealist poetry with their exploitation of the subconscious. ★Shelley called Coleridge "a mighty poet / And a subtle-souled psychologist" (Vinson, 1979). Although his prose writings were frequently fragmentary and unsystematic, "His insights were profound, if obscurely or imperfectly expressed" (Vinson, 1979). Coleridge's poetry has been set by Lee Hoiby, John Corigliano, Lennox Berkeley, and Benjamin Britten. PRINCIPAL WORKS: Verse: *Fears in Solitude; An Ode; Frost at Midnight*, 1798; *Lyrical Ballads with a Few Other Poems*, with William Wordsworth, 1798, revised and edited, 2 vols., 1800; *Christable, Kubla Khan: A Vision, The Pains of Sleep*, 1816; *Sibylline Leaves*, 1817, 1828, 1834. Plays: *The Fall of Robespierre*, with Robert Southey, 1794; *Remorse*, music by Michael Kelly, 1813. SELECTED READING: J. B. Beer, *Coleridge the Visionary*, 1959; Reeve Parker, *Coleridge's Meditative Art*, 1975. (SOURCES: Drabble, 1985; Vinson, 1979)

COLETTE, SIDONIE-GABRIELLE (1873–1954): French writer. Colette's position is that of a feminist in a culture controlled by men. She began her career under the guidance of her husband; her first novels were written with him and published under his name. After their divorce, she continued on her own. Essentially a turn-of-the-century writer, Colette captured the world called the *belle époque*. Her talent lay in the direction of exploring human relations, as a young man's love for a woman of fifty, or a husband's jealousy of his wife, but she also wrote with sensitivity about children, nature, and animals. Yet she was not a sentimental writer; she was severe in her analyses of her characters' moods. An actress and revue performer, a columnist, a literary editor, and a drama critic, she has been called a minor writer but a great woman. The French made her a Chevalier of the Légion d'honneur in 1920, an Officer in 1928, a Commander in 1936, and a Grand Officer in 1953. The words of Colette have been set by Francis Poulenc. PRINCIPAL WORKS: *Chéri*, 1920, trans. 1929; *L'Enfant et les sortilèges*, music by Ravel, 1925; *The Last of Chéri*, 1932; *Gigi*, with Anita Loos, 1951; *My Mother's House*, Eng. trans. 1953. SELECTED READING: *Colette: The Woman, The Writer*, ed. Erica M. Eisinger and Mari McCarty, 1981; Herbert R. Lottman, *Colette: A Life*, 1991. (SOURCE: Vinson, Kirkpatrick (1), 1984)

COLLIN, MATTHÄEUS VON (1779–1824): German poet, tutor of the son of Napoleon I, and brother of Heinrich von Collin, a renowned author for whose play *Coriolan* Beethoven composed the overture. Matthäeus von Collin was active in Austria as one of the early ★romantics. He and Schubert were friends, and Schubert set some of his poetry, notably "Nacht und Träume," "Der Zwerg," "Epistel," and "Wehmut." (SOURCE: Steinberg, 2, 1973)

COLOGNE CATHEDRAL: a magnificent cathedral near the Cathedral Bridge on the Rhein River in the city of Cologne. Distinguishing characteristics of the cathedral are the two 512-foot towers. Construction on the building was begun in the 1200s and not completed until 1880. It was damaged by the Allied bombings in World War II, but not destroyed.

SONG	COMPOSER	POET
1. "Die alten bösen Lieder"	Robert Schumann	Heinrich Heine
2. "Im Rhein, im heiligen Strome"	Robert Schumann, Robert Franz, Franz Liszt	Heinrich Heine

COLUM, PADRAIC (1881–1972): Irish poet and playwright. Son of a workhouse master, Colum was educated at Trinity College in Dublin, where he met James ★Joyce and became close friends with him. Colum was prominent in the Irish Revival and wrote several plays for the Abbey Theatre. In addition to his poetry, Colum wrote works on Irish and Hawaiian folklore and legends in diverse cultures. He was famous for his refined retelling of folktales for children. With his wife, Mary, he wrote *Our Friend James Joyce* (1958). The poetry of Padraic Colum was set by Arnold Bax. PRINCIPAL POETIC WORKS: *Wild Earth and Other Poems*, 1907; *Collected Poems*, 1953; *Images of Departure*, 1969. SELECTED READING: Zack Bowen, *Padraic Colum: A Biographical-Critical Introduction*, 1970. (SOURCE: Drabble, 2000)

COLUMBINE, COLOMBINA (It.): a stock character in old Italian ★*commedia dell'arte*, dating from about 1560, and transferred to French and English pantomime. A coquette and a keen wit, able to cope on her own in any situation, Columbine is the daughter of ★Pantaloon and the friend and sweetheart of ★Harlequin. Like him, she was invisible to mortal eyes. In Italian, Colombina is the pet name for a ladylove, *dovelike*, and takes its meaning from the word "colombina", *dove*. (SOURCE: Cooper, 1992)

SONG	COMPOSER	POET
1. "Pantomime"	Claude Debussy	Paul Verlaine
2. "Pierrot Lunaire"	Arnold Schönberg	Albert Giraud

"Come All, Come All to Me": a song composed by Henry Purcell to the words of Thomas ★Shadwell in his adaptation of William ★Shakespeare's *Timon of Athens*. For plot details and position of the song within the plot, *see* ★*Timon of Athens*.

"Come Every Demon": a song written by Henry Purcell to a text by ★D'Avenant in the 1677 production of ★*Circe*. For position of the song within the plot, *see* ★*Circe*.

"Come, Let Us Leave the Town": a duet composed by Henry Purcell to a text written by Elkanah ★Settle for his work *The Fairie-Queene*, produced in 1692 and 1693. For plot details and placement of songs, *see* ★*Fairie-Queene, The*.

"Come, Ye Songsters": a song composed by Henry Purcell to a text written by Elkanah ★Settle for his work *The Fairie-Queene*, produced in 1692 and 1693. For plot details and placement of songs, *see* ★*Fairie-Queene, The*.

COMMEDIA DELL'ARTE: a popular, improvised art form that flourished from the sixteenth through the eighteenth centuries, performed by a group of professional actors playing masked characters who were found in stock dramatic situations. The clown/jester enjoyed a long and distinguished history in the civilized world, no less so in Italy and Greece than in Asia and America. The clowns of Italy, *buffoni,* trace their history back to groups of mimes, jugglers, and acrobats performing in Greece before the birth of tragedy. These groups of mimes, performing for festivals in celebration of ★Dionysus, the god of wine and comedy, were enormously popular in Greece. Wearing grotesque masks and exaggerated padding on selected body parts—phallus, buttocks, and belly—they performed skits loosely based upon everyday life, such as domestic quarrels, thievery, fighting, sexual exploits, and trickery of all kinds. The characters in these scenes were familiar types: "braggart soldiers, pompous doctors and philosophers, larcenous slaves and servants, witchlike old women, rustics, go-betweens, bald-headed fools, bearded old men" (Towsen, 1976). Although the acting style was broad and exaggerated, it was considered by many to be more realistic than the style of the tragedians. These comic characters passed into the repertoire of the Greek dramatists, appearing in the works of Aristophanes. The Romans, who emulated all things Greek, adopted Greece's tragedies and comedies. The braggart soldier, the cunning slave, and the doddering old man all appear in the works of Plautus (whose plays served as the basis of Stephen Sondheim's *A Funny Thing Happened on the Way to the Forum).* From these early comic roots grew the *commedia dell'arte. Commedia dell'arte* translates literally to "comedy of professional actors." The name was used to distinguish it from the *commedia erudita,* "dilettantish amateurs who staged their own literary dramas for the intellectual elite" (Towsen, 1976). *Commedia dell'arte* was performed in courtyards and village greens, wherever the actors could find an audience. Although it involved masked characters in stock situations, it was an improvised art form, spontaneous and frequently vulgar. Most *commedia dell'arte* plays contained four types of characters: first, the lovers, *gl'innamorati,* who did not wear masks and were not necessarily funny; second, the old men*, I vecchi, Pantalone* and *il Dottore. Pantalone* was a lecherous old miser, a wealthy old merchant, wooing a young woman half his age. *Il Dottore* was his best friend and confidant, a character amusing because of his language, his absent-mindedness, and his use of malapropisms. Third was *il capitano* (the ★captain), a young man who boasted about his military and amorous adventures, only to be found out in the end—a faker. Fourth were the servants, *gli zanni,* ★*Harlequin,* and *Brighella* or *Francatrippa,* always comic, sometimes lazy, sometimes stupid, sometimes clever (Erenstein, 1989). Originally, the *zanni* were probably part of the entourage that traveled with quack healers, attracting audiences by singing and performing acrobatics. Each actor brought to his own performance a set of special effects called *lazzi* (songs, dances, magic tricks, sight gags, and elaborate speeches). Since many actors were acrobats, characters would turn somersaults or walk on their hands while holding a glass of water, which they would do whenever the scene began to drag. The success of a *commedia dell'arte* performance depended upon the improvised acting rather than the play. In tragedy the purpose of the play is to ennoble the audience by awakening in them sympathy for the plight of the hero or heroine. If sympathy is the aim of tragedy, the aim of comedy is contempt for the comic characters. The audience was meant to look down upon the foolishness of the character and thus avoid his or her shortcomings. Because of these differing goals, the types of characters appearing in tragedy and comedy diverged. Kings, queens, gods, goddesses, and assorted heroes from ancient epic poems and romances were the main characters of tragedy, but people of humbler birth—maids, men servants, members of the professional class, farmers—populated comedies. As a result, comedy was more natural and true to life than tragedy. Political satire was discouraged because the traveling companies did not wish to antagonize the authorities. The *commedia dell'arte* was dying out by the eighteenth century when ★Goldoni used a more elaborate psychology to refresh the types. (SOURCES: Towsen, 1976; Erenstein, 1989)

"Comment, disaient-ils": a song by Franz Liszt, written to a text by Victor ★Hugo. The great violin virtuoso ★Paganini had a strong influence upon Liszt, in the bravado of the composer's own performances and in his impressive techniques and tricks. In this song, Liszt's occasional imitation of a violin playing prompts one to imagine Paganini improvising.

CONGREVE, WILLIAM (1670–1729): English poet and dramatist. In his lifetime Congreve was considered the rival of practically every English dramatist except Shakespeare. He and Swift were fellow students at Trinity College, where Congreve gave up the law for literature. A master of Restoration comedy, he first achieved fame in 1693 with The ★*Old Batchelour* and The ★*Double Dealer*, in which he wrote of the social pressures on love and marriage with wit and subtlety. Henry Purcell set two songs from *The Old Batchelour*, one from *The Double Dealer*, and one from The ★*Maid's Last Prayer*. The poetry of William Congreve was also set by Handel, William Boyce, and John Eccles. SELECTED READING: John C. Hodges, *William Congreve, the Man*, 1941. (SOURCE: Drabble, 2000)

CONRADI, HERMANN (1862–1890): German poet and novelist. Conradi's start in literature was impassioned and perhaps overeager. He was a gifted poet, but the total effect of his verses was somewhat harsh and clumsy, and his constant struggles with ill-health and poverty contributed to his early burning out. Conradi's verses were set by Arnold Schönberg. (SOURCE: Steinberg, 3, 1973)

CONSTABLE, HENRY (1562–1613): English poet, political and religious prose writer. Henry Constable was born in England but died in France. He came from a line of distinguished ancestors on both sides of his family, members of his father's family having been constables since the time of William the Conqueror. After receiving his bachelor's degree from Cambridge (1579?), he became an emissary to the English ambassador in Paris. He was friendly with the Protestants of the Continent, including the followers of Henry of Navarre, but not long after 1591 he publicly became a Catholic. Thereafter he schemed to assure the safety of English Catholics and the return of England to the Roman Catholic Church. Following his return to England (1603) after James I became king, Constable was in and out of prison because of his political activities. He then returned to France and died there. Constable's major concerns were politics, theology, and justice, and he desired a union of

Protestant and Catholic churches. His religious interests affected his life and poetry; that is, his prose works showed commitment to Protestant causes, but he wrote religious *sonnets after his conversion to Catholicism. During the Elizabethan period, Constable was regarded as a major writer and admired for his simple, unaffected writing style. Despite the fact that *Shakespeare himself borrowed specific details from him and Ben *Jonson listed him as a great poet along with Homer, Ovid, *Petrarch, and *Ronsard, he is now considered to be a minor figure. The poetry of Henry Constable has been set by Francis Pilkington, Dominick Argento, and George Chadwick. PRINCIPAL POETRY: *Diana*, 1592, 1594; *The Poems of Henry Constable*, Joan Grundy, ed., 1960. SELECTED READING: Joan Grundy, *Henry Constable*. (SOURCE: Magill, 2, 1992)

CONSTANTINE, SAINT; AYIO CONSTANNDINA (ca.274–331): soldier and ruler of Gaul and St. Helena, then Roman emperor. Held as a hostage at the court of the emperor *Diocletian, Constantine escaped when the emperor died but returned to Rome as its conqueror (311). Two years after Constantine became commander of the western part of the Roman empire, he issued the Edict of Milan, lifting from Christian churches the classification of *religio illicita* once and for all. A successful military conflict with the emperor of the eastern part of the Roman empire left him as the sole ruler. His empire stretched all round the Mediterranean and north into much of Europe. Faced with the difficulty of maintaining all this territory, Constantine used the existing authority and communication system of the Christian churches as a kind of civil service. In 324 he convened and presided over the first ecumenical council of churches at Nicea, took up residence in Byzantium (the European part of modern Turkey), rebuilt the city, and named it Constantinople. The Eastern churches honor him as a saint because of his setting the churches free from the threat of active persecution. (SOURCE: Glazier, Hellwig, 1994)

SONG	COMPOSER	POET
"La-bas vers l'église"	Maurice Ravel	Greek folk poetry, French translation

CONSTRUCTIVISM: a Russian poetic movement that had its origin in architecture and the visual arts, but quickly spread to poetry, theater, and film, and lasted until 1930. The main concern of constructivists was that art should emphasize economy, simplicity, and expediency, thus quickly producing utilitarian verse. Its main practitioners were Vladimir *Mayakovsky, Nicolai Aseev, and Vasily Kamensky, who believed that poetry should be a tool for reducing the complexities of a modern world to simple terms accessible to the masses. (SOURCE: Terras, 1991)

COOPER, JAMES FENNIMORE (1789–1851): American poet and novelist. Cooper was born in Albany, New York. He graduated as a Phi Beta Kappa from Yale, received other literary and scholarly honors, and showed considerable promise. He spent 1808 to 1811 in the Navy, eventually writing an important history of that service. In the 1820s, with the awakening of curiosity about national culture, Cooper came into his own by giving meaning to the time and place in which he lived. At the age of thirty he began to produce an average of one novel every year. These were translated and appreciated abroad, but criticized at home. In 1828 he began to write in a political vein, which lost him some readers until he regained his popularity by returning to novels. One of the greatest of American writers of fiction, his work should be evaluated as art and as a historical document. His achievement goes beyond romance but stops short of realism and ★Symbolism. Intuitively, Cooper developed an American novel of manners that served as commentary as well as a record. His only published volume of verse appeared in 1918 as a memorial album. The work of James Fennimore Cooper was set to music by Charles Ives. PRINCIPAL WORKS: *Last of the Mohicans*, 1826; *The Pathfinder*, 1840; *The Deerslayer*, 1841; *The Leather Stocking Tales*, 1850. SELECTED READING: Warren S. Walker, *James Fennimore Cooper*, 1962. (SOURCE: *Americana*, 2001)

COPLAS: (Sp.), *couplets*, a Spanish stanza form, loosely used to describe any short stanza of eight-syllable lines, but generally applied to four-line stanzas of modern Spanish folk poetry. (SOURCE: Steinberg, 1, 1973)

SONG	COMPOSER	POET
"Coplas del pastor enamorado"	Joaquín Rodrigo	Lope de Vega

COPPÉE, FRANÇOIS EDOUARD (1842–1908): French poet, dramatist, and short story writer. Born in Paris of modest bourgeois parents, Coppée supported his mother and sister as an architect's clerk after his father's death. Later he found a position at the War Ministry, which afforded him the leisure with which to write verse. Coppée was a minor ★Parnassian who could be found at ★Leconte de L'Isle's famous Saturdays, where he acquired a sound technique. Although his verses were admired by his friends and by Victor ★Hugo, they went unnoticed by the public. Once encouraged by tying for the prize given by the Universal Exposition of 1867, Coppée tried the theater. He had a very sound success with *Le Passant* (1869), in which Sarah Bernhardt made her debut. Coppée's verse plays based on moral and patriotic themes were very popular in his time, but are now forgotten, perhaps because of their excessively maudlin character. At the beginning of his writing career Coppée was highly influenced by the principles of the Parnassians, but later turned to a simpler, more prosy form of verse after which he became known as the poet of the humble. He was elected to the French Academy in 1884. The poetry of François Coppée has been set in French by Reynaldo Hahn and Henri Duparc, in Russian translation by César Cui. PRINCIPAL WORKS: Poetry: *Les Humbles*, 1872; *Poésies Complètes*, 1923–25, 3 vols. English translations: *Fennet*, trans. J. Jerome, 1888; *The Days of my Youth*, trans. J. Jerome, 1888; *Ten Tales*, trans. W. Learned, 1890; *The Violin Maker of Cremona*, 1892; *True Riches*, 1893. Plays: *Le Passant*, 1869; *Le Luthier de Crémona*, 1876; *Severo Torelli*, 1883; *Pour la Couronne*, 1896. (SOURCES: Kunitz, Colby, 1967; Steinberg, 2, 1973)

COPTIC: the language of the Christian descendants of the ancient Egyptians. The two songs of Hugo Wolf are written to texts taken from an early five-act comedy of ★Goethe, *Der Grosskophta* (1791), based on a famous scandal concerning the theft of a priceless necklace. The Great Coptic was a preposterous quack who discoursed with invisible spirits and, with his initiates, conducted solemn investigations that echoed Masonic rituals.

SONG	COMPOSER	POET
"Kophtisches Lied I and II"	Hugo Wolf	Johann Wolfgang von Goethe

CÓRDOBA (Sp.), CORDOUE (Fr.): a Spanish city, a Middle Ages center for science. Algebra, trigonometry, and Arabic numerals were invented by the Moors, who also brought to Europe musical instruments such as the shawm (an oboe), kettle drums, the lute, and the oval guitar which gave Spanish music its exotic qualities. Once the beautiful and impressive capital of Moorish Spain because of its many mosques and public baths, Córdoba boasted a favorable comparison with the city of Baghdad. The magnificent mosque and the mezquita still remain. (SOURCE: Cockburn, Stokes, 1992)

SONG	COMPOSER	POET
1. "Soneto à Córdoba"	Manuel de Falla	Luis de Góngora
2. "Romance"	Joaquìn Turina	Duque de Rivas
3. "Zaïde"	Hector Berlioz	Roger de Beauvoir

"Corinna, I Excuse Thy Face": a song by Henry Purcell with lyrics by Thomas ★Southerne. *See* ★*Wives Excuse, The,* for plot details and position of the song within the plot.

CORINTHIANS: the seventh and eighth books of the New Testament, two letters written by St. ★Paul to the Christian Church in Corinth. The first of these letters contains the text of the fourth song of Brahms's *Vier ernste Gesänge,* "If I Spoke with the Tongues of Men," on the subject of love. The city of Corinth itself was founded in prehistoric times on the isthmus that connects the Peloponnesus with the rest of Europe.

SONG	COMPOSER	POET
1. "Wenn ich mit menschen"	Johannes Brahms	St. Paul, 1 Corinthians
2. "Familière"	Jacques Ibert	Philippe Chabaneix

CORNEILLE, PIERRE (1609–1684): French dramatist and poet. Corneille was educated at a Jesuit College and then studied law, graduating as a licensed lawyer in 1624. A member of the Rouen Parliament from 1629 to 1650, he became a king's advocate in the water and forests courts and in the Rouen port Admiralty court. Corneille was the earliest of the great French classical dramatists. His work was marked by grandeur, heroism, the subordination of passion to duty, and verbal display. His gift was for resolute and ponderous eloquence and revealed a fascination with human behavior in extraordinary and confused situations. Except for some lively personal pieces, his non-dramatic poetry is fairly uninteresting. Pierre Corneille's words were set to music by Jean-Baptiste Lully, and by Émile Paladilhe in a beautiful piece called "Psyché." PRINCIPAL WORKS: *Medée,* 1639, ed. André de Leyssac, 1978; *Le Cid,* 1637, trans. as *The Cid,* 1637; *Polyeucte, Martyr,* 1643; *Imitation de Jésus-Christ,* 1656; *Oedipe,* 1659; *Attila, Roi des Huns,* 1667; *Office de la Sainte Vierge,*

1670; *Psyché*, with Molière and Quinault, music by Lully, 1671. SELECTED READING: H.T. Barnwell, *The Tragic Drama of Corneille and Racine*, 1982. (SOURCE:Vinson, Kirkpatrick (1), 1984)

CORNUCOPIA: a container shaped like a horn, overflowing with fruit, flowers, and grain. The concept of a cornucopia is based on Greek mythology, wherein the infant ★Zeus was fed with goat's milk by ★Amaltheia, a she-goat or goat-nymph. In gratitude, Zeus placed Amaltheia's image among the stars as the constellation Capricorn. He also broke off one of the goat's horns, which resembled a cow's horn, and gave it to the daughters of Melisseus, a Cretan king. It became the famous Cornucopia, the Horn of Plenty, which was always filled with whatever food or drink its owner desired. (SOURCE: Delahunty et al., 2001)

CORYDON: a common name for a rustic, a shepherd, a brainless, lovesick fellow. A conventional name in pastoral poetry, the origin of the word is the shepherd in Virgil's Eclogue VII, also to be found in the *Idylls* of ★Theocritus. (SOURCE: Cooper, 1992)

SONG	COMPOSER	POET
"Phillis Was a Faire Maide"	Phillip Rosseter	Thomas Campion

COUPLET: a poetic pattern formed by a pair of rhyming lines. In France, the term *couplet* is sometimes used to mean a stanza.

COWLEY, ABRAHAM (1618–1667): English poet and playwright. The precocious son of a London stationer, Cowley started writing poetry at the age of ten, was a King's scholar at Westminster, and scholar and fellow of Trinity College, Cambridge. During the Civil War, Cowley went to Oxford, where he contributed his writing to the Royalist cause. At the Restoration, as a result of suspicions that he had been a spy, no official reward was given him for his services, but two noblemen saw to it that he was given a pension, and he was buried in Westminster Abbey. In 1815 Schubert set one of his poems from *The Mistress*, a collection of love poems, from which "Der Weiberfreund" was translated by Joseph Ratschky. PRINCIPAL WORKS: *Poetical Blossomes,* 1633; *The Mistress,* 1647; *Poems,* 1656; *Poems (Miscellaneous),* 1633; *The Guardian*, a play, 1650; *Poemata Latina,* 1668. (SOURCES: Reed, 1997; Drabble, 2000)

COWPER, WILLIAM (1731–1800): English poet. Son of an impecunious clergyman, descended from an ancient family, and related to John ★Donne through his mother's lineage, Cowper was an excellent scholar and a good athlete. His three-year apprenticeship to a solicitor depressed him and clouded the rest of his life. In 1754 he was called to the bar. Denied permission to marry his cousin and grieving the death of his best friend, Cowper sank into deep melancholy, but managed to write articles and translations of Homer. Despite glimpses of reason, three attempts at suicide caused him to be institutionalized twice. In 1779 he began to write poetry to preserve his sanity, beginning with hymns that are now studied as poems. A good craftsman in structuring his poetry, Cowper had a liking for literary experimentation and a preference for the rural over the urban. New directions suggested by Cowper were soon perfected by Wordsworth. Although his verse included landscape descriptions, character sketches, social criticism, and personal confessions, he searched for a point of balance as a unifying theme. The poetry of William Cowper was set by Charles Ives and Gordon Binkerd. PRINCIPAL WORKS: *Olney Hymns*, with John Newton, 1779; *Poems*, 1782; *The Task*, 1785; *Completed Poetical Works*, 1907. SELECTED READING: James King, *William Cowper: A Biography*, 1986. (SOURCE: Steinberg, 2, 1973; Magill, 2, 1992)

COWPIN: (Scot.), n. *a pen for cows*; v. *penning cows; overturning; coming to blows.*

SONG	COMPOSER	POET
"Black Day"	Benjamin Britten	William Soutar

CRABS: an expression used in Elizabethan lyrics, meaning *crab apples*.

SONG	COMPOSER	POET
"Winter"	Dominick Argento	William Shakespeare

CRAIGHER, JACOB DE JACHELUTTA (1797–1855): merchant and poet of Italian origin. In 1820 Craigher settled in Vienna, where he amassed a fortune. In his travels throughout Europe he gained an extensive knowledge of European languages and became well known to the ★Schlegel circle and all of Vienna. In addition to the agreement to translate Schubert's songs into Italian, he was also the poet for three Schubert songs: "Die junge Nonne," "Totengrabers Heimweh," and "Der blinde Knabe," which he translated from Colley ★Cibber's "The Blind Boy." (SOURCE: Reed, 1997)

CRAIGIE: (Scot.) (pr. kray-gee, hard g) diminutive of the word *crag*, a steep rugged rocky eminence, a rough broken cliff or projecting point of a rock; also, the *neck*, the *throat*.

CRANE, (HAROLD) HART (1899–1932): American poet. Crane was born in a small town in Ohio, the only child in a broken home, his father distant, his mother possessive. His parents separated in 1909, and Crane was sent to live with his maternal grandmother. In 1916, at the age of seventeen, he abandoned high school and went to New York to live, committing himself to poetry as a vocation. His most lucrative attempt at earning a living was as a copy writer, and he lived mostly in the then underground world of a homosexual. Crane made an early study of ★Plato, whose words, he said, taught him the necessity of madness in a true poet. He believed in ★Nietzsche's glorification of the artist, and he met and admired the Bengali poet Rabindranath ★Tagore in 1916. By 1921 he had reached full poetic maturity, but still had no economic or emotional stability. Although his work was given recognition in the form of a grant by the banker Otto Kahn and a Guggenheim Fellowship (1931), it is astonishing that his talent survived the extreme disorder of his life. Having spent some time in Mexico, suffering from his alcoholism and his unfulfilled ideals, he committed suicide by jumping overboard from a Caribbean ship. Both Crane and his poetry were intense, extreme, and uncompromising. His whole artistic effort was dedicated to using new poetic forms of expression as weapons against the philosophic trends of the period. One of his critics described his work as both contemporary and grandiose. Robert Lowell called him "the *Shelley of my age" (Unger, 1, 1974). The poetry of Hart Crane has been set by Elliott Carter. PRINCIPAL WORKS: *White Buildings*, 1926; *The Bridge*, 1930; *Collected Poems of Hart Crane*, ed. Waldo Frank, 1933. SELECTED READING: Vincent Quinn, *Hart Crane*, 1963; John E. Unterecker, *Voyager: A Life of Harte Crane*, 1969. (SOURCES: Drabble, 2000; Unger, 1, 1974)

CRANREUCH: (Scot.), *hoarfrost*.

CRAPSEY, ADELAIDE (1878–1914): American poet. Adelaide Crapsey was born in Brooklyn Heights, the daughter of a free-thinking minister father who had been deposed from the Episcopal Church. Soon after her birth the hectic but intellectual household was moved to Rochester, New York. After graduating from Vassar in 1901, Crapsey taught in prep schools. She attended Rome's School of Arches, studying archeology, and then spent two more years in Italy researching a study of English metrics. Originally her own poetry was conventionally *Romantic, but exposure to Japanese *tanka and *haiku and to the verse of Emily *Dickinson and Walter *Landor served to tighten up her poems. While teaching at Smith College in 1911, she invented a poetic form, the *cinquain*, an unrhymed, five-line poem with an accentual scheme of 1 2 3 4 1. The last year of her life she spent in a sanatorium, afflicted with tuberculin meningitis but doing her most significant writing, most of which was published posthumously. Although she is ranked a minor poet, she was a pioneer in shifting away from Victorian poetic modes. Adelaide Crapsey's poetry has been set by John Duke and Hugo Weisgall. PRINCIPAL WORKS: *Verse*, 1934; *Analysis of English Metrics*, 1918. SELECTED READING: *The Complete Poems and Collected Letters of Adelaide Crapsey*, 1976; Edward Butscher, *Adelaide Crapsey*, 1979; Karen Alkalay-Gut, *Alone in the Dawn*, 1989. (SOURCE: Hamilton, 1994)

CREEPIE: (Scot.), *a low, three-legged stool*.

SONG	COMPOSER	POET
"Bed-time"	Benjamin Britten	William Soutar

CREOLE: a person of French or Spanish descent born in Mexico, South America, or the West Indies, not to be confused with a child of a mixed race marriage.

CRESCENT: *see* *LUNA MORISCA.

CRIOLLA: a type of nineteenth-century Cuban song that is not an art song, yet is not a folk or popular song either, but a hybrid product of the tropics. Ernesto Lecuona is a well-known composer of such songs. The criolla produced many kinds of typical songs, such as the bolero, the *guajira, the guaracha, the punto, and the *habanera.

CRISPIAN, CRISPIN: shoemakers who became patron saints of their craft. The two brothers, Crispin and Crispianus, were born in Rome, but went to Soissons in France to proselytize for the Christian religion. They maintained themselves by making shoes and mending them. They were martyred in ca.286. St. Crispin's feast day is October 25, the day of the Battle of Agincourt, and Crispin's lance is a shoe-maker's awl. ★Shakespeare makes the brothers into one person, Crispin Crispian. "This day is call'd the feast of Crispian" comes from a speech by King Henry in act 4, scene 3 of the play *Henry V*. (SOURCE: Cooper, 1992)

SONG	COMPOSER	POET
"The Feast of Crispian"	Richard Cumming	William Shakespeare

CROMWELL, OLIVER (1599–1658): a Parliamentarian general in the English Civil War, later the lord protector of England, Scotland, and Ireland. As a general, Cromwell was a daring tactician, inspiring to his troops. As lord protector, he provided a stable government but failed to take it from a military basis to national consent. He was educated at Cambridge at one of its most Puritan colleges, where he made a better mark in sports than in his studies. During his twenties, Cromwell went through a period of melancholy and depression, but emerged with a strong, puritanistic faith. He believed that providence was guiding at all times, that God either blessed or severely judged every happening. In 1636 his uncle left him a comfortable estate near Ely, which district sent him to the Parliaments of 1640 where he allied himself with the anti-Royalists. In 1642 Cromwell helped to carry into law the radicals' reform measures. With the troops he raised, he fought until he was placed in command of all the cavalry of the eastern army (1644). By June of 1646 the war was won, and Cromwell lent all his weight in Parliament to the trial and execution of the king. In 1647 he and his son offered to restore Charles to his throne on more liberal terms than those of the Parliament. First Charles temporized and then fled to the Isle of Wight, from where he contracted with the Scots to help restore him. By 1649 the monarchy and the House of Lords were abolished. With his army Cromwell then worked to conquer Ireland. In 1651 he put an end to Charles II and the Scottish army's march into England. He was made lord protector in 1653. Cromwell never sought a dictatorship, nor did he accept Parliament's plan to make him king. Because he had no support base outside the army, he made England great abroad but unsettled at home. He gave England order without despotism, a remarkable degree of religious tolerance, and an improvement to educational opportunity, and he enforced greater social justice, to which the folk song "Oliver Cromwell" attests. (SOURCE: *Americana*, 2003)

CROS, ÉMILE HORTENSIUS CHARLES (1842–1888): French poet. Charles Cros was self-educated, never attending a school except as an auditor, but tutored by his father, who was a lecturer, writer, and philosopher. Both the arts and sciences interested Charles Cros. As a Bohemian, he became one of the circle that gathered around Countess Nina de Callias, known as Nina de Villard, whose circle included some ★Parnassians and was known for its gaiety and drinking. Cros was active in other literary circles as well: the self-styled hydropathes, hirsutes, zutistes, and chat-nouristes. Credited with inventing the satirical monologue, Cros recited his humorous pieces in cafés and the salons. He was a brilliant scientific theorist, but lacked the necessary perseverance to implement his ideas. He published a memoir on indirect color photography, one on interplanetary communication, a study on the phonograph that antedated Edison, and never made any money from his theories. Preferring to converse and improvise in cafés, Charles Cros died burned out by his own excesses. Yet he was respected and admired by his contemporaries: ★Verlaine, ★Villiers de l'Isle-Adam, and ★Salis-Seewis. The great number of poetical forms in which he wrote had versatility and sardonic humor. The verses of Charles Cros were set by Ernest Chausson. PRINCIPAL WORKS: *Le Coffret de Santal*, 1873, 1879; *Le Collier de Griffes*, 1908, ed. by Cros's son; *Poèmes et Proses*, ed. Henri Parisot, 1944. SELECTED READING: Aaron Schaffer, *The Genres of Parnassian Poetry*, 1944. (SOURCE: Kunitz, Colby, 1967)

CROSS OF LORRAINE: in modern times a symbol of the liberation of France, but once a symbol of the dread Holy League and its grim association with the French wars of religion. The cross of Lorraine has one long center bar and two cross bars near the top, the higher bar less wide than the lower one. The cross is one of the most ancient and universal symbols known to man. People of religious insight and those who have none have speculated endlessly on the hidden meaning attached to particular versions of the cross and have been willing to assign specific symbolism to their preferred form. (SOURCE: *Americana*, 2003)

SONG	COMPOSER	POET
"Chanson du clair-tamis"	Francis Poulenc	Maurice Fombeure

CROSS OF ST. GEORGE: a plain red cross set erect on a white background.

SONG	COMPOSER	POET
"Le Retour du sergent"	Francis Poulenc	Maurice Fombeure

CROW: *see* ★RAVEN.

CRUZ, SOR JUANA INÉZ DE LA (JUANA DE ASTAJE Y RAMÍREZ DE SANTILLANA) (1651–1695): Mexican poet and playwright. Born in a town southeast of Mexico City, the illegitimate child of a Spanish captain and a Creole mother, Juana de la Cruz learned to read at three. Her eight-year-old wish was to cut her hair and dress like a boy so that she could attend university classes, but, forbidden to do so, she educated herself. While a member of the vice-regal court, Juana de la Cruz was wooed by many, but entered a convent in 1669, declaring that she desired to be free to learn. For the next twenty-three years, she wrote extensively, from love ★sonnets to a treatise on music. A literary virtuoso, Sister Juana de la Cruz was termed "the tenth muse" by her public. Although she wrote 400 poems, twenty-three short plays, two comedias, and various prose works, her reputation was made by two dozen small poems, her lyric poems considered to be the best of her writing, which was always ingenious and sometimes moving in the seventeenth-century manner. Two years before her death, she sold her extensive library and scientific instruments and gave the money to the poor. Juana de la Cruz was first published in Spain, the first volume in 1689, the second in 1690, and the final one in 1700. Until a definitive study and compilation was produced in the twentieth century, there had been no effort to edit her works. The poetry of Sor Juana de la Cruz was set by Federico Mompou, Rodolfo Halffter, and Joaquín Rodrigo. PRINCIPAL WORKS:

El divino Narciso; *Respuesta de la poetisa a la muy illustre Sor Filotea de la Cruz*; Alfonso Méndez Plancarte, ed. *Complete works*, 1951–57. (SOURCE: Magill, 1, 1984)

CUARTO: a copper coin minted in Spain.

SONG	COMPOSER	POET
1. "El vito"	Joaquín Nin	popular song
2. "Vida del muchacho"	Amadeo Vives	Luis de Góngora

CUCKOLD: a man whose wife is unfaithful; a living horn supposedly growing upon the head of a cuckold and regarded as an emblem of his shameful state.

SONG	COMPOSER	POET
"Let the Dreadful Engines"	Henry Purcell	Thomas D'Urfey

CUCKOO: any member of the bird family *Cuculidae*. The cry of the cuckoo as it returns every year is greeted everywhere with anticipation and joy. In Germany peasants often cry happily, "Der Kuckuck hat gerufen!" (The cuckoo has called). In the British Isles, workmen stop work for a time to enjoy "cuckoo-ale." In different locales the bird is looked upon as a prophet, a love-oracle, a spirit of madness, or the devil.

CUCKOO, JUG-JUG, PU-WE, TO-WITTA-WOO: conventional Elizabethan rendering of bird songs, specifically that of the cuckoo, the nightingale, the lapwing, and the owl, as they appear in "Spring, the Sweet Spring," by poet Thomas ★Nashe. It was sung by the character Ver (Lat., *spring*) in Nashe's allegorical drama *Summer's Last Will and Testament*, which was performed in 1592 in the palace of the Archbishop of Canterbury. (SOURCE: *Norton*, 1996)

SONG	COMPOSER	POET
1. "Spring, the Sweet Spring"	Dominick Argento	Thomas Nashe
2. "Spring"	Ivor Gurney	Thomas Nashe

CUENCA: a medieval town in Spain situated on a romantic rocky projection of St. Christóbal. By carving deep gorges, the Júcar and the Huscar Rivers have cut the town of Cuenca off from the Serranía (plain) of Cuenca. Old walls and towers of Cuenca overhang both rivers. (SOURCE: Cockburn, Stokes, 1992)

SONG	COMPOSER	POET
"Iban al pinar"	Enrique Granados	Luis de Góngora

CULLEN, COUNTÉE (1903–1946): American poet, playwright, fiction writer, and editor. Born Countée L. Porter in New York City, the poet was adopted by the Cullens in 1918. He was educated at New York University, where he was a member of Phi Beta Kappa, and Harvard University, where he took a master's degree in English. In 1929 he held a Guggenheim Fellowship. Inspired by John ★Keats and other nineteenth-century ★Romantic poets, Cullen said, "Good poetry is lofty thought beautifully expressed" (Vinson, 1979). True to his words, he was a lyricist in search of beauty, despite the racial inspiration of much of his poetry. One of the modern African American poets who were part of the Harlem Renaissance of the 1920s, he was described as the least race-conscious of that group. As ever, the literary critics descried the effect of this conflict between black experience and universal experience. Cullen himself wished to have all poetry placed on the same level of achievement rather than have his "racial" poetry judged by one set of standards and his non-racial poetry judged by a more universal criterion. "Cullen was consistently absorbed by themes of love, the joy and sorrow of it, the beauty and evanescence of life as well as racial sorrow and racial problems" (Vinson, 1979). The poetry of Countée Cullen has been set by William Grant Still and George Walker. PRINCIPAL WORKS: *On these I stand*, 1947; *Black Voices*, Abraham Chapman, ed., 1968. SELECTED READING: Houston A. Baker, Jr., *A Many-Colored Coat of Dreams: The Poetry of Countée Cullen*, 1974; Nathan Irvin Huggins, *Harlem Renaissance*, 1971. (SOURCES: Vinson, 1979; Jason 2, 2003)

CULLODEN: the name of a moor 5 miles east of Inverness in north Scotland, on which the battle of Culloden was fought in April 1746. It resulted in the victory of the Duke of Cumberland, who was fighting in defense of the throne of his father, King George II, against Prince Charles, who was trying to place his own father, the pretender James III, on the British throne. This victory ended the armed revolt against the Crown and established the present dynasty upon the British throne.

cummings, e(dward) e(stlin) (1894–1962): American poet, playwright, novelist, travel writer, and painter. Cummings grew up in Cambridge, Massachusetts in a liberal household whose members prized ingenuity. His father, a Harvard lecturer and a Unitarian minister of renown, encouraged his son to paint and write. As a student at Harvard, Cummings helped found the Harvard Poetry Society. In 1917 when the work of eight Harvard poets was published, the printer made an error and set all the "I" pronouns and Cummings's name in lower case letters. Finding this pleasing, Cummings had his name legalized as *e. e. cummings*. Graduating from Harvard with honors, his commencement address defended Cubism, new music, the writings of Gertrude ★Stein and Amy ★Lowell. He started a job with a publishing house, but volunteered to go to France during World War I as an ambulance driver. After the war, going back to France to study art, he met Louis ★Aragon and ★Picasso and their circle of writers and painters including Archibald ★MacLeish and Ezra ★Pound. His first book of poetry, then rejected, is now one of the great classics of ★Modernist poetry. It was John Dos Passos who finally found a publisher for Cummings. His play, the forerunner of what is now called the Theater of the Absurd, was produced and acclaimed by the avant-garde critics. Absurdity was to startle readers into listening instead of merely hearing. This new art made spontaneous perception the basis of expression as did jazz. Critics were annoyed by the idiosyncratic typographical stylistic devices, but Cummings was admired by fellow innovators William Carlos ★Williams, Marianne ★Moore, ★Pound, and ★Eliot, eventually winning the critics' esteem. His devices were intended to show how outer appearance reinforces inner vision; his disorders and disarrangements were designed to heighten understanding. Cummings used as one method *tmesis* (the separation of parts of words by intervening words); he used space to indicate the tempo of reading—all to force the reader to weigh each syllable. The poetry of e. e. cummings has been set by John Duke,

Dominick Argento, Bernard Wagenaar, John Cage, Ned Rorem, Elie Siegmeister, Hugo Weisgall, William Bergsma, Marc Blitzstein, Howard Boatwright, and Aaron Copland. PRINCIPAL WORKS: Poetry: *Tulips and Chimneys*, 1923; *VV*, 1931; *No Thanks*, 1932; *Xaipe*, 1950; *95 Poems*, 1958. Travel: *The Enormous Room*, 1922; *Eimi*, 1933. SELECTED READING: Norman Friedman, *e. e. cummings: The Art of His Poetry*, 1960; Milton A. Cohen, *Poet and Painter: The Aesthetics of E. E. Cummings' Early Work*, 1987. (SOURCES: Unger, 1, 1974; Vinson, 1979; Hamilton, 1994; Jason, 2, 2003)

CUPID: Roman god of love, identified with the Greek ★Eros, usually represented as a beautiful winged boy, blindfolded and carrying a bow and arrows; also called *Amour* (Fr.) or *Amor* (It. and Ger.), Cupid's golden arrow stood for virtuous love. Cupid's lead arrow represented sensual passion. (SOURCE: Cooper, 1992)

SONG	COMPOSER	POET
1. "Un sonetto di Petrarca"	Norman dello Joio	Francesco Petrarca
2. "Dithyrambe"	Franz Schubert	Friedrich von Schiller
3. "Dans un bois solitaire"	Wolfgang Amadeus Mozart	Antoine Ferrand
4. "Amor"	Richard Strauss	Clemens Brentano
5. "Fairest Isle"	Henry Purcell	John Dryden
6. "La Ermita de San Simon"	Mario Castelnuovo-Tedesco	Romançero español
7. "Al Amor"	F. J. Obradors	Cristóbal de Castillejo
8. "Hark! the Ech'ing Air"	Henry Purcell	Elkanah Settle
9. "Tramontata è la luna"	Goffredo Petrassi	Sappho, tr. Quasimodo
10. "Sonst"	Hans Pfitzner	Joseph von Eichendorff
11. "Treibe nur mit Lieben Spott"	Hugo Wolf	Paul Heyse
12. "Liebe nur im Busen"	Hugo Wolf	Paul Heyse
13. "Trau nicht der Liebe"	Hugo Wolf	Paul Heyse
14. "Pace non trovo"	Franz Liszt	Petrarch
15. "Anacreótica"	Eduardo Toldrà	Clementina Arderiu
16. "Ballet"	Francis Poulenc	Pierre de Ronsard

CURLEW: a long-legged, wading bird with a long, slender curved bill. The French name, *curlu* or *curlieu*, is believed by etymologists originally to have described the cry of the bird, the word later developing into *courlieu*, a courier or messenger. The common European species is called *whaup* in Scotland. (SOURCE: *OED*, 1989)

SONG	COMPOSER	POET
"The Curlew"	Peter Warlock	William Butler Yeats

CYBELE: the mother goddess of Phrygia, associated with the Greek goddess Demeter, also goddess of fertility, of caverns, and of the mountains, whose priests were called Corybantes. Cybele personified earth in its primitive and savage state and was worshiped on the tops of mountains. The Greeks made her retain Asiatic characteristics: a turreted crown on her head, seated on a throne flanked by two lions or in a chariot drawn by two lions, sometimes holding a whip decorated with knuckle bones. Cybele united with Gordius, the king of Phrygia, to produce a son, ★Midas. (SOURCE: Cooper, 1992)

SONG	COMPOSER	POET
"Attributs"	Francis Poulenc	Pierre de Ronsard

CYCLE: a group of songs that hangs together as an entity through a dramatic unfolding of a kind of plot, similarity of subject matter, etc. A collection of separate songs is not, strictly speaking, a cycle. Beethoven's *An die ferne Geliebte*, generally termed the first cycle, represents in actuality the culmination of a long musical development. During the Renaissance, a circle was the symbol for perfection, eternity, and universal harmony. This idea originated from Phythagorean and Platonic writings, which in turn were derived from Oriental cults, who used the design of a serpent swallowing its tail. The trouvères also used cyclic forms. "Jeu de Robin et Marion" of Adam de la Halle is composed of a series of songs with an ideological center: love—divine, courtly, earthly. Along with early French ballet of the seventeenth century, allegorical song series originated, having a general subject, such as "night," together with anything that might be associated with night. In these, the visual or symbolic center was the king or a divine authority. Songs not associated with the dance began to conform to the concept. If flowers can be gathered for a wreath, so may songs be presented in attractive groups (to be known some years later as Liederkranz, song wreaths). Another ancestor of the song cycle was the double song. Two songs were related, the second often a ★parody of the first. Then additions began to form a suite, a cantata, and later a published song "collection," unified by a title or dedication expressing a loose overall theme—a girl's name, flowers, ideal love. The Liederkreis groups, soon prominent in Germany, were groups of music lovers who gathered at homes to enjoy the singing of songs and the playing of games related to songs. Generally speaking, a cycle can be any collection of songs that contains a unifying idea, such as Schubert's *Winterreise*. The degree to which a cycle utilizes extra musical or dramatic devices such as restatement of an opening musical theme toward the end of the work *(Fêtes galantes)*, or the following of a specific story outline song by song *(Frauenliebe und -Leben)*, indicate added artistic elements of cohesion chosen by the composer. (SOURCE: Emmons, Sonntag, 2002)

CYCLOPES (lit., *circle-eyed***):** the one-eyed giants of Greek mythology. According to ★Hesiod (700 B.C.E.), the Cyclopes gave to ★Zeus his weapons, thunder and lightning. Homer described them as ferocious, lawless, and given to cannibalism. By blinding Polyphemus, the leader, in his drunken sleep, ★Odysseus and his remaining men were able to escape from captivity. The two legends jar, and the Cyclopes remain forever mysterious.

SONG	COMPOSER	POET
"Hyde Park"	Francis Poulenc	Guillaume Apollinaire

CYNTHIA: the Moon, a surname of Artemis, or ★Diana, who represented the moon and was called Cynthia, the name taken from Mt. Cynthius in Delos where she was born. The name was one of those applied to Elizabeth I, virgin moon goddess, by ★Spenser and other contemporary English poets. (SOURCES: Drabble, 2000; *Norton*, 1996)

SONG	COMPOSER	POET
1. "Cynthia Frowns Whene'er I Woo Her"	Henry Purcell	William Congreve
2. "Bess o'Bedlam"	Henry Purcell	unknown

"Cynthia Frowns Whene'er I Woo Her": a song by Henry Purcell set to lyrics written by William ★Congreve for his play, *The Double Dealer*. For plot details and position of the song within the plot, *see* ★*Double Dealer, The.*

CYPRESS: a funeral tree often associated with cemeteries. Romans dedicated the cypress to ★Pluto, because, when cut, it never grows again. It is believed that cypress wood was once used for making coffins; the Greeks and Romans put cypress twigs into coffins. Traditionally ★Cupid's arrows were made from cypress wood. (SOURCE: Cooper, 1992)

CYPRIAN: lit., *of Cyprus*. Because Cyprus was formerly famous for the worship of ★Venus, this adjective is applied to lewd and profligate persons and prostitutes. (SOURCE: Cooper, 1992)

SONG	COMPOSER	POET
1. "Fairest Isle"	Henry Purcell	John Dryden
2. "Cyprian Songs"	Benjamin Lees	Richard Nickson

CYTHERA (Gk.), CYTHÈRE (Fr.): a Greek island on the coast of Laconia, now called Kithera. This island was sacred to the goddess ★Venus, whose surname was Cytheraea. It is said that she rose from the sea on the coast of the island. (SOURCE: Cockburn, Stokes, 1992)

SONG	COMPOSER	POET
1. "Las locas por amor"	Joaquín Turina	Ramón de Campoamor
2. "Anacreòntica"	Eduardo Toldrà	Clementina Arderiu

CYTHEREA, CYTHERÉE (Fr.): another name for Venus, referring to her island abode, Cythera.

SONG	COMPOSER	POET
"Attributs"	Francis Poulenc	Pierre de Ronsard

D ✑

DAHN, FELIX (1834–1912): German poet and novelist. Felix Dahn was born in Hamburg, his parents both actors. In order to work for the Bavarian Royal Theater, the family moved to Munich, where Felix had a private tutor and read voraciously in world history. His parents' divorce in 1850 resulted in an increase of his solitary study habits and took away his desire to write more poetry. After studying law, history, and philology at the University of Munich, he studied in Berlin (1852–53), where he met Theodor ★Fontane, who motivated Dahn to write heroic historical ballads. He also wrote love lyrics and didactic poems, taking his ideas from ★Scheffel, ★Geibel, and Paul ★Heyse. While a professor at the University of Würzburg in 1863, Dahn was rejected by the army for the Franco-Prussian War. He then joined the Red Cross as a nurse. During his fifteen years as professor of law at the University of Königsberg, he completed twenty volumes of scholarly writings and wrote his major literary works. The novel *Ein Kampf um Rom* (A Struggle for Rome) brought him his greatest success. He and Richard Wagner shared a common pursuit, the justification and promotion of nationalistic goals. In an attempt to create a national art, Dahn tried his hand at an operatic libretto, but was not successful. Dahn is generally considered one of the chief representatives of the archeological novel, fiction on topics that are based on academic research; this work was popular with the reading public. The lyrics of Felix Dahn were set to music by Richard Strauss and Max Reger. PRINCIPAL WORKS: *Harald und Theano*, 1855; *Gedichte*, 1857; *Sing Götter? Die Halfred Sigskaldsaga*, 1874; *Ein Kampf um Rom*, 1876. (SOURCE: Hardin, Mews, 129, 1993)

DAME DE MONTE CARLO, LA: a ★scena for soprano and orchestra or piano written by Francis Poulenc to a text by Jean ★Cocteau. Poulenc set Cocteau texts in a one-act opera, *La Voix humaine*, this scena, "La Dame de Monte Carlo," and *Cocardes*, a three-song set. Poulenc destroyed a collection of songs he had composed to Cocteau's verse collection, *Plain-Chant*.

DAMON, DAMIS (Fr.), DAMÖTAS (Ger.): the name of a goatherd in Virgil's *Eclogues* and the *Idylls* of ★Theocritus, used by pastoral poets for rustic swains. Also known as ★Corydon. (SOURCE: Cooper, 1992)

SONG	COMPOSER	POET
1. "Die betrogene Welt"	Wolfgang Amadeus Mozart	anonymous
2. "Die Bekehrte"	A. Knab, C. Zelter, H. Wolf	Johann von Goethe
3. "Die Verschweigung"	Wolfgang Amadeus Mozart	Christian Weisse
4. "Der Zauberer"	Wolfgang Amadeus Mozart	Christian Weissee
5. "Mandoline"	C. Debussy, G. Fauré, G. Dupont	Paul Verlaine
6. "Clair de Lune"	C. Debussy, G. Fauré	Paul Verlaine

| 7. "Fêtes galantes" | Gabriel Dupont, Reynaldo Hahn | Paul Verlaine |
| 8. "Phillis Was a Faire Maid" | Phillip Rosseter | Thomas Campion |

DAMÖTAS: *see* ★DAMON.

DAMOZEL: an older form of the word *damsel*, a young, unmarried lady. Damozel was preferred by ★Romantic and later writers because it avoids the simpler homelier associations of *damsel*. (SOURCE: *OED*, 1989)

DAN: an honorable title like *Don* (It. and Sp.), meaning master, sir, or used in addressing members of religious orders, also applied to distinguished men, knights, scholars, poets, etc. (★Spenser called ★Chaucer *Dan Chaucer*.) Also a small buoy, made of wood or sheepskin, supporting a stout pole carrying a flag by day, a lamp by night, to mark the position of deep-sea lines.

DANAË, DANAIDES, DANAES: various names for the fifty daughters of King Danaos, who murdered their husbands on their wedding night; also, a maiden whom Jove seduced by descending upon her as a shower of gold. Danaos, or Danaus, was the son of the king of Egypt and the brother of Aegyptus. Aegyptus suggested that his sons marry Danaos's daughters in order to unite the family, but Danaos, warned by the oracle that he would be murdered by a son-in-law, fled with his daughters to Argos. Aegyptus's sons followed and laid siege to the city until Danaos agreed to the marriages. Instructed by Danaos to behead their husbands on their wedding nights, all but Hypermnestra obeyed. Her husband, Lynceus, eventually killed Danaos and took the throne as foretold by the oracle. As punishment, the Danaë were required to fill leaky jars with water from a deep well. (SOURCES: Benét, 1, 1965; Mayerson, 1971; Cotterell, 1986)

SONG	COMPOSER	POET
1. "Fahrt zum Hades"	Franz Schubert	Johann Mayerhofer
2. "Consejo"	Fernando Obradors	Miguel de Cervantes

DANAIDES: *see* ★DANAE.

DANIEL, SAMUEL (1562?–1619): English poet, playwright, and historian. Samuel Daniel was the son of a music master. He entered Magdelan Hall, Oxford in 1581, but left after three years. In 1590 he became tutor to the third Earl of Pembroke, where the real attraction was the boy's mother, a patroness of literature. He dedicated fifty sonnets to the Countess of Pembroke in his collection, *Delia*, inspired by Tasso. Daniel's growing reputation attracted ★Spenser's attention. Owing to Spenser, he visited often at court while continuing to tutor other children. He spent his later years revising his earlier poetry, having rented a farm in Wiltshire, where he later died. Unfortunately, Samuel Daniel lived and wrote in an age of literary giants: ★Spenser, ★Jonson, ★Shakespeare, ★Campion. He always sought perfection at that calling, revising each piece four or five times, as can be seen by the sparse number of publications. A great patriot, he held the ideals of the Renaissance, to pursue learning and to reconcile the idea of action with that of culture. He was a true Elizabethan poet because he tried very hard to transcend the boundaries of his age. Ben Jonson called him "a good honest Man, but no poet" (Drabble, 1985), but Lamb, ★Coleridge, and Wordsworth were admirers. As he matured, he learned how to control the complex combination of poetry and history. The verse of Samuel Daniel has been set by Thomas Arne, Dominick Argento, and John Rutter. There has been no complete edition of his works since Grosart's (1885–96). PRINCIPAL WORKS: Poetry: *Delia,* 1592; *The Complaynt of Rosamonde,* 1592; *The First Fowre Bookes of the Civile Warres between the Two Houses of Lancaster and Yorke,* 1595; *Poeticall Essayes,* 1599; *The Works of Samuel Daniel,* 1601; *Certaine Small Poems,* 1605; *Songs for the Lute, Viol, and Voice,* 1606; *Works,* ed. Grosart, 1885–96. SELECTED READING: Cecil Seronsy, *Samuel Daniel,* 1967. (SOURCE: Drabble, 1985)

D'ANNUNZIO, GABRIELE (1863–1938): Italian poet, playwright, and novelist. D'Annunzio was born in Pescara and educated at the University of Rome. During World War I, he served his country in the Italian infantry, navy, and air force, leading to the loss of one eye. Although he married, his celebrated *affaire* with the actress Eleanora Duse lasted from 1895 to 1904. Elected to the Chamber of Deputies, he served from 1897 to 1900, when he was defeated. D'Annunzio lived in Tuscany but was forced by his debts to live in France from 1910 through 1915. After the Treaty of Versailles, he joined with other patriots in seizing Fiume, which city they held until 1920. As a supporter of the Fascists, he was granted a title by Mussolini. D'Annunzio was a major twentieth-century poet because his metric and linguistic innovations changed the way poetry was expressed and reflected a new way of writing verse. In his poetry from 1879 to 1936, the characteristic quality of his finest work was a joyful naturalism, the mastery of landscape descriptions, which he fused with spirituality and sensuousness. The verse of Gabriele d'Annunzio has been set by Ildebrando Pizzetti and Claude Debussy. PRINCIPAL WORKS: Poetry: *Primo vere* [Early Spring], 1879; *Laudi del cielo, del mare, della terra e degli eroi* [Praises of the Sky, the Sea, the Earth, and Heroes], 3 vols., 1903–12. Novels: *The Child of Pleasure,* 1898; *The Virgins of the Rocks,* 1899. Plays: *The Daughter of Jorio,* 1907; *Le Martyre de Saint Sébastien,* music by Debussy, 1911. SELECTED READING: Tommaso Antongine, *D'Annunzio,* 1936. (SOURCE: Vinson, Kirkpatrick (1), 1984)

DANSE DE SAING GUY: *see* ★VITUS, SAINT.

DANSE MACABRE: Dance of Death. The idea that Death made everyone equal first was made clear in France as a sermon in mime, in which figures from all parts of society were seized and hauled away, at first, each one by its own corpse, later, by a personification of Death. It is possible that this was a consequence of the plague that decimated Europe.

SONG	COMPOSER	POET
"Danse macabre"	Camille Saint Saëns	Henri Cazalis

DANTE ALIGHIERI (1265–1321): Italian poet. An enthusiastic student of philosophy and poetry, Dante was raised as a gentleman in Florence. Highly involved in the civic affairs of Florence, he was on a mission to Rome in 1301 while his party was defeated. Exiled from the city as a result, Dante sought refuge at courts of various Ghibelline noblemen in the north. Later he refused the offered conditional amnesty and is believed to have spent various amounts of time in Lucca, Mantua, Verona, and Ravenna. At the time of Dante's birth, Florence already had a literary tradition, into which Dante fit admirably. His first notable work was *La Vita Nuova*, the story of his idealistic love for Beatrice Portinari. In this composition, written after her death (1290), prose was interspersed with verse, in a combination of realism and intimated hidden feelings. Immersed in politics after Beatrice's death, after the banishment and consequent disillusionment he transferred his reading and writing into the study of philosophy. In 1301 Dante was one of three envoys sent to Rome to negotiate with the pope. He never returned to Florence but led a wandering life. Dante's *Divine Comedy*, which gave him a unique and long-lived prestige, was written in vernacular, not Latin, surprising as a choice but crucial in the development of Italian literature. The *Divine Comedy* enthralled the ordinary man and fascinated the intellectual. There were forty-seven translations into English alone. Dante himself held that the substance of his poem is simply an account of the state of souls after death. This substance possesses strength and beauty by virtue of Dante's rare technical artistry, his use of harmonious proportions, and a great variety of imagery. "It is a personal epic, a confessional autobiography, a lucid exposition of orthodox dogma, an encyclopedia, a love poem, a synthesis of medieval learning" (Vinson, Kirkpatrick (1), 1984). Francis Poulenc set Apollinaire's poem "Voyage," which speaks of Dante's many journeys. PRINCIPAL WORKS: *The Portable Dante*, ed. Paolo Milano, 1947; *La Vita Nuova*, ed. Michele Barbi, 1960, trans. D. G. Rossetti in *The Early Italian Poets*, 1861, by Longfellow, 1867, by Dorothy L. Sayers, 1949–62; *Rime*, ed. Michele Barbi and F. Maggini, 1965, trans. Patrick S. Diehl, 1979; *Eclogae Latinae*, ed. E. Pistelli, 1960, trans. W. Brewer, 1927; *Commedia*, ed. Giorgio Petrocchi, 4 vols., 1966–67, also ed. with trans. Charles S. Singleton, 6 vols., 1970–75; as *Divine Comedy*, trans. H. W. Longfellow, 1867, Laurence Binyon, 1933–46, L. G. White, 1948, Dorothy L. Sayers and Barbara Reynolds, 1949–62, and John Ciardi, 1954–70; *Lyric Poetry*, ed. Kenelm Foster and Patrick Boyde, 2 vols., 1967. SELECTED READING: Joseph Mazzeo, *Structure and Thought in the Paradiso*, 1958; William Anderson, *Dante the Maker*, 1980. (SOURCE: Vinson, Kirkpatrick (1), 1984)

DANUBE, DONAU (Ger.): a major European river, 1,750 miles long, rising in the Black Forest of southwest Germany, entering Austria at Passau, flowing between the hills of Bohemia and the most northerly ranges of the Alps. The beautiful Danube Valley boasts forested hills, castle ruins, and then the Vienna plain. In the marshy lowlands of Slovakia and Hungary the river subdivides into smaller streams, traversing the Great Hungarian Plain. In the plains of Yugoslavia, it crosses the Balkans in a series of spectacular gorges, then flows east for 300 miles as the border between Bulgaria and Romania before emptying into the Black Sea.

SONG	COMPOSER	POET
1. "Rückweg"	Franz Schubert	Johann Mayrhofer
2. "Prinz Eugen"	Carl Loewe	Ferdinand Freiligrath
3. "Auf der Donau"	Franz Schubert	Johann Mayrhofer

DANZIG (Ger.), GDANSK (Pol.): a port on the Vistula River, Poland's most important waterway, 4 miles from the Baltic Sea. Danzig is one of the leading ports of central Europe, with historic buildings of many styles. The Slavs founded Danzig in the 900s, and it became a rich trading center of the German Hanseatic League during the Middle Ages, later a vassal city of the Polish king in 1466. When Russia and Prussia divided the Polish territory late in the 1700s, Danzig fell into Prussian hands. The Free City of Danzig was set up after World War I, supervised by the League of Nations. In 1939 Germany demanded that Danzig be united with Germany, but Poland refused, with the result that Germany invaded their country. At the end of World War II, Danzig became part of Poland.

SONG	COMPOSER	POET
"In Danzig"	Hans Pfitzner	Joseph von Eichendorff

DAPHENEO, DAPHNE: in mythology a *nymph fabled to have been changed into a laurel; thus, also a laurel or bay tree. Daphne was the daughter of a river god and loved by *Apollo, who killed his rival Leucippus for her affections. Daphne escaped only to be changed into a laurel tree, which remained thenceforth the favorite tree of the sun god.

SONG	COMPOSER	POET
1. "Daphne am Bach"	Franz Schubert	Friedrich Graf Stolberg
2. "Daphne"	William Walton	Edith Sitwell
3. "Daphne"	John Dowland	Thomas Campion

DAPHNIS: a Sicilian shepherd who invented *pastoral poetry; also the lover of *Chloe in a pastoral romance of the fourth century, thus a name used often in pastoral poetry.

DA PISTOIA, CINO (pseudonym of Guittoncino de Sigibaldi) (1270–1336): Italian poet and jurist. Da Pistoia's father was a notary and his mother the daughter of a doctor. After studying under a grammarian, he began the study of law, following his teacher to Bologna and receiving his law teaching license about 1292. When he returned to Pistoia, he did not take an active part in the political warfare of the time, but the Black Guelphs exiled him for three years, during which time he is believed to have taught in Paris. Cino da Pistoia wrote legal works and lyrics and continued a voluminous correspondence with his friend *Dante. In 1330 da Pistoia was summoned to teach law in Naples. He and *Petrarch exchanged verses often, and, at the death of da Pistoia, Petrarch wrote a *sonnet in his honor. Some two hundred poems written by this member of the *stil nuovo* group of poets still survive. The poetry of Cino da Pistoia was set by Alfred Casella. (SOURCE: Rossetti, 1981)

DA PONTE, LORENZO (1749–1838): Italian poet, librettist, and founder of Italian culture in America. Born in Ceneda near Venice, the son of a Jewish tanner, Da Ponte was originally named Emanuele Conegliano. At fourteen Emanuele and his brothers turned to the Christian faith and were baptized by Monsignor Lorenzo da Ponte, the bishop of Ceneda. According to the customs of the time, Emanuele took the name of his spiritual father and was placed in a seminary, eventually taking ecclesiastical orders and becoming vice rector of the institution. Because of delusions of persecution that continued for his whole life, Da Ponte resigned his office and went to Venice. There followed a pattern of idling away a year or so in dissipation and then working for a few years. In 1779 da Ponte was part of so many public scandals that he was banished from Venetian territory for fifteen years. In this manner he ended up in Vienna, where he was appointed Poet to the Italian Theatre. Overnight he became a man of letters, sought out for his librettos. After Da Ponte collaborated with Mozart on *Figaro* (1786), *Don Giovanni* (1787), *Così fan Tutte* (1790), he was recognized as the foremost librettist in Europe, working also with Antonio Salieri, J. P. E. Martini, Vincenzo Righini, and Stephen Storace. Following another disgrace, Da Ponte was ordered to leave Vienna; he settled in London with his new wife. Thereafter the rest of his career was a story of misfortunes saved by his loyal wife. When a bookstore he had started went bankrupt, they sailed for America. Teaching Italian very successfully in New York led to his being appointed professor of Italian Literature at Columbia. During this time Da Ponte helped to spread Italian culture and the study of ★Dante in the United States, actually building an opera house in 1833, which also failed. Da Ponte died a poor man. PRINCIPAL WORKS: *Memorie*, trans. L. A. Sheppard, 1929. SELECTED READING: J. L. Russo, *Lorenzo da Ponte, Poet and Adventurer*, 1922. (SOURCE: Johnson, Malone, 3, 1930–31)

DARBIES: *see* ★DARBY.

DARBY: an English personal surname, also names of various things named after a place or person of that name; thus, *Darbies bands*, a rigid form of bond by which debtors were bound and put within the power of a moneylender. Therefore the slang term *in Darbies* means in handcuffs. The text of the Diamond song is taken from Melville's last novel, *Billy Budd, Foretopman* (1891). The handsome young sailor, Billy, is pressed into service aboard the *HMS Indomitable*. Being a natural leader, he is liked by all except the master-of-arms, Claggart, who slyly has Billy accused of mutiny. At the hearing before Captain Vere, Billy is tongue-tied. In frustration he strikes Claggart, killing him. For his crime he is sentenced to be hung from the yardarm. The captain is haunted by the memory of this good man, and the crew reveres the yardarm, from which Billy was hung, as holy as the cross. (SOURCE: *OED*, 1989)

SONG	COMPOSER	POET
"Billy in the Darbies"	David Diamond	Herman Melville

DARBY AND JOAN: a joking appellation for a husband and wife who are everything to each other, especially in advanced years and in humble life; a Darby and Joan club is a club for elderly men and women. These names appear in a ★ballad called "The Happy Old Couple" (1748), written by Henry Woodfall. (SOURCE: *OED*, 1989)

DARDANELLES: a strait that joins the Aegean Sea with the Sea of Marmara, part of a waterway that leads from the landlocked Black Sea to the Mediterranean. The name comes from the ancient Greek city of Dardanus on the Asian side of the strait. It is 37 miles long; its average depth is 200 feet; and at its narrowest it is one mile wide. Xerxes led an army across the Dardanelles and invaded Europe in 481 B.C.E. Alexander the Great led an army across a bridge of boats into Asia in 334 B.C.E.

DARGIE: (Scot.), *a day's work.*

SONG	COMPOSER	POET
"Bed-time"	Benjamin Britten	William Soutar

DARLEY, GEORGE (1795–1846): Irish poet, dramatist, and critic. Born in Dublin to an upper-class family who took him to America when he was three, Darley was then educated at Dublin's Trinity College (1815), where he acquired a severe stammer that never left him. He spent some time in France (1830) and ten years in London, where he died. His extreme poverty and the lack of recognition is not noticeable in Darley's poetry, which was seldom paid attention to or reviewed outside the circle of his friends, Charles Lamb, Thomas ★Beddoes, and John ★Clare. His continuing search for perfection gave his poetry an authentic style and tone, although it had a limited appeal. His best poetry is the work of a man seeking an escape from the world. Darley created a world of fantasy, benevolent nature, and beautiful maidens in an ordered universe that he never found in real life. Darley's verse was set by Bainbridge Crist and Henry Cowell. PRINCIPAL POETRY: *The Errors of Ecstasie: A Dramatic Poem, with Other Pieces,* 1822; *Nepenthe,* 1835; *Poems of the Late George Darley,* 1890; *The Complete Poetical Works of George Darley,* 1908. SELECTED READING: Claude Colleer Abbott, ed., *The Life and Letters of George Darley, Poet and Critic,* 1967. (SOURCE: Steinberg, 2, 1973)

DAUDET, LOUIS MARIE ALPHONSE (1840–1897): French man of letters, poet, novelist, and critic. Daudet was born in Nîmes; his parents were silk manufacturers from a peasant background. His father was a taciturn man, but his mother, who represented an ideal woman to her son, was imaginative and addicted to reading. Alphonse was an indifferent although precocious student, who drank to excess during his school days, but was already reading the ★Romantics and writing poetry and tales. Arriving in Paris, where his brother was an editor, Daudet formed a Bohemian clique with which members he made the rounds of salons and bars. In one of them he met Provençal poet Frédéric Mistral, the author of *Mireille* (set as an opera by Gounod). Mistral encouraged Daudet to use his southern background for his prose tales. Having spent three months in Algeria to recuperate from his drinking excesses, he contracted syphilis, which made his last twenty-five years a horror. During his travels Daudet wrote sketches, short stories, and three plays. His highly charged nature was stabilized by his marriage, allowing him to function as a drama critic and novelist. *L'Arlésienne,* one of his novels that he adapted for the stage (with music by Bizet), was not a success, although Zola and Anatole France praised his work. Daudet's realism was enhanced by his humor and warmth, his sensitive observations, and his compelling combinations of reality and dreams. Many of his works were translated into English. The poetry of Alphonse Daudet was set by Reynaldo Hahn. PRINCIPAL WORKS: *Les Amoureuses,* 1858; *La Double conversion, Contes en vers,* 1861; *L'Oeillit blanc,* a drama, 1865; *Le Petit chose,* trans. M. N. Sherwood, 1878; *Tartarin of Tarascon,* trans. R. S. Minot, 1880; *30 Years of Paris,* trans. L. Ensor, 1888; *Port-Tarascon*, trans. Henry James, 1891. SELECTED READ-ING: E. Gosse, *French Profiles*; G. Vera Dobie, *Alphonse Daudet*, 1975. (SOURCE: Kunitz, Colby, 1967)

DAUMER, GEORG FRIEDRICH (1800–1875): German poet and translator. Although Georg Daumer was a schoolmaster, he gave up his position to devote himself to writing, and, in 1859, he converted to Catholicism. In 1837 he wrote a poetic retelling of Bettina von Arnim's *Goether Briefwechsel mit einem Kinde*. Daumer was the author of pseudo-Oriental poetry such as *Orientalische Gedichte*, 1848, and the translator of the poetry of Hāfiz (*Liederblüten des Hāfis*, 1846–52). Johannes Brahms set a number of his poems and his translations of Hāfiz. (SOURCE: Garland, 1976)

D'AVENANT, SIR WILLIAM (1606–1668): English poet. Born and educated at Oxford, D'Avenant was rumored to be the natural son of ★Shakespeare. Actively supporting Charles II during the Civil War, he was the unofficial poet laureate (1638) and was knighted after the war. It is said that ★Milton saved him from his imprisonment in the Tower (1650–52). After the Restoration, D'Avenant obtained a patent from Charles II, giving him a monopoly of acting in London, where the innovations of the period were movable scenery and the use of actresses. Together with ★Dryden, D'Avenant adapted Shakespeare's The ★*Tempest* for the London stage. His own stage productions included ★*Circe*, and The ★*Rival Sisters*. The verse of William D'Avenant was set by Henry Purcell and Horatio Parker. PRINCIPAL WORKS: *Madagascar: With Other Poems*, 1638; *Gondibert*, 1651; *The Seventh and Last Canto of the Third Book of Gondibert*, 1685; *The Shorter Poems and Songs from the Plays and Masques*, 1972. SELECTED READING: Mary Edmond, *Sir William Davenant*, 1987. (SOURCE: Drabble, 2000)

DAVID, KING: biblical figure, the second king of Israel, author of several of the Psalms. In the Book of Psalms there are one hundred and fifty psalms, of which seventy-two are traditionally ascribed to David, among them the famous Twenty-third Psalm, "The Lord is my Shepherd." Two stories relate how David was introduced into the household of King ★Saul, the first king of Israel, who had been rejected by God. In the first, Saul, troubled by an evil spirit, was urged to send for a harp player, who could give him surcease from his troubled mind. So did David, a first-rate harp player, enter into Saul's service. The second story describes David's battle with the giant Goliath. Saul and the Israelite army were cowering before Goliath and the Philistine army. Goliath challenged the Israelites to send one man to do battle with him, the winner to decide the outcome of the war. After forty days of a standoff, David, delivering supplies, heard the challenge and offered to fight the giant, armed only with five stones and a sling-shot. After knocking Goliath unconscious with a stone, David killed him with Goliath's own sword. So did he enter King Saul's service, where he quickly became commander of the army. David's success and popularity caused Saul to feel great jealousy. Saul tried several times to have David killed, but was unsuccessful. When Saul met his doom in battle against the Philistines, David became king. (SOURCE: Metzger, Murphy, 1994)

SONG	COMPOSER	POET
1. "David Weeps for Absalom"	David Diamond	II Samuel 18.33
2. "Triste estaba el rey David"	Alonso Mudarra	anonymous
3. "Absalom"	Ned Rorem	Paul Goodman
4. "A Song of David"	Ned Rorem	from the Psalms
5. "David's Harp"	Anthony Strilko	Victor Reichert

"Dear Pretty Youth": a song written by Henry Purcell set to lyrics by ★D'Avenant and ★Dryden, adapted from William ★Shakespeare's *The Tempest*. For plot details and position of the song within the plot, *see The ★Tempest.*

DEATH, SONGS AND DANCES OF: a four-song cycle by Modest Mussorgsky to texts by his friend Arsenyi ★Golenishtchev-Kutúsov. Mussorgsky had originally planned to extend the cycle to include, among others, the following sketches: a monkish fanatic who dies in his cell to the heavy tolling of the monastery bell; a political exile who comes back, is wrecked within sight of home, and perishes in the waves; a dying woman whose fevered fancy calls up memories of love and visions of youth.

DECAMERON: one hundred stories by ★Boccaccio, probably completed after 1348, one of the great masterpieces of Italian literature. The tales of the *Decameron* are set in a narrative framework describing the time and location of the telling. The framework story relates how, to escape the plague of 1348 in Florence, seven young ladies and three young men go to ★Fiesole, a village above the city, to pass their time as pleasantly as possible. In order to accomplish this, each person agrees to tell one story every day for ten days (thus the title, meaning ten persons and ten days). This will take place under the rule of a "queen" or "king" elected from their group. Each day is given over to some special kind of story, for example, stories of love or adventure beginning in adversity and ending happily, or stories of tricks played by wives on husbands. Each day ends with a dance and a dance song. One such story is "The Patient Griselda." (SOURCE: *Americana*, 2003)

DEHMEL, RICHARD (1863–1920): German poet and writer of prose. The position Dehmel holds in German literature is as much for his unique personality as for his artistry as a poet. In 1895 Dehmel resigned his position in an insurance office to devote himself to writing. Although he was past fifty in 1914, he enlisted as a private, served in the trenches, was wounded, and given the Iron Cross. He believed that art was an expression of man's whole being, a creative energy, and called himself a realist and an idealist. In his most important work, *Zwei Menschen*, Dehmel attempted to find a synthesis between the physical and spiritual elements of love. He wanted to shock bourgeois sensibility with his frank sexuality. To him the essence of life is its joy and zest even through tears and suffering. As the product of both a naturalist (the son of a forest warden) and a visionary, his work was a forerunner of

*Expressionism. His poetry has many themes: the struggle between the generations, a healthy life in the country as opposed to cities, advocacy for Dionysian life. As a poet of social protest, he appealed to the German workers of his time, who called him Vater Dehmel, but his custom of going to extremes in both his poetry and prose diminished his ongoing appeal. Dehmel's verses were set by Sibelius, Reger, Webern, Schönberg, Pfitzner, Strauss, Armin Knab, and Ben Weber. PRINCIPAL WORKS: *Weib und Welt*, 1896; *Zwei Menschen*, 1903; *Schöne wilde Welt*, 1913; *Poet Lore*, selected verses, trans. E. H. Zeydel, 1920. SELECTED READING: P. Pollard, *Masks and Minstrels of Modern Germany*, 1911; H. Slochower, *Richard Dehmel der Mensch und Denker*, 1928. (SOURCES: Mathieu, Stern, 1987; Steinberg, 2, 1973)

DEIDRE: in Irish romances, such as The *Ulster Cycle, the daughter of the king of Ulster's storyteller. At her birth, it was prophesied that she would bring ruin to Ireland. She was brought up by King Conchobar, who kept her in hiding until he could marry her, but she fell in love with Naoise, the eldest of the three sons of Usneck. Deidre escaped to Scotland with the three brothers. King Conchobar lured them back with false promises and killed the three young men. Both *Yeats and J. M. *Singe wrote plays with this plot. (SOURCE: Cooper, 1992)

DEIL: (Scot.), *the Devil*.

DEINHARDSTEIN, JOHANN LUDWIG VON (1794–1859): Viennese critic. Deinhardstein was the editor of *The Yearbook of Literature* (1829). His poem "Skolie," was set by Schubert in 1815, although it is not included in the collected poems. (SOURCE: Reed, 1997)

DE LA MARE, WALTER (1873–1956): English poet, playwright, fiction and juvenile writer, critic, editor, and anthologist. Born in Kent, de la Mare attended St. Paul's Cathedral Choir School in London. He clerked for an oil company from 1890 to 1908 and then became a reviewer for the *Times* and the *Westminster Gazette*. De la Mare was the author of nineteen books of poems published between 1920 and 1953. He was made royal Companion of Honour in 1948 and awarded the Order of Merit (1953). It might be argued that de la Mare is even more interesting as a prose writer than as a poet, but his poems for children are models of their kind. He believed that man in his early years is closer than at any other time to understanding the truth of things. De la Mare retained a freshness of vision, to which he added wise maturity, not cynicism or disillusion. He was an inward-looking poet of escape, skilled at depicting atmosphere and mood. The word "strange" infuses de la Mare's work. His imagination inhabits a fantasy land between dreaming and waking. His writing is technically assured and conservative, yet capable of a wide range of virtuoso effects. Walter de la Mare's poetry has been set by John Duke, Lennox Berkeley, Sergius Kagen, Bainbridge Crist, Betty Roe, John Koch, Arthur Shepherd, and Theodore Chanler. PRINCIPAL WORKS: Poetry: *The Listeners*, 1912; *Peacock Pie*, 1913 (juvenile); *The Complete Poems*, 1968. Novels: *Henry Brocken*, 1904; *The Return*, 1910; *Memoirs of a Midget*, 1921, 1982. Criticism: *Pleasures and Speculations*, 1940; *Private View*, 1953. Anthologies: *Come Hither: A Collection of Rhymes and Poems for the Young of All Ages,* 1923; *Love*, 1943. SELECTED READING: Theresa Whistler, *Imagination* *of the Heart: The Life of Walter de la Mare*, 1993; *A Choice of de la Mare's Verse*, ed. W. H. Auden, 1963. (SOURCE: Hamilton, 1994)

DELVIG, BARON ANTON (1798–1831): Russian poet. A member of ★Pushkin's ★pleiad, Delvig was respected by his contemporaries, although his output, much of it derivative, was small. Despite his German name, Delvig was ignorant of German before he attended the Lyceum of ★Tsarskoe Selo. His forte as a poet was the Russian folk song. Although Delvig was notorious for his laziness, he edited the most successful literary ventures of the pleiad and was most remembered for his songs and romances, for example, "The Nightingale," set by Aleksandr Alyabiev. The poetry of Baron Delvig was set also by Nikolai Titov, A. P. Esaulov, Mikhail Glinka, Alexander Dargomizhsky, and Vladimir Mayakovsky. (SOURCE: Terras, 1991)

"Dernier poème": a song by Francis Poulenc set to the verse of Robert ★Desnos. The poem, intended for Desnos's wife, was written by the poet on a cigarette paper a few days before his death in a concentration camp during World War II.

DESBORDES-VALMORE, MARCELINE (1786–1859): French poet, actress, and singer. Marceline Desbordes was the daughter of an ornament painter who had been reduced to poverty as a result of the Revolution. Upon his death, his wife took Marceline to Guadeloupe in 1801, looking for some relatives in the colony. There the mother died and Marceline returned alone to France, where she tried to earn a living as an actress and singer. She played various operatic roles of Grétry and Rossini with distinction, as well as the classics of Molière and Marivaux. Her life was dominated at that time by an obsession for a man who may have been Henri de Latouche, a writer and a critic, and a counselor of the writer George Sand. This affaire Desbordes-Valmore kept a secret from her husband. He, too, was an actor, but his career came to an early end. The last years of Marceline Desbordes-Valmore were a long series of misfortunes, the loss of her two daughters and her husband, and her own developing cancer. The early poetry was in the style of the banal lyricism popular at the moment, derivative of ★Parny. In her collection, published in 1830, is seen a more personal manner that makes her a major romantic poet, before the work of ★Lamartine and ★Hugo. Using many verse forms, her ★elegies and other poems were recognized at once by critics and by such poets as ★Hugo, Sainte-Beuve, Lemaître, ★Baudelaire, and ★Banville. Her poems are still admired for their delicacy and simplicity of expression. The poems of Marceline Desbordes-Valmore have been set by Georges Bizet and César Franck. PRINCIPAL WORKS: *Collected Works*, 1830; *Un nom pour deux coeurs*, 1834. SELECTED READING: in *French Studies*, by Stefan Zweig and Charles Saint-Beuve, 1928. (SOURCE: Kunitz, Colby, 1967; Steinberg, 2, 1973)

DESNOS, ROBERT (1900–1945): French poet and novelist. Desnos earned a livelihood by working in the fields of publicity, advertising, and journalism, and he did his military service in Morocco. During World War II Desnos played a large part as a member of the Resistance and was always engaged with the political issues of his time. When he died of typhoid in the concentration camp Teresienstadt, he was working on poetry written in the classical mode. Chiefly memorable is his early poetry up to 1930, when he was connected with the ★Surrealists. The poetry of Robert Desnos has been set by Francis Poulenc. PRINCIPAL WORKS: *Les ténèbres*, 1926; *À la mystérieuse*, 1927; *Sirène-Anémone*, 1921; *Siramour*, 1931; *The Night of Loveless Nights*, original title, 1930 (the preceding were all written in honor of Yvonne George, a singer of chanties, hence the prominent images of sea, sailing, mermaids, etc.); *Choix de poèmes*, 1946; *Twenty-two Poems*, tr. Michael Benedikt, 1971; in English, *The Voice*, 1972; *Selected Poems of Robert Desnos*, 1991. SELECTED READING: M. A. Caws, *The Surrealist Voice of Robert Desnos*, 1977. (SOURCE: Serafin, 1999)

DEUTSCH, BABETTE (1895–1982): American poet. Deutsch was born in New York, educated at Barnard College, during which years she contributed to the serious periodicals of the time. She wrote an essay on Thorstein Veblen, who, admiring her work, took her on as his secretary while teaching at the New School for Social Research. After traveling in Europe and Russia, she devoted herself to writing, teaching courses at the New School on poetry, and translating from Russian and German. Deutsch was married to Avrahm Yarmolinsky, the critic and scholar. Critics have said that she did her best work in "loosely constructed free verse interspersed with regular rhymed poems where intensity is needed" (Kunitz, Haycraft, 1942). The poetry of Babette Deutsch has been set by David Diamond and Gordon Binkerd. PRINCIPAL WORKS: Poetry: *Fire for the Night*, 1930; *Take Them, Stranger*, 1944; *Animal, Vegetable, Mineral*, 1954; *Coming of Age*, 1959; *Collected Poems*, 1963, 1969. Novels: *Mask of Silenus*, 1933. Criticism: *Poetry in Our Time*, 1954. (SOURCE: Kunitz, Haycraft, 1973)

DIALOGUE: in music, the setting of a short, dramatized incident between two characters, biblical, mythological, or pastoral, as in Purcell duets for the Restoration theater.

DIANA, DIANE (Fr.): virgin goddess of the moon, sister to ★Apollo, who was god of the sun. Diana, daughter of Latona and ★Jupiter, was the goddess of hunting and woodlands, and is represented as a huntress whose bow was made of silver. Corresponding to the Greek goddess Artemis, she was the personification of feminine grace and vigor. Largely worshiped by women, she was associated with fertility and invoked by the Romans in all three of her aspects. (SOURCE: *Bulfinch*, 1978)

SONG	COMPOSER	POET
1. "Diane, Séléné"	Gabriel Fauré	Jean de la Ville de Mirmont
2. "Sombrero"	Cécile Chaminade	Éduard Guinand
3. "When Laura Smiles"	Phillip Rosseter	anonymous
4. "Cantilena"	Joaquín Turina	Duque de Rivas
5. "La Najade"	Ottorino Respighi	Gabriele d'Annunzio
6. "Der zürnenden Diana"	Franz Schubert	Johann Mayrhofer

DIAPHENIA: the name of the poet Henry Constable's beloved.

SONG	COMPOSER	POET
"Diaphenia"	Dominick Argento	Henry Constable

DIARY OF ONE WHO VANISHED: Leo Janáček's setting of twenty-two anonymous poems. His music was composed toward the end of World War I, at the time when the Czechoslovak Republic came into being (1917–1919). Originally, the police had found twenty-three poems in an exercise book belonging to a young Moravian peasant who had mysteriously disappeared. Seemingly the poems were autobiographical, telling the story of a young man's seduction by Zefka, a gypsy woman. When Janáček read them in a Brno newspaper, he was deeply moved. The poems had appeared under the title "From the Pen of a Self-Taught Man." They appealed to Janáček because they were written in Wallachian dialect, not unlike the dialect of his native district, Lachia, on the borders of Moravia and Silesia. The composer found in them reflections of his own life and love, for 1917 was the year in which he first met Mrs. Kamila Stössl, for whom he conceived a deep affection. The work contains one piano solo, the thirteenth song. The remainder of the cycle requires a solo mezzo soprano and three female voices who sing in ensemble. The words *Janicku* and *Janku* are diminutives for the name *Jan*.

DICHTERLIEBE: a song cycle by Robert Schumann with texts from Heinrich ★Heine's *Buch der Lieder* (Book of Songs). Within the *Buch der Lieder* are sixty-six short poems grouped under the heading *Lyrisches Intermezzo* (Lyric Intermezzo). From this collection Schumann chose twenty poems to set to music, four being omitted in later editions but available within a W. W. Norton publication, *Schumann's Dichterliebe*. Sentimental lament is the prevailing tone in the poems of the *Buch der Lieder*. Almost too romantic to facilitate interpretations by a modern singer, they become transformed when clothed in music by Schumann, Brahms, and Strauss. Schumann himself approved of the term *Dichtungen* (poetry, fine writing) as it referred to musical composition. He liked to think of himself as a *Dichter*, (inspired writer), thus bestowing upon the title, *Dichterliebe*, a more personal quality.

DICHTER UND IHRE GESELLEN (The Poet and His Temperaments): a novel written by Joseph ★Eichendorff (1833) in three volumes. The story is concerned with Baron Fortunat, who, during his travels, visits friends, meets various poets of varying temperaments, feels unrequited love, witnesses death, and finally experiences love fulfilled with Fiametta, the daughter of an Italian marquis. The song "Schöne Fremde," is prefaced by these lines: "Just then the moon came out and transformed everything into a dream. Then Fortunat, opening the folding doors, took his guitar and strode, singing, up and down through the long rows of rooms."

SONG	COMPOSER	POET
"Schöne Fremde"	Robert Schumann	Joseph Eichendorff

DICKEY, JAMES (1923–1997): American poet, novelist, and critic. Dickey's early life was dominated by an athletic career: football, physical contests of various sorts, and the tension of competition. In 1942 he interrupted his education to join the air force. During the bombing missions of the Pacific theater in which he participated, he started reading poetry and trying his own skill at the art. After the war he studied literature at Vanderbilt University and began an academic career. Disillusioned with graduate school, he returned to combat during the Korean War, after which he gave up teaching to make a good living at advertising. Subsequent to winning the National Book Award (1965), Dickey became poetry consultant to the Library of Congress. Dickey was a romantic, and his passionate and adventurous writing reveals no inhibitions; it is concerned with the basic emotions, death, and renewal. His literary invention was the "split line," marked by gaps between words instead of punctuation. The poetry of James Dickey was set by Ronald Perera. PRINCIPAL WORKS: *Poems: 1957–67*; *Into the Stone*, 1962; *Drowning with Others*, 1962; *Buckdancer's Choice*, 1965; *Deliverance*, 1970; *Self-Interviews*, 1970; *The Strength of Fields*, 1979; *The Early Motion*, 1981; *Falling, May Day Sermon, and Other Poems*, 1982; *The Eagle's Mile*, 1990; *The Whole Motion* (most comprehensive volume), 1992. SELECTED READING: Gordon Van Ness, *Outbelieving Existence: The Measured Motion of James Dickey*, 1992. (SOURCE: Serafin, 1999)

DICKINSON, EMILY (1830–1886): American poet. Emily Dickinson was born in Amherst, Massachusetts, and, except for brief visits to Washington, Philadelphia, and Boston, lived there for the rest of her life, a semi-invalid. She attended Amherst Academy, where she studied Latin, French, history, rhetoric, botany, geology, and mental philosophy, and later the Mt. Holyoke Female Seminary also in Massachusetts, where she confronted the large religious questions. Poor health often interrupted her education. During her life in Amherst, she chose loneliness and was fulfilled by seclusion. She did not roam; she saw from her window her garden, her church, what she needed to see. She tended her sick mother, baked bread, knitted, wrote poems and letters endlessly, played the piano, worked in the garden, and dreamed abundantly. She was moody; she gave herself to the moment; she tested everything. "Her special area of feeling was the great abstractions: pain, love, self, will, desire, expectation, and death" (Unger, 1, 1974). Among the major poets who have written in English, Emily Dickinson's place is secure. She meets all of T. S. ★Eliot's criteria by which all work of major poets should be judged: a body of work marked by distinctive style; all work possesses a "significant unity"; her seniority does not depend on having written lengthy works. The critics, however, have reproached her for her alleged whimsicality: bad grammar (she used the subjunctive mode frequently); irregularities in meter and rhyme (she felt no compunction to find exact rhymes); and childishness (she was childlike in her awareness). Emily Dickinson's poetry has been set by Thomas Pasatieri, Ronald Perera, George Perle, Ned Rorem, George Walker, Robert Ward, Ben Weber, Gordon Binkerd, Richard Hageman, Sergius Kagen, Otto Luening, Ernst Bacon, Robert Baksa, Howard Boatwright, Aaron Copland, Arthur Farwell, Vincent Persichetti, Lee Hoiby, William Bolcom, and John Duke. PRINCIPAL WORKS: *The Poems*, 3 vols., ed. Thomas H. Johnson, 1955; *Complete Poems*, ed. Thomas H. Johnson, 1960; *The Single Hound: Poems of a Lifetime*, ed. Martha Dickinson Bianchi, 1914. SELECTED READING: John J. Cody, *After Great Pain: The Inner Life of Dickinson*, 1971; Cynthia Griffin Wolff, *Emily Dickinson*, 1988; Judith Thurman, *Emily Dickinson: The Life of a Storyteller*, 1982. (SOURCES: Unger, 1, 1974; Vinson, 1979)

DIDO (ELISSA): founding queen of Carthage. Dido was the legendary daughter of Belus of Tyre, who became queen after Pygmalion murdered her husband,

Sichaeus. Virgil's *Aeneid* tells that she fell in love with Aeneas when he was driven to her shores by storms. Grieving at his departure, she committed suicide in the flames of a funeral pyre. An older legend claims that she did it to avoid marriage with the king of Libya. (SOURCE: Cooper, 1992)

DIE: in any Elizabethan poem this word is a metaphor for making love.

DIES IRAE: (Lat.) *day of wrath*; a thirteenth-century metrical sequence in the Roman Catholic requiem mass.

DINESEN, ISAK (KAREN CHRISTENTZE BLIXEN) (1885–1962): Danish writer of fiction, plays, and essays. Isak Dinesen was born in Denmark, educated privately, and studied art in Copenhagen, Paris, and Rome. After her marriage to the Baron Blixen-Finecke, she managed a coffee plantation near Nairobi, Kenya. After 1931 she returned to Rungsted, Denmark. She was awarded the Ingenio e Arte Medal in 1950 and was a founding member of the Danish Academy. Dinesen called herself a storyteller whose mission was to entertain people. This she did with sophisticated language, a painter's descriptions of nature, and elegant sensuality that took years of rewriting to achieve. Denmark accused her of indifference to social issues, and it is true that she herself "set her tales one hundred years in the past, and [defined] her period as the last great phase of aristocratic culture" (Vinson, Kirkpatrick (1), 1984). Her writing exhibited her aristocratic manner and made use of macabre, bizarre neo-Gothic fantasy. Dinesen's writing has been set by David Diamond. PRINCIPAL WORKS: *Seven Gothic Tales*, 1934; *Out of Africa*, 1937; *Babette's Feast*, 1955; *Last Tales*, 1957; *Letters from Africa*, 1981. SELECTED READING: Robert Langbaum, *The Gayety of Vision: A Study of Dinesen's Art*; Judith Thurman, *Dinesen: The Life of a Storyteller*. (SOURCE: Vinson, Kirkpatrick (1), 1984)

DIOCLESIAN: a 1690 adaptation of Massinger and *Fletcher's earlier play, *The Prophetess*, the first new semi-opera since 1677, for which Henry Purcell was appointed sole composer. An encapsulation of the plot is: "a debauched emperor and two aspiring ones try to reconcile their problems in the succession with the help of a blowzy prophetess" (Price, 1984). A satire on the poorly managed last years of the reign of Charles II, the parallels include Numerianus (Charles I), Aper (*Cromwell), the Emperor Charinus (Charles II), Princess Aurelia, sister to Charinus (Catherine of Braganza), Diocles (the Duke of York, later James II), Maximinian (The Duke of Monmouth). *Dioclesian* opens with a soprano singing "*Charon, the Peaceful Shade Invites" to the old emperor Numerianus, its music hinting that the dead emperor's shade is less than restful. When Diocles avenges the murder of Numerianus, Charinus gives him half the empire as a reward. A countertenor sings "Let the Soldiers Rejoice," followed by a chorus piece. The countertenor sings "With Dances and Songs" in honor of Diocles's ascent to the throne. Diocles renames himself Dioclesian and accepts Charinus's offer of Princess Aurelia, conveniently discarding the prophetess Delphia's ugly niece Drusilla. Displeased, Delphia conceives a plan to make Dioclesian return to Drusilla. Maximinian sings a song in an attempt to seduce Aurelia for his uncle, for which Purcell, in an effort to clarify the complex plot, wrote the virtuoso display piece "When First I Saw Bright Aurelia's

Eyes" to replace the original song. To humiliate Dioclesian, Delphia contrives to control the battle against the invading Persian army in which Charinus, Maximinian, and Aurelia are captured. Dioclesian then submits and repents. He is permitted a small victory over the Persians, after which there is a musical celebration. The countertenor sings "Sound, Fame, thy Brazen Trumpet" to Dioclesian. He, a fool, abdicates in favor of his nephew Maximinian. Scene 2 of act 5 is set in Lombardy, Dioclesian and Drusilla's country retreat, where Delphia sets up an entertainment by the peasants. Maximinian and Aurelia enter, determined to assassinate Dioclesian to prevent him from taking the throne back. Dioclesian reasons with them, and they, frightened by a flaming vision in the sky, apologize. Dioclesian requests that Delphia provide an entertainment for the emperor. The following forty-five-minute masque begins with a seductive duet for two sopranos, "Since from My Dear ★Astrea's Sight" (Astrea meaning Drusilla). The next song, "Tell Me Why," is a "clear depiction of amorous pursuit, submission and consummation" (Price, 1984). Next, a male trio sings "Triumphant, Victorious Love." Because the original play accepted music poorly, *Dioclesian* is generally considered to be the weakest of Purcell's major stage works. Nevertheless its success impelled the managers of the Theatre Royal to commission Purcell with two more semi-operas for the 1691 season, ★*King Arthur* and *The ★Faerie-Queene*. For more information about the history of the real-life emperor, *see* ★DIOCLETIAN. (SOURCE: Price, 1984)

DIOCLETIAN (245–313 c.e.): Roman emperor and reformer. Diocletian's full name was Gaius Aurelius Valerius Diocletianus, and he was born of an army father in poor circumstances. When the Emperor Numerian died, the soldiers chose Diocletian to be the next emperor. Principally concerned with assuring the stability of state and throne, he devised a system of government, a tetrarchy under the rule of four, two senior emperors and two junior emperors (caesars) who would rule simultaneously. Hoping to discourage rebellions, he reduced the power of provincial governors and regulated almost every human activity of his subjects. After he revived the ancient pagan religion of Rome, in 303 he began the active persecution of Christians. When Diocletian died, the tetrarchy system broke down.

DIOGENES (412–323 b.c.e.): a Greek Cynic philosopher. Diogenes was born in Sinope and lived in Athens where he became a student of Antisthenes. Contemptuous of worldly goods, Diogenes believed that the simple life was the best life. He lived in an ordinary barrel; when he saw a peasant drink by cupping his hands, he gave up using a cup. Legend says that Diogenes wandered through the streets of Athens with a lighted lamp during the daylight, in search of an "honest" man, clearly showing his contempt for his fellow citizens. ★Alexander the Great, a student of Aristotle, is said to have sought out Diogenes to offer him anything in this world that he might desire. Diogenes asked the conqueror to step aside and to stop blocking the sunlight. (SOURCES: Benét, 1965; Boardman, Griffin, Murray, 1986; Bridgwater, Kurtz, 1968)

SONG	COMPOSER	POET
"Genialisch Treiten"	Hugo Wolf	Johann Wolfgang von Goethe

DIONYSUS (BACCHUS, Roman): the god of wine in Greek mythology, son of ★Zeus and Semele. The name Bacchus is a subversion of the Greek Iacchus (from Iache, a shout). It was originally an epithet of Dionysus, the noisy and rowdy god. Originally Dionysus was represented as a bearded man, but later he appears as a beautiful youth with black eyes and flowing locks crowned with vine and ivy. The worship of Dionysus and Bacchus is associated with wild dancing, and later, because he was the god of wine, with loosened inhibitions and inspired creativity. (SOURCE: Cotterell, 1986)

SONG	COMPOSER	POET
1. "Dithyrambe"	Franz Schubert	Friedrich von Schiller
2. "Bacchus is Power Divine"	Henry Purcell	Thomas Shadwell
3. "Hence with Your Trifling Deity"	Henry Purcell	Thomas Shadwell
4. "The Capture of Bacchus"	Dudley Buck	Charles Swain
5. "Bacchus"	Arthur Shepherd	Frank Sherman

DIOSCURI: Castor and Polydeuces (Pollux to the Romans), from the Greek Dios Kouroi, meaning sons of ★Zeus. Homer calls them the brothers of ★Helen, whom they rescued after she had been carried off by ★Theseus. During this adventure Polydeuces killed Amycus, king of the Bebryces, with his bare hands. Their last exploit, an attempted abduction, ended in the death of Castor. Because the Spartans associated their worship with a tradition of dual kingship, the cult of the Dioscuri was very important to them. From the fifth century B.C.E. on, the Romans revered Castor and Pollux because the brothers had come to their aid on the battlefield. (SOURCES: Cotterell, 1986; Wells, 1988)

SONG	COMPOSER	POET
"Lied eines Schiffers an die Dioskuren"	Franz Schubert	Johann Mayrhofer

DIOTIMA: the nickname of a married woman with whom the poet Friedrich Hölderlin was in love.

SONG	COMPOSER	POET
"Geh unter, schöne Sonne"	Wolfgang Fortner	Friedrich Hölderlin

DITHYRAMB: a kind of poetry in honor of ★Dionysus, the god of wine. Dithyramb has its etymological roots in *di* and *rambos*, meaning "born twice," which was a title referring to Dionysus. It has to do with the legend that he was killed when his mother beheld ★Zeus in his complete glory and died, after which Rhea brought him back to life. During the spring in Greece the death and rebirth of Dionysus was marked in orgiastic celebrations featuring this particular type of wild passionate lyric poetry. (SOURCES: Benét, 1965; Murray, 1988; Boardman, Griffin, Murray, 1986; Bridgwater, Kurtz, 1968)

SONG	COMPOSER	POET
"Dithyrambe"	Franz Schubert	Friedrich von Schiller

DIVAN, DIWAN (Ger.): (Arab.), literally, *an account book* or *customs house*. Poetically: a collection of poems usually written by one author. Readers should not be mislead into conjuring up pictures of love seats or couches. Divan is derived from a Persian word, originally *devan*, now *diwdn*, an account book or customs house. For our purposes, a divan is a collection of poems usually written by one author. Schubert set two poems from ★Goethe's *Westöstlicher Diwan*, a collection of poems written while Goethe was under the influence of a German translation of the fourteenth-century Persian poet ★Hāfiz's *Divan*. The two poems, *Suleika I* and *Suleika II*, were not written by Goethe, but rather by Marianne von ★Willemer.

"Divine Andate! President of War": a song composed by Henry Purcell to words written by John ★Fletcher for his play *Bonduca*, produced in 1695. For plot details and placement of songs, *see* ★*Bonduca*.

DOBLÓN: a Spanish gold coin, at one time double the value of a pistole.

SONG	COMPOSER	POET
"Canción de la gitana habilidosa"	José Castel	Ramón de la Cruz

DOCTEUR BOLOGNAIS: a ★*commedia dell'arte* character, the Doctor, named Gracian Baloardo (last name meaning *dullard*), a philosopher, astronomer, man of letters, cabalist, barrister, grammarian, diplomat, and physician. Although spending all his time in his books, he seldom is able to quote anyone correctly. When he instructs, it generally results in his being beaten, his eloquence flowing all the while. Pompous, boastful, and incompetent, he has a gift for oratory and is a miser. His great friend is ★Pantaloon. The doctor is dressed entirely in black like a university professor, cheeks smeared red and nose black or flesh-colored.

SONG	COMPOSER	POET
"Fantoches"	Claude Debussy	Paul Verlaine

DODGER: a clever trickster, one who plays fast and loose in city life, who knows ingenious ways of doing things and profits by this knowledge; a name given by Dickens to such a rascal in *Oliver Twist,* Jack Dawkins, a clever young pickpocket, known for his quick-wittedness. Copland's song is a campaign song, believed to originate in the presidential campaign of 1884, when Grover Cleveland defeated James G. Blaine. (SOURCE: *OED*, 1989)

SONG	COMPOSER	POET
"The Dodger"	Aaron Copland, Ernst Bacon	folk song

DOGE OF VENICE: the chief magistrate of the Italian Republics of Venice and Genoa from the eleventh to the sixteenth century.

SONG	COMPOSER	POET
"Toréador"	Francis Poulenc	Jean Cocteau

DOGSTAR: the brightest star in the firmament, Sirius, in the constellation Canis Major (Large Dog). In ancient times its influence was supposed to cause great heat, pestilence, and so on.

SONG	COMPOSER	POET
"I'll Sail upon the Dog Star"	Henry Purcell	John Fletcher

DOIE: (Scot.), *does.*

DON JUAN: a character who first appeared in ★Tirso de Molina's play, *El Burlador de Sevilla y convidado de piedra* (The Jester of Seville and the Stone Guest). The Spanish playwright combined the essential elements of a callous seducer, a comic moralizing man-servant, and a religious lesson of a Hell's fire punishment delivered by a walking statue. The same characters were used by Mozart in his opera *Don Giovanni,* and by other dramatists and composers as well.

A *commedia dell'arte* version of the story can be found in *Gibaldone*, a collection of varied scenarios for comedies, transcribed by Antonio Passante, in which Tisbea, a fisher woman, is seduced by Don Giovanni. She wants to go with him, but he refuses, saying that it has been glorious enough for her to have enjoyed a cavalier of his quality. Anfreso, Tisbea's admirer, calls the fishermen and maidens out for dancing, not realizing what has happened to his Tisbea. They all sing and dance to a simple folklike verse that tells of a fisher maiden who has "cast her net."

SONG	COMPOSER	POET
"Serenade aus Don Juan aus der Jugendzeit"	Gustav Mahler	Tirso de Molina, Ludwig Braunfeis

DONNE, JOHN (1572–1631): English poet, priest, essayist, and prayer writer. Grandson of the writer John Heywood and great-grandson of John Rastell, another writer, John Donne was educated at Oxford and Cambridge. He took part in the Earl of Essex's expeditions to ★Cadiz in 1596 and to the Azores in 1597. He was a member of Parliament in 1601, but his secret marriage to the daughter of the Lord Keeper caused his dismissal and imprisonment, putting an end to his political advancement. Although he was born a Roman Catholic, King James asked him to be ordained in the Anglican Church in 1615, after which Donne attended James as Royal Chaplain. He served as dean of St. Paul's in London, as vicar of St. Dunstan's in the West of London (1624), as the governor of the Charterhouse in London (1626), and as a member of the Court of Delegates from 1622 to 1631. The seventeenth century was energized by a spirit of wide-ranging inquiry, both scientific and geographical, and the late Elizabethan voyages of discovery, in which Donne took part, expanded the frontiers of human consciousness. Donne was the leader of the Metaphysical school, which summed up the underlying unity of existence thus: "mathematics and love obey one principle . . . one law is at work in all experience" (Vinson, 1979). As a love poet, Donne displayed ranges of mood and concepts of passion more complex than his predecessors. The Elizabethans wrote of a faithful lover forever pining at the feet of a haughty mistress; one of Donne's most constant themes was the importance of a full relationship between man and woman, even suggesting an affinity between earthly and divine love. The power and passion of Donne's divine poems probably flowed from the tensions that his vocation imposed upon a sensual nature. The first edition of his poetry appeared only after his death. Three centuries after his death, Ernest Hemingway's *For Whom the Bell Tolls* owes its title and theme to one of Donne's *Devotions*. The verses of John Donne, in particular the *Holy Sonnets*, have been set by John Dowland, Ross Finney, Benjamin Britten, Douglas Moore, Virgil Thomson, Howard Boatwright, Alfonso Ferrabosco, Samuel Adler, William Flanagan, and Lee Hoiby. PRINCIPAL WORKS: Verse: *Holy Sonnets*, 1610–11; *Elegies, and Songs and Sonnets*, ed. Helen Gardner, 1965; *Satires, Epigrams, and Verse Letters*, ed. W. Milgate, 1967; *The Anniversaries, Epithalamiums, and Epicedes*, ed. W. Milgate, 1978. Other: *LXXX Sermons*, 1640; *Essays in Divinity, Interwoven with Meditations and Prayers*, ed. Evelyn M. Simpson, 1952. SELECTED READING: *Essential Articles for the Study of Donne's Poetry*, ed. John E. Roberts, 1976. (SOURCES: Vinson, 1979; Drabble, 1985)

DONNEYCARNEY: a rough, tough section in the northern part of Dublin, Ireland.

SONG	COMPOSER	POET
"O, It Was Out by Donneycarney"	John Duke	James Joyce

DON PEDRO D'ALFAROUBEIRA: a famed Portuguese traveler and explorer. According to the story written by Gomez de Santistevan, Don Pedro Alfaroubeira accompanied the ★Infante of Portugal on a three-year voyage to Egypt in the fourteenth century. ★Apollinaire found this information in a volume called *Le Monde enchanté du Moyen Age*, and, faithful to his predilection for scattering obscure allusions through his poetry, included this name as a divertissement in "Le Dromadaire," part of his ★*Bestiaire*.

SONG	COMPOSER	POET
"Le Dromadaire"	Francis Poulenc	Guillaume Apollinaire

DON QUIXOTE, THE COMICAL HISTORY OF: a Restoration theater trilogy in the form of a comedic semi-opera, based on ★Cervantes's work, written by Thomas ★D'Urfey (1694–95), for which the composed music was almost equally divided between Eccles and Purcell. Cervantes initially wrote his work in the form of a chivalric ballad burlesque. When the character of his hero developed, his work acquired depth and richness and supplied the plot for several seventeenth-century plays.

In Restoration drama, expressing in song anything better expressed in speech was believed to be absurd, unless it issued from magic or a state of madness. Restoration comedy, much more realistic than drama, rigorously restricted music that was an integral part of the plot. D'Urfey's solution to this problem was to make Don Quixote himself a fantastic and wildly irrational being. For this reason, although D'Urfey's dramatic works generally met with critical disdain, the response to his *Don Quixote* was more of a bewilderment.

Don Quixote, Part I

In act 1 Don Quixote, a gentleman of congenial disposition and otherwise sane, has had his wits befuddled by too great a devotion to chivalric tales. He imagines himself called upon to roam the world in search of adventure on his old horse, *Rosinante. He outfits himself with rusty armor and is accompanied by a squire, the rustic *Sancho Panza, who is both shrewd and innocent. In the best traditions of chivalry, Don Quixote designates a good-looking local girl as the mistress of his heart, dubbing her *Dulcinea del Toboso, despite the fact that she is unaware of the honor.

Act 2, scene 1 contains "Sing, All Ye Muses," a duet for countertenor and baritone that is delivered at the Don's bogus knighting. This song is both an invocation and a graphic battle song. After the duet, the innkeeper aims a blow at Don Quixote, cutting his head open, which explains the bandage that always adorns the Don's head in illustrations.

Act 3, scene 1 has one of the lengthy digressions interpolated by D'Urfey—that of *Cardenio and Lucinda. Believing that Lucinda has deserted him for his best friend, Cardenio has gone mad.

In act 3, scene 2 Don Quixote mistakes a barber for a noble enemy, and they do battle. Later in the same scene Sancho and Don Quixote free some galley-slaves, believing them to be political prisoners. One of them thanks the Don by singing "When the World First Knew Creation," a rollicking praise of criminal life.

Purcell's task in act 4 was to develop Cardenio's personality through music. The song "Let the Dreadful Engines" is one of the longest songs Purcell set and the musical high point of the semi-opera. Cardenio is tormented by the realization of his own insanity. Purcell shows his violent changes of mood and unfettered imagery with a series of wild recitatives, a lyric air full of pathos, some earthy ballads and highly ornamented declamations, all of which he made fit together coherently. The scheme for the aria is this: in part 1 are two recitatives in F major and F minor, followed by a ballad in F major. In part 2 are included a secco recitative in C major and a long pathetic air in C minor. In part 3 are, first, a secco recitative and arietta in F major, then a recitative in F minor, and a ballad in F major. It is generally accepted that F major indicates Cardenio's impulsive exterior, shown at the beginning by delusions of grandeur and at the end by a dismissal of all women as witches. The F minor sections equal Cardenio's inner despair, while the C major is reserved for brief moments of great rage, and C minor reveals Cardenio's recollection of lost youth.

In act 5 the characters of the subplot attempt to frighten Don Quixote into giving up his quest by convincing him that the inn is enchanted. For this section Purcell wrote a fine masque that knits all the themes of the play into a satisfying outcome. Cardenio is the principal figure of the masque. Together with Melissa and Urganda, two players from a carnival, Cardenio proposes bad ways to dispose of Don Quixote. With accompaniment of violins only, Cardenio sings a recitative, "With This Sacred Charming Wand," followed by a very serious recitative and air by Eccles, not Purcell. Melissa sings a slightly mischievous air and a teasing air, both by Eccles. Urganda and Melissa insist that the proposed death is too easy.

Don Quixote, Part II

Part II of *Don Quixote* has been called "an overblown and misguided display of patri-otism." At the end of act 4 a clown and his wife sing a Purcell dialogue, "Since Times Are So Bad," but Purcell's main contribution to part II is a trumpet song in act 5, "Genius of England." (*See* ★GENIUS.) In a disgraceful debate between heroes of England and France, St. ★George calls forth the Genius of England to sing his song.

Don Quixote, Part III

Because he was preoccupied at the time with his work on *Bonduca* and *The Indian Queen* as well as his fatal illness, Purcell wrote only one song for part III. Altisidora, the only important singing part, is encouraged in act 5 to make a more extravagant and cruel effort to seduce the Don, acting out a charade of teasing, singing, danc-ing, of which the climax is "From Rosy Bowers." This is Purcell's swan song, aiming at the heart of the human condition in a long lyric, only three or four lines shorter than "Let the Dreadful Engines," but more tightly constructed. D'Urfey wanted the song to be in five movements, Love, Gaily, Melancholy, Passion, and Frenzy, but Purcell changed this to six sections in three units, one recitative and one air each, concerning the power of music to move gods. All but the last declamatory part are decorated but with far less elaborate grace notes and more concentrated than earlier mad songs and dialogues, for Altisidora is only pretending to be mad. *See* ★MAD SONGS. (SOURCE: Price, 1984)

DOONEY: a huge rock located on the south shore of Lough Gill, which is a short distance southeast of the Irish town of Sligo. Here ★Yeats dreamed, imagin-ing a fiddler playing while standing on Dooney Rock. Yeats's poem, "The Fiddler of Dooney," was set by Charles Loeffler, Vittorio Rieti, Sidney Homer, Richard Hage-man, and Ivor Gurney.

D'ORLÉANS, CHARLES, DUC (1394–1465): French poet, fourth son of Louis, Duc d'Orléans, and the Duchess of Milano, nephew of Charles VI. When Charles's mother left the royal court, he went with her and was given an excellent education. When he was ten Charles's marriage was arranged to the widow of Richard II of England, and they were married in 1408. When his mother and father died, Charles was forced to defend his rights against many enemies. The early death of his wife left him free to make a new political marriage. His avid pursuit of the cabal that had murdered his father led to an invasion of France by Henry V of England and the disastrous defeat of the French at Agincourt in 1415, which made Charles a prisoner. Imprisoned for twenty-five years, he was a pawn in the political intrigues between France and England. Charles devoted himself to theological studies and wrote poetry to various ladies. Upon paying a huge ransom by pledging his own lands, he was released to settle down in Blois with cultivated friends and servants. Here Charles wrote most of his poetry, and here he died at seventy, leaving two daughters and a son who became Louis XII. Much of his poetry was autobiographical, reflecting the social life of the times and his complaints against bad fortune. He wrote a long series of ★*chansons* as well as ★*ballades*, which were his favorite poetic form, featuring the last line of each strophe cast as a refrain. D'Orléans's poetry was admired for its metrical skills, its broad vocabulary, and its personal warmth. It was set to music by Debussy, Poulenc, Reynaldo Hahn, André Caplet, Jean Françaix, Frank Martin, and Peter Warlock. PRINCIPAL WORKS: *Poésies*, ed. P. Champion, 1923–27; *English Poems of Charles d'Orléans*, ed. Robert Steele, 1941–46. SELECTED READING: R. L. Stevenson, *Familiar Studies of Men and Books*. (SOURCE: Kunitz, Colby, 1967)

DOUBLE DEALER, THE: a comedy by William ★Congreve with music by Henry Purcell, produced in 1693, the title meaning a person who tells selective truths. *The Double Dealer* was only Congreve's second comedy but his first masterpiece. It is frequently revived but without the music, reflecting the fact that Congreve was against combining music and plays. Lady Touchwood is an enthusiastic adulteress, determined to ruin Mellefont and obstruct his planned marriage with Cynthia. Lady Touchwood's frequent confederate, Maskwell, tries to deceive everyone by double dealing. Virtuous Mellefont and Cynthia, observing the marital dissension all around them (all the secondary characters are unfaithful also), have no hopes for their future. In act 2, when musicians cross the stage, Mellefont asks them to rehearse a song they intend to sing at Lord Touchwood's house, "Cynthia Frowns Whene'er I Woo Her." The song continues the simile between marriage and gambling that Cynthia begins with this remark: "Marriage is like a card game. One of us must lose." When it is sung (by a secondary character), the lovers pay no attention. In this song Cynthia's ambivalence toward the pleasures and pains of love are reflected by Purcell's tonal scheme of changes of key and frequent cross relations. No other lyrics in the play were set by Purcell. (SOURCE: Price, 1984)

DOUBLET: a jacket, sleeved or sleeveless, sometimes with a short skirt attached, worn by men in the Renaissance.

SONG	COMPOSER	POET
"Voice que le printemps"	Claude Debussy	Paul Bourget

DOUCE: (Scot.), *prudent*.

DOUGLAS, ARCHIBALD: one of the Scottish earls of Douglas. Nine earls of Douglas held the earldom for one hundred years from 1358 and were equally renowned throughout Europe for warlike exploits. Sir James had made a series of brilliant raids on the north of England and had been rewarded with broad estates. The second earl was mortally wounded at the battle of Chevy Chase, when the title passed to the illegitimate son of the first Sir James, Archibald the Grim (1328?–1400). His son Archibald held the title from 1369? to 1424. The third Archibald, the fifth earl (1391?–1439), claimed title to the royal succession through his mother and wife. Archibald's son William (1423?–1440), the sixth earl, was murdered at a dinner arranged in Edinburgh Castle by the courtiers of the six-year-old James II. The family history for three centuries was inseparable from the history of Scotland. (SOURCE: *Americana*, 2003)

SONG	COMPOSER	POET
"Archibald Douglas"	Carl Loewe	Theodor Fontane

DOUGLAS, LORD ALFRED (1870–1945): English poet, friend of Oscar *Wilde. Douglas translated Wilde's *Salome* from French to English. He published several volumes of verse, to which the critical reaction was that he had a minor talent. Nevertheless, his *sonnets have admirers. Douglas was given to litigation and in 1924 was himself imprisoned for libel. He wrote several accounts of his relationship with Wilde, defending Wilde and the relationship. PRINCIPAL WORK: Lord Alfred Douglas, *Oscar Wilde and Myself*, 1914. SELECTED READING: *Bernard Shaw and Alfred Douglas: A Correspondence*, ed. M. Hyde, 1982. (SOURCE: Drabble, 2000)

DOWLAND, JOHN (1563–1626): English composer and lutenist. Dowland is generally considered to be the best of all English songwriters of his age. Disappointed by his failure to receive the post of lutenist to Queen Elizabeth, Dowland traveled abroad (1594), visiting various German and Italian courts. When he returned to England (1597), he published his *First Book of Songes or Ayres of Fowre Parts with Tablature for the Lute.* Dowland returned to Germany when he was passed over again. By 1598 Christian IV of Denmark had made him lutenist at his court. Dowland's second and third books of airs were published in his absence from London. When he returned to England permanently, Dowland published his fourth collection of songs, *A Pilgrimes Solace*, 1612. Although he was famous all over Europe especially for "Flow my Teares," written in 1600, Dowland's ambition was not achieved until James I made him his lutenist, after which he, ironically, wrote little. Among others, Ben Weber and Ralph Vaughn Williams set his lyrics. READING: Diana Poulton, *John Dowland*, 2nd ed., 1982. (SOURCE: Drabble, 1985)

DRACHMANN, HOLGER (1846–1908): a Danish poet, novelist, and short story writer. Drachmann was born in Copenhagen. His father was a naval medical officer, later a professor. After his mother died early on, Drachmann accompanied his father on his business trips or stayed with his relatives. Although forced to end his painting studies without a degree because of his mercurial personality, Drachmann wrote subsequent articles on painting and poetry that drew praise from Georg Brandes, whose radical naturalistic aesthetics recruited Drachmann as a supporter. Between 1872 and 1879 he published five collections of poems. One of them, *Sange ved Havet* (Songs by the Sea) contains the greatest odes to the sea in Danish poetry. Some say that the early dissolution of his marriage caused by an affair with a young girl made him into a poet. Although a champion of radical ideas, Drachmann could not remain within the rules and was concerned with the erotic, exemplified by his collection *Ranker og Roser* (Vines and Roses). In the end he changed his writing again by transforming his conservative ideals into a partiality for liberal and lower-class interests, as in *Sangenes Bog* (Book of Songs), 1889. Edvard Grieg, Charles Kjerulf, Peter Heise, Peter Lange-Müller, and Christian Sinding set the verses of Holger Drachmann. SELECTED READING: John Volk, *Songs and Poems in Danish and English*, 1903; *A Book of Danish Verse*, trans. S. F. Damon and R. S. Hillyer, 1922.

DRAGONFLY: a large, harmless insect with a long slender body and four filmy wings that feeds on flies, gnats, and so on. It is known as "the devil's knitting needle."

The text of Ralph Vaughan Williams's much-admired song, "Silent Noon," mentions the dragonfly.

"Dream No More of Pleasures Past": a song composed by Henry Purcell, set to the words of Nathaniel ★Lee, from his heroic play *Theodosius*, produced in 1680. *See* *★Theodosius* for plot details and placement of songs.

DRIE: (Scot.), *suffer, bear.*

DRUIDS: an ancient Celtic order of priests, teachers, diviners, and magicians. The name is thought to relate to an oak tree or *Drus*. Druids studied the stars and believed in the transmigration of souls. Julius Caesar reported that they met annually at a site believed to be the center of Gaul. He also mentions a Chief Druid. The only detailed account of the Druid ceremony was recorded by another writer. The ceremony occurred at a time determined by the growth of the mistletoe on the oak trees. A Druid in a white robe climbed the tree and cut with a golden sickle the branch of mistletoe, caught on a white cloak as it fell. Two white bulls then were sacrificed and a feast took place. The meaning of this rite and everything about the priesthood is still obscure. (SOURCE: Cotterell, 1986)

DRYAD: a tree nymph in classical mythology, from the Greek *drus*, an oak tree. A dryad was supposed to die when the tree died. ★Eurydice, wife of ★Orpheus, was a dryad. (SOURCE: Cooper, 1992)

DRYDEN, JOHN (1631–1700): English poet, playwright, essayist, and critic. John Dryden was born in Northhamptonshire in England, but other facts of his life are rather obscure until he commenced his writing. Around 1646 he entered Westminster School as a King's Scholar and matriculated at Trinity College of Cambridge University about 1654. His activities for the next years are even more obscure, except for the 1659 publication of his *Heroique Stanzas* upon ★Cromwell's death. He is thought to have held a post in Cromwell's government. With the first period of the Restoration (1660–80), Dryden published poems on the new order, but his chief interest in these decades was the stage. He wrote one comedy first and then rhymed heroic plays, followed by serious and comic plots. Having been named poet laureate in 1668 and historiographer royal in 1669, he converted to Roman Catholicism around 1685. When King James II fled in 1688, Dryden entered into the most difficult period of his career. Stripped of his royal offices with the accession of William and Mary to the throne in 1689, Dryden turned back to the stage. In 1691 collaborated with Henry Purcell on a semi-opera, *★King Arthur*. In the last period of his life (1694–1700), Dryden worked through his problems successfully but died of degenerative diseases in 1700. Summarizing is made difficult by the diversity of Dryden's output—over thirty plays, operas, and cantatas alone. He was a poet gifted in the writing of odes rather than philosophical lyrics. He was a learned satirist and excelled in varieties of narration, having created a more natural language founded upon the actual speech of the time. His finest work came at the end of a lifetime, the end of a century, and the end of a distinct period of literature. T. S. ★Eliot has said, "Dryden found the English speechless, and he gave them speech" (Anderson, Buckler, 1966). John Dryden's poetry has been set by Henry Purcell, Henry and William Lawes, William Boyce, Ned Rorem, and Paul Nordoff. PRINCIPAL WORKS: Poetry: *Poems*, ed. James Kinsley, 4 vols., 1958; *An Ode on the Death of Henry Purcell*, 1696; *Alexander's Feast; or, The Power of Music: An Ode in Honour of St. Cecilia's Day*, 1697; *Hymns Attributed to Dryden*, ed. George Rapall and George Reuben Potter, 1937. Plays: The *★Indian Queen*, with Sir Robert Howard; The *★Indian Emperor*, 1667; The *★Tempest*, with William D'Avenant, from a play by Shakespeare, prod. 1670, ed. Vivian Summers, 1974; *★Tyrannic Love*, produced 1669. In *Works*, 10 vols., 1970: *★Aureng-Zebe*, prod. 1675, ed. Frederick M. Link, 1971; *★Oedipus*, with Nathaniel Lee, produced 1678; *Troilus and Cressida*, from a play by Shakespeare, prod. 1691; The *★Spanish Friar*, prod. 1694; *★Amphitryon*, prod. 1690; *★King Arthur*, music by Henry Purcell, prod. 1691; *★Love Triumphant*, produced 1694. SELECTED READING: Mark van Doren, *The Poetry of Dryden*, 1920, rev. ed., 1931; J. A. Winn, *John Dryden and His World*, 1987. (SOURCE: Vinson, 1979)

DUAN: (Eng.), *a little song.*

DULCINEA, DULCINÉE (Fr.): ★Don Quixote's beloved; a lady-love. The name taken from the lady to whom ★Cervante's Don Quixote paid knightly homage, whose real name was Aldonza Lorenzo, but whom the Don dubbed Dulcinea del Toboso. (SOURCE: Cooper, 1992)

SONG	COMPOSER	POET
"Chanson à Dulcinée"	Jacques Ibert	Alexandre Arnoux

DULE: (Scot.), *pain.*

DUMKA: from the Czech, an alternately melancholy and gay piece of music, found chiefly in the work of Slovanic composers.

DUNBAR, PAUL LAURENCE (1872–1905): American poet, playwright, novelist, and librettist. The son of a former slave, Dunbar was born in Ohio and educated at Dayton High School. He worked as an elevator operator but was encouraged in his writing by prominent Dayton men and by William Dean ★Howells. He joined the Pond Lecture Bureau in 1896 and enjoyed great popularity throughout the United States as the reader of his own works. From 1897 to 1898 he worked as an assistant at the Library of Congress. Suffering from tuberculosis, he died in 1905. It could be said that there were two Paul Laurence Dunbars. One was a writer supported by the interest of white Americans because some of his work was sufficiently faithful to the stereotypical black images designed by white Americans of that day. The other, more real Paul Laurence Dunbar was a writer of genuine literary talent and dramatic sensibility, whose true literary worth could not be assessed until the wide range of his work was gathered and published as late as 1975. As a dialect poet, Dunbar could not really be described as simply pandering to demands of white editors and the white reading public. He was also indulging his own natural interest in the rhythms of common speech and comedy. Late nineteenth-century America had an interest in local color, and Dunbar's use of dialect in literature was *au courant* with that interest. It was true that Dunbar had a gift as a dialect poet, but it was disappointing to him that his white audience could not accept him as more, as did William Dean Howells, who recognized that Dunbar, as the writer of fiction and essays, used the stuff of black lore to greater effect than any black writer previously, particularly the place of religion in African-American life and the implications of the black migration to American cities. "His material was mainly black, but his insights were universal" (Vinson, 1979). The poetry of Paul Laurence Dunbar has been set by William Grant Still, Howard Swanson, and George Walker. PRINCIPAL WORKS: Poetry: *Majors and Minors*, 1896; *Lyrics of Lowly Life*, 1896, 1897; *Lyrics of the Hearthside*, 1899. Novels: *The Sport of the Gods*, 1902 (reprinted as *The Jest of Fate: A Story of Negro Life)*, 1902. Short Stories: *Folks from Dixie*, 1898. Librettos: *Dream Lovers* (with Coleridge), 1898. SELECTED READING: E. W. Metcalf, *Paul Laurence Dunbar: A Bibliography*, 1975; Addison Gayle, Jr., *Oak and Ivy: A Biography of Paul Laurence Dunbar*, 1971. (SOURCE: Harris, 1986)

DÜNE: (Scot.) (pr. dyoon), *down;* v. *done.*

SONG	COMPOSER	POET
"Bed-time"	Benjamin Britten	William Soutar

DUQUE DE RIVAS (ÁNGEL DE SAAVEDRA) (1791–1865): Spanish poet and dramatist. Saavedra was a nobleman from Córdoba who became the Duke of Rivas. An officer of the Royal Guards, he distinguished himself in the War of Independence against the French at the age of seventeen. When he was condemned to death by Fernando VII because of his liberal activities, he fled Spain, spending the next ten years in England, Italy, Malta, and France. His most famous drama, *Don Álvaro, o la fuerza del sino*, was Verdi's inspiration for *La Forza del Destino*. The Duke of Rivas turned the focus of Spanish verse from the ancient Greek and Latin myths to Spain's own heroic past. He rejected the artificial syntax and Latinized vocabulary of previous generations and captured the country's customs in a lively language that complemented its exciting history. The verse of the Duke of Rivas was set by Joaquìn Turina. (SOURCES: Jason, 2, 2003; Cockburn, Stokes, 1992)

D'URFEY, THOMAS (1653–1723): English writer of songs, tales, satires, melodramas, and farces. Of French Huguenot descent and a friend to Charles II and James II, D'Urfey was still writing in the reign of Queen Anne. He made many adaptations and dramatizations of the work of other writers, such as ★Shakespeare. Many of D'Urfey's works were set to music by Henry Purcell. PRINCIPAL WORKS: *The ★Richmond Heiress; ★Sir Barnaby Whigg; The ★ Virtuous Wife*, 1679; ★*Don Quixote, Parts I, II, III*, 1694–96; *Wit and Mirth*, or *Pills to purge Melancholy*, 6 vols., 1719–20 (songs and ballads). (SOURCE: Drabble, 1985)

DURO: a Spanish coin, made of silver, worth five pesetas.

SONG	COMPOSER	POET
"Coplilla"	Oscar Esplà	Rafael Alberti

DURRELL, LAWRENCE (1912–1990): British poet and novelist. Born in India of Irish descent and educated in England, Durrell served as a foreign service press officer in Athens, Cairo, Rhodes, and Belgrade. In his self-description he said, "My poems constitute the only honest sketch of my self ever made." His poetry was distinguished by a rare purity of style, but, like his friend, Henry Miller, he made no attempt to cater to his wide, popular audience. In 1950 Durrell lectured in Argentina to an audience of graduate teachers of English, which lectures were published as *A Key to Modern Poetry*. The verse of Lawrence Durrell has been set by Richard Cumming. PRINCIPAL WORKS: *Ten Poems*, 1933; *Transition*, 1934; *A Private Country*, 1943; *Cities, Plains, and People*, 1946; *On Seeming to Presume*, 1948. (SOURCE: Kunitz, Colby, 1955)

"The Dying Nightingale": a song from a set of *Six Love Songs* by Norman Dello Joio set to a text by Stark ★Young (1881–1963). The song was originally to be an aria in a projected plan that dello Joio had for a never completed short opera based on Oscar Wilde's fairy tale, "The Nightingale and the Rose." In the Wilde story, a young student is desperate for the lack of a red rose to give to the lady of his choice. A nightingale who loves him sings all night, pressing her breast against a thorn so that her dying heart's blood may color the flower.

DYVEKE: a Danish woman who lived in Bergen, Norway, with her mother, Sigbrit, while Danish King Christian II was still a prince but ruler of Norway. Dyveke and the prince met around 1509, when she became his mistress. Although nothing is actually known about her character, she was said to be extremely beautiful. When Christian II became king, Dyveke and her mother moved to Copenhagen. As a residence Christian gave them the royal estate, Hvidøre, north of the city, and later a house at the corner of Amagertorv. Even when the king married in 1515, he kept Dyveke as his mistress, to the great indignation of his subjects. When Dyveke died in 1517, the rumor was that it was because of poisoned cherries. Danish composer Peter Heise set his song "Dyvekes Sange" to a text by Holger Drachmann and died while still working on redesigning the piano part to be very orchestral, something entirely new in the tradition of Danish romantic song at that time.

E

EBRO: a river in Spain, its source in the mountains below Santander, exiting near Barcelona at Cape Tortosa.

SONG	COMPOSER	POET
"Flutenreicher Ebro"	Hugo Wolf	Emanuel Geibel

ECCLESIASTICUS: a small book, belonging to the category of Wisdom literature, included in the Greek version of the Jewish Scriptures. Wisdom literature, such as Ecclesiasticus or the Old Testament books of Proverbs and Ecclesiastes, is not concerned with philosophy. Rather, it seeks to tell people how to live in proper relation to God and to each other. As such, Ecclesiasticus is an important link with ancient Judaism and the later developments of rabbinical Judaism. This Greek version of the

Jewish Scriptures, called the Septuagint, included fourteen books that are not found in the Hebrew versions of the Scriptures. In 90 C.E. the council of Jamnia eliminated these extra books from the Scriptures, but the Christian Church, which used the Septuagint, retained them. St. *Jerome, when he prepared the Latin Vulgate translation of the Old and New Testaments, compared the two versions and suggested that these extra books be kept in a separate section. Animosity between church and synagogue at this time was great. Christians believed that Jews had mutilated Christian scriptures so as to eliminate works that they felt testified to truths of Christianity. Not until Martin Luther prepared his German Bible were these books separated from the Old Testament and placed in a section of their own. To this day, divisions between Protestant and Catholic are evinced by the omission from Protestant Bibles of the fourteen apocryphal books. The Protestant singer will need to look hard for a Bible containing Ecclesiasticus. Ecclesiasticus, or the Wisdom of Jesus, the son of Sirach (or just plain Sirach in the Revised Standard Version), was the work of a Jewish scribe, an expert on the Jewish Scriptures and their interpretation. (SOURCES: Metzger, 1957; May, Metzger, 1977)

SONG	COMPOSER	POET
"Ernste Gesänge" 3	Johannes Brahms	Ecclesiasticus

ECHO, ECO: a Greek *nymph whom *Pan loved to chase. Echo's duty was to distract Hera's attention from *Zeus by talking incessantly as he pursued his amours. Hera discovered the plot and punished Echo by making her repeat the voices of others. Echo loved *Narcissus, who did not return the love, causing Echo to pine away until only her voice remained. (SOURCE: Kaster, 1964)

SONG	COMPOSER	POET
1. "L'Eco"	Gianfranco Malipiero	Angiolo Poliziano
2. "Paganini"	Francis Poulenc	Louise de Vilmorin
3. "The Dying Nightingale"	Norman dello Joio	Stark Young
4. "Das Echo"	Franz Schubert	Ignaz von Castelli

ECOLOGUE: any short poem with pastoral elements; specifically, a dialogue in verse. The participants are two shepherds or a shepherd and his mistress. The subjects of conversation range from the state of their hearts to that of the nation, from the management of sheep to that of poetry. (SOURCE: Drabble, 1985)

EDDIC POETRY: anonymous Scandinavian poems that were first transmitted by oral tradition, then written down, preserved primarily in the Codex Regius manuscript from the latter part of the thirteenth century. The gods of the Eddic poems were *Odin, *Thor, and a Germanic hero and heroine, Sigurthr (Siegfried) and Brynhildr (Brünnhilde). (SOURCE: Jason, 8, 2003)

EDWARD: an old Scottish ballad of domestic tragedy included in Percy's *Reliques*, a collection of *ballads, *sonnets, historical songs, and metrical romances published in 1765. Percy's version of the legend is the most popular. It is in a question and answer form telling of Edward's murder of his father. The mother's implication in the killing has been lost from several later versions.

SONG	COMPOSER	POET
1. "Edward"	Carl Loewe, Franz Schubert	Johann Herder, trans.
2. "Edward" (duet)	Johannes Brahms, P. I. Tchaikovsky	Johann Herder, trans.

EGLE: one of the many wood ★nymphs of mythology.

SONG	COMPOSER	POET
"Deità Silvane"	Ottorino Respighi	Antonio Rubino

EGMONT: a drama by ★Goethe, begun in 1775, finished in 1787. Egmont is the story of Count Lamoral Egmont, who, though born in Flanders, serves Spain as a capable general and urges King Phillip II to use patience in his dealings with Holland. Clärchen, a commoner of lowly station, loves and is loved by Egmont. When Egmont is arrested, Clärchen attempts to rally the people to rescue him, but when she fails, she returns to her house and drinks poison. When Egmont dies in the last scene of the drama, he realizes the deeper implications of his death: he is the victor, not the vanquished; he is one of the liberators of Holland; the end of his life signifies the dawn of Dutch independence. Beethoven set Clärchen's speech at the end of act 1 in his song "Die Trommel gerühret," wherein she thinks of her lover and wishes she could be a man to follow him into battle. Clärchen's beautiful love song at the closing of act 3, "Freudvoll und leidvoll," is set by Beethoven, Liszt, and Schubert ("Klärchen's Lied").

EICHENDORFF, JOSEPH VON (1788-1857): German poet. Born in the family castle in Silesia, Eichendorff had a carefree childhood, hunting and wandering the woods. His parents were more interested in entertainment and sports than the arts but gave their son a strict Catholic education from private tutors. Eichendorff read widely and had written a tragedy by the age of ten. In high school he read the Greek poets but wrote humorous articles for the school paper. At the University of Halle he came under the influence of the new ★Romanticism, which prompted him to move to Heidelberg, where he associated with Clemens ★Brentano and Achim von ★Arnim. Eichendorff had his first work published in 1808. He then moved to Vienna in 1810, where he found many friends among Catholic intellectuals. In 1813 he was called back to Silesia for military service in the war against Napoleon. In his career as a civil servant after the war, he eventually settled down in the ministry of cultural affairs and lived the life of a bureaucrat and family man, serene and good-humored. After 1844 Eichendorff devoted himself to writing. His reputation rests on two or three short novels and his poetry. The poetry was built on a small number of images, "a poet of the dim, mysterious forest, of the guitar-strumming wanderer, moonlit castles and marble statues, of yearning for a distant home—all these themes being unified by an almost pagan joy in nature and a simple faith in God." (Kunitz, Colby, 1967). PRINCIPAL WORKS: Novels: *Das Marmorbild*, 1819; *Aus dem Leben eines Taugenichts*, 1826. In English: The Marble Statue, trans. F. E. Pierce in *Fiction and*

Fantasy of German Romance, 1927; *Taugenichts*, trans. C. Marvel, 1864, C. G. Leland, 1886, A. L. Wister, 1889, B. Q. Morgan as *Memoirs of a Good-for-Nothing*, 1955. Poetry: *The Happy Wanderer*, trans. M. Rossy, 1925. (SOURCE: Kunitz, Colby, 1967)

ELCHE: a town in the Alicante province of Spain where a mystery play is performed every August 14 and 15. According the documents preserved in Elche, this play was found along with an image of the ★Virgin Mary in an ark that floated to the coast of Spain and was picked up by a coast watcher in 1370. During this famed piece of Spanish religious music, a song, "Ay, trista vida," is chanted by the one playing the part of the Virgin Mary.

ELDORADO: literally, *the gilded one*. Spaniards, reaching America in the sixteenth century, had heard rumors of a mysterious people whose cities were paved and plated with solid gold, and a kingdom ruled by a priest king called El Dorado because his body was covered in powdered gold. This garbled account of the Incas encouraged the conquistadors in their pursuit of wealth. The European explorers of the sixteenth century were driven by two overriding motives: greed and religious zeal. They sought a financial return for the dangers of battle and their voyage. The many casualties that were suffered by the army of Hernando Cortés resulted from soldiers loaded down with booty attempting to cross the swamps surrounding Tenochtitlán. Later the name was applied to any fabulously rich region. (SOURCE: Cotterell, 1986)

SONG	COMPOSER	POET
"El Dorado"	Jack Beeson	Edgar Allen Poe

ELÉGIE (Fr.), ELEGY (Eng.): from the Greek, a term used for a reflective poem, variously used in different periods from the sixteenth century on. Later this term was applied particularly to poems of mourning and later yet to reflective poems called *reveries.* (SOURCE: Drabble, 2000)

SONG	COMPOSER	POET
"Élégie"	Henri Duparc,	Thomas Moore, trans.
	Heitor Berlioz	to French

ELF: a dwarf of Teutonic birth. The elf was possessed of magical powers used for the good or ill of mankind. Later the name was used for a malignant imp, still later for fairy creatures that dance on the grass in the full moon. They have golden hair, sweet voices, and play upon magic harps. Legend has it that ★Eve had to show all her children to God, and those who were not good looking were hidden behind her, becoming the elves, also called "hidden people." (SOURCE: Cooper, 1992)

SONG	COMPOSER	POET
"Elfe"	Charles Griffes	Joseph von Eichendorff

ELIOT, T(HOMAS) S(TEARNS) (1888–1965): English poet, playwright, critic, editor, translator, and essayist. Born in Missouri in 1888, Eliot became a naturalized British citizen in 1927. He was educated at Harvard, a year (1910) at the Sorbonne, and later at Oxford. In England he worked as a schoolteacher, a bank clerk, and an editor for Faber and Faber. After Eliot and Ezra ★Pound met in 1914, their careers were profitably entwined despite periods of estrangement. Eliot was a Lecturer at Cambridge in 1926, the Charles Eliot Norton Professor of Poetry at Harvard (1932), a resident at the Institute for Advanced Study at Princeton (1950), and an Honorary Fellow at Oxford and Cambridge. He was awarded the Nobel Prize for Literature in 1948, made an Officer of the Légion d'Honneur, and given honorary degrees from fifteen American and European universities. In the period between the two world wars, Eliot's influence, together with that of Pound and *Joyce, was predominant in English poetry. His earliest verse was composed of observations that were detached, ironic, and alternately disillusioned and nostalgic. When *The Waste Land* was published in 1922, the first readers found the poem arid and incomprehensible, although in reality it was neither. He expressed himself solely through sense impressions, drawing upon his own social background and the surrounding squalor of an industrial age. After 1922 Eliot wrote little poetry but much critical prose, which writing profoundly affected the literary taste of his generation. In 1928 he declared himself Anglo-Catholic in religion, a royalist in politics, and a classicist in literature. The underlying philosophy of the important *Four Quartets* (1943) was this: there are two elements, temporal and timeless, that need to be woven together in a pattern of experience, the end to which the entire sequence points. Eliot's output was relatively small and extremely concentrated. In later years he devoted himself to writing verse plays, essays, and criticism. His verse has been set by song composers Howard Swanson and Arthur Bliss, among others. *Murder in the Cathedral* became an opera in the hands of Ildebrando Pizzetti, and the Broadway long-running show, *Cats*, was based on *Old Possum's Book of Practical Cats*. PRINCIPAL WORKS: Poetry: *Poems,* 1919; *The Waste Land,* 1922; *Old Possum's Book of Practical Cats,* 1939; *Four Quartets,* 1943. Plays: *Murder in the Cathedral,* 1935; *The Cocktail Party,* 1950. Essays and criticism: *The Use of Poetry and the Use of Criticism,* 1933; *The Idea of a Christian Society,* 1939; *On Poetry and Poets,* 1957. SELECTED READING: George Asher, *Thomas Stearns Eliot and Ideology,* 1995. (SOURCES: Vinson, 1979; Hamilton, 1994)

ÉLUARD, PAUL (pseudonym of Eugène Grindel) (1895–1952): French poet. Paul Éluard was born into modest circumstances, but his father later became a well-to-do estate agent. At the age of sixteen he spent a year in Switzerland recovering from a serious illness. Later, he was gassed in World War I. He began to read *Rimbaud and *Apollinaire and to write poetry, eventually signing the first *Surrealist manifestos. Éluard joined *Picasso in supporting the Republican cause when the Spanish Civil War broke out. In 1942 he joined the clandestine Communist Party and became, with Louis *Aragon, a leading poet of the Resistance. Before 1936 his poetry was based almost exclusively on a theme of man/woman affinity. Éluard used very simple, clear words; his images are unhackneyed but at times overelaborate; his rhythms are never declamatory, but strong and musical. The poetry of Paul Éluard has been set by Georges Auric and Francis Poulenc, to whom Éluard wrote a poem that said, "Francis, I owe it to you that I hear myself." PRINCIPAL WORKS: *Mourir de ne pas mourir,* 1924; *Capitale de la douleur,* 1926, *Capital of Pain,* 1973; *L'Amour la poésie,* 1929; *La Vie immédiate,* 1932; *La Rose publique,* 1934; *Les Yeux fertiles,* 1936; *Poésie et verité,* 1942; *Au rendez-vous allemand,* 1944; *Choix de poèmes 1914–41,* 1946;

Selected Poems, tr. Lloyd Alexander, 1946; *Oeuvres complètes*, 2 vols., 1968. SELECTED READING: M. A. Caws, *The Poetry of Dada and Surrealism*, 1970. (SOURCE: Steinberg, 2, 1973)

ELYSIUM, ELYSIAN FIELDS: the realm of the dead in Greek mythology, where the blessed are happy. The term "Islands of the Blessed" (Elysium) refers to that realm of the dead where the blessed are happy, as opposed to the realm of shadows (★Hades), where neither happiness nor pain is known, and as opposed to ★Tartarus, the land of torment. Elysium was said to be located in the furthest west regions of the world. In seventeenth-century Paris, the Champs Élysées was named for the Elysian Fields. The term "Elysium" is invoked to describe a place of perfect happiness that is the reward in afterlife for virtue or courage shown in earthly life. (SOURCES: Mayerson, 1971; Murray, 1988)

SONG	COMPOSER	POET
1. "Bess o'Bedlam"	Henry Purcell	anonymous
2. "An die Freude"	Franz Schubert	Friedrich von Schiller
3. "Das Rosenband"	Franz Schubert, Richard Strauss	Friedrich Klopstock
4. "Die Schale der Vergessenheit"	Johannes Brahms	Friedrich Hölty
5. "Orpheus"	Franz Schubert	Johann Georg Jacobi
6. "Il tuo sguardo"	Isaac Albéniz	Marquesa de Bolaños
7. "Elysium"	Franz Schubert	Friedrich von Schiller

EMERSON, RALPH WALDO (1803–1882): American poet, essayist, lecturer, translator, man of letters, and minister. Emerson was born in Boston and educated at Harvard, graduating in 1821. Although he worked for a time as a school master, he studied for the ministry and was a pastor from 1829 to 1832. Thereafter, he spent one year traveling in Europe and then returned to the United States, taking up residence in Concord, Massachusetts (1834). A leader of the ★Transcendentalist movement, Emerson was probably the most distinguished of that group and certainly one of the most brilliant American poets and thinkers of the nineteenth century. The importance of the Transcendental mode of ★Romantic thought has today been diminished by modern scientific theory, but even now Emerson's writings remain thought-provoking. Emerson's subjects were drawn from many sources: (1) the religious thought of both New England and seventeenth- and eighteenth-century England; (2) Scottish realism internalized at Harvard; (3) the skepticism of France and England; (4) Neo-Platonism, which was the dominant element in his thinking; (5) Oriental mystical writings; (6) Yankee pragmatism, which diluted his Romantic idealism (Vinson, 1979). When he discovered Coleridge's distinction between Reason and Understanding, his life was transformed. In his essays he stressed the unlimited potential of the individual. He was not against rule by the upper class so long as the upper-class persons were wise, temperate, and cultivated, possessing sufficient insight and courage to protect the poor and weak against the predatory. Further, because Emerson believed that the most a writer can do is to suggest his intuitions by a series of half-truths, the greatest writing must be provocative, not descriptive or explanatory. His prose style, stemming from this conviction, was epigrammatic, and he took liberties with poetic conventions. Emily ★Dickinson and Walt ★Whitman, and through them the modern writers, were influenced by Emerson's concentration on concrete images, by the simplicity of his symbols and words, and by his willingness to let form follow function. His philosophy is still found stirring today. Emerson's poetry was set by Charles Ives and Leslie Bassett. PRINCIPAL WORKS: Poetry: *Poems,* 1847; *May Day and Other Pieces,* 1867; *Complete Works,* 1884. Essays: *Essays: First Series,* 1841; *Second Series,* 1844; *The Conduct of Life,* 1860; *Society and Solitude,* 1870. SELECTED READING: Frederic I. Carpenter, *Emerson Handbook,* 1953; Charles J. Woodbury, *Talks with Emerson,* 1970. (SOURCES: Kunitz, Haycraft, 1938; Unger, 2, 1974; Vinson, 1979)

EMMET, ROBERT (1778–1803): an eloquent Irish patriot and an ardent but misguided partisan of Irish independence. Having put himself at the head of a party of insurgents consisting of the rabble of Dublin, Emmet was arrested at the age of twenty-five and tried for treason, even after delivering a famous impassioned speech in vindication of his actions.

EMPYREAN: in Ptolemaic philosophy, the last of the five heavens, made of pure elemental fire, the seat of the deity; also used in the Christian religion as the abode of God and the angels, for example, by ★Dante in his *Divine Comedy.* (SOURCE: *OED,* 1989)

ENCINA, JUAN DEL (1468?–1529): Spanish poet and dramatist. Encina is often called "the father of Spanish drama," being known for his dramatic pieces called *eglogas* or ★eclogues, which have religious themes. Its characters are usually Spanish peasants, realistically and humorously portrayed, who speak a rustic dialect, *sayagués.* At an early age Encina took minor orders and lived in Rome, after which he wrote three plays that reveal the influence of Italian pastoral poetry and represent an attempt to elevate the drama. ★Villancicos and Christmas carols written by him were often sung at the end of his plays. Robert Schumann set a translation by Emanuel ★Geibel of Encina's poem "Ojos garços ha la niña" in his op. 138, no. 9, called "Blaue Augen hat das Mädchen." (SOURCE: Cockburn, Stokes, 1992)

ENCOMIUM: a Greek choral song in celebration not of a god but of a hero, sung at the komos, a jubilant procession that celebrated the victor in the games.

ENDYMION: a beautiful shepherd boy of Asia Minor, beloved of the moon goddess ★Selene, who put him into a deep sleep so that she could embrace him continually. She took care that his fortunes should not suffer by his inactive life. She made his flock increase and guarded his sheep and lambs from wild beasts. Endymion represents the poetic one whose life is spent in dreams rather than reality. (SOURCE: Kaster, 1964)

ENGELHARDT, KARL AUGUST (1768–1834): German poet, novelist, and critic from Dresden. Engelhardt's pseudonym was Richard Roos. "Ihr Grab," his poem that was set by Franz Schubert, was published in *The Pocket-Book of Sociable Pleasures* (1822). (SOURCE: Reed, 1997)

ENOCH ARDEN: a narrative poem by Alfred, Lord ★Tennyson. Enoch, a fisherman, marries his childhood playmate Annie and has seven happy years of marriage with her. When he is injured, their happiness ends. Having sold his fishing boat to support his wife and three children, he sails away on a merchant ship only to be shipwrecked on a desert island where he worries constantly about his family. Years later, when he returns, he learns that Annie is remarried to a friend of his, Philip Ray, but does not reveal his identity until he is about to die. Richard Strauss set *Enoch Arden* as a ★melodrama.

EPHRAIM, MOUNT: a hymn tune by B. Milgrone (1731–1810).

SONG	COMPOSER	POET
"The Choirmaster's Burial"	Benjamin Britten	Thomas Hardy

EPICEDIUM: any work pertaining to funeral rites, or, a funeral.

ÉPIFANIE (Fr.): *see* ★EPIPHANY.

EPIGRAM (Eng.), EPIGRAMMA (Sp.), EPIGRAMME (Fr.): a short poem ending in an ingenious turn of thought, to which the rest of the composition is intended to lead up; or any writing achieving its point in a very brief space, in a strict verse pattern, with wit, or irony, for example, "Crying is the refuge of plain women, but the ruin of pretty ones." Coleridge defined it thus, epigrammatically: "What is an Epigram? a dwarfed whole / Its body brevity, and wit its soul." (SOURCE: Drabble, 2000)

SONG	COMPOSER	POET
1. "Epigram"	Benjamin Britten	Alexandr Pushkin
2. "Epigrammas ironicos e sentimentaës"	Heitor Villa-Lobos	Portuguese and Brazilian poets
3. "Epigram"	Jack Beeson	Francis Quarles
4. "Epigrams from Robert Burns"	Miriam Gideon	Robert Burns

EPILOGUE: the final part of a work of literature, completing it, as opposed to the preface that introduces it; after a play, a speech, usually in verse, addressed by an actor to the audience, the opposite of a prologue; in music, the final section of a composition.

EPIPALINODIE, PALINODIE: an ancient poetic form in which the author contradicts a previous poem. (SOURCE: Kimball, 1996)

SONG	COMPOSER	POET
"Epipalinodie"	Jacques Leguerney	Pierre de Ronsard

EPIPHANY: the Christian festival commemorating the showing of the infant ★Jesus to the ★Magi, usually celebrated on January 6; also, the appearance of a superhuman being. Traditionally, it was one of the important feasts of the Church, ranking only after Easter and Pentecost. In the Eastern Church it is believed that the Feast of Epiphany commemorates the date of the baptism of ★Christ. The Feast of Christmas was not added as an important feast until the fourth century, to supplant a pagan festival. Even in the Western liturgy, the Epiphany was of higher rank than Christmas until 1955. In the Eastern Church the feast has a broad concept commemorating the birth, the baptism (Christ's manifestation to the world), and the beginning of his public life. In the Western Church the emphasis is on Christ's revelation to the Gentiles, symbolized by the story of the *Magi. The Berio work is composed of seven short orchestral pieces and five vocal pieces that can be performed in ten different sequences, each combination appearing in a different light according to its position in the instrumental development. The Wolf piece was written for his friend Melanie Kochert as a special tribute at the time of her birthday, January 6, to be sung by her children dressed as the three Magi.

SONG	COMPOSER	POET
1. Epiphanias"	Hugo Wolf	Johann Wolfgang von Goethe
2. "Epifanie"	Luciano Berio	Marcel Proust, Bertolt Brecht, A. Machado, James Joyce, C. Simon, E. Sanguinetti

EPITAPH: a commemorative inscription on a tomb about the person buried at that site; a brief composition in praise of a deceased person.

SONG	COMPOSER	POET
1. "Epitaph"	David Diamond	Herman Melville
2. "The Epitaph"	David Diamond	Logan Pearsall Smith
3. "Eight Epitaphs"	Theodore Chanler	Walter de la Mare
4. "Epitaph of Timas"	Lennox Berkeley	Sappho
5. "Epitaph for a Poet"	Robert Fairfax Birch	Robert Nathan
6. "Epitaph on a Wife"	Richard Hundley	anonymous
7. "Épitaphe"	Francis Poulenc	François de Malherbe
8. "Epitaph"	Ned Rorem	anonymous, fifteenth century
9. "Epitaph"	Ned Rorem	Robert Herrick
10. "Another Epitaph"	Ned Rorem	Robert Herrick
11. "Epitaph on a Talkative Old Maid"	Ross Lee Finney	Benjamin Franklin
12. "Epitaph for a Wag in Mauchline"	Miriam Gideon	Robert Burns
13. "Epitaph for a Wee Johnnie"	Miriam Gideon	Robert Burns
14. "Epitaph on the Author"	Miriam Gideon	Robert Burns
15. "An Epitaph"	John Koch	Walter de la Mare
16. "The Astronomer: An Epitaph"	Richard Hundley	gravestone inscription
17. "Épitaphe"	Ildebrando Pizzetti	Victor Hugo

EPITHALAMIUM: a nuptial song or poem sung as a chorus by young men and women in honor and praise of a bride and bridegroom before the bridal chamber. This kind of writing was practiced by Latin poets. Its characteristics included an invocation to the *Muses, the bringing home of the bride, singing and dancing at the wedding party, and preparation for the wedding night. The *Fairie-Queene*, written by Elkanah *Settle, ends with a grand epithalamium, of which the song "Hark! Hark! the Ech'ing Air" is a part. (SOURCES: Kimball, 1996; Steinberg, 1, 1973)

SONG	COMPOSER	POET
1. "Hark! Hark! the Ech'ing Air"	Henry Purcell	Elkanah Settle
2. "Thrice Happy Lovers"	Henry Purcell	Elkanah Settle

EREBUS: in ancient Greek cosmology, the personification of primeval darkness. Erebus, son of *Chaos, was born together with his brother Nox (Night) from primordial chaos. In a later period Erebus was a dark region beneath the earth through which the shades were forced to pass to the realms of *Hades below. It is often used metaphorically for *Hades itself. (SOURCE: Kaster, 1964)

ERIS: the Greek goddess of discord and strife. Eris was the sister of *Ares and accompanied his group when in battle. It was Eris who threw the apple of discord into the midst of the assembled guests at the wedding of Peleus and Thetis. This act ultimately brought about the Trojan War. (SOURCE: Kaster, 1964)

SONG	COMPOSER	POET
"Warte, warte wilde Schiffsman"	Robert Schumann	Heinrich Heine

ERLAFSEE: a lake near Mariazell. Schubert's first published song, verse by Johann *Mayrhofer, it appeared (1818) as a supplement to Sartori's annual *Picturesque Album for Admirers of the most Interesting Sites and Most Noteworthy Works of Nature and of Art in the Austrian Monarchy.*

ERLKÖNIG (Ger.), ELFKING (Eng.): the king of the alders (a mistranslation of the Danish *ellerkonge*, king of the elves) or a malevolent goblin of the Black Forest, who lured people, especially children, to destruction. Previous to *Goethe's famous *ballad, goblins had never been a part of German folklore.

SONG	COMPOSER	POET
"Der Erlkönig"	Franz Schubert, Carl Loewe, Louis Spohr	Johann Wolfgang von Goethe

ERMIN: *see* *JOHANN KUMPF.

EROS: *see* *CUPID.

ERST: (Scot.), *once.*

ERYNNYS: one of the underworld *Furies who punish evildoers (plural: Erynnyes; in Greek: Eumenides). The names of these avenging spirits, when the number had been fixed as three, were *Alecto, Megaera, and *Tisiphone. Their task was to punish crimes not within the reach of human justice. Among those crimes were the killing of a family member by another from that family, blasphemy against the gods, and treachery to a host or guest. After the time when they intervened in the case of ★Orestes, the tradition had developed that their functions no longer covered cases of guiltiness that was free from moral guilt. In spite of their sternness, they wept when they heard ★Orpheus implore the underworld deities to restore ★Euridice to life. (SOURCE: *Bulfinch*, 1978)

SONG	COMPOSER	POET
1. "A Charm"	Benjamin Britten	Thomas Randolph
2. "Orest auf Tauris"	Franz Schubert	Johann Mayrhofer

ESENIN (YESENIN), SERGEI (1895–1925): a Russian poet. Esenin was one of the most controversial of all Soviet poets, even during the twenty-five years in which his work was suppressed and his character defamed. After this period (early 1950s) he became among the most popular of all Russian poets, his five-volume edition of works, *Sobranie sochinenii*, always selling out soon after publication. When his grandparents took their grandson in to live with them, they left an indelible impression on Esenin because of their interest in religious poems and folk songs, contributing to the ease with which the young man wrote poetry. At the age of sixteen Esenin decided not to continue his studies as a teacher and moved to St. Petersburg where the foremost Russian writers then lived. His first book was published with the help of Aleksandr ★Blok, who took him under his wing. After a stint in the army, Esenin founded a literary movement Imaginism, inspired by the ★Imagist movement of Ezra ★Pound, in which the image was the crucial component of poetry. An immediate mutual attraction between him and the dancer Isadora Duncan inspired his second marriage, a move to the United States, and a subsequent return to Russia, where Esenin was critical of the new order and unable to accept it. Blaming himself for personal failure and plagued by depression, he styled himself a hooligan, thus excusing himself for his drinking, barroom brawls, blasphemous verse, and all-night orgies. Depression caused him to hang himself on a radiator pipe of his hotel room. At his best, his poetry was a blend of deep lyricism, sincerity, melancholy, and nostalgia, longing for a rural utopia, and using folk and religious motifs, images of nature, scenes from everyday life. Esenin's verse was set by Russian composer Nechaev. PRINCIPAL WORKS: *Radunitsa,* 1915; *Goluben,* 1918; *Isproved' khuligana,* 1921, *Confessions of a Hooligan,* 1973; *All Souls' Day,* 1991; *Azure,* 1991; SELECTED READING: Gordon McVay, *Esenin: A Life,* 1976. (SOURCE: Magill, 2, 1984)

ESPRONCEDA, JOSÉ DE (1808–1842): Spanish poet. A disciple of ★Byron, Espronceda was a swaggering, adventurous revolutionary. He fought for the liberal cause in Holland (1828) and on the Paris barricades (1830). He returned to Spain in 1833, but was soon exiled because of his radical journalism. A born poet as well, his many activities were only one part of a fiery, gallant, impudent but deeply emotional nature, which he expressed more vividly than his fellow poets. The rebellious themes and motifs of Espronceda's poetry were defined by his unbounded love for freedom and spontaneity. He is remembered mostly for his patriotic poems calling for freedom. The verses of José de Espronceda were set by Joaquìn Turina. (SOURCE: Cockburn, Stokes, 1992)

ESTAMPIE: a Medieval dance song regarded as a difficult type of melody, because of which it is reputed to take command of the heart.

ESTREBILLO: a line or lines repeated as a refrain in Spanish lyrics and ballads.

ETNA: in Greek mythology, the name of a rock mass under which ★Zeus buried the fire-eating monster Typhon. It smoked and burned continually and was thought to be the workshop of Vulcan and the One-Eyed ★Cyclops. Mount Etna is one of the most famous volcanoes in the world, rising to 10, 868 feet on the east coast of Sicily. Part of its base, 100 miles around, lies in the Mediterranean Sea; the other part holds orange groves. The peaks are snow-covered; its slopes, containing forests, orchards, and vineyards, constitute the most thickly populated area of Sicily. (SOURCE: Kasper, 1964)

SONG	COMPOSER	POET
1. "Let the Dreadful Engines"	Henry Purcell	Thomas D'Urfey
2. "Mit Myrten und Rosen"	Robert Schumann	Heinrich Heine

EUGENE, PRINCE; PRINZ EUGEN (Ger.): a celebrated general, (1663–1736). His services having been refused by the king of France, the prince offered them to the emperor of Austria, who accepted them. Prince Eugene was a general-major in several campaigns against the Turks and the French. His success was due not so much to his skills in strategy as it was to his audacity and sharp decisions. The Loewe song has to do with army life and the activities within the Austrian camp between battles. Some of ★Freiligrath's German terms are specialized army vocabulary, for example: *Werdarufer* are sentries or guards; *Tschackos* is a German spelling for the British military cap in the shape of a truncated cone with visor and plume, that is, a *shako*; a *Kornet* is an officer of a cavalry troop who carries the colors; *Schecken* denotes a checked or dappled horse; *Knöchel* are literally knuckles or bones, meaning dice; a *Marketenderin* is a canteen woman, a troop follower. (SOURCE: *Americana*, 2003)

SONG	COMPOSER	POET
"Prinz Eugen, der edle Ritter"	Carl Loewe	Ferdinand Freiligrath

EUPHONIUM: a tenor tuba with a larger bore, a mellower quality, and usually a double bell.

SONG	COMPOSER	POET
"Euphonium Dance"	Betty Roe	Jacqueline Froom

EUPHRATES: the largest river in western Asia, beginning in east central Turkey. The Euphrates flows south to Syria, then southeast through Syria and Iraq, ending above Basra, where it joins the Tigris to form Shatt al-Arab. The Euphrates is 2,100 miles long. Forty percent of the river basin is in Turkey, fifteen percent in Syria, and the remainder in Iraq. The alluvial plain of the Euphrates forms part of the ancient civilization of Mesopotamia, the site of the ancient states of Sumeria, Babylonia, and Assyria.

SONG	COMPOSER	POET
"May the Tigris and Euphrates"	George Rochberg	Ancient Sumerian texts

EURIPIDES (ca.485 B.C.E. **– 406** B.C.E.**):** the last of the three great ★Attic dramatists. Euripides introduced to the theater heroes who were of common blood, women without virtue, and settings that were lowly, even though Euripides was not of lowly birth and not unhappy in his marriages. For this he was said to have debased the contemporary tragedy, but Euripides was simply interested in current politics and the social problems of his day. Of his ninety-two plays, the surviving nineteen were written in his middle and late years. Remaining within the traditional format, Euripides made changes of manner and substance: his *dramatis personae* were not typical; their language and grammar were not formal and grand; the plots were replete with intrigue. With Euripides's treatment, Greek tragedy changed from timeless to immediate. Yet, as a poet, Euripides saw and included in his writing the beauty and worth of life. The verse of Euripides's *Andromache* was set by Samuel Barber. EXTANT WORKS, in English translation: *Alcestis,* 1781; *The Children of Heracles,* 1781; *Hippolytus,* 1781; *Andromache,* 1782; *Hecuba,* 1782; *The Suppliants,* 1781; *Heracles,* 1781; *The Trojan Women,* 1782; *Iphigenia in Tauris,* 1782; *Electra,* 1782; *Helen,* 1782; *Ion,* 1781; *The Phoenician Women,* 1781; *Orestes,* 1782; *The Bacchae,* 1781; *Iphigenia in Aulis,* 1782. SELECTED READING: G. M. A. Grube, *The Drama of Euripides,* 1941. (SOURCE: *Americana,* 2003)

EURYDICE, EURIDICE (It.): a wood ★nymph, the wife of ★Orpheus, legendary Greek poet and hero. Son of ★Apollo and the muse ★Calliope, Orpheus was a great musician. His playing and singing moved not only animals and plants, but even rocks and the elements. One day his wife Eurydice stepped on a snake whose poisoned bite killed her. Overwhelmed with grief, Orpheus descended to the underworld, where his beautiful singing persuaded ★Hades, the god of death, to let Eurydice return, the condition being that Orpheus walk back to the land of the living without looking behind him at Eurydice. Overcome with anticipation, Orpheus looked over his shoulder at Eurydice, and she disappeared again. One of the most popular Greek myths, Orpheus and Eurydice has served Jacopo Peri, Claudio Monteverdi, and Christoph Gluck as a subject for their operas. (SOURCES: *Bulfinch,* 1978; Benét, 1, 1965; Mayerson, 1971)

SONG	COMPOSER	POET
"Die Schale der Vergessenheit"	Johannes Brahms	Ludwig Hölty

EVE: in the Bible, the first woman.

SONG	COMPOSER	POET
1. "Warte, wilde Schiffsman"	Robert Schumann	Heinrich Heine
2. "Songs for Eve"	Ezra Laderman	Archibald MacLeish

EVERYMAN: the most famous morality play. When Everyman received a summons from Death, he tried vainly to persuade his friends, Fellowship, Kindred, Worldly Goods, Beauty, and others to journey with him. Only Good Deed remains faithful. Hugo von ★Hofmannsthal put the story into German verse as *Jedermann* (1911), and Swiss composer Frank Martin wrote "Everyman."

EXISTENTIALISM: a name commonly given to a group of loosely associated philosophical doctrines and ideas of such men as ★Kierkegaard, ★Sartre, Heidegger, and Camus. Because their theories diverge in many important respects, there is not an actual philosophical "school" of existential writers. The themes that are characteristic are: emphasizing the unique in human experience; stressing the essential individuality of persons; abjuring a set of general laws or principles to which human beings conform; character or deeds are not predetermined by factors beyond man's control. (SOURCE: Drabble, 2000)

EXPOSTULATION: a speech of remonstrance or dissuasion, that reasons earnestly with someone in an attempt to dissuade or correct.

SONG	COMPOSER	POET
"The Blessed Virgin's Expostulation"	Henry Purcell	Nahum Tate

EXPRESSIONISM: a movement of the early twentieth century (1908–23) that commenced in art, then moved to literature, finally to the theater and cinema. Expressionism in poetry and music was characterized by fearlessness, distortion of word accents, and an emphasis on deep emotions. The earliest individuals to adopt expressionism were led by Schönberg, before serialism, in music; Kandinsky, Kokoschka, Klee, and Marc in art; Richard ★Dehmel and Stefan ★George in poetry; and Strindberg and early ★Brecht in the theater, all flourishing mainly in Germany. (SOURCE: Drabble, 2000)

F ✑

FA: (Scot.), *fall.*

FABLEAU: although opinion is sharply divided as to the origin of the *fableau*, there are two possibilities: a form of Medieval poetry dealing with stories of animals with some humorous insights into human character; or, a short story in verse relating a comic or bawdy incident from middle-class life.

FAGNES: a dialect word for peaty uplands in the European north, with heath, peat bogs, gnarled trees twisted by the wind. The fagnes of Wallonie are a high plateau in the Belgian Ardennes, where ★Apollinaire passed his holidays in 1899.

SONG	COMPOSER	POET
"Fagnes de Wallonie"	Francis Poulenc	Guillaume Apollinaire

FAHRENDEN GESELLEN, LIEDER EINER: a song cycle composed by Gustav Mahler. In 1884 at the age of twenty-four Mahler had fallen deeply in love but had been rejected. He abandoned himself to writing the verses of *Lieder einer Fahrenden Gesellen*, for which he borrowed only the first few lines from the first song in the folk-poetry collection, *Des *Knaben Wunderhorn*. Believing himself to be primarily a symphonist, he arranged the songs in a somewhat more elaborate form than was usual for Lieder. Although the cycle is usually sung by women today, the true emotions are masculine throughout.

FAIN: *with pleasure.*

"Fairest Isle": a song composed by Henry Purcell to a text by John *Dryden in their semi-opera *King Arthur*, produced in 1691. *See *King Arthur* for plot details and placement of songs.

FAIRIE-QUEENE, THE: a 1692 and 1693 adaptation of *Shakespeare's *Midsummer Night's Dream*, expanded to operatic proportions by means of five masques composed by Henry Purcell. The identity of the adaptor (*Dryden, *Settle, or Betterton) is in doubt, but Elkanah Settle is generally credited. The adaptation dispensed with most of Shakespeare's lyrics and concentrated the new music into four masques in 1692 and five in 1693. The cast was divided into actors and singers, and the incidental songs were set for non-speaking professional singers. It is difficult to weave together the pieces of the drama because the singing and speaking parts are segregated and the main musical entertainments do not advance the plot.

In act 1, "Come, Let Us Leave the Town," a duet for soprano and bass, urges that the urban hideaway be abandoned. A drunken poet enters, and Titania's fairies tease him until he admits to being a contemptible fellow.

In act 2, Titania, preparing for bed, requests an entertainment before sleeping. With the beginning of the masque, the scene is transformed into flowery grottos and bird sounds. A trio (ATB) singing "May the God of Wit Inspire" lulls Titania to sleep. With "Come, Ye Songsters," the fairies ask the birds to join in. Night, a soprano, sings "See, Even Night Herself Is Here." "One Charming Night" is a countertenor air sung by Secrecy. Sleep sings a bass aria, "Hush, No More, Be Silent All." Titania slumbers, but her dream begins with a dance for the followers of the Night.

In act 3, Titania's worship of Bottom begins in the dream. A soprano air, "If Love's a Sweet Passion," is a compliment to Titania's infatuation. In "Away, My Elves," Titania demands that this place be turned into an enchanted lake and that an entertainment be given for Bottom. Two swans gliding on the river turn themselves into fairies and dance. Four savages dance grotesquely, frightening away the fairies. "Ye Gentle Spirits of the Air," one of Purcell's few *da capo* arias, is sung by a soprano. "When I Have Often Heard," another soprano aria, follows. The final piece in the masque is a countertenor air, "A Thousand, Thousand Ways."

In act 4, Masque of the Seasons, "Now the Night is chas'd away," a soprano air, begins the chasing away of Night and Winter in its set of garden fountains and marble columns. Phoebus, a tenor, enters and sings "When a Cruel Long Winter Has Frozen the Earth," followed by a soprano aria, "Thus the Ever Grateful Spring."

A character without guile sings a countertenor air, "Here's the Summer, Sprightly, Gay." At the end, Autumn, a tenor, sings one of two minor key arias: "See My Many Colored Fields," and Winter, a bass, sings "Next Winter Comes Slowly."

In act 5, Juno appears in a peacock-drawn chariot and sings "Thrice Happy Lovers," cautioning lovers not to let jealousy invade their happiness. ★Oberon and Titania are reconciled. Oberon asks to hear "O Let Me Weep," which is a dramatically unmotivated song, probably inserted for a favorite singer. The masque: Oberon calls for a rehearsal of dreams passing into consciousness. The scene changes to a Chinese garden, where a Chinese man appears, singing a trumpeting song, "Thus the Gloomy World." Two songs, "Hark How All Things" and "Hark, the Ech'ing Air," followed by a chaconne for the Chinese man and woman, "Turn Then Thy Eyes," end the masque. Hymen enters and ignites a torch, ending the semi-opera with spoken words. (SOURCE: Price, 1984)

FAIRIES: one of a class of supernatural beings, generally conceived as having a diminutive human form, possessing magical powers, being fond of pranks, but pleasing. Some of the most popular forms of these beings are:

Banshie: an Irish fairy attached to a house.

Boggart: a Scottish hobgoblin or spirit.

Bogie: bugbear, Scottish form of bug.

Brownie: a Scottish domestic fairy, a servant friend if well treated.

Djinn: an Arabian fairy.

Duende: a Spanish house spirit.

Dwarf: a diminutive being, human or superhuman.

Elf: a small fairy, fond of practical jokes.

Elle-maid: a Scandinavian fairy.

Esprit-follet: a French house spirit

Familiar: an evil spirit attendant on witches.

Fata: an Italian fairy.

Fay: same as fairy.

Genii: good or bad eastern spirit.

Ghoni: a demon that feeds on the dead.

Ghost: the immaterial body of a human being, which is free to visit the earth at night.

Gnome: a guardian of mines, quarries, and so on.

Goblin: an evil or mischievous spirit.

Good folk: the brownies or house spirits.

Hag: a female fury.

Hamadryad: a wood nymph who dies when her tree dies.

Hob-goblin: hob is an old form of Rob, for Robin Goodfellow, an elf of English literature.

Imp: a puny demon or spirit of mischief.

Jack-a-Lantern: a marsh spirit, who likes to mislead.

Kelpie: an imaginary Scottish spirit of the water, formed like a horse.

Lamie: an African specter with the head of a woman and the tail of a serpent.

Leprechaun: an Irish fairy shoemaker.

Mab: the fairies' midwife, sometimes incorrectly called queen of the fairies.

Mermaid: a sea spirit whose upper part is that of a woman and lower, a fish.

Naiad: a water nymph.

Nix: a water spirit.

Ogre: an inhabitant of fairyland, said to feed on children.

Orend: a mountain nymph.

Pixy: a Devonshire fairy.

Shade: a ghost.

Stromkarl: a Norwegian music spirit.

Sylph: a spirit of the air.

Troll: a Norwegian hill spirit.

Undine: a water nymph.

Vampire: a spirit of a dead man that haunts a house and feeds on the blood of the living.

Will-o-the-wisp: a spirit of the bogs, whose delight is to mislead travelers.

Wraith: a ghost that appears to the survivors of a person about to die or recently dead.

FANFAN: (It. slang), *windbag*. (SOURCE: Lakeway, White, 1989)

SONG	COMPOSER	POET
"Keepsake"	Goffredo Petrassi	Eugenio Montale

FANTAISISTES, LES: a group of French poets who aimed for lighter, more tender, sometimes mocking poetry that would "flower the route where human grief passed" (M. Rat). The Fantaisistes came together about 1911 and included the poets Tristan ★Klingsor, Francis Carco, Jean-Marc ★Bernard, Tristan Dérème, and Jean Pellerin. (SOURCE: France, 1995)

FARANDOLA: an ancient dance in 6/8 time.

SONG	COMPOSER	POET
"La ausencia"	Roberto Gerhard	anonymous

FAREWELL TO ST. PETERSBURG, A: a cycle of twelve romances by Glinka with texts by Nestor V. ★Kukolnik. The songs are: "Romance from David ★Rizzio," "Hebrew Song," "Bolero," "Cavatina," "Cradle Song," "Traveling Song," "Fantasia," "★Barcarolle," "Virtus Antiqua," "The Lark," "To Molly," and "Song of Farewell," the piece that Glinka performed at a party his friends gave him before he left St. Petersburg.

FARGUE, LÉON-PAUL (1876–1947): French poet and columnist. Even as an adolescent, Fargue had close friends in the arts, which at that time were dominated by ★Symbolism and ★Impressionism. Due to a wealthy middle-class background, he enjoyed financial independence. Idiosyncratic, chronically late, and absent-minded, Fargue knew Paris so well that he was called "the Paris Stroller." On Fargue's list of favorite things were deer, the washing of Parisian streets, ears, kittens, frogs, and taxi-riding. At one time, Archibald ★MacLeish was dispatched to Paris to interview

Fargue for a biography, but could never manage to meet with him because the poet always arrived late to their appointments or forgot them. MacLeish went back to the United States without writing the book. A true Bohemian, concerned with the reality of a dream world, Fargue imbued his poetry with fantastic visions, dazzling creativity in words, and inventive images. The poetry of Léon-Paul Fargue was set by Erik Satie. WORKS: *Poèmes,* 1912, 1919, 1931, 1944, 1947; *Banalité,* 1928; *Vulturne,* 1928; *Haute solitude,* 1941; *Portraits de famille,* 1947. SELECTED READING: A. Beucler, *The Last of the Bohemians: Twenty Years with Léon-Paul Fargue,* 1954. (SOURCE: Steinberg, 2, 1973)

FARRUCA: a Spanish flamenco dance danced by gypsies in Triana. It has not only Galician roots but some Celtic undertones. Originally the theme derived from the Galician muñeira, the dance of the miller's wife. (SOURCE: Cockburn, Stokes, 1992)

SONG	COMPOSER	POET
"Farruca"	Joaquín Turina	Ramón de Campoamor

FASHED: (Scot.), *troubled.*

FATAL MARRIAGE, THE; OR, THE INNOCENT ADULTERY: a play by Thomas ★Southerne, produced in 1694, with one song by Henry Purcell. The play, one of the best plays of the period, was a domestic tragedy set in seventeenth-century Brussels. For this play Purcell wrote an ironic ★epithalamium. The plot was taken from a novel by Aphra Behn, an author of sentimental tales. Without knowledge of the plot, Purcell's music could easily be misinterpreted. Isabella, a former nun, a woman of low station, is married to Biron who is missing for years, supposedly killed in battle. Isabella, destitute and supporting a child, mourns her husband and rejects the advances of honest Villeroy, who wants to marry the "widow." Her father-in-law, wealthy Count Baldwin, refuses to remedy her poverty. The brother-in-law Carlos, a wolf in shepherd's clothing, knows that Biron is alive but in captivity. If Biron should buy freedom and return to Brussels, Carlos plans to murder him for the inheritance, but wants to see Isabella safely married and out of the family. Isabella is left with no choice but to marry Villeroy. The principal and subplots are parallel tales. Characters from both plots mingle in the wedding celebration. Isabella sings "I Sigh'd and Own'd My Love." The song is a long lyric of ecstatic love that turns sour. Aspirated off-beat sighs of the opening reveal Villeroy's emotions. The clash in bar 7 (F# and F) is "perhaps intended to reflect the underlying irony of the celebration" (Price, 1984). Purcell's song is both a "bitter harbinger of Isabella's fate and a soft engaging air" (Price, 1984). Biron returns, not knowing that Isabella participated in an innocent adultery the night before. Isabella's agony ends in madness and suicide. Biron discovers Carlos's treachery but is killed by him. Count Baldwin repents. (SOURCE: Price, 1984)

FATES, PARZEN (Ger.): the three Greek goddesses who controlled the birth, life, and death of all human beings. They were described as cruel because they paid no regard to the wishes of anyone. Clotho was the Spinner of the thread of life. Lachesis was the Disposer, who determines its length and course. Atropos was the Inflexible, who cuts it off. Three composers, Wolfgang Fortner, Paul Hindemith, and Hermann Reutter, set Friedrich Hölderlin's poem "An die Parzen," in which the Fates are the protagonists. (SOURCES: Kaster, 1964; Cooper, 1992)

FAUNE, LE: a pivotal song from the *Fêtes galantes* cycle written by Claude Debussy to poems of Paul ★Verlaine. The terra cotta statue of a faun is playing his traditional pipe. The *tambourin* is a small drum attached to the waist and played with a stick, seemingly imitated by the unrelenting rhythm in the left hand of the piano. In a recording with soprano Maggie Teyte, the pianist Alfred Cortot succeeds in translating the ostinato B flat and F to the sound of a small drum or tapping hooves.

FAUST: a legendary figure, the subject of many literary works; a verse tragedy by Johann Wolfgang von ★Goethe, published in two parts, *Der Tragödie erster Teil* (1808) and *Der Tragödie zweiter Teil* (1832). Before Goethe, before Marlowe, and before the numerous legends, there was a real Dr. Faust, a shadowy figure who was first mentioned in 1507 by his contemporaries. Records at the University of Heidelberg document his matriculation as a student of theology, and many contemporary accounts of the real Faust exist: "That he was widely known, fairly well educated, and extensively traveled; that he had pretty generally an evil reputation; that he was a braggart, a vagabond, and something of a mountebank; that his contemporaries had a great contempt for him not unmixed with fear, all this may be inferred from the extant documents without too much stretching of the imagination" (Palmer, Moore, 1936). A braggart he certainly was. He claimed the ability to duplicate the miracles of ★Christ (which he deemed inferior stuff). If all the works of ★Plato and Aristotle were somehow destroyed, he bragged, he would be able to restore them from memory (plus a few of his own improvements). The successful campaigns in Italy by imperial troops from 1525 to 1527 should be credited to him, said Faust.

The legend of Faust seems to have started even before his death. Contemporary accounts of his feats of magic and his dealings with the Devil abound. Alongside the tales of diabolical dealings were stories about Faust's inability to repent and beg for God's mercy. As a true tragic hero, Faust was unable to renounce the Devil. In one story Faust tells a monk that the Devil has been faithful to him for many years. To seek the mercy of God would be to become unfaithful to the Devil; this he could not bring himself to do. All such legends were extremely popular in Germany. In September 1587 the printer Johann Spies published *Historia von Dr. Johann Fausten*. This book enjoyed great popularity throughout Europe, and by 1592 Spies had produced over a dozen printings of his work. This book and others of its ilk traveled all across Europe to Great Britain. There Spies's Faust book, *The Historie of the Damnable Life, and Deserved Death, of Doctor John Faustus*, appeared in a 1588 translation by a certain P.F., self-described as a "gentleman." When Christopher Marlowe wrote his greatest work, *The Tragical History of the Life and Death of Doctor Faustus* (ca.1589), he was influenced by this translation. Marlowe's *Faustus* traveled back to Germany with groups of English actors, who introduced his play and those of William ★Shakespeare to the German public with great success. The actors performed in English, but the part of ★Mephistopheles was played in German. These roles were taken by the company's clowns, and Marlowe's tragedy was played for laughs as a comedy. This interpretation of *Faust*, in turn, influenced what are called the Faust puppet plays, which emphasized comedy and the most violent aspects of Faust's death. These puppet plays and Marlowe's works were certainly known to Johann Wolfgang von Goethe (1749–1832), whose *Faust* is the pinnacle of those works dealing with the life of the "bad" doctor. Goethe published Part I of his *Faust* in 1808, then worked on Part II while continuing to revise Part I until just before his death in 1832. As a work of art, Goethe's *Faust* has suffered the fate of many of the "great books" of the world. It has been more praised than read. Yet, this remarkable play has had a staggering influence on literature and music. The legend of Faust lives on today in such varied works as *The Devil and Daniel Webster* and *Damn Yankees*. Thomas Mann wrote his own version of the legend, *Doctor Faustus: The Life of the German Composer Adrian Leverkuhn as Told by a Friend* (1947). As for music, songs from *Faust* were set by Beethoven, Schubert, Schumann, Wagner, Wolf, and, in translation, Mussorgsky, Glinka, Berlioz, and Verdi, to name a few. Wagner wrote a *Faust Symphony* as did his father-in-law Franz Liszt, though Liszt's inspiration for the symphonies and the *Mephisto Waltz* came from Nikolaus ★Lenau's version of the legends. More tribute to the living legend of the Doctor who, bored with life, sells his soul to the Devil, were made in operas by Louis Spohr, Arrigo Boito, Hector Berlioz, Ferruccio Busoni, and Charles Gounod, whose *Faust* remains one of the most popular operas ever written. The real story, as told by Goethe, follows.

PART I

PROLOGUE IN HEAVEN

In a prologue, Mephistopheles speaks with God, who is attended by the Archangels. Mephistopheles finds the Earth a pitiful planet and man a puny "god" of that world. God points out his servant Faust, whom Mephistopheles finds amusing. He requests permission to tempt Faust. God, affirming his confidence in Faust's steadfastness, consents.

NIGHT

The scene entitled Night introduces us to Faust. Disconsolate, Faust begins to attempt suicide, but church bells and the singing of people on Easter Sunday stop him. Faust, returning to his study, has been followed by a poodle who is Mephistopheles in disguise. Mephistopheles appears and strikes up a bargain with Faust: as long as Faust continues to strive, the demon will serve him; if he ever stops striving, Mephistopheles will claim his soul forever.

AUERBACH'S CELLAR IN LEIPZIG

Faust observes Mephistopheles playing pranks on students at a drinking party. Brander sings "Es war eine Ratt im Kellernest," a tale about a rat. Here Mephistopheles sings "The Song of the Flea" ("Es war einmal ein König") for the amusement of the students.

WITCH'S KITCHEN

Faust is rejuvenated by a witch's potion.

A STREET

Faust first sees Gretchen. His immediate reaction is lust, but her innocence softens his attitude toward her.

EVENING

Mephistopheles leaves Faust in Gretchen's room and hides a casket of jewels for her to find. While preparing for bed, she sings "The King of Thule." Then, to her great surprise, she finds the jewels.

FOREST AND CAVERN

Faust interrupts the courtship to contemplate nature in the wilderness.

GRETCHEN'S ROOM

On his return, Mephistopheles prepares a sleeping potion to seduce Gretchen. Gretchen gives it to her mother. However, the potion is really poison, and her mother dies. In her room, Gretchen sings of her passion for Faust, "Meine Ruh ist hin." She becomes pregnant and despairs.

THE RAMPARTS

At the shrine of the Mater Dolorosa, Gretchen prays to the Virgin Mary, "Gretchen's Bitte." Her torment continues when her brother Valentine is killed by Faust in a duel.

CATHEDRAL

In the cathedral, Gretchen is denied the solace of prayer as she is plagued by Mephistopheles. Pregnant, alone, rejected—she swoons. (This scene inspired *Szene aus Faust*, a duet with chorus by Franz Schubert.)

WALPURGIS NIGHT

A year following Valentine's death, we meet Faust reveling at the festival of witches and spirits on the Brocken mountains. Here Faust is brought to the lowest state of sensuality. He sees a vision of Gretchen's execution but is diverted by Mephistopheles with *Walpurgis Night's Dream* or *Oberon and Titania's Golden Wedding Intermezzo*.

NIGHT IN AN OPEN FIELD

Mephistopheles and Faust race past the gallows to rescue Gretchen, who has been sentenced to death for the murder of the child she had with Faust.

IN PRISON

Faust and Mephistopheles arrive in time to rescue Gretchen, who, recognizing her tormentor, refuses to leave her cell. As she dies, invoking the mercy of God, she is saved. Mephistopheles drags Faust from the prison cell to escape.

PART II

In part II of the tragedy, Goethe took the opportunity to develop many of his ideas on mythology, cultural development, art, statesmanship, war, courtly life, economics, natural science, and religion to such an extent that the plot is lost from our view.

Songs inspired by Goethe's treatment of the Faust legend are numerous. (SOURCES: Boerner, Johnson, 1989; Grim, 1992; Newman, 1969; Palmer, More, 1936)

SONG	COMPOSER	POET
1. "Es war einmal ein König" (Song of the Flea)	Ludwig van Beethoven; Modest Mussorgsky; Richard Wagner	J. W. von Goethe
2. "Meine Ruh' ist hin"	Carl Loewe, Franz Schubert; Carl Zelter; Ludwig Spohr; Kreutzer; Hector Berlioz	J. W. von Goethe
3. "Ach neige, du Schmerzenreich"	Carl Loewe	J. W. von Goethe
4. "Wenn der Blüthen Frühlingsregen"	Carl Loewe	J. W. von Goethe
5. "Mächen, als du kamst ans Licht"	Carl Loewe	J. W. von Goethe
6. "Nur Platz, nur Blösse"	Carl Loewe	J. W. von Goethe
7. "Sei mir heute nichts zuwider!"	Carl Loewe	J. W. von Goethe
8. "Thurmwächter Lynceus zu den Füssen der Helena"	Carl Loewe	J. W. von Goethe
9. "Lynceus, der Helena seine Schätze darbietend"	Carl Loewe	J. W. von Goethe
10. "Lynceus, der Thürmer, auf Fausts Sternwarte singend"	Carl Loewe	J. W. von Goethe
11. "Gretchen am Spinnrade"	Franz Schubert	J. W. von Goethe
12. "Der König in Thule"	Franz Schubert	J. W. von Goethe
13. "Szene aus *Faust*: Wie anders, Gretchen, war dir's"	Franz Schubert	J. W. von Goethe
14. "Gretchens Bitte: Ach neige, du Schmerzenreiche"	Franz Schubert	J. W. von Goethe
15. "Sieben Kompositionen zu Goethes *Faust*," op. 5	Richard Wagner	J. W. von Goethe
16. "Gretchen vor dem Andachtbild"	Hugo Wolf	J. W. von Goethe

FEENEY, LEONARD (1897–1978): poet and Jesuit priest. Feeney was a friend of Theodore Chanler, who set many of Feeney's poems, including a cycle, "The Children." (SOURCE: Villamil, 1993)

FEIT: (Scot.), *feet.*

FELLINGER, JOHANN GEORG (1781–1816): Austrian poet. Born in the province of Styria, Fellinger studied law at Graz and served as an infantry officer during the war against Napoleon (1809), losing an eye in battle. After being released from his wartime imprisonment, Fellinger held various military positions until 1815, after which he committed suicide, depressed by being unable to continue in the military or get an appropriate civilian position. Two of Fellinger's poems were set by Franz Schubert in 1815: "Die erste Liebe" and "Die Sternenwelten," a setting of Fellinger's translation of a Slovene poem. (SOURCE: Garland, 1976)

FEMALE VERTUOSO'S, THE: an adaptation of Molière's *Les Femmes savantes* by Thomas Wright, a lesser light of Restoration drama, produced in 1693, containing one duet by Henry Purcell. Clerimont, in order to gain Mariana's hand, must prove to his future mother-in-law, Lady Meanwell, that he does not hate poetry. The matriarch will not admit into her family someone who does not value wit and who does not have the sense to ask her to read any of her works. Clerimont asks Lady Meanwell to hear a song he wrote yesterday, part of which says "only love can improve man's soul." Offended, she is determined to make an example of him by denying him her daughter in marriage. Purcell succeeds in using "Love, Thou Art Best" to cast Clerimont in a good light while showing disapproval of Lady Meanwell. (SOURCE: Price, 1984)

FERNANDO, FERDINAND V: Spanish king of Castile and Aragon, Spain's largest kingdoms. In 1469 Fernando married his cousin Isabella I. This marriage led to the unification of Castile and Aragon. During ten years of war, Fernando was very successful in battles against the Moors, regaining many cities that they had originally captured. One of the better known songs of the time, "Sobre Baça estaba el Rey," by an anonymous composer, recounts King Fernando's confrontations with the Moors.

FERNE GELIEBTE, AN DIE: a ★cycle of six musically connected songs composed by Beethoven in 1816 to poems by the little-known ★Jeitteles. It is often considered the first major song cycle because of the return of its opening melody toward the end and the unity of poetic themes. Composers were more inclined to seek expression by hammering material into enormous designs than to trust the simple thoughts required by songs; Beethoven characteristically contributed to the genre a cycle whose form was dependent upon a story in which the whole was greater than the parts. *See also* ★CYCLE.

FET (SHENSHIN), AFANASY (1820–1892): Russian poet. Born two months after his wealthy father brought his German wife to Russia, Afanasy Fet was declared illegitimate when the marriage was ruled invalid. Unable to inherit nobility or estate or name from his father, Afanasy was forced to take a Russianized name of his mother's first husband, Foeth. He was educated at the University of Moscow; even his extensive military service (1845–58) did not enable him to get the desired title of nobility. When he transferred to St. Petersburg, he did pursue a literary life, with Turgenev and ★Tolstoy being his closest friends. The books of poetry that Fet published in 1850 and 1856 brought him great success, after which he settled down on land in his native village (1860) and withdrew from literary life for twenty years, during which he managed his finances so successfully that he was able to buy an estate in the country and a mansion in Moscow. In 1873 he finally received the name of Shenshin by specific decree of Alexander II. In 1883 he began to publish his late poetry in four volumes, turning to darker, metaphysical subjects. He wrote his memoirs and translated the Latin poets as well as ★Goethe and Schopenhauer. Now his poetry, composed with natural ease and directness, rhythmic variety, nuances of feeling, and fleeting impressions made him a primary influence on the Russian ★Symbolist movement. His landscape poems were very popular and his love poetry was subtle but passionate. The poetry of Afanasy Fet was set by Rachmaninoff, Rimsky-Korsakov, Gretchaninov, Tchaikovsky, Nicolai Medtner, Anton Arensky, and N. N. Cherepnin. English translations of Fet's lyrics can be found in Oliver Elton's *A Sheaf of Papers*, 1923 and C. M. Bowra's *A Book of Russian Verse*, 1943. (SOURCE: Kunitz, Colby, 1967)

FÊTES GALANTES (Amorous parties): a special category of French painting practiced by Jean Antoine Watteau (1684–1721) among others such as Jean Fragonard, representing the essence of court life in eighteenth-century France. The *Fêtes galantes* theme—elegant couples in park-like settings, singing, dancing, and making love—was adopted by Paul ★Verlaine in a series of poems published under the title *Fêtes galantes* (1869). Written under the influence of ★Baudelaire's *Les fleurs du mal*, these poems are characteristic of Verlaine's ★Parnassian period and are not part of his more ★Symbolist works. Debussy chose six of the Verlaine poems to set in two groups, titled *Fêtes galantes Livre I* and *Fêtes galantes Livre II*. Selected poems from Verlaine's *Fêtes galantes* have also been set by Gabriel Fauré: *En sourdine, Clair de lune,* and *Mandoline*. Gabriel du Pont set *Mandoline*, and Reynaldo Hahn titled his setting of that poem *Fêtes galantes. Sur l'herbe* was set as a single song by Maurice Ravel. Francis Poulenc's ★parody *"Fêtes galantes"* is taken from *Deux Poèmes de Louis ★Aragon*.

"Feuerreitter, Der" (The Fire-Rider): a ballad-like Hugo Wolf song, words by Eduard ★Mörike. When Wolf wished to obtain a clear explanation of the poem before he set it to music, he consulted *Magikon*, a periodical of the day devoted to psychic research. There he learned about the Fire-seers, Fire-feelers, and Fire-riders, gifted with the power of detecting distant fires to which they were strongly drawn. Although the lore states that they were forbidden by magic to extinguish these fires, Mörike's fire-rider has ignored this injunction by using a chip of the true cross to extinguish the flames. As punishment for this, the mill collapses round him, and he is burned alive. A portion of the Feuerreitter poem appears in Mörike's novel ★*Maler Nolton*. (SOURCE: Glauert, 1999)

FIELD, EUGENE (1850–1895): American journalist, poet, and bibliophile. Eugene Field was born in Missouri. His light verse for adults and children were the most prized of his output. Field's poetry was set by Reginald de Koven, Arthur Foote, and George Chadwick. PRINCIPAL WORK: *A Little Book of Western Verses*, 1881. (SOURCE: Drabble, 2000)

FIESOLE: a small Italian hill village overlooking Florence. For centuries, Italian and foreign artists, writers, and musicians have been charmed by the entrancing quality of the place and by the views of the historic city of Florence. (SOURCE: Lakeway, White, 1989)

SONG	COMPOSER	POET
"La sera fiesolana"	Alfredo Casella	Gabriele d'Annunzio

FILLE (It.): *see* ★PHYLLIS.

FINGAL'S CAVE: a 227-foot long cave made of beautifully colored, bizarre rock formations. It is located on the uninhabited small island of Staffa in the Hebrides off the west coast of Scotland. Its handsome ★basalt columns are named after the Celtic hero, Fingal. The Gaelic name is Uaimh Binn, meaning musical cave, referring to the echo of the waves heard inside. Mendelssohn visited the cave and afterward composed his famous overture. (SOURCE: *OED*, 1989)

FIONA MACLEOD, THREE POEMS BY: a set of three songs composed by Charles Griffes to the verses of Scottish poet William ★Sharp, whose pseudonym is Fiona MacLeod. The text of one song, "Ian, the Proud," is from a set called *Foam of the Past—*★*Threnodies and Songs*, which is a part of a larger collection, *From the Hills of Dreams*. That work contains MacLeod's preface dedicated to W. B. ★Yeats, part of which reads: "Most of [the Threnodies and Songs] have their place in tales of mine, coloured with the colour of a lost day and a beauty that is legend and must suffer by severance from their context." Since the poem "Ian, the Proud" or "Ian Himself" is not to be found in the major MacLeod tales, it must be presumed that the character Ian is a solitary creation of fiction fashioned from familiar Scottish traditions, in which *the proud* is a romantic epithet for a man, and in which bards were often *blind* or thought to be. The music for "★Rose of the Night" is accompanied by an explanation of the allusion.

FLAMENCO: a form of Spanish music deriving from Berber/Sephardim roots. The rich heritage of flamenco has made itself a unique place in the history of the humanities and the arts. Its joys and sorrows are complex, at once introvert and extrovert, conveyed through dramatic rhythms and strong contrasts.

SONG	COMPOSER	POET
"Flamenco Meditations"	Carlos Surinach	Elizabeth Barrett Browning

FLASTER, KARL WEST (1905–1965): American poet, florist, and reporter. Nineteen of Vittorio Giannini's thirty-six songs are settings of the poems of Karl Flaster. Giannini and the poet met as young men while awaiting a trolley car, soon becoming lifelong friends. Their collaboration lasted forty years and included four operas. Julia Smith also set Karl Flaster. (SOURCE: Villamil, 1993)

"Fled Is My Love": a song composed by Henry Purcell, set to words by Thomas ★D'Urfey in his comedy, *A Fool's Preferment*, produced in 1688. *See* ★*Fool's Preferment, A* for plot details and placement of songs.

FLEMING, PAUL (1609–1640): German poet. Paul Fleming's exciting life began when he attended school in Leipzig, where he later returned to study medicine. He participated in a commercial expedition to Russia and Persia in 1634, and in the same year traveled to Moscow. While waiting in Reval for the second leg of the journey, he became engaged. The expedition continued to Ispahan in 1636, but returned unsuccessful in 1637. In his absence his fiancée married another, leaving Fleming to marry her sister upon his return. In 1639 he completed his medical studies at Leyden, moving to Hamburg thereafter to begin his practice, but died shortly after arriving. In his early works, Fleming wrote Latin poems, which were versions of the Psalms. His ★epitaph was a ★sonnet composed by him shortly before his death, and most of his poetry was published posthumously. Fleming's poetry was set by Johannes Brahms, Felix Mendelssohn, and Andreas Hammerschmidt. PRINCIPAL WORKS: *Prodromus*, 1641; *Deutsche Poemata*, 1642, reprinted 1965; *Deutsche und Lateinische Gedichter*, 3 vols., ed. J. H. Lappenberg, 1963–65. (SOURCE: Garland, 1976)

FLETCHER, JOHN (1579–1625): British dramatist. John Fletcher was born in Sussex, where his father was a rector. As Dean of Peterborough, the father had tormented Mary Queen of Scots in her last hours. John Fletcher was educated at Benet College, Cambridge. In London he joined a brilliant group of Elizabethan dramatists and collaborated with Francis ★Beaumont, whom he met in 1607. Enjoying a Bohemian lifestyle in a "perfect union of genius and friendship" (Untermeyer, 1959), Fletcher and Beaumont even shared a mistress. It is assumed that Fletcher was the creative force and Beaumont supplied the critical faculty. When Beaumont died in 1614, Fletcher collaborated with Philip Massinger. Fletcher died of the plague and was buried in the same mass grave as Massinger. Fletcher was known for his impecuniousness, personal modesty, and brilliant wit. He collaborated with ★Shakespeare himself on *Henry VIII*. The plays of Fletcher and Beaumont constitute the largest oeuvre in Elizabethan drama except for those of ★Shakespeare. Fletcher was not skilled at pure tragedy, but excelled at mixed comedy, no farce. Although he had a marked lyrical gift with a feeling for good theater, he was careless in his characterizations and inclined to leave gaping holes in his plots. Many of the song lyrics of John Fletcher were set by Henry Purcell, Ivor Gurney, and Arthur Bliss. One of Fletcher's more famous verses was "Take, Oh, Take Those Lips Away," which appeared in Shakespeare's *Measure for Measure*, and "Orpheus with His Lute," which was once attributed to Shakespeare, but now is credited to Fletcher (Untermeyer, 1959). PRINCIPAL WORKS: *The Tragedie of* ★*Bonduca*, 1718; *Comedies and Tragedies Written by Francis Beaumont and John Fletcher, Gentlemen*, 1647. SELECTED READING: E. H. C. Oliphant, *The Plays of Beaumont and Fletcher*, 1927. (SOURCE: Kunitz, Haycraft, 1952)

FLEUR DES BLÉS: *see* ★POPPY.

FLORA: the Roman goddess of flowers, especially associated with spring, whose festivals, the Floralia, took place from April 28 to May 3. Anyone carrying flowers can be described by invoking her name. (SOURCE: Cooper, 1992)

SONG	COMPOSER	POET
1. "Attributs"	Francis Poulenc	Pierre de Ronsard
2. "Madrigal"	Gabriel Fauré	Edmond Haraucourt
3. "Nymphs and Shepherds"	Henry Purcell	Thomas Shadwell

FLORIDA: the southern American state of Florida; also, the district around the church of Antonio de la Florida in Madrid, where Goya painted in the cupola his frescos of the Miracle of St. Anthony. The American poet Wallace ★Stevens first traveled to Florida in 1922 with a business acquaintance from Atlanta. Soon Stevens and his family were making annual winter visits to various Florida vacation spots, starting on Key Biscayne, eventually preferring southernmost Key West, where in 1936 he broke his right hand in a drunken fight with Ernest Hemingway. Although they made it up, Stevens wrote a lengthy poem called "Farewell to Florida" (1940), declaring Key West to be "too furiously literary." Frederick Delius also spent some years living in Florida and celebrated it in his music. (SOURCE: Hamilton, 1994)

SONG	COMPOSER	POET
1. "O Florida"	Lee Hoiby	Wallace Stevens
2. "La maja dolorosa 3"	Enrique Granados	Fernando Periquet

FLYING HART: an astrological reference used in Elizabethan lyrics, meaning *a male deer.*

SONG	COMPOSER	POET
"Winter"	Dominick Argento	William Shakespeare

FOMBEURE, MAURICE (1906–1981): French poet. From the very beginning of his career, Fombeure wanted to steer poetry toward simplicity and away from its abstractions and excesses of language. This effort paved his way into the literary circle of René-Guy Cadou and the poets of the École de Rochefort, with whom he collaborated. Later he blended his rude gusto with more poetic inspiration. Fombeure's love for his native Touraine caused his poetry to be principally rural, although he partook of the literary life with great enthusiasm and injected everyday living with humor. The poetry of Maurice Fombeure was set by Francis Poulenc. PRINCIPAL WORKS: *Silence sur le toit*, 1930; *À dos d'oiseau*, 1942; *Sortilèges vus de près*, 1947; *Le Vin de la Haumuche*, 1952; also *La Rivière aux Oies*, 1932; *Arentelles*, 1943; *Grenier des Saisons*, 1942; *A chat petit*, 1961. (SOURCE: France, 1995)

FONTAINE, JEAN DE LA: *see* LA FONTAINE, JEAN DE.

FONTANA: one of the original bathing places in Trieste, Italy, to which James ★Joyce was a regular summer visitor during his years living there. A description of holding his baby son Giorgio in the sea was Joyce's first mention of the Fontana baths, described in his *Trieste Notebook*. When Giorgio was older, Joyce wrote (1914) his lyric poem, "On the Beach at Fontana," which was included in his collection *Pomes Penyeach*. (SOURCE: Bowen, 1974)

SONG	COMPOSER	POET
"On the Beach at Fontana"	Roger Sessions	James Joyce

FONTANE, THÉODORE (1819–1898): German poet and writer of fiction and ballads. Fontane was a pharmacist, as was his father, before he became a freelance writer. The family was of French Huguenot descent. Fontane lived in Berlin (1833) with an uncle who introduced him to café life and witty conversation. A member of a literary club where ballads won acclaim, his first poetic writing was as a ballad writer. He wrote as a London correspondent for Berlin papers and as a theater critic, sympathetic to the rising democratic tide. Only in the late 1850s did he become a novelist, which in the last two decades of his life would bring him world fame. In his historical writing, his rather un-German goal was to present large-scale events through the details of everyday life. Fontane and ★Heine were alone among nineteenth-century writers in dealing with the politics of their country. In a sense, everything Fontane wrote was political, but linked private and public existence. Although he was a romantic at heart, he knew that an individual must exist within his or her given society. The ballads of Théodore Fontane were set by Carl Loewe. PRINCIPAL WORKS: Poetry: *Von der schönen Rosamunde,* 1850; *Männer und Helden,* 1850; *Gedichte,* 2 vols., 1851–75; *Balladen,* 1861. Fiction: *Die Poggenpuhls,* 1896, as *The Poggenpuhl Family,* 1979. SELECTED READING: G. Wallis Field, *A Literary History of Germany,* 1975. (SOURCE: Vinson, Kirkpatrick (1), 1984)

FOOL'S PREFERMENT, A: a comedy by Thomas ★D'Urfey, produced in 1688, that contains several songs composed by Henry Purcell. Price calls the play "brilliant, irreverent, cynical . . . couched in smutty language." D'Urfey begins the play with Lyonel, a poor eccentric young man who is in love with Celia, a maid of honor to the king. She has been pressed into the king's service. Frightened for Celia because of the king's philandering ways, Lyonel sings, "I Sigh'd and Pin'd." Although Lyonel speaks and sings only nonsense from here on, this song has a message: his insanity frees him, a sentiment used in other mad songs of the period. The song is easy and tuneful, capable of being sung by a person of moderate skill. (In fact, in comedies of Restoration theater the actors almost always sang their own songs, as opposed to the actors in tragedy, serious plays, and semi-operas, who were incapable of singing the difficult music that was then given to professional singers.) Celia protests. Lyonel pretends not to recognize her and sings "There's Nothing So Fatal as a Woman," its bitterness expressed by Purcell in wide vocal leaps and jagged rhythms. In act 2, Lyonel is falsely informed that the king will see him hanged for treason. Squire Cocklebrain is also falsely informed that the king is about to raise his position to a peerage and is told that he is preferred because the king is afraid of the squire's wrath if he is not elevated. Lyonel tries in vain to warn the squire of this elaborate scheme to trick him. In act 3, Lyonel wanders into the new duke's house, mumbling that Celia has married another or is dead, then sings, "Fled Is My Love," followed by "'Tis Death Alone," both of which show Lyonel's despair. Later in the scene as courtiers tease the "duke," it is believed that Lyonel, the madman, sang "I'll Mount to You, Blue Coelum." Price calls this song "fourteen bars of C major nonsense." Like "I'll Sail upon the ★Dog Star," the exact place where this piece was sung and by whom is not known. Since both pieces are longer and more difficult, perhaps the actor taking Lyonel's part was not up to the piece, and perhaps a professional singer performed "I'll Sail upon the Dog Star" between the acts. In act 4, the plot diverts to the squire's uncle, who comes to get honors for himself and to the tricksters who persuade the squire to offer his wife to the courtiers. In act 5, Lyonel has lost all reason, enters in madness, thinking that he has come to the underworld to find a bride. He sings "If Thou Wilt Give Me Back My Love." Finally Celia is returned to Lyonel, and the curtain falls. In the epilogue an actor asks the question "Are we not all a little mad?" (SOURCE: Price, 1984)

FORD, FORD MADOX (FORD HERMANN HUEFFER) (1873–1939): English poet and editor. Ford was the son of a music critic of *The Times* and spent his childhood in ★Pre-Raphaelite circles. He collaborated for a while with Joseph Conrad before their relationship deteriorated. He carried on an affair with the celebrated novelist Violet Hunt, which resulted in a scandalous divorce from Ford's wife. After taking part in World War I, he was invalided home from France in 1917 and in the same year changed his name. The war inspired a volume of poems (1918) and *Parade's End*. Founder of the *Transatlantic Review*, he published therein works by ★Joyce, ★Pound, Gertrude ★Stein, and e. e. ★cummings, publishing over eighty books in all. He spent his last years in France and America. Ford is generally appreciated mostly for his editing, wherein he influenced our appreciation of the originality of others. The poetry of Ford Madox Ford has been set by Paul Nordoff and Peter Warlock. PRINCIPAL WORKS: *The Good Soldier*, 1915; *On Heaven and Poems Written on Active Service,* 1918; *Parade's End*, 1924–28; *No More Parades,* 1925; *A Man Could Stand Up,* 1926; *The March of Literature,* 1938. SELECTED READING: Alan Judd, *Ford Madox Ford,* 1999. (SOURCE: Drabble, 2000)

"Forelle, Die": a song by Franz Schubert set to a poem by Christian ★Schubart. The poet had written a last stanza that Schubert omitted, in which there was a moral: a warning to maidens to avoid fishy young men, an important clue in the interpretation of the song.

"For Folded Flocks": a trio composed by Henry Purcell to text by John ★Dryden in their semi-opera *King Arthur*, produced in 1691. *See* ★*King Arthur* for plot details and placement of songs.

FORGES, ÉVARISTE DÉSIRÉ DE, VICOMTE DE PARNY (1753–1814): French elegist. The work of Évariste de Forges (or Parny, as he was often referred to) inspired a generation of Russian poets from Nicolai Karamazin to Evgenii Baratynsky. Parny's love poems, light but tinged with sadness, appeared as *Poésies érotiques*, some of which point forward to ★Romanticism. The poetry of Évariste de Forges was set by Maurice Ravel in his three *Chansons Madécasses.* The poet wrote in his preface a long description of Madagascar, its princes, and the people, but modern scholarship has established that Parny never set foot in Madagascar, nor was he acquainted with the language. Parny wrote his poetry in India in 1784–85, using the *hain-tenys* (popular Madagascan poems) as his models. PRINCIPAL WORKS: *Oeuvres élégies et poésies diverses*, 1875; *Oeuvres complètes*, 5 vols., 1805. (SOURCE: Brereton, 1967)

"Forgotten One, The": a song, subtitled "A Ballad," composed by Modest Mussorgsky, who was often inspired by the stories of ordinary folk. In the autumn of 1874, Mussorgsky saw and was deeply affected by a painting that showed a single dead soldier on a patch of battlefield with crows swarming around his body. This painting was done by Vassily Verestaghin, who later, in a fit of depression, destroyed his canvas. The same work inspired Count Arsenyi *Golenishchev-Kutúsov, to write a poem to which Mussorgsky, friend and collaborator, set one of his most powerful songs, a lullaby sung by the soldier's widow as she rocks her child, desolated by a grief she tries to hide from the infant.

"For Love, Ev'ry Creature": a duet composed by Henry Purcell to a text by John *Dryden from their semi-opera *King Arthur*, produced in 1691. *See* *King Arthur* for plot details and placement of songs.

FORT, PAUL (1872–1960): French poet, editor, and theater director. As a forum for the *Symbolist theater, Fort created both the Théâtre d'Art, sadly destined for a short life (1890–92), and the journal *Vers et prose*, an acknowledgment of *Mallarmé and his leadership. Between 1905 and the outbreak of World War I, Fort directed this journal, which brought together the literary avant-garde of *Montparnasse. As a poet, Fort's name was associated with the **ballade*. From the publication of his first collection (1896), he was never unfaithful to that form. Even when he wrote in prose, he maintained the sound forms and rhythms of poetry. It is generally agreed that his lyrics honor his subjects—love, nature, and death—with a kind of spontaneity that links French lyrical tradition with the popular song. The poetry of Paul Fort has been set by André Caplet. PRINCIPAL WORK: *Ballades Françaises*, 17 vols., 1922–58. (SOURCE: France, 1995)

FORTUNAT: *see* *DICHTER UND IHRE GESELLEN.

FOSCOLO, UGO (1778–1827): Italian poet, essayist, dramatist, and novelist. Foscolo was born in the Ionian Islands. After going to Venice about 1793, he joined the French army and fought against Austria and Russia. Foscolo first believed that Napoleon was the savior of his country, but, when the Veneto was handed over to Austria, he resigned from the army. The noble, patriotic ideals of his poetry inspired the generation that fought the battles of the Italian Risorgimento. Foscolo wrote only twelve *sonnets, which blended the Greek and Roman sensibilities. Believing that tombs link the living with the dead, he defended the right to burial in cities and the free decoration of tombs. Refusing to swear allegiance to the Austrians when they entered Italy in 1813, Foscolo fled to Switzerland, thence to London in 1816, where he died in great poverty. Forty-four years after his death, the remains of this patriot/poet were taken to Florence and interred in Santa Croce. Foscolo is generally considered the most important voice of *Romanticism in Italian literature.

The verses of Ugo Foscolo were set by Goffredo Petrassi. WORKS: *Poesie,* 1803; *Dei Sepolcri* [On Sepulchres], 1835, 1971; *Le Grazie,* 1914; *The Last Letter of Jacopo Ortis,* 1970. SELECTED READING: Glauco Combon, *Ugo Foscolo: Poet of Exile,* 1980. (SOURCE: De Lucchi, 1967)

FOUQUÉ, FRIEDRICH, BARON DE LA MOTTE (1777–1843): German *Romantic poet, novelist, and playwright. Having had a military career previous to his 1803 marriage, Fouqué devoted himself thereafter to literature and life on his wife's estate. He distinguished himself serving in the war against Napoleon (1813–15). Author of *Undine,* later an opera by E. T. A. Hoffman, he was a strong influence to many musicians and composers. Five of his poems were set by Franz Schubert. (SOURCE: Reed, 1997)

FRAE: (Scot.), *from.*

FRANCIS, SAINT (ca. 1181–1226): founder of the Franciscan order. Born in Assisi of a prosperous father and a mother from a distinguished French family, Francis was named John but acquired a nickname, Francesco the Freeman. High-spirited and delighting in revelry, Francis joined the army in 1205 to fight on behalf of the pope. In 1207 he had a second heavenly visitation while worshiping in a church. "Francis, repair my house," the voice said. Thereafter Francis made a project of repairing neglected churches. His warm personality and joyous asceticism drew men to be his followers. They lived as itinerant preachers, possessed no property, begging food when necessary. Although he was never a priest, the pope gave his approval to Francis's form of life. By 1220 his followers numbered more than 5,000. St. Francis's last years were spent in remote hermitages in the company of his early companions. (SOURCE: Grant, 1980)

FRAUENLIEBE UND -LEBEN: a cycle of eight songs by Robert Schumann and a cycle of nine songs by Carl Loewe (op. 60) with texts by Adalbert von *Chamisso. Chamisso's ninth poem is a lengthy poem spoken by the now aged girl of the first eight songs. She looks back many years and speaks to her granddaughter in "Töchter, meine Töchter." This epilogue was set by Loewe but not by Schumann.

FREE VERSE: a term used popularly but not accurately to describe the poems of Walt *Whitman and others, whose verse is based not on the recurrence of stress accent in a regular, strictly measurable pattern, but rather on the irregular rhythmic cadence of the recurrence, with variations, of significant phrases, image patterns, and the like.

FREILIGRATH, FERDINAND (1810–1876): German poet, translator, and editor. His father was a schoolteacher, but Freiligrath's formal education was abandoned because of financial difficulties. By the time he was apprenticed (1825), Freiligrath had already translated Greek and Latin poets. At eighteen he had published his lyrics and short stories in which he imitated the exoticism of Victor *Hugo. In 1838 Freiligrath published his *Poems* to great success. In 1844 he fled to Brussels after publishing a poem that affronted the king. There he met Karl Marx, became more radical, and soon moved to a city near Zurich that was a refuge for German exiles, where he published *Ça ira*, his own radical poetry. The general amnesty of 1848 brought Freiligrath back to Germany where he was acquitted of the former charges. Marx and Engels made him editor of their newspaper, which resulted in another warrant from the king. Again he fled, this time to London where he found a book-keeping job, doing his writing and translating after work hours. Having become a British subject in 1858, he was reintegrated into the establishment by means of an endowment donated by international admirers. He died three years after becoming the editor of a biweekly British literary magazine. Freiligrath was one of the most widely read poets of Germany in the middle of the nineteenth century, and one can trace in his poetry the transition in German literature from exotic ★romanti-cism to social commitment. His early poetry spoke of faraway places, foreign people, and strange customs. His later poetry calls for resistance and revolution. Freiligrath was the instigator of the most significant literary controversy of his day: the place of the poet in society. He introduced the German reading public to American writers like ★Longfellow and Bret ★Harte. The verse of Ferdinand Freiligrath was set by Carl Loewe and Franz Liszt. PRINCIPAL WORKS: *Gedichte* [Poems], 1838; *Die Kreuzigung* [The Crucifixion], 1841; *Ein Glaubensbekenntnis* [A Confession of Faith], 1844; *Ça ira!* [It will work out fine!], 1846; *Neuere politische und soziale Gedichte*, 1851. (SOURCE: Harden, Mews, 129, 1993)

FREMMIT: (Scot.), *foreign, estranged.*

FREY, ADOLF (1855–1920): Swiss poet, novelist, playwright, professor, and scholar. Frey was the son of a well-known Swiss journalist and author. After studying at Bern and Zürich, he worked as a schoolmaster before becoming a professor at the University of Zürich. In addition to writing biographies of Johann von ★Salis-Seewis and Christian ★Meyer among others, Frey wrote two novels and several plays. His poetry was set by Johannes Brahms. PRINCIPAL WORKS: Poetry: *Gedichte*, 1886; *Totentanz*, 1895, *Neue Gedichte*, 1913; *Stundenschläge*, 1920; *Aus versunkenen Gärter*, 1932; *Duss und unterm Rafe*, 1891, includes poems in Swiss dialect. (SOURCE: Garland, 1976)

FRIE: (Scot.), *good, fine.*

FRIGG (old Norse), FRIJA (Ger.), FRIG (Anglo-Saxon): the goddess who protected men's marriages and made them fruitful. The Scandinavians show Frigg as adventuresome, fond of ornaments and jewelry, and flagrantly unfaithful to her husband, ★Odin, who behaved similarly. The Romans identified Frigg with ★Venus. Whenever Frigg accompanied Odin into battle, she had the right to bring back to Valhalla half the warriors who had fallen. The son of Odin and Frigg, Balder, was the god of light. (SOURCE: Guirand, 1968)

SONG	COMPOSER	POET
"Till Frigga"	Jan Sibelius	Johan Runeberg

FRÖDING, GUSTAF (1860–1911): a Swedish poet and journalist. Born in pictur-esque and colorful Värmland, Fröding inherited great poetic talent but also mental instability from his parents, both of whom wrote amateur poetry and had religious, musical, and literary interests. Because both parents were often ill or in a sanitarium, the boy lived with relatives and had little interest in school work. He managed to be admitted to the University of Uppsala, where he became interested in radical ideas and activities but neglected his studies and led a dissipated life, drinking excessively. After writing for a radical newspaper for three years, his mental problems verged on insanity. In a German sanitarium Fröding read classical and romantic German (*Heine) and English literature (*Burns and *Byron), which gave him the courage to express his own feelings in poetry. His first collection of poems, *Guitarr och Drag-Harmonika* (Guitar and Concertina), 1891, was technically brilliant, containing playful songs and thought-provoking descriptions of people and nature. These made Fröding one of Sweden's most-read poets. Coming under the influence of *Nietzsche's anti-social philosophy posed a new danger to his emotional life. At first, his many stays in insane asylums from 1894 on did not impede his writing. His most splendid work, *Stänk och Flikar* (Splashes and Rags), issued from one such stay, although its erotic content, said the critics, gave evidence of his mental imbalance. The poetry of Gustaf Fröding was set by Selim Palmgren and Jan Sibelius. WORKS: *Poems*, trans. A. Björck, 1903; *Selected Poems*, trans. C. W. Stork, 1916. (SOURCE: Kunitz, Colby, 1967)

FRÖHLICH, ABRAHAM (1796–1865): Swiss poet, novelist, and writer of fables. Fröhlich was a pastor and schoolmaster. Robert Schumann set his poetry. PRINCIPAL WORKS: Poetry: *Schweitzerlieder*, 1827; *Trostlieder*, 1851; *Ausgewählte Werke*, 1884. Fables: *Fabeln*, 1825; *Hundert neue Fabeln*, 1825. (SOURCE: Garland, 1976)

"From Rosy Bowers": a song composed by Henry Purcell to a text written by Thomas *D'Urfey for Part III of his comedic semi-opera *Don Quixote*, produced in 1694–95. *See* *Don Quixote* for plot details and placement of songs.

FROST, ROBERT (1874–1963): an American lyric poet, born in San Francisco. Robert Frost was the son of a New England father and a Scottish mother who was fond of writing verse. When Frost's father died, the family moved back East, where young Robert attended Dartmouth for a while. Leaving college, Frost worked in a mill, tried his hand at newspaper writing, and in his leisure hours wrote poetry. After marriage, he tried to settle into a routine of school teaching while attending Harvard as a special student. Finding school unsatisfying again, he left Harvard and, for health reasons, pursued an outdoor occupation raising hens and selling eggs before moving his family to a farm in New Hampshire. Poetry was a consolation for his continuing illnesses. Frost then took his family to England for three years, while he concentrated on writing poetry. Returning to the United States when his wife died and after no public recognition for his work, he suddenly was given many honors, including honorary degrees from forty-four colleges and universities, Oxford and Cambridge among them. The early poetry—eleven volumes—began to emphasize the intonations of everyday conversational speech with a simple vocabulary of typical Yankee understatements. The later works present a variety of rural New England responses to the human predicament, frequently handled by means of inner and outer dialogue. Themes were fear, isolation, lostness, and not-knowing side by side with recurring elements of faith and love and continuity. Frost cherishes the humble beauties of nature, to which deeper levels of meaning are attached. His entire work is deeply rooted in the American idiom, native yet original. Robert Frost's poetry has been set by John Duke, Charles Naginski, John LaMontaine, and Elliott Carter, among other composers. PRINCIPAL WORKS: *Selected Poems*, 1923 (Frost's own selections); *Collected Poems*, 1930; *Complete Poems*, 1949; *Selected Poems*, 1955. SELECTED READING: Edward Connery Latham, *The Poetry of Robert Frost*, 1969; Lawrence Thompson and R. H. Winnick, *Robert Frost: A Biography*, 1981; Richard Poirier, *Robert Frost: The Work of Knowing*, 1977. (SOURCE: Vinson, 1979)

FROTTOLA: an old term for Italian street songs or music sung in a crowd of people. The starting point for Italian secular music was popular poetry, light verse that left musicians the task of heightening its emotional context or toning down its exaggerations as best they could. They used the *frottola* form for this purpose. Many of these early *frottole* have been republished in recent years, but they are never performed, perhaps because no one is sure of the correct manner of performing them, or because our ideas of solo song are limited. Emanuele Wolf-Ferrari's wrote two series of songs on *frottole* texts, for which no poet is named. (SOURCE: Stevens, 1970)

FUJI: a sacred mountain in south central Honshu, Japan; also a wisteria plant.

SONG	COMPOSER	POET
"O Lady Moon"	Alan Hovhaness	Lafcadio Hearn

FUNICULÌ, FUNICULÀ: a song by Luigi Denza (1846–1922). The song was written to celebrate the opening of the funicular cable car service that runs up to Mt. Vesuvius. More than a million copies were sold upon publication. Richard Strauss, believing it to be a Neapolitan folk song, quoted from it in his orchestral suite, *Aus Italien*.

FURDER: (Scot.), *succeed*.

FURIES: the avenging goddesses of guilt. The Furies avenge murder, perjury, violation of filial piety, and the laws of hospitality. They pursue and madden the perpetrators of these crimes. Their names are ★Alecto the uneasy, ★Tisiphone the blood-avenger, and Megaera the one who denies. They are represented as winged maidens with serpents in their hair and blood dripping from their eyes. *See* ★ERINNYS. (SOURCE: Kaster, 1964)

SONG	COMPOSER	POET
1. "The Charm"	Benjamin Britten	Thomas Randolph
2. "Misera, dove son?"	Wolfgang Amadeus Mozart	Pietro Metastasio

FUTURISM: a twentieth-century avant-garde movement in Italian art, literature, and music. Its intention was to break with the academic culture of the past and celebrate technology. In poetry it advocated the destruction of traditional syntax, meter, and punctuation. The Russian Futurists were led by Vladimir ★Mayakovsky, who hailed the revolution and expected the Futurists to lead the new poetry for the new state, but Lenin, among others of the new leaders, found their work to be "incomprehensible rubbish." Some years later Stalin declared Mayakovsky the most talented poet of the Soviet epoch. (SOURCE: Drabble, 2000)

G ✑

GABRIEL: an angel messenger of God, appearing in both the Old and New Testaments, whose name means *God is Mighty*. To the Hebrews Gabriel was the angel of death, the prince of fire and thunder. To the Muslims Gabriel was the chief of the four favored angels, the spirit of truth. In Medieval romances he was the second of the seven spirits that stand before the throne of God. God used Gabriel to deliver revelations to men and women. He revealed to Zacharias that his wife, Elizabeth, would bear a son called John, who became ★John, the Baptist (Luke 1.8–20). Gabriel also appeared to the ★Virgin Mary in the sixth month of her pregnancy. God sent him to Nazareth in Galilee to speak to Mary, who was engaged to ★Joseph, a descendant of King David. Gabriel told that her that she would bear a son called Jesus (Luke 1.26–38). In Islam, Gabriel appeared to Mohammed and revealed the ★Koran to him. In the Christian tradition Gabriel is thought to be the archangel who will blow his trumpet to announce a general resurrection. (SOURCE: Young, no date)

SONG	COMPOSER	POET
"The Blessed Virgin's Expostulation"	Henry Purcell	Nahum Tate

GALATEA: in Greek mythology, a ★Nereid noted for her beauty and her milk-white skin. Galatea's beauty attracted unwanted attention from the ★Cyclops Polyphemus. Galatea was in love with the handsome demi-god ★Acis who returned her feelings, but she was constantly pestered by Polyphemus. One day he saw the lovers together and, in a rage, smashed Acis with a huge boulder. The blood from Acis's broken body was transformed into a river. A second legend of Galatea concerns Pygmalion, a sculptor. He created a statue of a woman so lovely and lifelike that he fell in love with it. Pygmalion prayed to ★Aphrodite for a bride; Aphrodite brought the statue to life. In modern retellings the statue is named Galatea. (SOURCE: *Americana*, 2003)

SONG	COMPOSER	POET
"Galathea"	Arnold Schönberg	Franz Wedekind

GALINA, G. (1873–?): pseudonym of Glafira Adolfovna Einerling, poet, novelist, and translator. One of her poems whose theme was the unrest of students in 1901 was circulated in manuscript form for years, then printed abroad. Sergei Rachmaninoff set her "Zdes khorosho" (It's Lovely Here), as no.7 of his op. 21. (SOURCE: Miller, 1973)

GANG: (Scot.), *go.*

GANGES: a main river of India. Originating in the Himalayas, flowing for about 1,500 miles emptying into the Bay of Bengal, the Ganges is one of the two main rivers of India; the other is the Indus, which gives India its name. According to legend, the Ganges circles ★Brahma's city on Mount Meru. The Hindu religion regards streams and rivers as sacred places, and it is an act of devotion to travel a river or stream from start to finish, stopping at all the holy places along the waterway to pray or perform other acts of devotion. India's holiest river is the Ganges, called Mother Ganga and often personified as a river goddess. In Hindu mythology, the river originates at Vishnu's feet in heaven, flows across the sky via the Milky Way, and ends by pouring from Shiva's hair down to Earth. The steps at various sacred sites along the Ganges are called ghats. Here pilgrims enter the water and wash away their sins by bathing in the river. Other ghats are used for cremation, the ashes of the dead being scattered on the river water. (SOURCES: Ions, 1967; Basham, 1959; Noss, 1974)

SONG	COMPOSER	POET
1. "Abends am Strand"	Robert Schumann	Heinrich Heine
2. "Già il sole del Gange"	Alessandro Scarlatti	Felice Parnasso
3. "Auf flügeln des Gesanges"	Felix Mendelssohn	Heinrich Heine

GANYMEDE, GANYMED (Ger.): in Greek mythology, the cupbearer of ★Zeus, successor to ★Hebe. This Trojan youth was so beautiful that he was carried off by an eagle to be cup-bearer to Zeus; therefore his name is invoked to serve as an archetype of male beauty and desirable youth. (SOURCE: Cooper, 1992)

SONG	COMPOSER	POET
1. "Ganymed"	Franz Schubert, Hugo Wolf	Johann Wolfgang von Goethe
2. "Die Jugend"	Benjamin Britten	Friedrich Hölderlin

GAR: (Scot.), *to make*; *to do*; *to compel*; *to force*.

SONG	COMPOSER	POET
"Supper"	Benjamin Britten	William Soutar

GARBORG, ARNE (1851–1924): Norwegian novelist, poet, essayist, and playwright. Garborg was born on a farm in southwestern Norway. His mother was lighthearted and cheery, but his father's belief in God's punishment resulted eventually in his suicide. Son Arne had been educated at home for religious reasons, but eventually went to a regular school, later a teacher training school. After his father's death, Garborg enrolled in the university at Christiania, where, influenced by modern ideas, he soon became the leader of a national language movement, writing irreverent, biting articles on topics of the day. The neo-romantic philosophy and the influence of ★Nietzsche and ★Tolstoy persuaded him to leave naturalism. Remaining an agnostic, Garborg developed a philosophy based on the ethics of love in the Gospels, which attitude was expressed in his novel *Fred* (Peace), a chief classic of Norwegian literature. His faith in life produced a poetic cycle, ★*Haugtussa* (The Fairy), which was famously set to music by Edvard Grieg and also by Catharinus Elling. *Fred* was translated into English in 1929 by P. D. Carleton. SELECTED READING: H. Beyer, *A History of Norwegian Literature.* (SOURCE: Kunitz, Colby, 1967)

GARCÉS, TOMÀS (b.1901): Catalan poet, translator, and journalist. Garcés studied law and philosophy at the University of Barcelona, the city of his birth, before turning to literature as a career. His published musical and nature poetry includes *Vint cançons* (1922) and *L'ombra del lledoner* (1924), both of which show the influence of Juan Ramón ★Jiménez. Garcés is celebrated for his translation of Mistral. During the Spanish Civil War, he moved to France, where the poet Paul ★Verlaine's interest in musicality and form greatly influenced Garcés's work. The poetry of Tomás Garcés has been set by Eduardo Toldrà and Federico Mompou. (SOURCE: Cockburn, Stokes, 1992)

GARCHES: a small residential suburb of Paris.

SONG	COMPOSER	POET
"Montparnasse"	Francis Poulenc	Guillaume Apollinaire

GARCÍA LORCA, FEDERICO (1895–1936): Spanish poet and playwright. García Lorca was born and educated in Granada, studied the piano at the Granada Conservatory, and attended Columbia University for a year in 1929. During the 1930s he was the director of La Barraca, a traveling theater group, and formed friendships with Salvador Dali and with the cinema writer Luis Buñuel. Almost immediately after Franco's troops began the uprising of the Spanish Civil War, García Lorca was arrested and shot. He is one of the most widely read Spanish authors of the twentieth century. In the beginning he had humor, irony, and whimsy, but later lost them, emphasizing the demonic inspiration of his verse. Most of the characters in his plays exult in their pain and grief at the indifference of society and the silence of death. Often asked to read his poetry aloud, he did it to great effect. García Lorca was deeply moved by the pathos of the ★*cante hondo* introduced into Spain by oriental sources, and he tried to capture in his writing the impact of its monotonous chant. When he visited New York, he had found similarities between the spirituals of Harlem and the *cante hondo*. His ★modernism used the local Andalusian culture to express metaphorically the grief and frustration of the human predicament with an intense, dark, and somber voice. He explained himself as an Andalusian, thus: "The Andaluz is either asleep in dust or shouting at the stars." The poetry of Federico García Lorca has been set by Xavier Montsalvatge, Carlos Chavez, Silvestre Revueltas, Ramiro Cortés, Hermann Reutter, Lennox Berkeley, Joelle Wallach, Francis Poulenc, and Samuel Barber. PRINCIPAL WORKS: *Romançero gitano*, 1924, as *The Gypsy Ballads of Garçía Lorca*, 1951, 1953; *Obras completas*, as *Complete Works*, 2 vols., ed. Arturo del Hoyo, 1973. Plays: *Bodas de sangre, Blood Wedding*, 1935, in *III Tragedies*, 1947; *Yerma*, 1937, in *III Tragedies*, 1947; *La Casa de Bernardo Alba, The House of Bernardo Alba*, 1945, in *III Tragedies*, 1947. Poetry: *Libro de poemas, Book of Poems*, 1921; *Poema del canto jondo, Poem of the Deep Song*, 1931, in *Deep Song and Other Prose*, ed. Christopher Maurer, 1980; *Primer romancero gitano, Gypsy Ballads*, trans. Rolfe Humphries, 1963; *Lament for the Death of a Bullfighter and Other Poems*, trans. A. L. Lloyd, 1937. Prose: *Poeta en Nueva York, Poet in New York*, 1940, trans. Rolfe Humphries, 1940, trans. Ben Belitt, 1955. SELECTED

READING: Rupert Allen, *The Symbolic World of García Lorca*, 1972; Mildred Adams, *García Lorca, Playwright and Poet*, 1977; Candelas Newton, *Understanding García Lorca*, 1995. (SOURCES: Drabble, 2000; Vinson, Kirkpatrick (1), 1984)

GARCIA VILLA, JOSÉ (1914–1997): Philippine poet and short story writer. "I have no bio and shall have none," said the poet (Magill, 4, 1984). He wished to have his identity known solely in his poetry, his purer self. Born in the Philippines where his father was a physician and chief of staff for General Aguinaldo during the revolution of 1896, Garcia Villa himself identified with the power of the rebels. He studied at the University of the Philippines but was suspended for writing sexually explicit poetry, *Man Songs*. When he won a large poetry prize, he used the money to exile himself in the United States, where he took a B.A. from the University of New Mexico. After his short stories were published in 1933, he left for New York, where he was befriended by Mark van Doren and was in contention for a Pulitzer Prize. He did his graduate studies at Columbia University, began to paint geometric portraits, and later taught at the New School and City College, remaining a Philippine citizen during his sixty-seven years in New York. Garcia Villa's poetry is essentially inward, concerned with metaphysics, not descriptions, and attempts a mixture of light and dark. To express this fusion Garcia Villa created the word *doveglion*: dove, eagle, lion. His work was acclaimed critically by Marianne ★Moore and Edith ★Sitwell. Another of his creations was what he called his "Comma Poems" (between each two words was a comma, unsurrounded by space, used to regulate the poem's time movement). The verse of José Garcia Villa has been set by Samuel Barber and Francis Poulenc. PRINCIPAL WORKS: *Many Voices*, 1939; *Poems by Doveglion*, 1941; *Have Come, Am Here*, 1942; *Volume 2*, 1949; *Selected Poems and New*, 1958; *Poems 55*, 1962; *Poems in Praise of Love*, 1962. (SOURCE: Magill, 4, 1984)

GARCILASO DE LA VEGA (1540–?1616): Spanish poet and historian. Son of a Spanish father and a Peruvian mother, Garcilaso de la Vega went to Spain in 1560. He wrote the history of Peru, dating from before the arrival of the Spaniards, in his *Comentarios reales* (1604). It was natural that he should display a bias in favor of his mother's people. His narrative and descriptive skills were excellent, and he wrote a history of Florida that was well received. The work of Garcilaso de la Vega was set into music by Eduardo Toldrà. PRINCIPAL WORKS: *First Part of the Royal Commentaries of the Yncas*, trans. C. R. Markham, 2 vols., 1869–71; *A Critical Text with a Bibliography*, 1925; *The Incas: The Royal Commentaries*, trans. M. Jolas, 1963. (SOURCE: Steinberg, 2, 1973)

GARRIGUE, JEAN (1912–1972): American poet and fiction writer. Garrigue was born Gertrude Garrigus in Indiana of Huguenot, English, and Scottish ancestry. Her father was a postal inspector who wrote and published short stories. Both her mother and her sister were musical, the sister a concert pianist. At the University of Chicago, Garrigue discovered ★Shelley, ★Keats, and the ★Imagists. Having changed her name when she moved to New York in 1940, she was "broke most of the time since [she] decided not to sacrifice living . . . to the earning of a living" (Kunitz, Colby, 1955). Garrigue pursued a teaching career at the Universities of Iowa and Connecticut,

Bard College, the New School in New York, Smith College, and Queens College. Her verse was set by Gordon Binkerd. PRINCIPAL WORKS: *The Ego and the Centaur*, 1947; *The Monument Rose*, 1953; *A Water Walk by Villa d'Este*, 1959; *Country Without Maps*, 1964; *New and Selected Poems*, 1967; *Studies for an Actress*, 1973. SELECTED READING: Babette Deutsch, *Poetry in Our Time; Five Young American Poets*, 1944. (SOURCES: Kunitz, Colby, 1955; *American Poetry*, 1, 2000)

GASTIBELZA: a modification of the Basque term *gaste belza*, a young man of swarthy dark complexion, used in Victor ★Hugo's long poem of that name. Franz Liszt set the poem in his song "Gastibelza." Federico Mompou set four of the eleven verses to a song under the title "Gastibelza, le fou de Tolède," and Georges Bizet wrote a song derived from *Gastibelza*, which he called "Guitare." In the poem Hugo finishes each line with four stroke lines, meant to imitate the harsh sudden cadences of the Spanish guitar.

"Gate to Bliss Does Open Stand, The": a song composed by Henry Purcell to the words of Nathaniel ★Lee, from his heroic play *Theodosius*, produced in 1680. *See* ★*Theodosius* for plot details and placement of songs.

GATO: an energetic dance associated with the gauchos of Argentina.

SONG	COMPOSER	POET
"Gato"	Alberto Ginastera	anonymous traditional text

GAUTIER, (PIERRE JULES) THÉOPHILE (1811–1872): French poet, novelist, critic, and journalist. Gautier's family was of ★Avignon ancestry but moved to Paris when he was three years old. By the time he was six he had read *Robinson Crusoe* and ★*Paul et Virginie*. In school Théophile was an outstanding student, known for his quick, curious mind and extraordinary memory. Through Gérard de ★Nerval and his friends, Gautier became part of the circle that surrounded Victor ★Hugo, then the rising star of ★Romanticism. *Poésies*, published at the family's expense in 1830, contained all the verses written since the age of fifteen, but went unnoticed because it coincided with the uprising against Charles X. This revolution ruined Gautier's family, making it necessary for him to support his parents and sisters. In his youth Gautier was slender with an olive complexion, long chestnut hair, and black near-sighted eyes. Later, as he became corpulent and heavy-featured, his nickname was "the elephant." Many liaisons with actresses, singers, and models enlivened his private life, but financial need pushed his literary production. What he wrote before 1836 was voluntarily created, but, after that year, supporting his family dictated his 300 volumes and 2,000 articles written for some sixteen periodicals. His great fluency of expression and prodigious memory made it possible for him to work at night next to the printers, feeding his copy directly to the typesetters with no need for revisions. Gautier's vast output made him an outstanding literary figure but brought him no official honors except the Légion d'honneur. Although he was a force in the Romantic movement, his work was overshadowed by the giant, Victor Hugo. He was a strong influence on the ★Parnassians. ★Baudelaire dedicated *Fleurs du mal* (1857) to Gautier; ★Mallarmé was inspired by Gautier's death to compose a piece on poets' vocation. Gautier exploited the exotic, the macabre, and fantastic vein in many stories, but his real talent was for the pictorial and concrete; his poetic principles were careful artistry, clarity, and visual rendition. The verse of Théophile Gautier has been set by Bizet, Chausson, Fauré, Duparc, Édouard Lalo, Reynaldo Hahn, and Felipe Pedrell. Manuel de Falla set a Gautier translation of the verse of Manuel Bretón de los Herreros in his song "Séguidille." PRINCIPAL WORKS: *Mademoiselle de Maupin*, trans. E. Powys Mathers, 1938; *Émaux et Camées,* 1852; *Complete Works*, trans. F. C. de Sumichrast, 1900–1903; *Clarimonde*, trans. Lafcadio Hearn, 1899; *A Romantic in Spain*, 1926, many trans.; *Famous French Authors*, 1879; *The Evil Eye, A Square Game*, 1892; *Charles Baudelaire, His Life*, 1915. SELECTED READING: Albert Brewster Smith, *Théophile Gautier and the Fantastic*, 1977; L. B. Dillingham, *The Creative Imagination of Théophile Gautier*, 1927; J. G. Palache, *Gautier and the Romantics*, 1926. (SOURCE: Kunitz, Colby, 1967)

GAWK: (Scot.), v. *to stare*; n. *a fool, an awkward person.*

GEAN: (Scot.) (pr. jeen), *wild cherry tree, its fruit.*

SONG	COMPOSER	POET
"The Gean"	Thea Musgrave	Maurice Lindsay

GEAR: (Scot.), *wealth.*

GEIBEL, EMANUEL (1815–1884): German poet and dramatist. The son of a pastor, Geibel was born in Lübeck and studied theology and philology. When employed as tutor in the household of the Russian ambassador in Athens, Geibel met a former school friend with whom he traveled throughout Greece, later publishing a volume of translations from the Greek. In 1840 Geibel completed his first collection of poems, *Gedichte*, which enjoyed one hundred printings in his lifetime. A volume of affably political poems, *Zeitstimmen* (1841), made a favorable impression on King Frederick William IV, who granted the poet an annual stipend. In 1852 Geibel accepted an invitation from Bavarian King Maximilian II to become the honorary professor of aesthetics in Munich. Although he became a central figure among the Munich poets, the death of his wife made Munich an unhappy place for him. Geibel returned to Lübeck and became an ardent supporter of German nationalism before he died. His reputation has weakened somewhat since his death, but between 1848 and 1870 he was acknowledged as a representative poet of Germany. Geibel's works were dedicated to an ideal of aesthetic beauty. His sweet and sentimental verses are pleasant and melodious with great virtuosity of form but superficiality of content, lacking philosophical depth, derivative of ★Platen, ★Goethe, ★Heine, ★Lenau, and ★Hölderlin. ★Heyse and Geibel will be remembered for their work in translating into German the Italian and Spanish Song Books, a great reservoir of folk poetry. The verses and translations of Emanuel Geibel have been set by Mendelssohn, Wolf, Robert and Clara Schumann, Robert Franz, Max Reger, Charles Griffes, and Halfdan Kjerulf. PRINCIPAL WORKS: *Juniuslieder,* 1848; *Neue Gedichte*, 1856; *Gedichte und Gedenkblätter*, trans. Lucy H. Hooper as *Poems*, 1864; *Spätherstblätter*, 1877; selections, W. W. Caldwell, *Poems, Originals and Translations*, 1857. (SOURCE: Kunitz, Colby, 1967)

GELLERT, CHRISTIAN (1715–1769): German poet. Son of a Protestant minister, Gellert endured a youth of privation and strict discipline but was a poet by the age of thirteen. He matriculated in theology at the University of Leipzig and gave his first sermon from the cathedral four years later (1738). The failure of that sermon, owing to his excessive timidity, made him abandon hope of becoming a clergyman. Returning to Leipzig to study French and English literature, he began to publish his efforts. The light, natural tone of his fables and verse won him immediate popularity. In 1745 he became a faculty member at Leipzig where his lectures on aesthetics were popular. In his poetry Gellert seeks to amuse, to instruct, and to touch our hearts. There is in German poetry a dichotomy between sentiment and worldly wisdom. Gellert showed himself to be both a cynical showman ruled by baser instincts and a writer who could touch hearts with tales that attempted to show to what lengths generosity could go. Now we regard these traits as displaying a satirical writer who is sophisticated and world-wise, but also a sentimental man. His *Geistliche Oden und Lieder* (1757) contain some of the best-known German hymns. The poetry of Christian Gellert has been set by C. P. E. Bach and Ludwig van Beethoven. J. A. Nuske translated Gellert's *Fabeln* into English (1850). (SOURCE: Browning, 1978)

GENERAL WILLIAM BOOTH (1829–1912): an English revivalist preacher who founded the Salvation Army. General Booth went into the lowest depths of London to rescue the most degraded persons he could find. Determined to motivate them to a better life, he put them into uniform and under military discipline. Booth even chose the musical instruments and the tunes. Although his methods did exactly what he intended and very successfully, the Salvation Army was considered a scandal by the "respectable" religions. Charles Ives set the words of Vachel ★Lindsay's poem about Booth in his song "General William Booth Enters into Heaven." Vachel Lindsay says, in the preface of his *Collected Poems* published in 1923 (pp. 21–23), that he built his poem on certain adventures he had that were connected with the Salvation Army. When Lindsay was broke, he had slept in Salvation Army quarters more than once. He composed the poem all in one night while walking up and down in Los Angeles. Some of his public thought that he was making sport of Booth and the Salvation Army, but he was not. (SOURCE: Ellmann, O'Clair, 1973)

SONG	COMPOSER	POET
"General William Booth Enters into Heaven"	Charles Ives, Sidney Homer	Vachel Lindsay

GENEVIÈVE DE BRABANT: a medieval mystery play by J. P. Contamine de Latour that was originally acted by puppets. In a manuscript found behind his piano after his death, Erik Satie had scored it for two soloists and piano. In the plot Geneviève has been left by her noble husband in the charge of a wicked steward. To revenge himself for her refusal of his advances, the steward convinces her husband of her infidelity, and she is condemned to death. Geneviève protests her innocence in the song "Air de Geneviève." In another song, "Petit air," she rejoices in being proved innocent, thanks heaven that she will not die after all, and is restored to her husband.

GENIUS (pl., Genii): in Roman mythology, the spirit that tended a man from his cradle to his grave, governed his fortunes, determined his character. To "indulge one's Genius" meant to enjoy pleasure, since the Genius wished a man to enjoy pleasure in his life. The Genius tended only men; women had Juno. Another belief was that a man had two genii, one good and one evil. When a man was bad, it was due to his evil genius. The guardian angels referred to in Matthew 18.10 were similar to the Roman genii. The term is derived from the Latin *gignere,* to beget (in Greek, *gignesthai,* to be born), since the ancients believed that birth and life were due to these *dii genitales.* Thus the words described native intelligence and talent, a man's nature, the qualities possessed by the inner man. Eastern genii were *jinns,* who were fallen angels, not attendant spirits. A *genius loci* is an attendant deity of a place. In Restoration drama, the term was used often, as in Purcell's famous scene for The Cold Genius from *Don Quixote.* (SOURCES: Cooper, 1992; Jones, 1995)

SONG	COMPOSER	POET
"Genius of England"	Henry Purcell	Thomas D'Urfey

"Genius of England": a song composed by Henry Purcell to a text written by Thomas *D'Urfey for Part II of his comedic semi-opera *Don Quixote,* produced in 1694–95. *See* *Don Quixote* for plot details and placement of songs.

"Gentle Annie": a song by Stephen Collins Foster. According to his brother, "Gentle Annie" was inspired by an actual incident that occurred in Foster's neighborhood. On a stormy night, a little girl who had been sent on an errand was run over and killed. Foster, distressed, was about to go to a party when he learned of the tragedy. Instead, he went to the little girl's father, a poor working man, and stayed all night offering what comfort he could. (SOURCE: Preminger, 1986)

GEORGE, SAINT: Christian saint, martyr, dragon slayer, and patron saint of England. These are the facts of St. George's life: a native of Cappadocia and a Christian, St. George was martyred in Lydda in Palestine. The date of his martyrdom, as given by Farmer, was around 302 C.E. The most famous story about St. George concerns his killing of a poisonous dragon. A city in Libya called Silena was surrounded by a swamp, where there lived a huge dragon that attacked the city. Although the inhabitants tried to fight the dragon, all who inhaled his breath died of this poison. The city struck a pact with the dragon: in return for two sheep a day the dragon would not molest Silena or its inhabitants. When sheep became scarce, a human, selected by lot, was offered alongside the one sheep. In time, the lottery selected the king's daughter. The populace became enraged because the king did not want his daughter to be sacrificed when so many of their children had been. Traveling in the area, St. George met the princess, dressed in bridal clothing on her way to the rendezvous with the dragon. When the dragon appeared, he wounded it with his lance. He then had the girl tie her girdle around the dragon's neck and lead the dragon, now tame, into the city. St. George instructed the crowds that, if they were baptized as Christians, he would then kill the dragon. The *Golden Legend* claims that more than twenty thousand men, not counting women and children, converted. His purposes then achieved, St. George killed the dragon with his sword. It required four yokes of oxen to drag the body of the dragon away from the city. St. George refused all rewards, but instructed the king to maintain the churches, obey the priests, and remember the poor. During the reign of Diocletian and Maximian. St. George was martyred and condemned to torture. Several types of torture were tried, but each time the sign of the cross delivered St. George. He called down fire from heaven, which burned the pagan temple, the idols, and the priests. All that remained was swallowed up by an earthquake. In retaliation St. George was dragged through the city and beheaded. During the siege of Antioch, the Crusaders were encouraged by visions of St. George. It is possible that this was when King Richard the Lion Hearted put his men under St. George's protection. King Edward III founded the Order of the Garter, which was placed under St. George's patronage, and in 1415 Archbishop Chichele had St. George's feast day raised to a major holiday. Saint George was the patron saint of soldiers, knights, archers, and builders of armor. (SOURCES: De Voragine, 1993; Farmer, 1997; Walsh, 1991)

SONG	COMPOSER	POET
1. "Don Quichotte à Dulcinée"	Maurice Ravel	Paul Morand
2. "Canço de Bressol"	Eduardo Toldrà	Tomàs Garcés
3. "Christ's Sunday Morn"	Ernst Bacon	folk poetry

GEORGE, STEFAN (1868–1933): German poet and translator. George was born in the Rhine district of Germany and lived there till the age of 5. George's father then moved the family to nearby Bingen, whose beautiful environs had a lasting impact on the poet's imagination. At school he received broad humanistic training. He excelled in French, taught himself Norwegian and Italian, began to translate ★Ibsen, ★Petrarch, and Tasso, and wrote poetry by the age of eighteen. After finishing his schooling, George began the traveling that characterized his lifestyle from that time on. In Paris, he became a member of the circle of ★Symbolist poets surrounding ★Mallarmé. Returning to Germany, he studied Romance literature for three semesters in Berlin and began to experiment with language, developing his own Lingua Romana that combined Spanish and Latin words with German syntax. His translations now included ★Baudelaire, ★Shakespeare's sonnets, and ★Dante's *Divine Comedy*. Gradually George became the spokesman in Germany of a neo-Romanticism that grew into a new classicism. His work was almost entirely "hard, gem-like lyric poetry" (Kunitz, Haycraft, 1973), but very little was translated into English, it being utterly remote from our times and very difficult. Although George's fame grew, he refused almost all public honors because he was under great pressure from the National Socialists to accept awards that would dignify their cultural policies. In frail health, he left Germany for Switzerland in 1933, died and was buried there. Arnold Schönberg set the poetry of Stefan George, who has been described as equaled in artistic stature and scope of intelligence only by ★Rilke. PRINCIPAL WORKS: *Hymnen* (Odes), 1890; *The Books of Eclogues and Eulogies, of Legends and Lays, and of the Hanging Gardens*, 1895; *The Tapestry of Life, The Songs of Dream and Death*, 1899; *The Seventh Ring*, 1907; *The Works of Stefan George*, 1949. SELECTED

READING: George R. Urban, *Kinesia and Stasis: A Study in the Attitudes of Stefan George and His Circle to the Musical Arts*, 1962. (SOURCE: Magill, 2, 1997)

GERSTENBERG, GEORG VON (1780–1838): German poet. A government official in Weimar, Gerstenberg was a member of the ★Goethe circle. His name was originally Müller, but he later adopted his mother's last name. Some of his poems were included in Johanna Schopenhauer's novel *Gabriele*. Schubert set one Gerstenberg poem, "Hippolit's Lied." (SOURCE: Reed, 1997)

GHAZEL, GHAZAL: in Arabic, *love-making*, adapted in Persian, Turkish, Urdic, and Pashto languages from the eighth century on, as a name for short amatory poems, and used in that sense in the West. The poet signs his name in the final couplet. ★Hāfiz was one who used the form.

GIDE, ANDRÉ (1869–1951): French essayist, novelist, and dramatist. Three years spent in Algeria made an impression on Gide, causing him to react against the restraints imposed by a narrowly Protestant upbringing. Yet, closely bound to biblical characters and stories, he was to become one of the foremost modern representatives of the literature of introspection, self-confession, and moral and religious discomfort. SELECTED READING: George D. Painter, *André Gide: A Critical Biography*, 1968. (SOURCE: Jason, 3, 2003)

GIGUE: a lively, springy, irregular dance for one or more persons, usually in triple meter; a jig.

SONG	COMPOSER	POET
"Dansons la gigue"	Charles Loeffler	Paul Verlaine

GILM, HERMANN VON (1812–1864): Austrian poet. Member of an aristocratic family from the Tyrol, Gilm attracted political disfavor by his passionate anti-Jesuitical verse and by his labors on behalf of political awakening. Yet his lyrics and love poems reveal a sensitive ear, eye, and mind. The verses of Hermann von Gilm were set many times by Richard Strauss.

GIN: (Scot.) (pr. gin, as in be*gin*), *if*; *skill*; *scheme*.

SONG	COMPOSER	POET
"My Hoggie"	Benjamin Britten	Robert Burns

GIOVANITTI, ARTURO (1884–1959): an Italian poet, minister, editor, and socialist. Born in the small town of Campobasso, Italy, in the mountains of Abruzzi, Giovannitti immigrated to the United States in 1902. After studying theology at McGill University in Canada, he was ordained a Protestant Evangelical minister, and then moved to New York in 1906. Upon becoming the secretary of the Italian Socialist Federation in 1908, he edited their newspaper. He was arrested on charges of accessory to the murder of a striker while leading immigrant workers in a textile strike in Massachusetts. While awaiting his trial, he wrote *The Walker*, then was acquitted after ten months of incarceration. In 1917 he founded the Anti-Fascist Alliance of North America. He died while editing *The Complete Poems of Arturo Giovannitti*. His English verse was set by Charles Griffes. PRINCIPAL WORKS:

The Walker; Arrows in the Gale, 1914; *As it Was in the Beginning* (play), 1917; *Quando canta il gallo*; *The Complete Poems of Arturo Giovannitti*, 1962. (SOURCE: *American Poetry*, 2000)

GIPPIUS, ZINAIDA: *see* ⋆HIPPIUS.

GIRALDA, LA: a bell tower in Seville. The Giralda, the 318-foot bell tower dominating the skyline of the city of Seville, is so named because of Fides (Faith), its most elevated figure, whose banner serves as a weather vane or giraldillo. Eventually the entire tower, once a minaret attached to the mosque, became known as the Giralda. (SOURCE: Cockburn, Stokes, 1992)

SONG	COMPOSER	POET
"La Giralda"	Joaquín Turina	José Muñoz San Román

GIRAUD, ALBERT (1860–1929): Belgian poet. Giraud was the author of a collection of fifty poems titled *Pierrot Lunaire*, published in 1884. He was a member of La Jeune Belgique, one of the many youth movements that sprang up across Europe in defiance of oppressive political and cultural insularity. Many considered his rigid versification to be flat and labored, but Otto ⋆Hartleben, becoming interested in Giraud's peculiar combination of quasi-doggerel and parody, made a free German translation of the *Lunaire* poems. The then-current vogue for that reanimated Italian clown fired the imagination of *fin-de-siècle* Europe, including Debussy, who cites him in several works, and Arnold Schönberg, who adapted twenty-one of Hartleben's translations into his ⋆*Pierrot Lunaire*. (SOURCE: Steinberg, 2, 1973)

GIRAUDOUX, JEAN (1882–1944): French playwright, novelist, essayist, and diplomat. Giraudoux's theater dominated the French stage in the period between the two world wars. In the 1920s, at the age of forty-six, he first began writing for the theater with stylistic imagination, a witty sense of the contradictions of life, and a search for purity. These qualities made Giraudoux's work unique and brought him a worldwide fame. His works were translated and produced in English and other languages. In his novels, which he began to write later, his major theme was man's search for an ideal that was beyond the imperfections of reality. The public found this a touching point of view, and relished his wit, elegance, and civility, as well as his esteem for language itself with its verbal extravagance verging on poetic fantasy. Giraudoux delighted in depicting charming young girl characters who represent the innocence of nature. The writing of Jean Giraudoux was set by Arthur Honegger, who extracted from *Suzanne et le Pacific* five short morality tales that he called "Petit Cours de Morale" (A Small Course in Morality). PRINCIPAL WORKS: *Simon le pathétique*, 1918; *Suzanne and the Pacific*, 1921, English trans., 1923; *Juliette au pays des hommes*; *My Friend from Limousin*, 1923; *Bella*, 1926, English trans., 1927; *Siegfried*, 1928; *Amphitryon 38*, 1929; *Intermezzo*, 1933; *Ondine*, 1939; *La Folle De Chaillot*, 1945, as *The Madwoman of Chaillot*, 1949; *La Guerre de Troie n'aura pas lieu*, 1935, as *Tiger at the Gates*, trans. C. Fry, 1955. SELECTED READING: Paul A. Mankin, *Precious Irony: The Theatre of Giraudoux*, 1971. (SOURCE: Vinson, Kirkpatrick (1), 1984)

GITANJALI: a book of 159 poems by Rabindranath ★Tagore, Indian poet. This collection has been said to bring the poet into more familiar contact with the natural world than any previous book and brings us very close to a religious experience that is universal yet intensely individual. Although some have thought that *Gitanjali* had been influenced by the Bible, the poet himself said that when he tried to read the Bible, it was so violent that he could not. Poems from the *Gitanjali* have been set by John Alden Carpenter. (SOURCE: Thompson, 1992)

GLACÉ KID: leather made from the skin of a goat and finished to a shiny, glossy surface.

SONG	COMPOSER	POET
"Mon cadavre est doux comme un gant"	Francis Poulenc	Louise de Vilmorin

GLEIM, JOHANN WILHELM LUDWIG (1719–1803): German poet. Born in Thuringia, Gleim's elementary education was given to him by his father, a small town official. At ten years of age, he was sent to a neighboring pastor, who instructed Gleim in classical languages. After he was orphaned in 1734, some wealthy friends made it possible for him to attend the University of Halle, where he studied law (1738–40). He enjoyed a position as secretary to Prince Wilhelm von Schwedt in Berlin and took part in the Second Silesian War in his company. After the death of the prince and an unhappy period of service elsewhere, he was appointed secretary, later canon, to the cathedral chapter in Halberstadt (1747). This position gave him security as well as time to devote to his ★Anacreontic poetry writing, light, playful, and worldly verse. Gleim's real talent was for friendship, and he was on an intimate footing with almost the entire German literary world of the eighteenth century. He acted as a mentor to unknown, impoverished young poets and often supported them financially. His first collection of poetry (*Versuch*) was a popular and critical success; many of the poems were set to music. His most creative period occurred when he published *Preussische Kriegslieder von einem Grenadier* (1758), which made him famous. Many books were published subsequently, but "Vater" Gleim was chiefly remembered for the advice and encouragement he gave to other younger writers. The verse of Johann Gleim was set by Mozart and Haydn. PRINCIPAL WORKS: *Versuch in Scherzhaften Liedern* [A Sampling of Playful Songs], 2 vols., 1744–45; *Preussische Kriegslieder in den Feldzügen* [Prussian War Songs in the Field], 1758,; *Lieder für das Volk* [Songs for the Common People], 1772. SELECTED READING: *Klopstock and His Friends*, ed. Klamer Schmidt, trans. Elizabeth Ogilvey Benger, 1814. (SOURCES: Kunitz, Colby, 1967; Hardin, Schweitzer, 1990)

GLORIANA: ★Spenser's name for his representation of Queen Elizabeth I. Gloriana held an annual twelve-day feast, during which various adventurers appeared before her to be assigned tasks chosen by her. At one time twelve knights presented themselves to her. The exploits of these twelve form the scheme of Spenser's allegory.

GOD, M.: pseudonym invented by composer Erik Satie for a child whose full name was Mima Godebska.

SONG	COMPOSER	POET
"Daphénéo"	Erik Satie	M. God

GODE: (Scot.) (pr. good), *God*.

GODIVA, LADY: according to legend, Lady Godiva (ca.1010–67) rode naked through the streets of Coventry in order to persuade her husband, the local lord, to lower the taxes.

GOETHE, JOHANN WOLFGANG VON (1749–1832): a German poet, playwright, fiction and travel writer, scientist, statesman, and the first German poet to find an international audience during his lifetime. Calling Goethe "the German Shakespeare," as has been done, scarcely gives sufficient credit to this brilliant man and his remarkable career. As poet, novelist, playwright, philosopher, and scientist, Goethe achieved an influence on European culture and a popularity in his own lifetime never approached by the Bard of Stratford-on-Avon. Goethe was born in Frankfurt and educated at Leipzig University. The critic Herder, whom he met in 1770, introduced Goethe to ideas of spontaneous creation and inspiration, and the concept of a national character in literature, as well as the beauties of unsophisticated forms like folk songs.

Young Goethe was licensed in law in 1771, studied drawing as well, and after practicing law in Frankfurt for a time, became a writer. In 1775 he joined the small court of Weimar, becoming a member of the council (1776). He was granted a degree of nobility in 1782 and took over the finances of the court. As general supervisor for arts and sciences (1788), he was soon named director of court theaters (1791–1817), and became the chancellor of the University of Jena. In the history of modern German literature Goethe was the dominant figure. Before he was twenty-five years old, he had created models for the whole European ★Romantic movement: lyrical poetry on themes of nature, love, individuality, genius, and creativity; historical drama; and a tragic novel, ★*Werther*, which work created his European reputation in one stroke.

Goethe's creative life is generally divided into three periods: (1) his period of youth and early manhood, in which the poetry had spontaneity and empathy with nature and expressed his view of life by symbols taken from nature; (2) maturity and middle age, when the poetry had a more classical form and his outlook became more pagan; (3) the last quarter century of his life, after ★Schiller's death, in which Goethe worked with many forms of the world literature. One must remember that Goethe was not ever just wholly his Faust, but was always part Mephistopheles, that is, Goethe was sometimes portrayed as an ideal of decorum and a certain stodginess, but he never followed convention in things that truly mattered to him (Kaufman, 1962). Ever present in all of Goethe's work is nature, universal laws of evolution, death and rebirth, of which order man is a part. Despite the vicissitudes of his life, he remained an optimist. Faust is, after all, ultimately redeemed. A feature of his lyric writing is the mingling of sensuous and intellectual elements, and a sensitivity to irrational forces of existence. The verse of Goethe has been set by Schubert, Beethoven, Mozart, Schumann, Wolf, Mendelssohn, Liszt, Strauss, Brahms, Ferruccio Busoni, Carl Loewe, Louis Spohr, Armin Knab, Ottmar Schoeck, Hans Pfitzner, Carl Zelter, Fanny Mendelssohn Hensel, Louise Reichardt, Armin Knab, Johann Reichardt, Charles Griffes, Charles Ives, Edward MacDowell, Mary Howe, Mussorgsky, Tchaikovsky, Medtner, and Ildebrando Pizzetti. PRINCIPAL WORKS: Verse: *Neue Lieder,* 1770, New Poems, 1853; *Sesenheimer Liederbuch, 1775–89,* 1854, Sesenheim Songs, 1853; *Römische Elegien,* 1793, Roman Elegies, 1876; *Reinecke Fuchs,* 1794, Reynard the Fox, 1855; *Epigramme: Venedig,* 1790, Venetian Epigrams, 1853; *Xenien,* 1796 (with Schiller); *Epigrams,* 1853; *Balladen,* 1798, Ballads, 1853; *Neueste Lieder,* 1800, Newest Poems, 1853; *Gedichte,* 1812, 1815, The Poems of Goethe, 1853; *Sonette,* 1819, Sonnets, 1853; *Westöstlicher Divan,* 1819, West-Eastern Divan, 1877. Novels: *Die Leiden des jüngen Werthers,* 1774; revised 1787 as The Sorrows of Werther. Plays: *Iphigenie,* produced 1779; revised version in verse as *Iphigenie auf Tauris,* 1802; *Egmont,* produced 1784, trans. by Charles E. Passage, in *Plays,* 1980; *Faust,* part I, produced 1819; part II, 1833. SELECTED READING: F. J. Lamport, *A Student's Guide to Goethe,* 1971. (SOURCES: Vinson, Kirkpatrick (1), 1984; Kaufman, 1962)

GOLDEN FLEECE, THE: *see* ★JASON.

GOLDEN LEGEND, THE: a book containing stories of the lives of the saints, taken seriously only until the Renaissance. *The Golden Legend,* not to be confused with Longfellow's later work of the same title, was written by Jacobus De Voragine, archbishop of Genoa, and published in 1275. Its original title was *Legenda Sanctorum,* but was more popularly known as *Legenda Aurora.* It was very popular until the Renaissance, when its fantastic stories were ridiculed by the humanists, as being not serious work. William Caxton published an English translation in 1483. (SOURCE: Drabble, 2000)

GOLDONI, CARLO (1707–1793): Italian playwright and librettist. The works of Carlo Goldoni were one of the new influences upon literature during the eighteenth century. In his plays traditional masked ★*commedia dell'arte* figures were replaced with more genuine characters who were given complete dialogue, whereas previously there had been only improvisation upon stereotypical situations. Goldoni contributed much to *opera buffa.* He expanded the decorative elements, providing detailed descriptions of scenery and costumes. He reduced the amount of recitative, which speeded up the action, simplified the plot, thus approaching the continuous drama of the future. He also employed a greater variety of forms, allowing for larger and more interesting ensembles. He introduced the *arietta,* a short aria with no repeats, and the romantic or comic duet reconciling lovers, which became a fixed feature in act 3 of many of his librettos. His influence on the development of ensembles in *opera* *buffa* was probably greater than that of any composer. In the librettos one sees all the elements of a good *commedia dell'arte* scenario: mistaken identity, disguises, trickery, foolishness, stubborn old men standing in the way of true love, frauds and quacks, dialects, the conceited, the proud, the vain, the stupid, quick-witted servants and servant girls, frustrated love, and love triumphant. Goldoni was not only a playwright, but the leading librettist of his time. His works were set by Vivaldi (*La Cricolda*), Haydn (*Il mondo della luna, La Cantatrice*, and *Il Pescatrice*), Mozart (*La finta semplice*), and Baldassare Galuppi (*Il filosofo di campagna, Il mondo delle luna*, and *La Diavolessa*), Giovanni Paisiello (*Il mondo della luna*), Niccola Piccini (*La buona figliuola* and *La buona figliuola maritata*). Goldoni altered his approach to *opera buffa* and revolutionized the genre for those who followed. The more sentimental aspects of the later works of Bellini, Donizetti, and Rossini are unimaginable without the tenderness and care lavished upon *La Cecchina, ossia La buona figliuola* and its leading female role. After *La buona figliuola* a truly strong female character did not come into *opera buffa* until Mozart and Da Ponte created Susanna. Goldoni's significance to song literature lies in Salieri's setting of Goldoni's librettos, and his recommendation to his student Schubert, who set one Goldoni text (from act 3 of Goldoni's *Il filosofo di campagna*) first as a male quartet (D 513) and later as a solo song (D 528), and in Haydn's setting of Goldoni. SELECTED READING: *Memoirs of Carlo Goldoni*, trans. John Black, 1883; Joseph Spencer Kennard, *Goldoni and the Venice of his Time*, 1920, repr. 1967; Winifred Smith, *The Commedia dell'Arte*, 1980. (SOURCES: Goldoni, 1883; Kennard, 1920; Smith, 1980)

GOLENISHCHEV-KUTÚZOV, COUNT ARSENYI ARKADYEVICH (1848–1913): a Russian lyric poet. Golenishchev-Kutúsov was very popular at the end of the nineteenth century but not accepted by the literary establishment. He tried to revive a severe and classical style but could not breathe life into it. His principal title to glory was as a personal friend of Mussorgsky, who, when his former roommate Rimsky-Korsakov married, was unhappy living alone. At the age of twenty-four the count, as impoverished as the composer himself, became Mussorgsky's new roommate and his protégé. Mussorgsky found in Kutúsov's poetry "an unadulterated truth of sentiment" and in the count himself "spontaneity of artistic creation" (Riesemann, 1935). Mussorgsky used his verses for the "Songs and Dances of Death," the cycle "Sunless," and other songs. At the time when poet and composer crossed paths, Mussorgsky started to turn away from depicting the outside world and began to reach the inner depths of his own experience. Characteristic of Kutúsov's poems are themes of weariness, pessimism, and a desire to flee into the past. He is at his best when speaking of death and destruction. (SOURCES: Miller, 1973; Mirsky, 1958; Riesemann, 1935)

GOLIARD: a twelfth-century wandering scholar-poet noted for composing satiric and profane Latin verses.

GOMORRAH: *see* ★SODOM.

GONDOLA: a lightweight flat-bottomed boat used for travel in the *Venice canals, a cabin located in the center of the boat and at each end a rising point. The boat is rowed with a single oar by a gondolier.

SONG	COMPOSER	POET
1. "Barcarolle"	Gabriel Fauré	Marc Monnier
2. "Venezianisches Epigram"	Ottmar Schoeck	Johann Wolfgang von Goethe
3. "In a Gondola"	Alice Barnett, Ned Rorem	Robert Browning
4. "Toréador"	Francis Poulenc	Jean Cocteau

GÓNGORA (Y ARGOTE), LUIS DE (1561–1627): Spanish poet. Luis de Góngora was born in Córdoba. He was educated first at a Jesuit school and then, from 1576 to 1580, at the University of Salamanca, where he received no degree. He was given a stipend for his services to the Córdoba Cathedral from 1586 to 1617, ordained a priest in 1617, and made royal chaplain in Madrid (1617–1625). Luis de Góngora made significant contributions to a variety of poetic fields. As examples, his concept of the *ballad was a more sophisticated and artistically balanced form than the traditional one; he believed that the *burlesque* was a valid artistic form; he embraced many stylistic novelties. He originated new words; he took liberties with syntax and word order; he used complex metaphors. His major poems gave prominence to the world of nature, and he drew attention to the surprising patterns and relationships of the world with his metaphors. *Gongorismo* in Spanish literature is similar to the French *précieux*. His poetic style, so different from the norm, generated great controversy, and de Góngora never received the patronage he needed. The verses of Luis de Góngora have been set by Enrique Granados, Manuel de Falla, and Antonio Vives. PRINCIPAL WORKS: *Obras completas*, ed. Juan and Isabel Millé y Giménez, 1972; *Soledades*, ed. Dámaso Alonso, 1927, rev. ed. 1956 as *The Solitudes*, trans. Edward M. Wilson, 1931 and Gilbert F. Cunningham, 1977; *Góngora y el "Polifemo,"* ed. Dámaso Alonso, 1960, rev. ed., 2 vols., 1961, as *Polyphemus and Galatea*, trans. Gilbert F. Cunningham, 1977; *Sonetos completos* [The Complete Sonnets], ed. Biruté Ciplÿauskaite, 1969. SELECTED READING: M. J. Woods, *The Poet and the Natural World in the Age of Góngora*, 1978; Michael Woods, *Gracián Meets Góngora: The Theory and Practice of Wit*, 1995. (SOURCE: Vinson, Kirkpatrick (1), 1984)

GOODMAN, PAUL (1911–1972): American writer. Paul Goodman was born in New York City. He worked as a teacher in a progressive school and later as a lay psychologist. "Even his admirers often agreed that Goodman was a 'poor and intellectually fractured' writer, but provocative as a literary radical bohemian" (Hamilton, 1994). As a notorious dissident, he was a guru for young students in the 1960s. His eighteen collections of poetry are essentially just jotted down, awkward, and slangy bits of prose. Much of its appeal stemmed from Goodman's obsessive concern with homo-erotic problems, which he confronted directly. He was very much influenced by Wilhelm Reich and his ideas, despite the fact that Reich openly disliked homosexuality. Paul Goodman's writing has been set by Ned Rorem. SELECTED READING: *Collected Poems*, ed. Taylor Stoehr, 1974. (SOURCE: Hamilton, 1994)

"Good Neighbor, Why Do You Look Awry?": a duet for two women by Henry Purcell, set to words by Edward Ravenscroft. *See* ★ *Canterbury Guests, The* for plot details and position of the song within the plot.

GORGE: *throat.*

SONG	COMPOSER	POET
"A Divine Image"	Ralph Vaughan Williams	William Blake

GORGIO: a non-gypsy. The gypsy code mandates that their women have nothing to do with gorgios.

SONG	COMPOSER	POET
"Die Zigeunerin"	Hugo Wolf	Joseph von Eichendorff

GOTTER, FRIEDRICH (1746–1797): German poet and playwright. Gotter was the editor of the Göttingen *Musenalmanach*. Haydn set Gotter's poetry, and in 1816 his poem "Pflicht und Liebe" was set by Schubert. (SOURCE: Reed, 1997)

GOURMONT, RÉMY DE (1858–1915): French poet, novelist, and essayist. Gourmont's reputation was one of the most wide-ranging of the late nineteenth century. T. S. ★Eliot described him as "the critical conscience of his generation." Within the ★Symbolist movement, Gourmont was an important spokesman for the Idealism of ★Schopenhauer and its insistence upon individual subjectivity, which theme he explored in the novels, plumbing the relationship between sexuality and artistic creativity. Gourmont was co-founder of two ★Symbolist reviews, and his critical writing made a lasting impression, resulting in a theory of criticism that highly influenced his peers in many countries. André Caplet set the verse of Rémy de Gourmont. PRINCIPAL WORKS: Novels: *Sixtine*, 1890; *Lilith*, 1892. Criticism: *Livres des masques*, 1896–98; *Esthétique de la langue française*, 1899; *Le Problème du style*, 1902. (SOURCE: France, 1995)

GOWDAN: (Scot.), *golden.*

SONG	COMPOSER	POET
"A Laddie's Sang"	Benjamin Britten	William Soutar

GOWK: (Scot.) (pr. to rhyme with *cow*), adj. *cuckoo, crazy*; n. *a simpleton*; v. *to stare foolishly.*

SONG	COMPOSER	POET
"A Laddie's Sang"	Benjamin Britten	William Soutar

GOYA (1746–1828): Francisco José de Goya y Lucientes, an outstanding and celebrated Spanish artist. Goya's output included cartoons for the tapestry weavers (people at peace, at work, and at play), the horrors of the Napoleonic invasion (disasters of war), portraits of women and children, and pictures of sabbaths and witches. Goya was one of the strongest and most original painters in the history of Spanish art. He was born in a poor village of Aragón, apprenticed with a noted painter, finally taking a position as tapestry cartoonist when his painting was not initially successful. In 1786 he became a king's painter and later court painter to Ferdinand VII. Portraits were perhaps the most important part of Goya's painted work due to his ability to observe human nature. His representations of horror, hatred, and cruelty were intense and disturbing. Goya stated that he only recognized three masters: Velásquez, Rembrandt, and nature. (SOURCE: *Americana*, 2003)

SONG	COMPOSER	POET
"La maja de Goya"	Enrique Granados	Fernando Periquet

GRAIL: the cup or chalice traditionally believed to have been used by ★Christ at the Last Supper. Many medieval legends, romances, and allegories used the Grail as their subject. According to one account, Joseph of Arimathea preserved the Grail and collected into it some of the blood of the Savior at the Crucifixion. He then brought it to England, where it disappeared. According to other accounts, the Grail was brought from Heaven by angels and entrusted to a group of knights who guarded it in a safe place on top of a mountain, hence references to the Knights of the Grail. When the Grail was approached by someone of less than perfect purity, it vanished. The quest to find it became the source of most of the adventures of the Knights of the Arthurian Round Table. (SOURCE: Cooper, 1992)

SONG	COMPOSER	POET
"De Rêve"	Claude Debussy	Claude Debussy

GRANADA: a world-renowned Spanish city of Andalusia, near the southern coast bordering the Mediterranean Sea. Granada occupies a thirty-five-acre plateau on top of the last spur of the Sierra Nevada. The ★Alhambra, the last royal palace of the Moors, was occupied by twenty sultans for two and one half centuries. In the structures of the Alhambra, we see the likes and dislikes, aptitudes, and tastes of the Muslim civilization. Alhambra is known as the Red Citadel, made of red stone, and built in the thirteenth century. It is a naturally defensive position, with a sheer fall to the Darro River on the north side and a view across the plains on the south. The southern entry is approached by a long road ascending through tall elms planted by the Duke of Wellington during his war with Napoleon. The famous Court of the Lions contains the lion fountain surrounded by twelve roughly carved beasts spurting water from their mouths. (SOURCE: Casas, 1996)

SONG	COMPOSER	POET
1. "Pase abase el rey moro"	Luis de Narváez	anonymous
2. "Zaïde"	Hector Berlioz	Roger de Beauvoir

GRAND CANAL: the largest canal in Venice, winding through the heart of the city. Palaces built over a span of five centuries that represent a survey of the city's history line the waterway. Almost all the palaces bear the name of some once-great Venetian family. After the Grand Canal passes the ★Rialto Bridge, it doubles back on itself along a stretch known as La Volta (the bend), then widens out approaching Piazza San Marco.

SONG	COMPOSER	POET
1. "Barcarolle"	Gabriel Fauré	Marc Monnier
2. "Venezianisches Epigram"	Ottmar Schoeck	Johann Wolfgang von Goethe

GRANDMOUGIN, CHARLES JEAN (1850–1930): French poet and playwright. Grandmougin was known especially for his exploitation of patriotic themes, in such works as *Pour la patrie* (1902) and *Vengeons nos morts* (1916). Yet at the same time, his poetry has been described as pure, colorful, simple, and wise. The verse of Charles Grandmougin has been set by Gabriel Fauré.

GRAND OURSE: *see* ★GREAT BEAR.

GRAVES, ROBERT (1895–1985): English poet, novelist, and essayist. Robert Graves was born in London, son of a facile verse writer and translator from the Irish who was inspector of schools in Dublin. Graves's childhood and adolescence were typical of his class and time; he was educated at St. John's College, Oxford. He volunteered to serve in France with the Royal Welsh Fusiliers during World War I, a choice that reflected his desire to find his own Celtic roots outside Ireland. After the war he began to grapple with the difficulties of reality. As a poet he resisted any modernist breaking of meter, form, and linguistic propriety. The principal theme of Graves's poetry was the recording of romantic love, which he viewed as a transcendent ecstasy linked with doom. His body of love poetry is without rival in our time for intensity and elegance. As a novelist and essayist he demonstrates erudition and intellectual brilliance. Graves taught at Egyptian University in 1926, Oxford from 1961 to 1966, and at Boston's MIT in 1963. During the Spanish Civil War, he left Majorca where he had settled previously, only to return after World War II and remain until his death. The verse of Robert Graves has been set to music by Samuel Barber, John Duke, Hugo Weisgall, and Lee Hoiby. PRINCIPAL WORKS: Poetry: *Collected Poems*, 1948; *Collected Poems*, 1968; *Poems about Love*, 1969; *Collected Poems*, 1975. Novels: *I, Claudius: From the Autobiography of Tiberius Claudius, Emperor of the Romans, Born B.C.E. 10, Murdered and Deified C.E. 54*, 1934; *Claudius the God and His Wife Messaline: The Troublesome Reign of Tiberius Claudius Caesar, emperor of the Romans*; *Wife to Mr. Milton: The Story of Marie Powell*, 1944. Other: *Poetic Unreason and Other Studies*, 1925; *Goodbye to all That: An Autobiography*, 1929, revised ed. 1957, 1960; *Sergeant Lamb's America*, 1940. SELECTED READING: Martin Seymour-Smith, *Graves*, 1956; revised 1965, 1970; Douglas Day, *Swifter than Reason: The Poetry and Criticism of Graves*, 1963; Robert Graves, *Conversations with Robert Graves*, 1990. (SOURCE: Vinson, 1979)

GREASY JOAN: an expression referring to *the kitchen wench*.

SONG	COMPOSER	POET
"Winter"	Dominick Argento	William Shakespeare

GREAT BEAR, GRAND OURSE (Fr.): a constellation known as the Big Dipper, Ursa Major. The head of the Great Bear is the North Star, by which ships navigated in the past. A smaller constellation is known as the Little Dipper. According to the Greek legend, ★Zeus fathered a son, Arcas, with the nymph Callisto. Zeus's wife Hera changed Callisto into a bear. When Arcas was about to shoot Callisto,

Zeus changed them into the constellations Great Bear and Little Bear. (SOURCE: Bridgwater, Kurtz, 1968)

SONG	COMPOSER	POET
"Le Sommeil"	Francis Poulenc	Maurice Carème

"Great Love, I Know Thee": a song composed by Henry Purcell to a text by John ★Dryden from their semi-opera *King Arthur*, produced in 1691. *See* ★*King Arthur* for plot details and placement of songs.

GRECQUES, MÉLODIES POPULAIRES: a set of songs by Maurice Ravel with folk poetry translated by Michel Dimitri ★Calvocoressi. The poet called Ravel's attention to the Greek folk songs in February 1904 on the occasion of a lecture entitled *Songs of the Oppressed* that treated Greek and Armenian folklore. Luise Thomasset, a singer, was persuaded to collaborate, but her condition was that the songs be with piano accompaniment. Calvocoressi and Ravel chose four Greek poems from a Constantinople collection and one more, "Les Cueilleuses de lentisques" from a Pernot collection. Ravel composed piano accompaniments for all in thirty-six hours.

GREENAWAY, "KATE," CATHERINE (1846–1901): English illustrator of children's books. A painter of watercolors, Greenaway was particularly known for the quaint charm of her pictures, delicate paintings of flowers, gardens, and children who were themselves flowerlike. She often wrote verses to go with her drawings. Greenaway was born in London, the daughter of an engraver. The hats worn by her female subjects were very large with off-the-face brims, trimmed with flowers or feathers and voluminous veiling. (SOURCE: *OED*, 1989)

SONG	COMPOSER	POET
"La Diva de l'Empire"	Erik Satie	Dominique Bonnaud, Numa Blès

GREENE, ROBERT (1560–1592): English prose writer and dramatist. While in school in London, Greene was known as a wit. To his credit were thirty-eight publications—prose romances, pamphlets, and dramas. In his last pamphlet, *A Groatsworth of Wit*, Greene gives the first contemporary mention of ★Shakespeare, not entirely complimentary however. He warns his fellow playwrights to beware of the upstart actor who is encroaching on their territory and writing his own plays. PRINCIPAL WORKS: *A Maiden's Dream*, 1591; *Orlando Furioso*, 1588. SELECTED READING: Charles W. Crupi, *Robert Greene*, 1986. (SOURCE: Jason, 3, 2003)

GREENSLEEVES: the name of an inconstant lady love, the subject of a ballad published in 1580. This and the melody to which it was sung became very popular. Both are mentioned by ★Shakespeare in *The Merry Wives of Windsor*.

GRENADIER: a foot soldier in an elite unit, especially selected for strength and courage.

SONG	COMPOSER	POET
1. "Der Tambourgesell"	Gustav Mahler	Achim von Arnim, Clemens Brentano

| 2. "Die beiden | R. Schumann, | Heinrich Heine |
| Grenadiere" | R. Wagner | |

GRENOUILLÈRE, LA: the name of a small island in the Seine River in the suburbs of Paris, where writers and painters lived at the end of the eighteenth century, lit., *the froggery*. There was a restaurant there, where during the nineteenth century on Sundays writers and painters came boating. Renoir's famous picture *The Boatmen's Luncheon* shows the scene. (SOURCE: Bernac, 1977)

SONG	COMPOSER	POET
"La Grenouillère"	Francis Poulenc	Guillaume Apollinaire

GRILLPARZER, FRANZ (1791–1872): Austrian dramatist and poet. Many believe that the unstable heredity and political censorship endured by Grillparzer hampered his development. He became a civil servant in 1813, after much frustration was named director of archives, and retired in 1856. His private life was as difficult as his professional life. Grillparzer suffered much from the vacillating power of his creativity. Defeated by bitterness, he permitted no new play of his to be performed after 1838, although the old ones were produced. His most fertile period was 1816–1826. Even his posthumously published ★epigrams showed the characteristic gloom and the melancholy outlook that pervaded his plays. Nevertheless Grillparzer had a superb control of the medium and of his resources. The plays show also a characteristic Austrian musicality. His work was the last bastion of the eighteenth century, and he was the first Austrian writer to achieve international standing. Neither a romantic nor a realist, Grillparzer's work was the literary counterpart to the musical classicism of Haydn and Beethoven. Fanny Mendelssohn Hensel set his work, and, although Franz Grillparzer was very supportive of Schubert's work, his writing was set only once by Schubert. The two had met but once, but the epitaph on Schubert's tombstone was written by Grillparzer. PRINCIPAL WORKS: *Sappho*, 1817, trans. L. C. Cumming, 1855; *Das goldene Vlies*, 1818–20, trans. F. W. Thurstan and S. A. Wittman, 1879; *Tristia ex Ponto*, 1835; *Gedichte*, 1872. SELECTED READING: Douglas Yates, *Franz Grillparzer*, 1946; A. Burkhard, *Grillparzer in England and America*, 1961. (SOURCE: Steinberg, 2, 1973)

GRIMM'S FAIRY TALES: *see* ★KINDER- UND HAUSMÄRCHEN.

GRIS, JUAN (1887–1927): Spanish cubist painter, whose real name was José Victoriano González. Born in Madrid, Juan Gris had academic training at the School of Arts and Crafts in that city. For some years he earned his living doing commercial art, until he joined ★Picasso in Paris (1907). There Gris became interested in the development of Cubism done by Picasso and ★Braque. In 1912 Gris exhibited a monochromatic portrait, "Homage to Picasso," at the Salon des Indépendents, but then moved on to a coloristic style that anticipated the later synthetic cubist paintings of Braque and Picasso. The majority of Gris's paintings are still lifes that exerted a great influence within Cubism. In 1920, after a serious illness, Gris designed scenery and costumes for Diaghelev's Ballet Russe de Monte Carlo for a time. During his last years Gris produced many of his strongest, most simplified cubist paintings.

Carol Kimball informs us (*NATS Journal*, 1987) that: "Gris was interested in the counterplay between objects and their shadows; shapes in the paintings are reinforced by light and shade. . . . The concept of double objects joining to form a single form is further reinforced by the poem's allusion to day and night and shadows." (SOURCE: *Americana*, 2003)

SONG	COMPOSER	POET
"Gris"	Francis Poulenc	Paul Éluard

GROTH, KLAUS (1819–1899): poet of the Low German language and translator. Klaus Groth was born in Schleswig-Holstein, and he gave to his fellow citizens a cultural identity that helped them resist the Danish occupation of their country. Before the late *Romantic period and before Groth re-created it, the Low German language had been virtually extinct since the late Middle Ages. His industrious father was the owner of a windmill, a carpentry shop, a grain store, and a small farm, and Klaus's grandfather had recited local folklore and poetry to him during his childhood. Although he was not allowed to study another language, Groth became a schoolteacher (1842). While studying at the University of Berlin under Jacob Grimm, an unhappy love affair so depressed him that he left, but not before he became influenced by English Romantic literature. Soon he began to translate the works of Sir Walter *Scott, *Burns, and Lord *Byron into Low German, and his first published collection was much admired. Groth went to Bonn to learn from Karl *Simrock, and in 1856 he was given an honorary doctorate by Friedrich Wilhelm University. Holland, Denmark, and the United States translated much of his work into the local language. When Schleswig-Holstein was annexed by Prussia after its victory over Austria, Groth supported Bismarck's drive for German unification. Klaus Groth was Germany's most important dialect poet, and his poetry was set by Johannes Brahms, who appreciated its earnestness and sensitive qualities. PRINCIPAL WORKS: *Quickborn* (in Low German), 1853, 1854, 1856, as *Fountain of Youth*; *Hundert Blättern* (in High German) [One Hundred Pages], 1854; *Vertelln* (in Low German) [To Tell], 1855, 1859. (SOURCE: Hardin, Mews, 1993)

GROTTO: a hidden underground passage.

SONG	COMPOSER	POET
1. "La Grotte"	Claude Debussy	Tristan l'Hermite
2. "La Vie antérieure"	Henri Duparc	Charles Baudelaire

GRUN: (Scot.) (pr. to rhyme with *sun*), n. *ground, earth; a snare for catching birds*; v. *to grind*.

GUADALQUIVIR: a Spanish river that rises in the mountains in the south, flows through *Cordoba and Seville, and empties into the Gulf of *Cádiz at Jerez de la Frontera.

SONG	COMPOSER	POET
"Und schläfst du, mein Mädchen"	Hugo Wolf	Paul Heyse, Emanuel Geibel

GUAJIRA: a Cuban folk song and dance in 6/8 meter.

GUARD BLANCHE, LA: according to Pierre Bernac, "it is obvious that these Officers of the White Guard are angels." (SOURCE: Bernac, 1977)

SONG	COMPOSER	POET
"Aux officiers de la Garde Blanche"	Francis Poulenc	Louise de Vilmorin

GUID: (Scot.), *good.*

GUILLÉN, NICOLÁS (1902–1989): Cuban poet. Born in Camagüey, Nicolás Guillén wrote poems that are rooted in Cuba's own cultural and political circumstances, but possessed international appeal. They have been translated into thirty other languages. In 1937–38 Guillén was a war correspondent in Spain for *Mediodia* magazine. He was named Cuba's poet laureate and president of the National Union of Cuban writers and artists in 1961. Earlier he had been identified with the anti-imperialist movement that led to the 1959 Cuban Revolution. Guillén's later poems were dedicated to praising the achievements of Castro's regime, but his earlier poems had called for a classless and raceless society. As a whole, his poetry revealed the many disparate and conflicting parts that make up the Hispanic Caribbean and created a distinctive literature from the ingredients of "this cultural stew." Guillén was from one of Cuba's black middle-class families, but he was not interested in proclaiming black superiority or nostalgia for Africa. He was preoccupied with the cross-cultural phenomenon. In 1930 he wrote *Motivos de Son* (*son* being a pop musical form with a strong black component), eight short poems written in Afro-Cuban vernacular, which were set to music using poetic lines that end on a stressed syllable, a rhythmic effect that is not pleasing to Spanish readers. The verses of Nicolás Guillén have been set by Xavier Montsalvatge, Silvestre Revueltas, Alejandro García Caturla, and José Ardevol. PRINCIPAL WORKS: *Motivos de son*, 1930; *Sóngoro Cosongo*, 1931; *La paloma de vuelo popular*, 1958; *Tengo*, 1964; *El gran zoo*, 1967; *Canticle*, 1997; *Homage*, 1997; *Horses in the Air and Other Poems*, 1999. SELECTED READING: Dennis Sardinha, *The Poetry of Nicolas Guillén*, 1976. (SOURCE: Jason, 1, 2003; Steinberg, 2, 1973)

GURRE: a palace in the beautiful northern part of Seeland, the favorite residence of Danish King Valdemar Atterdag and his mistress Tove. The original story, dealing with King Valdemar the Great and the amorous relationship with Tove, was told in several twelfth-century ballads written in Icelandic and Danish. Two hundred years later another version of the legend inspired many Danish poets, such as J. P. ★Jacobsen (*Gurrelieder*), Ludwig Holstein (*Tove*), and Holger Drachmann (*Gurre*). In the original versions, Tove, a beautiful, self-confident young girl who is mistress of Valdemar the Great, challenges Queen Sofie when she reproaches Tove for wearing a provocative dress. The queen discovers that her husband not only has given Tove expensive gifts but has also made her mother of two sons. The queen's hatred and jealousy drive her to take a cruel revenge. She bids the servants overheat the palace bathroom. Then she lures Tove into it so that she perishes there.

SONG	COMPOSER	POET
"Gurrelieder"	Arnold Schönberg	Jens Peter Jacobsen

GYPSIES: a dark-skinned nomadic race that first appeared in England about the beginning of the sixteenth century. Because they were thought to have come from Egypt, they were referred to as *Egyptians*, the name soon corrupted to *gypcians*. They called themselves Romany (*rom* meaning a man or husband), which was also the name of their language. To the Portuguese they were *ciganos*; to the Spanish, *gitanos*; to the Dutch *heidens*; to the Danish and Swedish (who had the notion that gypsies came from Tartary) they were *Tartars*. Germans called them *Zigeuner*, the Italians called them *zingarelle*. They were called *Bohemians* by the French because the first gypsies who arrived in their country to present themselves before the gates of Paris came from Bohemia. Anton Dvořák's op. 55, seven *Gypsy Songs*, was identified with the typically romantic concept of gypsy life as a symbol of freedom and lack of bonds, an allegory of the fate of the Czech nation longing for liberation from Austro-Hungarian rule.

H

HA: (Scot.), *hall*.

HABANERA: a Spanish dance form and song introduced into Spain from Africa by way of Cuba and named after the capital city of that country, Havana. The Habanera is in a moderate 2/4 time. The dancers face each other, accompanying the singing with gestures. (SOURCE: Cockburn, Stokes, 1992)

SONG	COMPOSER	POET
"Punto de Habanera"	Xavier Montsalvatge	Néstor Luján

HADDAM: a town in Connecticut, located on the Connecticut River. The "thin men of Haddam" are fictitious. Wallace Stevens liked the name because it had a completely Yankee sound.

SONG	COMPOSER	POET
"13 Ways of Looking at a Blackbird"	Vincent Persichetti	Wallace Stevens

HADES: Homer's name for the god ★Pluto, who reigns over the dead. In later classical mythology, Hades was the dwelling place of departed spirits. It was a place of dark and gloom, but not necessarily a place of punishment and torture. The word "Hades" corresponds to the Hebrew word *Sheol*, which has been faultily translated to the word *Hell* in the authorized version of the Bible. For this reason Hades is often misused as a euphemism for Hell. (SOURCE: Cooper, 1992)

SONG	COMPOSER	POET
1. "An schwager Kronos"	Franz Schubert	Johann Wolfgang von Goethe
2. "Fahrt zum Hades"	Franz Schubert	Johann Mayrhofer
3. "My Crow Pluto"	Virgil Thomson	Marianne Moore

HĀFIZ (SHAMSU'D-DIN MUHAMMAD) (ca.1320–ca.1389): Persian poet and philosopher. Hāfiz is Persian for "rememberer." It is applied to one who has memorized the Qu'ran (★Koran) and who then recites and comments upon it for the general population. The fourteenth-century Persian poet, Shamsu'd-Din Muhammad, was such a "rememberer," who took Hāfiz as his pen name. Little factual knowledge about his life exists, though legends abound. We know that he married and had a son who died unexpectedly. He did work as a dough maker in a baker's shop and as a manuscript copyist. During his lifetime the city he loved was besieged and taken five or six times, but in his poems there was no mention of the fall of kingdoms and the clash of battles. Most of his important works were written by the time he was thirty. His poems were collected into a ★Divan (or Diwan) by his lifelong friend Muhammad Gulandam, who wrote in the preface of the poet's celebrity not only in Persia, but in India, Turkistan, and Mesopotamia. Hāfiz is buried in the city of his birth, Shiraz, where his tomb, marked with an alabaster tombstone, is situated in a garden named *Hafiziyya* and visited today by his countrymen and the more literate tourists. An elaborate system has developed whereby people seek guidance from Hāfiz *Divan* by turning to random passages, which practice is also currently used with the Qu'ran. Hāfiz is famous for perfecting the ★*ghazal*, a short lyric poem, considered to be related to the ★sonnet. In his ghazals, Hāfiz combined technical virtuosity with sublime poetic inspiration. In the midst of his "oriental" period ★Goethe read the first German translations of Hāfiz in 1814. Disillusioned by the French Revolution, and besotted with Marianne ★Willemer, the wife of Johann Jakob Willemer, he wrote the poems of his ★*West-östlicher Divan*. Invoking the name and spirit of Hāfiz's (in German, *Hafis*) poetry, Goethe wrote of his love for Marianne in the person of ★Suleika to his Hatem. Marianne was moved to write poetry of her own, which Goethe incorporated in the *West-östlicher Divan*, and Schubert set her "Suleika I and II." Johannes Brahms set several poems of Hāfiz (op. 32, nos. 7, 8, 9) translated into German; Robert Franz, Richard Strauss, and Adolf Jensen also set Hāfiz in German. Alan Hovhaness has set Hāfiz and written poetry about Hāfiz. Blair Fairchild has set English translations of Hāfiz verse; N. N. Cherpnin has set Russian translations; other poets have invoked his name in their poetry. PRINCIPAL WORKS: *Odes of Hāfiz*, trans. J. Richardson, 1774. SELECTED READING: Thomas R. Crowe, trans. *Drunk on the Wine of the Beloved: 100 Poems of Hāfiz*, 2001. The best summary of his life and works is by Gertrude Bell. (SOURCES: Arberry, 1947, 1958; Browne, 1928)

SONG	COMPOSER	POET
1. "Erschaffen und Beleben"	Richard Strauss	Johann Wolfgang von Goethe
2. "Love Songs of Hāfiz"	Alan Hovhaness	Hāfiz
3. "Hāfiz, like Lord Krishna, Darting"	Alan Hovhaness	Alan Hovhaness

HAGEDORN, FRIEDRICH VON (1708–1754): German poet. It is believed that Hagedorn's reflective poems are his best work, but his lighter verse is what makes him live on. Hagedorn admired the English sentimentalists, especially ★Milton, and defended ★Klopstock against his detractors, but he was a neo-classicist in his own work. His view was that clarity and reasonableness and avoidance of excess are most important. Hagedorn's role as a pathfinder showed an appreciation of the purely worldly. Previously, the only kind of poetry that was taken seriously was that oriented to religion. Here was a kind of verse that argued the benefits of sensuality in the name of truth and morality. The poetry of Friedrich von Hagedorn was set by Mozart, Schubert, Telemann, and Edward MacDowell. Very little by Hagedorn is available in English, but there are isolated poems in *The Poetry of Germany*, 1853. (SOURCE: Browning, 1978)

HAGS: *see* ★TARTARY.

HAIKU: a Japanese three-line poem with seventeen syllables, or an English poem imitative of that form. The haiku is a traditional form of Japanese poetry, still active. It originated as part of an older form called tanka (short song). The tankas usually had thirty-one syllables in five lines, arranged 5-7-5, 7-7. The dropping of the last two lines left 5-7-5, the normal seventeen syllable form of the haiku. The best-known writers from the golden age of haiku, the seventeenth century, were Bashō and Issa.

SONG	COMPOSER	POET
1. "Haiku Settings"	Ursula Mamlock	Japanese haiku poets
2. "Haiku"	Thomas Pasatieri	Louis Phillips
3. "A Net of Fireflies"	Vincent Persichetti	Haiku poets
4. "Haiku" (8 vols.)	Robert Fairfax Birch	Harold Stewart
5. "Three Hokku"	Richard Hundley, Mary Howe	various haiku poets, A. Lowell
6. "Songs of Love and Longing"	Stephen Paulus	Haiku poets, tanka poets

"Hail to the Myrtle Shade": a song composed by Henry Purcell, set to the words of Nathaniel ★Lee, from his heroic play *Theodosius*, produced in 1680. *See* ★*Theodosius* for plot details and placement of songs.

HALM, FRIEDRICH (pseudonym of Franz Joseph, Freiherr von Münch-Bellinghausen) (1806–1871): German poet and playwright. Halm's early education was at a monastery school. Later he studied at the Vienna Schottengymnasium (1816–22), where ★Lenau and ★Bauernfeld were his schoolmates. After further studies at Vienna University, he married a noblewoman, was appointed to the civil service in the same year, and attained senior rank soon after. In 1844 Halm was made custodian of the Court Library in Vienna, selected over the poet ★Grillparzer. By 1867 he was appointed intendant of the court opera theater and the Burgtheater. In his day Halm was considered a great poet, his poetry a self-conscious tribute to an ideal of beauty that excluded all that was crass or harsh. His reputation suffered at the end of the nineteenth century and never recovered. His verse was set by Brahms and Schumann. PRINCIPAL WORKS: *Gedichte*, 1850; *Neue Gedichte*, 1864. (SOURCE: Garland, 1976)

HAMADRYAD: a nymph from both Greek and Roman mythology, a beautiful and vigorous maiden who lived in a tree and died when the tree died. (SOURCE: Cotterell, 1986)

SONG	COMPOSER	POET
"Reflet dans l'eau"	Gabriel Fauré	Baronne de Brimont

HANGER: *a steep wooded slope.*

SONG	COMPOSER	POET
"On Wenlock Edge"	Ralph Vaughan Williams	A. E. Housman

HANGING GARDENS OF BABYLON, THE: a square garden, 400 feet each way, rising in a series of terraces, provided with earth of a sufficient depth to accommodate trees of great size. Water was lifted from the *Euphrates River by a screw, the gardens irrigated by a reservoir at the top. The hanging gardens were one of the seven wonders of the world, said to have been built by King Nebuchadnezzar to gratify his wife Amytis, who was weary of the flat plains of *Babylon and longing for something to remind her of her native Median Hills. Stefan *George's collection of poems was published in 1895. It presents a vision of an artificial paradise in the Babylon of the legendary, beautiful, self-centered Queen Semiramis. (SOURCE: Cooper, 1992)

SONG	COMPOSER	POET
"Das Buch den hängenden Gärten"	Arnold Schönberg	Stefan George

"Hang This Whining Way of Wooing": a song by Henry Purcell with lyrics by Thomas *Southerne in his play, *The Wives Excuse*. For plot details and position of the song in the plot, *see* *Wives Excuse, The.*

HANNAY, PATRICK (?1594–1665?): Scottish poet. Accurate information about Hannay is almost nonexistent. From the 1622 publication of his poetry collection, it is clear that he was educated to the master of arts level. The collection, *The Poetical Works of Patrick Hannay,* was published together with a memoir of the author written by David Laing, who repeatedly emphasizes the dearth of information. Even Seymour Barab mistakenly spelled his surname Hanney in his setting of Hannay's verse. The Hannay family was prolific and Patrick is such a common name that all of Laing's information is questionable. As a court poet of James VI of Scotland, Hannay may have relocated to London at the time of the king's accession to the English throne as James I. Hannay first appeared in print with the publication of *The Happy Husband* and two *Elegies on the Occasion of the Death and Funeral of Queen Anne of Denmark* (1619). From Hannay's dedication of his verse to General Sir Andrew Gray, Laing deduces that Hannay may have been a soldier in General Gray's army when it served King Fredericke of Bohemia in Europe. (SOURCE: Steinberg, 2, 1973)

HARDY, THOMAS (1840–1928): English poet, playwright, novelist, essayist, and literary critic. Hardy was born in Dorset, where he was educated in local schools and privately. From 1856 to 1861 he was apprenticed to an ecclesiastical architect, after which he settled in London, practicing architecture until 1867, when he gave it up to become a full-time writer residing again in Dorset. After an intense period of reading in London, he rejected belief in Providence for a scientific philosophy based on writings of Darwin, geology and astronomy readings, without giving up his belief in the Christian ethic. He was convinced that there was little hope for humanity without enlightened cooperation and charity. Hardy is a philosophic poet, struggling to answer questions like these: "What is the true nature of the relation between animate creatures and an apparently inanimate world . . .? Is it possible for conscious beings to imagine an absence of consciousness . . .? What is it of the dead that lives in us and in what forms does it manifest itself? These are the questions which his verse asks of itself and of its readers, even as it talks (or sings) of hedgehogs and thrushes, raindrops, birch trees, fresh love, embittered love, and a long-dead sister" (Hamilton, 1994). Hardy's earliest poetry suggests that he did not write it with ease. He rejected poetical lushness and achieved an independence of style that reflected his own observation, thought, vision, and feeling. Being impressed by the best of Wordsworth and ★Browning, he disciplined himself to write lyrical poetry that was as little removed as possible from the idiom of ordinary spoken English. This very quality explains his attraction to modern readers, who continually find something new to admire. Most of his best poems were composed after the age of seventy, and general critical acclaim came after his death. Many of his poems were composed with music in mind, reflecting his parents' lives as church musicians. Hardy has the distinction of being both a major poet and a major novelist. The poetry of Thomas Hardy has been set by Benjamin Britten, Ralph Vaughan Williams, Gordon Binkerd, Betty Roe, and David Diamond. Gerald Finzi, finding in Hardy his own philosophy and ideas about life, set forty-four of Hardy's sixty-one published poems. PRINCIPAL WORKS: Poetry: *Wessex Poems and Other Verses*, 1898; *Poems of the Past and the Present,* 1902; *Time's Lafingstocks and Other Verses,* 1909; *Satires of Circumstance,* 1914; *Selected Poems of Thomas Hardy,* 1916; *Moments of Vision and Miscellaneous Verses,* 1917; *Late Lyrics and Earlier,* 1922; *Human Shows, Far Fantasies, Songs, and Trifles,* 1925; *Winter Words in Various Words and Metres,* 1928; *Complete Poetical Works,* 1982–85. Plays: *The Dynasts,* 1904–8. Novels: *Under the Greenwood Tree,* 1872; *Far from the Madding Crowd,* 1874; *Tess of the D'Urbervilles,* 1891; *Jude, the Obscure,* 1896. SELECTED READING: Robert Gittings, *The Young Thomas Hardy,* 1975; Robert Gittings, *The Older Hardy,* 1978; Michael Millgate, *Thomas Hardy: A Biography,* 1982; Ellen Lanzano, *Hardy: The Temporal Poetics,* 1999. (SOURCES: Vinson, 1979; Hamilton, 1994)

"Hark, How All Things": a song composed by Henry Purcell to a text written by Elkanah ★Settle for his work *The Fairie-Queene*, produced in 1692 and 1693. For plot details and placement of songs, *see* ★*Fairie-Queene, The*.

"Hark How the Songsters": a duet composed by Henry Purcell to words by Thomas ★Shadwell, in his adaptation of William ★Shakespeare's play *Timon of Athens*. For plot details and position of the song, *see* ★*Timon of Athens*.

"Hark, the Ech'ing Air": a song composed by Henry Purcell to a text written by Elkanah ★Settle for his work *The Fairie-Queene*, produced in 1692 and 1693. For plot details and placement of songs, *see* ★*Fairie-Queene, The*.

HARLEQUIN, PIERROT (Fr.), ARLECCHINO (It.): in British, French, and Italian pantomime, a mischievous fellow supposed to be invisible to all but his faithful sweetheart, ★Columbine. Harlequin is a native of the lower town of ★Bergamo and considered to be a simpleton. Always in motion, Harlequin's function is to dance through his days and frustrate the tricks of the Clown, who is in love with Columbine. Harlequin is usually black-masked and wears a tight-fitting, spangled, or many-colored costume. His character is derived from the stock character of Italian *commedia dell'arte,* Arlecchino, whose name originally was probably that of a sprite or Hobgoblin, an insolent, arrogant, ribald character. In the *commedia dell'arte* Harlequin is a valet to ★Pantaloon and frequently takes advantage of him. One of the demons in ★Dante's work is named Alichino, and another devil of medieval demonology is Hennequin. (SOURCES: Cooper, 1992; Duchartre, 1966)

SONG	COMPOSER	POET
1. "Pierrot"	Claude Debussy	Théodore de Banville
2. "Pantomime"	Claude Debussy	Théodore de Banville
3. "Pierrot"	Gardner Read	Sara Teasdale
4. "Pierrot"	Howard Swanson	Langston Hughes
5. "Pierrot"	Wintter Watts, Charles Griffes	Sara Teasdale
6. "Pierrot"	Lee Hoiby	Adelaide Crapsey
7. "Colombetta: Serenata Veneziana"	Arturo Buzzi-Peccia	anonymous
8. "A Black Pierrot"	William Grant Still	Langston Hughes

HARMONIUM: a keyboard instrument, the tones of which are produced by free metal reeds, tongues, or vibrators set in action by a current of air from bellows, which are worked by treadles.

HARPALUS: the name commonly assigned in ancient times to a herdsman.

SONG	COMPOSER	POET
"Harpalus, an Ancient Pastoral"	Charles Ives	Thomas Percy

HARPER, THE: *see* ★WILHELM MEISTER.

HART, HEINRICH (1855–1906): German poet. Having studied at the universities of Halle, Munich, and Münster, Hart settled in Berlin (1877), where he worked closely with his younger brother Julius as a critical journalist. Being advocates of the new realism in literature and famous for their work on Naturalism, together they founded, edited, and produced several literary magazines. Although poetry was not an important part of his life, Heinrich Hart became known for his drama criticism. His poetry was set by Richard Strauss and Arnold Schönberg. PRINCIPAL WORKS: *Weltpfingsten* (poetry), 1872; *Sedan* (a tragedy), 1882; *Das Lied der Menschheit,* 1888–96; *Gesammelt Werke,* 4 vols., 1907–8. (SOURCE: Garland, 1976)

HARTE, BRET(T) (FRANCIS) (1836–1902): American novelist, short story writer, and writer of humorous verse. Harte was born in Albany and died in London. He was an Easterner who mined the literary wealth of the growing West and lived most of his life in New York and London. At nineteen he went with his mother to California, where he became a journalist. Harte had sudden fame with *The Luck of Roaring Camp* (1870), which was the first widely popular story of the West written with local color. After he left California (1871), he continued to write but with much repetition and a lack of inspiration. PRINCIPAL WORKS: *Plain Language from Truthful James (The Heathen Chinee)*, 1870; *Stories of the Sierras*, 1872; *A Millionaire of Rough and Ready*, 1887; *Poetical Works of Bret Harte*, 1896. SELECTED READING: M. Duckett, *Mark Twain and Bret Harte*, 1964. (SOURCE; Steinberg, 2, 1973)

HARTLEBEN, OTTO ERICH (1864–1905): German poet, playwright, translator, and writer of short stories. Hartleben studied law at the universities of Leipzig and Berlin, joined the civil service in 1889, but resigned a year later to pursue a career in writing. His early works were described as erotic comedies, and his style was ironic and mocking, he being anti-bourgeois and anti-philistine. His poetry, however, was mellifluous and charming. Hartleben's poetry was set by Alban Berg. PRINCIPAL WORKS: Poetry: *Meine Verse*, 1895, 1902; *Von reifen früchten*, 1902; *Ausgewählte Werke*, 3 vols., 1909. Plays: *Rosenmontag*, 1900. (SOURCE: Garland, 1976)

HAUGTUSSA: "Troll Maiden," a cycle by Edvard Grieg set to eight poems from the initial part of the collection of ninety-one poems of Arne ★Garborg. The story concerns Veslemoy, a shepherdess, who yearns for Jon "the nice lad from Skare-Bròt," but is jilted by him. Veslemoy, "little maiden," earned the nickname Haugtussa because of her gift for seeing and hearing the trolls. Grieg worked on more than twenty setting of the Garborg's epic collection, finishing only fifteen, from which he selected the eight songs included in the cycle.

HAUNS: (Scot.) (pr. hahnz), *hands*.

HAUTBOY: (Old French), *oboe*.

HAWTHORNE: a spiny shrub or tree of the rose family. Hawthorn means *good hope* because it shows that the winter has passed and spring is at hand. Athenian girls used to crown themselves with hawthorn flowers at weddings, and the Romans considered it a charm against sorcery.

"Hear, Ye Gods of Britain": a song composed by Henry Purcell to words of John ★Fletcher. *See* ★*Bonduca* for plot details and position of the song within the plot.

HEATH-STUBBS, JOHN, SIR (b. 1918): English poet, critic, and translator. Heath-Stubbs described himself as a traditionalist who believed that traditional values can only be maintained at the price of continual change and flexibility. Greece, Rome, Egypt, classical myths, and the Christian legend were his inspirations. Although he was a poet of the urban society of his time, his work includes translations from ★Hāfiz and ★Leopardi. Her Majesty's government gave him an OBE in 1989. The poetry of John Heath-Stubbs was set by John Duke. PRINCIPAL WORKS: *Wounded Thammuz*, 1942; *Beauty and the Beast*, 1943; *The Divided Ways*, 1946; *The Swarming of the Bees*, 1950; *The Blue-Fly in His Head*, 1962; *Artorius* (an epic), 1972; *Naming the Beasts*, 1982; *Collected Poems 1943–1987*, 1988; *Hindsights*, (an autobiography), 1993. (SOURCE: Drabble, 2000)

HEBBEL, FRIEDRICH (1813–1863): German poet, dramatist, and writer of fiction. Hebbel was born in Schelswig-Holstein, the son of a poor mason who was unsupportive of his son's ambitions and died when Friedrich was only fourteen. Hebbel then became the secretary to a local magistrate after which he read and wrote verses and drama under the influence of ★Uhland and ★Schiller's writing and participated in amateur theatricals. He spent a few years at the University of Heidelberg, and, in bitter poverty, developed his personal philosophy in Munich while lecturing, studying the law, and writing. Hebbel returned to Hamburg (1839), ready to start a career as a playwright, having written three plays before 1843. With money granted him by the king of Denmark he went to Paris, Rome, and Vienna. There he was received so warmly that he stayed, married one of his leading ladies, and died there. His reputation rests on his dramas, of which several describe the relationship between heroes of history and legend, male and female, in which the assertive male brings on his own destruction through his blindness to the real nature of women. *Maria Magdalena* (1844) is considered to be his dramatic masterpiece. ★Ibsen regarded Hebbel as one of his teachers. The lyric poetry of Friedrich Hebbel, powerful and deep, has been set by Brahms, Schumann, Liszt, Alban Berg, Hans Pfitzner, and Max Reger. PRINCIPAL WORKS: *Gedichte*, 1842; *Neue Gedichte*, 1848; *Gedichte von Friedrich Hebbel*, 1857; *Mutter und Kind*, 1859. SELECTED READING: Gunnar Flygt, *Friedrich Hebbel*, 1968. (SOURCE: Magill, 3, 1984)

HEBE, HÉBÉ (Fr.): the Greek goddess of youth, cup-bearer and servant to the Olympian gods. Hebe is the symbol for eternal youth. She has the power to restore youth and vigor to gods and men. The graceful young girl passes among the gods, offering a golden draught of life-preserving liquid. Once Hebe has passed by with her cup of youth, they cannot recall her. (SOURCE: Cooper, 1992)

SONG	COMPOSER	POET
1. "Dithyrambe"	Franz Schubert	Friedrich von Schiller
2. "Hébé"	Camille Chausson	Louis Ackermann
3. "1904"	Francis Poulenc	Guillaume Apollinaire
4. "When Forced from Dear Hebe to Go"	Thomas Arne	William Shenstone

HEBREW MELODIES: a set of poems by Lord ★Byron, based upon Old Testament characters such as ★David, ★Saul, and ★Jeptha. A number of them were set to music by Schumann, Wolf, Mily Balakirev, and Modest Mussorgsky. In the Schumann cycle, *Myrthen* (op. 25), is "Mein Herz ist schwer," a German version by Julius ★Körner of Byron's "My Soul is Dark." In the poem, King Saul, depressed and distracted, was unable to sleep. Only David's playing could console him and heal him of an evil spirit. At the end of 1849 Schumann wrote three more songs (op. 95) to Byron's *Hebrew Melodies*, all for harp or piano accompaniment: "Die Tochter Jepthas," "An den Mond" ("Sun of the Sleepless"), and "Dem Helden," all three translated by Körner. When Wolf set "Sun of the Sleepless," he used Otto Gildemeister's translation, called "Sonne der Schlummerlosen." (The biblical references are from 1 Samuel 17–19.)

SONG	COMPOSER	POET
"King Saul"	Modest Mussorgsky	Lord Byron

HECTOR: son of Priam, king of Troy, husband of ★Andromache, admirable as husband, father, and warrior. After killing Patrochulus, friend and chariot driver of ★Achilles, Hector was killed by Achilles and his body dragged three times round the walls of ★Troy. Achilles kept the body in the Greek camp, intending to feed it to birds and dogs, the ancient world's greatest indignity to the dead. The gods, moved by pity, sent Priam into the camp to plead for his son's body. In the ending to the *Iliad* the gods insisted that Achilles return Hector's body to his father for burial. (SOURCE: Cooper, 1992)

SONG	COMPOSER	POET
1. "Andromache's Farewell"	Samuel Barber	Euripides
2. "Hektor's Abschied"	Franz Schubert	Friedrich von Schiller

HEINE, HEINRICH (1797–1856): German poet, prose writer, and journalist, whose reputation abroad equaled that of ★Goethe. Heine grew up in Düsseldorf under the French occupation of the Rhineland. In his teens he was sent to live in Hamburg with a rich uncle, who, convinced of Heine's lack of business talent, sent him to study law at the University of Bonn. There he was encouraged by the critic Schlegel to write poetry. Heine transferred to Göttingen in 1821, but was expelled for challenging an anti-Semite to a duel. After three years in Berlin, where he met ★Chamisso and his ★Romantic circle, he returned to Göttingen and took a law degree (1825). Because Jews were not allowed in government service, Heine turned Christian. Although he did not get a job, his 1827 collection, *Book of Songs*, made him famous, showing him to be "a master of rhyme and rhythm, the most skillful manipulation of imagery, irony, facetiousness, resulting in bittersweet poetry full of surprises and sharp juxtapositions" (Flores, 1965). Germans both admired and mistrusted him, this brilliant chameleon. After the Revolution of 1830, Heine moved to Paris and wrote vitriolic satires, savage and witty attacks on German thought and literature. Paralyzed from spinal tuberculosis for the last eight years of his life, he was buried in Paris. He was a product of the ★Biedermeier period, an age of graceful resignation, of treating the adversities of life with sentimental sorrow. All Heine's poems that break the spell of sentimental poetry employ an identical technique: the effect of the first part, seemingly in the Romantic tradition, is suddenly destroyed by a cold shower of reason in the last part. ★Nietzsche said of Heine, "I seek in vain for an equally sweet and passionate music" (Kaufman, 1962). The poetry of Heinrich Heine has been set by Schubert, Brahms, Strauss, Wolf, Franz, Wagner (in French), Mendelssohn, Liszt, Tchaikovsky, Robert and Clara Schumann, Fanny Mendelssohn Hensel, Carl Loewe, Joseph Marx, Adolf Jensen, Peter Cornelius, Richard Trunk, Georges Hüe, Charles Griffes, Miriam Gideon, Henry Hadley, Charles Ives, César Cui, Reinhold Gliere, Aleksandr Borodin, Anton Rubenstein, Nicolai Medtner, and

Cesar Chavez. PRINCIPAL WORKS: *Gedichte,* 1822, Poems, 1937; *Tragödien, nebst einem lyrischen Intermezzo,* 1823, Tragedies together with Lyric Intermezzo, 1905; *Reisebilder,* 1826; *Buch der Lieder,* 1827, The Book of Songs, 1856; *Atta Troll,* 1843; *Neue Gedichte,* 1844, New Poems, 1858; *Deutschland: Ein Wintermärchen,* 1844, Germany: A Winter's Tale, 1892; *Romanzero,* 1851, trans. in Eng. as Romancero, 1905; *Ein Sommernachts Traum,* 1847, A Midsummer Night's Dream, 1876; *Paradox and Poet: The Poems,* trans. Louis Untermeyer, 1937; *Complete Works,* trans. C. G. Leland et al., 12 vols., 1891–1905. SELECTED READING: William Rose, *Heine: Two Studies of his Thought and Feeling,* 1956; Jost Hermand and Robert C. Holub, eds., *Heinrich Heine's Contested Identities: Politics, Religion, and Nationalism in 19th Century Germany,* 1999. (SOURCES: Mathieu, Stern, 1987; Flores, 1965; Kaufman, 1962; Vinson, Kirkpatrick (1), 1984; Steinberg, 2, 1973)

HEINRICH I (reign: 919–936): king of Germany, called *Heinrich der Vogler* because when his deputies arrived to announce his election to the throne, they found him fowling with a hawk on his fist. (SOURCE: *Americana,* 2003)

SONG	COMPOSER	POET
"Heinrich der Vogler"	Carl Loewe	Johann Nepomuk Vogl

HELEN: daughter of Tyndareus and Leda, or more popularly, of Leda and *Zeus, who visited her in the form of a swan; sister of *Castor, Pollux, and Clytemnestra. Helen was considered the most beautiful woman in the world. In her youth she was abducted by *Theseus but rescued by Castor and Pollux during Theseus's absence in *Hades. Later, Helen became the wife of *Menelaus, king of Sparta, and was carried off to *Troy by *Paris, which act brought on the Trojan War. (SOURCE: Kaster, 1964)

SONG	COMPOSER	POET
"Andromache's Farewell"	Samuel Barber	Euripides

HELIGOLAND: a German island in the North Sea, one-half square mile in size.

SONG	COMPOSER	POET
"Odins Meeresritt"	Carl Loewe	Aloys Schreiber

HELIOPOLIS: a biblical name; an ancient ruined city on the Nile delta in northern Egypt, once known as a center of sun worship. Its god Ra, or Re, was the state deity until *Thebes became the capitol (ca.2100 B.C.E.). Its schools of philosophy and astronomy declined after the founding of Alexandria in 332 B.C.E., but the city never wholly lost importance until the Christian era.

SONG	COMPOSER	POET
1. "Heliopolis"	Franz Schubert	Johann Mayrhofer
2. "Aus Heliopolis"	Franz Schubert	Johann Mayrhofer
3. "Freiwilliges versinken"	Franz Schubert	Johann Mayrhofer

HELIOS: the ancient Greek god of the sun. Helios was represented as a charioteer who each day drove the chariot of the sun pulled by four white horses across the sky from east to west. Later, Helios was supplanted by ★Apollo.

SONG	COMPOSER	POET
1. "Aus Heliopolis"	Franz Schubert	Johann Mayrhofer
2. "Freiwilliges Versinken"	Franz Schubert	Johann Mayrhofer

HELL, THEODORE: *see* ★WINKLER, KARL.

HELLESPONT: the sea of Helle, the ancient name of the ★Dardanelles. The Hellespont, located between Abydos on the Greek shore and Sestos on the Asian shore, is called the sea of Helle because Helle, the sister of Phrixus, was drowned there. Helle and her brother were fleeing to Colchis through the air on a golden ram in order to escape from her mother-in-law, Ino, who cruelly oppressed her. Turning faint, she fell into the sea near the Dardanelles. (SOURCE: Cooper, 1992)

SONG	COMPOSER	POET
"Seule!"	Gabriel Fauré	Théophile Gautier

HELOÏSE AND ABÉLARD: a classic romance of the Middle Ages. The tragedy of Heloïse and Abélard is the story of an arrogant scholar and a beautiful, brilliant young woman. Abélard (1079–1142), a teacher of logic and advocate of the rational, was overwhelmed by his passion for the beautiful Heloïse. Peter Abélard was a brilliant philosopher and theologian; his most famous work, *Sic et non*, was a collection of sayings by the Church Fathers, showing how each cleric had contradicted the others. (This book later formed the basis of Peter Lombard's *Sentences*, the basic theological textbook of the Medieval period.) While Abélard was a professor at the University of Paris, Canon Fulbert of Notre Dame Cathedral appointed him tutor to his niece Heloïse. As her tutor, Abélard made her seduction his most pressing goal. His success resulted in an extremely passionate love affair. Eventually a son was born to Heloïse, after which she and Abélard were secretly married. Denying that the marriage had taken place, Abélard had Heloïse placed in a convent to protect her from her uncle. Thinking that Abélard was going to abandon her, Canon Fulbert had a group of his men attack and castrate Abélard. (These events are covered in Abélard's *Historia Calamitatum*.) His teaching career ruined and a normal married life unthinkable, Abélard became a monk at Saint-Denis. He also insisted that Heloïse enter a convent. Imprisoned for heresy in 1121, he returned to Saint-Denis but soon, disagreeing with the other monks, he left to found a hermitage at Troyes. Followed by a number of students, he built a monastery, the Paraclete. Upon his appointment as Abbot of Saint-Gildas-en-Rhuys, he gave the Paraclete to Heloïse, who became the abbess of the convent there. Their celebrated correspondence took place after they had entered cloister life. These letters, full of passion and longing, find Heloïse still yearning to be with Abélard and dependent upon his guidance. Abélard, the forcibly reformed rake, counsels Heloïse to seek consolation as a bride of Christ. Abélard's woes were not over. His rationalistic theology was condemned by St. Bernard of Clairvaux, and eventually his teachings were declared heretical by the Council of Soissons (1121) and the Council of Sens (1141). Abélard's appeal to the pope was denied. A broken man, he capitulated to the Church's demands and retired to Cluny. Heloïse and Abélard were rejoined in death (Héloise living twenty-two years longer than Abélard), buried together at the Paraclete and, in 1817, eventually moved to Père-Lachaise Cemetery in Paris. (SOURCES: Gibson, 1951; Lloyd, 1971)

SONG	COMPOSER	POET
"Heloise and Abelard"	Thomas Pasatieri	Louis Phillips

"Hence! With Your Trifling Deity": a song composed by Henry Purcell to the words of Thomas ★Shadwell in his adaptation of William ★Shakespeare's play. *See ★Timon of Athens* for plot details and position of the song within the plot.

HENCKELL, KARL FRIEDRICH (1864–1929): German poet. Henckell, politically a socialist, was prominent in the left-wing literary movement of the 1890s. His proletarian poetry was forbidden in Germany as being too inflammatory. Strongly disapproving of Bismarck and the Prussians, he emigrated to Switzerland and set himself up as a publisher in Zürich, thus evading the authorities. The poetry of Henckell, occupying the space between delicate love lyrics and the bitterest socialist verse, was set by Richard Strauss. PRINCIPAL WORKS: *Umsonst*, 1884; *Strophen*, 1887; *Diorama*, 1889; *Trutzmachtigall*, 1891; *Zwischenspiel*, 1894; *Gedichte*, 1898; *Schwinggungen*, 1906; *Weltmusik*, 1918. (SOURCE: Garland, 1976)

HENLEY, WILLIAM ERNEST (1849–1903): English poet. Henley suffered from childhood with tubercular arthritis, because of which he eventually lost one foot. In order to save the other foot, he went to Edinburgh where he spent one year in the hospital under the care of Lister himself. This sojourn resulted in *Hospital Sketches*, which record his hardships. Most well known of all his poetry is "Invictus" (1875), which was set to music in a famous song at the turn of the century. Henley and Robert Louis ★Stevenson became close friends after they met in the hospital, ultimately collaborating on four unsuccessful plays. Henley had the opportunity to do much editing, in the course of which he helped make possible the publication of ★Hardy, ★Kipling, ★Stevenson, ★Yeats, and Henry James, and championed the work of the artist Whistler. A writer of ★ballads and free verse, Henley had a pronounced influence on his colleagues, mainly because of his forceful personality. His verse was set to music by Horatio Parker, Amy Beach, Sidney Homer, Frederick Delius, Theodore Chanler, and Charles Griffes. PRINCIPAL WORKS: *Hospital Sketches*, 1875; *A Book of Verses*, 1888; *The Song of the Sword and Other Verses*, 1892. BIOGRAPHIES: L. C. Cornford, 1913; J. H. Buckley, 1945. (SOURCE: Drabble, 2000)

HENRY THE SECOND, KING OF ENGLAND: a historical play by an unknown author, produced in 1692, containing music by Henry Purcell. Although historical plays were not fashionable in the 1690s, this is a fine drama; the action is exciting; the characters are strongly developed. Rosamond, the mistress of Henry II, is a victim of the king's desire, and Queen Eleanore's jealousy is made worse by the machinations of a traitorous abbot. The evil abbot draws the virtuous Rosamond into an affair with the king, who cannot stand up to his wife's insistence on preserving the royal marriage. Purcell's song was performed in scene 2 of act 3, where Rosamond resolves to resist the king's advances and preserve her honor. She asks an attendant to sing the song given her to charm her mistress to sleep. The song "In Vain 'gainst Love" debates love versus honor and makes love the winner. In the first four lines the singer lists what objections reason makes to her desire; in the second four lines the singer concludes that the heart has superior strength. The song then has five bars of alternating keys that reflect Rosamond's indecision and ambivalence about losing her innocence. At the finale Rosamond accedes to the notion that love is strongest. The song itself is left to the attendant, although sometimes sung by Rosamond herself, but it is a turning point of the main plot. (SOURCE: Price, 1984)

HERACLITUS: an ancient philosopher who lived ca.500 B.C.E. His changing and fleeting philosophy of life earned him the label "the weeping philosopher." In his work *Concerning Nature* he maintained that all things are in a state of flux, coming into existence and passing away, fire being their origin. From the passing impressions of experience the mind derives a false idea of the permanence of the eternal world. (SOURCE: *Americana*, 2003)

HERBERT, GEORGE (1593–1633): English poet. Herbert was born in Montgomery to a prominent family, and his mother was a patron of John Donne's. Herbert was a King's Scholar and later educated at Trinity College, Cambridge. He published his first poems (in Latin) in 1612. In 1618 he was elected a major fellow of Trinity and appointed reader in rhetoric. As a public orator at the university from 1620 to 1627, he was introduced to men of influence at court, but a brief experience in Parliament seemed only to disillusion him. He was ordained deacon, probably in 1624, and installed as canon of Lincoln Cathedral. Married in 1629, ordained a priest in 1630, Herbert died of consumption before his fortieth birthday. When he accepted the fact that he was dying, he sent all his English poems to a friend, asking him to publish them provided he thought they would help anyone, otherwise to burn them. He stated that his poems represented "a picture of the many spiritual conflicts that have passed betwixt God and my soul." After Herbert died, his much-admired poems collected as *The Temple* came out and enjoyed thirteen editions. Herbert went out of fashion in the eighteenth century but during the ★Romantic age revival he was again celebrated, his verse being found subtle rather than simple. The poems of George Herbert have been set by Ralph Vaughan Williams and Conrad Susa. PRINCIPAL WORKS: *Musae Responsoriae,* 1620, printed 1662; *Passio Discerpta,* 1623; *Lucus,* 1623; *Memoriae Matris Sacrum,* 1627; *The Temple,* 1633; *Poems,* 1958, 1961; *Works,* ed. F. E. Hutchinson, 1941. SELECTED READING: Helen Vendler, *The Poetry of George Herbert,* 1975; Amy M. Charles, *The Life of George Herbert,* 1977. (SOURCE: Drabble, 2000)

HERCULES (Lat.), HERACLES (Gk) (also called Alcides): a demigod, son of ★Zeus (★Jupiter) and Alcmene, wife of ★Amphitryon of ★Thebes. He was famous for his great strength from birth, when he strangled two serpents sent by Hera to destroy him. Hercules is most famous for the Twelve Labors, which he had to perform while serving Eurystheus, king of Tiryns. These were: (1) the killing of the monstrous

Nemean lion; (2) the slaying of the Lernean Hydra; (3) the capture of the ★Arcadian stag; (4) the capture of the Erymanthean boar; (5) the cleansing of the Augean stables; (6) the destruction of the Stymphalian birds; (7) the capture of the Cretan bull; (8) the capture of the man-eating mares of Diomedes; (9) the procuring of the girdle of ★Hippolyte, queen of the Amazons; (10) the capture of the oxen of Geryon; (11) the fetching of the golden apples of the Hesperides; (12) and the bringing up of ★Cerberus from ★Hades. (SOURCE: Cooper, 1992)

SONG	COMPOSER	POET
1. "Hercules"	Alan Hovhaness	Alan Hovhaness
2. "An die Leier"	Franz Schubert	Franz von Bruchmann

HERDER, JOHANN GOTTFRIED (1744–1803): German poet, translator, and dramatist. Herder was the son of a parish clerk, grew up under modest circumstances and studied theology at Königsberg University. After teaching at the cathedral school of Riga, he became a popular preacher (1764). In 1767 he published a work in three parts, *Fragmente*, a work assessing the current trends in German literature. Having taken up a position as traveling tutor to a Holstein-Eutin prince, Herder met poets ★Lessing and ★Claudius. While on a three-year tour with the prince, he married. When he became a court preacher (1771), Herder published a philological tract, a series of essays on German art, and a theological work. It was ★Goethe who then obtained for him the position of moderator in Weimar, where he remained for twelve years, producing a collection of German Volkslieder. Herder's contributions to the ★Sturm und Drang movement were an insistence on the perception of the entire personality, as opposed to the intellect, giving primacy to the Bible, ★Shakespeare, ★Ossian, and folk song, which he felt were closest to nature. In his historical works, he was the first to see progress as cyclical and not linear. Having traveled to Italy (1788), he returned to produce ten volumes of reflections of the French Revolution. In the 1790s Herder spent much time and effort on discrediting the philosophy of Emmanuel Kant. He considered his translations of foreign folk songs and the Greek Anthology to be more important than his own original poetry or plays. The poetry of Johann Herder was set by Beethoven, Schubert, and Carl Loewe. He translated into German two poems used by Schubert: "Verklärung" of Alexander Pope and "Eine altschottische Ballade," a version of the ballad "Edward" set by Loewe. PRINCIPAL WORKS: *Fragmente*, 1767; *Von deutscher Art und Kunst*, 1773; *Stimmen der Völker in Liedern*, 1778–79; *Ideen zu Philosophie der Geschichte der Menschheit*, 1784–91; *Adrastea*, 6 vols., 1801–4; *Sämtliche Werke*, 45 vols., 1805–20; *Historisch-kritische Ausgabe*, ed. B. Suphran, 33 vols., 1877–1913. (SOURCE: Garland, 1976)

"Here's the Summer, Sprightly, Gay": a song composed by Henry Purcell to a text written by Elkanah ★Settle for his work *The Fairie-Queene*, produced in 1692 and 1693. For plot details and placement of songs, *see ★Fairie-Queene, The.*

HERMETICISM: a ★Modernist trend in Italian poetry influenced by French ★Symbolism. The main practitioners were ★Ungaretti and ★Quasimodo, who concentrated on extremely precise language. This tended to produce obscure and drastically concise verse that isolated single images, which allowed the hermeticists to work through the Fascist period without political censorship, but reaped resentment from writers who allied themselves with the Resistance. (SOURCE: Drabble, 2000)

HERO AND LEANDER: in Greek legend, secret lovers, Hero the priestess of ★Aphrodite at Sestos and Leander as a youth of Abydos. Leander lived on the other side of the ★Hellespont, which he swam every night finding his way by the light of a lamp in Hero's tower. When a storm blew out the lamp, Leander drowned and Hero threw herself down from the tower and died beside his corpse. Many great writers dealt with the legend: ★Callimachus, Virgil, Ovid, ★Dante, ★Chaucer, ★Tasso, ★Marot, ★Marlowe, ★Schiller, ★Byron, ★Grillparzer, ★Keats, and ★Housman. (SOURCE: Steinberg, 1, 1973)

HEROD: name of a family that ruled in Palestine from 46 B.C.E. to about 100 C.E. The family had been forcibly converted to Judaism about 125 B.C.E. Herod the Great ruled Palestine from 37 B.C.E. to 4 B.C.E., maintaining his rule by keeping friendly with the Roman emperors. His cruelty is illustrated by the story of his massacre of children in Bethlehem, which caused ★Mary and ★Joseph to flee to Egypt with the infant ★Jesus, fearful of Herod's soldiers. His son Herod Antipas was the Tetrarch of Galilee (4 B.C.E. − 39 C.E.) and had married his brother's wife, Herodias. ★John the Baptist was imprisoned for denouncing the marriage, probably on the grounds of incest. Herod had John beheaded at the request of Herodias's daughter ★Salome after she danced the Dance of the Seven Veils. During Jesus' trial, Pilate sent him to Herod, who mocked him, wrapped him in a royal robe, and sent him back to Pilate.

SONG	COMPOSER	POET
1. "Chanson bretonne"	Francis Poulenc	Max Jacob
2. "The Flight"	Theodore Chanler	Leonard Feeney

HERRICK, ROBERT (1591–1674): English poet. Herrick's wealthy father was a goldsmith, who, two days after making his will and one and a half years after Robert's birth, fell to his death from the fourth floor window of his London house. After writing his earliest poem (1610), Herrick was released from an apprenticeship to his uncle, another goldsmith, and entered Cambridge, living opulently while taking two degrees. In 1623 he was ordained as a priest. Frequenting the literary circles gathered around Ben ★Jonson, by 1635 he became known as a poet. His friends included ★Fletcher and the Lawes brothers. Having accompanied as a chaplain the Duke of Buckingham's forces in his mission to aid the Protestants of La Rochelle, Herrick was rewarded with a living in the country (1630). He began to enjoy the folk festivals and folk customs, but was impelled to return to London (1647) as a loyalist. During the time of the Commonwealth he must have subsisted on the generosity of relatives. With the return of the monarchy, his living was reinstated and he went back to Devon to stay for the rest of his life. A fine lyric poet, Herrick wrote secular poems that are generally small-scale, refined, aesthetically graceful versions of a broad subject, such as sex or death. There are 1,400 pieces included in *Hesperides*, Herrick's only known publication of verse. Some have called his religious poems childish, "perhaps part of the seventeenth century Anglican attempt to idealize childhood in the face of the Puritan emphasis on original sin" (Drabble, 2000). Herrick's poetry has been set by Henry Lawes, Charles Horn, John Alden Carpenter, John Edmunds, Paul Hindemith, John Corigliano, John Lessard, Ned Rorem, Anthony Strilko, Miriam Gideon, Betty Roe, Gordon Binkerd, Lennox Berkeley, Leslie Bassett, Robert Fairfax Birch, and Judith Zaimont. PRINCIPAL WORKS: *Works*, ed. L. C. Martin, 1956; *Complete Poetry*, ed. J. Max Patrick, 1963. SELECTED READING: Leah S. Marcus, *Robert Herrick*, 1992. (SOURCE: Drabble, 2000)

HESIOD (ca.700 B.C.E.): Greek epic and didactic poet. According to the poet himself, he lived in Asera in Boeotia and tended sheep on Mt. Helicon. Roughly contemporary with Homer, Hesiod is said to have died in Locri or Orchomenus. He uses meter and dialect in much the same fashion as Homeric epics, but the background and subject matter is different. The works for which Hesiod is known are *Theogony* (an account of the origins of the world and the genealogy of the gods) and *Works and Days* (the story of a farmer's life that would later serve as a model for Virgil's *Georgics)*. Hesiod's style, like Homer's, was an oral-epic style. His catalogue poetry and his didactic verse are somewhat wearisome to moderns, but they contain exceedingly powerful sections of inspiration. ★Dryden, ★Spenser, and ★Milton referred to him and made use of his work; Charles Ives set some of Hesiod's poetry. PRINCIPAL WORKS: *Theogony, Works and Days*, trans. Dorothy Wender, 1973. SELECTED READING: Pietro Pucci, *Hesiod and the Language of Poetry*, 1976; Richard Gotshalk, *Homer and Hesiod: Myth and Philosophy*, 2000. (SOURCES: Vinson, Kirkpatrick (1), 1984; Drabble, 2000)

HESPER, HESPERUS: the evening star, son of ★Eros.

HESSE, HERMANN (1877–1962): Swabian poet. Hesse's father was a missionary to India and his son was born in Calw. The family moved to Calw so that the father could work with his father-in-law, an Orientalist. His family's pietistic strain and scholarly oriental background influenced Hesse's writing strongly. At the wish of his parents, he began to study theology, but his stay at the seminary lasted only six months. In 1899 Hesse began to work in a Basel publishing industry, but in 1904 determined to devote himself to writing. Further travels in India produced *Siddhartha, Eine indische Dichtung*, a poetic work of Indian philosophy. Until 1915 his poetry and novels were done in the romantic style. Thereafter, personal problems and the stresses of World War I, which Hesse strongly opposed, led to a period of psychotherapy with a disciple of C. J. Jung. This experience culminated in a collection of fairy tales (*Märchen*) that show his interest in psychotherapy. A popular success, *Der Steppenwolf*, revived public interest in Hesse's writing. In 1946 he was awarded the Nobel Prize and the Goethe Prize. Hesse's poetry was set by Richard Strauss. PRINCIPAL WORKS: *Peter Carmenzind*, 1904; *Märchen*, 1919; *Siddartha,* 1922; *Der Steppenwolf,* 1927; *Letzte Gedichte*, 1960; *Werkausgaber,* 12 vols., ed. V. Michels, 1970. (SOURCE: Garland, 1976)

HEYDUK, ADOLF (1835–1923): Czech poet. Heyduk was a member of a group of writers who founded an important almanac, and he is chiefly remembered for his lyrics, which were strongly influenced by Slovak folk poetry. The poetry of Adolf Heyduk was set by Charles Ives and Anton Dvořák. (SOURCE: Steinberg, 2, 1973)

HEYSE, PAUL (1830–1914): German poet. Heyse was born in Berlin, the son and grandson of well-known philologists. His father had been a tutor to Felix Mendelssohn. While Heyse was still in school he proofread his father's dictionary, wrote his first play, and began writing nature and love poems, influenced by *Heine and *Eichendorff. In 1846 *Geibel arranged a meeting with the young poet, having admired some of his work. Moving to Berlin to study classical philology at the university, Heyse came in contact with Liszt, Mendelssohn, Peter Cornelius, and the poet Théodor *Fontane, with whom he was friendly for the rest of his life. He transferred to the University of Bonn, changing his major to Romance languages and literatures, and completed a doctoral dissertation on the poetry of the *troubadours (1852). Heyse continued to make trips to Italy to observe the life of the people. King Maximilian II of Bavaria bestowed upon him a yearly stipend, which enabled Heyse to make his home on Lake Garda. Almost all of his most challenging works had a theme of the conflict between duties to self and society. Between 1873 and 1906 Heyse edited an important collection of German novellas and an anthology of modern Italian poets, as well as writing seven novels (of the more than one hundred written in the course of his life). In the 1880s and 1890s he suffered criticism from those who considered his works immoral, which position he attacked by taking a public stand against censorship and prejudice. Heyse was the first German literary author to receive the Nobel Prize for Literature, in his eightieth year. Brahms, Schumann, and Joseph Marx set his poetry. His many translations of Italian, Spanish, and French literature led him to the collection *Spanisches Liederbuch*, edited and translated by Geibel and himself, containing original poems by both poets under Spanish pseudonyms. Hugo Wolf set Heyse's own *Italienisches Liederbuch* as well as the *Spanisches Liederbuch*. PRINCIPAL WORKS: *Francesca von Rimini* (play), 1850; *Der Jungbrunnen* (fairy tales), 1850; *Spanisches Liederbuch* with Geibel, 1852; *L'Arrabiata* (novella), 1857; *Hadrian* (play), 1865; *Maria von Magdala*, 1899. (SOURCES: Hardin, Mews, 1993; Garland, 1976)

HIBOU: a word that forms its plural with a final letter x. (SOURCE: Kimball, 1996)

SONG	COMPOSER	POET
"Ba be bi bo bu"	Francis Poulenc	Guillaume Apollinaire

HIDALGO: a Spanish nobleman of secondary rank, a landowner.

SONG	COMPOSER	POET
1. "Les Filles de Cadix"	Leo Délibes	Alfred de Musset
2. "Der Hidalgo"	Robert Schumann	Emanuel Geibel

HILLYER, ROBERT (1895–1961): American poet. Robert Hillyer came from an old Connecticut family, but was born in New Jersey. He attended Harvard and the University of Copenhagen (1920–21). During World War I he was an ambulance driver with the French army, for which service he received a citation from the

French government. He transferred to the American army, in which he was a first lieutenant, after which he became a courier for the Peace Conference. In 1919 he taught at Harvard as the Boylston Professor of Rhetoric and Oratory. In 1934 Hillyer won the Pulitzer Prize for *Collected Verse*. By his own description he was a "conservative and religious poet in a radical and blasphemous age" (Kunitz, Haycraft, 1942). His poetry was always praised for its superior craftsmanship, although an air of loss and brooding hovers over his work. While Hillyer considered Robert Bridges to be the greatest poet of his era, he publicly attacked *Pound, *Eliot, *Joyce, Proust, and Gertrude *Stein as alien, decadent, and pretentious. The poetry of Robert Hillyer has been set by Norman dello Joio, Ned Rorem, and John Duke. PRINCIPAL WORKS: *Collected Verse*, 1933; *In Time of Mistrust*, 1939; *Pattern of a Day*, 1940; *Collected Poems*, 1961. (SOURCE: Kunitz, Haycraft, 1942)

HIPPIUS, ZINAIDA (1869–1945): Russian poet, short story writer, and critic. Zinaida Hippius came from an aristocratic family and was educated by tutors. She married another poet, Dmitry Merezhkovsky. Intellectually brilliant, Hippius's poetry is elegant and inventive, and, although it displays a highly idiosyncratic style, it has great thematic variety. Most of Hippius's love poems are addressed to women and are far from tame. Flowers, birds, and clouds have human emotions in her poetry, and death is a strong presence. On the opposite pole are many poems of religious content. The Revolution turned Hippius into a political poet, these verses stirring as well as stinging. The verses of Zinaida Hippius were set by Vladimir Mayakovsky. (SOURCE: Terras, 1991)

HIPPOLYTUS, HIPPOLIT (Ger.): son of *Theseus by *Antiope, queen of the Amazons. He lived at the court of Theseus when the queen was *Phaedra. She fell in love with him. When he refused her advances, she hanged herself, accusing Hippolytus of having seduced her. Theseus then called down upon Hippolytus the curse of his father *Poseidon, who sent a bull from the sea to frighten the horses of Hippolytus's chariot. When it overturned, Hippolytus was dragged to death. (SOURCE: Kaster, 1964)

SONG	COMPOSER	POET
"Hippolits Lied"	Franz Schubert	Johanna Schopenhauer

HISTOIRES NATURELLES: a set of five *mélodies* by Maurice Ravel, with texts by Jules *Renard. For a long time Renard refused to write these poems for Ravel. When he finally capitulated, he explained that he sought to write descriptions that would be pleasing to animals, in contrast to the work of Léclerc, an eighteenth-century French naturalist, the Comte du Buffon, who wrote a forty-four volume series called "Histories Naturelles" published between 1749 and 1804, and who had stated that he wanted his writing to give pleasure to men.

HISTORY OF KING RICHARD THE SECOND, THE: an adaptation of the *Shakespeare work by Nahum *Tate, produced in 1680, at first refused a license because it dealt with the deposition of an English king. Nahum Tate managed to soften Shakespeare's characters immeasurably. The only Purcell song is "Retired from Any Mortal's Sight." (SOURCE: Price, 1984)

"Hither This Way, This Way Bent": a song composed by Henry Purcell to a text by John ★Dryden from their semi-opera *King Arthur*, produced in 1691. *See* ★*King Arthur* for plot details and placement of songs.

HOARFROST: *a white frost.*

SONG	COMPOSER	POET
1. "Noël"	Gabriel Fauré	Victor Wilder
2. "Adieu"	Gabriel Fauré	Charles Grandmougin

HOB: a familiar or rustic variation of the Christian name Robert, or Robin, thus a generic name for a rustic or clown.

HODGSON, RALPH (1871–1962): American poet. Son of a coal merchant and brought up in the South, Hodgson learned to love and observe the natural world. He worked in the theater in New York and as an artist in London in the 1890s, where he was encouraged by his friends Walter ★de la Mare, Siegfried ★Sassoon, and T. S. ★Eliot. His reputation as a poet was established (1917) with his volume *Poems*, visionary and ambitious works. He spent the rest of his life in the United States. The verse of Ralph Hodgson was set by Samuel Adler. PRINCIPAL WORKS: *Poems*, 1917; *The Skylark and Other Poems*, 1958; *Collected Poems*, 1961. (SOURCE: Drabble, 2000)

HOFMANNSTHAL, HUGO VON (1874–1929): Austrian poet, dramatist, and essayist. Born in Vienna of a Spanish-Jewish family, Hofmannsthal studied the law and romance languages at the University of Vienna. Some of Hofmannsthal's best work, several plays as well as verse, was done before he was twenty. Even then his poetry had "music, sonorous sound, restraint, and somber seriousness" (Kaufman, 1962). Hofmannsthal had virtually no biography because external events did not influence his life at all. He lived removed from the world. After 1914 he sought to base his intellectual activity on spiritual motives, although he had previously been a romantic aesthete. His poetry is mystical, with color and melody. Death in his prime prevented further development. Although Hofmannsthal is greatly admired in German-speaking countries like Switzerland, where Frank Martin set his lyrics, he is best known outside Austria as the librettist for six operas by Richard Strauss and as the author of *Jedermann* (Everyman), which is done every year at the Salzburg Festival. PRINCIPAL WORKS: *Lyrical Poems*, ed. C. W. Stork, 1918; *Ausgewählte Werke*, ed. R. Hirsch, 2 vols., 1957; *Poems and Verse Plays*, 2000. SELECTED READING: *H. von Hofmannsthal: Selected Writings*, ed. M. Hamburger, 3 vols., 1959–63; Lowell A. Bangerter, *Hugo von Hofmannsthal*, 1977. (SOURCES: Kaufman, 1962; Flores, 1965; Mathieu, Stern, 1987)

HOGGIE: (Scot.) (pr. hahggee), *a hogget*, dim. of hog, *a young ewe.*

SONG	COMPOSER	POET
"My Hoggie"	Benjamin Britten	Robert Burns

HOKKU: *see* ★HAIKU.

HOLBORN: an area of London whose residents are wealthy and of high social position. (SOURCE: Friedberg, 1984)

SONG	COMPOSER	POET
"When I Died in Berners St."	Mary Howe	Elinor Wylie

HÖLDERLIN, (JOHANN CHRISTIAN) FRIEDRICH (1770–1843): German poet. Born in a village on the banks of the Neckar River, Hölderlin was educated for the church (Master of Philosophy, 1790), but declined orders and became a tutor to wealthy families in Frankfurt, Bordeaux, and in Switzerland (1793–1802). Partially as a result of a tragic love affair, he went mad (1805). After being confined to a clinic for a year, he spent the rest of his days lodged privately in Tübingen under the care of a local carpenter. His major writings were published by friends after he became mentally ill. Poetry was always Hölderlin's vocation, and Pindar, *Klopstock, and *Schiller were always his models. He shared with compatriot poets a passion for liberty and believed that poetry might serve the revolutionary cause. His early poems were often couched in violent terms, but his mature poetry was nourished by Greece and a belief that the spirit of civilization, having once flourished in the East and in Athens, might flourish in Germany. The theme of Hölderlin's poetry is how to continue to hold to ideals in times of their absence. His verses contain "subtle contradictions: despair with an insistence on hope, a longing for the past with a belief in a better future, sensuous language that is often simple and gains its effect through some peculiarity in the order of its words" (Vinson, Kirkpatrick (1), 1984). A poet of prophecy, he dreamed of a fusion of Apollo and Christ. Friedrich Hölderlin's poetry has been set by composers Wolfgang Fortner, Hans Pfitzner, Paul Hindemith, Hans Werner Henze, Hermann Reutter, and Benjamin Britten. PRINCIPAL WORKS: *Selected Poems*, trans. J. B. Leishman, 1944; *Poems and Fragments*, trans. Michael Hamburger, revised ed., 1980. SELECTED READING: Richard Ungar, *Hölderlin's Major Poetry*, 1984. (SOURCES: Vinson, Kirkpatrick (1), 1984; Flores, 1965)

HOLMES, OLIVER WENDELL (1809–1894): American poet, novelist, essayist, biographer, and editor. Born in Cambridge, Massachusetts, Holmes attended Harvard University, where he studied law, graduating in 1829. He studied medicine for two years in Europe and then at Harvard Medical School, getting his medical degree in 1836. After practicing medicine in Boston, he became professor of anatomy and physiology at Dartmouth from 1838 to 1840. Harvard Medical School named him Professor of Anatomy (1847–1882). Holmes's popular reputation was great in the nineteenth century, but when the general preeminence of New England writers lessened, Holmes's reputation suffered. Except for Whittier, Holmes was the most provincial of New England writers, but, unlike others, he did not espouse causes. Between 1830 and 1857 his work as a doctor and his professorships gave him little time for writing. He was brilliant talker, and it only remained for him to hit on a scheme for writing down his own talk, which then gave him material for an essay series. As a clear-headed rationalist, he disliked what he called the bullying of science and found the dogmatism of theology abhorrent. During his work as a doctor and professor he published important medical essays and a volume of poems, sixty-five of his poems being published by *Atlantic Monthly*. Holmes's Harvard lectures were celebrated for their wit and learning. His chief claim to medical distinction was generally agreed to be his excellence as a teacher. The poetry of Oliver Wendell Homes has been set by Charles Ives. PRINCIPAL WORKS: Poems: *Songs in Many Keys*, 1862; *Songs of Many Seasons*, 1875; *The Iron Gate and Other Poems*, 1880; *Before the Curfew and Other Poems*, 1888. Novels: *The Guardian Angel*, 1867; *A Mortal Antipathy*, 1884. Biographies: *Ralph Waldo Emerson*. Essays: *The Autocrat of the Breakfast Table*, 1857; *The Poet of the Breakfast Table*, 1872; *Over the Teacups*, 1890. SELECTED READING: J. T. Morse, Jr., *Life and Letters of Oliver Wendell Holmes*. (SOURCE: Vinson, 1979)

HOLT: *a wooded hill.*

SONG	COMPOSER	POET
"On Wenlock Edge"	Ralph Vaughan Williams	A. E. Housman

HÖLTY, LUDWIG (1748–1776): German poet. Hölty was a student of theology and lived for only a short time after his university days at Göttingen (1770–75), a literary center. Hölty and a friend, encouraged by ★Klopstock, Germany's foremost poet at the time, formed a literary society. Its members set themselves poetic tasks, criticized each other's work, and often produced poems of superior quality. Having steeped himself in Klopstock's verse early on, Hölty's poems reflect his love of nature, the fleeting character of life, and a foreshadowing of death. He found in his vision of death an affirmation of life, as did ★Herrick and ★Ronsard, his poetry singing of the simple pleasures of country life, the beauty of nature, and love. His work was a stepping stone to ★Romanticism, but he was overshadowed by ★Goethe. The poetry of Ludwig Hölty has been set by Schubert ("An die Nachtigall"), Mendelssohn, Brahms, Fanny Mendelssohn Hensel, and Václav Momášek. PRINCIPAL WORKS: *Werke*, ed. W. Michael, 2 vols., 1914–18. SELECTED READING: T. Oberlin-Kayser, *Ludwig Heinrich Christoph Hölty*, 1964. (SOURCES: Mathieu, Stern, 1987; Vinson, Kirkpatrick (1), 1984; Steinberg, 2, 1973)

HOMYAKOV: *see* ★KHOMYAKOV.

HOO: (Scot.), *how; a cry to attract attention.*

HOPAK: a hopping Ukranian folk dance with heel beats. ★Mei's poem "Hopak," set by Mussorgsky, was patterned after Tarás Schevtchenko's drama *The Haidamaks*, in which the Ukranian poet wrote poems in the local dialect, proselytizing for Ukranian liberty. Although the Russian intelligentsia had great sympathy for the movement, the government had responded by suppressing all of Tarás Shevtchenko's writing and forbidding the use of the Ukranian dialect. (SOURCE: Terras, 1991)

HOPE, LAURENCE (1865–1904): English poet, born Adela Florence Cory in Gloucestershire. The daughter of a colonel in the Indian Army, she went to join her parents after finishing her schooling at private institutions. In 1889 she married a colonel who was aide-de-camp to Queen Victoria and devoted her time to her marriage and her poetry. Her poetry was, for the time, torrid Swinburnian verse, her passion being expressed in the medium of Oriental imagery that was new in English literature, consequently very popular. The most famous of these poems, "Pale Hands I Loved Beside the Shalimar," was set to music. After her husband died, Hope committed suicide. Her poetry has been set most recently by Blair Fairchild. PRINCIPAL WORKS: *The Garden of Kama*, 1903; *Indian Love*, 1905; *Songs from the Garden of Kama*, 1908.

HOPKINS, GERARD MANLEY (1844–1889): English poet. Hopkins was born in Essex and educated at Oxford where religious uncertainties drove his studies. In 1866 he was received into the Roman Catholic Church. After taking a double degree in 1867, he taught for a year before joining the Jesuits as a candidate for the priesthood. Hopkins's pastoral capabilities, however, were not as pronounced as his religious faith. Ordained in 1877, he endured frequent transfers due to the fact that parish life overwhelmed him. He was elected to the chair of Greek and Latin at University College, Dublin, in 1884, but, saddened at being sent from his homeland, deprived of his friends and family, Hopkins caught typhoid and died in 1889. Hopkins never really reconciled the desire to write poetry with his desire to serve God, actually burning all his poems when he joined the Jesuits. Similarly, his poetry has a gift for fine aural and rhythmic effects, but this gift only intensified his aesthetic and moral questions. Among Hopkins's contributions to poetry were coined terms: *sprung rhythm*, indicating writing and scanning by the number of stresses rather than counting syllables; *inscape*, the individual or essential quality of a thing; and *instress*, the energy that maintains an inscape and flows into the mind of the reader. His response to nature and beauty was enthusiastic, and he found the visual arts important to his writing sensibilities. He was an admirer of the ★Pre-Raphaelites. Hopkins's poetic fame was posthumous. The poetry of Gerard Manley Hopkins has been set by Daniel Pinkham, Robert Baksa, Milton Babbitt, Ernst Bacon, Samuel Barber, Richard Cumming, David Diamond, John Duke, Vernon Duke, John Edmunds, Peggy Glanville Hicks, Lennox Berkeley, and Ralph Vaughan Williams. PRINCIPAL WORKS: *Poems*, 1918, 2nd ed., ed. C. Williams, 1930; *Poetical Works of Gerard Manley Hopkins*, ed. N. H. Mackenzie, 1990. SELECTED READING: Elisabeth W. Schneider, *The Dragon in the Gate: Studies in the Poetry of Gerard Manley Hopkins*, 1968; R. B. Martin, *Gerard Manley Hopkins*, 1991. (SOURCE: Drabble, 2000)

HOPKINSON, FRANCIS (1737–1791): American poet, musician, scientist, lawyer, painter, merchant, judge, designer of a flag for the United States, and a signer of the Declaration of Independence. Hopkinson graduated from the Academy of Philadelphia when fourteen and became the first scholar in the seminary, which by the time he graduated in 1757 had become the College of Philadelphia. In 1788 he published *A Set of Eight Songs*, both words and music written by him and dedicated to George Washington. As a scientist he experimented with the principles of aviation, designed a dirigible, invented a new method of quilling a harpsichord, developed a formula for coloring artificial pearls, wrote learned articles on education, designed border decorations for Continental currency, a Great Seal for the United States of America, and a seal for the Board of Admiralty. He wrote, "I shall ever esteem it the highest Honour of my Life that I have been instrumental in first announcing to the World the Freedom of my Country." (SOURCE: Essay contained in the Carl Fischer publication of Hopkinson's songs)

HORACE (65–8 B.C.E.): one of the most famous and admired of Latin lyric poets. Critics consider his poems to be perfect in form and phrasing. Horace was born Quintus Horatius Flaccus in Venusia, a city of southern Italy. While a student in Athens, Horace enlisted in Brutus's and Cassius's army against Octavian and Marc Anthony. When his side was defeated at Phillippi, Horace returned to Rome, impecunious. Virgil helped him by introducing him to Macaenas, a rich patron, who gave Horace an estate where he lived for the rest of his life. (SOURCE: Grant, 1980)

SONG	COMPOSER	POET
"Das Lied im Grünen"	Franz Schubert	Friedrich Reil

HORAE, HOREN (Ger.): the daughters of Themis, the Greek goddess responsible for order, justice, and the seasons. According to legend, these divinities received ★Aphrodite on ★Cyprus and covered her nakedness with proper attire. (SOURCE: Kaster, 1964)

SONG	COMPOSER	POET
"Es treibt mich hin"	Robert Schumann, Robert Franz	Heinrich Heine

HORIZON CHIMÉIRIQUE, L': a set of four songs with poetry by Jean de la ★Ville de Mirmont, set to music by Gabriel Fauré in his last opus for voice and piano. Ville de Mirmont, a young man killed in 1914 during World War I, treated the sea as a symbol of the undiscovered, not as a source of human tragedy. (SOURCE: Bernac, 1970)

HORNING: *becoming a crescent*, as: *a moon*.

SONG	COMPOSER	POET
"I'll Sail upon the Dog Star"	Henry Purcell	Thomas D'Urfey

HORN OF PLENTY: *see* ★CORNUCOPIA.

HOTTENTOT: a member of a race living in South Africa, or a boor, rude and uncultured. The Hottentots are one of two sub-races of the Khosanid race, characterized by short stature, yellow brown skin color, and tightly curled hair. Members of the Hottentot race are of Bushman-Hamite descent with some Bantu mixture and are now found mostly in Southwestern Africa. By 1640 the word was taken to mean a stammerer or stutterer, on account of the clicking speech. (SOURCE: *OED*, 1989)

SONG	COMPOSER	POET
"Les Illuminations"	Francis Poulenc	Arthur Rimbaud

HOUSATONIC: a Massachusetts/Connecticut river that rises in the Berkshire Hills near Pittsfield, Massachusetts, flowing southward to Long Island Sound. The Housatonic, 130 miles long, is an Indian word, meaning "great river of the mountains."

SONG	COMPOSER	POET
"The Housatonic at Stockbridge"	Charles Ives	Robert Underwood Johnson

HOUSE OF LIFE: a song cycle composed by Ralph Vaughan Williams to poems by Dante Gabriel *Rossetti (1828–82), who did several English translations of Dante's lyrics. The mythology and metaphors in Rossetti's *House of Life* sonnets came from Dante's *Vita Nuova*. A painter as well as a poet, Rossetti dealt in images that appeal to other senses in addition to that of hearing, as evinced by the imagery of "Silent Noon," the most well-known song of the group. (SOURCE: Stevens, 1970)

HOUSMAN, A(LFRED) E(DWARD) (1859–1936): English poet, editor, and classical studies scholar. A. E. Housman was born in Worcestershire and educated at St. John's College of Oxford University, where he took first class honors in classical studies (1879) but failed his final exams (1881). He clerked in the Patent Office in London (1882–92) while undertaking classical studies on his own. Subsequently, Housman chaired the Latin Department at University College in London from 1892 to 1911. A Fellow of Trinity College at Cambridge, he was made Kennedy Professor of Latin there (1911–36). "[Housman's] gifts as a poet seem to be much like his gifts as classical scholar: narrow, profound, isolated, brooding and ferocious" (Vinson, 1979). Condensed to the utmost and stripped of ornament, Housman's poetry reflects his classical scholar interests in its restraint, order, and balance. His apparently stark and simple verse stemmed from emotional wounds in his youth, of which he could not bear to speak openly. In his writing Housman refused to include intellect in what he saw as the basic purpose of poetry: to strike to the pit of emotions, bypassing thought. For him, his creative impulse was born of simple intuitiveness. "A Shropshire Lad," on which his reputation rests, was published at his own expense after being rejected. "His poems repeat again and again that love is fleeting, that lovers are fickle, that youth decays into age, and that death is final" (Vinson, 1979). Despite his harsh and austere point of view, Housman's work was very popular. Even professional literary critics may have found it difficult to account for the pleasure that reading Housman's poetry gave them. It has been set by Ernst Bacon, Robert Baksa, Arnold Bax, John Duke, Samuel Barber, George Butterworth, Lennox Berkeley, Ivor Gurney, E. J. Moeran, John Ireland, Graham Peel, Arthur Somervell, Ralph Vaughan Williams, Cecil Armstrong Gibbs, Vernon Duke, Celius Dougherty, George Walker, and C. Wilfred Orr. PRINCIPAL WORKS: *A Shropshire Lad*, 1896; *Last Poems*, 1922; *The Name and Nature of Poetry*, 1933. SELECTED READING: John Bailey, *Housman's Poems*, 1992; R. P. Graves, *A. E. Housman: The Scholar Poet*, 1979. (SOURCES: Vinson, 1979; Hamilton, 1994)

HOWELLS, WILLIAM DEAN (1837–1920): American journalist, poet, playwright, travel writer, critic, and novelist. Howells wrote professionally for nearly seventy years. His first poem was published at the age of fifteen, and he was still writing a column for *Harper's* magazine in the year of his death, having achieved his name and editorial power before his thirtieth birthday. His boyhood and early manhood in Ohio was filled with constant reading, the classical languages, and poetry writing, from which he established a circle of admirable culture heroes who taught him a Quaker dislike of violence and a devotion to principle. A friend to Henry James and Mark Twain, he knew and reviewed American writers for four generations and introduced American readers to many novelists from abroad. Howell's work as editor and reviewer earned him the praise of Turgenev, ★Tolstoi, ★Hardy, Shaw, and ★Kipling. In 1871 he fulfilled his dream and became editor in chief of *Atlantic*, which he made into a national magazine. After ten years, he resigned and returned to Europe, where the next ten years were to see his best writing. He began as a poet, but his novels and essays were more important than his poetry, which was weakened by formal clichés and Victorian sentimentality. At the turn of the century his power was waning and he was less often read, although often praised. His poetry was set by Edward MacDowell. PRINCIPAL WORKS: Travel: *Venetian Life*, 1866; *Italian Journeys*, 1867. Novels: *A Modern Instance*, 1885; *Indian Summer*, 1886; *A Hazard of New Fortunes*, 1890. Poetry: *Poems of Two Friends*, with John J. Piatt, 1860. SELECTED READING: Kenneth S. Lynn, *William Dean Howells: An American Life*, 1971. (SOURCE: Unger, 2, 1974)

"How Happy Is She": a song composed by Henry Purcell to the words of Robert Gould. For plot details and position of the song within the plot, see ★*Rival Sisters, The.*

"How Happy's the Husband": an ★epithalamium composed by Henry Purcell, set to the words of John ★Dryden in his drama *Love Triumphant*, produced in 1694. *See* ★*Love Triumphant* for plot details and placement of songs.

HUDSON RIVER: the largest river in New York State, 315 miles long. The Hudson River begins in the highest of the Adirondack Peaks, Mt. Marcy. Below Troy, it becomes navigable. From here on, its mountain waters are met and infiltrated by the salt tides of the Atlantic. From Haverstraw Bay downward toward New York City, the river is lined on the west bank by the Palisades, a sheer wall of ★basalt, 350–550 feet high. Because of its beauty, the arts began to flourish beside its scenic grandeur, for example, the writing of Washington Irving and the Hudson River School of painting. (SOURCE: *Americana*, 2003)

SONG	COMPOSER	POET
"The Lordly Hudson"	Ned Rorem	Paul Goodman

HUGHES, (JAMES MERCER) LANGSTON (1902–1967): a major African-American writer of poetry, fiction, short stories, newspaper columns, autobiography, and criticism. Hughes grew up first in Kansas and later in Lincoln, Illinois, where his grammar school elected him class poet, a fact that did not impress Hughes. He explained the honor with some irony: white people think that a black man (whom popular opinion decrees has rhythm) must be able to write poetry, since poetry has rhythm. Two summers with his father in Mexico introduced him to political ideas and gave him time to write a great deal of poetry. On a ride back to Texas from Mexico, Hughes wrote one of his most famous works, *The Negro Speaks of Rivers*. Colorful articles he wrote about Mexico were published by a children's magazine put out by the NAACP, establishing Hughes as one of the young articulate spokesmen for the African-American race. Attending Columbia briefly, he failed all his classes but fell in love with the streets and people of Harlem. He took a variety of jobs, finishing as a cabin boy/seaman on freighters to West Africa, which was a turning point in his life. Hughes gained support from Vachel *Lindsay and Carl Van Vechten, who introduced him to the publishing giants, the Knopfs. After he won first prize in a national poetry competition, the Knopfs published his first book of poetry. Before his death, he had received eight major awards and two honorary doctorates. In general, the poems of the 1920s concentrated on the appreciation of the black man's African heritage and the joys of the Harlem jazz age. In the 1930s Hughes's time in Spain as a journalist had convinced him to follow the communist ideological line, and his writing became more abrasive. In the 1940s he returned to his former successful subject matter—familiar themes of urban blues and street jazz—and wrote nine full-length plays as well as one-act plays, gospel musicals, opera librettos and one screenplay. After his death, admirers were distressed to see his lesser place in American literature: black critics disliked his early work for not presenting their race in an uplifting manner, while white critics termed the writing superficial. Hughes was content to let simple words come from the mouths of simple people. His poetry has been set by composers Herman Reutter, John Alden Carpenter, Jean Berger, Margaret Bonds, Betty Roe, William Grant Still, Sergius Kagen, John Musto, William Schumann, Ricky Ian Gordon, and Silvestre Revueltas, among others. PRINCIPAL WORKS: Poetry: *The Weary Blues*, 1926; *The Dream Keeper and Other Poems*, 1932; *Montage of a Dream Deferred*, 1951; *Selected Poems*, 1959; *Ask Your Mama: 12 Moods for Jazz*, 1961. Prose: *Not Without Laughter*, 1930; *Laughing to Keep from Crying*, 1952; *I Wonder as I Wander: An Autobiographical Journey*, 1956. SELECTED READING: Therman B. O'Daniel, *Langston Hughes, Black Genius*, 1971. (SOURCES: Vinson, 1979; Unger, 1974)

HUGO, VICTOR (1802–1885): French poet, playwright, novelist, and editor. Victor Hugo began his professional life as an editor in Paris, where he was heavily involved in politics. In 1848 he was elected to the assembly, only to be exiled in 1851, not returning to France until 1870. During a period of violent and frequent change in his country, his works dealt with all the major issues of individuals, society, literature, politics, and religion. In an output so monumental it is natural that, among evidence of genius, there should be a certain amount of material that was trite, simplified, and self-absorbed. Hugo was totally convinced of the validity of his own vision, of his belief that creation was a composite of good and evil forces. "It is not a distortion to describe the fundamental Hugolian experience as a play of day and night on the edge of an abyss" (Vinson, Kirkpatrick (1), 1984). Victor Hugo wrote in order to manipulate material things into revealing spiritual truths. His exile allowed him the necessary time to reflect on the moods and movements of his times. In his work the *Romantics, the *Symbolists, even the *Surrealists found examples of their beliefs. He brought a new freedom of subject matter and verse forms to French poetry. The poetry of Victor Hugo has been set by Britten, Saint-Saëns, Gounod, Bizet, Pizzetti, Carlos Chavez, Felipe Pedrell, Reynaldo Hahn, and Russian composers Rachmaninoff, Cesar Cui, and Alexandr Dargomizhsky. PRINCIPAL

WORKS: Poetry: *Les Orientales*, 1829, ed. Pierre Albouy; *Les Feuilles d'automne,* 1831; *Les Voix intérieures*, 1837. Plays: *Cromwell*, 1827; *Hernani*, 1830; *Le Roi s'amuse*, 1832; *Ruy Blas*, 1838. SELECTED READING: Henri Peyre, *Hugo: Philosophy and Poetry*, 1980. (SOURCE:Vinson, Kirkpatrick (1), 1984)

HULDER: in Norse popular lore, *the spirits of the waterfall*, from whom a musician can learn the most precious secrets of his art, although at the risk of losing his peace of mind forever.

SONG	COMPOSER	POET
"Spellemaend"	Edvard Grieg	Henrik Ibsen

HUNGARIAN FOLK SONGS: a collection of twenty peasant songs, most of which were taken down in the field by Béla Bartók and Zoltán Kódaly, each one of whom arranged his own selections. The publication was intended to show Hungarians the purity and artistic value of these neglected parts of their culture and to replace the cheap popular music then in general favor.

HUNTER, ANNE (1742–1821): English poet. Anne Home was the eldest daughter of Robert Home, the surgeon of Burgoyne's Regiment of Light Horse. After a long engagement, she married John Hunter, a distinguished surgeon. Anne Hunter became well known in the fashionable literary society in London where her obsessively hard-working husband left his wife to her own devices. She occupied herself by writing poetry. Hunter's friend Horace Walpole described her behavior as a poet: "she never assumed, or in the least affected, the character of a poetess, but with modesty delivered her productions in manuscript to a favoured few" (Lonsdale, 1989). Several of her efforts found their way into print. In the 1790s Hunter's position in London society made it possible for her to become friendly with Haydn during his visits to England. With typical modesty she anonymously provided words for his *Six Original Canzonettas* (1794), which Haydn dedicated to her. The *Second Set of Canzonettas* (1795) contained some poems by Hunter and a few selected from other poets. Two more Hunter poems were adopted by Haydn for the separate songs, "O Tuneful Voice," and the highly dramatic "The Spirit's Song." When John Hunter died in 1793, his complicated will forced his widow to leave her home and depend on the sale of other parts of the estate in addition to a pension from the queen. In 1799 when Parliament voted to purchase the Hunter Museum and establish it in the Royal College of Surgeons, she was finally able to live in comfort and security. Hunter's collected *Poems*, dedicated to her son, were published in 1802, and *The Sports of the Genii*, although written in 1797, was finally published in 1804. The most famous of her poems remains one of several that was set to music by Haydn in the first group of Canzonettas, "A Pastoral Song," perhaps better known by its first line, "My Mother Bids me Bind my Hair." PRINCIPAL WORKS: *Poems*, 1802; *The Sports of the Genii*, 1804. (SOURCE: Lonsdale, 1989)

HUNTLY CASTLE: a Scottish castle, once the home of the Gordons, located in the county of Aberdeen, one of many local castles belonging to the Huntly, Forbes,

Fraser, and Farquarson families, who busied themselves with warfare against each other, infrequently in the name of the king.

SONG	COMPOSER	POET
"Tom der Reimer"	Carl Loewe	Theodor Fontane

HURLY-BURLY: derived from an Old English word *hurly*, confusion, uproar, tumult. It in turn was derived from the French *hurler*, meaning to howl or yell.

SONG	COMPOSER	POET
"Sailor's Song"	Franz Joseph Haydn	anonymous

"Hush, No More, Be Silent All": an aria composed by Henry Purcell to a text written by Elkanah *Settle for his work *The Fairie-Queen*, produced in 1692 and 1693. For plot details and position of the song, *see *Fairie-Queen, The*.

HUSSAR: a soldier in one of many European cavalry regiments.

SONG	COMPOSER	POET
"Trost im Unglück"	Gustav Mahler	Des Knaben Wunderhorn

HÜTTENBRENNER, HEINRICH (1799–1830): Austrian journalist and poet. He studied law at Graz and the University of Vienna (1819), eventually securing a position as professor of Roman and ecclesiastical law at Graz. His two brothers, Anselm, a composer, and Josef, who was Schubert's secretary, were acquainted with Schubert. Heinrich made Schubert's acquaintance when he went to Vienna to study law, and it was the three brothers who hid the "Unfinished" Symphony. Schubert set Heinrich Hüttenbrenner's poem "Der Jüngling auf dem Hügel" in 1820 and a partsong, "Wehmut." (SOURCE: Clive, 1997)

HUXLEY, ALDOUS (1894–1963): English poet and novelist. Huxley developed serious eye trouble at the age of sixteen. His near blindness meant no scientific career, but he recovered sufficiently to be educated in English at Balliol College, Oxford. The important figures he met appeared, not to their satisfaction, in his early satirical novels, which foretold his future writing habits. By 1919, when he began to write for *Athenaeum*, he had already published three volumes of verse and a volume of stories. During the 1920s and 1930s, he and his wife lived in Italy and France, where he wrote fiction. In 1937 he left for California for the sake of his eyes, also because he was disillusioned with the failure of peace movements, and partly because he was searching for a new spiritual direction. Huxley wrote in many genres: poetry, novels, essays, historical studies, and travel works. He was interested in mysticism and experimented with mescaline and LSD. His writing was a mixture of irony and sincerity, heartlessness and charity, which made it difficult to judge. Some saw it as shallow, some as fascinating. The verse of Aldous Huxley was set by John Ireland. PRINCIPAL WORKS: *Chrome Yellow*, 1921; *Antic Hay*, 1923; *Point Counterpoint*, 1928; *Brave New World*, 1932; *The Devils of Loudon*, 1952. SELECTED READING: S. Bedford, *Aldous Huxley*, 2 vols., 1973–74. (SOURCE: Drabble, 2000)

HYACINTHUS, HYACINTH (Fr.): a beautiful youth who was beloved by both *Apollo and *Zephyrus. He disdained Zephyrus's love but returned the love of Apollo. As Hyacinthus and Apollo were throwing the discus together, Zephyrus blew

Apollo's discus off-course, causing it to strike Hyacinthus' head, killing him. From Hyacinthus's blood, Apollo created the flower that bears his name, Hyacinthus. The petals of the flower were inscribed with the letters A I, meaning woe. The Debussy song refers to the ceremonial day that honors the deity. (SOURCE: Kaster, 1964)

SONG	COMPOSER	POET
1. "La Flûte de Pan"	Claude Debussy	Pierre Louÿs
2. "Hyazinthen"	Hermann Reutter	Theodor Storm

HYDE PARK: a beautiful 630-acre park in central London, the largest of the royal parks, entered through four great gates. The park's original purpose was to glorify Britain's victories in the Napoleonic War, whose hero was the Duke of Wellington at the Battle of Waterloo. The royal family won Hyde Park in 1536, as part of the loot from the dissolution of the monasteries. Henry VIII preserved it for his private hunting, but James I opened it to the public. The park proper is separated from the Kensington Gardens by the Serpentine, a body of water with one curve, used for boating and swimming since 1730. In or near its environs are found the Marble Arch, the Wellington Monument, Hyde Park Speakers' Corner, Kensington Palace, the Albert Memorial and the Royal Albert Hall.

SONG	COMPOSER	POET
"Hyde Park"	Francis Poulenc	Guillaume Apollinaire

HYLAS: a companion of *Hercules, the name referring to his death in a fountain and the cries made by those seeking him, which were compared to the choral calling of tree frogs, since the word *hylas* is also the plural of *hyla*, a tree frog.

SONG	COMPOSER	POET
"Die zu späte Ankunft der Mutter"	Franz Joseph Haydn	Christian Weisse

HYMEN, HYMENAEUS: the ancient Greek god of marriage, a personification of the marriage song, represented as a handsome youth, son of *Apollo and one of the *Muses.

SONG	COMPOSER	POET
"Das Lied im Grünen"	Franz Schubert	Friedrich Reil

HYMN, HYMNE: from the Greek *hymnos*, a song in praise of a hero or one of the gods, thus a religious song of praise, devotion, or thanksgiving. *Abélard was a prolific and original author of hymns, and Hildegard of Bingen (ca.1150) used a rich gamut of visionary imagery in her hymn writing. Both writers used accented verse forms alongside orthodox imagery and themes, into which classical and contemporary allusions were incorporated. The influence of Latin hymnody on secular poetic forms is best illustrated in *Carmina Burana*. *Ronsard's two books of *Hymnes* (1555–56) were miniature epics after classical models and were written as celebrations of powerful figures, natural phenomena, and abstractions like philosophy and justice. (SOURCE: *OED*, 1989)

SONG	COMPOSER	POET
1. "Hymne"	Gabriel Fauré	Charles Baudelaire
2. "C'est l'extase"	Claude Debussy	Paul Verlaine
3. "Les Cloches"	Claude Debussy	Paul Bourget

HYPERION: in Greek mythology, one of the ★Titans, the son of Uranus and Gaea and father of ★Helios, ★Selene, and ★Eos (Sun, Moon, and Dawn). Poets sometimes give the name Hyperion to the sun itself. (SOURCE: Cooper, 1992)

I ✍

"I Attempt from Love's Sickness to Fly": a song from the tragic extravaganza *The Indian Queen*, written by John ★Dryden and Sir Robert Howard, first produced in 1677, then altered in 1695 to include music by Henry Purcell. *See* ★*Indian Queen, The* for plot and placement of the songs.

IBSEN, HENRIK (1828–1906): a Norwegian poet and playwright, the most famous writer and dramatist of his era. Ibsen began as a stage manager, where he learned a lot about the practicalities of the theater. Although his dramas were criticized for their outspokenness, they had great influence on social reform. The dramas *Brand* and *Peer Gynt*, for which he is best known, established his reputation in his native land. His early works were historical dramas, often in verse, tales of Norway's heroic past, lofty in style with a tendency toward melodrama. Ibsen found his natural idiom when he turned his attention to contemporary society and wrote in modern prose. From 1877 the plays, in prose only, centered on a small group of people. The late plays, obscure and disturbing, often ending in death and despair, puzzled audiences and critics alike. Yet there are few European dramatists, since his day, who do not owe something to Ibsen's controlled forms and sense of theater. Ibsen's poetry was set by Edvard Grieg. (SOURCES: Miller, 1973; Vinson, Kirkpatrick (1), 1984)

IDA: a mountain in a ridge of mountains near Troy, scene of the Judgment of ★Paris. At the marriage of Thetis and Peleus, at which all the gods and goddesses had assembled, Discord (Eris), looking for revenge because she had not been invited, threw on the table a golden apple intended to be a prize for the most beautiful goddess. Hera (Juno), Pallas Athene (Minerva), and ★Aphrodite (★Venus) entered the competition. Paris, as judge, gave the prize to Aphrodite. Thus he brought upon himself the vengeance of Hera and Pallas Athene, whose spite was said to precipitate the fall of Troy. (SOURCE: Cooper, 1992)

SONG	COMPOSER	POET
"From Rosy Bow'rs"	Henry Purcell	Thomas D'Urfey

IDOL: an image of God, used as an object of worship; a person or thing that is the object of intense admiration or devotion.

SONG	COMPOSER	POET
"Hymne"	Gabriel Fauré	Charles Baudelaire

IDYL: a short poem or prose composition that deals charmingly with rustic life. It usually describes a picturesque rural scene of gentle beauty and innocent tranquility, narrating a story of some simple sort of happiness.

"If Love's a Sweet Passion": an air composed by Henry Purcell to a text written by Elkanah ★Settle for his work *The Fairie-Queen*, produced in 1692 and 1693. For plot details and position of the song, *see* ★*Fairie-Queen, The.*

"If Thou Wilt Give Me Back My Love": a song composed by Henry Purcell, set to the words of Thomas ★D'Urfey in his comedy *A Fool's Preferment*, produced in 1688. *See* ★*Fool's Preferment, A* for plot details and placement of songs.

ILKA: (Scot.), *every.*

"I'll Mount to You, Blue Coelum": a song composed by Henry Purcell, set to words of Thomas ★D'Urfey in his comedy, *A Fool's Preferment*, produced in 1688. *See* ★*Fool's Preferment, A* for plot details and placement of songs.

"I'll Sail upon the Dog Star": a song composed by Henry Purcell, set to words by Thomas ★D'Urfey in his comedy *A Fool's Preferment*, produced in 1688. *See* ★*Fool's Preferment, A* for plot details and placement of songs.

ILLUMINATIONS, LES: *The Illuminations*, settings of nine poems written by Arthur ★Rimbaud (1854–91), composed by Benjamin Britten. *Les Illuminations* is one of Rimbaud's major works; it also includes *Une saison en enfer*. These poems were published in *La Vogue* in 1886. According to Paul ★Verlaine, who did the original editing, they were written between 1873 and 1875. Rimbaud's work as a poet was done between the ages of sixteen and nineteen; with *Une saison en enfer* (1873), he stopped writing. Rimbaud's work is much more extensive than the nine poems selected by Britten would suggest. *Les Illuminations* contains forty-two poems and is divided into five different sections. Written in prose, they are considered hallmarks of the ★Symbolist movement. The title was suggested by Verlaine and refers not only to an illuminated medieval manuscript, but to throwing light upon an obscure scene. The nine songs chosen by Britten for his cycle are for high voice and string orchestra. They have French texts, although the titles of the individual pieces vary between French and English: 1. Fanfare; 2. Villes; 3. Phrase, Antique; 4. Royauté; 5. Marine; 6. Interlude; 7. Being Beauteous; 8. Parade; 9. Départ. (SOURCE: Flowlie, 1966)

ILMENAU: a German city in Thuringia, located 60 miles from the Czech border. ★Goethe wrote his poem "Über allen Gipfel ist Ruh" (Wanderers Nachtlied II), of which the Ives song is a translation, on a mountain hut wall near Ilmenau.

SONG	COMPOSER	POET
"Ilmenau"	Charles Ives	Johann Wolfgang von Goethe

IMAGISM: principally a movement of English and American poets in revolt against
★Romanticism in the early twentieth century. Some Imagists were Ezra ★Pound,
Amy ★Lowell, James ★Joyce, Ford Madox ★Ford, and William Carlos ★Williams.
Imagist poems have a tendency to be short, with short lines, their metrics musical rather than regular, clearly influenced by the Japanese ★haiku and ★tanka forms.
These poets avoid abstraction and use images that are clear and devoid of symbolic
intent. One of their practitioners, Ezra Pound, said: "The natural object is always the
adequate symbol" (Drabble, 2000). The Russian imagists, ★Esenin and Ivnyov among
them, insisted that art was independent of and superior to real life. Determined to
delete any intellectual or moral message from content, the movement was destined
for a short life in Russia. (SOURCES: Drabble, 2000; Terras, 1991)

IMMERMANN, KARL (1796–1840): German poet, playwright, writer of fiction, travelogues, and memoirs. Born in Magdeburg, his father a Prussian civil servant, Immermann studied law at the University of Halle until Napoleon closed the
university, but returned there three more times during the wars. In 1823 he met
★Heine and remained friends with him until his own death. In 1827 he passed his
exam to be district judge in Düsseldorf, where he established a theater association
for which he directed. Many of his dramas were produced during his lifetime, but
they did not endure. Immermann enjoyed only a relatively short life and his work
had an uneven quality, probably due to his position in the generation after that of
★Goethe and ★Schiller. It forced him to try to cope with their legacy. Immermann,
primarily a dilettante, did not realize until ten years before his death that his strength
lay in a kind of prose writing that used his keen powers of observation and analysis
and his natural gift for satire. The poetry of Karl Immermann was set by Schumann,
Schubert, and Mendelssohn. PRINCIPAL WORKS: *Gedichte*, 1822; *Gedichte: Neue
Folge*, 1830; *Gedichte*, 1834. (SOURCE: Hardin, Mews, 133, 1993)

IMPRESSIONISM: a name given scornfully to the work of a group of French
painters who held their first exhibition in 1874. To render the effects of light on
objects rather than rendering the objects themselves was the artistic goal of this
group, which included Claude Monet (1840–1926), Alfred Sisley (1839–99), Camille
Pissarro (1831–1903), Auguste Renoir (1841–1919), and Paul Cézanne (1839–1906).
The term transferred into literature and music. Soon composers created a similar movement, the most important practitioner of which was Claude Debussy.
(SOURCE: Drabble, 2000)

INANNA AND DUMUZI: a pair of deities worshiped in Sumeria. The temples in
Sumeria were located in groups of two. At first the mother goddess and her consort
were worshiped without names; later they were called Inanna and Dumuzi. Inanna
was the most important goddess in the pantheon; a variant of her name was Ninanna,
"mistress of heaven." She was identified with the planet Venus and overcame the
mountain god Ebeh (probably a reference to the victory over the encroaching Sem-
ites). Inanna was best known as the goddess of fertility and love. In metamorphoses
central to thought in West Asia Inanna was Ishtar, ★Astarte, ★Cybele, ★Aphrodite, and
★Venus. Dumuzi's significance is uncertain. He was Inanna's shepherd lover, whom

she preferred over all others. This 5,000-year-old story is very close to the origin of symbols fundamental to West Asian thought. (SOURCE: Cotterell, 1986)

SONG	COMPOSER	POET
"Songs of Inanna and Dumuzi"	George Rochberg	Ancient Sumerian texts

INCENSE: powder or small crystals made from resins, which when burned give off an aromatic smoke; or the smoke itself. Incense burned over charcoal in a container called a thurible is used at High ★Mass, Benediction, and other ceremonies. Incense symbolizes the sacrifice for God as well as prayers and good works ascending to God. (SOURCE: Nevins, 1964)

SONG	COMPOSER	POET
1. "Noël"	Gabriel Fauré	Victor Wilder
2. "Le Secret"	Gabriel Fauré	Armand Silvestre

INDIAN QUEEN, THE: a tragic extravaganza by John ★Dryden and Sir Robert Howard, first produced in 1664, then altered in a 1695 production to include music by Henry Purcell, whose music and dialogue worked together as equals. The plot begins with a war between the Incas of Peru and the Aztecs of Mexico. Montezuma, having defeated Acacis, son of the Mexican queen, Zempoalla, is asked by the Inca to choose his reward. When his request for the hand of the Inca's daughter Orazia is refused, Montezuma deserts to join the Mexicans to seek revenge for the insult. He finds that Queen Zempoalla is infatuated with him, but he wants to remain faithful to Orazia. Act 2, scene 2 begins with the masque of Fame (countertenor) and Envy (a bass). Envy and two other basses sing a trio, "What Flatt'ring Noise Is This?" In act 3, scene 2, Zempoalla complains of nightmares and asks her priest magician, Ismeron, to relieve her troubled heart. Ismeron begins his conjuration, "Ye Twice Ten Hundred Deities," to which there is no answer, and follows up with his aria, "By the Croaking of the Toad," an effective acting piece. The conjurer refuses to reveal in words what fate awaits the queen, but no doubt is left by the music and words, a catalogue of chromatic and dissonant symbols for death that hovers over gloomy words. Eventually the God of Dreams appears and sings "Seek Not to Know," sending the unspoken message: Zempoalla is doomed. To alleviate the queen's depression a duet, "Ah, How Happy Are We," is sung. Ismeron asks the spirits to restore the harmony of Zempoalla's soul, but they are infected with her melancholy. The precise location in this scene of "I Attempt from Love's Sickness to Fly," is unknown. The sentiments are the queen's but the original Zempoalla was not a singer. It was probably sung off stage before the queen entered. "They Tell Us That You Mighty Powers Above" was also sung in an unknown place in the plot, but it was designed for Orazia. At the end of the play the final chorus makes Zempoalla into a genuine tragic figure, although the final masque supplies a happy ending. (SOURCE: Price, 1984)

INDRA: a pre-Hindu Indian god of heroes and of war, who used a thunderbolt as a weapon. Pleasure-loving and quite amoral, Indra was a perfect counterpart for the cheerful optimists who worshiped him. His fondness for feasting and drinking, for gambling and dancing, and for making war, reflected the character of a robust, extroverted people who had little of the spirituality and none of the pessimism that are now commonly associated with India. Also the title of one of the songs in Gustave Holst's *Vedic Hymns, translated from the *Rig Veda by Holst. (SOURCE: Schulberg, 1971)

INFANTA: a daughter of the king and queen of Spain or Portugal, but not the heir to the throne. Neither is the *infante*, a royal son, the heir to the throne in these countries.

SONG	COMPOSER	POET
1. "La Grace exilée"	Francis Poulenc	Guillaume Apollinaire
2. "Infanta Maria"	Vincent Persichetti	Wallace Stevens

"Ingrateful Love! Thus Every Hour": a song by Henry Purcell with lyrics by Thomas *Southerne. For plot details and position of the song within the plot, *see* *Wives Excuse The.

INNISFAIL: lit., *island of destiny*, an Irish poetic name.

SONG	COMPOSER	POET
"Innisfail"	Blair Fairchild	W. B. Yeats

INNISFREE: an island in Lough Gill, which is located a short distance southeast of the Irish town of Sligo. The word *Innisfree* means *heather island*. Both Blair Fairchild and Alan Hovhaness set William B. Yeats's poem "The Lake Isle of Innisfree."

"In Vain, Clemene": a song by Henry Purcell, set to the words of Thomas *Southerne in his play, *Sir Anthony in Love*, produced in 1690. *See * Sir Anthony in Love* for plot details and placement of songs.

"In Vain Are All Our Graces": a trio composed by Henry Purcell to a text by John *Dryden in their semi-opera *King Arthur*. *See *King Arthur* for plot details and placement of songs.

"In Vain 'gainst Love": a song composed by Henry Purcell with words by an unknown author. *See *Henry the Second* for plot details and position of the song within the plot.

INWOOD: a section of New York in the extreme north of Manhattan Island, along the Henry Hudson Parkway, where the *Cloisters are located.

SONG	COMPOSER	POET
"Christmas at the Cloisters"	John Corigliano	William Hoffman

IPHIGENIA: the daughter of *Agamemnon who was offered as a sacrifice at the start of the Trojan expedition, but carried away to *Tauris by *Diana. Acting as a priestess of Diana, Iphigenia freed two prisoners whom she had recognized as her brother *Orestes and his friend, Pylades.

SONG	COMPOSER	POET
"Iphigenia"	Franz Schubert	Johann Mayrhofer

IRIS: the Greek goddess of the rainbow, or the rainbow itself, regarded as the messenger of the gods to mankind. The rainbow is the bridge or road that was let down from heaven to accommodate her. (SOURCE: Cooper, 1992)

SONG	COMPOSER	POET
"Fair Iris and her Swain"	Alan Hovhaness	Alan Hovhaness

IRISH REVIVAL, THE: a movement that revitalized Irish nationalism and culture. It began at the end of the nineteenth century and lasted until the 1920s, promoted by many recountings of Irish legends and folklore. The Irish Literary Theatre, founded by W. B. ★Yeats and others in 1899, soon became the Abbey Theatre Company, featuring plays by Yeats, John Millington ★Synge, George Bernard Shaw, and Sean O'Casey that bestowed their renown upon the Abbey. James ★Joyce and others gave Irish writing a new stature. (SOURCE: Drabble, 2000)

IRLANDE (Irish Melodies): a collection of five songs by Hector Berlioz, settings of French translations of Thomas ★Moore's poems, "L'Origine de la harpe," "Adieu, Bessy," "La Belle voyageuse," "Le Coucher du soleil," and "Élégie." For "Élégie" Berlioz wrote a preface with an account of the 1803 execution of the Irish patriot, Robert ★Emmet, an event that inspired Moore to write the poem.

IRMELIN: a steel-hearted princess, who found fault with her hundreds of noble suitors, yet fell in love with a wandering troubadour. (SOURCE: Kimball, 1996)

SONG	COMPOSER	POET
"Irmelin Rose"	Frederick Delius, Carl Nielsen, Alexander Zemlinsky	Jens Peter Jacobsen

"I See She Flies Me": a song by Henry Purcell set to the words of John ★Dryden. *See ★Aureng-Zebe* for plot details and position of the song within the plot.

"I Sigh'd and Own'd My Love": a song composed by Henry Purcell to the words of Thomas ★Southerne for his drama, *The Fatal Marriage. See ★Fatal Marriage, The* for plot details and position of the song within the plot.

"I Sigh'd and Pin'd": a song composed by Henry Purcell, set to the words of Thomas ★D'Urfey in his comedy *A Fool's Preferment*, produced in 1688. *See ★Fool's Preferment, A* for plot details and placement of songs.

ISIS: the most important female goddess of ancient Egypt. She was both sister of and wife to Osiris, and the mother of Horus. By about 100 B.C.E. her worship had spread throughout all Egypt and reached to Greece and Rome, where she was a popular god during the period of the empire. Isis was always represented in human form and was pictured wearing a crown made of cow's horns and a sun disk. (SOURCE: *Americana*, 2001)

ISLAM: the Muslim religion. About the year 610, the beliefs of the Jews and Christians struck a chord in Mohammed, a prophet of Islam, who began to see visions during his walks among the hilltops of Mecca. Visited by ★Gabriel, the "spirit of holiness," Mohammed was commanded to proclaim "there is no God but ★Allah." Legend tells that on a certain night, the Prophet was conducted through the air, riding on the back of a winged steed Burak, first to Jerusalem, then up through the seven heavens, in which he met the patriarchs ★Adam and ★Jesus, to the throne of Allah, where the mysteries of divinity were revealed to him. Although Mohammed drew on other West Asian traditions, the god he called upon was an unmistakably Arabian one, whose scriptures were direct and straightforward. He sought to replace the divisive tribal loyalties with membership in a universal way of life. There was little room for myth. Within twenty years Mohammed established himself as the leading chieftain of Arabia. To his followers fell the task of world conquest. The people of West Asia passed under Islamic control, ending a heritage that went back to the ancient Sumerians. Arab armies pushed out in every direction. In 751 Central Asia was wrested from Chinese influence. The region ceased to be Buddhist and was added to the Muslim world. (SOURCE: Cotterell, 1986)

ISLE OF PORTLAND: a peninsula linked to the mainland of the southern coast of England near the town of Weymouth. The Chesil Bank, the link, is a long spit of land with a remarkable beach on which pebbles decrease in size from east to west. The limestone of the island itself, which is famous for its quarries, was used in the construction of St. Paul's Cathedral as well as many other important buildings in Europe. At the southern tip of the island is a lighthouse, and Portland Castle, built by Henry VIII, occupies the site of an earlier Saxon stronghold.

SONG	COMPOSER	POET
"The Isle of Portland"	John Edmunds, Charles Orr	A. E. Housman

ISPAHAN, ISFAHAN (English transliteration): a city in Persia, modern-day Iran. "Persia, that imaginary seat of Oriental splendor! That land of poets and roses! That cradle of mankind" (Morier, 1937). "Gardens, palaces and pavilions, mosques and masdrasahs, bazaars, splendid bridges, and above all a magnificent Royal Square— these are the impressions which the traveler carries away from Isfahan . . . Isfahan retains its traditional title, Nisf-I-Jahan, 'half the world'" (Jackson, 1906). Celebrated as half the world, Isfahan was a great center of learning and culture, equally famous for the beauty of its architecture and gardens. The rose, like the tulip, is said to have come originally from Persia, where gardening has long been considered an art form and where roses were a favorite object for the decoration of Persian tiles. Ispahan was the capital of Persia during the Safavid dynasty. Shah Abbas (1587–1629) had the city constructed around a *maidan* (a large grassy field), also used as a polo field. The city, once the most beautiful flower of the Persian Orient, has a wide, two-mile long avenue running through it, in the middle of which is a shaded promenade that is said to have been the inspiration for the Champs Élysées in Paris. The grave of the great Persian poet ★Hāfiz is situated in a modern park in Isfahan and surrounded by a plot filled with rose bushes. Ispahan (Isfahan) is pronounced [i]s-fa-[ã].

(SOURCES: Jackson, 1906; Morier, 1937; Herbert, 1929; Christopher, 1972; Harvey, Heseltine, 1959)

SONG	COMPOSER	POET
"Les Roses d'Ispahan"	Gabriel Fauré	Leconte de L'Isle

ITA, SAINT: one of the most revered of Irish female saints. Born 570 C.E. near Waterford, also called Ida and Mida although probably named Deidre, Ita was of royal descent and committed to living her life as a virgin. When a suitor presented himself, she commenced three days of fasting and praying. The angelic help that arrived in answer to her prayers convinced her father to allow her to take the veil. Ita then dedicated her life to fasting and prayer, remaining in solitude for long periods of time and becoming much sought after for advice. In County Limerick she founded a community of nuns; she ran a school for boys at which one of her students was the famed St. Brendan. A lullaby to the baby ★Jesus is attributed to her. St. Ita's feast day is January 15. (SOURCES: Walsh, 1991; Farmer, 1997)

SONG	COMPOSER	POET
"St. Ita's Vision"	Samuel Barber	anonymous medieval Irish poet

IWASZKIEWICZ, JAROSLAV (1894–1980): Polish poet, prose writer, dramatist, and translator. Friend and relation of composer Karol Szymanowski, Iwaszkiewicz had a solid education and made youthful attempts at composition. His literary creations often had musical themes. Iwaszkiewicz was the author of the libretto for Szymanowski's opera "King Rodger," as well as "Meetings with Szymanowski," a book of reminiscences, and monographs on J. S. Bach and Frederick Chopin. (SOURCE: Steinberg, 2, 1973)

"I Wonder as I Wander": a song by John Jacob Niles, based on a fragment of music Niles heard in the town square of Murphy, North Carolina. It was being sung by a "blue-eyed girl with a mop of tousled blond hair," who seemed to be a part of a group of traveling evangelists. She sang only the first two lines and refused to go beyond those lines. "I Wonder as I Wander" was first published in a book titled *Songs of the Hill-Folk*. (SOURCE: Preminger, 1986)

J ✍

JABBERWOCKY: the central figure of a strange, almost gibberish poem in Lewis ★Carroll's *Through the Looking Glass*. It contains many significant words that are subsequently explained to Alice by Humpty Dumpty: *brillig*, 4P.M. when one begins broiling things for dinner; *slithy*, lithe and slimy; *toves*, animals like badgers, lizards, or corkscrews; *gyre*, to go round and round like gyroscopes; *gimbel*, to make holes like a gimlet; *wabe*, grass around a sundial, before or behind it; *mimsy*, flimsy and miserable; *borogove*, a thin, shabby-looking bird with feathers sticking out all around; *rath*, a green pig; *mome*, from home; *outgrabe*, a bellow and a whistle with a sneeze in the middle. (SOURCES: Cooper, 1992; *Norton*, 1996)

SONG	COMPOSER	POET
"Jabberwocky"	Lee Hoiby	Lewis Carroll

JACK O'LANTERN: a hollowed pumpkin with openings cut to represent a human face, traditionally displayed at Hallowe'en, with a candle or other light inside; any phenomenon of light, as a corona discharge (*Irrlicht*).

SONG	COMPOSER	POET
1. "Des Fischers Liebesglück"	Franz Schubert	Karl von Leitner
2. "Irrlicht"	Franz Schubert	Wilhelm Müller

JACOB, MAX (1876–1944): French poet. A Breton of Jewish origin, Jacob arrived in Paris in 1894. Several years later he was fortunate to meet ★Picasso and ★Apollinaire. He welcomed the experiences that came to him after 1904, which led at first to an understanding of Cubism and ★Surrealism, but within five years he experienced a vision of ★Christ while drawn to religion and bohemian life. In 1915 he converted to Catholicism, after which his writing had a greater depth and power. To his contemporaries he became an inexplicable character, a clown or a mystic, yet his influence on young writers was great, although he never achieved the fame of Picasso or Apollinaire. Twice he retired to seclusion, once in 1921–27, and again from 1936 to World War II. Arrested with other Jews by the Germans in February 1944, he died of pneumonia in a concentration camp. Jacob's interests in painting and in literature were united in his poetry. His contributions to French literature were many, expanding lyricism to include those elements previously associated with prose writing: humor, ★parody, wordplay, fragmented images, satirical sketches, dream sequences, hallucinations, and irony. Jacob experimented with biography, art criticism, tales, and drama, and his last works turned toward spirituality. The poetry of Max Jacob has been set extensively by Francis Poulenc, also by Henri Sauguet and Vittorio Rieti. PRINCIPAL WORKS: *Le Cornet à dés*, 1917; *Le Laboratoire central*, 1921; *Visions infernales*, 1924; *Les Pénitents en maillots roses*, 1925; *Rivage*, 1931; *Le Bal masqué*, 1932; *Derniers poèmes en vers et en prose*, 1945; *L'Homme de cristal*, 1946; *For Max Jacob*, tr. Andrei Codrescu, 1974; *The Dice Cup*, ed. Michael Brownstein, 1979; *Selected Prose Poems*, 1980. (SOURCE: Serafin, 1999)

JACOBI, JOHANN GEORG (1740–1814): German poet and writer on the arts. Jacobi was born in Düsseldorf and studied at several universities. An *Anacreontic poet, Jacobi enjoyed a position as Professor of Philosophy at Halle and at Freiburg, and edited a literary journal that published a number of *Goethe's poems. Jacobi's collected poetry, mixed with rhythmic prose, was published in Vienna in 1816. His verse was set by Mozart, Mendelssohn, and Schubert, who set seven of his poems, including "Litanei." PRINCIPAL WORKS: *Poetische Versuche*, 1764; *Abschied an den Amor*, 1769; *Die Sommerreise*, 1770; *Die Winterreise*, 1769; *Iris*, 1803. (SOURCE: Reed, 1997)

JACOBSEN, JENS PETER (1847–1885): Danish poet and novelist. Jacobsen began his career as a student of botany and zoology, and his subject matter as a poet was naturalistic. Early poetic attempts met with little critical success until his cycle, *A Cactus Blooms*, was published. His independence from tradition is in evidence in the cycle of lyric monologues, *Gurresang*. This work has a Medieval *ballad motive, which was in high favor with Danish poets of the early nineteenth century. Jacobsen's poetry is written in a careful, precise style with a skillful use of language, although his creative output was small. His poetry was set, among others, by Arnold Schönberg in the composition *Gurrelieder*. (SOURCES: *Americana*, 2003; Kunitz, Colby, 1967)

JALEO: a Spanish dance in moderate tempo, 3/8 time, often accompanied by castanets; also the clapping of hands to spur the dancers on; (lit.), *a scuffle, quarrel, commotion*. (SOURCE: Cockburn, Stokes, 1992)

SONG	COMPOSER	POET
"Anda jaleo"	Federico García Lorca	traditional song

JAMMES, FRANCIS (1868–1938): a French pastoral poet of the Pyrenees region. The admiration with which Jammes's poetry was regarded did not come from Paris, but from the rest of France, because he brought a popular appeal into French poetry after the stylized work of the *Symbolists. Jammes's Catholicism was particularly strong, as was his love of familiar, natural things and his contempt for artifice. He saw God in all natural things but did not use the verbosity of the Romantic *pantheists, who believed that God is everything and everything is God. Although disconcertingly sincere, Jammes was not naive, possessing wit and refinement, and writing about nature, animals, and rustic life with a deliberate charm. The poetry of Francis Jammes was set by Arthur Honegger and Lili Boulanger. PRINCIPAL WORKS: *Vers*, 1892–94; *La Naissance du poète*, 1897; *De l'Angélus de l'aube à l'angélus du soir*, 1898; *Le Deuil des premevères*, 1901; *Tristesses*, 1905; *Clairières dans le Ciel*, 1906; *Poèmes mesurés*, 1908; *Rayons de miel*, 1908; *La Vierge et les sonnets*, 1919; *Livres des quatrains*, 1922–25; *Diane*, 1928; *Alouette*, 1935. (SOURCE: Rees, 1992)

JANÉS, CLARA (b. 1940): Spanish poet, novelist, essayist, biographer, and translator. Clara Janés is the daughter of the publisher/poet Josep *Janés. Her father wrote in Catalan, but she wrote in Spanish and translated many of her father's works. Her many volumes of poetry, translated into twenty different languages, were published to great success and awarded prizes. As a translator she put Czech verse into Spanish. She also wrote a biography of Mompou, *La vida callada de Federico Mompou* (The Silent Life of Frederic Mompou). The verse of Clara Janés has been set by Federico Mompou. WORKS: *The Stars Overcome*, 1964; *Human Limit*, 1974, *Personal Anthology*, 1979; *Kampa*, 1986; *Pink of Fire*, 1996; *Parallaxes*, 2002. (SOURCE: Cockburn, Stokes, 1992)

JANÉS, JOSEP (1913–1959): Catalan poet and publisher. Born in L'Hospitalet near Barcelona, Janés wrote three books of poetry, of which the best known is *Combat del Somni* (Dream Combat), 1937. The poetry of Josep Janés was set extensively by Federico Mompou. (SOURCE: Cockburn, Stokes, 1992)

JASON: a hero of Greek legend, who led the Argonauts in the quest for the ★Golden Fleece of the winged ram Chrysomallus. When Jason demanded his kingdom from his uncle Pelias, who had deprived him of it, and when he was told he could have it in return for the Golden Fleece, Jason gathered around himself the chief heroes of Greece and set sail in the ship *Argo*. After many tests and trials, Jason was successful through the help of ★Medea, whom he married. (SOURCE: Cooper, 1992)

SONG	COMPOSER	POET
"Le Chèvre du Thibet"	Francis Poulenc	Guillaume Apollinaire

JAW-BONE: an instrument made from the actual jawbone of a horse or ass, which the end men in an old time minstrel show shook like a tambourine. When the bone was dried thoroughly, the teeth became so loose that they rattled and produced a sound like a pair of castanets. (SOURCE: Preminger, 1986)

SONG	COMPOSER	POET
"Angela Baker"	Stephen Collins Foster	Stephen Collins Foster

JEAN-AUBRY, GEORGES (1882–1949): French poet. During Manuel de Falla's first sojourn in Paris, Jean-Aubry, then writing articles on French music, became a friend of his. He organized a concert of Falla's work, the first devoted to Spanish music given in France. He arranged for Falla to make his first visit to London (1911). Jean-Aubry himself lived in England from 1915 to 1930. His poetry was set by Falla in his composition titled *Psyché,* and by Albert Roussel, Jacques Ibert, and Antony Arensky. (SOURCE: Cockburn, Stokes, 1992)

JEAN MARTIN: (Fr.), *everyman.*

SONG	COMPOSER	POET
"Le Mendicant"	Francis Poulenc	Maurice Fombeure

"Jeg Elsker Dig" (I Love Thee): a song by Edvard Grieg set to a poem by Hans Christian ★Andersen. Owing to the fact that a German translator chose to add a second verse, singers frequently sing this song through twice. The manuscript in Bergen makes it clear, however, that neither a repeat nor a second verse was intended by the composer.

JEHOVAH: a hybrid form of Yahweh, the name by which the God of Israel identified himself to his people, according to Ex. 3.14. The name Jehovah is sometimes referred to as the Tetragrammaton (in Greek, *four letters*), since the name is composed of four Hebrew consonants, YHWH, a form of the Hebrew infinitive *to be*. The exact meaning of the word is much disputed, but it very likely refers to the divine creative force. (SOURCE: Nevins, 1964)

SONG	COMPOSER	POET
1. "Jehovah"	Franz Schubert	Johann Mayrhofer
2. "Die Allmacht"	Franz Schubert	Johann Pyrker
3. "Belsazar"	Robert Schumann	Heinrich Heine
4. "Die ihr des unermesslichen Weltalls"	Wolfgang Mozart	Franz Ziegenhagen

JEITELLES, ALOYS (1794–1858): Czech poet and playwright. Jeitelles was born in Brno, Czechoslovakia, and died there. His medical studies took place in Prague, Brno, and Vienna (M.D., 1825). In 1848 Jeitelles took an active part in the revolutionary movement. He was a writer for periodicals and a musical amateur. As a playwright he was the author of comedies, but he is best remembered as the romantic poet of the first song cycle "An die ferne Geliebte," set by Ludwig van Beethoven in 1816. Little is known about Beethoven's association with the poet other than the composer's sincere gratitude for the inspiration afforded him by Jeitelles's cycle of poems. (SOURCE: Garland, 1976)

JEPTHA: the illegitimate son of Gilead in the Old Testament. Driven out of his father's house by his legitimate brothers, Jeptha went to live in the land of Tob. When a war with the children of Ammon arose, the Gilead elders went to Jeptha to ask him to become their leader. During the war Jeptha swore to sacrifice, as an offering to God, the first living creature that came forth from his house, should he return home victorious. Upon his return, he was greeted by his only daughter, whom he sacrificed according to his vow. (SOURCE: *Americana*, 2003)

JÉRICA, PABLO DE (1781–1831?): Spanish fable writer. Jérica was born in Victoria, educated at the University of Oñate, finally entered a business firm in Cádiz. Having become involved in liberal politics, he was forced to go into exile in France. His fable writing is humorous but biting. The writing of Pablo de Jérica has been set by Eduardo Toldrà. (SOURCE: Cockburn, Stokes, 1992)

JERICHO, JERICO: name of a town in Israel where David bade servants tarry until their beards were grown; used in colloquial phrases for a place of retirement or concealment, or a place far distant, out of the way (2 Samuel 5.5). Jericho was the first city conquered by the Israelites under Joshua after they crossed the Jordan River into the Promised Land.

JEROME, SAINT (ca.347–419/20): saint, born at a fortress on the border between Dalmatia and the former Yugoslavia. Jerome studied in Rome, where he was baptized in 366. In Trier he was exposed to monasticism, which probably caused him to choose an ascetical life. Traveling east ca.372, Jerome studied Greek in Antioch, then moved to the Syrian desert where he lived as a hermit and studied Hebrew. When he returned to Antioch, he was ordained a priest and became secretary to Pope

Damasus I. Because of his sarcastic criticism and self-centeredness, he encountered animosity wherever he went. After the death of Pope Damasus, Jerome established in Bethlehem (386) a double monastery for men and women and devoted the remainder of his life to study and writing. With his knowledge of languages, he worked at an accurate biblical text based on original languages. (SOURCE: Glazier, Hellwig, 1994)

SONG	COMPOSER	POET
"La Ermita di San Simon"	Mario Castelnuovo-Tedesco	Romançero Español

JESUS: Lat. form of the Greek *Iesous*, derived in turn from the Aramaic *Yeshu*, meaning "Yahweh is salvation." The name of her son was announced to ★Mary by the angel ★Gabriel.

SONG	COMPOSER	POET
1. "Noël"	Gabriel Fauré	Victor Wilder
2. "En prière"	Gabriel Fauré	Stephen Bordèse
3. "Jesus bettelt"	Arnold Schönberg	Richard Dehmel

JEU DE TONNEAU: a garden game played at the end of the nineteenth century. In this game a bronze frog with an open mouth sat upon a cabinet that had compartments numbered to count scored points. Players threw metal discs that fell through holes into the compartments or into the frog's mouth, which gave the player the highest score. The bored frog dreams of being set free from her pedestal, of being able to use her open mouth to utter "the word." "Le mot," the word, stands for "Le mot de Cambronne," a polite way of saying the French expletive *merde*, derived from the fact that Cambronne was a famous French general who said *merde* when asked to surrender. (SOURCE: Kimball, 1996)

SONG	COMPOSER	POET
1. "La Statue de bronze"	Erik Satie	Léon Paul Fargue
2. "La grenouille Ameouicane"	Erik Satie	Léon Paul Fargue

JEUNESSE, QUATRE CHANSONS DE: a collection of four songs by Claude Debussy, with texts by Paul ★Verlaine and Stéphane ★Mallarmé. The songs were originally to be found in the so-called Vasnier series ("Clair de lune," "Pierrot," "Pantomime," and "Apparition") as well as other early Debussy songs. These four songs were published posthumously in the *Revue Musicale* of May 1926 and sometime later in an American publication. They were finally printed under the title *Quatre Chansons de Jeunesse* and enjoyed great success with high sopranos. Of the four affairs of the heart that played any real part in Debussy's life, the one with Madame Vasnier, the young wife of a not so young Parisian architect, was most important in so far as his composing was concerned. The Vasnier home was open to the twenty-year-old composer, and he spent as much of his time there as with his parents in Clichy. He admired Mme. Vasnier's sweet but fragile soprano, but chiefly as it expressed for him her very winning personality. (SOURCE: Meister, 1980)

JEZEBEL: in the Old Testament, the daughter of the Phoenician king Ethbaal, and the wife of Ahab, king of Israel. As queen, Jezebel introduced the worship of Baal into Israel. The prophet Elijah opposed this as idolatrous and sinful. Jezebel persecuted the prophets of *Jehovah, many of whom she had slain. So that her husband Ahab could have the vineyards that belonged to Naboth the Jezreelite, Jezebel falsely accused Naboth of treason. As a result he was stoned to death. When Ahab took possession of the vineyard, Elijah prophesied that God would punish both of them. Jezebel was murdered in Jezreel, but Ahab repented and was spared. The name Jezebel came to stand for a wicked and depraved woman, as written in 1 Kings 18 and 19, and 2 Kings 9. (SOURCE: *Americana*, 2003)

JIMÉNEZ, JUAN RAMÓN (1881–1958): Spanish poet. Juan Ramón Jiménez was born in Moguer, Spain. His education began with a Jesuit School in *Càdiz (1891–1896) and concluded at the University of Seville. Some years after being released from the sanatoriums that his ill health had forced him to live in from 1901 to 1905, he settled in Madrid, having become a professional writer. In 1936, sent into exile, he left Spain to teach in Puerto Rico, Cuba, North Carolina, and Florida until 1942 when he went to Washington, D.C. where he remained until 1951. He then became a member of the faculty of the University of Puerto Rico at Rio Piedras (1951–1958), during which time he received the 1956 Nobel Prize for Literature. Jiménez's first two books, published in 1900, were written in a highly sentimental form of end of the century decadence. Soon, however, he became an adapter of *Verlaine's *Symbolism and a follower of *Becquer. During his time in the United States he became acquainted with free verse, of which he made a version of short stanzas he called *verso desnudo* (naked verse). His work titled *Espació* (space) was inspired by the Florida Everglades. The themes that most inspired his work were the confluence of past and present, memory, spiritual versus carnal love, destiny, and morality. His poems express states of mind through lyricism of landscapes and put him in a key position in the evolution of contemporary Spanish poetry, his aim being "pure" poetry, free verse, short compressed poems, and simplicity in describing deep emotion. Jiménez was sensitive and solitary, a scrupulous critic of his own work, revising and rewriting much of his poetry and destroying his older books so as to leave a better legacy. The poetry of Juan Ramón Jiménez has been set by Gottfried von Einem, Federico Mompou, Jesús Bal y Gay, and Joaquín Rodrigo. PRINCIPAL WORKS: *Libros de poesía* (*Books of Poetry*), ed. Agustin Caballero, 1957; *Rimas*, 1902; *Arias tristes*, 1903; *Diario de un poeta recién casado*, 1917, rev. ed. as *Diario de poeta y mar*, 1948, 1955; *Eternidades,* 1918; *Belleza,* 1923; *Animal de fondo*, 1949; *300 Poemas: 1903–1953*, trans. Eloise Roach, 1962; *Platero y yo: Elegía andaluza*, 1914, as *Platero and I,* 1956. SELECTED READING: P. Olsen, *Circle of Paradox: Time and Essence in the Poetry of J. R. Jiménez,* 1967; Donald F. Fogelquist, *Jiménez*, 1976. (SOURCE: Vinson, Kirkpatrick (1), 1984)

JINGLE: any verse that pleases the ears by a catchy rhythm and sound repetitions, usually at the expense of sense. Good examples are: "Eeny meeny miny mo" and "Hickory dickory dock."

JO: (Scot.), *joy*.

JOHN THE BAPTIST, SAINT: New Testament figure, Christian saint. According to the gospel of St. Luke, John was the son of the ★Virgin Mary's cousin Elizabeth and her husband Zachariah. John lived in the wilderness, dressed in camel skins and ate locusts (or grasshoppers) and wild honey. A powerful speaker, John preached about the kingdom of Heaven being close at hand and attracted many people, who came to be baptized by him at the River ★Jordan. John told these people that a prophet who would come after him would baptize not with water but with the Holy Spirit. The Church regards John as the one who prepared the way for the Messiah. All four gospels tell of ★Jesus beginning his public ministry with his baptism by John, whom Jesus referred to as Elijah. When John first saw Jesus, he uttered the famous words, "Behold the lamb of God, that takest away the sins of the world." Although John acknowledged Jesus as the greatest prophet at the baptism, he did not become one of the followers. Later, John was imprisoned by King ★Herod for condemning him, but not executed. At Herod's birthday his stepdaughter, ★Salome, danced for him. So enthralled with her dancing was Herod that he promised to give Salome anything she wanted. Herodias prompted her to ask for the head of John the Baptist, and accordingly Herod ordered John beheaded. June 24 is the feast day of John the Baptist. (SOURCES: Metzger, Murphy, 1994; Thurston, Attwater, 1963)

SONG	COMPOSER	POET
1. "La Sauterelle"	Francis Poulenc	Guillaume Apollinaire
2. "Christ's Sunday Morn"	Ernst Bacon	folk poetry
3. "Mens jeg venter"	Edvard Grieg	Vilhelm Kraz
4. "Mañanita de San Juan"	Jesús Guridi	Castilian folk poetry
5. "Aserrín, aserrán"	Federico Mompou	folk poetry

JOHNNY APPLESEED: an eccentric, wandering pioneer nurseryman of historical and folk traditions. Johnny is usually pictured as a barefoot, bearded, kindly hermit or a tramp. He left a trail of legends and anecdotes throughout the Midwest. Hailed as a saint in action, he is a poetic symbol of plain living and high morality.

SONG	COMPOSER	POET
"Johnny Appleseed"	Elie Siegmeister	Rosemary Benét

JOHNS, ORRICK (1887–1946): American poet and critic. Born in St. Louis, Johns was educated at the University of Missouri and Washington University. He made his living as an ad man, reporter, and a man of all trades, including deputy city marshal. He reviewed plays, books, music, and fine arts, and helped to found the Players' Club of St. Louis. When Johns moved to New York to write advertising copy, he wrote poetry on the side, winning a national poetry prize in 1912. After three years in Italy, he returned to New York, where he became Director of the Federal Writers Project and interested himself in the labor movement. Johns was a pioneer of the "New Poetry" movement, his own writing being intensely readable and filled with charm. The verse of Orrick Johns has been set by Richard Hundley. PRINCIPAL WORKS: *Asphalt*, 1919; *Black Branches*, 1920; *Wild Plum*, 1926; *The*

Time of our Lives, 1937. SELECTED READING: Louis Untermeyer, *American Poetry Since 1900*, 1923. (SOURCE: Johns, 1973)

JOHNSON, ROBERT UNDERWOOD (1853–1937): American poet, diplomat, and editor. Johnson was born in Washington, D.C. One of his first jobs was as an assistant editor of *Century Magazine*, later editor-in-chief. His poetry was fluent yet conventional, but his services to establishing international copyright laws were of great value to the profession. Ambassador to Italy for many years, Johnson also started a movement that resulted in the creation of Yosemite National Park. His verse was set by Charles Ives. PRINCIPAL WORKS: *Italian Rhapsody and Other Poems of Italy*, 1917; *Poems of Fifty Years*, 1931. (SOURCE: Kunitz, Haycraft, 1942)

JOHNSON, SAMUEL (1709–1784): English man of letters. Johnson, the son of an elderly bookseller, was born in Litchfield and educated at Pembroke College, Oxford, where he took no degree because his Oxford days were marred by poverty and bouts of melancholia. After leaving Oxford he moved to Birmingham, where he contributed to newspapers and did translations from the French. After he married, Johnson started a private school, unsuccessful partly because of his lack of a degree. In addition to writing essays, poems, Latin verses, and biographies for the *Gentleman's Magazine* in London, he also worked as an editor. In 1747 he began work on what would be the first English dictionary (containing 40,000 definitions and without a rival until much later). *A Dictionary of the English Language* was published in 1755 and brought him his Oxford degree. In 1762 he was given a Crown pension, and in 1763 he met his famous biographer, Boswell. So did he become one of the most eminent literary figures of the day. Johnson and Boswell traveled to Scotland, Wales, the Hebrides, and Paris. In 1777 Johnson undertook *The Lives of the English Poets*, as requested by London booksellers. Upon his death, Johnson was buried in Westminster Abbey. His reputation rests on his works but also on Boswell's telling of Johnson's brilliant conversation and oversized personality. Samuel Johnson's writing has been set by Dominick Argento. Yale University (A. T. Hagen and J. H. Middendorf) has published Vols. 1–15 of Johnson's *Works*, a continuing project. W. J. Bate wrote a biography in 1978. (SOURCE: Drabble, 2000)

JONGLEUR: a member of the troubadour groups of the twelfth and thirteenth centuries, essentially an instrumentalist who often played and sang at the same time and was skilled in acrobatics and dancing.

JONSON, BENJAMIN (1572–1637): English writer of plays and masques, poet, actor, and literary critic. Ben Jonson was born in London and educated at the Westminster School. He fought for the Dutch against the Spanish in the Low Countries. A playwright and actor from 1595 on, he killed a fellow actor in a duel in 1598 but escaped the gallows. Jonson was appointed poet laureate of England in 1616. Many of the fifty-three plays and masques Jonson wrote and presented at court (1616–25) were in collaboration with scenic designer and architect Inigo Jones. During this period he gained a reputation as the literary dictator of London. Later on, he attracted a circle of young writers who styled themselves the "Sons of Ben." Jonson was elected burgess of Edinburgh in 1619 and appointed city chronologer of London in 1628.

"Jonson designated himself the arbiter of true critical taste, the upholder of classical standards of decorum and morality against the undiscriminating popular appetite for sensation and extravagant spectacle, the champion of high erudition against barbarous ignorance" (Vinson, 1979). Since Jonson made no efforts to disguise his true opinions from the public, much was made of the contrast between the warm, generous ★Shakespeare and the cold-bloodedly perfect Jonson. The distinction was faulty, however. Jonson's fertile creative imagination contributed to his comic theatrical creations, his tender lyrics, and savagely satirical ★epigrams. His last years presented a sad picture of commercial failure, declining creative powers, and increasing physical problems. The poetry of Ben Jonson has been set by Benjamin Britten, Alfonso Ferrabosco, Geoffrey Bush, Arthur Bliss, Leslie Bassett, and Marc Blitzstein. One of Jonson's poems, "To Celia," better known as "Drink to Me Only with Thine Eyes," is a vocal staple. PRINCIPAL WORKS: Plays: *Every Man out of His Humour*, 1600; *Every Man in His Humour*, 1601; *The Poetaster*, 1602; *Volpone; or, the Foxe*, 1609; *The Alchemist*, 1612; *Epicoene; or, the Silent Woman*, 1620. Poetry: *The Workes of Ben Jonson* (the 1616 and 1640 folios); *Epigrams*, 1616; *The Forest*, 1616; *Underwoods*, 1640. Other: *Horace, His Art of Poetrie*. SELECTED READING: A. C. Swinburne, *A Study of Ben Jonson*, 1889; G. B. Johnston, *Ben Jonson: Poet*, 1945. (SOURCE: Vinson, 1979)

JORDAN: an Arab kingdom in the Middle East, now bordered by Israel on the west, Syria on the north, Iraq on the east, and Saudi Arabia on the southeast and south. On parts of its Israeli border lie the Dead Sea and the Sea of Galilee; the rest of Jordan is composed of sandy desert, rocky plains, and green hills. Jordan was once part of ancient Palestine, but it is now the Hashemite Kingdom of Jordan, Hashemite being the family name of its kings.

SONG	COMPOSER	POET
"Die Könige"	Peter Cornelius	Peter Cornelius

JOSEPH, SAINT: Christian saint, husband of the ★Virgin Mary, foster father of ★Jesus (although the Bible refers to Jesus as the son of Joseph, and although he was regarded by Jesus's contemporaries as his legal father). When the Bible traces the genealogy of Jesus (Matthew and Luke), it is through Joseph that Jesus is said to be a descendant of ★King David. Legends about Joseph abound; in some he was seen as a comic figure. He worked as a carpenter, but he is better described as a builder or artisan. Matthew portrays Joseph as a "just man." When Joseph learned that Mary was pregnant, he had intended to divorce her quietly, but two angels came to him in visions; one assured him that the baby was of divine origin and another warned that ★Herod planned to harm the baby Jesus, thus precipitating the flight of Joseph and his family to Egypt. When Herod died, an angel appeared to tell Joseph that it was safe to return to Israel. To explain Joseph's other children, referred to as brothers and sisters of Jesus, it is said that Joseph, considerably older than Mary, had children from a previous marriage. Some of the apocryphal gospels portray Joseph as ineffective in dealing with the infant and toddler Jesus, who was petulant and a general nuisance. Yet, in his last illness Joseph was comforted by both Mary and Jesus. Since the Bible does not mention Joseph as present during the public ministry of Jesus, we must assume that he had died. Based upon the legend of Joseph's fear of his own death and judgment, Joseph is the patron saint of those seeking a holy death. He was also the patron saint of families, bursars and procurators, manual workers, and carpenters. (SOURCES: Walsh, 1991; Farmer, 1997; Thurston, Attwater, 1963; Glazier, Hellwig, 1994)

SONG	COMPOSER	POET
1. "Nun wandre, Maria"	Hugo Wolf	Paul Heyse
2. "Der heilige Josef singt"	Hugo Wolf	Emanuel Geibel, Paul Heyse
3. "San José y Maria"	Joaquín Rodrigo	Victoria Kamhi
4. "Villancico Castellano"	Joaquín Nín	Castilian carol
5. "Epiphanias"	Hugo Wolf	Johann Wolfgang von Goethe
6. "Mariae Heimsuchung"	Paul Hindemith	Rainer Maria Rilke
7. "Argwohn Josephs"	Paul Hindemith	Rainer Maria Rilke

JOSEPHSON, ERNST (1851–1906): a Swedish painter and poet. Born into a middle-class Jewish family in Stockholm, Josephson started at the Academy of Fine Arts at the age of sixteen and later studied in Paris and the Netherlands. Successful as an artist, he was awarded a royal medal. He was famous for his oil portraits before the onset of his mental illness. Afterward, his art was dominated by historical motives and pictures from myths and fairy tales, which ★Picasso and Matisse knew and appreciated. Josephson published two collections of poetry, from one of which Sibelius set "Svarta rosor" (Black Roses). (SOURCE: Kunitz, Colby, 1967)

JOTA: a Spanish dance form, common to Navarre, Castile, and Valencia but danced mostly in Aragon, usually in a fairly fast 3/4 time and often accompanied by castanets. Dating from the twelfth century, the dance is thought to be connected with the Moor, Aben Jot. (SOURCE: Cockburn, Stokes, 1992)

SONG	COMPOSER	POET
"Jota"	Manuel da Falla	Spanish folk song

JOVE: another name for ★JUPITER.

JOYCE, JAMES (1882–1941): Irish poet and novelist. Joyce was born in a Dublin suburb and attended Jesuit private schools followed by the University College in Dublin, where he also had a Jesuit education. Although he eloped with his fiancée in 1904, his contempt for convention meant that they would not marry for twenty-seven years. Joyce lived abroad in Trieste (where he taught English to foreigners), Paris, and Zurich, where he died in 1941. Joyce's preeminence in modern fiction writing relegated his verse to obscurity, although he regarded himself as a poet. In an essay Joyce said, "Poetry, even when apparently most fantastic, is always a revolt against artifice, a revolt in a certain sense, against actuality. It speaks of that which seems unreal and fantastic to those who have lost the simple intuitions which are the tests of reality" (Ellmann, O'Clair, 1973). Joyce began to write poetry under the shadow of ★Yeats about 1900. Soon he modeled himself on the Elizabethan lutenists like ★Dowland. Music is important in Joyce's writings; he gave some of his poems musical titles and intended for them to be set to music. The composer Dallapiccola maintains that various words and sounds in the Circe episode of *Ulysses* correspond to the twelve-note scale. Joyce wished poems to be free of conscious purpose, but he did not underestimate those difficulties. He actually put his lines together letter by letter and read ★Blake and ★Rimbaud on the value of letters in an effort to recover more singable poetry. James Joyce's poetry was set many times by Samuel Barber, and also by Roger Sessions, Sergius Kagen, Conrad Susa, Israel Citkowitz, David Del Tredici, Donald Martino, Richard Cummings, Miriam Gideon, John Cage, David Diamond, Albert Roussel, Albert Reimann, and Karol Szymanowski. PRINCIPAL WORKS: Poetry: *Chamber Music*, 1907; *Pomes Penyeach*, 1927. Novels and Short Stories: *The Dubliners*, 1914; *Ulysses*, 1922; *Finnegan's Wake*, 1939. Fictionalized Autobiography: *A Portrait of the Artist as a Young Man*, 1914; *Stephen Hero*, 1944. SELECTED READING: Richard Ellmann, *James Joyce*, rev. ed., 1982; *James Joyce: Poems and Shorter Writings*, ed. R. Ellmann, A. Walton Litz, and John Whittier-Ferguson, 1991. (SOURCES: Ellmann, O'Clair, 1973; Hamilton, 1994)

JUBAL: a biblical figure, the son of Lamech, the grandson of Methuselah, the great grandson of Enoch, the great, great grandson of ★Cain, who was the son of ★Adam. Genesis 4.21 credits Jubal with being the first musician. "He was the father of all those who play the lyre and pipe" (The Holy Bible, 1611). The name Jubal means "he who runs" or "he who is pursued," though it can also mean "a trumpet." After Cain murdered his brother ★Abel and was driven from the presence of God, he settled in the land of Nod, east of the Garden of Eden. There he married and had children. Jubal is referred to in a soprano solo from Handel's oratorio *Joshua*, "Oh, had I Jubal's lyre." (SOURCES: Cruden, 1953; May, Metzger, 1977)

JUDAH: a biblical personage, son of Jacob and Leah; also the name of one of the twelve tribes of Israel. Once Jacob had passed over his unstable oldest son Reuben and given Judah the authority, Judah proposed to his brothers that they sell their father's favorite son Joseph to merchants rather than kill him. The tribe of Judah outnumbered all other Hebrew tribes in captivity in Egypt. The tribe led the Exodus and the conquest of Canaan, settling in the dry hill country and wilderness of Judah west of the Dead Sea. Under the leadership of ★David, Judah was incorporated with other Hebrew tribes into a united monarchy and its territory took the name ★Judea.

SONG	COMPOSER	POET
1. "The Blessed Virgin's Expostulation"	Henry Purcell	Nahum Tate
2. "Die Könige"	Peter Cornelius	Peter Cornelius

JUDEA: the name of a country in the southern part of ancient Palestine. Judea was originally named for the tribe of ★Judah. King ★David came from Judean territory and united all Israel into one kingdom, making Jerusalem its capital. The state of

Judea came to an end in 70C.E. when the Romans captured Jerusalem and destroyed the temple.

SONG	COMPOSER	POET
1. "Die Könige"	Peter Cornelius	Peter Cornelius
2. "Mariae Heimsuchung"	Paul Hindemith	Rainer Maria Rilke

JUG-JUG: *see* ★CUCKOO.

JULIA, TO: title of a set of songs by British composer Roger Quilter put to the poetry of Robert ★Herrick. Therein Quilter uses an interesting format (used also by Joaquín Turina in his *Poema en forma de canciones* with texts by ★Campoamor), a melodic link between the songs and the inclusion of two piano solos, one as introduction and one as an interlude.

JULY 14: Bastille Day, a French national holiday marking the storming of the Bastille at the beginning of the French Revolution. The Bastille was a state prison and citadel in the eastern part of Paris, a symbol of the absolute power of the French monarchs.

SONG	COMPOSER	POET
"Fête nationale"	Jacques Ibert	Philippe Chabaneix

JUNG VOLKER: an outlaw character in ★Mörike's novel, ★*Maler Nolten*.

SONG	COMPOSER	POET
"Jung Volker Lied"	Robert Schumann	Eduard Mörike

JUPITER, JOVE: the supreme deity of the ancient Romans, associated with the sky and rain; identified with the Greek god, ★Zeus; also a planet in the solar system having seven moons.

SONG	COMPOSER	POET
1. "Dithyrambe"	Franz Schubert	Friedrich von Schiller
2. "Oh, the Sweet Delights of Love"	Henry Purcell	Philip Massinger and John Fletcher
3. "Jupiter Has Seven Moons"	Leonard Bernstein	Leonard Bernstein

K

KADDISCH: an ancient Aramaic prayer set to a Sephardic melody, intended to be recited by mourners as part of the synagogue service and by the congregation at High Holiday services. The text has four versions, of which Ravel set the one known as the Half Kaddish. Not a prayer for the dead, the Half Kaddish is an affirmation of the belief of the devout that their mission is to bring about the advent of God's kingdom by proclaiming and sanctifying the name of God. (SOURCE: Kimball, 1996)

SONG	COMPOSER	POET
"Kaddisch"	Maurice Ravel	Traditional

KAIL: (Scot.) (pr. kale), *a reheated broth or soup made with kale or cabbage.*

SONG	COMPOSER	POET
"Black Day"	Benjamin Britten	William Soutar

KALEVALA: the national epic of the Finns. *Kalevala* was compiled from popular songs and oral tradition by the Finnish philologist Eliaskø Lonnroth (1802–84), who published his first edition of 12,000 verses (1835), the second of some 22,900 verses (1849). The name was taken from the three hero sons of Kalewa (Finland): Väinäøinen, Ilmarinen, and Lemminkäinen. The action features the Sampo, a magical mill that grants all wishes. The *Kalevala* is written in unrhymed alliterative trochaic verse. In form and content, it is a prototype of ★Longfellow's *Hiawatha*. (SOURCE: Cooper, 1992)

KANA: *see* ★CANA.

KANT, IMMANUEL (1724–1804): a German philosopher whose subject was nature and the limits of human knowledge. Kant believed that the mind organizes experience into different patterns and arrangements even if it cannot yet experience them. In aesthetics and ethics he believed that doing one's duty was more important than being happy, that scientific predictions do not conflict with the use of free will. Kant never traveled; he was born and lived in East Prussia, teaching school near there until his death. (SOURCE: *Americana*, 2003)

SONG	COMPOSER	POET
"Das Lied von Grünen"	Franz Schubert	Friedrich Reil

KANTELE: (Finn.), a form of zither still used in Finland and Karilia, a large wooden box, pentagonal and tapering at one end. Although originally it had only five strings stretched the length of the instrument in a zither-like manner, today it may have as many as twenty-five made of metal and plucked with a plectrum. (SOURCE: *OED*, 1989)

KASHMIR: the northernmost region of the Indian sub-continent, administered jointly by India, Pakistan, and China, who are in a bitter dispute over the territory. Kashmir is 86,000 square miles in size and strategic largely because of the mountains and high plateaus with deep narrow valleys. There are two small cultivated plains, one of which is the Vale of Kashmir, five or six thousand feet high and celebrated for its beauty, in which is located the largest city, Srinagar. Kashmir's people are of the Hindu and Muslim religions. Although many languages are spoken, Kashmiri, an Indo-European language, is spoken by most inhabitants. (SOURCE: *Americana*, 2003)

SONG	COMPOSER	POET
"Kashmir"	Harry T. Burleigh	Laurence Hope

"Kathleen Mavourneen": a song by Frederick Crouch to poetry by Mrs. Julia Crawford. Mrs. Crawford, a native of County Cavan, had written several poems on

Irish themes. Crouch had spied the poem in *Metropolitan Magazine*, a London publication, and set it to music in 1835. The song sold twenty thousand copies in the first year of publication. In fifteen years the number had reached over a half a million, not one penny of which accrued to Crouch. (SOURCE: Preminger, 1986)

KEATS, JOHN (1795–1821): English poet. Son of a livery stable manager, John Keats lost both parents by the time he was fourteen. Although he was apprenticed to an apothecary-surgeon (1810), he cancelled the fifth year of his apprenticeship and took an apothecary's license (1816), but soon abandoned that profession for poetry. After meeting ★Shelley, he began to plan *Endymion*. His first volume of poems were ★sonnets, epistles, and poems. Keats's thought was influenced by Wordsworth and by his own travels in the Lake District, Scotland, and Northern Ireland, whose rough, majestic terrain moved him. Attacked on his published *Endymion* (1818), he continued to turn out his best work in this, his greatest writing year. Financial problems and tuberculosis signaled the end of his great creative work and propelled him to move to Rome, where he died within the year. As a principal figure of the ★Romantic movement, Keats grew in fame steadily despite changes of fashion. ★Tennyson thought him the greatest poet of the nineteenth century. Keats's letters (1848, 1878), containing his professional thoughts on love, poetry, and the nature of man, were almost as admired as his poetry. T. S. ★Eliot considered his work to be "the most notable and most important ever written by an English poet" (Drabble, 2000). The verse of John Keats has been set by Charles Ives, Benjamin Britten, Paul Hindemith, Jack Beeson, David Diamond, Jan Meyerowitz, and Mario Castelnuovo-Tedesco. PRINCIPAL WORKS: *Poems*, 1817; *Endymion*, 1818; *The Fall of Hyperion*, 1818; *The Use of Poetry and the Use of Criticism*, 1933. SELECTED READING: Andrew Motion, *John Keats*, 1997. (SOURCE: Drabble, 2000)

KECSKEMÉT: a town located 40 miles southeast of Budapest on the Great Hungarian Plain, which is formed by the ★Danube River flood plain (a combination of level arid land without forests and cultivated land).

SONG	COMPOSER	POET
"Zigeunerlieder #6"	Johannes Brahms	Hugo Conrat

KEEL HER POT: an expression used in Elizabethan lyrics, meaning *to cool a boiling pot by adding cold liquid.*

SONG	COMPOSER	POET
"Winter"	Dominick Argento	William Shakespeare

KELLER, GOTTFRIED (1819–1890): Swiss poet, novelist, and short-story writer. Born in Zürich, his father died when Keller was only five, but his mother provided him a good elementary education. After studying painting in Munich for two years, Keller decided that this was not the right calling and returned home (1842). During the next six years Keller's interests gradually turned to literature. He published a small volume of poems, *Gedichte*, which stirred no notice. Helped by a government stipend, he went first to the University of Heidelberg (1848) and then to Berlin (1850), where the next five years were the most fruitful of his career. His second collection of poetry, *Neuere Gedichte* (1851) was outstanding. Returning to Zürich

(1855), Keller was given a position as canton secretary that he held until 1876. In this period he wrote many short stories and published a collection of his poetry, *Gesammelte Gedichte* (1882). Although his reputation had spread slowly, by the time of his death Keller was regarded as an outstanding figure in nineteenth-century German literature and Switzerland's leading poet of that century. Keller's stories often pointed a moral but one that is softened with wit. His writing talent was for characterization and description in a direct and original style, his art based on resolute sophistication. The poetry of Gottfried Keller was set by Brahms, Wolf, Hans Pfitzner, Arnold Schönberg, and Ottmar Schoeck. Many of his short stories were translated into English, and his *Romeo und Julia auf dem Dorfe* was made into an opera by Frederick Delius. SELECTED READING: J. M. Lindsay, *Keller: Life and Works*, 1968. (SOURCE: Kunitz, Colby, 1967)

KERMESS: a festival in honor of a local saint, of Dutch and Belgian origin. Kermess is also the title of a large painting of such a festival by Breughel.

SONG	COMPOSER	POET
"The Dance"	Ned Rorem	William Carlos Williams

KERNER, JOSEF (1794–1868): Austrian sometime poet. Kerner studied at the University of Vienna and at the Imperial College in Vienna, where he met Schubert. Kerner returned to Linz after his studies, assuming his duties as a public servant. Nevertheless, he remained in contact with the Schubert circle. In 1858 Kerner wrote his memoirs, in which he stated that Franz von Schober was responsible for Schubert's illness. The ★Ossian poems strongly influenced Kerner's own poetry. Three of those were set by Schubert. (SOURCE: Reed, 1997)

KHAMHI, VICTORIA (1905–1997): Turkish pianist and text-writer. Khamhi was a talented Turkish pianist who, after meeting the blind composer Joaquín Rodrigo at the Paris Conservatoire where they were both studying (1928), married him in 1933 against her parents' opposition. She spoke several languages and had an extensive knowledge of different cultures. After their marriage Khamhi supported Rodrigo in every way, performing his piano music, editing his music, helping with his compositions, and writing texts for his songs. Their daughter, born in 1941, became a ballerina at the London Royal School of Ballet. The texts written by Victoria Khamhi were set by her husband, Rodrigo. She wrote an autobiography recounting her childhood, her marriage to Rodrigo, and the story of their lives, *De la mano de Joaquín Rodrigo: Historia de nuestra vida*. (SOURCE: Cockburn, Stokes, 1992)

KHAYYAM, OMAR (1048–1131): Persian poet and mathematician. Omar Khayyam, whose name, too famous to change, was faultily transliterated from the Persian, was well educated in geometry and astronomy. A Shi'ite Muslim, he worked for the chief magistrate and ruler of Bokhara in Samarkand. Later he entered the service of Sultan Malikshah, where he helped construct an observatory and compile the tables of astronomical figures that served as a basis of the new calendar era. He was summoned because he had produced work on algebra that established him as a pioneer of cubic equations that are still accessible to scholars. In 1095 he journeyed to Mecca and Baghdad and then returned to his birth city, where he was buried

(1131). The times he lived in were extremely perilous. In the year of his birth the Turks from central Asia were finishing off their conquest of Iran, Mesopotamia, and Asia Minor. By the time he died, they had almost made their great empire secure, even as far as Syria, where they engaged the Crusaders from Europe. Contemporaries extolled him as a mathematician and philosopher, not as a poet who wrote four-part stanzas of irreligious poetry. His contemporaries probably circulated his quatrains clandestinely without crediting him with their composition. Ninety years after his death, a Muslim writer spoke of Omar only to castigate his verses as evil and depraved. These verses were titled *Rubaiyat,* which means *quatrains. Omar Khayyam's quatrains were set by Francesco Santoliquido. PRINCIPAL WORKS: *Rubaiyat*, ed. Foroughi and Quasim Ghani, 1942; as *The Rubaiyat of Omar Khayyam*, trans. Edward Fitzgerald, 4th ed., 1964; also trans. John C. E. Bowen, 1961; Parichehr Kasra, 1975; and Peter Avery and John Heath-Stubbs, 1979. SELECTED READING: Ali Dashti, *In Search of Omar Khayyam*, 1971. (SOURCE: Vinson, Kirkpatrick (1), 1984)

KHOMYAKOV, HOMYAKOV, ALEKSEI (1804–1860): Russian poet and dramatist. Khomyakov graduated from the University of Moscow in mathematics (1821) but soon became an important theologian and the leader of the *Slavophile poetic movement. In the 1820s and 1830s Khomyakov published poetry describing his exalted view of a poet's calling and wrote many religious poems. Two Slavophile essays written in 1845 and 1846 stated his position that Russians, in trying to be like Europeans, would enhance their resulting feelings of inferiority. A thinker and competent lyricist, Khomyakov wrote plays and poems that served the expression of his ideas. Aleksei Khomyakov's verse was set by Rachmaninoff, Mussorgsky, Tchaikovsky, and Mily Balakirev. WORKS AVAILABLE IN ENGLISH: *The Poet*, 1827; *A Wish*, 1827; *Ode*, 1831; *The Eagle*, 1832; *Dimitri the Pretender* (a play), 1833; *A Fantasy*, 1834; *The Island,* 1836; *To Russia*, 1839; *The Laborer*, 1858. (SOURCE: Terras, 1991)

KIERKEGAARD, SØREN AABYE (1813–1855): Danish philosopher and theologian. Kierkegaard's father, already retired when his son was a boy, seemed obsessed with remorse over some obscure sin and fearful that his children would be punished. Upset by his father's attitude, Søren rebelled against society and studied theology at the University of Copenhagen. Upon the death of his father, Kierkegaard became a man of means whose writing was his pulpit. Subject to severe melancholia, Kierkegaard was convinced that his life was meant to serve God. Except for infrequent, short visits to Berlin, he stayed home and wrote feverishly, chiefly about man confronted with a moral choice between two kinds of life: aesthetical (life of the senses and material gratification) and ethical (life devoted to the attainment of spiritual insight). His inner life was turbulent, his outer life uneventful. Kierkegaard was the greatest modern exponent of *Existentialism, which emphasizes man's active will and freedom of choice and his obligation to meet moral experience totally and completely. The group of French existentialists, headed by Jean Paul Sartre and Albert Camus, were described as "Kierkegaard without God." Kierkegaard's hymn verses were set by composer Howard Boatwright. Most of Kierkegaard's principal works were translated by Walter Lourie. SELECTED READING: P. P. Rohde, *Søren Kierkegaard: The Father of Existentialism*. (SOURCE: Kunitz, Colby, 1967)

KINDERTOTENLIEDER: a cycle of songs by Gustav Mahler with texts by Friedrich ★Rückert. The poet had lost his two younger children in a scarlet fever epidemic. Two years after the first performance of the cycle, Mahler tragically lost his eldest daughter.

KINDER- UND HAUSMÄRCHEN: a collection of German stories known in the English-speaking countries as *Grimm's Fairy Tales*. Jacob and Wilhelm Grimm collected more than two hundred tales and put them into literary form, published in two volumes (1812, 1814).

KING ARTHUR; OR, THE BRITISH WORTHY: an essentially comedic semi-opera written by John ★Dryden with music by Henry Purcell, produced in 1691. (There are nine worthies, or heroes from history, of whom the British Worthy is King ★Arthur.) Purcell worked all winter and early spring of 1690 on this, his first unmitigated triumph, although, in the end, *King Arthur* was a somewhat perplexing and patchy work. Act 1 of the opera, whose essential business is the battle, opens in the camp of Oswald, king of the Saxons. A heathen sacrificial scene transpires during which priests invoke deities. Arthur, leading the Britons, wins a last battle after many against Oswald, whom he then allows to leave the island. In act 2, we are witness to ★Merlin's supernatural powers, as he descends in a chariot drawn by dragons. He recruits Philidel, an airy spirit, who is to help him protect the Britons, by steering them away from the bogs. Oswald has his own magicians, Grimbald and Osmond, whose duty it is to harass the Britons and lead them into swamps. Philidel, a soprano, sings "Hither This Way, This Way Bent," and Grimbald sings in response "Let Not a Moonborn Elf Mislead Ye," with the result that Arthur does not know which group to trust. Philidel leads the Britons to safety. Merlin is in charge of the love plot for both Arthur and Osmond, who are rivals for Emmeline, blind daughter of the Duke of Cornwall. In scene 2 two women entertain her with "Shepherd, Shepherd, Leave Decoying." In act 3 Emmeline, abducted by the Saxons, is made to witness the Frost Scene (a ★masque titled "Prospect of Winter in Frozen Countries"), one of the first masques composed for opera, this fine one written by Purcell. ★Cupid, descending in a machine, sings "What Ho! Thou Genius of This Isle." "What Power Thou Art," a tour de force, is sung by the hoary Cold ★Genius, followed by Cupid singing "Thou Doting Fool, Forbear," in which he derides the Cold Genius for exaggerating his condition. The Cold Genius acknowledges his extravagance in "Great Love, I Know Thee." In the rest of the Frost Scene, the Cold Genius, aided by dancers and a chorus, warns other inhabitants of the frozen landscape by singing "No Part of My Dominion." In act 4, Emmeline still being Oswald's prisoner, Arthur must attempt another rescue. Merlin warns Arthur that he will encounter only illusion. Tempted by an illusion of two river sirens, Arthur listens to them as they sing "Two Daughters of This Aged Stream Are We," a threat of death masked by explicit eroticism. As Arthur sets off in search of Emmeline, ★nymphs and sylvans appear; two of them (soprano and bass) sing "For Love Ev'ry Creature" and three sopranos sing "In Vain Are Our Graces," a piece that symbolizes the three graces. Arthur finds a tree that controls the enchantment of the grove and begins to hack away at it. Emmeline's voice is heard, but Arthur is not fooled. He breaks the spell. (In Restoration theatre, after the usual splendid fourth act, the spoken plots seemed insipid, so it was customary to lift the story with stagecraft. *King Arthur* was no exception.) In the final masque of act 5, following Emmeline's rescue and the restoration of her sight, Merlin foretells Britain's glory in scenes of health, wealth, and love making. All this is eclipsed by the final tableau, the patriotic "Order of St. *George and the Garter." In this, the god *Aeolus appears in a cloud machine to sing "Ye Blustering Brethren of the Skies," a graphic description of the winds and waves as they abate, after which there is a duet and chorus for *Pan, a *nereid, and their followers, "Round Thy Coast," a tribute to the land of plenty. The scene continues on an island bearing the figure of Britannia, seated. A male trio sings "For Folded Flocks," followed by a jolly but blasphemous folk song, "Your Hay is Mowed." *Venus sings, "Fairest Isle," a shepherd and his love sing "Love Has a Thousand Ways to Please," and Honour and the chorus sing "You Say, 'tis Love." (SOURCE: Price, 1984)

KIPLING, RUDYARD (1865–1936): English poet, novelist, and journalist. Born in Bombay, Kipling was the son of an author/illustrator. In 1871 he was brought to England, where he lived without his parents for five unhappy, bitter years. Later he worked as a journalist in India (1882–89), where many of his early poems and stories were published in newspapers. In 1889 he achieved instant literary celebrity when he returned to London where his poems (later collected as *Barrack Room Ballads*) had been published. Kipling married the sister of his American publisher (1892), with whom the couple lived for four years in Vermont. They then settled in Sussex, although Kipling spent much time in South Africa during the Boer War. Despite being regarded as an unofficial poet laureate, he refused many honors. In 1907 Kipling was the first English writer to receive the Nobel Prize. Kipling's output was vast and varied, and judged variously. Soldiers and ordinary readers made his writing popular, but accusations of jingoism and vulgarity were leveled by others. Even admirers such as Henry James, *Yeats, and T. S. *Eliot were made uneasy by the nature of his art. Perhaps his most uncontroversial achievements were his tales for children. The poetry of Rudyard Kipling was set by Oley Speaks, Frederick Ayres, Gordon Binkerd, Betty Roe, and Charles Ives. PRINCIPAL WORKS: *Barrack Room Ballads*, 1892; *Kim*, 1901. Juvenile: *The Jungle Book*, 1894; *Just So Stories*, 1902. SELECTED READING: *Something of Myself* (autobiography), 1937; Lord Birkenhead, *Rudyard Kipling*, 1978. (SOURCE: Drabble, 2000)

KLÄRCHEN: *see* *CLÄRCHEN.

KLEE, PAUL (1879–1940): Swiss artist, born in Berne but lived in Germany for many years. Klee was one of the most original artists of his time and very productive. His work comprised thousands of paintings, drawings, and prints, small masterpieces of poetic invention, wit, and fantasy that express his highly imaginative vision of the world and its inhabitants, its tiny symbols giving a strong feeling of lively movement. Klee, considered a forerunner of *Surrealism, was associated with many German expressionist artists, although his work was independent. He taught at the Bauhaus, Germany's famous school of design. (SOURCE: *Thames Hudson*, 1994)

SONG	COMPOSER	POET
1. "Paul Klee"	Francis Poulenc	Paul Éluard
2. "Homage to Paul Klee"	David Diamond	Babette Deutsch

KLINGSOR, TRISTAN (pseudonym of Leclère) (1874–1966): French poet, painter, musician, and art critic. Klingsor's work is distinguished by his love of legends and by his many experiments with meter and with traditional French popular verse forms. His mastery of those verse forms and rhythms, including *vers libre*, produced very personal, light, witty, and pliant poetry, whether the legends were those of the ★Symbolist movement or those of oriental literature. Klingsor's verse was of great influence upon the ★Fantaisistes in the period that preceded World War I. The verse of Tristan Klingsor was set by Maurice Ravel, Gabriel Pierné, Georges Hüe, and Gabriel Grovlez. PRINCIPAL WORKS: *Filles-Fleurs*, 1895; *Shéhérazade*, 1903. (SOURCE: France, 1995)

KLOPSTOCK, FRIEDRICH GOTTLIEB (1724–1803): German poet. Klopstock, son of a Lutheran pastor in Prussia, received a classical education at Schulpforta (1739–45), where he came under the influence of pietism, a movement in the Lutheran Church against Lutheran orthodoxy and scholasticism. It was a deeply felt, personal religion that emphasized personal piety, prayer, and study of the Bible. After studying theology at Jena and Leipzig, Klopstock lived in Copenhagen on a royal pension (1751–70), given partly to allow him time to finish *Der Messias,* The Messiah. He then moved to Hamburg where he remained until his death, March 14, 1803. "[He is] of towering importance in the history of Modern High German. . . . He freed the language from the countless restrictions of syntax dictated by the grammarians, rhetoricians, and philosophers" (Waterman, 1966). *Der Messias*, begun when Klopstock was a student and finished twenty-five years later, is an epic poem on the life of Christ, written in hexameter, six-foot lines. When a student, Klopstock first became acquainted with ★Milton's *Paradise Lost* and vowed to write a religious epic in German. The appearance of the early sections of *Der Messias* established Klopstock's reputation as a poet, but it was with his odes, wherein he drew upon a fervent personal religion, that his influence became greatest. The poetry of Friedrich Klopstock was set by Mahler (Symphony No. 2), Schubert, who set thirteen of Klopstock's poems, including "Dem Unendlichen," Ildebrando Pizzetti, Christoph Gluck, Johann Reichardt, Ernst Krenek, Carl Loewe, Richard Strauss, and Carl Zelter. PRINCIPAL WORKS: Poetry: *Der Messias*, 1770; *Oden*, 1771. Plays: *Bardiets* (trilogy), 1769–87. (SOURCES: Waterman, 1966; Demetz, Jackson, 1968; Swales, 1987)

KNABEN WUNDERHORN, DES: the first comprehensive anthology of German folk song. This anthology was collected and edited by poets Clemens Maria ★Brentano and Ludwig Joachim (Achim) von ★Arnim. The folk songs of this collection dated from the Middle Ages to the editors' own time, were gathered together from earlier books and imprints, and then published in three volumes, volume 1 in 1805, volumes 2 and 3 in 1808. The songs fell under six headings: 1. Sacred songs

(*Geistliche Lieder*); 2. Work songs (*Handwerkslieder*); 3. Historical romances (*Historische Romanzen*); 4. Love songs (*Liebeslieder*); 5. Drinking songs (*Trinklieder*); 6. War songs (*Kriegslieder*). Brentano and von Arnim edited the materials to match their own tastes, even writing additional verses to several songs. This personal touch was criticized as unscholarly. Yet the volumes made the folk songs available in one collection, and, as a consequence, better known by the public. Many later romantic poets studied and reworked poems from the anthology. The first poem of the first collection, "Das Wunderhorn," inspired the title of the anthology. This poem tells of a boy holding a beautiful horn and riding a horse. Decorated with four golden rings and precious gems, the horn was even larger than an elephant's tusk. The boy presented the horn to the empress as a tribute to her beauty and virtue. One touch of the empress's hand set the hundred golden bells of the horn to ringing, a sound more beautiful than that of a harp or singing women. Mahler set several songs from the collection, and Brahms set five songs, including "Marienwürmchen," "Wiegenlied," and "Liebesklage des Mädchens." (SOURCES: Garland, 1976; Atkins, 1969; Grabert, Mulot, 1971)

KNÖCHEL: lit., *knuckles, bones*, meaning *dice*. *See* ★EUGENE, PRINCE.

SONG	COMPOSER	POET
"Prinz Eugen, der edle Ritter"	Carl Loewe	Ferdinand Freiligrath

KOCH, KENNETH (1925–2002): American poet, playwright, novelist, opera librettist, and editor. Koch was born in Cincinnati, Ohio, where he began writing verse at the age of five, but he did not become serious about it until he read John Dos Passos at seventeen. At eighteen he went into the army and served for three years in the Pacific theater as a rifleman. When he returned, he took a B.A. at Harvard (1948), where he became friends with poet John ★Ashbery. More important were the three years he spent in France and Italy. There he discovered the humorous ★surrealistic verses of Jacques Prévert and found that he had an affinity with this French poet. Thereafter he tried to re-create in his own writing the excitement he felt when he read French poetry. After a time, he began to teach, at several colleges and at Columbia University, and his poetry became more realistic. Koch is perhaps best at shorter poems, but he has written longer ones, such as "Ko," a comic epic modeled on ★Byron's "Don Juan," and a sequence of twenty-four-line poems such as "When the Sun Tries to Go On," illustrated by Larry Rivers, the collaboration demonstrating Koch's close connection to modern painting. His poetic credo declares his independence from traditional poetry. He made a point of teaching poetry to children in the New York public schools as he had taught poetry to French children. This teaching to those considered to be uninterested in poetry has brought him as much renown as his own poetry. Critical neglect of his work is probably traceable to Koch's own strong belief that humorous literature is serious and to the defiantly anti-academic stance of his poetry. The poetry of Kenneth Koch has been set by Virgil Thomson, Paul Reif, and Ned Rorem. PRINCIPAL WORKS: *Ko, or A Season on Earth*, 1959; *Thank You and Other Poems*, 1962; *The Pleasures of Peace and Other Poems*, 1969; *The Art of Love*, 1975; *The Burning Mystery of Anna in 1951*, 1979. SELECTED

READING: Paul Zweig, "The New Surrealism," in *Contemporary Poetry in America: Essays and Interviews*, ed. Robert Boyers, 1974, pp. 315–24. (SOURCE: Greiner, 5, 1980)

KOLTSOV, ALEXEY (1809–1842): Russian poet. Born in south central Russia where his father was a cattle dealer, Alexey Koltsov's family was middle class and wealthy. Although he read a great deal (*The Arabian Nights,* ★Zhukovsky, ★Pushkin), his education was neglected because, at twelve, he was forced to leave school to help his father. During his business trips to Moscow and St. Petersburg, Koltsov met the greatest Russian writers in the literary circles he frequented. ★Krylov, ★Pushkin, and ★Zhukovsky were friendly and helped him to bring out a collection of his poems in 1835, after which Koltsov became known as a poet of the middle classes and "the poet-cattle dealer." Despite his habitual wide reading, Koltsov was uncultured on the whole, torn for his whole life between literary art and his family. His poems show a deep understanding of peasants and of nature, his language sometimes archaic, sometimes popular or sophisticated. Called by some "the Russian Burns," the themes of his lyrics, both literary and folkloristic, were sadness, frustrated love, the search for freedom, the desire for adventure, and the solace of nature—both passionate and realistic. The great Moscow literary critic Belinsky had this to say, "All this dirt has become through him the pure gold of poetry" (Kunitz, Colby, 1967). His poetry was translated into English, French, German, Czech, Bulgarian, and other languages, and set to music by Mussorgsky, Rimsky-Korsakov, Gretchaninoff, Glinka, Rachmaninoff, Mily Balakirev, and Aleksandr Dargomizhsky. English translations can be found in *A Book of Russian Verse,* ed. C. M. Bowra, 1943; *Russian Poets and Poems,* ed. N. Jarintzov, 1917; and *A Treasury of Russian Verse,* ed. A. Yarmolinsky, 1949. (SOURCE: Kunitz, Colby, 1967)

KOPISCH, AUGUST (1799–1853): German poet. Kopisch was born in Breslau and studied painting in Dresden until an accidental injury to his right hand handicapped him. In 1823 he settled in Italy, remaining there for five years. While swimming in Capri, Kopisch discovered the now celebrated Blue Grotto. Away from Italy, he translated ★Dante's *Divina Commedia* (1837). Humorous fairy tales, and elfin stories written by Kopisch include "Der Nöck," set by Carl Loewe. His verse was also set by Johannes Brahms. (SOURCE: Garland, 1976)

KORAN: *see* ★QU'RAN.

KÖRNER, THEODOR (1791–1813): Born in Dresden, Körner studied law in Leipzig, from which he was expelled for fighting a duel. He became a resident dramatist at the Burgtheater when he settled in Vienna in 1811. His friendship with ★Spaun, who encouraged the young composer to pursue music, effected an introduction to Schubert. Commissioned in the army in 1813, Körner died from wounds received at Gadebusch. It remained for his father to collect his poems and patriotic songs and publish them as *Leyer und Schwert.* From this volume, a best seller in 1814, Schubert set fourteen poems including "Auf der Riesenkoppe" and "Das war ich." Körner's verse was also set by Robert Franz. (SOURCE: Reed, 1997; Garland, 1976)

KORNET: an officer in a troop of cavalry who carries the colors. *See* ★EUGENE, PRINCE.

SONG	COMPOSER	POET
"Prinz Eugen, der edle Ritter"	Carl Loewe	Ferdinand Freiligrath

KOSEGARTEN, LUDWIG (1758–1818): a German poet. Born in North Germany, Kosegarten studied at Mecklenburg, where he eventually became professor of theology. Schubert composed twenty-one songs to texts by Kosegarten, (twenty in 1815 and one in 1817), among which were "Die Täuschung," "Die Mondnacht," "Die Sterne," "Schwanengesang," and "Luisens Antwort." The text in Schubert's songs differs in many instances from the published works. (SOURCE: Reed, 1997)

KOZLOV, IVAN (1789–1840): Russian poet and translator. Kozlov was the child of an aristocratic family. Brilliantly educated, he had read the literature of several languages and was acquainted with many literary figures. In the 1820s he was afflicted with blindness and without the use of his legs, but he overcame these difficulties splendidly. The public, knowing his misfortune, admired his fortitude. It soon became apparent, however, that, although he constructed verse well, most of his better poems were translations or imitations of the poets he had read: ★Petrarch, Thomas ★Moore, Tasso, ★Ariosto, ★Byron, Walter ★Scott, and others. When his own narrative and confessional poems were compared with his versions of the renowned poets, the lack in his poetic imagery was apparent. The poetry of Ivan Kozlov was set by Aleksandr Alyabiev, Michael Glinka, and Aleksandr Dargomizhsky. PRINCIPAL WORKS: *The Blackfriar*, 1824; *The Madwoman*, 1830; *My Prayer*, 1833; *Prayer*, 1839. (SOURCE: Terras, 1991)

KRAG, VILHELM (1871–1933): a Norwegian poet, novelist, and playwright. Miller states that Krag's writing was admired for its "fine landscape painting, . . . truth in depicting the life of simple fisher folk, . . . humor, and . . . human sympathy." Krag's poetry was set extensively by Edvard Grieg and also by Christian Sinding and Sigurd Lie. (SOURCE: Miller, 1973)

KRILOV: *see* ★KRYLOV.

KRISHNA: a popular Hindu deity (*the black one*) and an earthly, visible incarnation of the god Vishnu. He is decorated with jewels and peacock feathers and wears a trouser-like wrapping of yellow silk. A complex character who fulfilled various roles, Krishna is of importance in the great Indian epic *Mahābhārata*, where he is a warrior. His consort is Rādhā. Later he is the charioteer of his friend Arjuna, but even later a universal deity, Lord Vishnu. Vishnu takes human form as Krishna in order to defend the underlying moral order in the universe. One myth says that Vishnu plucked out two of his own hairs, one white and one black, which became Krishna. In another myth, Krishna is the son of Vasudeva and Devaki, born at Mathura between Delhi and Agra. His uncle was King Kamsa, who had been warned that one of his nephews would kill him, and that he must murder Devaki's child on birth. Therefore Krishna was taken away, hidden among cowherds who brought him up, from whence he lived to kill his uncle, fulfilling the prophecy. Krishna was the ★Apollo of India and the idol of women. He is generally depicted as standing with one foot bent in front of the other as if in a dance step, his flute raised to his lips. (SOURCES: Cooper, 1992; Cotterell, 1986)

SONG	COMPOSER	POET
1. "Songs in Praise of Krishna"	George Rochberg	Bengali poets
2. "Hāfiz, like Lord Krishna, Darting"	Alan Hovhaness	Alan Hovhaness

KRONOS: *see* ★CHRONOS.

KRYLOV, KRILOV, IVAN A. (1769–1844): Russian poet. Krylov was born to the family of an army captain but left fatherless at the age of nine, therefore home educated, while his mother worked as a servant in rich households. At an early age Krylov was working as a scribe for the Town Council. His passion for reading and his mother's fervent request allowed him to attend lessons with the children of the rich landowners for whom she worked. Krylov's constant desire for independence impelled him to move to St. Petersburg, where he became interested in the theater and literature, writing an operatic libretto that went unpublished in his lifetime. He turned to literature in 1788. First he worked as a journalist, founded two unsuccessful journals, which were banned as anti-government. His interest in the theater and journalism passed, and Krylov began to devote all his attention to fables. Some were derivative of ★Fontaine and the best ones were socially satirical, making him a prominent figure in St. Petersburg literary circles and resulting in his election to the Russian Academy. The verse of Ivan Krylov was set by Anton Rubenstein and Sergei Rachmaninoff. (SOURCE: Levitt, 1995)

KUBLA KHAN: the first khan (ruler) of the Mongol dynasty in thirteenth-century China.

KUGLER, FRANZ (1808–1858): German poet, dramatist, and art historian. Kugler was born in Stettin and studied literature and architecture before becoming a professor (1835) at the Berlin Akademie der Künste. Among his friends and colleagues in a literary club, Der Tunnel über der Spree, were the poets ★Eichendorff and ★Reinick. Together Kugler and Reinick wrote a *Liederbuch* (1833). An outstanding art historian, Kugler published several works on that subject, but he was best known for his popular biography of Frederick the Great. The verse of Franz Kugler was set by Johannes Brahms. WORKS: *Skizzenbuch*, 1830; *Legenden*, 1831; *Gedichte*, 1840. (SOURCE: Garland, 1976)

KULMANN, JELISAWETA (ELIZABETH) (1808–1825): Russian poet and translator. Born in St. Petersburg, Kulmann was the daughter of a bilingual (German and Russian) officer, and a child prodigy proficient in all the principal European languages. She translated ★Milton, ★Metastasio, Alfieri, and ★Camões into German, as well as translating ★Anacreon into several languages. Kulmann's own poetry was written in German and Russian. The verse of Elizabeth Kulmann was set by Robert Schumann. WORKS: *Sämtliche Dichtungen*, 1835. (SOURCE: Garland, 1976)

KUMPF, JOHANN (pseudonym Ermin) (1781–1862): a German poet, doctor, and journalist. Kumpf was born in Klagenfurt. Schubert set two of his poems, "Der Mondabend" (D141) and "Mein Gruss an den Mai" (D305). (SOURCE: Reed, 1997)

L ✑

LABÉ, LOUISE (1524–1566): French poet. Although her father was a wealthy but illiterate ropemaker, Labé was given an education typically lavished only upon court ladies of the Italian Renaissance. Labé knew Latin and Italian, was an accomplished lute player and singer, and a fine horsewoman. After her much older husband died, she carried on a love affair with the poet Olivier de Magny, who was not only unfaithful but tactless. Because of his indiscreet talk, Labé was often considered to be a kind of cultivated courtesan. Her admirers included many philosophers and poets, but the bourgeoisie of Lyons were scandalized by her behavior. By 1553 her fame was such that she had a street named for her, owing to her beauty, knowledge, and elegant conversation. In 1555 she published her *Oeuvres*, which contained a prose debate, three ★elegies, and twenty-four ★sonnets. This work brought her immediate recognition in France and translations into English. The main themes of her poetry are love and descriptions of her feelings about sensuality, desires, and regrets, genuine analyses of her sentiments. Information about her life after 1555 is hard to come by; she retired to a country estate near Lyons where she died. Rainer Maria ★Rilke translated her sonnets into German. The verses of Louise Labé have been set by Darius Milhaud and Lennox Berkeley. PRINCIPAL WORKS: *Love Sonnets with Translations*, trans. Frederick ★Prokosch, 1947. SELECTED READING: L. E. Harvey, *The Aesthetics of the Renaissance Love Sonnet*, 1959. (SOURCE: Kunitz, Colby, 1967)

LADY OF THE LAKE: a narrative poem by Sir Walter ★Scott, told in six cantos, first published in 1810 (not to be confused with the Arthurian legend in which the supernatural figure offered Arthur the sword Excalibur). The locale of the story is Loch Katrine in the western highlands of Perthshire at the close of the Middle Ages. The action spans six days, each day told in one canto. Canto 1, The Chase: A Scottish nobleman is riding in a stag hunt when his fatigued horse falls, forcing the rider to go on foot to Loch Katrine. A little skiff appears, containing a young woman, who is Ellen, daughter of James of Douglas, an outlaw and enemy of the king. Ellen cordially invites the man, James FitzJames, to rest in her island home before proceeding. The Schubert song "Raste, Krieger," describes this moment, followed by another Schubert song, "Jager, ruhe von der Jagt." Canto 2, The Island: FitzJames leaves the island the next morning. Ellen and her father are guests of Roderick, the Black, a hated member of the rebels. Ellen's beloved, Malcolm Graeme, appears. Roderick also hopes to marry Ellen, although she gives him no encouragement. Canto 3, The Gathering: Roderick sends a messenger to announce a gathering of the clans. The wedding of a young clansman, Normann, is interrupted by this announcement. His farewell song, sung to his betrothed, Mary, is "Die Nacht bricht bald herein." Ellen and her father leave the island to avoid Roderick, taking refuge in a cavern on the side of the mountain. Here Ellen prays to the ★Virgin Mary and asks for guidance. Franz Schubert set this prayer in his celebrated "Ave Maria." The poem is completed in three more cantos.

LA FONTAINE, JEAN DE (1621–1695): French poet and fable writer. Jean de La Fontaine was the son of the master of waters and forests in the region of Château Thierry. No vocation seemed to interest La Fontaine until he heard an ode by ★Malherbe. Then, fired with admiration, he studied Malherbe's work and tried to imitate it. Encouraged to read ★Horace, Virgil, Terence, ★Rabelais, and ★Marot, La Fontaine was pleased by the noble simplicity of these works. Jean's father, trying to provide his son with a livelihood, gave Jean his own mastership of waters and forests, but the young man was indifferent to his duties. La Fontaine moved to Paris (1656), where he found a long series of distinguished patrons, including noblewomen who were attracted by his lack of practicality. The court left him free for his creative work, and the French Academy elected him to membership (1684), but La Fontaine's placidity and laziness continued. Although he left works in several genres—novels, verses, *Contes* (65 licentious tales based on ★Boccaccio), and six plays—his fame rests on the *Fables*, of which two volumes were published in 1668. The sources for his renewal of this neglected category were Aesop, the medieval Phaedrus, and the Oriental Bidpai. With pessimistic attitudes toward human nature, fables, in which animals play human roles and reveal human foibles, were typical of this time. The writings of Jean de La Fontaine were set by Camille Saint-Saëns, Benjamin Godard, David Diamond, Virgil Thomson, and André Caplet. Several operas based on tales by Jean de La Fontaine were composed by David Diamond, André Caplet, Virgil Thomson, Camille Saint-Saëns, André Grétry and Pierre Monsigny. PRINCIPAL WORKS: *Fables choisies, mise en vers*, 1668; *Fables and Tales*, 1734, 1806. The *Fables* were retranslated during the last century by E. Wright, F. Tarver, E. Marsh, most recently by Marianne Moore, 1955. SELECTED READING: M. Guiton, *La Fontaine: Poet and Counterpoet*. (SOURCES: Kunitz, Colby, 1967; Magill, 3, 1997)

LAFORGUE, JULES (1860–1887): French poet and critic. Born in Uruguay, Laforgue moved to Paris at a young age. Laforgue's poetry exhibits a steady development from his early ★Baudelaire imitations to his death, which came before he reached complete artistic maturity. The virtuosity with which he presented his verse differs from its content. The free verse of *Les Derniers Vers* was an important technical innovation in French poetry. Laforgue's experiments helped to liberate and rejuvenate French prosody; they had the effect of establishing free verse as a legitimate and viable poetic mode in England and the United States as well as France. Laforgue's work challenged middle-class ideas about marriage and the Church but also the stability of the language itself by using puns, disruptive and unconventional rhymes, by controlled disturbance of metrical expectations, and by the invention of new forms, all of which influenced Jules ★Supervielle, James ★Joyce, T. S. ★Eliot, Ezra ★Pound, and Hart ★Crane. Laforgue's essay on ★Impressionism explains the painters brilliantly but is also essential for an appreciation of his poetry, which held a tantalizing amalgam of irony and sentiment. He was interested in anything new and different like the theory behind Impressionism, photography, contemporary sculpture, and the works of Monet, Sisley, and Pissarro; he had translated Walt ★Whitman and heard Wagner's music. The volumes on which his reputation rests are *Les Complaintes* and *Les Derniers Vers*. The poetry of Jules Laforgue was set by Arthur Honegger and Henri Sauguet, and inspired Arnold Schönberg and Darius Milhaud as well. PRINCIPAL WORKS: *Les Complaints*, 1885, trans. Michael Collie, 1877, ed. Pierre Reboul, 1981; *Les Derniers Vers de Jules Laforgue*, 1890, crit. ed. M. Collie and J. M. L'Heureux, 1965; as *The Last Poems*, ed. Madeleine Betts, 1973. SELECTED READING: W. Ramsey, *Jules Laforgue and the Ironic Inheritance*, 1953; Elizabeth Howe, *Stages of Self: The Dramatic Monologues of Laforgue, ★Valéry, and ★Mallarmé*, 1990. (SOURCES: Steinberg, 3, 1973; Magill, 3, 1997)

LAHOR, JEAN (pseudonym for Henri Cazalis) (1840–1909): French poet and medical doctor. Jean Lahor practiced medicine in Paris, wrote poetry, studied occult philosophy such as the Cabala (a Jewish mystical interpretation of the Scripture), and had a substantial interest in contemporary French painting. He was dubbed "hindou du Parnasse contemporain" because of his predilection for oriental subjects and philosophy. Because of his well-developed visual sense, Lahor was attracted to the imagery of the ★Parnassian poets, even though they were philosophically opposed to including ★transcendental elements in their work. Lahor's best poems were in the collection *L'Illusion*, 1875, but "even these fail to solve the problem of reconciling the elusiveness and inexpressiveness of mysticism with the love of painterly concreteness" (Beum, 2000). Lahor admired Stéphane ★Mallarmé and enjoyed his Tuesday evening seminars (1885–94), but Lahor's poetry lacked Mallarmé's ability to evoke musicality. The poetry of Jean Lahor has been set by Camille Saint-Saëns, Henri Duparc, Ernest Chausson, and Blair Fairchild. (SOURCE: Beum, 2000)

LAHOR, LAHORE: now the second largest city of Pakistan, the capital of a Punjab province also called Lahore, near the Ravi River, 640 miles northeast of Karachi (Pakistan's largest city) and 10 miles from the Indian border.

SONG	COMPOSER	POET
"Le Parfum impérissable"	Gabriel Fauré	Charles Leconte de L'Isle

LAI (Fr.), LAY (Eng.): a short, lyrical or narrative poem. The lai is addressed to an earthly lady or to the ★Virgin Mary.

LAIGH: (Scot.), *low*.

LAIR, LAIRED: (Scot.), v. *to bury, to cause to sink into the mire*; also, n. *a bed, a burial place, a sleeping place*.

SONG	COMPOSER	POET
"A Riddle"	Benjamin Britten	William Soutar

LAMARTINE, ALPHONSE DE (1790–1869): French poet, biographer, writer of political and historical works, novelist, and travel writer. Born of a family of minor nobility, brought up as a strict Catholic at the family country estate, Alphonse de Lamartine was tall and attractive to women. Until 1814 he led the life of an aristocrat, running up debts, reading the libertine poets, ★Rousseau, and the philosophers, while writing verses that imitated these. After his marriage to an Englishwoman, he lived in Naples where friends had obtained for him a position in the embassy. Lamartine tended to his diplomatic duties and wrote lyrics occasionally while devoting himself to developing his metaphysical epic, guided by the works of Thomas ★Moore and ★Byron. With the death of his daughter, Lamartine became disappointed in the limitations of the Catholic religion. His contact with Islam had persuaded him that it was closer to true religion than his own. The Church's response put a curb on the popularity of his poetry, and Lamartine entered a period of financial difficulty and political activity. Most of his works of this period were below his former standard, twenty-eight volumes that could only be described as hackwork. His beloved estate had to be sold, but he solicited a pension from Napoleon III. His poetry is heavily autobiographical, a mix of politics, religion, and the love of women and nature. Lamartine is regarded as a link between pre-romanticism and the full flowering of ★Romanticism. The verses of Lamartine were set by Georges Bizet, Erik Satie, Benjamin Godard, and Charles Gounod. PRINCIPAL WORKS: *Méditations poétiques*, 1820, as *The Poetical Meditations*, trans. Rev. Henry Christmas, 1839, and J. T. Smith, 1852; *Nouvelle méditations poétiques*, 1823; *Harmonies poétiques et réligieuses*, 1830; *Recueillements poétiques*, 1839; *Jocelyn, A Romance in Verse*, trans. H. P. Stuart, 1854; *Graziella*, trans. S. C. Barney, 1872 and J. B. Runnion, 1876. SELECTED READING: H. R. Whitehouse, *Life of Lamartine*, 1918. (SOURCES: Kunitz, Colby, 1967; Magill, 3, 1997)

LAMENT: a non-narrative type of poetry, arising as part of oral tradition, expressing profound regret, sorrow, or concern for the loss of a person, or sometimes the loss of a position. The lament, having risen alongside heroic poetry, exists in all languages, including Hebrew, Chinese, and Zulu.

LANDOR, WALTER SAVAGE (1775–1864): English poet, playwright, and essayist. Landor was born in Warwick and studied at Trinity College, Oxford. His inheritance of considerable wealth upon his father's death in 1805 made it easier for him to pursue the writing career that he had commenced in 1793. In 1808 Landor led a private regiment against Napoleon in Spain. He lived in France during 1814, then in Italy from 1815 to 1835. Returning only once to England, he resided again in Italy until his death. Although Landor was admired by Robert ★Browning, although Ezra ★Pound was convinced that the decline of England began the day when Landor departed for Tuscany, although ★Yeats himself admired Landor to the extent of including him in one of his poems, still Landor was actually little read. His writing life was completely different from his public behavior; for example, he sought a writing style that would embody classical ideas of lucidity and balance, but during his school years he committed many obstreperous acts. He best achieved his goal in prose, not poetry, writing several "Imaginary Conversations." In them he brought together related or contrasting historical characters and used their juxtaposition to express significant ideas about life and conduct with his unique combination of scholarship, irascibility, and humanity. The poetry of Walter Landor has been set by Ned Rorem, Charles Ives, and Leslie Bassett. PRINCIPAL WORKS: *Poems*, a selection, ed. Geoffrey Grigson, 1964; *Imaginary Conversations of Literary Men and Statesmen*, 5 vols., 1824–29, ed. R. H. Boothroyd, 1936; *Imaginary Conversations of Greeks and Romans*, 1853. SELECTED READING: Robert Pinsky, *Landor's Poetry*, 1968. (SOURCE: Vinson, 1979)

LANDSMÅL: a rugged and sonorous Norwegian language based on regional dialects, first systematized in 1848 by Ivar Aasen, who called it the rural language, as distinct from the Dano-Norwegian ★riksmål of the urban educated classes.

LANIER, SIDNEY (1842–1881): American poet and musician. Sidney Lanier was born in Macon, Georgia, to a lawyer father who sent him to Oglethorpe University for his education. Lanier volunteered during the Civil War, and his health was poor ever after he was put in a Union prison upon being captured. His lifelong struggle with tuberculosis never abated and caused his death before the age of forty. Until seven or eight years before his death, Lanier had followed a multitude of interests: studying science, playing the flute, composing, teaching, the law, and writing boys' books and poetry. Even when he decided to make art his career, music was his primary interest. He was a masterful flutist and enjoyed a position with the Peabody Orchestra in Baltimore as well as the admiration of professional musicians. Lanier believed that the function of a poet is to suggest the beauty and truth that lie beyond the physical world: "[A]ll that poetry and science have to say can best be said in music. And since poetry and science both attempt to reveal the existence and benevolence of God, music should always be regarded as an act of worship" (Unger, 1, 1974). Reading ★Emerson, ★Whitman, Darwin, ★Spenser, and ★Huxley during his last years of life turned his career in a different direction. A series of lectures on poetry at Johns Hopkins University resulted in his writing *The Science of English Verse*, which expressed his conviction that when poetry is repeated aloud, "The ear accepts as perfect verse a series of words from which ideas are wholly absent, that is to say, a series of sounds" (Unger, 1, 1974). Lanier's interest in the sounds of poetry together with his knowledge of music allowed him to point out the similarities between the two arts as well as any American critic ever has. Sidney Lanier's poetry has been set by American composers Charles Griffes and Dudley Buck, among others. PRINCIPAL WORKS: Poetry: *Centennial Edition of the Works of Sidney Lanier*, ed. Charles R. Anderson, 10 vols., 1945. Novels: *Tiger-Lilies*, ed. Garland Griever, 1867. SELECTED READING: Aubrey Harrison Starke, *Sidney Lanier: A Biographical and Critical Study*, 1933; Jack de Bellis, *Sidney Lanier*, 1972. (SOURCES: Vinson, 1979; Unger, 1, 1974)

LAPPE, KARL (1773–1843): Pomeranian schoolmaster and poet. Although Karl Lappe's works were not collected and published during Schubert's lifetime, Schubert set two of Lappe's texts, "Im Abendrot" and "Der Einsame." WORKS: *Gedichte*, 1801; *Blüten des Alters*, 1841. (SOURCE: Reed, 1997)

LAPRADE, VICTOR-RICHARD DE (1812–1887): French poet and critic. Laprade was born on the Loire River west of the city of Lyons, where he became a professor of French literature (1847–61). Laprade was a fine human being, a Catholic poet with a strong understanding of the power of external nature. He combined a romantic sensibility with powerful classical influences to produce a major poem, *Psyché* (1841), and a large quantity of other, rather mediocre poetry. After 1848 Laprade's conservatism increased. He formed a conclusion that the crisis of the present sprang from three causes, which he labeled as: the egalitarianism of the revolution, industrialism, and the rehabilitation of flesh proclaimed by the Utopian scientists. The lyrics of Victor de Laprade were set by Éduard Lalo. PRINCIPAL WORKS: *Odes et Poèmes*, 1844; *Les Symphonies*, 1855. (SOURCE: France, 1995)

LARKY: (Scot.) (pr. larkee), *sportive, frolicsome*.

SONG	COMPOSER	POET
"The Larky Lad"	Benjamin Britten	William Soutar

LAUCHIN: (Scot.) (pr. as in Ger. "lachen"), *laughing*.

SONG	COMPOSER	POET
"A Laddie's Sang"	Benjamin Britten	William Soutar

LAUDA: an intimate prayer addressed to the Madonna. Many Italian song composers wrote laude to the ★Virgin Mary. They were addressed to Maria, Mater Dolorosa (★Mary, mother of sorrows) rather than to Maria, Regina Coeli (Mary, queen of heaven). The laude celebrate the intimate connection between Mary, the mother of God, and all mothers. An example of a lauda text is this: "Madonna, I knew you when my mother joined my hands in prayer for the first time. . . . Sweet Mary, one day may I see in you the face of my mother again." (SOURCE: Lakeway, White, 1989)

SONG	COMPOSER	POET
1. "Preghiera alla Madonna"	Franco Alfano	Luigi Orsini
2. "Inna à Maria Nostra Donna"	Gian Francesco Malipiero	Angelo Poliziano

LAURA: the beloved of ★Petrarch.

SONG	COMPOSER	POET
1. "Benedetto sia'l giorno"	Franz Liszt	Petrarch
2. "O, quand je dors"	Franz Liszt	Petrarch

LAVAPIÉS: a district in the East End of Madrid.

SONG	COMPOSER	POET
"El majo discreto"	Enrique Granados	Fernando Periquet

LAVEROCK: (Scot.) (pr. leverik), *a skylark*.

SONG	COMPOSER	POET
"A Laddie's Sang"	Benjamin Britten	William Soutar

LAWRENCE, D. H. (1885–1930): English novelist, poet, essayist, and playwright. Lawrence was the son of a coal miner father and a schoolteacher mother. A frail and studious child, he grew up in the midst of poverty, brutality, and drink. Lawrence was writing verse even as he was obtaining his teaching certificate at twenty. Ford Madox ★Ford introduced him to a publisher, and Lawrence decided to live by literature. Although the love of his life, Frieda, was the wife of a professor whom Lawrence knew, he and Frieda lived together abroad. During that time, he published his first book of poems and the novel *Sons and Lovers*. His troubles during World War I included his own ill health and the fact that Frieda, now his wife, was the cousin of Baron von Richtofen, the brilliant German airman. Upon returning to reside near the coast of England, they were asked to leave because they sang German songs and left lights openly burning at night. His novel *The Rainbow* (1915) was condemned as obscene and destroyed. *Women in Love*, at first rejected by publishers, was finally put out to private subscribers in New York. After living in Australia, Lawrence and Frieda lived in Taos, New Mexico (1923–28), then returned to Italy, where he wrote *Lady Chatterley's Lover*, which contained the utmost physical detail, causing it to be prohibited in England and the United States, but distributed by means of pirated editions. All of Lawrence's literary power was devoted to pursuing a fuller, freer, more intense life than that permitted by the social system of his day, but personally, he was actually a puritan, living frugally, not smoking, and drinking very little. The poetry of D. H. Lawrence was set by Vittorio Rieti and Arnold Cooke. PRINCIPAL WORKS: Novels: *Sons and Lovers*, 1913; *Women in Love*, 1920. Poetry: *Love Poems and Others*, 1913; *Amores*, 1916; *New Poems*, 1918; *Birds, Beasts, and Flowers*, 1923; *Collected Poems*, 1928; *Pansies*, 1929; *Nettles*, 1930; *Last Poems*, 1933. SELECTED READING: F. Carter, *Lawrence and the Body Mystical*. (SOURCE: Kunitz, Haycraft, 1942)

LAZARUS: biblical character from the New Testament, in which Lazarus is mentioned twice. In the Gospel According to Luke, ★Jesus tells the parable of the Rich Man and Lazarus the Beggar (Luke 16.19–31). Tradition calls the rich man Dives, although Jesus never names him. Outside a rich man's house waited Lazarus, a poor beggar whose body was covered with sores, waiting for crumbs from the rich man's table. Lazarus was rewarded for his misfortunes in life by being taken to Heaven by ★Abraham after his death. The second reference found in the Gospel according to John (John 11.1–44) calls Lazarus the friend of Jesus, brother of ★Mary and Martha. When Lazarus became ill, his sisters sent for Jesus to come and heal him. When, after waiting for two days, Jesus arrived in Bethany, he discovered that Lazarus was dead and had been buried for four days. As Jesus called Lazarus to come out of the tomb, his friend emerged from the grave still wrapped in burial clothes. Lazarus is alluded to in literature in the context of a literal or metaphorical resurrection. (SOURCE: Farmer, 1997)

SONG	COMPOSER	POET
"Rimas de Bécquer"	Isaac Albéniz	Gustavo Adolfo Bécquer

LEA: (also lay, lae, leye); a tract of open ground, meadow, pasture, or arable land; chiefly found in poetical or rhetorical use (as in "Linden Lea"), a term ordinarily applied to grassland.

LEA: a character from Thomas ★Moore's *Loves of the Angels*. Lea is "one of the daughters of men beloved by one of the songs of God." An angel saw Lea bathing and fell in love with her, but she wanted only to dwell in purity. He became mad with passion; she floated to heaven and vanished. The angel lost his ethereal nature and became earthly. This theme is a forerunner of "reverse" character stories such as *Miss Thompson* by Somerset Maughan (1921), *Thaïs* by Anatole France, and *Summer and Smoke* by Tennessee ★Williams.

LEAR, EDWARD (1812–1888): English writer, artist, and traveller. Lear was the twentieth child of a stockbroker, brought up by his sister. While working as a zoological draftsman, his work was noticed by the earl of Derby. Lear wrote *A Book of Nonsense* (1845), containing limericks and illustrations, for the earl's children. Traveling widely, he published his impressions and sketches of Italy, Albania, Calabria, Corsica, Egypt, the Holy Land, Greece, and India. In 1871 he settled in San Remo and died there, a lonely man. As an artist he is known for his watercolors; as a writer he is remembered for the linguistic inventiveness of his nonsense verses. Lear's verses have been set by John Koch, Margaret Ruthven Lang, Igor Stravinsky, and Robert Fairfax Birch. PRINCIPAL WORKS: *A Book of Nonsense*, 1845; *Nonsense Songs, Stories, Botany and Alphabets*, 1871; *Laughable Lyrics*, 1877. SELECTED READING: Vivien Nokes, *Edward Lear*, 1968. (SOURCE: Drabble, 2000)

LECONTE DE L'ISLE, CHARLES MARIE RENÉ (1818–1894): French poet. Leconte de L'Isle was born on an island in the Indian Ocean. His father was an army doctor who had immigrated to the island of Réunion after the defeat of Napoleon. Leconte de L'Isle was strongly influenced by his artistic mother who was related to the eighteenth-century poet, Évariste Parny. Although little was known about his life on the island until 1837, he is said to have been interested in Sir Walter ★Scott's work, writing elegies and romances at an early age. Returning to Brittany to finish his education, he neglected his studies at Rennes University, preferring to edit more than one unsuccessful literary periodical. After playing a minor role in the June Revolution (1848), he became disillusioned and withdrew from active political participation. Leconte de L'Isle's reputation was upheld by *Poésies complètes* (1858), and this publication established him as the leader of a new school of poetry called ★Parnassian, in which his friends Catulle ★Mendès and Théodore de ★Banville also believed. Leconte de L'Isle put his trust not in the solace of religion but in the beauty of the arrangement of word, sound, and image in poetry. Scorning the multitudes, he embarked upon a twenty-year effort to translate the Greek and Roman poets such as Homer, ★Hesiod, and ★Horace. In 1886 Leconte de L'Isle was elected to replace Victor ★Hugo in the French Académie. His lifetime output of 23,000 verses reveals sensitivity under a cold exterior. The poetry of Leconte de L'Isle was set by Fauré, Chausson, and Duparc. PRINCIPAL WORKS: *Poèmes antiques*, 1852; *Poèmes barbares*,

1862; *Poèmes tragiques*, 1884; *Derniers poèmes*, 1995. SELECTED READING: I. H. Brown, *Leconte de L'Isle: A Study on the Man and His Poetry*; I. Putter, *Leconte de L'Isle and His Contemporaries*. (SOURCES: Kunitz, Colby, 1967; France, 1995)

LEE, NATHANIEL (1653?–1692): English playwright and poet. Born in London, Lee was educated at Trinity College, Cambridge (1668). When he returned to London, he attempted to become an actor but failed because of severe stage fright. He went so far down hill as an alcoholic that in 1684 he was committed to ★Bedlam. Even there he was known for his witty conversation. The Royal Theatre gave him a pension, but he died of alcoholism before the age of forty, his writing merely a source of income for him. Lee's plays were mostly drawn from historical sources, The ★*Rival Queens* and ★*Theodosius* being his most successful plays. Even these plays included constant hysterical ranting and absurd confusion, but Lee must have had some element of literary talent to attract ★Dryden as a collaborator. Dryden wrote prologues and epilogues for Lee's plays and spoke affectionately of him. Having written whatever was fashionable, Lee today is close to unreadable. The lyrics written by Lee for songs that appeared in his plays were often set by Henry Purcell. PRINCIPAL WORKS: *The Rival Queens; or, The Death of Alexander the Great*, 1677; ★*Oedipus* (with Dryden), 1679; *Theodosius; or, The Force of Love*, 1680. SELECTED READING: G. Langbaine, *Account of the English Dramatic Poets.* (SOURCE: Kunitz, Haycraft, 1952)

LEEZ ME ON: (Scot.), *blessings on*.

LE GALLIENNE, RICHARD (1866–1947): English journalist, poet, and novelist. Le Gallienne's early verse and epigrammatic prose show the influence of Oscar Wilde. After settling in the United States (1903), he modified his early affected style to some extent, while still remaining essentially British. He returned to Europe in 1927 to spend his last years in the south of France. The verse of Richard Le Gallienne was set by Wintter Watts and Seymour Barab. (SOURCE: Jason, 4, 2003)

LEIER: a hurdy-gurdy, a Medieval stringed instrument shaped like a lute or viol in which the strings are put in vibration not by a bow, but by a wheel that is operated by a handle at the lower end of the instrument's body, which is turned by the player's right hand. The rosin on the wheel creates the typical whining and abrasive sound. (SOURCE: *Harvard Dictionary of Music*)

SONG	COMPOSER	POET
"Der Leiermann"	Franz Schubert	Wilhelm Müller

LEILAH: a beautiful young slave girl, the concubine of Hassan, Caliph of the Ottoman empire. Leilah falls in love with the Giaour, flees from the seraglio, is overtaken by an emir, and cast into the sea in *The Giaour* by ★Byron.

SONG	COMPOSER	POET
"Les Roses d'Ispahan"	Gabriel Fauré	Charles Leconte de L'Isle

LEITNER, KARL VON (1800–1890): an Austrian poet and teacher from Graz. Leitner was an avid admirer of Styrian culture, the section of Austria whose principal city is Graz. Schubert set eleven of Leitner's rather sentimental verses, including "Die Sterne," "Der Kreuzzug," and "Der Winterabend." (SOURCE: Reed, 1997)

LEMCKE, KARL VON (1831–1913): German poet, novelist, and lecturer. Lemcke used a pseudonym for his published novels and his books on aesthetics and poetry. He lectured at Heidelberg, Munich, Amsterdam, and Stuttgart. Johannes Brahms set his "In Waldeinsamkeit."

LENAU, NICHOLAUS (pseudonym for N. Niembsch von Strehlenau) (1802–1850): a Hungarian-German poet. Lenau was born of the German-Austrian nobility in Hungary and deeply attached to music and to the Hungarian landscape. His father, a gambler, a spendthrift, and a consumptive, passed on his instability to his son, who frittered away an impoverished youth in Vienna and Heidelberg. Lenau, moving without rest between Hungary and Germany, changed his studies very often, the law, philosophy, agriculture, and medicine, finishing none. As a handsome nobleman, he was welcomed to Stuttgart by the circle of Swabian poets who published his poems in 1832. In the same year, he bought a 400-acre farm in the American state of Ohio, but was disillusioned with man and nature in one year. By 1844 he was incurably insane, his poetry reflecting his despair and morbid longings. Convinced that in every joy was a threat, Lenau sought inner harmony in a world that was out of joint. The longer epic poems that he preferred were not as successful as his lyric poetry, which reflects his melancholy attitude to life, the same despair that ★Byron made fashionable. Lenau is a poet of despair with a feeling for nature that is deep but subjective. Lenau's poetry has been set by Schumann, Liszt, Mendelssohn, Robert Franz, Alban Berg, Fanny Mendelssohn Hensel, Anton Rubenstein, Ottmar Schoeck, Charles Griffes, and Miriam Gideon. PRINCIPAL WORKS: *Faust*, 1836; *Neuere Gedichte*, 1838; *Gedichte*, 1844; *Die Albigenser*, 1842. No complete volume of Lenau's poetry exists in English translation, but in small collections in these anthologies: H. D. Wireman, *Gems of German Lyrics,* 1869; K. Francke, *The German Classics* vol. 7, 1913. SELECTED READING: T. S. Baker, *Lenau and Young Germany in America*, 1897; C. von Klenze, *The Treatment of Nature in the Works of Lenau*, 1902. (SOURCES: Flores, 1965; Mathieu, Stern, 1987; Kaufman, 1962; Kunitz, Colby, 1967)

LENT: from *lencten* (spring), a penitential season preceding Easter that begins on Ash Wednesday and ends with Easter. Lent contains forty days for fasting in remembrance of the forty-day fasting of ★Jesus Christ. (SOURCE: Nevins, 1964)

SONG	COMPOSER	POET
"1904"	Francis Poulenc	Guillaume Apollinaire

LEOPARDI, GIACOMO (1798–1837): Italian poet. Leopardi was born in Recanati and, upon the death of his father, inherited the title of count. He was educated at home by tutors until 1822, then lived in Rome, Bologna, Florence, Pisa, and in Naples from 1833 on. Leopardi, seeking a union between poetry and critical philosophical thought, lived up to ★Coleridge's statement that a great poet is also a profound philosopher. He was not as romantic as contemporary English ★Romantic poets, nor was he as classical as his contemporaries ★Goethe and ★Hölderlin. Although plagued with ill health and increasing blindness all his life, he rose above

these difficulties, transforming his pain into poetic and philosophical contempla-
tions. *I Canti* reveal his poetic genius and anticipate poetry of the twentieth century,
although his themes are the conventional ones of love, death, youth, nature, and the
transitory quality of life. Admired by ★Pound, a modern poet, and also by Bertrand
Russell, a modern philosopher, Leopardi's poetry was set by Goffredo Petrassi, Mario
Castelnuovo-Tedesco, and Ildebrando Pizzetti. PRINCIPAL WORKS: *The Poems*,
trans. Francis H. Cliffe, 1893; *Poems,* trans. John Heath-Stubbs, 1946, J.P. Barricelli,
1963. SELECTED READING: Giovanni Carsaniga, *Leopardi: The Unheeded Voice*,
1977. (SOURCE: Vinson, Kirkpatrick (1), 1984)

LERBERGHE, CHARLES VAN: *see* ★CHANSON D'ÈVE.

LERMONTOV, MIKHAIL (1814–1841): Russian poet and novelist. Born in Moscow, Mikhail Lermontov was the direct descendent of a Scottish soldier of fortune.
His father was a retired army captain. After the death of his mother, Lermontov
was raised by a wealthy grandmother, who fought constant custody battles with
Lermontov's father. She spared no expense, providing foreign tutors for the boy,
even moving to Moscow (1827) so that he could attend a preparatory school for
the University of Moscow. Lermontov duly entered the department of literature at
the university (1830), where he learned English and came under ★Byron's considerable personal influence. ★Pushkin, too, had lasting effects on Lermontov's writing.
Because of his openly contemptuous attitude toward the faculty, Lermontov was
asked to leave the university, after which he entered the School of the Guard in Saint
Petersburg. The dramas and the historical novel that he wrote here were permeated
with loneliness, disillusionment with life, and spiritual agitation. As he grew older,
he lost his enthusiasm for Byron and wrote more realistically. Lermontov wrote
an elegy for Pushkin that mourned his death and savagely criticized his slayer and
the authorities. They then arrested Lermontov and sent him to prison. Despite his
acceptance by society, he insisted upon writing pessimistically of Russian society.
His many brave actions under fire in the Caucasus did not elicit any decorations, on
orders of the czar. He was angered by Lermontov's epigrammatic wit and cutting
satires that created enemies, among them one who challenged the poet to a duel and
killed him. Lermontov is considered to be second only to Pushkin. His fame rests
on a small body of lyric and narrative works written during the last five years of his
life. These works were marked by technical perfection and unusual emotional depth,
great scorn for the cringing of society before autocracy, richly poetic language, and
innovative rhymes and meters. The poetry of Mikhail Lermontov was set by Alexsandr Alyabiev, Alexsandr Dargomizhsky, Nicolai Rimsky-Korsakov, Mily Balakirev,
Sergei Rachmaninoff, Alexsandr Gretchaninoff, Aram Khachaturian, Antony Arensky, Boris Asafiev, and Manuel Ponce. English translations of Lermontov include *A
Hero of Our time*, trans. I. Nestor-Schurmann, 1899, V. and D. Nabokov, 1958, and
others; *The Demon*, trans. F. Storr, 1894, G. Shelley, 1930. SELECTED READING:
J. Lavrin, *Lermontov*, 1959. (SOURCE: Kunitz, Colby, 1967)

LE ROY, GRÉGOIRE (1862–1941): Belgian poet. Le Roy and Maurice ★Maeter-
linck were schoolmates; both abandoned the law for literature. Further similarities

were the gentle melancholy and delicate lyricism that characterized the writings of both and elicited the admiration of Claude Debussy, who set the verses of Grégoire Le Roy as well as those of Maeterlinck. SELECTED READING:V. Mallinson, *Modern Belgian Literature, 1830–1960*, 1966.

LESBIA: the Roman poet ★Catullus (87?–54 B.C.E.) sang the praises of his beloved Lesbia in a poem imitated and partly translated by Thomas ★Campion in his "My Sweetest Lesbia." (SOURCE: *Norton*, 1996)

LESLEY: daughter of the poet Robert ★Frost, born in 1899, probably at the time of the writing of Frost's poem "The Last Word of a Blue Bird."

SONG	COMPOSER	POET
"The Last Word of a Blue Bird"	John Duke	Robert Frost

LESSING, GOTTHOLD (1729–1781): German dramatist and critic. Enrolled at the University of Leipzig studying theology (1746), Lessing was soon introduced to the worlds of journalism and the theater. This prompted him to transfer to philosophy and literature, after which he supported himself as a journalist, publishing his first collection of verses, *Kleinigkeiten*, in 1751. In the preface of a theater journal that Lessing founded, he articulated his conviction that the future of German drama lay in an imitation of English, not French theater writing. His play, *Miss Sarah Sampson*, which used prose, not ★alexandrine verse, marked the beginning of modern drama in Germany. Macaulay named Lessing beyond all dispute the first critic in Europe. Lessing defended the rights of free criticism and open inquiry, emancipating German literature from the narrow conventions of the French classical school, suggesting that German writers look to ★Shakespeare and English literature for better models. Lessing's work was set by Haydn and Beethoven. PRINCIPAL WORKS: *Minna von Barnhelm*, 1767; *Emilia Galotti*, 1772; *Nathan der Weise*, 1779; *Miss Sarah Sampson*, 1775. SELECTED READING: H. B. Garland, *Lessing: The Founder of Modern German Literature*, rev. ed., 1962. (SOURCE: Kunitz, Colby, 1967)

LETHE: in Greek mythology, one of the rivers of ★Hades, running partly underground, which the souls of the dead are obliged to taste so that they may forget everything said and done when they were alive. The word means *forgetfulness*. (SOURCE: Cooper, 1992)

"Let Me Weep, O": a song composed by Henry Purcell to a text written by Elkanah ★Settle for his work *The Fairie-Queene*, produced in 1692 and 1693. For plot details and placement of songs, *see* ★*Fairie-Queene, The.*

"Let Not a Moonborn Elf Mislead Ye": a song written by Henry Purcell, with words by John ★Dryden, for their semi-opera *King Arthur*, produced in 1691. *See* ★*King Arthur* for plot details and placement of songs.

"Let the Dreadful Engines": a song composed by Henry Purcell to a text written by Thomas ★D'Urfey for Part I of his comic semi-opera *Don Quixote*, produced in 1694–95. *See* ★*Don Quixote* for plot details and placement of songs.

"Let the Soldiers Rejoice": a song from the 1690 semi-opera *Dioclesian* with music solely by Henry Purcell, set to the words of Massinger and ★Fletcher. *See* ★*Dioclesian* for plot details and placement of songs.

LIBERO, LIBERO DE (1906–1981): Italian poet, critic, translator, and novelist. Born in Ciocaría, an area between Rome and Naples, Libero de Libero was a member of a large, impecunious family that prized books over food. After pursuing classical studies, Libero moved to Rome ostensibly to study law, but really to introduce himself to the artistic life of the big city. He was active as an art critic and, from 1941 on, taught art history in Rome. His poetry is of the ★hermetic school and was influenced by the French ★Symbolists. Libero seemed to find inspiration in his native land, which he depicted with deep emotion. Moved by the events of World War II, he wrote poems describing both German and Italian deaths. "Lamento d'Arianna" is the penultimate poem in *Proverbi* and dedicated to Goffredo Petrassi, who set the poem to music. WORKS: *Proverbi: 1930–34*, 1937; *Epigrammi*, 1942; *Ascolta la Ciocaría*, 1953; *Scempio e lusinga: 1930–1955*, 1976. (SOURCES: Wedel et al., 1992; Golino, 1977)

LIBERTINE, THE: a play by Thomas ★Shadwell, the first version of which was produced in 1675 and a revival produced in 1692. The music was originally written by William Turner; the date of the revival for which Henry Purcell wrote music is not known. Price considers Shadwell's play to be "a complete perversion of Molière's libertine and even of its source: *Le Festin de pierre* by Dorimon." Shadwell reveals a Don Giovanni who is a rapist of nuns and a murderer, the governor of Seville among his victims, in the goriest version of the many versions of this story. In the first two acts Don Giovanni kills the brother of a woman he is trying to seduce; he makes crude jokes while his fourth wife commits suicide; he encourages his companions to burn a nunnery and massacre a band of shepherds. In act 4, a ★pastoral ★masque (a play within a play) takes place, in which we hear Purcell's "★Nymphs and Shepherds" sung by a soprano at a merry festivity that honors ★Flora, the goddess of flowers. Flora is also the name of a servant whom Don Giovanni kills in act 2. "Nymphs and Shepherds" is generally regarded as a piece of hackneyed innocence, but Purcell intends it to be a genuine moment that is all too short. The celebration is soon brought to an end by the arrival of a band of ruffians who ravish the shepherdesses, and in the next act the shepherds are massacred. (SOURCE: Price, 1984)

LIDO: a stretch of grand hotels, entertainment emporia, and beautiful beaches on a thin peninsula of land in Venice, accessible only by boat.

SONG	COMPOSER	POET
"Barcarolle"	Gabriel Fauré	Marc Monnier

LIEDER EINER FAHRENDEN GESELLEN: *see* ★FAHRENDEN GESELLEN.

LIEDERKREIS: the title of Robert Schumann's op. 24, a song cycle, and also of his op. 39, not strictly a cycle, but possessing a unifying theme. The nine poems in op. 24 are taken from Heinrich ★Heine's *Buch der Lieder*. This set was dedicated to the daughter of the elder Garcia, soprano Pauline Viardot, who was then at the height of her career. The songs of op. 39, written within a month's time, are closely allied with nature. All twelve songs are set to poems of ★Eichendorff, including several texts from his ★*Ahnung und Gegenwart*.

LIÈGE: in the Poulenc song, the word Liège means *cork*, thus the boy of cork, *light as the wind*.

SONG	COMPOSER	POET
"Le Garçon de Liège"	Francis Poulenc	Louise de Vilmorin

LILIENCRON, DETLOV VON (1844–1909): German poet, novelist, short story writer. Born in Kiel and descended from an impoverished baronial family, Liliencron became an officer in the Prussian army, fighting in the wars against both the Austrians and the French. In 1875 Liliencron resigned his commission "because of wounds and debts," as he said. After two years of trying to make a fresh start in the United States as a painter, horse trader, piano teacher, and beer hall pianist, he returned disillusioned and took a government position briefly before becoming a church warden. Again accumulating debts, Liliencron moved to Munich where he tried unsuccessfully to make a living from his writing. At the age of sixty he was finally given a small government stipend, but had to supplement his income by giving public readings in cabarets. The unhappiness caused by the constant strain of financial needs made him pessimistic and was reflected in his poetry. Yet he was a virile person whose life was centered on war, the hunt, nature, and love. Although he belonged to no literary group and was without training, Liliencron was one of the forerunners of the modern period. He wrote with a mastery of technique and was tireless in polishing his work. A theme that appeared frequently in his collected poems, which ran to four volumes, was the contrast between the permanence of nature and the transient nature of human existence. The lyrics of Detlev von Liliencron were set by Brahms, Hans Pfitzner, Anton Webern, Max Reger, and Richard Strauss. PRINCIPAL WORKS: *Adjuntantengeritte und andere Gedichte*, 1883; *Poggfredo*, 1896–1908; selections in *Contemporary German Poetry*, trans. Jethro Bithell, 1909. SELECTED READING: O. E. Lessing, *Masters in Modern German Literature*, 1912. (SOURCE: Kunitz, Colby, 1967)

LILITH: a demon in the Talmudic tradition, said to haunt wildernesses and to be dangerous to children and pregnant women. As Jewish legend has it, Lilith was the first wife of ★Adam, created from the same dust as he. Lilith refused to be subject to Adam's will, claiming that their common origin made them equal. In an escape attempt, she fled from the Garden of Eden. Three angels sent by God found Lilith in the Red Sea, but they were unsuccessful in their attempt to compel her to return to Adam in Eden. The angels threatened that one hundred of her demon children would die daily. In retaliation to the threat, Lilith preyed on human children, boys on the first night after their birth and girls on any night up to their twentieth. An amulet that contained the three angels' names was fastened to children to protect them from her. Arab legend contains clear parallels to this story: Adam and his first wife Quarina were created simultaneously, joined at the hip. Over a period of time the bodies separated. Quarina refused to let Adam rule over her, since they were both made by the same creator from the same dust. Considering this rebellion a serious one, *Allah drove Quarina from the Garden of Eden, after which she became the mate of Satan. Feeling enmity toward all of Adam's descendants, especially the males, Quarina tried to lure them into wickedness. In George Bernard Shaw's play, *Back to Methusala*, Lilith is portrayed as the mother of both Adam and Eve. As Shaw has written it, Lilith went through agony attempting to shed her skin only to split into Adam and Eve. "And when she cast the skin, lo! There was not one new Lilith but two: one like herself, the other like Adam. You were the one. Adam was the other." She also appears in *Goethe's *Faust*. (SOURCES: Ginzbert, 1913; Gaer, 1951; Shaw, 1963)

LILLIBULERO: a political song of sheer doggerel in pseudo-Irish, known during the English revolution of 1688, still known as one of the most effective and bombastic English marching songs, words written by Thomas Wharton, said to have been used as a watchword by Irish Catholics in their 1641 massacre of the Protestants.

LILLYGAY: five songs by Peter Warlock set to Victor Neuburg's *Anthology of Anonymous Poems*. Neuburg added several of his own poems to the set. It is probable that numbers 1, 2, 3, and 5 are Neuburg's. The poems are written in Old English and Old Scottish.

LIMERICK: a verse form composed of five lines, the rhyme scheme AABBA. As example: There was an old man of the Dee / Who was sadly annoyed by a flea / When he said, "I will catch it / They gave him a hatchet / Which grieved that old man of the Dee. (SOURCE: Preminger, 1986)

LIMOUSIN: a region and former province in south central France, located west of the *Auvergne mountains. Limoges, the historic capital of this arid, hilly country, is the center of the ceramic industry, and both Limoges and Tulle are important markets for the cattle raised in most of Limousin. The *Chants d'Auvergne*, folk songs of this region, are arranged by Joseph Canteloube.

LINDA M. DE S.: a shortened name for the sister of Guillaume *Apollinaire's comrade, Linda Moline de Silva, whom Apollinaire tried unsuccessfully to seduce.

SONG	COMPOSER	POET
"Dicts d'amour à Linda"	Francis Poulenc	Guillaume Apollinaire

LINDSAY, MAURICE (b. 1918): Scottish poet. Born in Glasgow, Lindsay became a radio broadcaster after serving in World War II. Later he was made programme controller at Border Television. Lindsay was appointed as director of the Scottish Core Trust and awarded a CBE in 1979. The University of Glasgow made him an honorary doctor of letters in 1982. His poetry has been set by Thea Musgrave. PRINCIPAL WORKS: *Robert Burns: The Man, His Work, the Legend*, 1968; editor, *Modern Scottish Poetry*, 1976; editor, *A Book of Scottish Verse*, 1983; *History of Scottish Literature*, 1977; poetry, *Walking without an Overcoat*, 1977; *Scottish Comic Verse*, 1981. (SOURCE: Wikipedia)

LINDSAY, VACHEL (1879–1931): American poet. Vachel Lindsay was born and grew up in Springfield, Illinois, which he idolized because Lincoln had lived there, his hope being to bring glory as an artist to his birthplace. He became a fanatical prohibitionist, and, seeing himself as a missionary, tramped through the South and Middle West, going from door to door exchanging his verse and stories for a night's lodging. His first book, published at the age of thirty-four, was a new experiment in the American idiom, *General William Booth Enters into Heaven*. It was a combination of religion, ragtime, and what he called "higher vaudeville." Lindsay incorporated poems like "The Congo," "The Santa Fe Trail," "The Booker Washington Trilogy," "The Daniel Jazz," and "John L. Sullivan, the Strong Boy of Boston" into public recitals that were performances, not lectures. The visionary teacher had become an entertainer. Lindsay failed to get the understanding he craved and began to despise the audiences who did not want to listen to his quieter work. He fell in love with Sara ★Teasdale and wooed her with an unwelcome enthusiasm. Eventually he married an old schoolmate, who tried but failed to restore his self-confidence. In his early fifties, sinking deeper into debt and despair, he took his own life. Lindsay brought into his verse the raucous but exciting blare of military bands, the rhythms of popular dances such as the Charleston, the beat of jazz sessions, the noise of racing automobiles, express trains, and torchlight parades. In the end, however, a discouraged Lindsay acknowledged the failure of his vision to make over America and raise the common man into an uncommon hero. Sidney Homer and Howard Swanson set Vachel Lindsay's verse and Charles Ives set his powerful poem, *General William Booth Enters into Heaven*. PRINCIPAL WORKS: *General William Booth Enters into Heaven*, 1913; *The Congo and Other Poems*, 1914; *The Chinese Nightingale and Other Poems*, 1917; *The Golden Whales of California and Other Rhymes in the American Language*, 1920. SELECTED READING: Edgar Lee Masters, *Lindsay: A Poet in America*, 1935; Eleanor Ruggles, *The West-Going Heart: A Life of Lindsay*, 1959. (SOURCE: Untermeyer, 1959)

LINLITHGOW: a district and a city of the mid-Scotland county of West Lothian, northeast of Glasgow, west of Edinburgh, just off the Firth of Forth. Located in a hollow, hidden from the Firth (a long, narrow indentation of sea coast) of Forth (a river), Linlithgow has an ancient castle and church that command the land route. On the edge of the small ★loch is the famous palace where Mary, Queen of Scots was born.

SONG	COMPOSER	POET
"Archibald Douglas"	Carl Loewe	Theodore Fontane

LINN: (Scot.), *a waterfall*.

SONG	COMPOSER	POET
"My Hoggie"	Benjamin Britten	Robert Burns

"L'Invitation au voyage": a song composed by Henri Duparc to a poem by Charles ★Baudelaire. The original poem had three stanzas, but Duparc set only two. The country the poet speaks of is Holland. Bernac suggests that the singer not perform this *mélodie* with sadness as many do, but rather "with an ecstatic sense of joy in the imagined realization of the vision." (SOURCE: Bernac, 1970)

LITANY: a form of a prayer-dialogue in which worshipers take responsive parts. A minister or priest recites its separate sentences and the congregation responds. A litany may be said at any religious service as a request for grace and mercy, or for deliverance from danger, pestilence, or sin. The congregation replies "Kyrie Eleison" or similar response. (SOURCE: *Americana*, 2003)

SONG	COMPOSER	POET
"Litanie"	Franz Schubert	Johann Jacobi

LIZBIE BROWN: the pretty daughter of a gamekeeper, Elizabeth Browne, with whom Thomas ★Hardy believed himself to be in love. He admired her beautiful bay-red hair. She rejected him because Hardy was several years her junior and already married.

SONG	COMPOSER	POET
"Lizbie Brown"	Gerald Finzi	Thomas Hardy

LOCH: (Scot.) (pr. as in Ger. "Lach"), *a lake or arm of the sea.*

SONG	COMPOSER	POET
"Archibald Douglas"	Carl Loewe	Theodor Fontane

LOCH LOMOND: a Scottish lake featured in the poetry of Robert ★Burns. The tale goes that a Scottish soldier about to be executed in England was visited by his girlfriend, who had journeyed from Scotland on foot. Her one wish was to see her lover once more. His parting words to her were, "O, ye'll take the high road and I'll take the low road." They imply that she will return to Scotland, and he will take the road to death, where his liberated spirit would meet her. Although there is little to be learned of its origin, fragments of the song were found on the streets of Edinburgh.

LOIRE: a French river, whose source is in the high Vivarais Mountains of southeastern France, flowing east past the great chateaus of Nantes, Angers, Saumur, Vouvray, Chaumont, Blois, and Orléans. Since ancient times the Loire Valley has been known as the "garden of France." The Seine is more beautiful but the Loire Valley was, until Louis XIV moved his residence to Versailles, the home of the French nobility, the center of commerce, the center of religious and intellectual life, and a battlefield. Serene today, the Loire Valley had a bloody past. Among the famous names connected with this territory are Julius Caesar (52 B.C.E.), the ★Saracens (defeated in Tours in 732 C.E.), Norse pirates (who settled on the northwest coast and became the Normans), the Hundred Years' War (which began in the valley), and Joan of Arc. In short, the Loire Valley embodied the history of France from the Celtic dawn through the Bourbon kings.

SONG	COMPOSER	POET
"C"	Francis Poulenc	Louis Aragon

LONGFELLOW, HENRY WADSWORTH (1807–1882): American poet. Longfellow was born in Portland, Maine, son of an attorney, a member of Congress, a trustee of Bowdoin College from which he graduated in 1825, already a published author. After he spent 1826 to 1829 in France, Spain, Italy, and Germany, a chair was created for him at Bowdoin. There he stayed until 1835, when his first book of poems, *Voices of the Night*, appeared. Harvard appointed him to be Smith professor of modern language in 1836. He wrote prolifically, and his fame grew; he became a friend to *Lowell and Hawthorne. In 1854 he resigned from Harvard to spend more time writing and, after the tragic death of his second wife, lost himself for a time in the mechanical work of translating. At the time of his sudden death, his fame was worldwide. He was the only American poet whose body was placed in the Poet's Corner at Westminster Abbey. Longfellow's poetry had melody and sweetness and clarity of expression, and his *ballads and *sonnets had dramatic power. His long poem, "Evangeline," has been force fed to American children, but it is not his best work. Walt *Whitman said, "He is the poet of the mellow twilight of the past." Longfellow's poetry has been set by Charles Ives, Franz Liszt, and David Diamond. PRINCIPAL WORKS: *Voices of the Night*, 1839; *Evangeline,* 1847; *The Song of Hiawatha*, 1855; *The Courtship of Miles Standish and Other Poems*, 1858. SELECTED READING: E. S. Roberton, *Life and Writings of Henry Wadsworth Longfellow*, 1972. (SOURCE: Kunitz, Haycraft, 1938)

LORCA, GARCÍA: *see* ★ GARCÍA LORCA.

LORELEI: the name of a steep rock, 430 feet high, located on the right bank of the Rhine River opposite St. Goar, and noted for its extraordinary echo. Clemens *Brentano in his novel *Godivi* was the first to associate the rock with a woman of the same name. Tradition now has it that this location, celebrated by *Heine and other poets, is the dwelling place of one or more seductive sirens. It was Heine who had added the element of seductress to the legend, depicting her as sitting on a rock, singing siren songs that lure ships to their destruction, thus revenging herself on mankind. Max Bruch made these alluring creatures the subject of his opera *Die Lorelei*, produced in 1864, and Mendelssohn failed to complete an opera of the same name. (SOURCE: Cooper, 1992)

SONG	COMPOSER	POET
1. "Die Lorelei"	Franz Liszt	Heinrich Heine
2. "Waldesgespräch"	Robert Schumann	Joseph von Eichendorff

LOTHARIO: in modern usage, a libertine, a rake. Originally the name of one of the characters in Nicholas Rowe's *Fair Penitent* and Philip Massinger's *Fatal Dowry*, then often used in the phrase "gay Lothario." Another reference is to a mysterious old harper in Thomas's opera *★Mignon*, who is Mignon's father. Lothario is also a character from *Goethe's novel *★Wilhelm Meister's Lehrjahre*. (SOURCE: *OED*, 1989)

LOTOSBLUME: *see* *LOTUSFLOWER.

LOTUSFLOWER, LOTOSBLUME (Ger.): a plant referred to in Greek legend, believed to be a jujube or elm, producing red, yellow, pink, or white flowers, blooming at night in answer to the rays of the moon and avoiding the sun, referred to as yielding a fruit that induced in those who ate it a state of dreamy and contented forgetfulness.

SONG	COMPOSER	POET
"Die Lotosblume"	Robert Schumann, Robert Franz	Heinrich Heine

LOUNS: (Scot.), *rogue.*

LOUŸS, PIERRE (pseudonym of Pierre Louis) (1870–1925): French poet. A friend of André *Gide and Paul *Valéry, Pierre Louÿs founded a literary magazine with them. Louÿs led a sophisticated, scintillating life up to the time he fell ill, became semi-blind, and was forced to live in partial seclusion. Louÿs, a classical scholar of the first rank, was intrigued by ancient Greece and in his writings attempted to re-create the pervading tone of that libidinous culture. An exacting artist, Louÿs had literary interests and style that were totally imbued with Greek literature, a fixation that resulted in his novels being regarded as threats to the Protestant morality of his time. Yet, he claimed to be a strict moralist whose writings showed the ravages caused by passion. His poems had brilliant color and displayed the pictorial qualities of the *Parnassians and the *Symbolist poets. The verses of Pierre Louÿs were set by Claude Debussy. PRINCIPAL WORKS available in English: *The Songs of *Bilitis,* 1904; *Aphrodite,* 1925; *Psyché,* 1928; *Satyrs and Women,* 1930; *The Collected Tales of Pierre Louÿs,* 1930; *Collected Works,* ed. M. S. Buck and J. Clugh, 1932. (SOURCE: Steinberg, 3, 1973; Kunitz, Haycraft, 1942)

"Love, Thou Art Best": a duet for two women, composed by Henry Purcell to words by Thomas Wright in his play, *The Female Vertuoso's.* For plot details and placement of songs, *see* *Female Vertuoso's, The.*

"Love Has a Thousand Ways to Please": a song composed by Henry Purcell to a text by John *Dryden for their semi-opera *King Arthur,* produced in 1691. *See* *King Arthur* for plot details and placement of songs.

LOVELACE, RICHARD (1618–1656 or 1657): English poet. There are no records of Lovelace's childhood, but he was born either in England or in Holland of a Dutch mother and an English father. He entered Oxford University as a commoner in 1634 but spent only two years there before moving to Cambridge. Subsequently, Lovelace joined the royal court, which sent him on the first expedition against the Scots (1639), where he rode with fellow poet Sir John *Suckling. Lovelace remained a literary amateur, but his sensibilities were deepened by the war experiences of his king and himself. After being confined to prison for two months, he spent the greater part of 1643–46 in France and Holland, where he learned his appreciation for art. Wounded at the siege of Dunkirk, he then withstood a second period in prison, mandated largely as a precaution against his past political activities, from which time issued a well-known poetic line, "iron bars do not a prison make." His poetry, mostly written during the Civil War and indebted to Ben *Jonson and John *Donne, displays the age that produced him, but he is chiefly remembered for a handful of exquisite lyrics that celebrate beauty, honor, and love. The verse of Richard Lovelace has been set by Richard Cumming. (SOURCE: Jason, 4, 2003)

"Lovers Who to Their First Embrace Go": a song composed by Henry Purcell to the text written by Thomas *D'Urfey for his play, *Circe*, produced in 1677. For plot details and placement of songs, *see* *Circe.

LOVE TRIUMPHANT: a play written by John *Dryden, produced in 1694, containing one song by Henry Purcell, for whom this play was the last full-length drama. The first scene of act 5 shows Sancho and Carlos, rivals for Dalinda. Carlos withdraws with mock horror from the rivalry when he learns that Dalinda is the mother of two illegitimate children, but he allows Sancho to marry her without telling what he knows. When the stepchildren appear on the wedding day, Sancho is furious, but the little boy and girl win him over with a dance. Carlos composes an *epithalamium, "How Happy's the Husband," which ribald verse the Purcell Society censored. (SOURCE: Price, 1984)

LOWELL, AMY (1874–1925): American poet. Lowell was born in Massachusetts, educated privately, and traveled extensively abroad. She was strongly associated with the *Imagists in London (1913) and was awarded a Pulitzer Prize in 1926. Amy Lowell played a large part in the poetic renaissance that lasted for some ten years after 1912. With her great wealth, flamboyant persona, her big, black cigar, her flair for organization and promoting, she was a major force in the new poetry. Her work, including experiments in "polyphonic prose," reflects a strong feeling for her native New England. The poetry of Amy Lowell has been set by Richard Owens, Stephen Crane, Celius Dougherty, Mary Howe, Virgil Thomson, and Alexander Steinert. PRINCIPAL WORKS: *Complete Poetical Works*, 1955; *Sword Blades and Poppy Seed*, 1914; *Men, Women, and Ghosts*, 1916; *What's O'Clock*, 1925. SELECTED READING: S. Foster Damon, *Amy Lowell: A Chronicle, with Extracts from her Correspondence*, 1935; Horace Gregory, *Lowell: Portrait of the Poet in Her Time*, 1958. (SOURCES: Waggoner, 1984; Unger, 3, 1974)

LOWELL, ROBERT (1917–1977): American poet, translator, and playwright. Lowell was born in Boston of old New England families, both father's and mother's. He was educated at Kenyon College, which, according to him, determined the kind of poet he became. "From the beginning, I was preoccupied with technique, fascinated by the past, tempted by other languages" (Drabble, 2000). In 1940 he became a fanatical convert to Roman Catholicism and was jailed for six months during World War II as a conscientious objector. The height of Lowell's public acclaim took place during his opposition to the Vietnam War and his support of Senator Eugene McCarthy's campaign for the presidency. Lowell had been suffering bouts of manic-depressive illness and heavy drinking for many years. Following a 1970 trip to England at the invitation of several prestigious schools, he returned to America, where he died. Lowell's work was compared favorably to that of *Yeats. An ironic intellectual, Lowell wrote complex imagery that was admired by the New Criticism movement (1935–60). These critics considered that a poem should not be reduced to content, but understood on its own terms as a complex unity of verbal ironies and paradoxes. The verse of Robert Lowell has been set by Benjamin Britten, Arthur Shepherd, Elliott Carter, and Carl Engel. PRINCIPAL WORKS: *Lord Weary's Castle*, 1946; *Life Studies*, 1959; *For the Union Dead,* 1964; *The Dolphins*, 1973; *Day by Day*, 1977. SELECTED READING: a biography by Ian Hamilton, 1982. (SOURCE: Drabble, 2000)

LUCASTA: a nickname for Lucy Sacheverell given by the poet Richard *Lovelace (1618–58), who wrote poetry to her during his imprisonment of 1648. Lovelace was a romantic figure, wealthy, handsome, and well-mannered. His army exploits were numerous; but when Lovelace was reported to have been killed in action, Lucy married another man. Lovelace had chosen to call her Lucasta, invoking the Latin *lux casta, pure light*, therefore "chaste Lucy."

SONG	COMPOSER	POET
"Going to the Warres"	Richard Cumming	Richard Lovelace

LUCY, SAINT, SANTA LLÚCIA (Catalan), SANTA LUCIA (It.) (d. 304): a Christian saint and martyr. According to historically suspect tradition, Saint Lucy was born in Sicily to wealthy parents and raised a Christian. Early in life she dedicated her virginity to God but kept it a secret. Her father having died, she made a pilgrimage to St. Agatha's shrine to seek healing for her mother. St. Agatha revealed to Lucy that her prayers had already healed her mother. Upon their return home, Lucy and her mother began selling their possessions, giving the proceeds to the poor. Because Lucy tricked her wealthy suitor into believing that she was selling her belongings to make purchases for their marriage, he willingly helped her sell many items. When the suitor realized that he had been duped, he turned her in to the governor of Syracuse, Paschias, who had her taken to a brothel and abused until she died. The many tortures left her resolute, prophesying Paschias's arrest and death. St. Lucy died of her injuries, but not before receiving Holy Communion. Actual facts about her life are unclear. She was martyred during the persecution under the rule of Emperor *Diocletian. On St. Lucy's Day, December 13, celebrated in Scandinavia as a festival of lights, a Christmas crèche fair is held in Barcelona, Spain. The chapel of Santa Llúcia in the Barcelona Cathedral looks out on the Plaça Nova. There, artisans sell statues of the Holy Family as well as bushes and branches with which the people can decorate their mangers at home. (SOURCES: Cockburn, Stokes, 1992; Farmer, 1997; Thurston, Attwater, 1963; de Voragine, 1993)

SONG	COMPOSER	POET
"Romanç de Santa Llúcia"	Eduardo Toldrà	José de Sagarra

LUDIONS: bottle imps. Ludions are small figures suspended in a hollow ball that descends or rises in a vase filled with water when one presses down on the elastic membrane covering the mouth of the vase. (SOURCE: Bernac, 1970)

SONG	COMPOSER	POET
"Ludions"	Erik Satie	Léon Paul Fargue

LUJÁN, FERNANDEZ NÉSTOR (1922–1995): Spanish journalist. Néstor Luján, who lived in Barcelona, wrote on art, politics, sport, art, and gastronomy, having produced the formidable *Historia del torea* (1954) and *Historia de la cocina española* (1970), written with a co-author, Joan Perucho. The texts of Néstor Luján have been set by Xavier Montsalvatje. (SOURCE: Cockburn, Stokes, 1992)

LUKE HAVERGAL: one of the characters, like Miniver Cheevy and Richard Cory, invented by American poet Edward Arlington ★Robinson as living in his own town of Gardiner, Maine, which he renamed "Tilbury Town." Robinson's characters were tormented by modern anxieties as was the poet, who had a tendency to make every sentence repeat key words and then proceed to worry their meaning at length. Robinson "offers a deeply felt account of the indignities of living and of its occasional mysterious rewards" (Ellmann). "Luke Havergal," and "Miniver Cheevy," were set to music by John Duke. "Richard Cory" was set by John Duke, Paul Reif, and Charles Naginski. (SOURCE: Ellmann, O'Clair, 1973)

LUNA: moon, in Latin, used poetically as the personification of Earth's moon, or as the name of the Moon Goddess in Roman mythology, and interchangeably with ★Selene, Artemis, ★Diana, Phoebe, and ★Cynthia. (SOURCES: Hamilton, 1969; Mayerson, 1971)

SONG	COMPOSER	POET
"Bess o'Bedlam"	Henry Purcell	anonymous
"Dämmrung senkte sich von oben"	J. Brahms, O. Schoeck	Johann Wolfgang v. Goethe
"Nachtstück"	Franz Schubert	Johann Mayrhofer
"Abendlied unterm gestirnten Himmel"	L. van Beethoven	H. Goebel

LUNA MORISCA: the Turkish sultans' emblem of a Moorish moon, or crescent. The crescent moon is the attribute *par excellence* of the Great Mother, the lunar queen of heaven, and all lunar goddesses. It is also the emblem of the Sumerian moon god, Sin, of Islam, Byzantium, and the Turks, and can be represented by cows' or bulls' horns. Tradition has it that Philip, the father of ★Alexander, having great difficulties during his siege of Byzantium, set his workmen to undermining the walls. After a crescent moon revealed the strategy to them, the Byzantines erected a statue to ★Diana, goddess of the moon. Thus did the crescent become the symbol of the state. Yet another legend is that Sultan Othman saw a crescent moon in a vision. The crescent increased in size until its horns extended from east to west. So did he adopt the crescent moon as his standard. This symbol was used by the Seljuk Sultan Ala-ud-din in the mid-thirteenth century. Reputedly, it was then adopted by Osman, who founded the Ottoman dynasty in ca. 1281. Supposedly, it was after the capture of Constantinople in 1453 that Mohammed II placed the crescent on the Turkish flag. (SOURCES: Cockburn, Stokes, 1992; Cooper, 1992)

SONG	COMPOSER	POET
"Romance"	Joaquín Turina	Duque de Rivas

LYONESSE: a mythical country from which King ★Arthur came in the legend. Lyonesse is a rich tract of land fabled to stretch between Land's End and the Scilly Isles, on which stood the City of Lions and some one hundred and forty churches.

According to ★Spenser in his ★*Faerie-Queene*, "that sweet land of Lyonesse" was the birthplace of Tristram. According to ★Tennyson, it was the scene of King Arthur's death. The battle of Lyonesse was the final conflict between Arthur and Sir Mordred. ★Hardy's poem recalls his first trip to St. Juliot in Cornwall, his falling in love, and his return home. Clearly, for Hardy, his trip had a relationship to the legend of King Arthur. (SOURCE: Cooper, 1992; Kimball, 1996)

SONG	COMPOSER	POET
"When I Set Off for Lyonesse"	Gerald Finzi	Thomas Hardy

LYRE: a stringed instrument, the body of which has two extensions that connect to a crossbar above. The strings are stretched between the two extensions from the body. It is played either with the fingers or a plectrum. Lyres were played throughout northern Europe until the eleventh or twelfth centuries. Ancient poets called the lyre a "shell" because the cords of the lyre, supposedly used by ★Orpheus, ★Amphion, and ★Apollo, were stretched on the shell of a tortoise. Amphion built ★Thebes with the music of his lyre, for the very stones moved of their own accord into walls and houses. Orpheus charmed savage beasts and even the infernal gods with the sublime music of his lyre.

M ✍

MAB: the fairies' midwife, employed by them to deliver man's brain of dreams. When Romeo says, "I dreamed a dream tonight," then Mercutio replies, "Oh, then I see Queen Mab hath been with you." When Mab is called queen it does not mean sovereign, because ★Titania, as wife of King ★Oberon, was queen of the fairies, but means simply "female." Shakespeare gives an excellent description of Mab in *Romeo and Juliet*, act 1, scene 4; Ben ★Jonson, Robert ★Herrick, and Michael Drayton also describe Mab well. (SOURCE: Cooper, 1992)

SONG	COMPOSER	POET
"Bess o'Bedlam"	Henry Purcell	anonymous

MACARENA: the Virgin of the Macarena, La Macarena, patron saint of Seville.

SONG	COMPOSER	POET
1. "Semana Santa"	Joaquín Turina	José Muñoz San Román
2. "Sevillanas del siglo XVIII"	Federico García Lorca	Federico García Lorca

MACDONALD, ANDREW (1757–1790): a Scottish dramatist. Macdonald, the son of a gardener, settled in London, where he wrote for newspapers and theater under the pen name of Matthew Bramble and died, in poverty, of tuberculosis. Schubert's setting of "Lied der Anne Lyle" was to Macdonald's text "Wert Thou, Like Me, in Death's Low Vale," translated into German by Sophie May, from Sir Walter Scott's opera libretto *Love and Loyalty*. (SOURCE: Reed, 1997)

MACKAY, JOHN HENRY (1864–1933): German poet and novelist. Born of a Scottish father and a German mother, Mackay was an infant when his father died. Shortly after that, he was taken by his mother to Germany, where he spent the rest of his life. Often in disfavor with the authorities, he was a born rebel and a tough man. *Sturm* (1887), his volume of poetry, was a source of texts for the songs of Richard Strauss, the most well known being "Morgen" and "Heimliche Aufforderung." (SOURCE: Beum, 2000)

MACLEISH, ARCHIBALD (1892–1982): American poet and dramatist. MacLeish was born in Illinois, educated at Yale and Harvard, and spent some time in the U.S. Army. Living in Paris in the 1920s, he was strongly influenced by Ezra ★Pound and T. S. ★Eliot. When he returned to the United States at the end of the 1920s, he became more and more a public figure. MacLeish served as Librarian of Congress (1939–44), assistant secretary of State (1944–45), and Boylston Professor at Harvard (1949–62). He received the Pulitzer Prize for drama in 1933 and 1953. MacLeish participated in every movement and learned from every poetic generation, never appearing to be old-fashioned or out of touch with the times. His quick fame of the 1920s also marked his best work. In another period he wrote imaginatively of the space-time cosmos just being revealed, and many of his poems depended upon technical knowledge. In the next period, his Pulitzer Prize-winning *Conquistador*, occupying one hundred pages at the end of *Collected Poems 1924–1933*, exemplified his poems and radio plays that were written against Fascism. In the 1950s, his fourth phase, he wrote *Songs for Eve*, in which his thesis was that we must set about finding meanings that science cannot be bothered with. At every stage of his career, MacLeish "gave expression to the historical situation as thoughtful people immersed in it saw it" (Unger, 3, 1974). The poetry of Archibald MacLeish has been set to music by William Schumann, Richard Cumming, John Duke, Ross Finney, Theodore Chanler, Miriam Gideon, and Ezra Laderman. PRINCIPAL WORKS: *A Pot of Earth*, 1925; *New Found Land*, 1930; *Conquistador*, 1932; *Frescoes for Mr. Rockefeller's City*, 1933; *Songs for Eve*, 1954; *Collected Poems 1924–1933*, 1933. SELECTED READING: J. G. Southworth, *Some Modern American Poets*, 1950; H. H. Waggoner, *The Heel of Elohim*, 1950. (SOURCE: Unger, 3, 1974)

MACLEOD, FIONA: *see* ★SHARP, WILLIAM.

MACPHERSON, JAMES (1736–1796): a Scottish poet and novelist. In 1760 Macpherson published poems that he claimed were the works of an ancient bard named ★Ossian, titling them *Fragments of Ancient Poetry Collected in the Highlands of Scotland from the Gaelic or Erse Language*. These and subsequent works enjoyed great popularity in Europe, especially Germany, and were greatly admired by ★Herder. Today they are denigrated by many as a hoax perpetrated by Macpherson, although a battle still rages as to the authenticity. Schubert set ten German translations of Macpherson by Edmund von Harold, including "Die Nacht," D534. (SOURCE: Reed, 1997)

MAD HATTER: a character from Lewis ★Carroll's *Alice in Wonderland*. The text of the Satie song is an adaptation of Carroll, and the melody is taken from a tenor aria from Gounod's opera *Mireille*, characteristic of Satie's wit.

SONG	COMPOSER	POET
"Le Chapelier"	Erik Satie	adapted by René Chalupt

MADONNA: (Lat.), *mea domina* (my lady), a title used for a representation of the ★Virgin Mary in art.

SONG	COMPOSER	POET
1. "Madrigal"	Gabriel Fauré	Edmond Haraucourt
2. "Pierrot Lunaire 6"	Arnold Schönberg	Albert Giraud

MAD SONGS: the stock in trade of most important actor-singers of the English Restoration theater. Also, feigned madness was a common form of begging in early times. Theatrical mad songs came in two basic types: (1) a vehicle for truly insane characters, to which the audience and other characters attend seriously, in which the singer is intended to be demented (e.g., Bess o'Bedlam, ★Cardenio in *★Don Quixote*) and (2) a soliloquy in which the character shares his or her innermost thoughts, or explains the cause of his madness, or why he is pretending to be mad (e.g., Lyonel in *★A Fool's Preferment*, "From Rosy Bow'rs" in *The Comical History of Don Quixote*). The English have more songs on the subject of madness than any of their neighbors.

MAENADS: frenzied women, the Bacchae, or Baccantes, female attendants of ★Bacchus (Roman), or the female participants in the orgiastic rites of ★Dionysus (Greek). The name arises from their extravagant gestures and frenzied rites, and is invoked to illustrate chaos and disorder. (SOURCE: Cooper, 1992)

MAETERLINCK, MAURICE (1862–1949): Belgian poetic dramatist and essayist. Maeterlinck wrote in French and was a leading figure of the ★Symbolist movement. He is now remembered chiefly for *Pélleas et Mélisande*, which was the source of Debussy's opera, but his great contemporary popularity was related to *L'Oiseau bleu* (The Bluebird). Maeterlinck received the Nobel Prize in 1911. Romances and fairy tales were the source for his work, and its originality lies in his transposition of Symbolism to the stage. The characteristic tone of his poetry was "doom-laden mystery and timeless melancholy," albeit with the "sense of fatality exquisitely constructed and simplified" (Drabble, 2000). The poetry of Maurice Maeterlinck has been set by Chausson, Schönberg, Debussy, Nadia Boulanger, and Paul Dukas. PRINCIPAL WORKS: *Serres chaudes,* 1889, trans. B. Miall, 1915; *Pélleas et Mélisande*, 1892, trans. 1894; *L'Oiseau bleu*, 1908, *The Bluebird*, 1909. SELECTED READING: *Vie des abeilles*, 1901, as *Life of the Bee*, 1901. (SOURCE: Drabble, 2000)

MAGELONE LIEDER (*Die schöne Magelone***):** a cycle of fifteen songs composed by Johannes Brahms, set to texts by Johann ★Tieck and interspersed with Tieck's narration. Originally the following narration was not used, but in 1886 Brahms changed his mind and decided that it should be read during performances of the cycle. The following translation is adapted from that published by Ronald A. Turner, "Johannes Brahms and *Die Schöne Magelone*."

"Dear friends: This is an old legend about the knight Peter and the beautiful Magelone.

Narration 1:

"Once upon a time in Provence there lived a nobleman whose son Peter was handsome and accomplished. Being very strong, Peter's skill with lance, sword, and horse was unequaled by anyone in his father's kingdom. Invitations had been sent out for a great tournament to be held at the father's court. Knights from many distant regions came to take part in the event, but all marveled at the way Peter distinguished himself. Among the guests was a minstrel who had travelled widely and was knowledgeable in the ways of the world. Sensing young Peter's restless nature, he took up a harp and tried to encourage Peter to discover life beyond the confines of his native land, singing thus:"

Song 1: "Keinen hat es noch gereut"

Narration 2:

"Peter, deciding to follow the advice of the minstrel, approached his father, hoping for permission to make an extended journey. When the count approved, the young prince began preparations for travel and his search for adventure. On the day of departure the father's blessing included a reminder that a noble character was a greater weapon in adversity than a bow and arrow. Peter's mother presented him with three precious rings to serve as engagement gifts, should he find a worthy young maiden. Peter embraced each of his parents, mounted his horse, courage high, and rode off, spurring his horse and singing lustily:"

Song 2: "Traun! Bogen und Pfeil!"

Narration 3:

"After many days of travel, Peter reached Naples, enticed by stories he had heard of the king of Naples's beautiful daughter, Magelone. When a series of tournaments was announced shortly after his arrival, Peter resolved to compete, seeing this as a way to appraise Magelone's beauty for himself. On the first day of the tournament, Peter was a prominent competitor, victorious over all who rode against him. He won recognition and respect from contestants and spectators alike. Although the king sent for Peter in order to learn his name and nationality, Peter asked for permission to keep his identity to himself. He wanted to make his reputation by accomplishment, not by parentage. Magelone found herself anxious to make the acquaintance of the victorious knight whose face remained a mystery hidden by his visor. After the banquet held for the winning knights that evening, where Peter was

seated at the king's table opposite Magelone, he walked home intoxi-
cated by the rapture of a first love:"

Song 3: "Sind es Schmerzen, sind es Freuden"

Narration 4:

"When sleep finally came to Magelone that night, she dreamed of the
tournament and felt a longing to see the unknown knight again. In
the morning, she confided to her nurse Gertrude her wish to learn
the identity of the handsome young knight who had appeared in her
dreams. When Gertrude happened to see Peter in church that morning, she gave him Magelone's greetings. Overjoyed at Magelone's
interest, Peter sent her a poem he had written that morning. He said it
would answer many of Magelone's questions. To Gertrude, he gave one
of the three rings:"

Song 4: "Liebe kam aus fernen Landen"

Narration 5:

"Having persuaded the nurse to exchange Peter's ring for an equally
attractive one, she hung Peter's ring on a golden chain around her
neck. That night, the ring lying warm on her breast, sent dreaming
Magelone a vision of her beloved. Coming through a beautiful garden,
he embraced her with great tenderness and slipped yet another ring,
more precious than the first, on her finger. Waking, Magelone recalled
her dreams to Gertrude, who realized that the princess's whole life
now centered on the stranger. That morning at church Gertrude again
met Peter, who sent Magelone the ring of which she had dreamed and
with it another poem:"

Song 5: "So willst du des Armen"

Narration 6:

"The next morning Gertrude told Peter that she wanted to be assured
of his honorable intentions. When Peter vowed eternal fidelity and
constancy, Gertrude described a secret passage to her room, where
Magelone would be waiting for him the next morning. Sitting alone
later that evening, Peter's yearning for Magelone drove him out into
the dark street, where he wandered, accompanied only by his lute:"

Song 6: "Wie soll ich die Freude"

Narration 7:

"At the hour of their meeting Peter found Magelone waiting alone
as arranged. The two lovers exchanged their passionate vows of love.
As they parted, Peter gave Magelone the third ring, most precious of
all. Magelone took the golden chain from her neck to hang it around
Peter's and kissed him. Overwhelmed with happiness, Peter wandered
the streets, remembering the bliss of Magelone's first kiss. He picked up
his lute and, releasing his bursting heart, began to sing:"

Song 7: "Was es dir, dem diese Lippen bebten"

Narration 8:

"Although the king wished Magelone to marry Henry of Carpone, Peter had again defeated all opponents at another tournament. Peter knew that it was time to begin his homeward journey, but feared that Magelone might be forced into marrying Sir Henry in his absence. After tearful indecision, Magelone at last agreed to flee from Naples with Peter, as soon as the arrangements could assure secrecy. As he awaited the hour of rendezvous, Peter bade a symbolic farewell to the lute that had won him treasures he would guard with his life:"

Song 8: "Wir müssen uns trennen"

Narration 9:

"Following the plan, one evening Magelone slipped through the palace guard and found Peter waiting on the other side of the wall. By morning they were well on their way toward Provence. When the king heard of the lovers' escape, he ordered his troops to search for them. Peter's route took them through thick forests, and the king's troops were thwarted by the less-traveled route. At midmorning, wearied by traveling through the night, Magelone begged to rest for a while. Peter laid his cloak on the ground in a shady spot and sang to Magelone as she dropped off to sleep:"

Song 9: "Ruhe, Süssliebchen, im Schatten"

Narration 10:

"Curious about the contents of a small red bag that hung around Magelone's neck, Peter opened it as she slept. There he found the three rings given him by his mother. Intending to replace it later, he put the bag on the ground beside him. A raven swooped down and snatched it up, flying off toward the seashore. On a rock out in the sea, positioned not far from shore, the raven alighted, red bag still in his beak. Distracted by an approaching storm and discovering that its supposed meal was not food, the bird dropped the bag and flew off. Peter set out toward the rock in a small boat he had found along the shore. The storm broke violently; the winds whipped the waves into a seething cauldron; Peter was driven far out to sea. Despairing of seeing Magelone again, Peter challenged the sea to do its worst:"

Song 10: "So tönet denn, schäumende Wellen"

Narration 11:

"Awaking to find Peter gone and fearful at the thought of spending the night alone, Magelone wept bitterly. Determined nevertheless to seize her courage, Magelone climbed into a tree where she spent the night. Then, after a few days of walking, she came upon a lovely meadow. As she approached a small hut, an old shepherd and his wife came out to greet her. Her pitiable story prompted them to offer her refuge with them for as long as she cared to remain. When she found herself alone, Magelone would pass her solitude sitting in the doorway, spinning, or singing to herself:"

Song 11: "Wie schnell verschwindet"

Narration 12:

"Meanwhile, the morning after Peter had been carried out to sea, he was picked up by a large ship manned by Moorish sailors and bound for an African port. The ship's captain saved Peter's life, reasoning that he would make a fine slave for the house of their sultan. When the ship docked, Peter was taken to the sultan. Impressed by his new slave's fine appearance, the sultan appointed Peter head gardener of the palace. Heart heavy with sadness at thinking of his beloved Magelone, Peter would often wander into the darkening gardens at night, singing quietly to himself:"

Song 12: "Muss es eine Trennung geben"

Narration 13:

"Loved by the Sultan, both respected and envied by the court servants, Peter would have had a happy life had it not been for his constant thoughts about Magelone and his lost homeland. Time passed until he had been at the sultan's court for nearly two years. Hope of returning to his homeland had died, and a conviction that Magelone was dead saddened him. The sultan's daughter, Sulima, famous throughout the countryside for her beauty, had often seen the stranger and, without realizing it, had fallen in love with him. One day she bade a slave bring an embarrassed and astonished Peter to a meeting with her in the garden. Although he was taken by Sulima's beauty, Peter's heart remained with Magelone. When Sulima suggested that they flee together in a boat owned by a friend, Peter agreed to the idea because of his desire to see his native land again. Hiding in the garden, Peter sang the song Sulima had sung to him, the prearranged signal for their meeting:"

Song 13: "Geliebter, wo zaudert"

Narration 14:

"The strains of Sulima's song drifting out of the garden brought to Peter a vision of Magelone. She reproached him for having deserted her and forgotten their loving vows to one another. This dream made Peter realize the strength of his longing for Magelone. Thus did he resolve to escape alone. Untying the boat, he pushed it out to sea. The sighing of the wind muted Sulima's song. As Peter set his sails with the prevailing wind, his courage revived and he sang to himself, adrift on the sea:"

Song 14: "Wie froh und frisch mein Sinn sich hebt"

Narration 15:

"Soon a ship manned by a friendly crew picked Peter up. He was overjoyed to learn that their destination was southern France. En route, the ship dropped anchor near a small, uninhabited island to freshen their water supply. Peter wandered away on his own, became drowsy, and fell asleep in a pleasant meadow. On awakening, Peter hurried back to the ship's anchorage, but found himself left behind. He fell to his knees, despondent. The next morning a fisherman happened to find him. Recognizing that Peter was of noble birth, the fisherman took him to the mainland and set him on the road to Provence. Peter followed a twisting path as he passed through a pleasant forest. Suddenly he came upon a broad meadow where the sun shone. As Peter drew closer, he heard the sweet voice of a young girl singing. The shepherd and his wife invited the weary traveler to rest awhile in their home. At the sight of a noble stranger the young girl disappeared. She changed from her peasant dress into a beautiful gown, loosed her tightly braided hair, letting it fall down around her shoulders, came out to Peter, and embraced him. Peter's astonishment and joy were joined to self-reproach for the years of misery he had caused her.

"The young couple journeyed on to his father's court, where they were joyously welcomed. Soon they were married, and the king of Naples became reconciled to his son-in-law and the marriage. On the spot where the shepherd's hut had stood, Peter built a magnificent house. In front of it Magelone and Peter planted a tree that symbolized their reunion. With each new year they returned to this spot to celebrate by singing this song in praise of enduring love:"

Song 15: "Treue Liebe dauert lange"

(SOURCE: Turner, 1979)

MAGGIE: a character in a Stephen Collins Foster song, "Maggie by My Side." Because women other than captains' wives (who were frequently allowed to sail on their husband's ships) never lived on sailing ships, Maggie is apparently the sailors' protective dog, not a woman.

MAGI: (Lat., plural of *magus*) lit., *wise men*; specifically the three wise men of the east who brought gifts to the infant savior. Tradition calls them Melchior, Gaspar (or Caspar), and Balthazar, the three kings of the East. The first offered gold, the emblem of royalty; the second, frankincense in token of divinity; the third, myrrh, in allusion to the persecution unto death that awaited the "Man of Sorrows." Melchior was the king of light; Caspar, the white one; Balthazar, the lord of treasures. Medieval legend calls them the three kings of Cologne, and the cathedral of ★Cologne claimed their relics. They are particularly commemorated on January 2, 3, and 4, particularly at the Feast of the ★Epiphany. Among the ancient Medes and Persians, the Magi were members of a priestly caste credited with great occult powers. (SOURCE: Cooper, 1992)

SONG	COMPOSER	POET
1. "Noël"	Gabriel Fauré	Victor Wilder
2. "Journey of the Magi"	Benjamin Britten	T. S. Eliot

MAGPIE: one of two corvine (crowlike) birds, black-billed or yellow-billed, with long graduated tails, black and white plumage, known for their noisy, mischievous habits.

SONG	COMPOSER	POET
1. "Cinq chansons de Lise Hirtz"	Georges Auric	Lise Hirtz
2. "Margot la pie"	Federico Mompou	anonymous

MAGYAR NÉPDALOK: title of the volume of ★*Hungarian Folk Songs* collected and arranged by Béla Bartók and Zoltán Kodály.

MAIDENHEAD: an English town located 30 miles west of London.

SONG	COMPOSER	POET
"Tell Me the Truth about Love"	Benjamin Britten	W. H. Auden

MAID'S LAST PRAYER, THE; OR, ANY, RATHER THAN FAIL: a play by Thomas ★Southerne with some music by Henry Purcell, produced in 1693. Herein Southerne rails at contemporary immorality, and the humor reveals his knowledge of the practice of music. Act 1 opens with a concert scene directed by Sir Symphony. The musicians are dilettantes who, after much confusion, finally play a piece, followed by a song called for by Sir Symphony: "Though You Make No Return to My Passion," an enthusiastic acceptance of adultery. The next event is a duet for two women, "No, Resistance Is But Vain," whose lyrics tell of the power of love. Although most scholars have concluded that the song is not appropriate there, it is one of Purcell's longest and most passionate compositions, marked by great tension between the harmonies and the appearance of six different keys in fourteen bars (Price, 1984). There is one more Purcell song in the last act, "Tell Me No More I am Deceived," with lyrics by ★Congreve, sung by a woman who is accompanied by Sir Symphony's musicians on their way to a masquerade (almost a cliché in Covent Garden comedies of that time). (SOURCE: Price, 1984)

MAIK: (Scot.) (pr. meck), *halfpenny.*

MAIKOV, APOLLON: *see* ★MAYKOV.

MAIR: (Scot.), *more.*

MAIST: (Scot.) (pr. mest), *most; almost.*

SONG	COMPOSER	POET
"My Hoggie"	Benjamin Britten	Robert Burns

MAJA: a glamorously dressed female companion of a ★*majo.* (SOURCE: Cockburn, Stokes, 1992)

SONG	COMPOSER	POET
1. "La maja de Goya"	Enrique Granados	Fernando Periquet
2. "La maja dolorosa"	Enrique Granados	Fernando Periquet

MAJLÁTH, JOHANN, COUNT (1786–1855): a Hungarian poet and journal-ist. Count Majláth left his job as a civil servant because of an eye injury and went to Vienna for medical treatment. There he remained, making his living as a writer. A member of the Schubert circle in the 1820s, he later moved to Munich. There, depressed by the fact that he was unable to support himself or his daughter, he com-mitted suicide. Schubert set one song by Majláth, "Der Blumen Schmerz," D731 (1821). (SOURCE: Reed, 1997)

MAJO: (Sp.), a term used at the end of the eighteenth century to describe a man of the working-class population of Madrid in areas such as ★Lavapiés. Socially, a majo is at the bottom of the scale while a *señor* is at the other end. A majo is usu-ally described as rowdy, boastful, handsome, and egotistical. Majos and majas were often depicted in the paintings and tapestries of the great Spanish artist Goya. The poetry of ★Periquet invoked those canvases, of which Granados set four that invoked the majo: "Amor y odio," "El majo discreto," "El majo olvidado," and "El tra la la y el punteado." He called them *Tonadillas Escritas in Estilo Antiguo*. For Granados the term did not mean the theatrical form of the ★tonadilla, but rather simply a kind of romantic song associated with eighteenth-century Madrid. (SOURCE: Cockburn, Stokes, 1992)

MALAGUEÑA: (Sp.), an Andalusian song or instrumental piece originally from Malaga.

SONG	COMPOSER	POET
1. "Malagueña"	Joaquín Nin	popular song
2. "Malagueña de La Madruga"	Fernando Obradors	classical Spanish song

MALER NOLTEN: title of a two-volume novel by Eduard ★Mörike, containing many poetic song texts interpolated throughout the work. The song texts remained untitled until they were set by several composers: "Rosenzeit, wie schnell vorbei" (Brahms, Robert Franz, and Hugo Wolf under the title "Agnes"); "Elfenlied," "Das verlassene Mägdelein," "Er ist's," "Im Frühling," "Gesang Weylas," "An die Geliebte," "Lied vom Winde," a part of "Der Feuerreiter," set by Wolf, and "Der Jäger" set by Brahms. *Maler Nolten* is a confused novel in which the principal characters are depressives and hypochondriacs. Mörike believed in the reality of an invisible world, in the fusion of those things familiar to us with the supernatural, the mysterious, and the incomprehensible. Book 1 contains the shadow play, *Der letzte König von ★Orplid*. The character of Agnes, the heroine of the novel, is based on a pastor's daughter with whom Mörike had fallen in love. Poems written about her were set by Hugo Wolf under the titles "Peregrina I and II." In the novel she is the painter's sweetheart, who at first appears to be a simple country girl, but later submits to the machinations of a gypsy woman.

MALHERBE, FRANÇOIS DE (1555–1628): French poet and theorist. Born into a noble but modest Protestant family, as a child François was put in care of a Hugue-not tutor and then sent to the universities of Basel and Heidelberg. Malherbe's own religious feelings were swayed by his opportunism, and he had little affinity for any sect. He began to write poetry at the university, but destroyed most of it as unworthy. In 1576 Malherbe left home and went to Aix, where he worked as a secretary and became active in poetic circles. Five years later he returned to Normandy to remain for ten years and published the poetry written to that date. Malherbe's unremitting but unfruitful search for patrons inspired many a work written as a homage to a royal personage. While he remained in civil service, he made advances in his poetic technique. Malherbe is now remembered as a founder of a new school of purism and precision. A classicist, he censured ★Ronsard's innovations and those of the ★Pléiade, attacking all flaws of grammar and versification techniques, himself preferring a stately but stiff and colorless type of verse, the ★alexandrine. Malherbe was a chronic opportunist, using poetry for political advantage. Yet he did express serious ideas, and his narrow views on poetry did move the neoclassical period toward clarity. The verses of François de Malherbe have been set by Francis Poulenc. PRINCIPAL WORKS: *Consolation à Cléophon*, 1627; *Prière pour le Roi Henri le Grand*, 1627; *Ode au Roi Louis XII allant Châtier les Rochelois*, 1627. SELECTED READING: *Studies in Seventeen Century French Literature*, ed. J. J. Demorest, 1963. (SOURCE: Kunitz, Colby, 1967)

MALLARMÉ, STÉPHANE (1842–1898): French poet. Mallarmé was one of the founders of modern European poetry and one of the prominent members of ★Structuralism. After spending some years in London (1862–63), he taught English in various schools in Paris and, with his later verse, became an object of a cult. His poetry spoke of deferred gratification and paucity of possessions as superior to wealth and worldly goods. Mallarmé sought perfection that demanded a new effort in language. Inventing his own vocabulary, he wanted to produce poetry that had a suggestive kind of writing through ambiguous language that used the aural elements of verse. Poetry, he said, must not be fettered by words used in customary contexts. An object must not be named because a name destroys it; it must be evoked by analogy. He preached the importance of ideas and of the existence of an ideal with which to combat the terrible errors of a scientific age. As a consequence, his output was small but his influence great. The poetry of Mallarmé has been set by Maurice Ravel, Henri Sauguet, and Claude Debussy. PRINCIPAL WORKS: *L'Après-midi d'un faune Eglogue*, 1876; *Mallarmé in English Verse*, trans. Arthur Ellis, 1927; *Poems*, trans. Roger Fry, 1951; *Selected Poems*, trans. C. F. MacIntyre, 1957; *Poems*, trans. Keith Bosley, 1977. SELECTED READING: Malcolm Bowie, *Mallarmé and the Art of Being Difficult*, 1979; Ursula Franklin, *The Anatomy of Poesis: The Prose Poems of Mallarmé*, 1976. (SOURCE: Drabble, 2000)

MANDALAY: the second largest city in Burma, now Myanmar, situated on the central Irrawaddy River, 370 miles north of Rangoon, now Yangón. From 1860 to 1885 it was the capital of the Burmese kingdom. Then as now Mandalay was noted for music, dance, its ornate Burmese pagodas, and fine buildings of teak and other woods. (SOURCE: *Americana*, 2003)

SONG	COMPOSER	POET
"On the Road to Mandalay"	Oley Speaks	Rudyard Kipling

MANGER: a long open trough or box in a stable for horses or cattle to eat from. The most famous manger is the one, according to the Bible, in which the baby ★Jesus was placed after his birth.

SONG	COMPOSER	POET
"Noël"	Gabriel Fauré	Victor Wilder

"Man is for the Woman Made": a song by Henry Purcell to words written by Thomas Scott for the play *The Mock Marriage*, produced in 1695. For plot details and placement of songs, *see* ★*Mock Marriage, The.*

MANOIR DE ROSAMONDE, LE: *see* ★ROSAMONDE.

MANOLA: a street girl of Madrid.

SONG	COMPOSER	POET
"Séguidille"	Manuel de Falla	Théophile Gautier

MANTILLA: a high-born Spanish woman's black, lacy head covering, usually heightened at the top of the head with a decorative comb.

SONG	COMPOSER	POET
"La Ermita di San Simon"	Mario Castelnuovo-Tedesco	Romançero español

MANZANARES: a river that runs through the city of Madrid.

SONG	COMPOSER	POET
"La maja de Goya"	Enrique Granados	Fernando Periquet

MARIE MADELEINE: the French name for the biblical personage, ★Mary Magdalene.

SONG	COMPOSER	POET
"Paganini"	Francis Poulenc	Louise de Vilmorin

MARJORAM: the popular name of a group of herbaceous plants belonging to the mint family. They grow wild in the Mediterranean region and in Asia, where they are sometimes given the name oregano. Several other kinds are cultivated in America. The plant stands one to two feet tall, bearing small white or purplish flowers. The sweet marjoram grown in American gardens can be used to flavor food and to perfume some soaps. (SOURCE: *Americana*, 2003)

SONG	COMPOSER	POET
"La Belle au bois dormant"	Claude Debussy	Vincent d'Hyspa

MARLING, BELLS OF: referring to the church bells in the town of Marling, which is located southwest of Merano, once part of Austria, now in the South Tyrol area of Italy, still disputed. Kuh spent the last years of his life in Marling. (SOURCE: Kimball, 1996)

SONG	COMPOSER	POET
"Ihr Glocken von Marling"	Wolfgang Fortner, Franz Liszt	Emil Kuh

MARMOTTE: (Fr.), a little monkey, puppet, grotesque figure, little chap.

SONG	COMPOSER	POET
"Lied der Marmottenbuben"	Ludwig van Beethoven	Johann Wolfgang von Goethe

MAROT, CLÉMENT (1496–1544): French poet. Marot was the son of a member of the Rhétoriqueur group, bourgeois poets who shared a preoccupation with rhetoric. Marot spent a great part of his life in the service of the French court, serving as *valet de chambre* to Francis I from 1527. Because of his Protestant sympathies he was arrested and exiled several times. After spending some time in Italy and Geneva, he enjoyed great popularity in the sixteenth century. Marot is credited with developing the ★rondeau and ★ballade form. In addition he introduced the ★elegy, eclogue, ★epigram, ★epithalamium and perhaps even the Petrarchian ★sonnet. For some two hundred years after his death his translation of the Psalms were frequently reprinted and also much admired by Calvin. By the end of his life he had written fifty-seven épîtres (epistles), ten satirical poems, ninety formally lyrical poems, a large number of epigrams, ★epitaphs, rondeaux, and chants royaux. Essentially a court poet, his writing is light, graceful, and amusing, with artificial simplicity. The poetry of Clément Marot was set by Maurice Ravel, Jean Françaix, and George Enescu. PRINCIPAL WORKS: *L'Adolescence Clémentine*, 1532; *Oeuvres*, 1538; *Trente psaumes de David*, 1587. SELECTED READING: George Joseph, *Clément Marot*, 1958; Robert Griffin, *Clément Marot and the Inflections of the Poetic Voice*, 1974; G. Hanisch, *Love Elegies of the Renaissance: Clément Marot, Louise Labé, and Pierre Ronsard*, 1979. (SOURCES: Steinberg, 3, 1973; Magill, 3, 1997)

MARRIED BEAU, THE; OR, THE CURIOUS IMPERTINENT: a play by John Crowne with music by Henry Purcell and John Eccles, produced in 1695 or 1696. The play was not much of a success, but the musical scenes played an important role, Crowne being more amenable than others to including music in his plays. In general, Purcell supplied music for the professional singers, and Eccles wrote simpler music for the actor/singers. Since the actor/singers could not manage to sing together, it was Purcell's task to write the many duets, unhampered by their limitations. Act 1 begins with Mr. Lovely, newly married, asking his friend Polidor to test his new wife's fidelity by trying to seduce her. She fails the test. Act 2: Squire Thorneback sings and dances, making Sir John envious and impressing Mrs. Lovely. Sir John humiliates Mrs. Lovely by exposing her adultery, and she leaves. Act 5: Mrs. Lovely is discovered alone and worried. She asks her maid, who is also alone in the world and thus sympathetic, to sing a reassuring song, "See Where Repenting Celia Lies," Purcell's only solo song for the play. The song is a passionate lament that puts the singer in the depths of despair, after which Mrs. Lovely is reborn through repentance. (SOURCE: Price, 1984)

MARTIN, SAINT; SANT MARTÍ: Spanish saint, the patron saint of social justice. Martin de Porres (1579–1639) was the illegitimate son of a Spanish grandee and a free black woman of Lima, Peru. First apprenticed to a barber surgeon, Martin later became a lay brother in the Dominican order. His nights were spent in prayer and his days in devotion to the poor of all races. His charity and holiness were recognized by all who knew him. Saint Martin died at the age of sixty and was beatified in 1887. (SOURCES: Thurston, Attwater, 1963; Farmer, 1997)

SONG	COMPOSER	POET
1. "Sant Martí"	Federico Mompou	Père Ribot
2. "Euphonium Dance"	Betty Roe	Jacqueline Froom

MARTIN, SAINT (ca. 316–397): French saint, one of the patron saints of France, former Roman legionary who converted to Christianity. Martin was born in Hungary, was educated in Italy, where he joined the Roman army, and was sent to Gaul. There legend has it that, coming across a beggar shivering in rags, Martin cut his cloak in half and wrapped the beggar in half of it. Two years later he converted and spent a period as a recluse on Gallinaria, a desert island near Genoa. Then he joined the followers of St. Hillary, bishop of Poitiers as an exorcist, founding the first monastery in all Gaul. His fame as a preacher was so great that the Christians of Tours invited Martin to be their bishop (371). Having spent the remaining years of his life in prayer and contemplation, Martin died in his small cell in 397. As his followers took his body to the final resting place, dead foliage turned green, flowers appeared, birds sang. It was the first "St. Martin's Summer." (SOURCE: Delaney, 1980)

SONG	COMPOSER	POET
"Le Disparu"	Francis Poulenc	Robert Desnos

MARTÍNEZ SIERRA, GREGORIO (1881–1947) AND MARÍA (1874–1974): Spanish dramatists and poets. Gregorio Martínez Sierra was born and educated in Madrid. After graduation he joined the semi-professional Spanish Art Theatre as an actor, remaining with it for ten years, during which time he worked as a journalist and turned out a series of novels. After marriage, he and his wife María Lejarrada, a poet born in Argentina, wrote jointly for a time and then collaborated under the husband's name in plays and two volumes of verse. During 1907 and 1908 Martínez Sierra traveled widely, returned to Madrid, writing his own plays, adapting and translating fifty plays by foreign dramatists. With the success of his 1911 play *The Cradle Song*, Martínez Sierra organized his own theater company, for which he wrote forty plays with and without his wife. In 1927 he brought his company to New York and in 1931 spent some time in Hollywood. During the Civil War his sympathies were with Franco, and he exiled himself to Buenos Aires. After the war he returned to Madrid, where he died. His warm, unabashedly romantic writing and his strong leaning toward realistic mysticism were influenced by the works of ★Maeterlinck. Manuel de Falla set some of the Martínez Sierras' writings to music and collaborated with him on *El amor brujo*, 1915, and *El sombrero de tres picos*, 1949. PRINCIPAL WORKS in English translation: *The Cradle Song*, 1917; *Theater of Dreams*, 1918; *Poor John*, 1920; *The Kingdom of God,* 1922; *The Road to Happiness*, 1927; *A Lily Among Thorns*, 1930; *Spring in Autumn*, 1933. SELECTED READING: A. F. G. Bell, *Contemporary Spanish Literature*. (SOURCE: Kunitz, Haycraft, 1942)

MARUTS: storm clouds, one of Gustave Holst's *Vedic Hymns*.

SONG	COMPOSER	POET
"Maruts"	Gustave Holst	*Rig Veda*, trans. G. Holst

MARY, MARIA: *see* ★VIRGIN MARY, THE.

MARY MAGDALENE: a saint, follower of ★Jesus. The name Magdalene recalls her town of origin, Magdala in Galilee. The New Testament singles her out among the women who accompanied Jesus from Galilee. It points out the role she played as witness to the death. Two gospels specify her personal encounter with the risen Jesus and her report of the resurrection to others. Some have been led to connect her to the sinful woman of Luke 7.36–50, but modern authorities find no basis for this belief. (SOURCE: *Americana*, 2003)

SONG	COMPOSER	POET
1. "Jesus bettelt"	Arnold Schönberg	Richard Dehmel
2. "Paganini"	Francis Poulenc	Louise de Vilmorin

MASEFIELD, JOHN (1878–1967): English poet, playwright, novelist, born in Herefordshire. His parents having died when he was young, he was brought up by an aunt who was unsympathetic to Masefield's literary ambitions. He enlisted in the merchant navy and was positioned on a training ship, on whose second voyage Masefield left the ship in New York City. In the United States he worked as a bartender and in a carpet factory. In 1897 he returned to London, determined to be a writer. While struggling to make a living in his twenties, he had the friendship of William Butler ★Yeats, Lawrence Binyon, and John Millington ★Synge. He began to write poems with the flavor of his youthful experiences. In 1911 he achieved fame with the publication of his narrative poem "The Everlasting Mercy," in which he used brawls and lusty language new to poetry of the time. In World War I he worked with the Red Cross. His prose studies that followed were "Gallipoli," 1916, "The Old Front Line," 1917, "Battle of the Somme," 1919. Masefield settled near Oxford and continued his prolific output of plays and novels. He was named poet laureate in 1930. The poetry of John Masefield has been set by John Ireland, A. Walter Kramer, Charles Griffes, and Robert Ward. PRINCIPAL WORKS: Poetry: *Salt Water Ballads*, 1902; *Ballads*, 1903; *Collected Poems*, 1923; *In the Mill*, 1941; *New Chum*, 1944. Novels: *Sard Harker*, 1924; *Odtaa*, 1926. SELECTED READING: Paul Binding, *An Endless Quiet Valley*, 1998; Constance Babbington, *John Masefield*, 1978. (SOURCE: Hamilton, 1994)

MASQUE: a form of elaborate entertainment of the sixteenth and seventeenth centuries. It consisted of scenes on allegorical, mythological, or humorous subjects that contained singing, dancing, dialogue, and instrumental accompaniment. During the sixteenth century the music was largely in the style of madrigals. By the end of that century a new style of writing, monodic with a melody and accompaniment, was utilized. Recitative made its first appearance during the seventeenth-century masques, becoming very popular. Later in that century masques were often interpolated into Restoration plays, the music of many being composed by Henry Purcell. Ben ★Jonson was perhaps the most celebrated of the writers of masques.

MASS: (Lat.), *missa*, from the mass dismissal, "*Ite missa est*," (Go, it is ended). *Mass* is the word commonly used to designate official worship in the Catholic Church, the gathering together of worshipers around the altar to hear the word of God. (SOURCE: Nevins, 1964)

SONG	COMPOSER	POET
"Berceuse"	Francis Poulenc	Max Jacob

MASSACRE OF PARIS, THE: a play by Nathaniel ★Lee, produced in 1689, with one song by Henry Purcell. The plot concerns the final scenes of the extermination of the Huguenots during the reign of Charles IX. The king, filled with guilt, tries to oppose his mother's plan to annihilate the Huguenots, but realizes, after a wakeful night, that he cannot stave off the vast conspiracy. A ★Genius appears, telling Charles that divine power will intercede if he repents. Lee did not ask for music for the Genius, but Purcell transformed his act 5 speech into a song, "Thy Genius, Lo!" "Thy Genius, Lo!" is a set piece for the baritone who plays the Genius, in which the king is given good advice and a warning. The second version (1695) for treble voice, set entirely in recitative, is not as effective a concert piece as the first. The Genius is meant to model Charles's guilty conscience. (SOURCE: Price, 1984)

MATINS: the first of the canonical hours of the Divine Office, composed of psalms, scriptural readings, lessons, homilies, antiphons, responses. It is sometimes called the night office and dates back to vigils that preceded the Eucharistic Assembly in Lille, France in 1881, held as a means of answering growing secularism in the Catholic Church. (SOURCE: Nevins, 1964)

SONG	COMPOSER	POET
"Les Angélus"	Claude Debussy	Guy le Roy

MATTHISSON, FRIEDRICH VON (1761–1831): a German poet. Born in Magdeburg, Matthisson studied at Halle and acquired Duke Friedrich of Württemberg as a patron. He supported himself as a private tutor, theater director, and librarian. In Schubert's time, Matthisson was a very popular poet whose works were admired for their elegance and sentiment, prompting Beethoven, Weber, Hugo Wolf, and Johann Reichardt to set his poetry and inspiring Schubert to set twenty-nine texts by him, including the celebrated "Adelaide," D95 (1814), "Andenken," and "Der Geistertanz." (SOURCE: Reed, 1997)

MAUCLAIR, CAMILLE (pseudonym of Camille Faust) (1872–1945): French poet, novelist, art critic, and travel writer. Mauclair championed ★Impressionism and ★Symbolism and was a prolific author of great flexibility. Eventually he abandoned poetry and the novel to produce books on writers, musicians, painters, and interesting places. Mauclair co-founded the Théâtre de l'Oeuvre. His novel *Le Soleil des morts*, 1898, is a worshipful picture of ★Mallarmé still in print. The poetry of Camille Mauclair was set by Ernst Bloch, Ernest Chausson, and Gustave Charpentier. (SOURCE: France, 1995)

MAUNDY THURSDAY: Thursday of Holy Week, which encompasses the days from Palm Sunday to Easter Sunday. Maundy Thursday refers to the events of the night of the Last Supper: ★Jesus washes the feet of his disciples; Jesus institutes Holy Communion during the Last Supper; the agony in the Garden of Gethsemane; Jesus' betrayal by ★Judas; Jesus' arrest, trial, and torture.

SONG	COMPOSER	POET
"Trova"	Fernando Obradors	folk poetry

MAUPASSANT, GUY DE (1850–1893): French writer of short stories and novelist, born in Normandy. Maupassant wrote vivid, brutal stories that made him one of the most popular French writers with the English-speaking public. His short stories were dramatic, restrained, and rich in surprise effects. Often called the father of today's short story, he wrote in a tense, impatient style. Many of his most memorable stories present greedy Norman peasants, thrifty farmers, and women of low moral character. Maupassant died in an insane asylum. (SOURCE: *Americana*, 2003)

SONG	COMPOSER	POET
"La Grenouillère"	Francis Poulenc	Guillaume Apollinaire

MAXIMIN: a literary creation of Stefan ★George, commonly recognized as the key to George's mature poetry, "the embodiment of a primeval force, a universally present ★Eros" (Jason, 5, 2003). George used *Maximin* in his work *The Seventh Ring* as a symbol for the manner in which eternal, divine forces were manifest in the modern world. (SOURCE: Jason, 5, 2003)

MAY: a kinsman, a relative by marriage; also, hawthorn blossoms.

SONG	COMPOSER	POET
1. "Spring, the Sweet Spring"	Dominick Argento	Thomas Nashe
2. "The Faucon"	John Edmunds	sixteenth-century English traditional song

MAYAKOVSKY, VLADIMIR (1893–1930): Russian poet and dramatist. Mayakovsky was the son of a forest ranger in Georgia. Later living in Moscow, Mayakovsky became involved in the Bolshevik movement and had been arrested three times by the age of sixteen on charges of anti-tsarist activities. He began to write verses while serving five months in prison in solitary confinement. When released, his talent for drawing led him to the Moscow School of Painting, Sculpture and Architecture (1910). His next step was to enter into the ranks of the cubo-★futurists who were interested in avant-garde painting and freeing the arts from academic tradition. When the Bolsheviks came to power (1917), he was enthusiastic. In his first play, *Vladimir Mayakovsky, A Tragedy*, he performed the title role. He wrote various verses—poems, marches, children's poetry, communist jingles for the state, and several film scenarios. His goal was to bring art closer to normal speech, in which effort he mixed rhythmic patterns, creative typesetting styles on the page, his view influencing Louis ★Aragon and Pablo Neruda greatly. When, in 1935, Stalin proclaimed that a lack of admiration for Mayakovsky's work was a crime against the state, his place in the literary history of Russia was secure. His poetry was set by Anton Rubenstein. PRINCIPAL WORKS: *Oblako v shtanakh*, 1915, *The Cloud in Trousers*, 1933; *Fleyta– pozvonochnik*, 1915, *The Backbone Flute*, 1960; *Lyublyu*, 1922, *I Love*, 1960.

SELECTED READING: L. Stahlberger, *The Symbolic System of Mayakovsky*, 1964; W. Woroszylski, *The Life of Mayakovsky*, 1970. (SOURCE: Rees, 1992)

MAYKOV (MAIKOV), APOLLON (1821–1897): Russian poet and translator. Maykov was born in Moscow of a noble, cultured family, his painter father a member of the Academy of Arts, his mother a writer of verse and prose, and one of his brothers a noted literary critic. In 1834 his family moved to St. Petersburg, where their house became a famous salon. Initially Maykov wanted to be a painter, but he began to write poetry at fifteen. Commencing his study of law at the University of St. Petersburg, he then turned to ancient history and the Latin poets. Maykov remained an amateur poet after serving in the guards and holding important civil service posts. He tried his hand at odes, fables, ★epigrams, occasional poetry, and wrote two tragedies. His versions of psalms and spiritual odes are the best of these works. However, he is best known for his epics that follow French and Italian models but have Russian detail and vernacular language to enliven them. Readers who enjoyed these epics most were those who were familiar with Greek mythology, its French treatment in ★parody, and the Russian literature. Maykov was given the ★Pushkin Prize in 1880, after which religious themes dominated his late work. Highly revered during his life, Maykov was given only a modest place in Russian letters after his death. He strove for harmony, beauty, and objectivity, but much of his poetry was static, although he was at his best in idyllic genres and songs about harvesting or haymaking. The poetry of Apollon Maykov has been set by Rimsky-Korsakov, Rachmaninoff, Tschaikovsky, César Cui, and Mily Balakirev. WORKS in English: *From Apollodorus Gnosticus*, 1877–93; *On Angling*, 1855. Some antiquated translations appear in John Pollen's *Russian Songs and Lyrics*, 1917. (SOURCE: Kunitz, Colby, 1967)

MAYRHOFER, JOHANN (1787–1836): a melancholy Austrian poet, friend of Franz Schubert and one of the early members of the Schubert circle. If it is true, as Dietrich Buxtehude is reputed to have said, that a professional composer should be able to set a menu to music, Mayrhofer could be described as a menu writer. Mayrhofer's poetry is certainly not doggerel, but he remains essentially a minor poet. His works are not quoted in anthologies of "great" German poetry; his activities are not chronicled in textbooks treating German Romantic poetry. Were it not for his friendship and collaboration with Schubert, he would be totally forgotten. Mayrhofer provided Schubert with texts for forty-seven songs, one singspiel, and one opera. He supplied more poetic texts for Schubert than did ★Heine (6), ★Klopstock (13), ★Schiller (31), or Wilhelm ★Müller (45). In 1817 alone, Schubert set twenty Mayrhofer poems. Only the fifty-eight poems of ★Goethe set by Schubert exceed this number. Mayrhofer was born in Steyr, Austria on November 3, 1787. His first studies were undertaken for the purpose of entering the priesthood. Later, however, having left the church, he studied law at the University of Vienna and became a minor government official. He and Schubert met and became friends in August 1814, sharing rooms in Vienna from 1818 to 1820. The lack of creativity in his job, his severely depressed nature, and, possibly, his supposed homosexuality, overwhelmed Mayrhofer. He committed suicide in 1836, by jumping from the third story window of his office building. Inspired by Goethe and ★Schiller, Mayrhofer made extensive use of the themes of classical mythology in his poetry. While most German scholars would consider his works second rate, the poems made first-class *Lieder* in some cases. Schubert's first published song was "★Erlafsee," text by Mayrhofer. Other well-known Schubert songs with texts by Mayrhofer are "Auflösung," "Fahrt zum ★Hades," and "Nachtviolen." PRINCIPAL WORKS: *Gedichte*, 1824; *Erinnerungen an Franz Schubert*, 1829. SELECTED READING: Otto Erich Deutsch, *Schubert Memoirs by His Friends*, 1958. (SOURCES: Capell, 1957; Garland, 1976)

"May the God of Wit Inspire": a trio composed by Henry Purcell to a text written by Elkanah ★Settle for his work *The Fairie-Queene*, produced in 1692 and 1693. For plot details and placement of songs, *see ★Fairie-Queen, The*.

MAZURKA: a Polish dance resembling the polka, with two sliding steps instead of one.

SONG	COMPOSER	POET
"Mazurka"	Francis Poulenc	Louise de Vilmorin

McCULLERS, CARSON SMITH (1917–1967): American novelist and short story writer. McCullers was born in Georgia and wrote from the age of sixteen on. Having gone to New York to study music, she soon became more interested in writing, studying at Columbia and New York University at night (1934–36) and working at part-time jobs during the days. Once two of her short stories were bought, McCullers settled down to write as a profession. She met and married McCullers but separated from him after the success of her novel *The Heart is a Lonely Hunter*. By 1942 her career was flourishing but poor health dogged her. After finishing her successful play *The Member of the Wedding* (1946), McCullers suffered a series of strokes, but continued to write. The final plays were not admired or financially successful. The writing of Carson McCullers has been set by David Diamond. PRINCIPAL WORKS: *The Heart is a Lonely Hunter*, 1940; *Reflections in a Golden Eye*, 1941; *The Member of the Wedding*, 1946; *The Ballad of the Sad Café*, 1951; *The Mortgaged Heart* (short fiction, poetry, and essays), ed. Margarita G. Smith, 1971. SELECTED READING: Virginia Carr Spencer, *The Lonely Hunter: A Biography of Carson McCullers*, 1975. (SOURCE: Jason, 5, 2003)

MEANDER: a river-god of Phrygia. In ancient times every river had its own divine personality. The wandering Meander River owed its name to Maender, king of Pessinonte, who in the course of a war made a vow that, if he were victorious, he would immolate the first person who came to congratulate him. That first person was his son. Meander fulfilled his vow but, in his despair, threw himself into the river that took his name. (SOURCE: Cooper, 1992)

SONG	COMPOSER	POET
"Ballet"	Francis Poulenc	Pierre Ronsard

MEDEA: in Greek legend a sorceress. The daughter of Acetes, the king of Colchis, Medea married the leader of the Argonauts, ★Jason, whom she helped to obtain the ★golden fleece.

MEI, LEV (1822–1862): Russian poet and dramatist. Mei was born in Moscow, son of an impoverished country squire of German descent. He was first educated at the private boarding school of the nobility of Moscow, later at the *Tsarskoe Selo Lyceum. After completing his studies, he served in the office of the Moscow governor general. As a writer of elegiac, idyllic, and nature poetry, he was basically skilled at versifying but without originality. His ballads in the style of folk poetry, based sometimes on medieval chronicles and saints' lives are undistinguished compared to those of Aleksei *Tolstoi. The verse of Lev Mei was set by Rimsky-Korsakov, Tchaikovsky, Mily Balakirev, Aleksandr Borodin, César Cui, and Modest Mussorgsky. PRINCIPAL WORKS in English: *To the Departed*, 1856; *The Village*, 1858; *Will-o'-the 'Wisp*, 1861. (SOURCE: Terras, 1991)

MÉLODIE: a distinct type of French song composition, markedly different from the earlier *romance*. There were two types of *romance*: in the first, expression has first place, structure is freer, and the piano part (revealing German influence) underlines the meaning of the words; in the second, the melodic line has a purely musical character (more Italian) that does not specially underline its meaning, but does not contradict it either. The *mélodie* form emerged at the end of the nineteenth century owing to three factors: the lowering of the artistic level of the *romance* making evident the need for another vocal form; the popularity of Schubert's songs said to have "killed" the *romance*; and the new romantic poetry whose texts inspired new styles and techniques. The *romance* was at one time a literary form only, the text naive and usually a sentimental love story meant solely to charm for a moment. Martini raised the artistic level of the romance with "Plaisir d'amour," but after 1815 the serious composers became disinterested in the triviality of the *romance*. The *mélodie* was at first considered to fall midway between a *romance* and a *lied*. Later, free structure took the place of strophic form, recitatives were added to the square phrase, and the piano took on a more important role in interpreting the text. Berlioz was the first French composer to title his songs *mélodies*. Meyerbeer and Liszt soon followed. (SOURCE: Noske, 1970)

MÉLODIES POPULAIRES GRECQUES: *see* GRECQUES, MÉLODIES POPULAIRES.

MELODRAMA, MÉLODRAME (Fr.): from the Greek μέλος, *tune* and δράμα, *action*; originally an eighteenth-century operatic term to indicate a composition with music accompanying either dialogue or mime, this done by the protagonist in the pauses of, and later during the musical accompaniment. The Italian term *melodramma* meant simply a musical drama or opera, such as the dungeon scene from *Fidelio* or the Wolf's Glen scene in *Der Freischütz*. In song literature examples are: "Abschied von der Erde" by Schubert, "Die Flüchtlinge" by Robert Schumann, "Enoch Arden" by Strauss, and "Music" from *Love's Labor Lost*, by Gerald Finzi. *Expressions lyriques* (1913), a work of great originality by Jules Massenet, contains ten pieces in which sung passages alternate with declaimed sections. (SOURCE: Steinberg, 1, 1973)

MELUSINA, MÉLISANDE (Fr.): the most famous of all fairies of French romance. Melusina enclosed her father in a high mountain for offending her mother, who was condemned to become every Saturday a serpent from the waist down. Her mother, after her marriage, had asked her husband for a vow that he would never visit her on a Saturday. The husband hid himself on the forbidden day and saw his wife's transformation. The mother was obliged to leave her husband and was destined to wander as a specter until the day of doom. (SOURCE: Guirand, 1968)

SONG	COMPOSER	POET
"Sonetti delle Fate"	Gian Francesco Malipiero	Angelo Polizano

MELVILLE, HERMAN (1819–1891): American novelist and poet. Born in New York City, Melville left school and educated himself after the failure of his father's mercantile business in 1832. In 1839 he sailed on a merchant ship to Liverpool, next shipped on a whaler to the South Seas (1841), then jumped ship and joined the U.S. Navy. Three years later he began writing, using his plentiful experiences. *Typee* and *Omoo* (1847), fictionalized travel narratives, were very popular with the reading public. Married with four children and forced to support his family, he wrote sea stories that he called "potboilers," after which he changed his next sea tale into an unsuccessful novel, *Moby-Dick.* When writing anonymous magazine stories and doing lecture tours failed to succeed, Melville worked as a customs officer at the New York harbor. He died forgotten, with *Billy Budd, Foretopman,* a long short story, still in manuscript form. *Billy Budd* was adapted by Benjamin Britten's librettists for the opera of that name. Melville enlarged the range of American fiction and created a national prose epic for America: *Moby-Dick.* Hugo Weisgall and David Diamond have set the words of Herman Melville in songs. PRINCIPAL WORKS: *Typee, or a Peep at Polynesian Life,* 1846; *Omoo: A Narrative of Adventures in the South Seas,* 1847; *Moby-Dick,* 1851; *Clarel,* 1876; *Billy Budd,* 1924. SELECTED READING: Leon Howard, *Herman Melville: A Biography,* 1951; Warner Berthoff, *The Example of Melville,* 1962. (SOURCES: Drabble, 2000; Unger, 3, 1974)

MEMNON: an Ethiopian prince, son of Tithonius and *Aurora, ally of the Trojans in their war against the Greeks. Memnon was slain by Achilles. The statue of Amenhotep III at *Thebes on the banks of the Nile was associated with him and is known as the "vocal Memnon." When the first rays of the morning sun fall upon this statue, a sound is heard to issue from it, which is compared to the snapping of a harp string. (SOURCE: *Bulfinch,* 1978)

SONG	COMPOSER	POET
1. "Four Ladies"	David Diamond	Ezra Pound
2. "Memnon"	Franz Schubert	Johann Mayrhofer

MENDÈS, CATULLE (1841–1909): French poet, dramatist, novelist, and critic. Catulle Mendès led an uneventful personal life. An unhappy first marriage, to Théophile *Gautier's daughter, was followed by a second, successful one. The periodical he founded, *La Revue fantaisiste,* served as a center for poetic discussion among the older and younger members of the *Parnassian group: *Gautier, *Baudelaire, *Leconte de L'Isle, *Banville, *Claudel, and *Sully Prudhomme. One of the most active of the Parnassian poets and a prolific writer, Mendès insisted that his group was not a school or an official movement, but that it sought full use of artistic techniques rather than the romantic expressions of emotion. A partisan of verse drama, he was further distinguished by the wide range of his subjects as well as his devotion to the works of Richard Wagner in France. Catulle Mendès wrote several librettos for Chabrier, Massenet, and Hahn, and his verse was set by Gabriel Fauré and Émile Saint-Saëns. PRINCIPAL WORKS: *Philoméla*, 1864; *Soirs moroses*, 1876; *Poésies*, 1876; *Richard Wagner*, 1886; *Poésies nouvelles*, 1893; *La Grive des vignes*, 1895. (SOURCES: Steinberg, 3, 1973; Kunitz, Haycraft, 1942)

MENELAUS: son of ★Atreus, younger brother of Agamemnon, king of Sparta, and the husband of ★Helen, by whom he became the father of Hermione. When Paris, prince of Troy, abducted Helen, Menelaus called for aid from his brother Agamemnon, who organized an expedition against Troy. After the death of Paris, Menelaus and Helen reconciled and returned to Sparta, the first to leave Troy. (SOURCE: Kaster, 1964)

MENTIDERO: a small eighteenth-century square in the city of Madrid, which now serves as the entrance to the Calle del León.

SONG	COMPOSER	POET
"La maja dolorosa, 3"	Enrique Granados	Fernando Periquet

MEPHISTOPHELES, MEPHISTO: the fabricated name of a devil or familiar spirit, appearing first in the late medieval ★Faust legend. It is possible that the name was created from three Greek words meaning "not loving the light." In ★Goethe's *Faust*, Mephistopheles is the evil spirit who, with wit and charm, persuaded Faust to sell his soul. His name and the adjective *Mephistophelean* are often used to describe a fiendish but sophisticated tempter.

SONG	COMPOSER	POET
"Flohlied des Mephisto"	L. van Beethoven, M. Mussorgsky, F. Busoni	Johann Wolfgang v. Goethe

MEREDITH, GEORGE (1828–1909): English poet, novelist, and writer of short stories. Meredith was the son of an indigent Portsmouth tailor, educated in Portsmouth and Southsea, and in Germany at a Moravian school. He himself published his first book of poems (admired by ★Tennyson) in 1851. His first major novel caused scandal but brought him the friendship of Carlyle and the ★Pre-Raphaelites. In 1860 Meredith became a reader for a publishing firm, which job lasted until 1894. His steady output of poetry and novels caused his reputation to grow with the public. By the time he died, Meredith had been writing for fifty years and had become a revered man of letters, sought out by younger writers such as Henry James, Thomas ★Hardy, and Robert Louis ★Stevenson. Meredith garnered most praise for his perceptive portrayal of women, his narrative skills, and his incisive dialogue. These days neither his poetry nor his novels have enjoyed popular or critical approval due to the intricacy of his prose. The poetry of George Meredith has been set by Aaron Copland and Margaret Ruthven Lang. PRINCIPAL WORKS: *The Egoist*, 1879; *Poems* *and Lyrics of the Joy of Earth*, 1883; *Diana of the Crossways*, 1885. SELECTED READING: G. Beer, *Meredith: A Change of Masks*, 1970. (SOURCE: Drabble, 2000)

MEREZHKOVSKY, DIMITRI (1865–1941): Russian poet and religious philosopher. Born in St. Petersburg, Merezhkovsky studied at the university there and began a literary career as early as 1883, when his verse began to appear in liberal magazines. He was recognized as the most promising of the younger ★civic poets, his early verse showing a care for form and diction and more elegance than his contemporaries. His popularity was very great among the advanced thinkers and the young. Merezhkovsky was a minor poet of substantial skill but without a unique voice; his favorite words were *mystery, polar,* and *synthesis.* He began writing with some competent nature poetry and narrative verse, moved on to programmatic poems, then in later poems progressed to ★Symbolist verse, which now appears shallow. The poetry of Dimitri Merezhkovsky was set by Tchaikovsky, Rachmaninoff, and Aleksandr Cherepnin. PRINCIPAL WORKS: *Poems: 1883–1887,* 1888; *Symbols, Songs, and Poems,* 1892; *Leonardo da Vinci,* 1895; *Children of Night,* 1896. (SOURCE: Terras, 1991; Mirsky, 1958)

MERLIN: Historically a Welsh or British bard born near the end of the fifth century. Merlin is said to have become a bard of King ★Arthur and to have died after the terrible battle that took place around 570 between the Britons and their Saxon enemies. The real Merlin's story has been intermixed with that of the magician Merlin in Arthurian romance. This Merlin was the son of a maiden who had been seduced by a friend. By being baptized he was rescued from Satan's power and became adept at Necromancy. The enchantress Nimue charmed him and then shut him up in a rock. Later, the Lady of the Lake used her spells to ensnare Merlin in a thornbush, where he still sleeps, his voice sometimes heard by passers-by. (SOURCE: Cooper, 1992)

SONG	COMPOSER	POET
1. "Koptisches Lied I"	Hugo Wolf	Johann Wolfgang Goethe
2. "Le Carafon"	Francis Poulenc	Maurice Carême

MESSALINA, VALERIA (ca. 18–48): the third wife of Emperor Claudius and the mother of his children Octavia and Britannicus. Messalina's father was a relative of Claudius and her mother the aunt of ★Nero. She and Claudius were married a few years before his accession to the throne in 41. Sources who disliked her painted Messalina in the blackest colors. They stated that Claudius was so blinded by his love that he overlooked her plots and frequent unfaithfulness, that she took bribes, promoted executions, indulged in sexual excesses so flagrant that the palace became almost a brothel. She even held a public wedding ceremony with Gaius Silius, mocking or defying Claudius, that was perhaps a prelude to an attempted coup against the emperor. When Claudius got word of the plot, he ordered Messalina's execution in 48. (SOURCE: *Americana,* 2003)

SONG	COMPOSER	POET
"Messalina"	Benjamin Britten	W. H. Auden

METASTASIO, PIETRO ANTONIO (1698–1782): Italian poet and dramatist. Pietro Metastasio was born in Rome. His original name was Antonio Domenico Bonaventur Trapassi, but it was changed by his adopted father, who was in the papal service. Metastasio's talent at improvisation and singing was apparent at an early age. He studied in Calabria and in Rome; then in 1715 he began the study of law. Metastasio's first writing was published in ★Naples in 1717, *Poesie*. With the death of his patron Metastasio received a bequest of his library and a large sum of money. He practiced law in Naples and became at the same time the most renowned poet of this period. With a constant presence in the salons and academies, Metastasio encountered members of the imperial Austrian court who were to be his future protectors. Having met the composers Alessandro Scarlatti and Nicola Porpora as well as Marianna Bulgarelli, a great singer, he created his first melodrama, *Didone*, in 1723. *Didone* was to have a lasting success and be set by forty some composers. Persuaded by Bulgarelli, Metastasio left for Vienna, where he enjoyed the favor of Emperor Charles VI. Here his operatic masterpieces *Adriano in Sirio* and *Attilio Regolo* were to be successful. He continued his success during the reign of Maria Teresa. With her death in 1780, Metastasio no longer was considered the most brilliant of playwrights. Metastasio's greatest works were done during the rule of Charles VI, with more human situations and improved verse, resulting in some 800 opera librettos. His work *La Clemenza di Tito* (set to music by Mozart) was much admired by Voltaire. When Schubert began formal studies with Salieri in 1812, he was assigned various passages from Metastasio to set as solos and ensembles. In 1827 Franz Schubert wrote his op. 83, a set of three Italian songs for bass on Metastasio texts. They were intended for Luigi Lablache (1794–1858), an Italian bass of French/Irish descent, the greatest basso of his age, with a prodigious technique and famous for both his dramatic and comic performances. They are "three wonderful bass studies, three completely untypical, technically skilled works, which stand outside the Schubertian canon" (Fischer-Dieskau, 1987). Only the first and second songs are credited to Metastasio, despite the dedication. Metastasio's verses also were set in songs by Mozart, Haydn, Schubert, Beethoven, Rossini, Louise Reichardt, Johann Hasse, and Thomas Arne, who also set Metastasio's libretto *Artaxerxes* as an opera. PRINCIPAL WORKS: *Poesie*, 6 vols., 1717; *Opere*, 12 vols., 1780–82, newest ed. Brunelli, 3 vols., 1943–52; *Dramas and Other Poems*, trans. J. Hoole, 3 vols., 1800. SELECTED READING: Charles Burney, *The Life and Letters of Metastasio*, 3 vols., 1943–52. (SOURCE: Kunitz, Colby, 1967)

MÉTRO: a slang word for the Paris subway, the Métropolitain.

SONG	COMPOSER	POET
"Vous n'écrivez plus"	Francis Poulenc	Max Jacob

MEYER, CONRAD (1825–1898): Swiss poet and novelist. Meyer was born in Zürich and died there. Having been afflicted with neuroses and delusions as a young man, Meyer finally suffered a breakdown. He consented to be committed to an asylum (1852), then returned home after seven months. After his mother was sent to the same asylum, she drowned herself; her death appeared to liberate Meyer. In 1892 he once again was sent back to the asylum he had left forty years before. Released after a year, he spent the last five years of his life at home. Among those poets born in the first half of the twentieth century, he achieved the stature he did because of his originality, which imparted a richer quality to German literature. His style aimed at concreteness of presentation and the absorption of the visual arts into literature; his supreme craftsmanship was balanced by aloofness, stemming from his hypersensitivity. Conrad Meyer's poetry was set by Hans Pfitzner and Ottmar Schoeck, a fellow Swiss. PRINCIPAL WORKS: *Huttens letzte Tage*, 1871; *Gedichte*, 1882; *Jürg Jenatsch* (a novel), 1874; *Collected Poems*, 1892. SELECTED READING: A. Burkhard, *Conrad Ferdinand Meyer: The Style and the Man*, 1936. (SOURCE: Kaufman, 1962)

MÌ: Olivier Messiaen's nickname for his wife.

SONG	COMPOSER	POET
"Poèmes pour Mì"	Olivier Messiaen	Olivier Messiaen

MICHAEL, SAINT; SAINT MICHEL (Fr.): a biblical figure, an archangel, and a saint. In the Old Testament, St. Michael appears as the angel who speaks to Daniel and who takes particular care of the people of Israel (Daniel 10.13ff. and Daniel 12.1). In the New Testament, the Epistle of Jude (verse 9) recounts that St. Michael and Satan fought over the body of *Moses and that St. Michael defeated Satan by saying, "The Lord rebuke thee." In the book of Revelations (12.7ff.), St. Michael and his angels fought against the dragon, a symbol of Satan, and his fallen angels. St. Michael finally defeated the dragon, which was then cast out of Heaven. In Christian art St. Michael is depicted as a beautiful young man with a severe countenance, winged and lithe, clad in white or in armor, carrying a sword and a shield with which he fights a dragon. Mont-Saint-Michel, the most famous European shrine to St. Michael, is located in Normandy. There, a Benedictine abbey is dedicated to him in honor of an earlier apparition. St. Michael's feast day is September 29. (SOURCE: Farmer, 1997)

SONG	COMPOSER	POET
1. "Chanson épique"	Maurice Ravel	Paul Morand
2. "Christ's Sunday Morn"	Ernst Bacon	Old English
3. "Schmerzliche Morn"	Hugo Wolf	Emanuel Geibel, Paul Heyse
4. "Michaelskirchplatz"	Hans Pfitzner	Karl Busse
5. "Four Ladies"	David Diamond	Ezra Pound

MICHELANGELO: *see* *BUONARROTI.

MICKIEWICZ, ADAM (1798–1855): the national bard and prophet of Poland, comparable to *Goethe and *Pushkin. Mickiewicz embodied the soul of the Polish people, although he never saw them or their cities. Son of a lawyer and small landowner, Mickiewicz was born on a farm in a part of Lithuania that was populated predominantly by old Polish gentry. While studying philology at the University of Wilno, he belonged to a secret society that tried to influence public affairs. The Russian police arrested him for plotting to spread Polish nationalism and sent him to St. Petersburg, where he stayed for four years. He was accepted into literary circles and befriended by Pushkin. He settled in Paris—where he met Chopin during the 1830s—just after the Polish Insurrection was defeated but spent his last years working for Polish independence and aiding the exiles who had escaped to France. His early poetry, written to be understood by the common man, symbolized the land, history, and daily life of the Polish. The last twenty years he wrote only a handful of poems, turning instead to religious and political works and to literary criticism. He died in Constantinople while trying to raise a Polish brigade to fight Russia in the Crimean War. By his efforts, Polish literature was elevated to a prominent place in world literature. His poetry was set by Tchaikovsky, Carl Loewe, and César Cui. PRINCIPAL WORKS in English translation: *Pan Tadeusz*, 1917; *Poems by Adam Mickiewicz*, 1944; *Adam Mickiewicz: Selected Poetry and Prose*, 1955; *Selected Poems*, 1956. SELECTED READING: David Welsh, *Adam Mickiewicz*, 1966. (SOURCE: Magill, 3, 1984)

MICKLE: (Scot.), *great in size or number.*

MIDAS: legendary king of Phrygia in Asia Minor. Because Midas had helped Silenus, Dionysus's old teacher, ★Dionysus (★Bacchus) offered the king anything he wanted. Midas asked that all he touched might be turned to gold. At first, Midas's power pleased him, but soon it became a curse, because even his food turned to gold the moment he touched it. When he prayed to Dionysus to help him, Dionysus said to go bathe in the river Pactolus. Midas washed himself and the magic touch left him, but the sands of the river turned to gold. According to legend, Midas acted as a judge at the musical contest between ★Apollo and ★Pan. When he awarded the prize to Pan, Apollo turned Midas's ears into those of an ass. Midas kept his ears covered because he was ashamed. Yet he could not hide his ears from the slave who acted as his barber. The slave, not daring to tell anyone, dug a hole in the ground and whispered the truth into it. Reeds grew out of the soil and spread the secret, whispering it when the wind blew. The phrase to "have the Midas touch" describes a person who makes money in everything he does. (SOURCE: Guirand, 1968)

SONG	COMPOSER	POET
"King Midas"	Ned Rorem	Howard Moss

MIGNON: a young girl character in ★Goethe's ★*Wilhelm Meister*. Mignon is described as "a girl in boy's clothes, about thirteen years of age, her body well formed. Her countenance was not regular but striking, her brow full of mystery, her nose extremely beautiful, her mouth, although it seemed too closely shut for one of her age and though she often drew it to a side, had yet an air of frankness and was very lovely." Mignon is the daughter of the ★Harper and his own sister. Guilt over this sin had caused the Harper, then mad, to wander about the world far from Italy. Mignon, although born in Italy, was abducted by nomads and carried to Germany, where she sings and dances in a traveling troupe of entertainers. Here Wilhelm finds her singing with the Harper. Neither has deduced that she is his daughter from his former illicit relationship with his own sister. "Nur wer die Sehnsucht kennt," known as "Mignon's Song," was set by Beethoven, Schumann, Wolf, Tchaikovsky, Carl Loewe, Carl Zelter, and forty-nine others. Schubert called it "Lied der Mignon," Loewe and Zelter titled it "Sehnsucht," and it was named "None but the Lonely Heart" by Tchaikovsky. "Kennst du das Land," another of Mignon's songs, was set by eighty-four composers, Schumann and Zelter among them. It was called "Mignon" when set by Beethoven and Wolf, titled "Mignon's Gesang" by Schubert, and set under the name "Mignon's Lied" by Liszt and Tchaikovsky. "So lasst mich scheinen" was set by Robert Schumann, Johann Reichardt, John Duke, and seventeen other composers under various titles, by Schubert under "Mignon II," and by Wolf as "Mignon III." Among the seventeen who made settings of "Heiss mich nicht reden" were Wolf, Reichardt, Zelter, Beethoven, Loewe, Schubert, Schumann, Liszt, Tchaikovsky, John Duke, Gaspare Spontini, Nicolai Medtner, and Erich Wolff. The poet Victor Wilder wrote, in the style of Goethe, a poem called "Romance de Mignon," which was set by Henri Duparc. *See also* ★HARPER, THE. (SOURCE: Drabble, 1985)

MILLAY, EDNA ST. VINCENT (1892–1950): American poet and playwright. Edna Millay (known to her family as Sefe or Vincent) was born in Rockland, Maine. Her parents separated when their three talented daughters were tiny, and it was the mother who brought up the family. Edna Millay had no formal education until, in her twenties, she was sent for a short time to Barnard College and then to Vassar, from which she graduated in 1917, already an established poet after the publication of *Renascence and Other Poems*. When Millay moved to New York City, she quickly became the darling of Greenwich Village, a bohemian rebel, a new "free" woman, an actress, a playwright, and a satirist. She was famous for her many love affairs, especially the one with young Edmund Wilson. It was her second book, *A Few Figs from Thistles*, that included her most famous quotation: "My candle burns at both ends; / It will not last the night / But ah, my foes, and oh, my friends— / It gives a lovely light." Millay published two more collections of verse. *The Harp-Weaver and Other Poems* won the 1923 Pulitzer Prize. At the end of 1923 she married a business man with whom she lived in New York. After her several nervous breakdowns, the couple moved to a farm in upstate New York, where Millay wrote steadily. She lived in seclusion until her death. Between the two world wars Millay's reputation was roughly what Sylvia ★Plath's is today. Millay's verse boasted a firm, musical, economical line, but to the modern ear her ★sonnets sometimes exhibit excessive pathos. Her one-act plays are still performed in American schools. Edna St. Vincent Millay's poetry has been set by John Duke, Miriam Gideon, Sven Lekberg, Judith Zaimont, John Musto, and William Bolcom, among other composers. PRINCIPAL WORKS: *A Few Figs from Thistles*, 1920; *The Harp-Weaver and Other Poems*, 1923; *The Buck in the Snow*, 1928; *Wine from These Grapes*, 1934; *Conversation at Midnight*, 1937; *Bright these Arrows*, 1940. (SOURCE: Hamilton, 1994)

MILONGO: a type of Argentine popular dance song that employs the familiar habanera rhythm.

MILOSZ, CZESLAW (1911–2004): Polish poet, novelist, essayist, and translator. Milosz was born in Lithuania, which was the last European country to adopt Christianity. This meant a survival of pagan attitudes toward nature that Milosz adopted in his writings. His father was a civil engineer who was drafted into the Russian army in World War I; therefore he stayed in Russia for the conflict. After the Bolsheviks seized power, the Milosz family went to the Polish city Wilno. The boy went to Catholic school for eight years, then to the University of Wilno where he took a master's degree, soon receiving a fellowship from the government for study in Paris (1934–35). When Lithuania became a republic of the Socialist Soviet movement (1940), Milosz went to Warsaw, where he wrote poetry and studied English. After Warsaw was virtually destroyed, he was selected for the diplomatic corps and worked in Washington, D.C. (1946–50). Milosz broke with the Warsaw regime in 1951 and worked as a freelance journalist in Paris, then lectured at the University of California, Berkeley (1960–61), settling thereafter in Berkeley and taking American citizenship in 1970. In 1978 he retired as professor emeritus. Milosz's poetry earned him a Nobel Prize for literature in 1980, the culmination of a life spent in scholastic and literary efforts. His other efforts, however, were more widely known to the international reading public. Only a small amount of his poetry was translated into other languages, partially because it is so complex. The best way to appreciate Milosz's poetry is to read his other writings, such as his 1968 autobiographical *Native Realms: A Search for Self-Definition*. Other works of this type are *The Witness of Poetry* (1983) and the Charles Eliot Norton lectures at Harvard (1981–82). The wide scholarship and knowledge exhibited in these essay collections shows Milosz to be one of the leading polymaths of his time, historical circumstances having placed him at the center of the political and intellectual turmoil. More impressive is the fact that his poetry still affirms the beauty of the world and the value of life, despite his experiences of Nazi barbarism and Soviet tyranny. Eventually he moved back to Krakow, Poland, and remained there. The poetry of Jerzy Harasymowicz translated by Czelaw Milosz was set by Samuel Barber. PRINCIPAL WORKS in English: *Selected Poems*, 1973; *Bells in Winter*, 1978; *The Separate Notebooks*, 1984. SELECTED READING: Madeline G. Levine, *Contemporary Political Poetry, 1925–1975*, 1981. (SOURCE: Magill, 3, 1984)

MILTON, JOHN (1608–1674): English writer of sacred and secular themes. Son of a writer and composer of music, Milton was educated at St. Paul's School and Cambridge, where he began to write poetry while studying for the ministry. Upon leaving Cambridge, Milton began a course of private study for a future as a poet or a clergyman, while attempting to convince his father that the two vocations were compatible. After traveling in Italy (1638–39) where he met Galileo, Milton returned to London and spent many years writing pamphlets in defense of religious, domestic, and civil liberties. By 1652 he had become totally blind. Having publically tried to halt the tide of Royalism, Milton was arrested and fined at the time of the Restoration. When released, he returned to poetry for the first time in twenty years. Milton is appreciated as a writer of polemical prose and for his subtle lyricism, but his reputation rests primarily on *Paradise Lost*. A notion that Satan is the true hero of this poem has persisted despite the efforts of important writers to dismiss it. Others, including T. S. ★Eliot, complained of Milton's sensuousness. ★Dryden, however, described *Paradise Lost* as "one of the most noble and sublime poems." John Milton's poetry has been set by Haydn, Charles Ives, Ross Finney, Henry Lawes, and Thomas

Arne. PRINCIPAL WORKS: *L'Allegro and Il Penseroso*, 1631–32; *Comus*, 1637; *Poems*, 1645, 1673; and *Paradise Lost*, 1671. SELECTED READING: S. Davies, *John Milton*, 1991; C. Ricks, *Milton's Grand Style*, 1963. (SOURCE: Drabble, 2000)

MIMAAMAQUIM: the Hebrew name for the first line in Psalm 130, "Out of the depths have I cried unto thee, O Lord."

SONG	COMPOSER	POET
"Mimaamaquim"	Arthur Honegger	Psalm 130

MINERVA: Roman goddess of wisdom and patroness of the arts and crafts. In fable, Minerva sprang, with a tremendous battle cry and fully armed, from the brain of ★Jupiter, for which reason she is invoked to illustrate a sudden appearance. Later the Romans classified her together with the Greek Athene (Athena) as one of the three chief deities, the others being Jupiter and Juno. Minerva, also goddess of war, is represented as grave and imperial, wearing a helmet, and clad in drapery over a coat of mail. Minerva is believed to have invented the flute. While playing the flute before Juno and ★Venus, the goddesses laughed at the distorted face she made while blowing on the instrument. This caused Minerva to throw the flute away indignantly. (SOURCE: Cooper, 1992)

SONG	COMPOSER	POET
"Attributs"	Francis Poulenc	Pierre de Ronsard

MINIVER CHEEVY: *see* ★LUKE HAVERGAL.

MINNE: an obsolete word that means more than just *love*, rather love in its purest, noblest sense.

SONG	COMPOSER	POET
"Ich trage meine Minne"	Richard Strauss	Karl Henckell

MINNESINGER: the author of Minnesang, the first body of German poetry to rank as a part of world literature. The earliest traces of songs set to German texts in the manner of courtly love date from the end of the twelfth century. By the fourteenth century the Minnesang tradition was superseded by the more bourgeois Mastersinger rules.

MIRÓ, JUAN (1893–1983): Spanish artist. Miró was born near Barcelona. His art was influenced by the carnivals and the Catalonian street festivals of his boyhood. He became a leader in the ★Surrealist art movement in 1924. In great contrast to the Cubists who made art formal and severe, Miró made his paintings imaginative and gay. His playful subjects were freely drawn, sometimes growing out of accidental splashes of color. Miró sprinkled childlike symbols of men, women, even dogs on gaily colored landscapes, whose titles were often humorous, such as "Still Life with Old Shoe." To his images of space Miró adds lines and tiny blobs of color that are echoed by ★Éluard's word images in the Poulenc song. During Franco's regime Miró's painting became darker, dominated by night and by dream motifs with bold black strokes. (SOURCE: *Americana*, 2003)

SONG	COMPOSER	POET
"Juan Miró"	Francis Poulenc	Paul Éluard

MOABITE: an inhabitant of Moab. Moab was an ancient Near Eastern kingdom consisting of a fertile plateau blessed with abundant water that lay between the Dead Sea and the Arabian Desert. Moab formed what is now the southwest part of modern *Jordan. Settling the area before 1200 B.C.E., the Moabites reached a high level of culture by the 800s B.C.E. Their language and customs were similar to those of the Israelites, their neighbors. The supreme god of the Moabites was Chemosh. What is known of the Moabites comes from the Old Testament. The biblical personage Ruth, an ancestor of *David, was a Moabite. Moab was conquered by the Babylonians in 582 B.C.E. and then faded from history. (SOURCE: *Americana*, 2003)

SONG	COMPOSER	POET
"Miel de Narbonne"	Francis Poulenc	Jean Cocteau

MOCK MARRIAGE, THE: a play by Thomas Scott, produced in 1695, with two (one disputed) songs by Henry Purcell. Scott, an inexperienced playwright, followed a popular formula. Willmot is a ladies' man who needs reform; Clarinda is a match for him, even wears pants. Lady Barter (unfaithful wife), Marina (witty, inexperienced), and Sir Arthur (a fop) fill out the cast. Willmot hopes to take up his affair with Lady Barter again, but she is unhappy that he is infatuated with Clarinda. Act 3: Willmot hires musicians to serenade Lady Barter with "'Twas within a Furlong of Edinboro' Town." There is some doubt that this was written by Purcell. Act 4: Sir Arthur boasts that he composed a piece and arranges a private concert for friends, asking a pretty girl to sing "Man is for the Woman Made." Included in the song is a list of rude metaphors with which Purcell musically exposes Sir Arthur as a fool, writing at the same time one of his funniest songs. (SOURCE: Price, 1984)

MODERNISM: a literary movement that belonged to the period from 1875 in France, from 1890 in Great Britain and Germany; up to the start of World War II, a collective term for the large variety of contending groups in literature, art, and music across Europe in the same period. These movements included *Symbolism, Post-Impressionism, Decadence, Fauvism, Cubism, Expressionism, *Imagism, Vorticism, *Futurism, Dada, *Surrealism, and so on. It was a period during which artists confronted the public and disseminated avant-garde works and ideas across national and linguistic borders. (SOURCE: Drabble, 2000)

MODINHA: a traditional Brazilian romantic, sentimental, and Italianate song with erotic context, apt for a salon performance, which had great influence on the modern Brazilian art song.

SONG	COMPOSER	POET
"Modinhas e Canções"	Heitor Villa Lobos	traditional children's songs

MOLONDRÓN: (Sp.), *a lout* or *boor*.

SONG	COMPOSER	POET
"El molondrón"	Fernando Obradors	classical Spanish song

MOMUS: the Greek deity of mockery and fault finding, called by ★Hesiod the son of Night (Nox). Momus found fault with the man made by Hephaetus because he had not created little doors in his breast through which his secret thoughts might be seen, and he was angry with ★Aphrodite for talking too much and because her sandals creaked. In Puccini's *La Bohème* the second act café is called Cafè Momus. (SOURCE: Kaster, 1964)

MONCLOA: a district in Madrid surrounding the square of La Moncloa.

SONG	COMPOSER	POET
"Las currutacas modestas"	Enrique Granados	Fernando Periquet

MONIE: (Scot.) (pr. *moh*-nee), *many.*

SONG	COMPOSER	POET
"The Larky Lad"	Benjamin Britten	William Soutar

MONODY: originally in Greek lyric poetry, an ★ode sung by a single voice, for example, by one of the characters in a tragedy. It came to be associated with the lamentation of a single mourner, hence a dirge or a funeral song. The poem of Diamond's song is from ★Melville's *Timoleon*, one of his poetry collections. It is widely believed to refer to the writer Nathaniel ★Hawthorne. He and Melville were friends around 1850, although they became estranged later. "Monody" is a ★lament for a beloved friend.

SONG	COMPOSER	POET
"Monody"	David Diamond	Herman Melville

MONSTRANCE: a tall vessel, generally silver- or gold-plated, used to expose the blessed sacrament (a title given to the sacrament of the body and blood of ★Jesus Christ). The top is usually circular with simulated sun rays coming from the center where the lunette (the circular receptacle holding the consecrated host) is inserted so that the host can be seen by the people. Below the circular part is a handle for carrying and lifting the monstrance. On the bottom is a base on which it stands. Sometimes called an ostensorium (from Lat., to show). (SOURCE: Nevins, 1964)

SONG	COMPOSER	POET
"Harmonie du soir"	Claude Debussy	Charles Baudelaire

MONTALE, EUGENIO (1896–1981): Italian poet. Montale was born in Genova and studied to be an opera singer. He served in the Italian army as an infantry officer (1917–19). In 1922 he founded a literary journal in Turin. From 1928 to 1938 he was the curator of the Florence book collection. Montale served as literary editor for one Milan newspaper (1955–67), then music critic for a second. He was made a life member of the Italian senate, won many literary prizes, was given several honorary degrees and the Nobel Prize for Literature in 1975. Montale was generally regarded as Italy's greatest twentieth-century poet. He was held in wide esteem despite his personal austerity, high morality, and the metaphysical difficulty of his verse. Montale believed that poetry was a means of understanding rather than a means of representation. Many of his poems, about small personal defeats and the anxieties of everyday life, brought with them new and dissonant harmonies, a posture of doubt and skepticism. His later works became more informal and contained more wit and insight together with gentle humor. The verses of Eugenio Montale were set by Goffredo Petrassi. PRINCIPAL WORKS: *Poesie di Montale* (bilingual), trans. Robert Lowell, 1960; *Provisional Conclusions: A Selection of the Poetry of Montale 1920–1970*, trans. Edith Farnsworth, 1970; *The Storm and Other Poems*, trans. Charles Wright, 1978. SELECTED READING: Glauco Cambon, *Montale's Poetry: A Dream in Reason's Presence*, 1982; Rebecca J. West, *Montale: Poet on the Edge*, 1981. (SOURCE: Vinson, Kirkpatrick (2),1984)

MONTAÑES, JUAN MARTINEZ (1568–1649): a Spanish sculptor. Juan Martinez Montañes was a master of polychrome sculpture, perhaps the greatest in Spain. The poem of Muñoz San Román refers to a crucifix that hangs in the cathedral of Seville, called The Christ of Clemency. Montañes produced sculptures for palaces, convents, and churches in Andalusia, where he was very active. (SOURCE: Cockburn, Stokes, 1992)

SONG	COMPOSER	POET
"Semana Santa"	Joaquín Turina	José Muñoz San Román

MONTE PINCIO: a hill near Rome featured in a poem by Björnstierne ★Björnson, "Fra Monte Pincio" (From Mt. Pincio). A lover of political freedom and independence, Björnson wrote it as a celebration of the year during which Rome was liberated from the French military dominance and Italy was united.

SONG	COMPOSER	POET
"Fra Monte Pincio"	Edvard Grieg	Björnstierne Björnson

MONTPARNASSE: a quarter of Paris where a large population of artists lived at one time.

SONG	COMPOSER	POET
1. "Montparnasse"	Francis Poulenc	Guillaume Apollinaire
2. "Jour des morts"	Paul Nordoff	Charlotte Mew

MONTROSE: an ancient royal burgh of the Scottish county of Angus. It was Montrose from which Sir James Douglas embarked for the Holy Land.

MOORE, MARIANNE (1887–1972): American poet and essayist. Marianne Moore was born in a suburb of St. Louis, Missouri. Her mother, who was a housekeeper for her own father, a Scotch-Irish minister, moved with her children to Pennsylvania when he died. Marianne went to Bryn Mawr as a biology major. After she graduated in 1909, she taught business skills to Native Americans in her hometown. In 1918, when her brother became a chaplain in the Navy, she and her mother moved to New York, eventually to Brooklyn. The poems that were published early on attracted praise from Ezra ★Pound. When *Poems* was published in 1921, her reputation was already substantial with the avant-garde. During and after World War II, Moore's reputation was that of the leading American woman poet. She won several awards and then a Guggenheim Fellowship in 1945. At least four honorary degrees were given to her in the 1950s including the National Book Award and the Pulitzer

Prize. Marianne Moore's achievement is unique within the modernist movement. "She withstood sentimentality and self-indulgence, literariness and philistinism, and survived the worst intellectual plagues of the post-Romantic period. She was the founder of a woman's poetry that showed traces neither of self-aggrandizement nor of hysteria" (Hamilton, 1994). She combined abstract language with a fresh-eyed observation of the natural world. Marianne Moore's poetry has been set by Virgil Thomson and William Bolcom. PRINCIPAL WORKS: Poetry: *Observations*, 1924; *Selected Poems*, 1935; *Like a Bulwork*, 1956; *O To be a Dragon*, 1960; *The Fables of La Fontaine* (her own version), 1954; *The Poems of Marianne Moore*, 2003. Essays: *Predilections*, 1955. SELECTED READING: *A Marianne Moore Reader*, 1961 (both poetry and essays). (SOURCE: Hamilton, 1994)

MOORE, THOMAS (1779–1852): Irish poet and musician. Moore was born in Dublin, the son of a grocer. He was educated at Trinity College, having already published poems in Irish periodicals as an undergraduate. Moore became an enthusiastic Irish patriot, and his personal charm and musical ability made him welcome in society. With the publication of his *Irish Melodies* (music by Sir John Stevenson), he began to earn a good living and became Ireland's national singer. In 1811 Moore met ★Byron, whose friendship would prove very important. He was influenced by Lord Byron to choose an eastern subject for *Lalla Rookh*, which publication made Moore known over all of Europe. His series of humorous skits and his *Life of Byron* were very successful, but failing energy and several deaths in the family left him living alone in degenerating mental health. An amiable man with ingenuous charm, Moore had many friends and was worshiped by women. It was said that his own singing of his songs was extremely sweet and touching. He was not one of the great poets, more a drawing-room variety of poet, but he had an ability to combine words and music happily. Among the most popular of his songs is "The Last Rose of Summer," for which he wrote both words and music. The poetry of Thomas Moore has been set by Duparc, Berlioz, Mendelssohn, Schumann, Paul Hindemith, Adolf Jensen, Halfdan Kjerulf, Thomas Attwood, Peter Warlock, Henry Bishop, Miriam Gideon, Charles Ives, and Samuel Coleridge-Taylor. PRINCIPAL WORKS: *Intercepted Letters: or, The Two-Penny Post-Bag*, 1813; *A Selection of Irish Melodies*, 1807–34; *Lalla Rookh*, 1817; *Legendary Ballads*, 1830. SELECTED READING: W. Hazlitt, *Spirit of the Age*, 1922; H. R. Montgomery, *Thomas Moore: His Life, Writings, and Contemporaries*, 1860. (SOURCE: Kunitz, Haycraft, 1936)

MORA: *blackberry, mulberry, or a Moorish girl.*

MORAND, PAUL (1888–1976): French poet, short story writer, essayist, and novelist. Born in Russia into a bourgeois family with artistic, political, and literary interests, Paul Morand was a sophisticated man. He studied at the University of Paris and spent one year at Oxford, later making a career as a diplomat until after World War II. His extensive travels that began early on would dominate his life and works. He commenced his literary career with two volumes of strongly modern poetry (1920): *Lampes à arc* and *Feuilles de température*. As a stylist, he produced work that resembled the work of his friend ★Giraudoux. Morand was best known for his travel fiction of the 1920s and excelled in the portrayal of the cities of New York, London, and Bucharest. He wrote seriously about the contrast between the eastern and western civilization, but his literary reputation suffered from having served as a Vichy ambassador during World War II. Some dismissed his work as superficial, too rapid, too aloof, too ironic, but he was a moralist, influencing the younger generation of French writers. The poetry of Paul Morand was set by Maurice Ravel. PRINCIPAL WORKS: Travel: *New York City*, 1929; *Londres*, 1933; *Bucarest*, 1935. Short stories: *Ouvert la nuit*, 1922; *Fermé la nuit*, 1923. Novels: *L'Europe galante*, 1925; *Bouddha vivant*, 1927. SELECTED READING: M. Schneider, *Morand*, 1971. (SOURCE: Serafin, 1999)

MORÉAS, JEAN (1856–1910): French poet. Moréas was born Johannes Papadiamantopoulos in Athens. His father was prominent in the Greek military and judiciary, but absent much of the time. Jean was brought up by a French governess who inspired his love of French poetry, of which he read more than 2,000 volumes from the Renaissance and Classical periods. In 1872, Moréas was sent to study in Bonn and Heidelberg, where he gallicized his name, taken from Morea in the Peloponnesus. After visiting Austria, Switzerland, and Italy and settling in Marseilles for a time, Moréas returned to Greece, devoting himself to translations from the French and German and editing anthologies of modern Greek verse. Following the publication of a volume of Greek and French poems, he returned to the literary circles and café life of Paris, founding (1884) the Cercles des Jemenfoutistes (persons who are without interest in anything). Moréas's greatest popularity was gained with *Le Pèlerin passioné*, in which he expertly wove together antiquity and modernity. At this time his desire was that poetry might return to Medieval and Renaissance materials with freedom in the verse forms, but he soon abandoned this credo for true classicism, in which he combined his personal viewpoint with a theme of sadness in a traditional mode of expression. At the end of his life Moréas wrote little, but he became a French citizen in the year of his death. His poetry was set by Carl Engel, Francis Poulenc, and Reynaldo Hahn. PRINCIPAL WORKS: *Le Pèlerin passioné*, 1891; *Les Syrtes*, 1892; *Iphyigénie*, 1894–1900; *Les Stances*, 1897–1905. SELECTED READING: G. R. Turquet-Milnes, *Some Modern French Writers*, 1921. (SOURCE: Kunitz, Colby, 1967)

MORGAN, SIR HENRY (1635–1688): a Welsh buccaneer. Sir Henry's name has often appeared in songs and literary works. His wartime feats and adventures during the hostilities between England and Spain, when he captured Portabelo and Panama and ravaged the coast of Cuba and Maracaibo, established his name.

MORGANATIC: pertaining to a marriage between a man of high rank and a woman of low rank, whose children have no claim to the father's possessions or title.

SONG	COMPOSER	POET
"Paganini"	Francis Poulenc	Louise de Vilmorin

MORGENSTERN, CHRISTIAN (1871–1914): German poet and epigrammist. Born in Munich, Morgenstern was the son and grandson of well-known painters.

Afflicted as a child with tuberculosis, a disease that would cause his premature death, he was confined to his room where he voraciously read writers like Schopenhauer and *Nietzsche. His lyric poems written after 1906 reflect his turn to mysticism, but the love poems and nature lyrics tend toward sentimentality. He is best remembered for his nonsense verse, ironic comic lyrics, and *epigrams that are characterized by a mastery of humorous fantasy. In these he played games with conventional language that anticipated the *Surrealists, and used distortion in a way that anticipated the *Expressionists. Morgenstern's poetry was set by Paul Hindemith, Willi Burkhard, Yrjö Kilpenin, and Ernest Toch. PRINCIPAL WORKS: Poetry: *Melancholie*, 1906; *Ich und Du*, 1911; *Wir fanden einen Pfad*, 1914. Epigrams and Nonsense: *Galgenlieder* [Gallows Songs], 1905; *Palmström*, 1910; *Palma Kunkel*, 1916; *Gingganz*, 1919; coll. in *Alle Galgenlieder*, 1951, trans. 1963. SELECTED READING: W. Witte, "Humour and Mysticism in Christian Morgenstern's Poetry," in *German Life and Letters*, Vol. 1, 1936. (SOURCES: Kaufman, 1962; Steinberg, 3, 1973)

MÖRIKE, EDUARD (1804–1875): German poet and novelist. Son of a Swabian district doctor, Mörike was educated at seminaries, although he passed a stormy youth in his preferred company of poets and musicians rather than his fellow theological students. His mother possessed a lively sense of humor and fantasy that her son inherited. He entered the University of Tübingen, where he and friends formed a literary circle, to which they sometimes invited an aging and already insane *Hölderlin. After his strange romance with a mystic and sensual girl, who appears in his early poetry as Peregrina, Mörike led a placid life as pastor of Swabian country parishes. During his absences from pastoring, he wrote some of the most perfect lyrics in the German language, evincing his introspective involvement with nature and achievement of childlike effects. Their flowing rhythms, humor, realistic pictures of abstract thoughts, imaginative mood swings, and musically sonorous language were greatly appreciated by composers. Fifteen years after his death "Das verlassene Mägdlein" had been set by fifty-odd composers. Mörike's early poetry had much in common with the *Romantics but later he became form-conscious and adopted classical meters. His last years were troubled by domestic unhappiness and frequent illness, which robbed him of the former balance between impish good humor and irritability that had characterized his periods of creativity. The poetry of Eduard Mörike has been set by Schumann, Brahms, Wolf, Hans Pfitzner, Robert Franz, Max Reger, and Josef Marx, who responded to Mörike's personality and creative work. PRINCIPAL WORKS: *Poems of Eduard Mörike*, trans. N. K. Cruikshank and G. F. Cunningham, 1959; *Maler Nolten* (prose), 1832; *Mozart auf der Reise nach Prague* (prose), trans. W. and C. A. Phillips, 1934. SELECTED READING: M. Mare, *Eduard Mörike, The Man and the Poet*, 1957. (SOURCES: Mathieu, Stern, 1987; Kunitz, Colby, 1967)

MORRIS DANCE: a rural folk dance originating in northern England, performed in costume, traditionally on May Day, by men who originally represented characters of the Robin Hood legend.

SONG	COMPOSER	POET
"Ho, Who Comes Here?"	Gordon Jacob	Thomas Morley

MORRISON, TONI (b. 1931): American novelist and poet. Born Chloe Anthony Wofford in an Ohio steel town, Morrison graduated from Howard University, where she was affiliated with the Howard University Players. There she married Harold Morrison. After taking a bachelor's degree at Howard (1953), Morrison did graduate work at Cornell University, taking a master's degree (1955). She served as an editor with Random House, enjoyed several academic posts, and was a recipient of the National Book Critics Circle Award and the Pulitzer Prize for fiction. Morrison's verse has been set by André Previn. WORKS: *The Bluest Eye*, 1970; *Sula*, 1974; *Song of Solomon*, 1977; *Tar Baby*, 1981; *Beloved*, 1987; *Jazz*, 1992; *Paradise*, 1998. (SOURCE: *Americana*, 2003)

MOSEN, JULIUS (1803–1867): German poet and playwright. Much of Mosen's writing centered around and culminated in the two revolutions (1830, 1848). He and other young German poets attempted to use their work to reform the political and social conditions of their time. Typically, their militantly political attitudes resulted in many poems written on behalf of the suppressed Greeks and Poles. Mosen was a prolific writer of both plays and poems, some of which have passed into German folk song. The poetry of Julius Mosen was set by Charles Griffes, and by Robert Schumann in the celebrated "Der Nussbaum." (SOURCE: Garland, 1976)

MOSES: a great leader, chosen by God to deliver the Israelites from slavery in Egypt, and to give them a code of laws by which they could govern themselves in their new home, Palestine. Moses was born to Israelite parents during the period when Pharaoh ordered all baby boys born to Israelites killed. Moses's parents kept him alive in their own home for three months. Then they placed him in a waterproof basket in the rushes along the River Nile. Pharaoh's own daughter found him and raised him. When Moses was forty, he ran away from Egypt to save his own life. The Lord asked him to go back and lead the Israelites out of Egypt into Palestine. For forty years Moses wandered in the wilderness of the Sinai, during which years he wrote the book of Exodus. (SOURCE: *Americana*, 2003)

SONG	COMPOSER	POET
"The Song of Moses"	Richard Cumming	Exodus

MOSLEMIN: Muslim.

SONG	COMPOSER	POET
"Ob der Koran von Ewigkeit sei?"	Hugo Wolf	Johann Wolfgang von Goethe

MOSS, HOWARD (1922–1987): American poet, critic, playwright, and editor. Moss, son of a Lithuanian immigrant, grew up in Rockaway Beach outside New York City. His Lithuanian grandparents, brought to the United States by Moss's father, added a continental touch to his childhood. First educated in local schools, he took his B.S. from the University of Wisconsin and did his graduate work at Harvard and Columbia. Influenced by once a week attendance at the theater in Manhattan from the age of twelve, Moss began writing as a child and was published before finishing his undergraduate degree. Having worked first as a book reviewer for *Time* magazine, for forty years he held a very influential position as poetry editor for the *New Yorker* magazine (1948–87). His teaching positions included Vassar and Barnard Colleges, Columbia University, the University of California at Irvine, and the University of Houston. Moss was given a National Book Award for *Selected Poems* (1972) and was made chancellor of the Academy of American Poets (1987). He admired the work of Proust, ★Chekhov, and John ★Donne, distrusting all writing theories. "Though I respect and sometimes envy spontaneity in writing, I revise my work a good deal" (Wakeman, 1975). The verse of Howard Moss has been set by Ned Rorem. PRINCIPAL WORKS: Poetry: *The Toy Fair*, 1954; *A Winter Come, A Summer Gone*, 1960; *Selected Poems*, 1976; *Rules of Sleep*, 1984; *New Selected Poems*, 1987. Criticism: *Minor Monuments: Selected Essays*, 1986. Plays: *The Oedipus Mah-Jongg Scandal*, 1968; *Two Plays*, 1981. Satire: *Instant Lives*, 1974. Juvenile: *Tigers and Other Lilies*, 1977. Translations: *The Cemetery by the Sea*, by Paul Valéry. Editor: *The Nonsense Book of Edward Lear*, 1964. SELECTED READING: *World Authors 1950–70*, ed. John Wakeman, 1975. (SOURCE: Wakeman, 1975)

MOSUL: a city, whose modern name is Al Mawsil, located near Nineveh on the Tigris River in the northwest corner of Iraq.

SONG	COMPOSER	POET
"Les Roses d'Ispahan"	Gabriel Fauré	Charles Leconte de L'Isle

MOTHER GOOSE: a mythological little old lady who is supposed to have told nursery stories and rhymes that children loved very well. Whether she was a real person is a mystery. In an old graveyard in Boston, there are several tombstones with the name Goose. Some claim that one of them is Mother Goose. Her real name was supposed to have been Elizabeth Vergoose. Her son-in-law, a printer named Thomas Fleet, is supposed to have published in 1719 the songs and rhymes she sang to her grandchild, but no copy of the book was ever found. Mother Goose is translated from a French collection, *Mère d'Oye*. In 1697 a Frenchman, Charles Perrault, published the first book in which the name Mother Goose was used, *Contes de ma Mère d'Oye*. There were no rhymes, but eight tales including Cinderella, Sleeping Beauty, and ★Puss in Boots. (SOURCE: *Americana*, 2003)

SONG	COMPOSER	POET
1. "Chinese Mother Goose Rhymes"	Bainbridge Crist	Chinese poems
2. "New Songs of Old Mother Goose"	John Koch	nursery rhymes

MOZÁRABE, MOZARABIC: a Romance dialect spoken in southern Spain as early as the tenth century.

MUCKLE: (Scot.), *great; large; much.*

SONG	COMPOSER	POET
"The Larky Lad"	Benjamin Britten	William Soutar

MUEZZIN: in Muslim countries a public crier who proclaims the regular hours of prayer from a minaret or the roof of a mosque.

SONG	COMPOSER	POET
"Songs of the Infatuated Muezzin"	Karol Szymanowski	Jaroslav Iwaszkiwicz

MÜLLER, WILHELM (1794–1827): German poet, journalist, and philologist. Müller was the son of a shoemaker. He served as a volunteer soldier of the Prussian army (1813) during the Wars of Liberation. From 1815 to 1817 he studied philology in Berlin, where he was a leading figure in the literary and social life of the ★Romantics, becoming associated with ★Arnim and ★Brentano. After traveling in Italy (1817–18), Müller became a *Gymnasium* teacher in Dessau, then in 1820 was given the position of librarian of the ducal library. His son was for many years a professor at Oxford University. Although Fanny Mendelssohn Hensel set his work, Müller is most famous for his lyric poetry set in two song cycles by Franz Schubert, *Die schöne Müllerin* (1824) and *Die Winterreise* (1828). These forty-four lyrics were originally written for a Berlin play with songs and set by Ludwig Berger. "Der Hirt auf dem Felsen" is derived from two of his poems, "Der Berghirt" and "Liebesgedanken." The hallmark of Müller's verse was simplicity and a love of nature. His interests lay in Romanticism, folk poetry, and also translations of foreign works. PRINCIPAL WORKS: *Poems from the Posthumous Papers of a Traveling Horn-Player*, 1824; *Works*, 5 vols., 1830; a critical edition by J. T. Hatfield, 1906. SELECTED READING: P. S. Allen, *Wilhelm Müller and the German Volklied*, 1901. (SOURCE: Kunitz, Colby, 1967)

MUMMELSEE: *a water lily lake*, fictitious name invented by ★Mörike.

SONG	COMPOSER	POET
"Mummelsee"	Hugo Wolf	Edouard Mörike

MUN: (Scot.) (pr. to rhyme with *sun*), *must*.

MÜNE: (Scot.) (pr. as in Ger., mön), *moon; a long time*.

SONG	COMPOSER	POET
"Bed-time"	Benjamin Britten	William Soutar

MURNAN: (Scot.) (pr. marnin), *mourning*.

MUSES: the nine daughters of ★Zeus and Mnemosyne in Greek mythology, identified with individual arts and sciences. The Muses are patron goddesses of intelligence and creative ability—literature, music, dance—providing inspiration. Originally the Muses were goddesses of memory only, but later each was identified with an individual art or science. The paintings of the Herculaneum show all nine in their respective attributes: ★Calliope (epic poetry), Clio (history), Erato (lyre and lyric love poetry), Euterpe (lyric poetry and the flute), Melpomene (tragedy), Thalia (comedy and bucolic poetry), Terpsichore (dancing and the singing that accompanies it), Polyhymnia (songs to the gods), and Urania (astronomy). Sometimes three earlier Muses are added: Melete (Meditation), Mneme (Remembrance), and Aoide (Song). Various places that are associated with the worship of the Muses, therefore places of inspiration, are: Pieria on Mt. Olympus, Mt. Helicon, Beotia, Mt. Parnassus, Aganippe, Castalia, Hippocrene, and the Pierian spring—all waters associated with Music—are supposed to give poetic inspiration to those who drink of them. (SOURCE: Cooper, 1992)

SONG	COMPOSER	POET
1. "La Rose, Ode Ancréontique"	Gabriel Fauré	Charles Leconte de L'Isle
2. "La Cigale"	Ernest Chausson	Charles Leconte de L'Isle
3. "Auf einer Wanderung"	Hugo Wolf	Eduard Möricke
4. "Zur Warnung"	Hugo Wolf	Eduard Möricke
5. "Der Musensohn"	Franz Schubert	Johann Wolfgang von Goethe
6. "The Muse"	Nikolai Medtner	Aleksandr Pushkin

"Music for a While": an air composed by Henry Purcell to the words of John ★Dryden in the revival of the play *Oedipus*, produced in 1678. For plot details and placement of songs, *see ★Oedipus*.

MUSSET, ALFRED DE (1810–1857): French poet and playwright. Musset was the brilliant second son of cultivated parents. By the age of eighteen he was a favorite in a circle of young romantics, whose worship of Victor ★Hugo his early poems reflect. Soon he liberated himself and began to prefer ★Byron, as can be seen by his first published work, a fairly notorious free translation of De Quincey's *Opium Eater* (1828). Later in his career his reputation was invigorated by another factor, the famed and emotionally dangerous liaison with George Sand (1834–35). His most famous poem was inspired by a chance meeting of her in a theater foyer. By the age of thirty his fragile mental health, undermined by sexual excesses and alcoholism, was further demoralized by another love affair. Musset's most inventive work is in his plays. His serious poetry tends to feature lost love and fantasy, although written with irony, impish wit, and psychological acuity. The poetry of Alfred de Musset has been set by Gounod, Saint-Saëns, Liszt, Franck, Offenbach, Tchaikovsky, Isaac Albéniz, Mario Castelnuovo-Tedesco, Léo Délibes, Darius Milhaud, Josef Marx, and César Cui. Like ★Gautier, Musset never expressed his opinions of the songs written to his verses. PRINCIPAL WORKS: Poetry: *Première poésies*, 1829; *Poésies nouvelles*, 1836; *Les Nuits*, 1835–37; *Souvenir*, 1841. Plays: *Fantasio*, 1834; *On ne badine pas avec l'amour*, 1834; *Lorenzaccio*, 1834. SELECTED READING: Charlotte Haldane, *The Passionate Life of Musset*, 1960; Margaret A. Rees, *Musset*, 1971. (SOURCE: Steinberg, 2, 1973)

MYRRH: a kind of gum resin used in perfumes, medicines, and incense.

SONG	COMPOSER	POET
"Noël"	Gabriel Fauré	Victor Wilder

MYRTLE: a tree whose leaves figure largely in many of the world's mythologies. The myrtle is the flower of the gods, a magic herb, having an essence that transmits the breath of life. When viewed in a strong light, the myrtle leaf can be seen to be pierced with innumerable little punctures. In Greek fable ★Phaedra, wife of ★Theseus, fell in love with ★Hippolytus, her stepson. When Hippolytus went into the arena to exercise horses, Phaedra repaired to a myrtle tree in Troezen to await his return. To pass the time she pierced the leaves with a hairpin. Ancient Jews believed that the eating of myrtle leaves conferred the power of detecting witches, and that, if the leaves crackled, the person's beloved would prove faithful. In Mandaean rites the myrtle is a sacred plant. It is part of a priest's ritual headdress. Myrtle is placed on the heads of the newborn and the baptized, and used at marriage and at death. In Egypt the myrtle was sacred to Hathor. In Greco-Roman myth, the myrtle is sacred to Adonis, ★Aphrodite/★Venus, Artemis, Europa, and to ★Poseidon/ Neptune. Both myrtle and laurel were traditional materials for constructing poetic garlands. (SOURCE: Cooper, 1992)

N ✍

NABAB (Fr.), NABOB (Eng.): originally a native viceroy in India or one who returns to Europe from the east with great riches, later describing a man of great wealth or prominence in a particular field and sometimes used as a generalized expression of disapproval.

SONG	COMPOSER	POET
"Le Joueur de bugle"	Francis Poulenc	Max Jacob

"Nachtigall, An die": a poem by Ludwig ★Hölty set by Brahms and Schubert. When Hölty's poems were collected after his death, his friend Johannes ★Voss edited them for publication, making extensive changes. "An die Nachtigall" was incomplete as Voss found it, and he wrote a good half of the poem himself. Brahms and Schubert used the Voss edition of the poem. Schubert wrote another "An die Nachtigall," this one with a text by ★Claudius.

NACHTVIOLE: a violet with a very sweet perfume, called *dame's violet* in English-speaking countries.

SONG	COMPOSER	POET
"Nachtviolen"	Franz Schubert	Johann Mayrhofer

NADSON, SEMËN (1862–1887): Russian poet. A revival of poetry in Russia just before 1881 affected both literary schools, the so-called "★civic" school and the art-for-art's-sake schools. During the 1880s and 1890s there was general agreement that the only legitimate subject for poetry was beauty and melancholy. Among the "civic" poets the most famous was Nadson, a young man of partly Jewish descent, who died of consumption at an early age. His poetry was inspired by "an unrealized desire to make the world better and by the consciousness of his failure" (Mirsky, 1958). Nadson's poetry is smooth, without irregularities that disturb, and it is pretty but lacking strength. Although it is considered to be a measure of the worst Russian poetical technique, it gained a great popularity with the public. Nadson's verse has been set by Anton Arensky and Sergei Rachmaninoff. (SOURCE: Mirsky, 1958)

NAE: (Scot.), *no.*

NAIAD: in Greek mythology, water nymph, *nymphs of the liquid element, daughters of *Zeus. The Naiads were styled as "fostering nymphs," and for this reason were commonly found in the company of Zeus, *Poseidon, and *Aphrodite, and were also looked upon as deities of marriage and sacred rites. "Generally speaking, the Nymphs were a kind of middle beings between the gods and men, communicating with both, loved and respected by both; gifted with the power of making themselves visible or invisible at pleasure; able to do many things only permitted to be done by the gods; living like the gods on *ambrosia; leading a cheerful happy life of long duration, and retaining strength and youthfulness to the last, but not destined to immortality, like the gods" (Murray, 1988). Strictly speaking, Naiads were water nymphs, beautiful, long-haired, and associated with lakes, rivers, and fountains. Sometimes, when circumstances were sufficiently extraordinary, they were permitted to take part in the councils of the *Olympian gods. Usually, however, they stayed in their usual habitats—hidden grottoes and bucolic pastures—where they danced and gamboled with those deities who passed through their domains. (SOURCES: Graves, 1960 (2); Murray, 1988)

SONG	COMPOSER	POET
1. "Le Tombeau des Naïades"	Claude Debussy	Pierre Louÿs
2. "Les Naïades"	Charles Gounod	François Ponsard
3. "La Najade"	Ottorino Respighi	Gabriele d'Annunzio

NAIDU, SAROJINI (1879–1949): Indian poet, political leader, and social reformer. The daughter of a Bengali Brahman, Naidu graduated from Madras University and studied in England, after which she broke caste barriers by marrying a man of lower status. Working particularly to raise the status of Indian women, Naidu joined Gandhi's movement in 1919, was jailed often, but by 1925 was elected the first woman president of the Indian National Congress, later the first woman governor of an Indian state. Although her poetry was written in English, the themes were Indian. The verse of Sarojini Naidu was set by Ernest Charles and Frederick Jacobi. PRINCIPAL WORKS: *The Golden Threshold*, 1905; *The Bird of Time*, 1913; *The Broken Wing*, 1917. (SOURCE: *Americana*, 2001)

NAIGE: (Scot.), *nag.*

NANCY HANKS: mother of Abraham Lincoln, American president during the Civil War. Lincoln was the second son of Nancy Hanks and Thomas Lincoln.

SONG	COMPOSER	POET
"Nancy Hanks"	Elie Siegmeister, Katherine Davis	William Rose Benét

NANTES: a French city located east of the Atlantic coast on the Loire River. Although it is not nominally part of Brittany, Nantes has strong ties to the Bretons. The medieval sector has cobbled streets, a cathedral, and a castle built by the dukes of Brittany, a massive fifteenth-century fortress.

SONG	COMPOSER	POET
"Souric et Mouric"	Francis Poulenc	Max Jacob

NAPLES: an Italian city, the third largest city and the second busiest port in that country. With a population of more than one million, Naples is located on the north shore of the Bay of Naples 120 miles south of Rome. The view from the bay is dominated by the volcano, Mount Vesusius. The city extends along the bay and up the slopes of the surrounding hills, where the modern section is found. The Old Quarter is the heart of old Naples, with narrow crowded streets, picturesque squares, small shops of local artisans. Homes of the working people sporting lines of drying laundry and strings of lemons can be seen. Shoeshine boys compete for business, and street vendors sell tortoise jewelry, glowworms, and peanuts. Settled by the Greeks, built on the site of ancient ★Partenope, Naples was later occupied by the Ostrogoths, Lombards, and Byzantines until Neapolitans acquired their own dukes and kings. In 1860 Garibaldi made Naples part of a unified Italy.

SONG	COMPOSER	POET
"Naples"	Wintter Watts	Sara Teasdale

NARCISSUS: in Greek mythology, the son of Cephisus, a youth of great beauty who cruelly spurned many admirers including the ★nymph ★Echo. Bending down one day to drink from a pool, he fell in love with his own reflection. Thinking it to be the presiding nymph of the place, he jumped into the fountain to reach it, but died there. When the nymphs came to take the body to pay it funeral honors, they found only a flower, which they called by his name. The name Narcissus and its adjectival form, narcissistic, are used to illustrate excessive physical vanity. (SOURCE: Cooper, 1992)

SONG	COMPOSER	POET
1. "Venise"	Charles Gounod	Alfred de Musset
"La Grotte"	Claude Debussy	Charles, Duc d'Orléans
3. "Auprès de cette grotte somber"	Claude Debussy	Tristan l'Hermite
4. "The Death of St. Narcissus"	Benjamin Britten	T. S. Eliot

NASH, OGDEN (1902–1971): American poet, librettist, editor, and illustrator. Ogden Nash was born in Rye, New York, the son of well-to-do parents. In 1921 Nash left Harvard, after having been enrolled for one year. He then worked as a teacher, a bond salesman, a writer of streetcar ads, and finally in the publicity and editorial departments of publishers Doubleday and Rinehart. In 1929 he joined the staff of *The New Yorker*, his favorite publication, although he regularly contributed to more than thirty journals. In the same year that Nash married, 1931, he published both *Hard Lines* and *Free Wheeling*. Nash began to write lyrics for Broadway musicals, among them the 1943 production of Kurt Weill's *One Touch of Venus* and the 1962 production of Vernon Duke's *Two's Company*, starring Bette Davis. Tall, spectacled, elegantly dressed with fair curling hair and a toothy but intelligent smile, Nash did urbane public readings of his verse. These created a strong following, as did his clever illustrations. Although Nash belonged to the entertainment business, he always used his poetic resources, as an example, finishing his poems in surprising couplet-rhymes. He constantly and meticulously revised his puns, witty *epigrams, and lyrical verse. At his best, Nash belongs with Lewis *Carroll, Edward *Lear, and W. S. Gilbert. The verses of Ogden Nash have been set by Stephen Paulus, Jacob Avshalomov, and Samuel Adler. PRINCIPAL WORKS: *I Wouldn't Have Missed It*, 1975, 1983; as *Candy is Dandy: The Best of Ogden Nash*, 1985. (SOURCE: Hamilton, 1994)

NASHE, THOMAS (1567–1601?): English poet, pamphleteer, dramatist, novelist, and editor. Thomas Nashe was educated at Cambridge. In 1588 he went to London where he became associated with professional authors. Although Nashe was one of the first English prose eccentrics, he did collaborate on Marlowe's play, *Dido, Queene of Carthage*. Like Ben *Jonson, Nashe could be both acrid and lyrical in his writing. Some commentators see him as an Elizabethan *Rabelais, for he was in revolt against the approved conventions and fed up with affected civility. He indulged in attacks that were purposefully crude and corrosive. Some of his writing savagely exposed abuses in the state. Because of his political activities, the archbishop of Canterbury ordered all his books taken and none to be printed thereafter. As a consequence, Nashe spent several months in prison. His prose was the very opposite of the usual sugary romances; his plays, instead, related sordid and violent adventures. Nashe's poetry, although not as racy as his prose, took account of the Londoners' predilection for hasty pleasures but put them against a background of plague and terror. One of the modern composers who set Thomas Nashe's verses was Dominick Argento. PRINCIPAL WORKS: *Works*, ed. R. B. McKerrow, 5 vols., 1904–10; revised and ed. F. P. Wilson, 1958. SELECTED READING: C. Nicholl, *A Cup of News*, 1984 (a biography). (SOURCES: Untermeyer, 1959; Drabble, 1985)

NASOBEM: an imaginary animal that walks on its nose.

NATHAN, ROBERT (1894–1961): American novelist and poet. Robert Nathan was the nephew of two uncles, one the founder of the Consumers' League and the other a founder of Barnard College. He was also a direct descendent of Rabbi Gershon Seixas, one of the incorporators of Columbia College in the eighteenth century. Nathan was educated at a Swiss private school, Phillips Exeter Academy, and Harvard. Except for a two-year period as a solicitor for a New York advertising firm, as a teacher at the New York University School of Journalism, and seven years in Hollywood writing for films, Nathan devoted all his time to writing. The true Nathan touch appeared with his third book, *Autumn*, but he did not become well known until the publication of *One More Spring* in 1933. Nathan was a painter, an accomplished and passionate cellist and pianist, and a composer. He did not limit himself to prose, publishing several volumes of poetry. A hallmark of Nathan's writing is low-key, deceptive understatement. His style is highly individual, dealing in fantasy but not whimsical. His interest lay in obscure people, very plain human beings, and children. His attitude was gently ironic, always nearly sentimental, sometimes becoming so. The poetry of Robert Nathan was set by John Duke, Robert Fairfax Birch, and Richard Hageman. PRINCIPAL WORKS: Poetry: *Youth Grows*

Old, 1923; *The Cedar Box*, 1930; *Winter Tide*, 1940. SELECTED READING: *The New Yorker*, January 20, 1940; *The New York Times Book Review*, April 20, 1941; R. Van Gelder, *Writers and Writing*, 1946; H. R. Warfel, *American Novelists of Today*, 1972. (SOURCE: Kunitz, Haycraft, 1942)

NATURALISM: a tradition often considered to be a crude movement, an exaggerated successor to Realism, nourished by the pseudo-scientific theories of its chief exponent, Zola. Associated with Zola in this movement were major writers *Daudet, *Goncourt, and *Maupassant. Zola used the term to denote the heritage of realist literature, inspired by a positivist tradition in philosophy, science, and the arts that rejected the idealistic aspirations of the *Romantic movement and embraced the aesthetic principle of an exact imitation of Nature. (SOURCE: France, 1995)

NAXOS: the island where *Theseus abandoned *Ariadne, Princess of Crete, who had gone with him after they escaped from the labyrinth with the aid of a ball of thread. She sings her lament alone on Naxos. (SOURCE: Lakeway, White, 1989)

SONG	COMPOSER	POET
1. "Lamento di Arianna"	Goffredo Petrassi	Libero de Libero
2. "Arianna à Naxos"	Franz Joseph Haydn	anonymous

NECKAR: a southern German river that rises at Baden-Württemberg and flows 230 miles north and west into the Rhein River at Mannheim. As the Neckar runs north, it creates a scenic valley through vine-clad hills, orchards, and woods, then follows a winding gorge and emerges at Heidelberg.

SONG	COMPOSER	POET
"Rheinlegendchen"	Gustav Mahler	Des Knaben Wunderhorn

NECTAR: in classical mythology the drink of the gods. Nectar was a sweet liquid secreted by the nectaries of a plant and the chief material used by bees in the production of honey. Like the gods' food, *ambrosia, nectar conferred immortality. (SOURCE: Cooper, 1992)

SONG	COMPOSER	POET
"Bess o'Bedlam"	Henry Purcell	anonymous

NEGRI, ADA (1870–1945): Italian poet and novelist. In Italian literature Ada Negri was one of the first poets from the working class who had grown up in poverty in Milano. Negri described her widowed mother and their domestic difficulties arising from the desertion of the father in an autobiographical novel *Stella mattutina*. Through her strength and her mother's, Negri became a teacher. In 1896 she entered into a marriage that proved unsustainable. The birth of her daughter resulted in a collection of poetry written in a *Romantic manner, *Maternità*, which celebrated both her child's birth and her mother's death. Soon her poetry, beginning with *Fatalità* (1892), began to explore social and political protest, criticizing all but the poorest working women. Negri won the Mussolini prize for artistic achievement and was made the first woman member of the Accademia d'Italia. A gradual but steady evolution of style and content was noticeable, beginning with early socialistic humanitarian themes, and ending with somewhat bland content reflecting more personal aspects. Negri's best prose was autobiographical, in old age displaying a new spirituality. Many of the verses of Ada Negri were set by Ottorino Respighi. PRIN-CIPAL WORKS: *Tempeste*, 1895; *Fatalità*, trans. A. M. von Blomberg as *Fate*, 1898; *Dal profondo*, 1910; *Esilio*, 1914; *Le solitarie*, 1917, rev. 1945; *Il libro di Mara*, 1919; *Stella mattutina*, 1921, trans. Anne Day as *Morning Star*, 1930; *I canti dell'isola*, 1925; *Il dono*, 1936. SELECTED READING: Simonetta Grilli, *Ada Negri: La vita e l'opera*, 1953. (SOURCES: Hainsworth, Robbey, 2002; Wedel et al., 1992)

NÉGRITUDE: a term used to denote a literary movement from the 1930s. The word was coined by the French-speaking African and Caribbean writers. The movement undertook to recover their rich black cultural heritage, which had been over-whelmed by the values of European colonialism. In seeking to define these qualities, the movement emerged as a protest against French colonial rule and the French pol-icy of assimilation. Jean-Paul Sartre's essay, "Black Orpheus," published as a preface to Léopold Sédar Senghor's anthology of black poets in French (1948), called atten-tion to the racial themes in West Indian and African poetry in French. (SOURCE: Drabble, 2000; Kennedy, 1975)

NEKRASOV, NIKOLAI (1821–1877): Russian poet. Nekrasov published his first volume of verse in 1840; it showed little promise. Because his father, a brutal bully, would not support him, Nekrasov had to give up his studies at the University of Petersburg and do hack work, both literary and theatrical. By 1845 he had become the principal published poet of the young literary school. A good businessman and an efficient editor, Nekrasov acquired ★Pushkin's literary review in 1846, and turned it into the rallying ground of the extreme Left. He published ★Tolstoy, Turgenev, and other major figures until the review was suppressed during the official panic of 1866. Nekrasov gambled heavily and regularly, spent all his money on food and on mis-tresses, and was a snob who liked the company of his social superiors. An excellent judge of others' verses, he had no judgment of his own work. He did have a facility for writing verse that he had developed during his years of hack work, and his best work was the bold creation of new poetry unfettered by traditional standards of taste. His idealization of people tended to be sentimental, but he did have poetic energy and sincerity. Nekrasov's work can be divided into two types: (1) poetic forms gov-erned by the development of poetry, in which he was subjective, and (2) what he wrote in the spirit of folk song, in which he was objective. It was this combination that made him unique. He is considered to be the greatest of Russian "civic" poets. The poetry of Nikolai Nekrasov was set by Tchaikovsky, Modest Mussorgsky, Alek-sandr Borodin, and César Cui. PRINCIPAL WORKS: *Poems*, trans. J. M. Soskice, 1929; *The Peddlers*, 1861; *Red-Nosed Frost*, 1862, trans. J. Sumner Smith, 1886; *The Railway*, 1864; *Who Can be Happy and Free in Russia*, trans. J. M. Soskice, 1865–77; *Russian Women*, 1872. (SOURCE: Mirsky, 1958)

NEMEROV, HOWARD (1920–1991): American poet, writer of fiction and non-fiction. Born in New York, Nemerov attended Harvard, then spent 1941–45 flying for both the Royal Air Force and the U.S. Air Force in England, where he married. After the war, he lived in New York while he completed his first book of verse

(1947). In 1948 he moved his family from New York, going to Bennington College to teach. There he stayed for many years, during which he contributed short stories, poems, and essays to distinguished journals and wrote two novels. Nemerov's verse was the work of an original and sensitive mind alive to the anxieties and agonies of his age. Critics considered his work vigorous and original. He was awarded the Pulitzer Prize in 1978, and he was the poet laureate of the United States (1988–90). The verse of Howard Nemerov has been set by Louis Calabro. PRINCIPAL WORKS: *The Image and the Law*, 1947; *Guide to the Ruins*, 1950; *The Salt Garden*, 1955; *Mirrors and Windows*, 1958; *The Next Room of the Dream*, 1962; *The Blue Swallows*, 1967; *Gnomes and Occasions*, 1973; *The Western Approaches*, 1975; *Sentences*, 1980. (SOURCE: Kunitz, Haycraft, 1938)

NEO-CLASSICISM: in literature, the habit of imitating great authors of antiquity as a matter of aesthetic principle.

NEREIDS: the sea-nymphs of Greek mythology, the fifty daughters of Nereus. Best known are Amphitrite, Thetis, mother of Achilles, and ★Galatea, all of whom figure in ★Spenser's *Faerie-Queene*, book 4. (SOURCE: Cooper, 1992)

NERO (37–68 C.E.): emperor of Rome (34–68 C.E.), known for his depravity and cruelty, the husband of Poppea. Ottavia sings "Disprezzata regina" in act 1 of Monteverdi's drama after learning of Nero's affair with Poppea.

SONG	COMPOSER	POET
"Disprezzata regina"	Claudio Monteverdi	G. F. Busenello

"Next Winter Comes Slowly": an aria composed by Henry Purcell to a text written by Elkanah ★Settle for his work *The Fairie-Queene*, produced in 1692 and 1693. For plot details and song placements, *see* ★*Fairie-Queene, The.*

NICHOLAS, SAINT: fourth-century Christian saint and bishop. Born in the town of Patara, in a province of Asia Minor, St. Nicholas was known for his piety and zeal as well as the many miracles he performed. When his parents died, they left him well off, and he used his money for good works, but was imprisoned during the persecution ordered by the Emperor ★Diocletian. Nicholas was the patron saint of Greece and Russia, of sailors, merchants, and apothecaries. An act of charity he performed in Patara was responsible for his being the patron saint of unmarried girls and pawnbrokers: a Patara man had lost all his money and was about to let his three unmarried daughters become prostitutes because he could not support them or find them husbands. When Nicholas heard of this predicament, he threw a bag of gold into the man's window on three separate occasions, giving dowries that saved the three daughters. Today the three bags of gold are represented by the three gold balls outside pawnshops. Another kindly and generous act accounts for Nicholas's being the patron saint of children: he is believed to have raised from the dead three children whom an evil butcher had murdered in a brine tub. The custom of giving presents in his name on Christmas may link him to Santa Claus, the name derived from the Dutch translation, Sinter Klaas. Upon his death, Nicholas was buried in the cathedral of Myra (capital of his province), but after the Moslems overran Myra in 1087, his relics were taken to Bari, Italy. There his shrine produced an aromatic substance, which accounts for his being the patron of perfumers. Saint Nicholas's feast day is December 6. (SOURCES: Walsh, 1991; Farmer, 1992; Thurston, Attwater, 1963; De Voragine, 1993)

SONG	COMPOSER	POET
1. "Guten Morgen, 's ist Sankt Valentinstag"	Richard Strauss	William Shakespeare
2. "A Prayer to St. Catherine"	Virgil Thomson	Kenneth Koch

NIETZSCHE, FRIEDRICH WILHELM (1844–1900): German philosopher and poet. Nietzsche was born in Prussian Saxony, although tradition claimed the family to be of Polish aristocratic origin. King Frederick William IV of Prussia gave him a scholarship to attend a fashionable school with high academic standards. His early talent for humanistic subjects was at the mercy of his many doubts about religion. Nietzsche enrolled at the University of Bonn (1864) and followed the great classical philologist Ritschl, to the University of Leipzig a year later. Two discoveries made at Leipzig were to influence him for years to come in his position as professor of classical philology at the University of Basel: the melancholy philosophy of Schopenhauer and the music of Wagner, so much so that his first works came under attack as nothing more than Wagnerian propaganda. When he realized that the building of Bayreuth, which he had admired, was nothing more than a typical expression of decadent late *Romanticism that led straight back to the Church of Rome, he broke with Wagner. He then published works that mercilessly attacked all self-lies and all forms of idealism, finding them to be egoism at their core. The public ignored his shrill books, and many saw signs of his approaching madness (1899), although his works were the precursor of all modern philosophies concerned with the problem of decadence, of philosophy of life, many of which insights pointed ahead to Freud. Nietzsche's poetry has been set by Nicolai Medtner, Arnold Schönberg, and Anton Webern. PRINCIPAL WORKS: *Also sprach Zarathustra*, 1883. SELECTED READING: D. Halévy, *The Life of Friedrich Nietzsche*, 1911. (SOURCE: Vinson, Kirkpatrick (1), 1984)

NIGER: a principal West African river, 2,500 miles in length, running through Guinea, Mali, Niger, Benin, and Nigeria, discharging through a massive delta into the Gulf of Guinea. Its source is just 150 miles inland from the Atlantic, but it runs eastward away from the sea into the Sahara Desert, then taking a sharp right turn and heading southeast. The true course of the river was known only to locals until westerners established its path in the late nineteenth century. Its flood plain permits the cultivation of crops like rice, sugarcane, and cereals as well as the raising of livestock. Thus it is a vital source of life for the more than twenty African tribes who rely on it.

SONG	COMPOSER	POET
"Der Mohrenfürst"	Carl Loewe	Ferdinand Freiligrath

NIGHTINGALE: *see* *PHILOMELA, PHILOMEL.

NIHILISM: (Lat., *nihil*, nothing) a term introduced by Turgenev, originally a Russian movement that rejected social institutions such as marriage and parental authority. Eventually in the nineteenth century the movement transformed itself to a secret revolutionary sect, with social and political interests. (SOURCE: Drabble, 1985)

NIX, NÖCK (Ger.): a supernatural creature, a water spirit with green teeth, wearing a green hat originally in German folklore. The Nix was conceived of in many forms, but usually as having the form of a beautiful woman, or half-woman and half-fish, that dwelled in fresh water, living usually in a beautiful palace, and usually unfriendly to men.

SONG	COMPOSER	POET
1. "Der Nöck"	Carl Loewe	August Kopisch
2. "Nixe Binsefuss"	Hugo Wolf	Eduard Mörike

"No, No, Poor Suff'ring Heart": a song composed by Henry Purcell to the words written by John *Dryden for his play *Cleomenes, the Spartan Hero*. For plot details and placement of songs, *see* *Cleomenes, the Spartan Hero*.

"No, Resistance Is but Vain": a song by Henry Purcell with words written by Thomas *Southerne for his play *The Maid's Last Prayer*, produced in 1693. *See* *Maid's Last Prayer, The* for plot details and placement of songs.

NOAH: very early Old Testament figure, descendant of *Adam, son of Lamech, grandson of Methuselah. In Genesis 6.1–8.22, God decides that men are living too long and sets their life span at one hundred twenty years. God sees the wickedness of mankind, excepting only Noah, a righteous man, and decides to destroy all people and animals. He announces that he intends to destroy all life with a great flood, and he instructs Noah to make an ark of cypress, covered with pitch, to be three hundred cubits long, fifty cubits wide, and 30 cubits high (a cubit was about 18 inches long). The ark was to have a door, a window, three levels, and a roof. Noah was to bring two of each animal, male and female, into the ark, and provisions for humans and animals. After seven days of preparing, all enter the ark, and God himself shuts the door. He causes it to rain for forty days and forty nights, and the water rises, covering the highest mountaintops and killing everything that lived on dry land. Water covers the earth for 150 days; God stops the rain, and the water recedes for 150 days. The ark comes to rest on Mount Ararat. After forty days, Noah sends out a raven, then a dove; neither can find dry land. In another seven days, Noah sends the dove out again and it returns with an olive branch. Noah was 601 years old when he and his cargo left the ark and eventually repopulated the earth. Noah became a father at the age of five hundred and died at the age of 950. (SOURCE: Metzger, Murphy, 1994)

SONG	COMPOSER	POET
"Erschaffen und beleben"	Richard Strauss	Johann Wolfgang von Goethe

NÖCK: *see* *NIX.

"Nocturne": a song by Samuel Barber with text by Frederic ★Prokosch. The original poem includes the following four lines, which were cut by Barber in order to soften the disaster that was looming within the poem, thereby to concentrate on the poem's allusions to love as a refuge from pain. "Condors of the future rise / Through the stupor overhead / And a million shaking sighs / Spring from the insulted dead."

NOGGIN: (Scot.) (pr. nahgin), *a small amount of drink; a small drinking vessel.*

SONG	COMPOSER	POET
"Supper"	Benjamin Britten	William Soutar

"No More, Sir, No More": a dialogue composed by Henry Purcell, set to words by Thomas ★Southerne in his play *Sir Anthony in Love*, produced in 1690. For plot details and placement of songs, *see* ★ *Sir Anthony in Love.*

NONSENSE VERSE: humorous verse that abandons all attempts at intellectual justification. Two masters of this genre were Edward ★Lear and Lewis ★Carroll, and the first Italian to embrace nonsense poetry was ★Burchiello. In Carroll's *Jabberwocky* he invents his own words, and Lear, in his *The Pobble who has not Toes*, uses ordinary words to express absurd ideas.

"No Part of My Dominion": a song composed by Henry Purcell, words written by John ★Dryden for the semi-opera *King Arthur*, produced in 1691. *See* ★*King Arthur* for plot details and song placements.

NORDENEY: a town on the island of the same name, one of the East Frisian Islands in the North Sea.

SONG	COMPOSER	POET
"Odins Meeresritt"	Carl Loewe	Aloys Schreiber

NORNA: a character in the novel *The Pirate* by Sir Walter ★Scott (1821). Half-mad Ulla Troil, known as Norna, believes herself endowed with supernatural power. Norna was of a brooding and superstitious nature, trained by her father in the legendary lore of the old sagas. She performed with such dignity and confidence that most people acknowledged her to be what she claimed to be, the Sovereign of the Seas and Winds. Schubert's song is taken from chapter 19 of the novel.

SONG	COMPOSER	POET
"Gesang der Norna"	Franz Schubert	Sir Walter Scott

NOVALIS (FRIEDRICH VON HARDENBURG) (1772–1801): German poet, novelist, essayist, and philosopher. Novalis studied at the universities of Jena, Leipzig, and Wittenberg, completing his law studies in 1794. After studying mining for two years, he worked as an actuary and as an assistant in the Freiberg salt works (1797–99), living as both a mining engineer and a religious mystic. Novalis was an important figure of early German ★Romanticism, combining strong philosophical inclinations with his poetic gift. The poet for him was "both seer and scientist, priest and craftsman, whose ability to harmonize and unify can overcome the divisions of human knowledge" (Vinson, Kirkpatrick (1), 1984). Because of his gift for symbolic statement, Novalis became important to the *Symbolist movement in France. He created the Blue Flower as a symbol of romantic longing, the color blue standing for the infinity of the sky, while Night was the symbol of death that bears life anew, therefore of religious significance. His influence on neo-Romanticism of the later nineteenth century was also important even though he died at the age of twenty-eight. The poetry of Novalis was set to music by Joseph Marx, Louise Reichardt, Hans Georg Nägeli, and Schubert, who set six of his poems. PRINCIPAL WORKS: *Devotional Songs*, ed. Bernard Pick, 1910; *Hymns to the Night*, trans. Mabel Cotterell, 1948; *Sacred Songs*, trans. Eileen Hutchins, 1956. SELECTED READING: Bruce Haywood, *Novalis: The Veil of Imagery*, 1959. (SOURCES: Vinson, Kirkpatrick (1), 1984; Mathieu, Stern, 1987; Kaufman, 1962)

"Now the Fight's Done": a song composed by Henry Purcell to words of Nathaniel *Lee, from his heroic play *Theodosius*, produced in 1680. For plot details and placement of songs, *see *Theodosius*.

"Now the Night Is Chas'd Away": an air composed by Henry Purcell to a text written by Elkanah *Settle for his work *The Fairie-Queene*, produced in 1692 and 1693. For plot details and song placements, *see *Fairie-Queene, The*.

NUITS D'ÉTÉ, LES: a set of six songs by Hector Berlioz to poems written by Théophile *Gautier in his *La Comédie de la mort*. These songs marked the evolution of French song from the *romance* form to the *mélodie*. "Berlioz displayed the kind of artistic devotion usually reserved for operas and symphonies. . . . All ties with the dying *romance* are broken; the *mélodie* has become a serious genre." (Noske, 1970)

NURSERY, THE: a set of seven songs by Modest Mussorgsky with texts by the composer. In 1870 Mussorgsky wrote four songs that, with the addition of the previously written "Child and Nurse," he made into a cycle called *The Nursery*. In 1872 he added two more songs, making seven in all. According to contemporaries, a few other songs were so near completion that the composer could play them for friends. Unfortunately, they were never written down.

"Nussbaum, Der": a song by Robert Schumann to a poem by Julius *Mosen. The song is frequently translated as "The Hazel Tree" or "The Almond Tree." It is, however, a walnut tree.

NUVOLETTA: a loving but seductive character in James *Joyce's *Finnegans Wake*. The structure of *Finnegans Wake* is cyclic, lacking a beginning or end, set during one day and night in the life of the Mooske and Gripes clans. Nuvoletta herself is one of the characters. She fails to win the attention of either warring family, never dies, but turns herself into another character during the course of the novel. The half-Italian, half-English words coined by Joyce can be attributed to his facility with the Italian language gained during years of teaching English to residents of Trieste. In her 2003 book, *Lucia Joyce*, Carol Loeb Shloss explored the belief that Nuvoletta, in the person of Joyce's beloved daughter Lucia, was "his second self, a pathetic, vanishing figure, flitting through her father's book." The Barber song is a condensation of the lengthy fantasy of Nuvoletta in *Finnegans Wake*. The composer admitted that he, although knowledgeable of Joyce, when faced with these words, was forced to set them as abstract music like a vocalise. (SOURCE: Kimball, 1996; *The New York Times Book Review*, December 28, 2003)

SONG	COMPOSER	POET
"Nuvoletta"	Samuel Barber	James Joyce

NYMPHS: in classical mythology, young and beautiful maidens, minor female divinities of nature, of woods, groves, springs, streams, rivers, and so on. The nymphs, friendly toward mortals, were not immortal, but their life span was usually several thousand years. Each particular kind of nymph was associated with a certain domain of nature. Nymphs are classified according to the place of their abode. They had the gift of prophecy, cured the sick, watched over flowers, fields, and flocks. Generally benevolent, they could become dangerous to the mortals whom they distinguished with their favors, for example, the Rusalki of the Slavs, who sometimes dragged such mortals down into the depths of water. *See* ★Dryads, ★Hamadryads, ★Naiads, and ★Nereids. (SOURCE: Cooper, 1992)

SONG	COMPOSER	POET
1. "Nymphs and Shepherds"	Henry Purcell	Thomas Shadwell
2. "Le Tombeau des Naïades"	Claude Debussy	Pierre Louÿs
3. "Attributs"	Francis Poulenc	Pierre de Ronsard

"Nymphs and Shepherds": a song written by Henry Purcell to the words written by Thomas ★Shadwell for his play, *The Libertine*, produced in 1692. For plot details and placement of songs, *see* ★*Libertine, The*.

O

OBERON: king of the fairies, husband of ★Titania, introduced by ★Shakespeare in *Midsummer Night's Dream*. The name is probably connected with Alberich, king of the Elves. At Oberon's birth fairies bestowed their gifts: insight into men's thoughts; power of transporting the self into any place instantaneously; the eventual conveyance of his soul into Paradise. (SOURCE: Cooper, 1992)

SONG	COMPOSER	POET
"Bess o'Bedlam"	Henry Purcell	anonymous

OBOLUS: the coin ★Charon received for ferrying shades of the newly dead across the River ★Styx to ★Hades.

OCAÑA: a Spanish city that is located a short distance northeast of Toledo.

SONG	COMPOSER	POET
"La Buenaventura"	Amadeo Vives	Miguel de Cervantes

ODALISQUE: (Turk.), *a female slave or concubine in a harem.*

SONG	COMPOSER	POET
"The Odalisque"	John Alden Carpenter	Yü-hsi (772–842)

ODE: a musical setting of a nonreligious poem, in particular one written in honor of a famous person or special occasion. In the seventeenth and eighteenth centuries, odes were usually written for soloists, chorus, and orchestra. Examples are: the final movement of Beethoven's Ninth Symphony (*Ode to Joy*), Brahms's setting of ★Schiller's *Nänie*, and Schönberg's setting of a ★Byron text, *Ode to Napoleon*.

ODIN: the principal god of pagan Scandinavia, associated especially with warfare, also with magically acquired knowledge, poetry, and agriculture. Odin became all-wise by drinking from Mimir's fountain, but at the cost of one eye. His wife was Frigga, his sons, Thor and Balder, his court, Valhalla. His two black ★ravens were called Hugin (thought) and Munin (memory). Gugnir was his spear that never failed to hit the mark.

SONG	COMPOSER	POET
"Odins Meeresritt"	Carl Loewe	Aloys Schreiber

OEDIPUS: son of Laius, king of ★Thebes, and of Queen Jocasta. Oedipus unwittingly killed his own father. In order to avoid fulfilling the prophecy that his son would murder him and marry the queen, King Laius had left the infant Oedipus exposed on a mountain. Shepherds took him to the king and queen of Corinth, who brought him up. Grown to manhood, Oedipus traveled to Delphi. The oracle told him of the prophecy and warned him to stay away from "his own land," which he interpreted wrongly to mean Corinth. On his way to ★Thebes he killed King Laius in a right-of-way dispute. Oedipus became king of Thebes, gaining in marriage the hand of his mother, Jocasta, both ignorant of their true relationship. After learning the facts, Jocasta hanged herself, and Oedipus tore out his own eyes. Oedipus is alluded to as a symbol of someone predestined to act in a particular way and powerless to act otherwise, and also as the idea of incestuous love of a son for his mother and jealousy of a son toward his father. (SOURCE: Cooper, 1992)

SONG	COMPOSER	POET
"Antigone und Oedip"	Franz Schubert	Johann Mayrhofer

OGARYOV, NIKOLAI (1813–1877): Russian poet. Ogaryov was a fine romantic poet, whose private life was scarred by tragedy. He being a melancholy pessimist, it broke his spirit. Ogaryov lacked political tact and was personally awkward in his relationships, not retaining respect from his acquaintances. His poetry is depressing, expressing boredom, hopelessness, and self-hatred, made greater by the autumn and winter backdrops he used. Ogaryov was a sensitive and gentle person, but he lacked a musical voice. He was torn between his love for Russia and his hatred for its government. Since he spent many years abroad even before he emigrated, his poetry features foreign landscapes and traditions. The poetry of Nikolai Ogaryov was set by Aleksandr Alyabiev and Tchaikovsky. (SOURCE: Terras, 1991)

"OH" AND "AH": *see* "★AH" AND "OH."

O'HARA, FRANK (1926–1966): American poet, art editor, and assistant curator of New York's Museum of Modern Art. Frank O'Hara was born in Baltimore, Maryland, but grew up in Massachusetts. After serving in the U.S. Navy, he attended Harvard as a music major from 1946 to 1950. He returned to New York, where he was employed by the Museum of Modern Art directly after graduate school at the University of Michigan. For the rest of his life, O'Hara was deeply involved in the New York art scene, especially with the work of abstract expressionist painters such as Willem de Kooning, Jackson Pollock, and Franz Kline. Between 1953 and 1955 he worked as an editorial associate for *Art News*, for which his poet colleagues John ★Ashbery and James Schuyler also wrote. In 1955 O'Hara rejoined the MOMA staff and was appointed assistant curator in 1960. Early in a July morning of 1966 he was struck and gravely injured by a beach buggy on Long Island. The next day he died from his wounds. O'Hara's poems are a potent mix of enthusiasm and ★surrealism. For him, as for his friends the abstract expressionist painters, art is a process. His airy poetic structures are full of casual details of his own life, love affairs, friendships, responses to paintings, movies, and literature. O'Hara refused to take his poetry seriously and often gave away copies of his poems. Yet, some of his later and longer poems have been influential for many younger poets. The poetry of Frank O'Hara has been set by Stephen Paulus. PRINCIPAL WORKS: *Collected Poems*, ed. Donald Allen, 1971, 1991; *Selected Poems*, 1974. SELECTED READING: Brad Gooch, *City Poet: The Life and Times of Frank O'Hara*, 1993. (SOURCE: Hamilton, 1994)

"Oh, the Sweet Delights of Love": a soprano duet from the 1690 semi-opera *Dioclesian*, music solely by Henry Purcell, set to the words of Massinger and ★Fletcher. *See* ★*Dioclesian* for plot and placement of songs.

OLD BATCHELOUR, THE: the first comedy written by William ★Congreve, produced in 1693, containing two songs by Henry Purcell. The "batchelour" is old, ill-tempered Heartwell, who pretends to be a woman-hater. Heartwell falls in love with Silvia, ignorant of the fact that she is the discarded mistress of Vainlove. He arranges a musical entertainment, which has as its main event, a song, "As Amoret and Thyrsis Lay." Heartwell hopes that it will please Silvia. In act 2, Araminta is conversing with an old friend, Belinda. They have quarreled over Bellmour. In order to console her friend, Araminta asks her music master to sing "Thus to a Ripe and Consenting Maid." A vain and foolish target, Heartwell is inveigled into marrying Silvia, only afterwards to discover her true nature. The parson who marries them is, in fact, Vainlove's friend Bellmour, who allowed himself to be used for the purpose only so that he can intrigue with Laetitia, the young wife of an old banker, Fondlewife. In act 5, Heartwell is much relieved to discover that his marriage was a pretense and returns to the joys of bachelorhood. (SOURCE: Price, 1984)

"O Lead Me to Some Peaceful Gloom": a song composed by Henry Purcell for inclusion in John ★Fletcher's play *Bonduca*, produced in 1695. For plot details and placement of songs, *see* ★*Bonduca*.

OLUF, OLOF, OLAF: a literary character in a play by August Strindberg, based on King Olaf, the first Christian king of Norway, slain in battle by his pagan subjects in 1030 during his struggle to free Sweden from the foreign ruler who had deposed him. In Johann ★Herder's poem, Sir Olaf is a character in a folk tale, a young man riding in the forest where he comes upon a ★Lorelei figure.

SONG	COMPOSER	POET
"Sir Oluf"	Carl Loewe	Johann Herder

OLYMPUS, OLYMPE (Fr.): a mountain about 9,800 feet high between Macedonia and Thessaly, home of the gods of ancient Greece. The adjective "Olympian" can refer to anyone or anything superior to or more important than lesser mortals. (SOURCE: Cooper, 1992)

SONG	COMPOSER	POET
1. "La Rose, Ode Anacréontique"	Gabriel Fauré	Charles Leconte de L'Isle
2. "Dithyrambe"	Franz Schubert	Friedrich von Schiller

OMPHALE: the masculine but beautiful queen of Lydia, to whom ★Hercules was bound as a slave for three years. He fell in love with her and was forced to lead an effeminate life spinning wool, while Omphale wore the lion's skin.

OMPHALOS: literally, *navel*, and the reputed center of the earth; the sacred oval or hemispherical stone marking that spot at the temple of ★Apollo at Delphi. According to the myth, ★Zeus determined the spot by sending forth two eagles at once to fly from the eastern and western ends of the earth. They met at Delphi. (SOURCE: Kaster, 1964)

"One Charming Night": an air composed by Henry Purcell to a text written by Elkanah ★Settle for his work *The Fairie-Queene*, produced in 1692 and 1693. For plot details and placement of songs, *see* ★*Fairie-Queene, The.*

ONOMATOPOEIA: the spelling and formation of words in such a way as to imitate the sound of the object or action expressed, as *buzz, boom, whisper, cuckoo.*

ON THIS ISLAND: a cycle composed of five songs by Benjamin Britten to the texts of W. H. ★Auden. Auden is often difficult to understand, his work being filled with allusions that made sense to Auden and his close associates, but not to the general public. The cycle is a compendium of difficult styles, each different from the other. "Let the Florid Music Praise" is composed in Purcellian manner. "Now the Leaves are Falling Fast" is in a contemporary style. "Seascape" and "Nocturne" are more easily accessible poems. "As It Is Plenty" is written in a cabaret style.

ON WENLOCK EDGE: a song cycle for tenor, string quartet, and piano by Ralph Vaughan Williams, text by A. E. ★Housman. *A Shropshire Lad* appealed strongly to the entire generation of British composers represented by Vaughan Williams. The pessimism and cynicism of the words set against a background of one of England's loveliest parts was hard for the composers to resist. Housman himself was not at all pleased by composers' desire to set his poetry. Vaughan Williams chose the poetry for his work skillfully, avoiding mentions of "soldiers marching" and a "hangman's noose."

OPHELIA, OPHÉLIE (Fr.): a character in ★Shakespeare's *Hamlet*. Daughter of Polonius and in love with Hamlet, Ophelia sings her famous mad scene to the queen in act 4, scene 5 of *Hamlet*, accompanying herself by strumming on a lute. After her father is murdered by Hamlet, her grief drives her out of her mind. Later, while making garlands of flowers by the side of a stream, she falls in and is drowned. Ophelia is the subject of a famous painting by John Everett Millais, in which she is pictured floating face-up in a stream, surrounded by flowers, about to slip under the water. She is often portrayed with flowers entwined in her hair. Strauss set her "mad" songs. (SOURCE: *Bulfinch*, 1978)

SONG	COMPOSER	POET
1. "Chanson d'Ophélie"	Ernest Chausson	trans. Maurice Bouchor
2. "Drei Lieder der Ophelia"	Richard Strauss	William Shakespeare
3. "La Mort d'Ophélie"	Hector Berlioz	trans. Ernest Legouvé
4. "These, My Ophelia"	Theodore Chanler; Ross Finney	trans. Archibald MacLeish

OPHIR: an unidentified region in the Bible, famous as the source of gold and precious stones brought to King ★Solomon (1 Kings, 9.28, 10.10). It is possible that the location of Ophir was in Southeast Arabia. (SOURCE: Cotterell, 1986)

SONG	COMPOSER	POET
"Sanglots"	Francis Poulenc	Guillaume Apollinaire

ORCUS, ORKUS (Ger.): the death god of Roman mythology, eventually the realm of the dead, comparable to ★Hades in Greek mythology. Later, Greek mythology identified ★Pluto with the god of death, and the Roman god of death became Dis. Eventually Hades and Orcus were used to designate the realm of the dead ruled over by Dis and Pluto, respectively. (SOURCE: Mayerson, 1971)

SONG	COMPOSER	POET
1. "An die Parzen"	W. Fortner, P. Hindemith, H. Reutter	Friedrich Hölderlin
2. "An Schwager Kronos"	Franz Schubert	Johann Wolfgang von Goethe

ORESTES, OREST (Ger.): the son of Agamemnon and Clytemnestra and brother of Electra and ★Iphigenia. All strangers who were shipwrecked on the shores of ★Tauris were sacrificed to Artemis, ★Iphigenia presiding over these sacrifices. When Orestes's father was murdered by his mother and her lover Aegisthus, Electra sent him to be brought up in Phocis. Upon his return, Electra persuaded him to murder his mother and Aegisthus. For this, he was driven mad and pursued by the ★Furies. In another tradition Orestes went to fetch the statue of Artemis from ★Taurus, where he went accompanied by his faithful friend Pylades. Arriving there, they were seized to be sacrificed to the goddess. Iphigenia, the priestess, recognized the two, and all three escaped with the statue, which finally found sanctuary on the Acropolis in Athens. Upon their return to Mycenae, Orestes took over the kingdom and married Hermione, daughter of ★Menelaus. (SOURCES: Kaster, 1964; Guirand, 1968)

SONG	COMPOSER	POET
1. "Orest auf Tauris"	Franz Schubert	Johann Mayrhofer
2. "Der entsühnte Orest"	Franz Schubert	Johann Mayrhofer

ORGEL, IRENE (d. 1960): English poet. Irving Fine met Irene Orgel when she was at the MacDowell Colony with him the summer that he composed his song cycle *Mutability*. (SOURCE: Villamil, 1993)

ORION: a giant hunter in Greek mythology, noted for his beauty. During his attempt to kidnap his beloved Merope, Orion was blinded by her father Oenipion, but Vulcan sent Cedalion to be his guide. Cedalion restored Orion's sight by exposing his eyeballs to the sun. Having been slain by ★Diana at the urging of her brother ★Apollo, Orion was made one of the constellations in the heavens. He is said to be attended by stormy weather. Orion the constellation is pictured as a giant hunter with a belt and sword, surrounded by dogs and animals. The stars that outline Orion's shoulders are Betelgeuse and Bellatrix, and three bright stars appearing in a line represent his belt. (SOURCE: Kaster, 1964)

SONG	COMPOSER	POET
1. "Nocturne"	Samuel Barber	Frederic Prokosch
2. "Euphonium Dance"	Betty Roe	Jacqueline Froom

ORKENISE: a road leading to the Roman gate by the same name in the imaginary town of Autun. There are huge city gates, guarded over by large mustached guards who knit while questioning people who enter and leave. (SOURCE: Bernac, 1970)

SONG	COMPOSER	POET
"Chanson d'Orkenise"	Francis Poulenc	Guillaume Apollinaire

OROONOKO: a tragedy produced in 1695, adapted by Thomas ★Southerne from a novel. He brought together comic and serious plots at various points to give a different perspective on the tragic activities. Purcell made one contribution to the drama, "Celemene, Pray Tell Me," an erotic dialogue about children that was introduced into the tragic plot, which is a strong attack on slavery. Oroonoko, heir of an African king, loves and weds Imoinda, daughter of a white European. The king, also in love with Imoinda, angrily orders her to be sold as a slave. His son is trapped as a slave and carried off to Surinam, where he incites his fellow slaves to rebellion. In the upper society level of Surinam are a tyrannical governor, the Welldon sisters, who have immigrated to the island to search for husbands, the Widow Lackitt and her foolish son, Daniel, and a vile slave trader, Captain Driver. In the slave society are Oroonoko and several other lower station black men, among them Aboan and Hottman, who betray Oroonoko's rebellion. In act 2 singing and dancing black slaves appear, just as shepherds and shepherdesses appeared in pastoral Restoration plays. The plot centers on Celemene, who is actually Imoinda, desired by the evil governor. Because she has not seen her husband since their wedding day, she is sad. The governor tries to ease her melancholy by ordering some slaves to perform a musical show (act 2, scene 3). The text of Purcell's "Celemene, Pray Tell Me," which is sung in this scene, is made purposely tasteless in order to reveal the governor's boorish nature. The dialogue describes the innocent arousal of a pubescent boy and girl. (The text was too erotic for the Purcell Society, who inserted other words in their edition.) In act 4, Oroonoko abandons his rebellion and surrenders because Imoinda is now pregnant. Oroonoko and Imoinda part and die by their own hands in the last act. (SOURCE: Price, 1984)

ORPHEUS: in Greek legend, a Thracian poet, son of Oeagrus and *Calliope (often said, son of *Apollo), whose music could move even inanimate things. While taking part in the Argonautic expedition, he appeased a storm. When Orpheus's wife *Eurydice died, Orpheus went into the infernal regions. He so charmed *Pluto that Eurydice was released on condition that Orpheus would not look back until they reached the earth, but when Orpheus was about to place his foot on earth, he turned around. In that moment Euridice vanished instantly, and Orpheus perished, torn to pieces by infuriated Thracian *maenads. (SOURCES: Cotterell, 1986; *Bulfinch*, 1978)

SONG	COMPOSER	POET
1. "Orpheus with His Lute"	Arthur Sullivan, William Schumann, Ralph Vaughan Williams	William Shakespeare
2. "Die Schale der Vergessenheit"	Johannes Brahms	Friedrich Hölty
3. "Orpheus"	Franz Schubert	Johann Georg Jacobi
4. "When Orpheus Played"	Richard Hundley	William Shakespeare

ORPHEUS BRITANNICUS: the great collection of Henry Purcell's works in two books (1698, 1702). The collection contains songs from plays and operas as well as songs with no theatrical connection, also pieces from occasional music such as *odes, birthday songs, and *welcome songs. In addition there are duets, trios, songs with chorus, and songs with instrumental ritornellos and obbligato accompaniments.

ORPLID: the name of an island created in the imaginations of poet Eduard *Mörike and his friend L. A. Bauer, when they were boys at school in Urach. The history of Orplid is outlined by a character in book 1 of Mörike's novel *Maler Nolten.* The imaginary island was located in the Pacific between New Zealand and South America; its principal city also bore the name Orplid. The island was protected by the goddess *Weyla, and its inhabitants included human beings, elves, and *fairies. When the island became too civilized, it incurred the wrath of the gods. With the exception of one survivor, its people died out, and Orplid, except for the castle, fell into ruins.

SONG	COMPOSER	POET
"Gesang Weylas"	Hugo Wolf	Eduard Mörike

ORVIETO: an ancient Italian town in central Umbria, built atop an enormous plateau of volcanic rock, first settled by the Etruscans, destroyed by the Romans in 283

B.C.E. From the Etruscan settlement there remain walls, a fortress, and the magnificent cathedral, built between 1290 and 1580 to celebrate the Feast of Corpus Christi. The facade is made of black and white marble, containing mosaics, sculptures, and frescoes by Signorelli and Fra Angelico.

SONG	COMPOSER	POET
"Ihr seid die Allerschönste"	Hugo Wolf	Paul Heyse

OSIER: a rod used in basketry; any of the willows used for furniture and basketry.

SONG	COMPOSER	POET
"Come, You Pretty False-Eyed Wanton"	Thomas Campion	Thomas Campion

OSIRIS: the ancient Egyptian god of fertility and lord of the afterworld. As the eldest child of Geb (Earth) and Nut (Sky), he was given lordship over the earth. He ruled with his sister and consort ★Isis as the first king of Egypt, teaching mankind the arts of agriculture. His evil brother Set, jealous of his power, ambushed and killed him, then either cast his body into the Nile or cut it into pieces, scattering the parts throughout Egypt. Isis searched for and finally found Osiris's body. With her magic powers she reconstituted it and restored enough life that Osiris could impregnate her. He then departed into the other world, becoming Lord of Eternity and ruler of the departed. Isis gave birth to their child Horus, who engaged Set in a bloody struggle for the kingdom and won, becoming the heir to Osiris, named the justified legitimate ruler of Egypt. (SOURCE: Kaster, 1964)

OSSIAN, OISIN: a legendary bard from Gaelic Scotland and Ireland. Frequently represented as an old blind man surviving both his father and his son, Ossian sang of the deeds of Finn (or Fingal) his father, king of the Fenians, who were a roving group of warriors that protected Scotland and Ireland from Scandinavian marauders. A young Scottish schoolteacher, James ★Macpherson, produced a series of "translations" of what purported to be an actual manuscript written in Gaelic, describing the epics of Ossian. Macpherson published this poetry of Ossian, mostly in prose (1760–63). Some compared his poems to Homer and the Bible, while others, like Dr. Samuel ★Johnson, believed them to be fraudulent. The controversy raged on for many years. Today it appears that there did exist in Scotland, during Macpherson's time, several orally transmitted songs and poems of varying lengths attributed to Ossian. While Macpherson may have used these poems as the basis of his "translations," his *Poetry of Ossian* is primarily an original work and not the result of serious scholarship. Nevertheless, these torrid, bloody poems became the rage in Germany and the rest of Europe. In *The Sorrows of Young Werther* ★Goethe described Charlotte and ★Werther as reading Ossian. The brooding quality of the works with their description of sweeping panoramas was exactly of a sort to attract poets of the ★Sturm und Drang period. The Ossian poems, widely read in Germany, were translated by ★Herder and Edmond von Harold, and read by Franz Schubert. Between 1815 and 1817 Schubert set nine of them to music. Brahms and Saint-Saëns also set poems from Ossian. (SOURCE: Stafford, 1988)

OSTENSOIR: *see* ★MONSTRANCE.

O'SULLIVAN, SEUMAS (pseudonym of James Starkey) (1879–1958): Irish poet. O'Sullivan was born in Dublin. His physician father wrote poetry and contributed to the *Dublin University Magazine*. O'Sullivan's own first published poems appeared in journals in 1902. O'Sullivan was one of the original members of W. G. Fay's Irish National Dramatic Company, later the Irish National Theatre Society. He acted with these companies between 1902 and 1905, then resigned his membership and founded with others the Theatre of Ireland. In 1939 he took a doctorate of literature from Trinity College in Dublin and became one of the first to be elected to the Irish Academy of Letters. O'Sullivan is a poet of the melancholy and graceful "Celtic Twilight School." He is admired for his mastery with rhythms and the "certainty with which a personal music, elusive yet definite and quite unforgettable is caught and sounded" (Kunitz, Haycraft, 1942). In America he is best known for his musical poetry, which is steeped in Celtic spirit, in the tradition of ★Yeats. Seumas O'Sullivan's verse has been set by Michael Head, E. J. Moeran, Arthur Shepherd, and John Duke. PRINCIPAL WORKS: Poetry: *The Twilight People*, 1905; *Verses Sacred and Profane*, 1908; *Selected Lyrics*, 1910; *Poems*, 1912; *Poems*, 1923; *Selected Poems*, 1940. Essays: *Impressions*, 1912; *Mud and Purple*, 1914; *Common Adventures*, 1926. SELECTED READING: E. A. Boyd, *Ireland's Literary Renaissance*, 1968; Padraic Colum, *Road Round Ireland*, 1926. (SOURCE: Kunitz, Haycraft, 1942)

OTTAVA RIMA: an Italian stanza composed of eight eleven-syllable lines (a b a b a b c c) used by Tasso, ★Ariosto, and others. (SOURCE: Drabble, 2000)

OWEN, WILFRED (1893–1918): English poet, killed in France at the age of twenty-five, one week before the Armistice to World War I. A dreamy and precocious boy, Owen was a poet and a lover of poetry from childhood. At the outbreak of the war he enlisted in the British army and, after sustaining a wound, was sent to a hospital in Scotland, where a fellow patient was Siegfried ★Sassoon, who encouraged Owen in his poetic pursuits. Recovered, Owen was sent back to France where he was named company commander and later died. In 1920 Sassoon collected his friend's poems and saw to it that they were published. Owen's war poems were the protest and testament of a potentially great poet caught in a disaster from which there was no escape. In his verse he made use of assonance rather than rhyme. Critics agree that none of the war poets were equal to him in pure genius. As such, he was the ancestor of the generation of poets defined by ★Auden and Stephen Spender. The poetry of Wilfred Owen has been set by Benjamin Britten and Hugo Weisgall. PRINCIPAL WORKS: *Poems*, 1920; *Poems*, 1931. (SOURCE: Kunitz, Haycraft, 1938)

OWRE: (Scot.) (pr. oar), *over; down.*

SONG	COMPOSER	POET
1. "A Laddie's Sang"	Benjamin Britten	William Soutar
2. "Black Day"	Benjamin Britten	William Soutar

OZYMANDIAS: the Greek name for the Egyptian monarch Ramses II, who erected a huge stone statue of himself in the thirteenth century B.C.E.; also, the fictional King of Kings, whose ruined statue ★Shelley describes in his sonnet so titled. The face of the statue, revealing an arrogant and cruel tyrant, is ruined but the legs remain standing. (SOURCES: Benét, 1965; *Norton*, 1996)

SONG	COMPOSER	POET
"Ozymandias"	Richard Bales, Alexander Steinert	Percy Bysshe Shelley

P

PAESTUM: an ancient site in Italy, located 62 miles southeast of Naples, lying on the edge of a flat coastal plain. Its Greek temples are well preserved. The site is that of the ancient city of Poseidonia, founded by Greek colonists in the seventh century B.C.E. and taken over by the Romans in 273 B.C.E.

SONG	COMPOSER	POET
"The Ruins at Paestum"	Wintter Watts	Sara Teasdale

PAGANINI, NICCOLÒ (1782–1840): an Italian virtuoso violinist, whose astonishing virtuosity gave birth to the legend that he was in league with the devil. Not surprisingly, Paganini was a poor ensemble player. In spite of his erratic brilliance as a performer, his own compositions show considerable beauty.

SONG	COMPOSER	POET
"Paganini"	Francis Poulenc	Louise de Vilmorin

PALADIN: a palace officer, a knight, any of the twelve peers of Charlemagne's court. When used in medieval romantic poetry, it represents a matchless, elegant man.

PALANQUIN: in the Orient, a covered litter for one person, sitting atop poles, and carried on men's shoulders.

SONG	COMPOSER	POET
"Song of the Palanquin Bearers"	Martin Shaw	Sarojini Nardu

PALINODE, PALINODIE or EPIPALINODIE (Fr.), : from the Greek, *singing over again*, a poem of recantation.

SONG	COMPOSER	POET
"Épipalinodie"	Jacques Leguerney	Pierre Ronsard

PAN: in Greek mythology, the god of nature, pastures, forests, flocks, and herds, also the universal deity, literally in Greek: *all, everything*. Pan's name was probably derived from the same root as the Latin word *pascere*, to graze. Pan was born of ★Jupiter and Callisto, or of Hermes and Penelope. He is represented with the upper torso of a man and the horns, ears, and legs of a goat. A lustful nature was characteristic of

Pan, and he was the symbol of fecundity. On one occasion he pursued the ★nymph ★Syrinx, who escaped him by turning into a reed. Since he could not tell her from the other reeds, he cut several and made them into Pan pipes, converting his sexual desires into art. As legend (and a poem by Elizabeth Barrett ★Browning) have it, at the time of the Crucifixion, when the veil of the temple was rent in twain, a cry swept across the ocean: "Great Pan is dead!" At the same time, responses from the oracles ceased forever. (SOURCE: Cooper, 1992)

SONG	COMPOSER	POET
1. "La Flûte de Pan"	Claude Debussy	Pierre Louÿs
2. "Crepuscolo"	Ottorino Respighi	Antonio Rubino

PANDERO: a tambourine-like musical instrument.

SONG	COMPOSER	POET
"Klinge, klinge mein Pandero"	Hugo Wolf	Emanuel Geibel, Paul Heyse

PANEGYRIC: a speech or poem in praise of an individual, institution, or group. Originally it was a rhetorical style of oratory. Much primitive poetry is panegyric, consisting of the praises of heroes, armies, and victories.

PANTALOON: a *commedia dell'arte* character. Pantaloon is from Venice, dressed in breeches made of a single piece of cloth (called pantaloons), a loose black cape, Turkish slippers, and a red woolen bonnet, his legs in red stockings. Pantaloon is always old, retired, a father or an old bachelor. When married, the wife is young and pretty, deceives him and mocks him. He is duped by the women he falls for, by his rivals, his son, and his servant girls (who include Zerbinette). When he is wealthy, Pantaloon is called *Don* or *Magnifico*. Excessively miserly, he is a slave to money and is prone to giving useless or misguided advice. The French Pantaloon is called Gaultier-Garguille, "great, greedy mouth." (SOURCE: Duchartre, 1966)

PANTHEISM: from two Greek words, *all* and *God*, the belief that everything is God. Pantheists identify all or part of God with all or part of the universe. This belief is monotheistic, holding that deity is impersonal, that only nature should be worshiped. The origins of the pantheistic belief are in religious mysticism and philosophic speculation. There are several varieties of pantheism. First, western thought is more philosophical than religious; its followers include Giordano Bruno, Benedict de Spinoza, Johann Wolfgang von ★Goethe, William Wordsworth, Samuel Taylor ★Coleridge, Georg Hegel, and Ralph Waldo ★Emerson. Contemporary pantheism is predominantly genetic, that is, God's primordial nature is an eternal infinity of possibilities of what the world could become; therefore his consequent nature is what the world actually is. Both atheists and theists object to pantheism on this basis: evil is a problem if the universe is identical with God. Evil is either a part of God or an illusion.

SONG	COMPOSER	POET
"Sacred Songs for Pantheists"	Robert Ward	G. M. Hopkins, R. L. Stevenson, E. Dickenson

PANTOUM: a Malayan verse pattern in which the second and fourth lines of each stanza become the first and third lines of the following stanza, creating the effect of musical harmony.

SONG	COMPOSER	POET
"Le Jet d'eau"	Claude Debussy	Charles Baudelaire

PANZACCHI, ENRICO (1840–1904): Italian poet. A classicist, Panzacchi was a follower of the great Giosuè ★Carducci. He is noted for being rebellious, republican, anti-clerical, and hostile to Romantic emotionalism, which he considered deficient of formal expression. He equated ★Romanticism with the Middle Ages, and tried to subdue his and others' romantic impulses. His verse was set by Ottorino Respighi. (SOURCE: Jason, 5, 2003)

PAPAVERACAE: a plant of the poppy family.

SONG	COMPOSER	POET
"Chanson du clair tamis"	Francis Poulenc	Maurice Fombeure

PAPHOS: the ancient name of two cities in Cyprus, usually called the "old" and the "new" Paphos. Situated close to the southwestern coast of Cyprus, the old Paphos contained a famous temple for ★Aphrodite (★Venus), who was said to have taken up residence there after rising from the foam of the sea, and the new Paphos is the modern city of Papho.

PAPINI, GIOVANNI (1881–1956): Italian poet, editor, and essayist. Papini was awarded no university degree, but managed to acquire formidable literary and philosophic knowledge by means of his own wide reading and auditing of university lectures. He published dozens of books during his lifetime, founded more than one periodical, and worked as chief editor of a national publication. His autobiographical work, *Un uomo finito* (The Failure), chronicled what he saw as his failure to join his intellectual activity to his political affairs. The controversy that always grew up around his writings did not dismay Papini; he enjoyed it, being a genuine man of letters. More a man of the Enlightenment than a narrow academic, he made a substantial contribution to twentieth-century Italian culture. The verse of Giovanni Papini was set by Ildebrando Pizzetti. PRINCIPAL WORKS: *Un uomo finito,* 1912; *Pane e Vino* [Bread and Wine], 1926; *Imitazione del padre* [Imitation of My Father], 1942; *Il libro nero* [The Black Book], 1951; *La spia del mondo* [The Spy of the World], 1955. SELECTED READING: G. Papini, *Storia della letteratura Italiana* [History of Italian Literature], 1937; *Lettere à Giovanni Papini: 1915–1948* [Letters to Giovanni Papini], ed. Giuseppe Ungaretti, 1988. (SOURCE: Donadoni, 1969)

PARABLE: a saying to illustrate a moral or spiritual truth.

PARACELSUS: a dramatic poem in blank verse by Robert ★Browning (1835). The career of the historical Paracelsus served Browning's exploration of the conflict between Love (self-forgetting) and Knowledge (self-assertion) in the mind of an artist. Theophrast Bombast von Hohenheim (1493–1541)—Paracelsus—was a Swiss-born physician attracted to alchemy, astrology, philosophy, and mysticism. His was a first-class mind, creative, but he was arrogant and unconventional, although he influenced the thinking of sixteenth-century intellectuals in significant ways. His writings remain important for understanding early modern science. Paracelsus's concept of magic was a universal system of scientific and theoretical inquiry into the relationship between God, nature, and humanity. (SOURCE: Drabble, 2000; Reinhart, Hardin, 1997)

SONG	COMPOSER	POET
"Paracelsus"	Charles Ives	Robert Browning

PARIGOT: a type of Parisian slang used on occasion in French poetry. Poulenc was particularly fond of this kind of verse.

SONG	COMPOSER	POET
"L'Anguille"	Francis Poulenc	Guillaume Apollinaire

PARKER, DOROTHY (1893–1978): American poet and short prose writer. Dorothy Parker was born in New York City and, as a member of the celebrated Algonquin Hotel Round Table group, famous in the 1920s and 1930s as the foremost American wit and as a writer of short prose pieces for *The New Yorker* magazine. She was justifiably praised for her light prose, although the serious love poems were regarded as overemotional. She adopted sharp, ★epigrammatic verse to punish her own unsatisfactory lovers and all men, and published several books of verse, legendary for their satirical wit. Dorothy Parker's verse has been set by Richard Cumming and Seymour Barab. SELECTED READING: *The Penguin Dorothy Parker*, 1991 (poems and best prose). (SOURCE:Vinson, 1979)

PARNASSIANS: a group of French poets who embraced restraint, precision, and objectivity. The Parnassians, essentially miniaturists, were reacting to the emotional excesses of ★Romanticism, seeking to purify French poetry and restore it to a calm attitude and a technical precision of metrics. The movement was headed by ★Leconte de L'Isle, whose associates were ★Baudelaire, ★Banville, ★Mendès, and ★Sully Prudhomme. The name of the group came from a collection of their joint work, *Le Parnasse contemporain*. (SOURCE: Drabble, 2000)

PARNY, ÉVARISTE DÉSORÉE, VICOMTE DE: *see* ★FORGES.

PARODY: from the Greek, a song sung counter to or alongside another song, originally referring to a narrative poem in epic meter. Now, a parodist must imitate the pretext as well as create a contradiction in relation to the original, generally with comic attributes. The difference between a parody and a satire is important: a parody aims at a pre-existing text; a satire aims at persons or events of the real world.

SONG	COMPOSER	POET
"Parodie"	Seymour Barab	parodies of G. F. Handel, G. Donizetti, H. Wolf, M. Mussorgsky, H. Duparc, M. de Falla

PARRITCH: (Scot.) (pr. pahritch), *porridge, oats boiled in water.*

SONG	COMPOSER	POET
"Supper"	Benjamin Britten	William Soutar

PARSON'S SAW: an expression used in Elizabethan lyrics, meaning a wise saying.

SONG	COMPOSER	POET
"Winter"	Dominick Argento	William Shakespeare

PARTENOPE: an ancient name for the modern city ★Naples. When Odysseus escaped the lure of the sirens' song, they had drowned themselves in despair. One of them, Partenope, had thrown herself into the sea out of love for Ulysses (Odysseus). She was cast up on the shore of the Bay of Naples, a Greek settlement at the time. Thus her name was given to the city. (SOURCE: *OED*, 1989)

SONG	COMPOSER	POET
"Antica Ninna Nanna Partenopea"	Franco Alfano	anonymous

PARZEN, DIE: *see* ★FATES.

PASCOLI, GIOVANNI (1855–1912): Italian poet and translator, the forerunner of ★Modernism in Italian poetry. When Giovanni was twelve years old, his father was murdered; his mother died a year later. These tragedies are reflected by Pascoli in his gentle pastoral poetry, a return to the primordial aspects of life, caused by his awe before the forces within man. Called the son of Virgil, Pascoli had a talent for exploiting all the beauties of sound: extensive use of alliteration, animal and baby talk, and unusual word combinations that capture the most intimate meanings of nature. According to Pascoli, a child remains within all adults, and this innocent child is free from the influence of society. A socialist sympathizer, he was imprisoned for some months after the 1879 demonstrations. By 1905 Pascoli had succeeded ★Carducci as Professor of Literature at the University of Bologna. His verse was set by Pietro Cimara and Jacopo Napoli. WORKS: *Myricae*, 1891–1905; *Canti di Castelvecchio*, 1903. (SOURCE: Smith, 1974)

PASTONCHI, FRANCESCO (1877–1953): Italian poet, playwright, and writer of short stories. Pastonchi published his first volume of verse, *Saffiche,* in 1892. It was strongly influenced by ★D'Annunzio, like much of Pastonchi's later work. He also showed a disposition toward decadence in *Il Violinista* (1908). Born near Imperia, Pastonchi served as Professor of Italian Literature at the University of Torino from 1935. His poetry was set by Franco Alfano. (SOURCE: Hainsworth, Robbey, 2002)

PATCHEN, KENNETH (1911–1972): American poet, novelist, and dramatist. Patchen was born and reared in Ohio, the son of a steelworker, grandson of mill workers and coal miners. He attended Columbia University but was largely self-taught, publishing a sonnet in the *New York Times* as a teenager. His formative years were spent on the road, crossing the country back and forth, always writing. Originally his output was in the form of proletarian poetry but by 1937 he had embraced anarchy. Thereafter his poetry centered upon love, social protest, and visual art. His belief in pacifism was a response to a world he considered to be mad. During an exploratory operation for back surgery, he fell off the operating table and was left an invalid. Patchen wrote forty books, read angry poems with jazz bands as he explored the relationship between poetry and jazz and the visual arts. Although a real iconoclast, he defied categorization and joined no school of writing. His work was vilified by critics and the poetry establishment as well. The poetry of Kenneth Patchen was set by Richard Hundley. PRINCIPAL WORKS: *The Journal of Albion Moonlight* (journal/novel), 1941; *Memoirs of a Shy Pornographer* (novel), 1945. Poetry: *Sleepers Awake*, 1946; *Hurrah for Anything*, 1957; *Because It Is*, 1960; *Hallelujah Anyway*, 1967; *Wonderings* (picture poems), 1971. SELECTED READING: L. R. Smith, *Kenneth Patchen*, 1978. (SOURCE: Serafin, 1999)

PATER NOSTER (Our Father): A Christian prayer, the Lord's Prayer. The Gospel according to St. Matthew says that ★Jesus taught his disciples how to pray in the Sermon on the Mount. *Pater noster* is, therefore, merely the Latin rendering of the opening words of the Lord's Prayer. It occupies an important place in both Protestant and Catholic liturgies and devotions.

PATMORE, COVENTRY (1823–1896): English poet, essayist, biographer, and nonfiction writer. He was born in Essex, and the first period of Patmore's life was dominated by his father, a man devoted to the arts and a practiced social climber. Patmore published his first book of poems at twenty-one, after which his father sent him to Paris to improve his French. When the elder Patmore lost money speculating, he left his twenty-two-year-old son without support, although he did encourage his son's poetic gifts. Once happily married (1847), young Patmore was able to entertain Robert ★Browning, Lord ★Tennyson, Thomas Carlyle, John Ruskin, Dante Gabriel ★Rossetti, and other ★Pre-Raphaelites. After his wife died, he married twice more but his poems never displayed the same emotional and spiritual fulfillment, although he now embraced Catholicism. His reputation as a writer enjoyed odd extremes: he spoke to the common reader intelligibly but spoke of mystical and esoteric subjects. John Edmunds set his verse. PRINCIPAL POETRY: *Poems*, 1844; *Tamerton Church-Tower and Other Poems*, 1853; *The Betrothal*, 1854; *The Espousals*, 1856; *Faithful For Ever*, 1860; *The Victories of Love*, 1862; *The Angel in the House*, 1863; *Collected Odes*, 1868; *The Unknown Eros and Other Odes*, 1877; *Amelia*, 1878; *The Poems of Coventry Patmore*, 1949. SELECTED READING: E. J. Oliver, *Coventry Patmore*, 1956. (SOURCE: Jason, 5, 2003)

PATRICK, SAINT (ca.381–461): the patron saint of Ireland. Patrick was born in Bannavem, which may have been in England near the ★Severn River estuary, or in Scotland, near the modern city of Dunbarton. Patrick's British name is said to have been Sucat, Patrick being the English form of his Latin name, Patricius. Patrick had a romantic life, full of adventures. At the age of sixteen he was captured by Irish pirates, who took him to Ireland and set him to tending the flocks of an ★Ulster chieftain. Six years of slavery made him a devoted Christian. After he escaped to France, he became a monk. In 432 a vision led him to return to Ireland as a missionary bishop. He worked in various parts of the island for the rest of his life. It is said that "he found Ireland all heathen and left it all Christian." Patrick founded over 300 churches and baptized over 120,000 persons. There are many legends surrounding the name of St. Patrick. In one he charmed the snakes of Ireland, bringing them to the sea shore so that they were driven into the water and drowned. His *Confession*, written in crude Latin, is a kind of autobiography. St. Patrick's relics were held for 1,000 years, but some were destroyed during the Reformation. His feast day is celebrated all over the world on March 17. (SOURCE: *Americana*, 2003)

SONG	COMPOSER	POET
"At St. Patrick's Purgatory"	Samuel Barber	Irish monks and scholars of eighth to thirteenth centuries

PATTER SONG: a song in which the melody of many rapid notes is matched to a text containing a separate syllable for each note. "Patter" vocal music is not restricted to Mozart, Rossini, and Gilbert and Sullivan. Art songs such as Saint-Saëns's "Danse Macabre" and Poulenc's "Fêtes galantes" or Rossini's "La Danza" qualify as patter songs, providing vocal contrast in a song recital.

PAUL, SAINT: Christian missionary, theologian, saint, and martyr. Originally named Saul, Saint Paul changed his name when he converted to Christianity. Paul wrote thirteen of the twenty-seven books of the New Testament, thus was considered the father of Christian theology and highly influential in the Christian Church. Passages from his writing have been cited to justify arguments that slavery is acceptable, that women should not be priests or ministers, that clergy might be celibate or married. The sixteenth-century Reformation was a result of Martin Luther's discovery of Paul's teaching on salvation by grace through faith. Born a Roman citizen in Tarsus, Saint Paul died about 65 C.E. As an employee of the high priest in Jerusalem, having participated in the stoning of the first Christian martyr, he was on his way to Damascus to arrest Christians, when he had a vision of Christ, was struck down by a bright light, and blinded. He was healed by Ananias, who baptized him in the Christian faith. After this Paul stayed in Arabia for a three-year period of reflection and prayer, which led to three missionary journeys into Asia Minor and Greece. Upon his return to Jerusalem he was taken prisoner for preaching against the Jewish law. He successfully claimed his right to a trial in Rome before the emperor. Tradition says that, after remaining under house arrest for two years, Paul was acquitted, then traveled to Spain and Ephesus. Later, having returned to Rome during the reign of *Nero, he was beheaded as a martyr. The patron saint of Malta and Greece, Saint Paul shares the same feast day as St. Peter, June 29, because they are believed to have been martyred on the same day. (SOURCES: Walsh, 1991; Farmer, 1997; Metzger, Murphy, 1994)

SONG	COMPOSER	POET
1. "Wenn ich mit Menschen"	Johannes Brahms	St. Paul
2. "Letters of St. Paul"	Daniel Pinkham	The Holy Bible

PAUL ET VIRGINIE: the masterpiece (1788) of Jacques Henri Bernardin de Saint-Pierre, a French natural philosopher and novelist, who was a friend and follower of *Rousseau. *Paul et Virginie* tells the story of the childhood of two French children, brought up as brother and sister by both mothers on Mauritius, a tropical island. The mothers, who have suffered social disgrace in France, are determined to rear their children in a simple, frugal, and hardworking existence that has no social prejudice, religious superstition, or fear of authority. They are all too successful. Virginie, at adolescence, visits a rich Parisian aunt who wishes to bestow her fortune upon the girl. On the way back to the island, Virginie's vessel is struck by a hurricane and thrown onto the reefs within sight of shore. Virginie drowns because she refuses to undress to save herself. Paul and the two mothers die of grief soon after. (SOURCE: Drabble, 2000)

SONG	COMPOSER	POET
"Paul et Virginie"	Francis Poulenc	Raymond Radiguet

PAUSANIAS: a play by Richard Norton (1695), containing a song by Henry Purcell. The play has been forgotten, but its one Purcell song, "Sweeter than Roses," has not. Pausanias, the regent of Sparta, is lured by the promise of marriage with a Persian princess into considering an overthrow his own government. Even after his counselor Argilius has warned Pausanias of a pending double cross, his mistress Pandora betrays him. The character Pandora, the only one of note, is set apart from the usual leading woman in the 1690s by her ambition and lack of sentimentality. Her affair with Pausanias approaching an end, Pandora has now set her sights on Argilius, intending to blackmail him into cooperating with the Persians. At the beginning of act 3, Pandora is awaiting Argilius while "Sweeter than Roses" is sung by an attendant. The song is not intended, say the knowledgeable, to be the palely pretty, gentle piece that is often performed, but rather an aphrodisiac for the listening Pandora. The duet that follows, "My Dearest, My Fairest," in which lovers ask why love's rapture is so short and sweet, is ascribed to Daniel Purcell, Henry's brother. (SOURCE: Price, 1984)

PEELE, GEORGE (1556–1596): English poet and playwright. Son of a hospital clerk who authored city pageants, Peele was educated at Pembroke College, Oxford. From 1581 on he resided mainly in London, pursuing a literary career. His work was dominated by patriotic themes in which he extended the range of nondramatic blank verse. The verse of George Peele has been set by John Bartlet, John Dowland, Jack Beeson, Peter Warlock, and William Bergsma. PRINCIPAL WORKS: *Polyhumnia,* 1590; *The Honour of the Garter,* 1593. SELECTED READING: *Life and Works,* ed. C. T. Prouty, 1952–70. (SOURCE: Drabble, 2000)

PEER GYNT: a story by Henrik *Ibsen set to music by Norwegian composer Edvard Grieg. *Peer Gynt* is the story of a loutish, ruthless young peasant, whose childish ambition is to become emperor of the world. He abandons his ailing old mother, Ase, and then runs away from home. Peer invites himself to a rustic wedding celebration and succeeds in abducting the bride, Ingrid. Although he carries her off to the mountains, he soon tires of her, taunting her with her failure to compare favorably to Solveig, a girl he noticed in the wedding party. Bored, Peer deserts the unhappy Ingrid. Traveling, he comes upon the palace of the king of the trolls. The king is angered at his refusal to pay court to the troll princess, and the troll court abuses him. About to be tortured, he is saved by the peal of church bells that shatter the palace into ruins. Peer, wandering on, builds himself a little wooden hut. Here Solveig comes to him, believing him to be a fine young man. Giving up everything for love of Peer, Solveig has left her family. In fear of the trolls, Peer abandons Solveig and runs to seek protection with his mother. It is too late; Ase is dying. Her lifeless body falls into his arms. Next, Peer is seen in North Africa where he has several adventures. He is entertained by local Bedouins; he enjoys the performance of the dancing ★odalisques; he courts Anitra, the daughter of the chieftain. She accompanies him into the desert, but robs him and gallops off. Homesick, he embarks for the north, where his ship is wrecked among the fjords. Although wounded, he manages to get to his little hut, where he finds the patient Solveig still waiting for him. Peer sinks down to the ground, putting his head in Solveig's lap. She sings her lullaby (*Solveig's Song*), and he dies before she can finish it.

PEESIES: (Scot.) (pr. *peezeez*), child's word for *excellent*; also, vulgar expression for *frequent urination*.

SONG	COMPOSER	POET
"A Laddie's Sang"	Benjamin Britten	William Soutar

PEGASUS: the winged horse of the muses, born of the sea-foam and the blood of the Gorgon Medusa after ★Perseus cut off her head. Pegasus is the horse on which Perseus came to rescue ★Andromeda, who had been tied to a rock and left to be devoured by a sea monster. Another myth concerning Pegasus is that it was caught by Bellerophon, who mounted him and went to destroy the Chimaera. When Bellerophon attempted to ascend to heaven, he was thrown from the horse, and Pegasus mounted alone to the skies to become a constellation of the same name. When the ★Muses contended with the daughters of Pi'eros, Mount Helicon rose heavenward. Pegasus gave the mountain a mighty kick, and out of the mountain flowed the inspiring waters of the fountain of Hippocrene. (SOURCE: *Bulfinch*, 1978)

SONG	COMPOSER	POET
1. "Pegasus Asleep"	Giancarlo Menotti	Giancarlo Menotti
2. "Love Went a-Riding"	Frank Bridge	Mary E. Coleridge

PENTHESILEA: the daughter of ★Ares, and the queen of the Amazons. She fought against the Acheans as an ally of Troy, but was slain by ★Achilles, who mourned the beauty, youth, and valor of the dying warrior queen. (SOURCE: Kaster, 1964)

PEREDA VALDÈS, ILDEFONSO (1899–?): Cuban poet. The poetry of Pereda Valdès contained the vanguard poems that integrated their vision of blacks within the Communist movements. This important contribution incorporated Afro-Hispanic literary works into Latin American literature. The poetry of Ildefonso Pereda Valdès has been set by Xavier Montsalvatje.

PEREGRINA: a pseudonym given by the poet Eduard ★Mörike for Maria Meyer, a beautiful but half-crazy girl, with whom he fell in love. Of the five poems written by Mörike about his Peregrina, the first and fourth were later set to music by Hugo Wolf. These poems tell of Mörike's love for the girl and his final renunciation of her. Either he discovered that she was morally irresponsible or, according to another theory, he learned that she had formerly been in a convent. Peregrina appears in Mörike's novel ★*Maler Nolten* as the mysterious gypsy, Elizabeth. (SOURCE: Whittinger, 2005)

SONG	COMPOSER	POET
"Peregrina I and II"	Hugo Wolf	Eduard Mörike

PERI, PÉRI (Fr.): originally a beautiful but malicious elf of Persian mythology; later, delicate, fairylike beings. The lovely but malevolent sprite was of a class that was responsible for natural disasters such as comets, eclipses, failure of crops, and so on. The beautiful, gentle creatures were begotten by fallen spirits who direct the pure in mind on their way to Heaven. As the ★Qu'ran (and a poem by Elizabeth Barrett ★Browning) would have it, the later peaceful and docile sprites are under the sovereignty of Eblis, and Mohammed was sent for their conversion as well as for that of man himself. The name *peri* is sometimes applied to any beautiful girl. (SOURCE: Cooper, 1992)

SONG	COMPOSER	POET
"Enchantement!"	Jules Massenet	Jules Ruelle

PERIQUET Y ZUAZNABAR, FERNANDO (1873–1940): Spanish journalist, poet, and librettist. Periquet's great interest in Spanish popular song produced *Apuntes para la historia de la tonadilla y de las tonadilleras de antaño* (Notes on the History of the Tonadilla and its Singers of Old). This work of Periquet spurred a revival of interest in the art of the past and encouraged Granados to compose his own ★tonadillas. Periquet was the librettist for Granados's opera *Goyescas*. The poetry of Fernando Periquet was set by Enrique Granados, Isaac Albéniz, and Tomas Bréton. (SOURCE: Cockburn, Stokes, 1992)

PERSEPHONE, PROSERPINA, PROSERPINE: the Greek goddess, queen of the infernal regions, wife of ★Pluto, daughter of ★Zeus and Demeter. Poets relate Persephone to the daffodil because of this myth. The daffodil, or Lent lily, was once white, called an *affodil* by the British. Persephone had wreathed her head with the white lilies and fallen asleep in a meadow. She was captured by Pluto and carried off in his chariot. During the ride she let fall some of the lilies, which promptly turned to a golden yellow that delighted the spirits of the dead. Demeter, distraught at her daughter's disappearance, wandered weeping through the world until, discovering her location, she retaliated by turning the earth barren. Zeus persuaded Pluto to return Persephone, but she was tricked into eating pomegranate seeds that are sacred to the lower world. Therefore she was obliged to return there for one-third of each year, this being interpreted as the course of the seasons. (SOURCE: Cooper, 1992)

SONG	COMPOSER	POET
1. "Persephone"	Alan Hovhaness	Consuelo Cloos
2. "O, Proserpina"	Mary Howe	Shakespeare

PERSEUS: a legendary Greek hero, the son of the Argive princess ★Danaë and ★Zeus himself, who came to her in the form of a golden shower. Medusa, one of the three frightful sisters who had snakes for hair and who turned all who looked upon them into stone, was killed by Perseus. He did so by never looking directly at her, but at her reflection in his shield. (SOURCE: Cotterell, 1986)

SONG	COMPOSER	POET
"Ah, lo previdi"	Wolfgang Amadeus Mozart	V. A. Cigna-Santi

PESETA: a Spanish coin, the word a diminutive of *pesa* (weight). A peseta was equivalent to the French franc, divided into one hundred centavos, which has been the unit of value in Spain since 1868 until recently with the use of the Euro. (SOURCE: Cockburn, Stokes, 1992)

SONG	COMPOSER	POET
"Seguidilla murciana"	Manuel de Falla	folk song

PETER, SAINT: originally named Simon but renamed by ★Jesus. Peter worked as a fisherman with his brother Andrew, they being the first disciples called by Jesus to follow him. Directly after the miracle in which the five thousand were fed, Jesus and the disciples crossed the Sea of Galilee in a boat. While Jesus went up into the mountains to pray, the disciples remained in the boat. During the night a storm caused the boat to end up far from the land. Early in the morning the disciples saw Jesus walking toward them on the water. Jesus called Peter to walk out that they might meet. Peter began to walk on top of the water toward Jesus, but the high wind disturbed him and he began to sink. Jesus took his hand and saved him. Matthew 16.13–23 is frequently cited as proof that Peter was to lead the church with extraordinary powers over it. As Jesus taught the disciples that he would eventually go to Jerusalem and be crucified, Peter took him aside and insisted that this could never happen to him. Jesus' reply was the well known "Get thee behind me, Satan." Jesus related to the disciples that they would scatter and betray him once he was arrested. Peter claimed that he would be faithful even if it meant death. Jesus told him that Peter, that very night, would deny knowing him three times before the rooster crowed. After Jesus' arrest, Peter was identified twice by a servant girl of the high priest as someone who was with Jesus. He denied it twice, then, as bystanders made the same observation, he denied it for the third time. Tradition has Peter in Rome, founding the church there as the first pope. During Peter's flight from Rome, legend says that he met Christ and asked him the famous question, "Quo vadis?" Jesus said that he was going to Rome. Peter returned with him to meet his fate. He was martyred under the emperor ★Nero around 64 C.E., hung with his head downward because he thought himself unworthy of dying in the same manner as Jesus. Traditionally, St. Peter is seen as the tender of the gates to heaven. St. Peter's feast day is June 29, a date shared with St. Paul. (SOURCE: Delaney, 1980)

SONG	COMPOSER	POET
1. "Alte Weisen"	Hugo Wolf	Gottfried Keller
2. "Wie glänzt der Helle"	Hugo Wolf	Gottfried Keller
3. "Es sungen drei Engel"	Gustav Mahler	Des Knaben Wunderhorn
4. "Monsieur Sans-Souci"	Francis Poulenc	Jean Nohain

PETERISMS: the title of a collection of songs by Peter Warlock (Philip Heseltine). At one time a well-known British brewing firm had invented a character named Peter, a perky errand boy who uttered jaunty and amusing remarks in their advertisements. They were referred to as Peterisms, a word that appealed to Warlock's sense of fun. He adopted the title for a collection of his more frivolous compositions.

PETITE SIRÈNE, LA: the title of a set of three songs by Arthur Honegger, with a text by René Morax, adapted from Hans Christian ★Andersen's tale for children, *The Little Mermaid.* The story tells of a young and beautiful mermaid who is in love with a handsome prince. During a storm at sea she succeeds in saving his life, only to witness his marriage to the daughter of a neighboring king. Upon her death the unhappy mermaid is transformed into a spirit of the air, instead of dissolving into sea foam, the normal fate of mermaids.

PETRARCA, FRANCESCO (1304–1374): Italian poet and scholar. Petrarch (English spelling) was born in Arezzo where his father was a notary attached to the Florentine government. When the elder Petrarca was banished from Florence for political reasons, he took his family to Incisa di Valdarno where he owned property, and then, when the papal court was transferred, to ★Avignon, France. The young Petrarch entered the University of Montpelier and began the study of law around 1316. He showed a marked love of classical literature and continued his studies at Bologna, learning the Italian vernacular poets and the Tuscan idiom. Upon returning to Avignon, he glimpsed his beloved Laura for the first time (1327). She remained the chief subject of his verse until long after her death in the plague of 1348. In fact, Petrarch worked on his *Canzoniere* (Song Book) intermittently until his death in a small village near Padua. His large output includes epic poems, ★dialogues, treatises, guide books, and poetry. ★Sonnets and odes were the only works he wrote in Italian, believing that he would win fame for his Latin writings, but the opposite happened. The minor ecclesiastical post that was given him made time for his writing possible. Petrarch is regarded as the first modern man because his writings are a record of an endless self-analysis, in which he examined his spiritual dilemma (the conflict between flesh and spirit). In the year 1341, on Capitoline Hill, Petrarch received his crown as poet laureate. His speech on that occasion has been called "the first manifesto of the Renaissance." The Italian vernacular verses of Francesco Petrarca have been set by Haydn, Liszt, Schönberg, and Schubert, who set three of his sonnets in German translation, and by Robert Jones, Norman dello Joio, and Ildebrando Pizzetti. TRANSLATED WORKS: *Secretum* [Petrarch's Secret], trans. William Draper, 1911; *De Vita Solitaria* [The Life of Solitude], trans. Jacob Zeitlin, 1924; *Petrarch's Sonnets and Songs*, trans. Anna Maria Armi, 1946. SELECTED READING: J. H. Robinson and H. W. Rolfe, *Petrarch: The First Modern Scholar and Man of Letters*, 1899; E. H. Wilkins, *Studies in the Life and Works of Petrarch*, 1955. (SOURCE: Kunitz, Colby, 1967)

PETRARCH SONNETS, THREE: a group of three Petrarch ★sonnets set to music early in Franz Liszt's composing career while on his second "year of pilgrimage" in Italy (1838). On the way to Italy, Liszt concertized with his friend, the singer

Adolphe Nourrit, whose tenor voice clearly influenced the dramatic and operatic quality of Liszt's early songs. (Nourrit was famed for being the first tenor to sing the high C in full voice, not falsetto.) Liszt's subsequent revision of the songs for lower voice was deemed to have weakened them.

PHAEDRA, PHÈDRE (Fr.): the daughter of Pasiphaë and King Minos of Crete, the sister of *Ariadne, who became another wife of *Theseus. Phaedra, although the wife of Theseus, fell in love with her stepson, *Hippolytus. When her advances were repulsed, she aroused the jealousy of her infatuated husband and Hippolytus was killed. When Theseus's innocence became apparent, Phaedra committed suicide and Aesculapius, with the help of *Diana, restored Hippolytus to life. (SOURCE: *Bulfinch*, 1978)

SONG	COMPOSER	POET
1. "Air de Phèdre"	Virgil Thomson	Jean Racine
2. "Phaedra"	Benjamin Britten	Robert Lowell

PHAETON: lit., *the shining one*; an epithet of Helios (the Sun) in Greek mythology, but, according to a more commonly known myth, the son of Helios by *Clymene. Phaeton asked to drive his father's sun chariot for a day, but he did not have the strength to control the horses. The horses, feeling their reins held by a weaker hand, ran wildly out of their course and came close to the earth, almost destroying it by fire. In retribution *Zeus slew him with a lightning bolt. (SOURCE: *Bulfinch*, 1978; Kaster, 1964)

SONG	COMPOSER	POET
"Let the Dreadful Engines"	Henry Purcell	Thomas D'Urfey

PHILADELPHIA: a conjurer whose feats entertained Frederick the Great. In Schiller's poem, set by Schubert, "Laura am Klavier," Philadelphia's magic powers are compared to Laura's piano playing.

PHILINE: a character from *Goethe's *Wilhelm Meister's Lehrjahre*. During Wilhelm's travels, he meets two stranded actors, Laertes and Philina. She is a light-hearted, shallow girl, who is serious about nothing, living solely for pleasure and flattery. It is she who speaks about her philosophy in "Singet night in Trauertönen." (SOURCE: Blackall, 1989)

SONG	COMPOSER	POET
"Singet nicht in Trauertönen"	Robert Schumann	Johann Wolfgang von Goethe

PHILIPS, AMBROSE (1674–1749): British poet. Philips was born in Shrewsbury of a Midland family, his father a draper who died at thirty-three, leaving his wife with five sons to bring up. Philips attended St. John's College, Cambridge. Later, a long-lived quarrel developed between Philips and Alexander Pope as to who was the best pastoral poet. When his position as paymaster of the lottery ceased, Philips turned to writing *A Collection of Old Ballads* and made unsuccessful proposals for printing an English dictionary. In Ireland, he became secretary to Boulter, the new

Primate of All-Ireland. Philips did, despite malicious attacks by Swift, manage to get a seat in the Irish House of Commons, retaining it until his death in London at the age of seventy-four. He wrote little in his later years, having had many careers: don, soldier, diplomat, royal tutor, poet, journalist, secretary, legal officer. Concerned with the main literary and political movements of history, Philips was successful as a poet describing external nature, writing *epigrams, *epitaphs, translating Pindar, *Anacreon, and *Sappho. The poetry of Ambrose Philips was set by Gordon Binkerd, and by Handel for his "Ode for the Birthday of Queen Anne." WORKS: *The Poems of Ambrose Philips*, ed. M. G. Segar, 1969. (SOURCE: Jason, 5, 2003)

PHILOMEL, PHILOMELA: lit., *lover of song*; a bird of spring, said never to sleep. In Greek legend, Philomela was the daughter of Pandion, king of Athens, and sister to Procne, wife of Tereus, king of Thrace. Tereus brought Philomela to visit his wife, Procne, but when he reached Helleas, he dishonored Philomela, then cut out her tongue so that she could not reveal what he had done. Although Tereus told Procne that her sister was dead, Philomela made the story of his evil deed known by weaving it into a robe and sending it to Procne. In revenge, Procne and Philomela cut up Itys, product of the illicit union, and served his flesh to Tereus. Since Tereus was about to kill the sisters, the gods changed him into a hawk to be forever in pursuit of the birds, Procne into a swallow, and Philomela into a nightingale, which is the way poets still refer to her. A medieval story says that the nightingale is afraid of snakes and keeps awake all night by pressing her breast against a thorn, singing mournfully because of the pain. Another legend says that, if the nightingale's eyes and heart are dissolved and given in a drink, the drinker will never sleep again as long as he lives. (SOURCE: Cooper, 1992)

SONG	COMPOSER	POET
"Philomel"	Ned Rorem	Richard Barnefield

PHOEBUS: in Greek, *the shining one*, an epithet for *Apollo, god of the sun; in poetry the name is sometimes used for the sun itself, sometimes for Apollo as leader of the *Muses. (SOURCE: Cooper, 1992)

SONG	COMPOSER	POET
1. "Attributs"	Francis Poulenc	Pierre Ronsard
2. "Dithyrambe"	Franz Schubert	Friedrich von Schiller
3. "Ständchen"	Franz Schubert	William Shakespeare, trans. Schlegel
4. "When a Cruel Long Winter"	Henry Purcell	Elkanah Settle

PHOENIX: a fabled bird that supposedly lived for 500 years, after which it destroyed itself by fire and rose from the ashes to start life anew. The name is thought to be of Phoenician or Greek origin. In Egypt the bird was sacred to the sun god Re (or Ra) and worshiped at *Heliopolis. The purple-red bird was a symbol of the rising sun and the hieroglyph for the sun. The original legends date from the fifth century, but in Christian lore and later literature it is the symbol of resurrection and immortality. (SOURCE: Cotterell, 1986)

SONG	COMPOSER	POET
"Phoenix Afire"	Herbert Elwell	Robert Liddell Lowe

PHOSPHOR: the morning star.

PHYLLIS, FILLE (It.), FILLI, FILLIDA, FILLIDE: a generic name for shepherdess in pastoral poetry. Phyllis's interest was not in her sheep, but in love and poetry. (SOURCE: Marinelli, 1971)

SONG	COMPOSER	POET
1. "Pastorella, ove t'ascondi"	Filippo Vitale	anonymous
2. "Dolente imagine"	Vincenzo Bellini	anonymous
3. "Torna vezzosa Fillide"	Vincenzo Bellini	anonymous
4. "Zefiro, torna"	Claudio Monteverdi	Francesco Petrarca
5. "Phyllis, We Don't Grieve"	Thomas Arne	anonymous

PIBROCH: a piece of music for bagpipe, usually martial, but often dirgelike. With reference to Stanford's song, Gerald Moore, the great British accompanist, advises that the pianist should keep feet off the sustaining pedal for most of the composition, since bagpipes do not possess a sustaining element.

SONG	COMPOSER	POET
"The Pibroch"	Charles Villiers Stanford	Murdoch MacLean

PICASSO, PABLO (1881–1973): a Spanish-born painter and sculptor, who moved from Málaga to Paris in the early 1900s. Picasso was one of the most familiar and controversial artists of the first part of the twentieth century. His genius inspired many other artists and movements. Soon after arriving in Paris (1904), Picasso won recognition with his paintings of the Blue Period. The Rose Period followed, mostly paintings of circus people. In 1907 Picasso and ★Braque opened the Cubist movement with Picasso's painting *Les Demoiselles d'Avignon*. At the same time Picasso was painting neoclassic giant nudes and mythological subjects. In the late 1920s he influenced and was influenced by the ★Surrealists. When, in 1937, General Franco ordered German bombers to destroy the Spanish town of Guernica, it inspired Picasso's angry, symbolic mural *Guernica* and his joining of the Communist Party. In the late 1940s he moved to Vallauris, where he revived the pottery-making industry by designing ceramics. In 1955 Picasso settled in Cannes. ★Éluard's description of his understanding of Picasso, as quoted by Kimball (*NATS Journal*, 1987), states, "Beginning with Picasso, the walls crash down. The painter renounces his reality no more than the reality of the world. He dreams, he imagines, he creates. . . . And suddenly the potential object is born from the real object and it in turn grows real." (SOURCE: *Americana*, 2003)

SONG	COMPOSER	POET
"Picasso"	Francis Poulenc	Paul Éluard

PICCADILLY: open paved area called Piccadilly Circus, a busy, crowded major hub in London city center near Haymarket, the center of the theater district. Haymarket Street extends northward, ending at Piccadilly Circus, which serves as a link between daytime shopping areas and the gay evening entertainment area. The street called Piccadilly runs through a fashionable shopping area, ending at ★Hyde Park Corner, an open-air forum.

SONG	COMPOSER	POET
"La Diva de l'Empire"	Erik Satie	Dominique Bonnaud, Numa Blès

PICHLER, KAROLINE (1769–1843): a Viennese poet, novelist, and playwright. In 1796 she married Andreas Pichler, a civil servant. Together they maintained a literary salon that was frequented by all the literary lights of Vienna. Franz Schubert was a frequent visitor (1820–21), and he set three of her poems, including "Der Unglückliche," D713 (1821). (SOURCE: Reed, 1997)

PICKLE: (Scot.), *a very small amount.*

PIED: variegated, having two or more colors in patches or blotches, as in ★Shakespeare's "When Daisies Pied." (SOURCE: *Norton,* 1996)

PIED PIPER OF HAMELIN: a mythological character made famous by Robert ★Browning in a poem based upon a legend. According to the legend, the German town of Hamelin was infested by rats. One day a strange man, dressed in a suit of many colors, walked into Hamelin and offered to rid the town of its pests for a sum of money. When the lord mayor agreed, the man drew out a pipe, and walked along the streets playing haunting tunes. All the rats came tumbling out of the houses, following the piper to the Weser River, where they drowned. When the piper claimed his reward, the mayor refused to pay. The piper swore vengeance. He walked along the streets playing the same melodies. This time the children ran from their homes and followed him to a cave in nearby Köppen Hill. The cave closed in, and the children were never seen again. The legend is based at least in part on fact. Old writings on the walls of several houses of Hamelin say that, on July 26, 1284, a piper led 130 children out of town and lost them on Köppen Hill. Some believe that the piper was an agent of the bishop of Olmütz, who in the late 1200s drew many Hamelin lads to Moravia, where they settled. Others claim that the children were kidnapped by robbers. ★Goethe's poem on the subject adds maidens to the piper's conquests. (SOURCE: *Americana,* 2003)

SONG	COMPOSER	POET
"Der Rattenfänger"	Hugo Wolf	Johann Wolfgang von Goethe

PIERROT: lit., *little Peter,* a traditional character in French pantomime, kind of an idealized clown. Pierrot is generally represented as tall and thin, his face covered with white powder or flour, wearing a white costume with very long sleeves and a row of big buttons down the front. *See also* ★HARLEQUIN. (SOURCE: Cooper, 1992)

SONG	COMPOSER	POET
1. "Pierrot"	Claude Debussy	Théodore de Banville
2. "Pantomime"	Claude Debussy	Paul Verlaine
3. "Pierrot"	Wintter Watts	Sara Teasdale
4. "Pierrot Lunaire"	Arnold Schönberg	Albert Giraud, Otto Hartleben, trans.

PIERROT LUNAIRE: a collection of fifty poems by the Belgian ★Symbolist poet, Albert ★Giraud, pseudonym of Albert Kayenberg (1869–1921). Arnold Schönberg set twenty-one of the fifty poems, translated by Otto Hartleben, in a composition that featured the device of ★Sprechgesang. The formal structures were derived from popular dance forms.

PIPPA: the heroine in a poetic drama by Robert ★Browning, *Pippa Passes* (1841). Pippa is a poor child who works all year in the silk mills of Asolo in Italy. In the play she makes chance appearances at critical moments in the spiritual lives of the leading characters. She passes, singing, and her voice and her song alter the destinies of the people who overhear her. Her own life is changed by her final song, "God's in His Heaven. All's Right with the World."

SONG	COMPOSER	POET
"Pippa's Song"	Ned Rorem	Robert Browning

PITCHFORD, KENNETH (b. 1931): American poet, novelist, playwright, translator, and essayist. Pitchford graduated from the University of Minnesota summa cum laude, served in the infantry during the Korean War, won prizes for his work during his stay at Magdalen College as a Fulbright scholar, later becoming a resident of New York City. His play *The Wheel of the Murder* was produced by Joseph Papp; his play *Shellac for the Gears of Progress* was produced in Paris; his ballet *Triptych* was staged by the San Francisco Ballet. His work has appeared in numerous magazines, his writing has been anthologized widely, and he has taught extensively. Pitchford is generally considered to have broken the mold of conventional poetry as he invented a new one and is known for his mastery of lyrical and metaphysical forms. His verse has been set by Ned Rorem (*Poems of Love and the Rain*, a cycle), in a cantata by Robert Phillips, and in songs by Lockrem Johnson. PRINCIPAL WORKS: *The Blizzard Ape*, 1958; *A Suite of Angels*, 1967; *Color Photos of the Atrocities*, 1973; *The Contraband Poems*, 1976; *The Sonnets to Orpheus of Rainer Maria Rilke* (translation), 1981 Novels: *The Temple Wall*, 2001; *The Zipper Mask*, 2004. (SOURCE: Hardison, 1958)

PLATEN-HALLERMÜNDE, KARL GRAF VON (1796–1835): a German poet and playwright. Platen-Hallermünde received a commission in the army (1814), but found himself unsuited for military service. After his discharge (1818), he devoted his life to travel and the ancient Greek and Roman forms of poetry. Brahms and Schumann set the verse of Platen-Hallermünde, whose poems Franz von ★Bruchmann introduced to Schubert, who set two of them, including "Die Liebe hat gelogen." PRINCIPAL WORKS: *Ghaselen; Sonetti aus Venedig* [Sonnets from Venice]; *Gedichte*. (SOURCE: Reed, 1997)

PLATH, SYLVIA (1932–1963): American poet, short story writer, and novelist. Sylvia Plath was born in Boston and spent her childhood in Winthrop, Massachusetts. At the age of eighteen her professor father died. Her mother then moved the family to Wellesley, where she struggled to give Sylvia and her younger brother every advantage of superior education. Plath's anxiety about status and money during her adolescence contributed to a profound insecurity that she concealed all her life. By the time she was at Smith College in the early 1950s, Plath had published poems in newspapers and written over fifty short stories, some of which were prize winners. Working too hard at Smith pushed her to attempt suicide in her junior year. After graduating summa cum laude in 1955, she went to Cambridge University in England on a Fulbright Scholarship. There she met Ted Hughes, a poet, whom she married in 1956. Supremely dedicated writers and believers in each other's literary gift, they lived in Massachusetts and London for six years. After 1960 her poems presented "the surreal landscape of her own damaged psyche" (Drabble, 1985). Her sad novel, *The Bell Jar* (1963), and her first book of poems, *The Colossus* (1962), were informed by a preoccupation with death and rebirth. Her mature poetry became not merely confessional but also an attempt to redeem a meaningless life with art. In the spring of 1962, the deathly *Ariel Poems* appeared. In October 1962, learning of her husband's infidelity, she asked him to leave permanently. After Hughes's departure, Plath produced forty poems of rage, despair, love, and vengeance in less than two months. These have been responsible for her immense posthumous fame. In December 1962 she moved from Devon to London, and in January she descended into deep clinical depression until, on the morning of February 11, she gassed herself. She became the heroine and martyr of the feminist movement. The poems of Sylvia Plath have been set by Ned Rorem. PRINCIPAL WORKS: *Collected Poems*, 1981. SELECTED READING: Lindsay Wagner-Martin, *Sylvia Plath*, 1987; Anne Stevenson, *Sylvia Plath*, 1989. (SOURCE: Drabble, 1985)

PLATNER, ANTON OR EDUARD (1786–1860): Austrian poet and priest. Born near Innsbruck, where he studied philosophy, Platner participated in the uprising of Tyrol against Bavaria (1809) and, after the failure of the revolution, lived the life of an adventurer in southern Germany, Bohemia, Vienna, and Hungary. Returning to the Tyrol, Platner was ordained a priest (1819). In the course of his serving several parishes, his bizarre behavior led to his being incarcerated in lunatic asylums several times. Although a large quantity of his poetry was published posthumously, "Die Blumensprache," which Franz Schubert set in 1817, had been published in 1805. (SOURCE: Garland, 1976)

PLATO (427?–347 B.C.E.): one of the greatest philosophers of western culture. At the age of twenty-one Plato came under the influence of *Socrates, thereafter devoting himself to philosophy. In 397 B.C.E. Plato opened a school called The Academy because of its location in the Grove of Academus. It became the intellectual center of Greece and the first university in the history of Europe. Never allowing his lectures to be written down, he made a distinction between opinion and knowledge, saying that the realm of nature and human experience were in constant flux. If man's mind could ascend from specific objects and ideas to the universal, he could have an unchanging formal object of knowledge. Plato was born in Athens of an aristocratic family. "Plato" was a nickname, meaning broad-shouldered, for his real name Aristocles. When Socrates was executed, Plato left Athens to travel and study in Greece, Italy, Sicily, North Africa, and Egypt, after which he returned to Athens where he died. (SOURCE: Grant, 1980)

SONG	COMPOSER	POET
1. "Das Lied im Grünen"	Franz Schubert	Friedrich Reil
2. "Vilse"	Jan Sibelius	Karl Tavaststjerna

PLATONIC LOVE: a Renaissance concept that beauty is an outer sign of the moral and spiritual beauty of the soul. Platonic love was based on an idea of *Plato that a proper Platonic lover adores the beloved's physical beauty only as a manifestation of his or her inner beauty. (SOURCE: *OED*, 1989)

PLEIADES: the seven daughters of *Atlas and Pleione and the virgin companions of Artemis. When they and their mother were pursued by *Orion, they prayed to the gods for rescue. In answer to their prayer, they were changed into doves and later into stars, forming the constellation named for them. Also, the name of a literary group of seven French poets (La Pléiade) of the sixteenth century, led by *Ronsard. They were inspired by the literature of antiquity and the Italian Renaissance. The name had originally been applied to a group of seven poets from the reign of Ptolemy II. La Pléiade did much to create the modern poetry of France. Russian poet *Pushkin's group of followers were often called "the Pushkin pleiad." Their life and works were inseparably linked with Pushkin's. They included Nikolai Ryléev, Kondraty Yazykov, and Anton *Delvig. (SOURCES: Kaster, 1964; Drabble, 2000; Terras, 1991)

SONG	COMPOSER	POET
"Oscuro è il ciel"	Ildebrando Pizzetti	Giacomo Leopardi

PLESHCHEYEV, ALEKSE NIKOLAYEVICH (1825–1893): Russian poet, prose writer, critic, journalist, and translator of western poets into Russian. Pleshcheyev came from a noble family and was educated at St. Petersburg University. He began his career in 1845 by attending meetings of the Petrashevsky Circle. With other members of the Circle he was arrested and tried (1849). His death sentence was commuted to exile in Orenburg Province. Returning in 1859, he continued his literary activities. Pleshcheyev's translations from Heinrich *Heine, Taras Shevchenko, and Johann Wolfgang von *Goethe were set by Tchaikovsky, and by Rachmaninoff in his op. 8, no. 1– 8. Gretchaninov set Pleshcheyev in his op. 5, no. 1, "Stepye idu ya unylyu" (Over the Steppe). (SOURCE: Miller, 1973; Mirsky, 1958)

PLISKY: (Scot.) (pr. plisskee), *practical joke, dirty trick*; adj. *mischievous*.

SONG	COMPOSER	POET
"The Larky Lad"	Benjamin Britten	William Soutar

PLUTO: *see* *HADES.

"Pluto, Arise!": a song composed by Henry Purcell, to the text written by Thomas *D'Urfey for his play *Circe*, produced in 1677. For plot details and placement of songs, *see *Circe*.

POE, EDGAR ALLAN (1809–1849): American poet, essayist, short story, and fiction writer. Poe was born in Boston, Massachusetts, during a trip that his itinerant actor parents had made. His father disappeared soon after Edgar, the second son, was born. A year later his mother died after the birth of a daughter. The children were separated, Edgar being taken in by a Richmond merchant and his childless wife, who were indulgent to the boy, sending him to a fine school in England. When Poe entered the University of Virginia, he gave way to the weakness and restlessness that were to plague him all his life. When, within a year, the university expelled him for drinking, Poe quarreled with his foster father and ran away from home. He changed his name and enlisted in the U.S. Army. Although his foster father procured his discharge and brought him back to Richmond, the old excesses made for clashes between the two. Allan got his stepson an appointment at West Point, but he was dismissed within six months for disobedience. At twenty-two Poe came to New York and worked as a proofreader, fighting his struggle against poverty, illness, and alcohol. By the time he was thirty-eight, he had married and become a widower, and was violently neurotic and depressed. A compositor on the *Baltimore Sun* found him in a tavern, hallucinating and inarticulate, and took him to the hospital. After four days in delirium, he died, not yet forty-one. Although a discerning critic of other poets' work, Poe could "never separate the genuinely inspired from the ornate and essentially shallow. . . . He was drawn to the tawdry, which he embellished with tinsel, and to the morbidly melancholic" (Untermeyer, 1959). Some literary historians believe that Poe inspired the *Symbolist movement. His best poems are vague, but as persistent as a recurring dream. Poe's popularity in Europe, fed by *Baudelaire's translations and admiration, was very great. The poetry of Edgar Allan Poe was set by Jack Beeson and American composer Charles Martin Loeffler, whose link to Poe was France. Loeffler studied with Debussy's teacher and was an admirer of French literature, setting *Verlaine and Baudelaire as well. PRINCIPAL WORKS: *Tales of the Grotesque and Arabesque*, 1840; *The Raven and Other Poems*, 1845. SELECTED READING: K. Campbell, *The Mind of Poe*, 1962; J. A. Marks, *Genius and Disaster*, 1968. (SOURCE: Untermeyer, 1959)

POÈME: a word used in France, specifically by composer Jules Massenet, to denote a true song cycle. Massenet might be said to have established this cycle form in France: always a sensitive feeling for the words, musical interest divided equally between voice and accompaniment, rhythmic declamation used as a contrast to singing. His oeuvre contains eight such cycles.

POET'S ECHO, THE: a cycle of six songs by Benjamin Britten with texts by *Pushkin. Britten felt throughout his life a need to search out other cultures and languages. He believed that friendship and music made the most powerful combination. In 1960 Britten and the composer Shostakovich had attended a recital by cellist Mstislav Rostropovich, where an immediate rapport was established. Directly after this meeting, Britten wrote several works for cello. A 1965 holiday in the Soviet Union with the Rostropoviches was the final incentive the composer needed to set Russian verse to music. Thus was "The Poet's Echo" written for Galina Vishnevskayha, the wife of Rostropovich.

POIRE: (Fr.), as a slang word, *mug, simpleton.*

SONG	COMPOSER	POET
"Chanson de la Poire"	Arthur Honegger	René Morax

POLICHINELLE: *see* ★PULCINELLA.

POLIZIANO, ANGELO (1454–1494): Italian poet. Angiolo Ambrogini called himself Poliziano, taken from the name of his birthplace, Montepulciano. Poliziano was the tutor to the sons of Lorenzo de Medici. By 1480 he had become the dominant scholar of the Italian Renaissance, holding the position of Professor of Greek and Latin Literature at Florence. His first masque was a long and melodious poem about a tournament in which Giuliano de Medici won a prize in 1475. Poliziano wrote also many popular poems, *ballate*, and ★*rispetti,* which were related to the earlier Sicilian ★*strambotto.* His love of nature and joy in earthly things were combined with a sophisticated polish. Writing lyrics and stanzas in praise of the de Medici family's exploits, he perfected the ★*ottava rima* form. The verse of Angelo Poliziano was set by Gian Francesco Malipiero and Arthur Bliss. (SOURCES: De Lucchi, 1967; Lind, 1954)

POLO: a Spanish dance form native to Andalusia, probably of Moorish origin, danced in a moderately fast 3/8 time, often syncopated, adorned with periodic ornamental phrases on such words as ¡Ay! and ¡Olé! (SOURCE: Cockburn, Stokes, 1992)

SONG	COMPOSER	POET
1. "Polo"	Manuel de Falla	folk song
2. "Polo"	Joaquín Nin	popular song
3. "Polo del contrabandista"	Fernando Obradors	classical Spanish song

POLONSKY, YAKOV (1819–1898): Russian poet, novelist, and librettist. Polonsky was descended from a noble family of modest means, studied law at St. Petersburg University, spent a period in the civil service, and held the post of censor at one time. He was a conservative, less politically committed than some of his contemporaries, and an enthusiastic supporter of science, yet he refrained from any social protest. Polonsky worked in many genres: novels in prose and poetry, short stories, plays in prose and verse, epics serious and satirical, essays, memoirs, opera libretti. Russians remember Polonsky principally as a lyric poet whose poems have a wide range: love poems, Gypsy romances, idylls, ★sonnets, biblical themes, and popular ★ballads. Most of his themes are typical of the romantic period and somewhat banal. The verse of Yakov Polonsky was set by Rimsky-Korsakov, Tchaikovsky, and Rachmaninoff. (SOURCE: Terras, 1991)

POLYCRATES: the tyrant of Samos. Terrified of the good luck that constantly befell him, and wishing to forestall the jealousy of the gods, Polycrates threw into the sea a priceless ring of which he was very fond. When a fisherman returned the ring, having found it in the body of a fish, Polycrates knew that he had offended Nemesis, who punished mortals who transgressed moral law or attained too much happiness or good fortune. (SOURCE: Guirand, 1968)

SONG	COMPOSER	POET
"Orest auf Tauris"	Franz Schubert	Johann Mayrhofer

POMES PENYEACH: a collection of thirteen disparate poems written by James ★Joyce after *Chamber Music* (1913–15 in Trieste, 1915–19 in Zürich, after 1920 in Paris). When asked by Joyce to read the poems, Archibald ★MacLeish encouraged him to publish them under this modest title. Shakespeare and Company duly published the tiny volume (1927) with a cover in the pale green of Joyce's favorite apple (*pomme* is the French word for apple), illuminated by Joyce's daughter. The volumes sold for a shilling or twelve francs "each." The title evokes the slurred pronunciation of a street hawker crying his wares. The poems were mostly about personal subjects, for example, "She Weeps over Rahoon," which was written after Joyce and his wife had paid a visit to the grave of her former early sweetheart, "Simples," which arms the speaker against nostalgia for the simplicity and trust of childhood, "I Hear an Army," which speaks of the loss of peace and security. When Oxford later published Herbert Hughes's *The Joyce Book*, it included settings of all the poems by thirteen different composers: Ernest Moeran, Arnold Bax, Albert Roussel, Herbert Hughes, John Ireland, Roger Sessions, Arthur Bliss, Herbert Howells, George Antheil, Giosuè Carducci, Eugene Goosens, Charles Orr, and Bernard Van Dieren. (SOURCE: Fargnoli, Gillespie, 1996; Litz, 1966)

SONG	COMPOSER	POET
1. "She Weeps over Rahoon"	Miriam Gideon, David del Tredici	James Joyce
2. "Simples"	Arthur Bliss	James Joyce
3. "I Hear an Army"	Samuel Barber	James Joyce

POMONA: the Roman goddess of fruits and fruit trees, hence fruit generally. (SOURCE: Cooper, 1992)

SONG	COMPOSER	POET
1. "Attributs"	Francis Poulenc	Pierre de Ronsard
2. "Madrigal"	Gabriel Fauré	Edmond Haraucourt

PONSARD, FRANÇOIS (1814–1867): French dramatist. Although Ponsard was trained in the law, he began his life as a man of letters with a translation of *Manfred* (1837). In 1845 Ponsard received a prize awarded by the Académie for a tragedy in which he made a stand against ★romanticism. He adopted the unities of time and place as used by the romantics, but wrote in the more serious style of earlier French drama. Although Ponsard's plays reveal a high level of literary and dramatic ability, he owed his popularity to a public dislike of the extravagant style used in the 1830s. He was elected to the Académie in 1885, after which he did less writing. Then in 1866 he achieved a great success with *Le Lion amoureux* (1867), a play about the revolutionary epoch, which encountered great opposition from the clergy. In the same year he was made a commander in the Légion d'honneur. His *Complete Works* were published in three volumes (1865–76). Ponsard's verse was set by Gounod. (SOURCE: France, 1995)

PONT D'IÉNA: one of the bridges that cross the Seine River in Paris. It is located between the Chaillot Palace (near the Place du Trocadéro) on one side of the Seine and the Tour Eiffel (near the Champs de Mars) on the other bank.

SONG	COMPOSER	POET
"Le Joueur de bugle"	Francis Poulenc	Max Jacob

PONTE VECCHIO: lit., *old bridge*, the bridge that spans the Arno River linking the Italian city of Florence to San Miniato, where ★Michelangelo's statue of ★David stands. The Ponte Vecchio, originally built by the Romans and rebuilt in 1345 with tiny gift shops built into its walls, is the only Florentine bridge that the Germans did not blow up during World War II. The bridge now is the bustling location for many small retail shops that sell Florentine leather goods and jewelry. (SOURCE: *Americana*, 2003)

SONG	COMPOSER	POET
"Ponte Vecchio"	Wintter Watts	Sara Teasdale

POPE, ALEXANDER (1688–1744): English poet. With Jonathan Swift, Alexander Pope was one of the two preeminent satirists of the Augustan age. Born in London, his father a linen merchant, Pope suffered from poor health all his life. His formal education was at the hands of priests, but he studied and read by himself. His bent for satire began early, as in *The Rape of the Lock*, a mock heroic poem. Pope began by writing pastoral lyrics and proceeded to verse and critical essays. His mock-heroic poems were popular. From 1713 to 1726 there was a period of translations and editing. From forty to fifty years of age, he wrote one brilliant poem after another. Laboring over each ★couplet, searching for just the right word in order to bring it to perfection as he did was evidence of his single-minded devotion to poetry. The ★romantic poets, with the exception of ★Byron, attacked him for the humor and wit of his verse, but he rose again to eminence in the twentieth century. He died at his villa beside the ★Thames River in Middlesex. The verse of Alexander Pope was set by Franz Schubert. PRINCIPAL WORKS: *The Rape of the Lock*, 1712 and 1714; *The Dunciad*, 1728–43; *Works*, 6 vols., 1939–61, ed. John Butt. SELECTED READING: Maynard Mack, *Alexander Pope: A Life*, 1985. (SOURCE: Drabble, 1985)

POPPY, FLEUR DES BLÉS (Fr.): the common name for several related groups of flowers, the most important of which is the white opium poppy of China, India, and Iran that has been raised in the Orient since ancient times. A flower of delicate beauty and grace, its tiny seeds are sold for bird food, and they yield an oil used in the preparation of food. (SOURCE: *Americana*, 2003)

SONG	COMPOSER	POET
"Phidylé"	Henri Duparc	Charles Leconte de L'Isle

PORTER, KATHERINE ANN (1890–1980): American writer of fiction and movie scenarios. Born in Texas (1894) and educated in small Southern convent schools, Porter had begun to write stories by the time she was three. She was admired for the precision, subtlety, and poetic sensibility of her writing, which she always did at a very slow pace. The work of Katherine Ann Porter has been set by David Diamond. PRINCIPAL WORKS: *Flowering Judas*, 1930; *Hacienda*, 1934; *Noon Wine*, 1937; *Pale Horse, Pale Rider*, 1939; *No Safe Harbor*, 1942; *The Leaning Tower and Other Stories*, 1944. (SOURCE: Kunitz, Colby, 1955)

POSEIDON: the Greek god of the sea and creator of waters, the son of *Kronos and Rhea and brother of *Zeus and *Hades. As lord of the waves, he splits the earth and rocks with his trident, and his epithet in Homer is "the earth-shaker." His power of making the earth quake explains his attribute as ruler of horses. Dolphins and bulls are also sacred to him. Poseidon is equated by the Romans with their sea-god *Neptune. (SOURCE: Kaster, 1964)

POUND, EZRA WESTON LOOMIS (1885–1972): American poet of Quaker ancestry. Having finished his education at the University of Pennsylvania, Pound went to Europe (1908), where he published his first book of poems, then moved to London. He soon became prominent in literary circles, founding with colleagues the *Imagist School. These poets advocated free rhythms and concise language and imagery. His tart pronouncements included: "Use no superfluous word; go in fear of abstractions; don't be descriptive; only emotion endures." Pound championed the work of *Joyce and *Eliot early on. By 1920 he had turned away from the strictness of Imagism. He freed himself through translating early Italian works, works in Provençal and Chinese, and began composing his most serious project, the *Cantos*. Pound left London for Paris and joined the literary scene surrounding Gertrude *Stein. In 1925 he settled permanently in Rapallo, Italy, where he continued work on the *Cantos* until they were finished (1970). Pound's interpretation of the evils of credit capitalism led him into anti-Semitism and some support of Mussolini, such as some partisan broadcasts. He was arrested in Genoa for his activities, delivered into the hands of the U.S. Army but found unfit to stand trial, and sent to a mental institution in Washington. When released, he returned to Italy, where he lived at the time of his death. Pound's literary reputation was lessened by the last decades of tragedy and by the formidable difficulty of his work. The poetry of Ezra Pound has been set by Lee Hoiby, John Koch, Thea Musgrave, and David Diamond. PRINCIPAL WORKS: *Pisan Cantos,* 1948; *Literary Essays of Ezra Pound,* 1954; *Cantos,* 1970. SELECTED READING: N. Stock, *The Life of Ezra Pound,* 1970. (SOURCE: Drabble, 2000)

POW: (Scot.), *head*.

PRADERA: a park near Madrid.

SONG	COMPOSER	POET
"El majo celoso"	Fernando Obradors	classical Spanish song

PRAYER: a solemn request of or thanksgiving to an object of worship. The two types of prayer are a prayer of worship and a prayer of petition. The method of praying may be either mental or vocal. (SOURCE: Nevins, 1964)

SONG	COMPOSER	POET
"En prière"	Gabriel Fauré	Stephen Bordèse

PRÉCIEUX: a popular French literary tradition that governs word choices. The goal of the *précieux* tradition is to elevate the banal to the level of art through use of "conceits." An example of such a conceit is chosen by Paul ★Verlaine in his poem set by Claude Debussy as "Fantoches": the use of *à tue-tête* in place of the more literal *à voix haute.*

"Prepare, the Rites Begin": an invocation set by Henry Purcell to words by Nathaniel ★Lee, author of the heroic play *Theodosius,* produced in 1680. For plot details and placement of songs, *see* ★*Theodosius.*

PRE-RAPHAELITE BROTHERHOOD: a group of artists, poets, and critics who first met in 1848. The group had admiration for the Italian quattrocento and disdain for the authority of Raphael and for academic nineteenth-century writing. Their fidelity was to nature and moral seriousness; they were against the ugliness of modern life and dress. (SOURCE: Drabble, 2000)

PRIAM: the king of Troy during the ★Trojan War. Priam and his wife, Hecuba, had fifty sons of which Paris and ★Hector are the best known. (SOURCE: Kaster, 1964)

SONG	COMPOSER	POET
"Miniver Cheevy"	John Duke	Edwin Arlington Robinson

PRIBAOUTKI: (Russ.), lit., *a telling,* by connotation, *humorous sayings.* Robert Craft repeats Stravinsky's definition as "a form of popular Russian verse to which the nearest English parallel is the limerick." They are seldom more than four lines in length. (SOURCE: Kimball, 1996)

SONG	COMPOSER	POET
"Pribaoutki"	Igor Stravinsky	traditional Russian

PRIEF: (Scot.) (pr. preef), n., *cloth of the best quality, proof;* v. *prove.*

SONG	COMPOSER	POET
"Birthday Song"	Benjamin Britten	Robert Burns

PRINKIN' LEDDIE: *primping lady.*

SONG	COMPOSER	POET
"Prinkin' Leddie"	Mary Howe	Elinor Wylie

PROKOSCH, FREDERIC (1906–1989): American poet, novelist, and translator. Frederic Prokosch was born in Wisconsin and educated at Haverford College, King's College, Cambridge, and Yale. His father, a professor at Yale, pushed for his son to take up an academic career, but following the success of his novel *The Asiatics* in 1930, Prokosch devoted himself entirely to his writing. A handsome, athletic man, he traveled widely, even to Egypt, which is the setting for the song "Nocturne," put to music by Samuel Barber. His first book of poems, *The Assassins*, published in 1936, was followed by several others. Prokosch is probably best known for his numerous novels. His translations include *Some Poems of Friedrich *Hölderlin* (1943), and *Medea* of *Euripides (1947). Prokosch's poetry is accomplished and impressive at first glance. His diction is fresh and contemporary and has a kind of unease reminiscent of W. H. *Auden, the sense of things happening in a dream. The poetry of Frederic Prokosch has been set by Samuel Barber and John Duke. PRINCIPAL WORKS: *The Asiatics*, 1930; *The Assassins*, 1936; *The Carnival*, 1938; *Death at Sea*, 1940; *Common Poems,* 1944, 1948; *Voices*, 1983 (memoirs). SELECTED READING: *Common Poems*, 1944 (best for sampling); Radcliffe Squires, *Friedrich Prokosch*, 1964. (SOURCE: Hamilton, 1994)

PROMENOIR DES DEUX AMANTS, LE: song cycle by Claude Debussy with texts from an extended poem of twenty-eight verses written by *Tristan L'Hermite. The first song, "Auprès de cette grotte sombre," is the setting for the rendezvous that follows. The red flower, *cette fleur vermeille*, refers to the ruddy complexion, *teint cramoisi*, of a faun who looks into the water to see whether his red blush has disappeared. In the original poem, the verses that follow (5 to 13), which Debussy chose to ignore, deal with the countryside, the mountains, the forests, *nymphs, and nightingales. Debussy's second song, "Crois mon conseil," sets the fourteenth stanza of the original poem. The twenty-fourth stanza, "Je tremble en voyant ton visage," provides the composer with his third song. The lover looks into *Clymène's eyes and sees his own reflection in her eyes, just as *Narcissus in the first song looked into the pond to see his reflection.

PROMETHEUS: a demi-god, son of the *Titan Iapetos and *Clymene, brother of *Atlas. Prometheus, whose name means "forethought," taught mankind the useful arts and crafts, particularly the use of fire, which had been zealously guarded by *Zeus. Prometheus stole the fire from *Olympus, hiding it in a stalk of fennel, and brought it down to man. For this act Zeus cast him out of Olympus and had him fastened to a rock in the Caucasus, where daily an eagle fed upon his liver, which then grew again during the night. After many thousands of years, the eagle was killed by Heracles and Prometheus was set free. Some legends have Prometheus as the creator of man, whom he formed out of earth and water. *Goethe's poem "Prometheus" was set by Schubert, Johann Reichardt, and Hugo Wolf. (SOURCE: Kaster, 1964)

PROSERPINA: *see* *PERSEPHONE.

PSALM: an invention of the ancient east, a song to the accompaniment of a plucked instrument, such as a harp, the term derived from the Greek *psalmos*. Psalm writing associated with temple cults was an important literary activity of Mesopotamia, Egypt, and Israel. The biblical Book of Psalms is an anthology, a wedding together of what were originally four smaller anthologies, compiled some time in the Second Temple Period. There have been some shifts in language and poetic structure over the centuries, but the continuity of style and convention in biblical Psalms is remarkable. The beauty and simplicity of these Psalms, such as the compositions of King *David, have made them a recurrent source of inspiration to later poets, among them Clément *Marot and John *Milton.

PSAUMES, TROIS: Swiss-born composer Arthur Honegger's three settings of the French metrical versions of Psalms 34, 140, and 148, all dealing with King *David.

PSYCHE, PSYCHÉ (Fr.): lit., in Greek, *breath,* hence *life,* or *the soul itself.* In the latest of the myths, *Cupid and Psyche, Psyche is a beautiful maiden beloved by Cupid, who visited her every night but left at sunrise. Cupid warned her never to seek to know who he was. One night her curiosity was so intense that she lit the lamp to look at him. A drop of hot oil fell on his shoulder; he awoke and fled. Abandoned, Psyche then wandered far and wide in search of her lover. Later, she became a slave of *Venus, who treated her cruelly and demanded that she perform difficult tasks. Ultimately Psyche became immortal. The text of Paladilhe's song is taken from act 3, scene 3 of the drama *Psyché*, written as a joint project of Molière, Philippe Quinault, and Pierre *Corneille, who limited his contribution to verses for acts 2 and 5. (SOURCE: Cooper, 1992)

SONG	COMPOSER	POET
1. "Psyché"	Édouard Paladilhe	attributed to Pierre Corneille
2. "Guitare"	Édouard Lalo	Pierre de Ronsard
3. "Adieu de l'hotesse Arabe"	Georges Bizet	Victor Hugo
4. "Psyché"	Manuel de Falla	G. Jean-Aubry

PUCKLE: (Scot.) (pr. to rhyme with buckle), *a small amount.*

PUKHTIN, A. N.: *see* *APUKHTIN.

PULCINELLA (It.), POLICHINELLE (Fr.), PUNCH (Eng.): a combination of two characters from Roman comedy, quick, witty, impertinent, slightly crude Maccus, and self-sufficient, fawning, silly, timid, boastful, thieving Bucco. Pulcinella gets his hooked nose, hunched back, and long spindly legs from Maccus. From Bucco he inherits flabby cheeks and an enormous mouth. Hunchbacked and potbellied, he is frequently shown as an old bachelor, eccentric and selfish, sensual and a glutton, witty, but very cruel. Often he is represented as eating macaroni from a chamber pot. In French farce, Polichinelle is more like the *Captain than Pulcinello. Polichinelle had a pot belly and a hunched back. Punch is a seducer of young girls. (SOURCE: Duchartre, 1966)

SONG	COMPOSER	POET
1. "Fantoches"	Claude Debussy	Paul Verlaine
2. "È morto Pulcinella"	Francesco Tosti	Ferdinando Fontana

PURDY, JAMES (b. 1923): American poet, novelist, playwright, short-story writer, and screen writer. James Purdy graduated from a Chicago high school, the University of Chicago and the University of Puebla, Mexico. He later taught English in a private boys' school in Havana, Cuba. In 1953, after graduate study and travel abroad, he spent four years on the faculty of Lawrence College in Wisconsin, after which he devoted himself to writing full time and lived abroad for some years. Having been rejected for years by American publishers, his works were first published privately and then, with the support of Dame Edith ★Sitwell and Angus Wilson, were published publicly in England under the title *63: Dream Palace*. In 1957 the collection was published in the United States as *Color of Darkness*. Recipient of both Ford and Guggenheim grants, he lived in New York. Purdy's work is linked to the Southern Gothic tradition with elements such as: loveless and barren marriages, estranged children unable to communicate or find their identity, perverse love, and violent sexuality. Purdy's first and most popular novel was *Malcolm*, an allegory of black humor, published in 1959 and made into a play by Edward ★Albee. His works show the anguish and suffering of the human condition while exploring the theme of homosexuality. He uses bizarre incidents to underscore ideas, and the eccentric nature of his works lies in the originality and power of his dour vision. Purdy remains what Gore Vidal, an admirer, calls "an outlaw" from the literary establishment. His verse has been set by Richard Hundley. PRINCIPAL WORKS: *Color of Darkness*, 1957; *Malcolm,* 1959; *Cabot Wright Begins*, 1964; *An Oyster is a Wealthy Beast*, 1967; *Eustace Chisholm and the Works*, 1968; *On the Rebound: A Story and Nine Poems*, 1970; *The Running Sun*, 1971; *Sunshine is an Only Child*, 1973; *In a Shallow Grave*, 1975; *Narrow Rooms*, 1978; *On Glory's Course*, 1984; *Moe's Villa and Other Stories*, 2003. SELECTED READING: S. Adams, *James Purdy*, 1976. (SOURCE: Serafin, 1999)

PURGATORY: a place or condition in which souls undergo purification by temporary punishment. The first circle of purgatory is the ★*whinny muir*, the second is the ★*brig o'dread*.

SONG	COMPOSER	POET
"Serenade"	Benjamin Britten	anonymous fifteenth-century poet

"Pursuing Beauty": a song composed by Henry Purcell, set to words by Thomas ★Southerne in his play *Sir Anthony in Love*, produced in 1690. For plot details and placement of the song, *see* ★ *Sir Anthony in Love*.

PUSHKIN, ALEXANDR (1799–1837): generally regarded as the greatest Russian poet. Born into the landed nobility of Russia, one of Pushkin's maternal ancestors was an Abyssinian (Hannibal) who had been in the service of Peter the Great. Pushkin's early education was French, and his nanny was his only link to the Russian people. After finishing his schooling, he settled in St. Petersburg, where he divided his time between dissipating and writing poetry that was even then of high quality. His favorite French authors had given him ease, lucidity, and a sparkling wit, but his biting ★epigrams caused his exile to the south of Russia, where he was introduced to ★Byron. In 1826 Nicholas I pardoned him, but offered to be the only censor of his coming works, which tied Pushkin to the court and the tsar against his will. After his marriage, his wife was so openly pursued by a French court diplomat that Pushkin was forced to issue a challenge to a duel, during which he died. In spite of his ever-present problems, Pushkin never ceased his artistic activities. The naked beauty of his lyric poetry was influenced by Byron, his 1826 *Boris Godunov* by ★Shakespeare, and other works by Sir Walter ★Scott. Pushkin mastered classical economy and all the western literary forms, but he integrated them with the spirit of the Russian language; that is, his verse was thoroughly European but essentially Russian. Pushkin's verse was set by Tchaikovsky, Borodin, Shostakovich, Stravinsky, Glinka, Liszt, Mussorgsky, Prokofiev, Rachmaninoff, Rimsky-Korsakov, Aleksandr Alyabiev, Nicolai Medtner, Aleksandr Gretchaninov, Mily Balakirev, César Cui, Aleksandr Dargomizhsky, Aleksandr Glazounov, Nicolai Titov, A. P. Esaulov, Marion Koval, Yuri Shaporin, Nicolai Nabokov, Nicolai Mednikof, Fridtjof Backer-Grøndahl, Franz André Messager, Émile Pessard, Joseph Marx, Anton Rubenstein, and Benjamin Britten. PRINCIPAL WORKS: *Poems*, trans. M. Baring, 1931; *Pushkin's Poems*, trans. W. Morison, 1945; *The Fairy Tales*, trans. T. Pancheff, 1947; *Poems*, trans. V. Nabokov, 1947; *A Pushkin Verse Reader*, ed. I. P. Foote, 1962. SELECTED READING: several English biographies: N. L. Brodsky, 1937; S. L. Frank, 1957; L. M. Toibin, 1964. (SOURCE: Steinberg, 3, 1973)

PUSS IN BOOTS, LE CHAT BOTTÉ (Fr.): a nursery tale from Straparola's *Nights* (1530). Constantine's cat procures a fine castle and the king's heiress for his master, a young miller without a penny to his name. The story traveled from Italy to France (1585), where it became part of Perrault's *Les Contes de ma Mère d'Oye* (The Stories of Mother Goose), finally making its way to England. (SOURCE: Cooper, 1992)

SONG	COMPOSER	POET
"Paganini"	Francis Poulenc	Louise de Vilmorin

PYRKER, JOHANN (1772–1847): a Hungarian poet and dramatist. Pyrker was ordained a priest in 1796, named patriarch of Venice in 1820, and named archbishop of Erlau in 1827. Schubert met Pyrker in 1820 and dedicated op. 4 to him. In 1825 they met again at a meeting that Schubert considered to be the most inspiring of his life. In that year he set two of Pyrker's poems: "Das Heimweh" and "Die Allmacht." (SOURCE: Reed, 1997)

PYROGÈNE: a little stoneware pot to be found in all cafés, holding matches upright, their heads looking like red hair, matches to be struck on the rough sides of the pot.

SONG	COMPOSER	POET
"Un poème"	Francis Poulenc	Guillaume Apollinaire

PYTHAGORAS: a Greek sage of the sixth century B.C.E. Born on the Greek island of Samos off the coast of Asia Minor, he emigrated to Crotone, Italy in 530 B.C. Pythagoras was a teacher of great charisma who founded a society of religious-ethical orientation. Pythagoreanism became greatly influential politically and was often attacked, even bodily, by those of other persuasions. Pythagoras believed in metempsychosis, the transmigration of souls from one body, human or animal, to another. His beliefs and his work transformed him into a Greek shaman. Modern scholars discount the tradition that he was the founder of Greek mathematics or that he proved the geometric theorem named for him. (SOURCE: *Americana*, 2003)

SONG	COMPOSER	POET
"Dans le jardin d'Anna"	Francis Poulenc	Guillaume Apollinaire

PYTHIA: the priestess of ★Apollo at his oracle at Delphi. The Pythia officiated and uttered the words of the Delphic oracle.

SONG	COMPOSER	POET
"Orest auf Tauris"	Franz Schubert	Johann Mayrhofer

Q

QUARLES, FRANCIS (1592–1644): English poet, playwright, writer of biblical paraphrases, and political pamphlets. Francis Quarles was born in Essex and was educated at Christ's College, Cambridge (1608). He was the father of eighteen children. Quarles worked as private secretary to the archbishop of Armagh (1626–30) and as the chronologer of the City of London (1639–44). At the beginning of the English Civil War, Quarles wrote in defense of Charles I. A voluminous writer, he was most famous for the poems *Emblems* and *Hieroglyphics*. Each emblem includes a picture, a biblical motto, a poem, a quotation from the Church Fathers, and a four-line ★epigram. The engravings were taken from two continental Jesuit collections, most concerned with the soul's struggle for salvation. The poetry of Francis Quarles has been set by Henry Purcell, John Rutter, Benjamin Britten, and Jack Beeson. PRINCIPAL WORKS: *Complete Works in Prose and Verse*, ed. Alexander B. Grosart, 3 vols., 1880–81; *A Feast for Worms: A Poem of the History of Jonah*, 1620; *Argalus and Parthenia*, 1629; *Emblems*, 1635; *Hieroglyphiks of the Life of Man*, 1638; *The Virgin Widow* (play), 1649. SELECTED READINGS: Masodul Hasan, *Quarles: A Study of His Life and Poetry*, 1966. (SOURCE: Vinson, 1979)

QUASIMODO, SALVATORE (1901–1968): Italian poet and translator. Born in Siracusa, Sicily, Quasimodo received a haphazard education because of the hardships of his early life. In the 1920s he traveled over Italy as an employee of the State Civil Engineers Bureau, and in the 1930s he moved to Milano and stayed there. The Nobel Prize for Literature, awarded him in 1959, made him the best-known Italian poet outside Italy and secured his reputation. Quasimodo's early poetry reveals his membership in the *hermetic movement. Although the poetry of his first period was characterized by economical idiom, the war brought changes. His poetry became more concrete, more bound to the human condition and the reality of events, poetry of a social conscience, and it appealed more broadly than that of *Montale. He survived the last polemic between hermetics and their enemies to become a chief figure in Italian literature. In his *Discorso sulla poesia* he stated that the poet's responsibility is in direct ratio to his achievement of beauty, and that the poet cannot separate himself from the age in which he lives (Golino, 1966). The verse of Salvatore Quasimodo was set by Goffredo Petrassi and Elizabeth Lutyens. WORKS: *Acque e terre* [Water and Land], 1930; *Oboe sommerso* [Sunken Oboe], 1932; *Ed è subito sera* [And It's Suddenly Evening], 1942; *Con il piede straniero sopra il cuore* [With the Alien Foot on Our Heart], 1946; *La vita non è sogno* [Life is not Dream], 1949; *Dare ed avere* [Giving and Having], 1966. Quasimodo has been translated by R. Wilbur. (SOURCE: Golino, 1977)

QUATRAIN: a four-line stanza form, used widely in the French *mélodie.

QUEEN OF HEAVEN: *Astarte to the ancient Phoenicians; Hera to the Greeks; *Juno to the Romans; the *Virgin Mary to the Catholics. Also called by this epithet were Trivia, Hecate, *Diana, and the Egyptian *Isis.

QUEEN OF THE SEAGULLS: according to Pierre Bernac, the queen is "undoubtedly a delicate and charming lady, blinking under her grey muslin veils" in Poulenc's song collection titled *Métamorphoses*.

SONG	COMPOSER	POET
"Reine des mouettes"	Francis Poulenc	Louise de Vilmorin

QUEVEDO Y VILLEGAS, FRANCISCO GÓMEZ DE (1580–1645): Spanish novelist, satirist, moralist, and poet. In his youth Quevedo pursued theological studies at Vallodolid and Alcalá. He then did special missions for the Duke of Osuna in Madrid and Naples. In 1620 he was banished to his estates until he returned (1623), becoming royal secretary in 1632. Again in 1639 he was in disfavor, suffering four years in prison, after which he spent his last years in retirement. Quevedo's talents were many and varied: novels, political works, verse translations of Epicetetus, theological works, polished and intense love poems, satire in verse, and good burlesque verses, in addition to *sonnets on the vanity of life. The verses of Francisco Quevedo y Villegas were set by Eduardo Toldrà. PRINCIPAL WORKS: *The Visions of Quevedo*, trans. Sir R. L'Estrange, 1667; *The Life and Adventures of Buscon*, 1657, 1660. SELECTED READING: *The Choice Humorous and Satirical Works*, ed. C. Duff, 1926; L. Nolting-Hauff, *Satire and Pointe in Quevedo's* Sueños, 1968; O. H. Green, *Courtly Love in Quevedo*, 1952. (SOURCE: Steinberg, 3, 1973)

QUIMPER: a French city on the Atlantic coast of Brittany. Quimper is the ancient capital of Cornouaille, founded by King Gradlon 1,500 years ago. Its name stands for "confluence," and the city is located at the confluence of the Odet and Steir rivers.

In the old town is the Gothic Cathedral of St. Corentin, the second largest cathedral in Brittany.

SONG	COMPOSER	POET
"Souric et Mouric"	Francis Poulenc	Max Jacob

QUINTERO, SERAFÍN and JOAQUIN: *see* ★ALVÁREZ QUINTERO

QUIXOTE, DON: the hero of *Miguel de* ★*Cervantes's* famous romance, which was published in Madrid, the first part in 1605, the second in 1615; also, title of the Restoration drama in two parts ★*Don Quixote*, adapted by Thomas ★D'Urfey, containing music by Henry Purcell and John Eccles. Cervantes ridicules the other tedious romances of chivalry from the period. Don Quixote is a country gentleman from La Mancha, gentle, dignified, affectionate, and simple-minded, but driven so mad from reading books of knight errantry that he believes he is called upon to make right the wrongs of the entire world. Early in the twentieth century, a film company made a simultaneous proposal to Manuel de Falla, Maurice Ravel, Darius Milhaud, Jacques Ibert, and Marcel Delannoy that they compose music to be sung by Feodor Chaliapin in a movie based upon the Cervantes story, but in the end Ibert's music alone was used for the film. One of the Ibert songs, "Chanson du Duc," presents a question. Exactly why it was called "Song of the Duke" is a puzzle. In the film Quichotte and Sancho have been invited to the duke's palace so that the duke may play a cruel joke on them. Chaliapin sings this song while at the table of the duke and duchess. (SOURCE: Cooper, 1992)

SONG	COMPOSER	POET
1. "Don Quichotte à Dulcinée"	Maurice Ravel	Paul Morand
2. "Chansons de Don Quichotte"	Jacques Ibert	Pierre Ronsard, Alexandre Arnoux

QU'RAN: the Holy Book of Islam, its name previously transliterated from the Arabic as *Koran*. In Arabic Qu'ran means "recital." In a dream the Angel ★Gabriel commanded the prophet Mohammed to recite. Mohammed asked what he should recite. Again the Angel ordered Mohammed to recite in the name of ★Allah, who made man from clots of blood. Waking from the dream, Mohammed found the message completely contained in his memory. Following his first vision and message, other visions with their messages led Mohammed to found Islam, the third great monotheistic religion in the world and one of the most influential today. First he converted his wife, next several kinsmen. In a later military conquest, he and his followers claimed most of the Near East, Northern Africa, Spain, and Turkey. In the east the religion spread rapidly to India. Today it has made significant progress in the western world, especially in the United States. Just like the works of the Hebrew prophets, the Qu'ran claims to be not merely the words of Mohammed, but the actual words of God, Allah. Throughout the work Allah speaks to Mohammed and the world in the royal plural. The Qu'ran, containing the basic tenets of Islam, was transmitted orally by professional reciters until an authoritative written version was established in the mid-seventh century. The reciter, who had memorized the Qu'ran, remained an important figure in Islamic culture for many years. Such a reciter was the poet ★Hāfiz. The Qu'ran has two basic teachings: the Oneness of God, Allah, and God's mercy and forgiveness. The faith of a Muslim involves five things: 1. Faith in Allah, the one God of all, and in his prophet Mohammed; 2. Daily prayers said at specific times of the day, when the faithful in all lands prostrate themselves facing the holy city of Mecca; 3. Fasting during Ramadan, a month long period similar to the Christian season of Lent, where the faithful fast, pray, and meditate on their sins, from sunup to sundown, after which believers are allowed to take enough nourishment to sustain life; 4. A pilgrimage to Mecca, considered to be a religious obligation of all Muslims, wherever possible; 5. The giving of alms, charity, and hospitality, a reglious obligation.

SONG	COMPOSER	POET
1. "Ob der Koran von Ewigheit sei"	Hugo Wolf	Johan Wolfang von Goethe
2. "Tres Moricas m'enamoran"	anonymous	anonymous

R ✍

RACINE, JEAN (1639–1699): French poet and dramatist. Racine's parents died soon after his birth, after which he was brought up by Jansenist parents. Still in his teens, he wrote passable ★odes in Latin and French. One of these odes, written in honor of the marriage of the king, brought Racine 600 gold livres from Louis XIV. The critic Nicolas Boileau, having become a friend to Racine, behaved as his mentor for most of his life. Between 1664 and 1673 two of Racine's plays, one of them *Alexander the Great*, were given excellent reception by the public, although the Jansenists hated the theater and Racine's place in it. His drama ★*Andromache* displayed the elements of his genius, his ability to combine those strict requirements of formalized French drama together with human motivations and characterizations. ★*Phaedra* (1677) used the Greek theme and followed the Aristotelian dramatic unities. Remembered with ★Corneille as two leaders of classical revival in the drama of seventeenth-century France, Racine devoted his skills to the creation of warm human characters. His declining years were marked by a loss of friends and royal favor. The poetry of Jean Racine was set by Francis Poulenc. PRINCIPAL WORKS: Poetry: *Cantiques spirituels*, 1694. Drama: *Andromaque*, 1667; *Andromache*, 1674, *Mithridate*, 1673, *Mithridates*, 1926; *Phèdre*, 1677; *Phaedra*, 1701; *Idylle sur la paix*, 1685 (libretto with Lully); *The Best Plays of Racine*, 1936. SELECTED READING: Jean Giraudoux, *Racine*, 1950; Roland Barthes, *On Racine*, 1992. (SOURCE: Magill, 4, 1997)

RĀDHĀ: the consort of ★Krishna.

SONG	COMPOSER	POET
"The Call of Rādhā	Harriet Ware	Edwin Markham

RADIGUET, RAYMOND (1903–1923): French poet and novelist. Radiguet was born in a meteorology station 8 miles from Paris; his father was a newspaper cartoonist. By the age of fourteen, Radiguet had written poems worthy of being included in an anthology of contemporary verse. At fifteen (1918) Radiguet arrived in Paris, where he wandered about without literary connections, but was eventually taken under the protection of Max ★Jacob and Jean ★Cocteau. Soon he was invited to contribute to the literary magazine *Sic*, alongside Louis ★Aragon and other young poets. Despite all the new trends in Paris, Radiguet was not interested in any of the *isms*; he simply reverted to the classic poetic tradition. When his first collection of poetry was published (1920), he moved to a fishing village. This first period of Radiguet's life produced poetry that was serious but with a background of cynicism surprising in a teenage boy. *Devil in the Flesh*, his first novel (1923), was branded immoral by the critics, but Aldous ★Huxley found that Radiguet possessed those qualities that most poets achieve only at the end of their lives. Radiguet's second novel, *The Count's Ball*, was hailed as remarkable. At the age of twenty he contracted typhoid fever and died, having written two or three dozen poems, published under the title, *Les Joues en feu*, two short novels, and an unproduced play. His verse has been set by Georges Auric, Erik Satie, and Francis Poulenc. WORKS in English translation: *The Count's Ball*, 1929; *Devil in the Flesh*, 1932. SELECTED READING: H. Massis, *Raymond Radiguet*, 1927. (SOURCE: Kunitz, Haycraft, 1936)

RAGWORT: any of several herbs of the genus Senecio with leaves of a ragged shape; a rubble of thin, small stones. Ragwort is one of five injurious weeds covered by the provisions of The Weeds Act of the United Kingdom. Ragwort is poisonous to horses, ponies, donkeys and other livestock, and causes liver damage. Under the Weeds Act 1959, the secretary of state may serve an enforcement notice on the occupier of land on which injurious weeds are growing, requiring the occupier to take action to prevent the spread of injurious weeds.

SONG	COMPOSER	POET
"The Ragwort"	Arthur Bliss	Frances Cornford

RANDOLPH, THOMAS (1605–1635): English poet and playwright. Randolph was educated at Westminster School and Trinity College, Cambridge, where he became known as a writer of English and Latin verse. After returning to London in 1632, he wrote pastoral, satiric, and comedic plays and poems. One of his dramatic sketches proposes that the study of a philosophy of drinking be added to the university syllabus. The poetry of Thomas Randolph was set by Benjamin Britten in his *Charm of Lullabies*. (SOURCE: Drabble, 2000)

RAPUNZEL: a character in the fairy tale of the same name. Rapunzel is the beautiful long-haired girl who is locked up at the top of a tall tower by an ugly witch. The witch, and before long a handsome prince, are able to climb up to her, using her hair as a ladder, after calling out, "Rapunzel, Rapunzel, let down your long hair." After several evil machinations perpetrated by the witch, the story ends happily ever after for Rapunzel and her prince.

SONG	COMPOSER	POET
"Rapunzel"	John Duke	Adelaide Crapsey

RAVEN: a bird considered to be a bad omen. The notion that ravens foretell death and bring infection probably stems from the belief that they follow armies in order to feed on dead bodies. In Christian art, however, the raven is an emblem of God's providence. In Scandinavian folklore there are allusions to "fatal ravens." Schubert's song "Die Krähe" is often translated "The Crow," but the raven, the rook, and the jackdaw are all crows by definition. (SOURCE: *Americana*, 2003)

RAVENNA: a small Italian city with brick palaces and cobbled streets, located on the Adriatic Sea, east of Bologna, 32 miles northwest of Rimini. The high point of its history was 1,500 years ago when it was the capital of the Roman Empire. Ravenna had been ruled by Constantine in the fourth century, taken by the Ostrogoths in the fifth century, then conquered by the Byzantines, hence the many mosaics. ★Dante's tomb is in Ravenna, where he died in 1321.

SONG	COMPOSER	POET
"Ravenna"	Othmar Schoeck	Hermann Hesse

REAL: a silver coin minted in Spain.

SONG	COMPOSER	POET
"El vito"	Joaquín Nin	popular song

REAM, REAMAN: (Scot.) (pr. reem, reeman), n. *cream, froth*; v. *to foam, to skim cream off milk, to arouse confusion.*

RÉGNIER, HENRI DE (1864–1936): French lyric poet. Régnier's verse is a harmonic blend of ★Romantic, ★Parnassian, and ★Symbolist influences, yet the symbolist features of Régnier's verse did not overwhelm his capacity for sentiment and eroticism. He wrote metric verse and free verse with a delicate musicality. His predilection for imagery never allowed the emotional element to disappear from his work. The verse of Henri de Régnier was set by Roussel and Ravel. PRINCIPAL WORKS: *Poèmes anciens et romanesques*, 1890; *Tel qu'en songe*, 1892; *Jeux rustiques et divins*, 1897; *Les Médailles d'argile*, 1900; *La Cité des eaux*, 1902; *La Sandale ailée*, 1906; *Le Miroir des heures*, 1910. (SOURCE: Rees, 1992)

REGULUS: a play by John Crowne, produced in 1692, containing one song by Henry Purcell. *Regulus* has one low comic plot and two serious ones. Because an invading Roman army is keeping Carthage under siege, some of its citizens attempt to capitalize on this unexpected event: Prince Asdrubal is encouraged to overthrow the government while the city is distracted; Batto sells arms and supplies to the enemy, making a great deal of profit. The arrival of the Roman invaders, among whom is Regulus, is delayed until act 2, scene 3, which opens with "Ah, Me! Too Many Deaths Decreed," sung to entertain Regulus's mistress, Fulvia. On the surface it speaks of the mixture of pain and joy that comes to a woman who is the companion of a soldier; she suffers while waiting for the battle to conclude, but she will hate him if he should prove to be a coward. Near the end of the song Fulvia tries to ignore the message and command the servant to cease singing. The words are passion overblown, and the last lines of each verse express the exact opposite sentiments. The melismas on the word *war* suggest Fulvia's conversion to a warrior in act 5, and the repeated figures in the final section may be an augury of Fulvia's later madness, since Purcell uses such figures in other mad songs. (SOURCE: Price, 1984)

REID: (Scot.), *red*.

REIL, JOHANN (1773–1843): a German playwright, poet, and actor. Reil was a member of the Burgtheater Company, having joined in 1801. Schubert, a friend of Reil, set his "Das Lied im Grünen" in 1827 and used Reil's translation of two additional verses of "Hark, Hark, the Lark." He was also the poet of Schubert's male quartet, "Glaube, Hoffnung und Liebe" (1828). (SOURCE: Reed, 1997)

REINE DES MOUETTES: *see* ★QUEEN OF THE SEAGULLS.

REINICK, ROBERT (1805–1852): German author of children's works, painter, and illustrator. Reinick was the librettist for Robert Schumann's "Genoveva," which was based on *Das Leben und Tod der heiligen Genoveva* by Ludwig ★Tieck and *Genoveva* by Friedrich ★Hebbel, as well as several songs including "Ständchen." His verse was also set by Brahms ("Liebestreu" and "Juchhe!") and Wolf ("Morgenstimmung"). (SOURCE: Garland, 1976)

REISSIG, CHRISTIAN (1783–1822): an Austrian poet and soldier. Reissig, a cavalry officer in the Austrian army from 1808, was passionately opposed to Napoleon. His poetry, which was set by Beethoven and Schubert, was published in various periodicals. (SOURCE: Reed, 1997)

REJA: a window beautified and protected by a grille, behind which a woman was seated, in which setting a traditional Spanish courtship took place. (SOURCE: Cockburn, Stokes, 1992)

SONG	COMPOSER	POET
"El majo olvidado"	Enrique Granados	Fernando Periquet

RELLSTAB, LUDWIG (1799–1860): a German poet, novelist, and music critic. Rellstab, born in Berlin, was a talented pianist, but had started his career as an artillery officer. When he turned to writing, he became one of the first music critics. After a meeting between him and Beethoven in 1825, there was talk of their collaborating on an opera, but it did not materialize. Anton Schindler had discovered a number of poems by Rellstab among Beethoven's effects, where the master had marked those that he intended to set. Upon his death, they were returned to Rellstab, who sent them to Schubert. Subsequently, Schubert set ten of Rellstab's poems, including the first seven songs of *Schwanengesang*. (SOURCE: Reed, 1997)

RENARD, JULES (1864–1910): a French man of letters. Both of Jules Renard's parents were harsh and demanding, his father brusque and satirical, his mother prone to punish. Renard wrote verses, renounced his preparation for an academic career, but took a degree in 1883. He was forced by his lack of qualifications to do odd jobs, military service, ghost writing, and tutoring. Subsequent to the publication of his *Les Roses*, early verses, Renard began to move in literary circles. After marriage, his wife's dowry allowed them to live a modest Parisian life. He published at his own expense a book of short stories, a novel, and *Histoires naturelles* (on behavior and personality of animals). In 1896 he added forty more to the original forty-five stories of *Histoires naturelles*, in which he tried for the most condensed, striking descriptions possible. Renard made a popular success as a critic and in the theater, mainly one-act plays, which gave him some financial security. His effort was toward direct, simple, and economical statements, and he was admired for the pithiness and irony of his observations. His animal stories were set to music by Maurice Ravel, after the composer's lengthy and forceful persuasion. PRINCIPAL WORKS: *Les Roses* (verse), 1886; *Poil de Carotte*, 1893 (a play, then a film), trans. Alfred Sutro as *Carrots, a Play*, 1904; *Histoires naturelles*, trans. G. W. Stonier and T. W. Earp, 1948, as *Hunting with the Fox*; *The Journal of Jules Renard*, trans. Louise *Bogan and E. Roget, 1964. SELECTED READING: H. B. Coulter, *The Prose Work and Technique of Jules Renard*, 1935. (SOURCE: Kunitz, Colby, 1967)

RESTORATION DRAMA, MUSIC OF THE: the theatrical period that came directly after the years of the Commonwealth when the Stuarts, in the person of Charles II, were restored to the British throne in 1660. From 1660 to 1705 English plays were performed with rather large amounts of music. During the reign of James II, however, English composers were relegated to the sidelines until 1688 because the king preferred French theater.

In early classic rhymed drama the characters were put into crises and forced to choose painfully between love and honor. The characters are exalted and the action often unbelievable; the language was rhymed *couplets. This made for tedium and soporific regularity in the poetry. To relieve the audience of these burdens, music was injected into two kinds of scenes: (1) ceremonial processions and (2) conjurations that made for great dramatic possibilities.

Comedies and semi-operas soon arrived on the scene. Songs and dances for serenades, entertainments, and toasts were interpolated. Purcell himself wrote music for twenty comedies. Music was associated with madness, battles between the sexes, and eroticism. In comedies the actors usually performed their own songs, thus found great parts for themselves. Comedic characters were ranked by wit and social position. Clever couples were at the top, followed by married couples, who were foolish city cuckolds with affected wives. On the next level were found pompous or uncouth fools, rustics, and fops. After a big gap came servants, prostitutes, and criminals. Music was introduced into the stories of the second rank characters as truncated serenades, incompetent concertizing, and ridiculous love songs. Only when pretending madness were clever women allowed to sing. Songs sung by second rank characters and servants often instructed or entertained the leading ladies. (SOURCE: Price, 1984)

"Retir'd from Any Mortal's Sight": a song written by Henry Purcell to words of Nahum *Tate, in an adaptation of *Shakespeare's work, *The History of King Richard the Second*, produced in 1680. For plot details and placement of songs, *see *History of King Richard the Second, The*.

RHADAMANTHUS: the son of *Jupiter and Europa, brother of Minos, ruler and judge in the underworld. Rhadamanthus reigned in the Cyclades with such impartiality that, at his death, he was made one of the three judges of the infernal regions who passed sentences and sent the wicked to everlasting torment. So renowned for his justice was Rhadamanthus, that his name and the adjective Rhadamanthine came to mean stern and incorruptible in judgment. (SOURCE: *Bulfinch*, 1978)

SONG	COMPOSER	POET
"A Charm"	Benjamin Britten	Thomas Randolph

RHYMER, TOM THE: a Scottish poet who flourished between 1250 and 1300, whose reputation was that of a prophet.

SONG	COMPOSER	POET
"Tom der Reimer"	Carl Loewe	Theodor Fontane

RIALTO: the name of a stone bridge that crosses Venice's Grand Canal; its name is adapted from *rivo alto* (high bank). The environs of the Rialto Bridge comprise one of the first areas of Venice to be inhabited, now one of the city's busiest and most bustling areas. A banking area first, it then became and remained a market district—an *erberia* (fruit and vegetable market) and a *pescheria* (fish market). Stone bridges were built in Venice as early as the twelfth century, but in 1588, after the collapse, decay, or sabotage of the earlier wooden structures, a solid stone bridge was designed for the Rialto. Completed in 1591, the new bridge remained the only means of crossing the Grand Canal until 1854, when the Accademia Bridge was built.

SONG	COMPOSER	POET
"Barcarolle"	Gabriel Fauré	Marc Monnier

RICHARD CORY: *see* *LUKE HAVERGAL.

RICHEPIN, JEAN (1849–1926): French poet. Richepin was born in Algeria, but lived most of his life in France. After finishing his schooling, he no longer kept up his relationship with university colleagues. A short imprisonment was brought about by the publication of his *Chansons des gueux*, which were violent and, said the government, nihilistic. Richepin eventually publicly expressed his regret about his former unconventional views. With this apology, he finally received official recognition. The verses of Jean Richepin have been set by Gabriel Fauré, César Cui, and Ernest Chausson. PRINCIPAL WORKS: *Les Blasphèmes*, 1884; *La Mer*, 1886; *Poèmes durant la guerre*, 1914–18. (SOURCE: Steinberg, 3, 1973)

RICHMOND HEIRESS, THE: a play written by Thomas *D'Urfey, produced in 1693, containing one duet composed by Henry Purcell. Tom Quickwit, feigning madness and slow-wittedness, makes fools of everyone. He offers to help his friend Frederick, a rake, win the hand of a shrewd heiress, Fulvia. To avoid her arranged marriage to Tom Romance, a vain and dishonest man, Quickwit persuades the heiress to pretend to be mad. Act 2 takes place in the home of Dr. Guiacum, a society faker, more amused by his patients than interested in their recovery. The doctor suspects that Fulvia is getting better. Quickwit coaches Fulvia to enter "madly dress'd" and mouthing nonsensical phrases. This mad act is interrupted by Purcell's bizarre long duet for a man and woman, "Behold the Man." The two singers barely acknowledge each other. The man thinks he's engaged in combat with *Jupiter and *Pluto; the woman imagines that she has been *Jove's mistress. Since the dialogue is supposed to demonstrate Guiacum's cure, the singers should appear to become more rational as the song continues. At the end, the ex-soldier and the woman speak to the gods, not to one another. Quickwit wanders in during the end of the duet, intending to help Fulvia convince her suitors that she is mad. (SOURCE: Price, 1984)

RIKSMÅL: the Dano-Norwegian language of the urban educated classes of Norway.

RILKE, RAINER MARIA (1875–1926): Austrian poet, novelist, and short-story writer. Rilke was born in Prague in the days of the Austro-Hungarian Empire. His childhood was colored by the collapse of his parents' marriage. While in school during his fragmentary education, Rilke published his first book of poetry. He then made a living writing naturalistic dramas as well as newspaper reviews. In 1896 he began a life of restless wandering. Twice he traveled to Russia where he became acquainted with ★Tolstoy and other Russian writers, and he drew inspiration for the rest of his life from the Russian landscape and the people. As a young man he had written anti-Christian poems in rebellion against the Catholic Church, but after being impressed with the piety of the Russian people, his personal religious convictions started to change. In 1902 he moved to Paris, which became the focus of his life and work. There he formed friendships with the sculptor August Rodin, who taught him artistic discipline, and Paul ★Cézanne, whose paintings influenced the visual elements in Rilke's poetry. He spent the unproductive war years in Munich and served briefly in the Austrian army, but moved to Switzerland after the war, where he spent the rest of his life. Rilke has been described as a poet of inner experience. His language is often musical and sometimes playful. The poems abound with internal and end rhymes, alliteration, assonance, consonance. His verses captured his own internal life, common elements being experiences of suffering, an infatuation with individual objects, the harmony of love and death, and an overpowering loneliness. When contemplating the secrets of existence, Rilke maintained a deep humility. The verses of Rainer Maria Rilke have been set by Paul Hindemith, Hank Badings, Ernst Toch, Frank Martin, Alban Berg, Donald Martino, Leonard Bernstein, Stephen Paulus, Samuel Barber, Richard Cumming, Ben Weber, and Lee Hoiby. PRINCIPAL WORKS: *Das Stundenbuch*, 1905 [The Book of Hours], 1961; *Das Buch der Bilder* [The Book of Pictures], 1902; expanded edition, 1906; *Neue Gedichte* [New Poems], 2 vols., 1907–8; *Das Marienleben*, 1913 [The Life of the Virgin Mary], 1947; *Sonette an Orpheus*, 1923 [Sonnets to Orpheus], 1936. SELECTED READING: S. Mandel, *Rainer Maria Rilke: The Poetic Instinct*, 1965; H. E. Holthusen, *Portrait of Rilke*, 1971; D. Kleinbard, *The Beginning of Terror: A Psychological Study of Rainer Maria Rilke's Life and Work*, 1993. (SOURCE: Serafin, 1999)

RIMAS: (Sp.), *rhymes, verses.* When a poet calls his work *rimas*, it indicates that he regards the poetry as modest in nature. (SOURCE: Cockburn, Stokes, 1992)

SONG	COMPOSER	POET
"Rimas de Bécquer"	Isaac Albéniz	Gustavo Adolfo Bécquer

RIMBAUD, ARTHUR (1854–1891): French poet. Rimbaud was brought up by his mother, whom his army captain father had abandoned. Revolting against the tight motherly control and the hated provincial life, Rimbaud went to Paris (1871). His first influences were ★Hugo and ★Baudelaire. In 1871 he formulated a new poetic theory, which was that a poet's task is to become a seer; the poet must disorder his senses in order to perceive and describe a totally new understanding of the universe. The poems that make up *Les Illuminations* are a series of miniatures and visions projected on Rimbaud's pure but chaotic universe of adolescent genius. These part-verse, part-prose poems have had an immense influence on modern literature; they changed the course of the ★Symbolist movement and are still felt in literature today. Rimbaud spent one year in Paris literary circles before setting off for Belgium and London with Paul ★Verlaine, his new friend. During a quarrel in Brussels, Verlaine wounded Rimbaud with a revolver. Three months later, Rimbaud published *Une saison en enfer* (1873), forever giving up literature directly after the publication. After living all around the world, he ended up in Abyssinia, where he made his living by gun running, the coffee business, and the slave trade, finally dying in Marseilles. The verse of Arthur Rimbaud has been set by Willem Andriessen, Benjamin Britten and Darius Milhaud. PRINCIPAL WORKS: *Une saison en enfer*, 1873, 1932, crit. ed. H. de Bouillane de Lacoste, 1941; *Les Illuminations*, 1887, 1932; *Poésies complètes*, 1895. SELECTED READING: Enid Starkey, *Rimbaud*, 1947; Marjorie Perloff, *The Poetics of Indeterminacy: Rimbaud to Cage*, 1981. (SOURCE: Steinberg, 3, 1973; Magill, 4, 1997)

RING A DING-DING: a reference to the several removals of Charles I, from one place of captivity to another, till finally he was brought to the block. The Parliament Party laughed at their success, the Royalists wept to see the king thus treated. The doggerel was: "Ring a ding-ding, ring a ding-ding / the Parliament soldiers are gone to the king / Some they did laugh, and some they did cry / To see the Parliament soldiers go by." (SOURCE: Cooper, 1992)

RINNAN: (Scot.), *running*.

RISPETTO: an Italian verse form of eight lines of ten or eleven syllables: the first four lines rhyme alternately; the last four lines rhyme in pairs. In his *Italienisches Liederbuch*, Hugo Wolf set many *rispetti* that have only six or eight lines, but a few are somewhat longer. Many *rispetti* say the same thing more than once in different words, or the same words in a different order. (SOURCE: Lakeway, White, 1989)

SONG	COMPOSER	POET
"Quattro rispetti"	Ermanno Wolf-Ferrari	anonymous

RIVAL SISTERS, THE; OR, THE VIOLENCE OF LOVE: a play by Robert Gould, produced in 1695, containing three songs by Henry Purcell. The play examines the tragic results of a Portuguese custom that the eldest sister in the family must marry first. Vilarezo, a rich landowner, has promised his daughter Catalina that she may take the dashing Spaniard, Antonio, as a husband, but Antonio has already fallen in love with Catalina's younger sister, Berinthia. Antonio has suggested his sister Alaphanta, a decidedly unvirtuous adolescent, as a lover for Berenthia's brother Sebastian. Much of the music stems from Alaphanta's fiancé, Alonzo, and his attempts to retrieve the changeable affections of Alaphanta. Two of the songs are delivered by attendants, but their sentiments reveal the unspoken thoughts of the principal characters, a common practice in the Restoration theater. Act 2 opens in a grove where Sebastian rests after the hunt. Here Alonzo, disguised and traveling with a little boy whom he occasionally asks for music, arrives in search of Alaphanta. Alonzo is babbling like a lunatic, but the boy's intelligible songs impart his master's real emotions. Purcell's much-admired song, "Celia Has a Thousand Charms," says that lying in arms of a beloved is ecstasy, but that one must be on guard against her treachery. Critics suggest that Purcell deliberately overstated the affectations of the first section and contrasted those sentiments with the simpler and more direct emotions expressed in the air itself. In act 4, "Take Not a Woman's Anger Ill," a loud, rollicking song, is performed by Gerardo, a comic servant. The exact location for "How Happy Is She," delivered by Alaphanta, is not known. Its vaguely pornographic lyrics reflect a vogue of the times. (SOURCE: Price, 1984)

RIZZIO, DAVID: Mary Stuart's Italian secretary, murdered at Holyrood House in 1566.

SONG	COMPOSER	POET
"David Rizzio's Song"	Mikhail Glinka	Nestor Kukolnik

ROBINSON, EDWIN ARLINGTON (1869–1935): American poet, novelist, and playwright. Robinson was born in Maine, where his father was a grain merchant, bank director, and owner of the general store. The youngest of three sons, Edwin, the quiet one, read and wrote poetry by the age of eleven. Robinson was determined to be an author, but, upon entering Harvard, had seen all his poems rejected by the *Harvard Monthly*. Two years later he was forced to give up Harvard and support himself. He attempted to make a living writing short stories, and later plays as well, but he had no talent for anything but poetry. In 1897, financed by a Harvard friend, his *The Children of the Night* was published. Determined to live by poetry alone, he worked on the subway construction crew to pay the rent. Hermann ★Hagedorn, poet, critic, and first biographer of Robinson, brought him to the MacDowell Colony, a haven for creative artists. A dozen books followed, filled with the poetry made possible by the security and calm of his position as a revered artist. Robinson's *Collected Poems* won the Pulitzer Prize in 1921 and twice again during the next six years. At sixty, loneliness was the leading theme of his work; he rarely left his rooms; he suffered physically. Robinson created an entire gallery of untypical American figures: Richard Cory, Miniver Cheevy, Fernando Nash, Mr. Flood, some of which were set to music by American composers. Robinson's personality and that of his brothers, one a drug addict and the other an alcoholic, served as material for Richard Cory and Miniver Cheevy, while Luke Havergal is believed to have been derived from Robinson's strong unrequited feelings for his sister-in-law. "He made the unusual and eccentric seem familiar, and exposed the dilemmas of modern life, the essential character of the failures, the discarded and dispossessed, and triumphed in a poetry of defeat" (Untermeyer, 1959). Edwin Arlington Robinson's verse has been set by John Duke and also by Wintter Watts. "These poems are all psychological portraits of people from the fictional Tillbury Town, which some believe was actually Robinson's home town, Gardiner, Maine" (Villamil, 1993). PRINCIPAL WORKS: Poetry: *The Torrent and the Night Before*, 1896, revised as *The Children of* *the Night*, 1897; *Captain Craig*, 1901, revised ed. 1915; *The Man Against the Sky*, 1917; *Avon's Harvest*, 1921; *Tristram*, 1927; *Collected Poems*, 1937; *Selected Poems*, 1965. Fiction: *Amaranth*, 1934; *King Jasper*, 1935. Plays: *Van Zorn*, 1914; *The Porcupine*, 1915. SELECTED READING: Hermann Hagedorn, *Robinson: A Biography*, 1938; Wallace L. Anderson, *Robinson: A Critical Introduction*, 1967. (SOURCES: Untermeyer, 1959; Vinson, 1979; Villamil, 1993)

ROCCHI, FRANCESCO (1902–1978): Italian poet, painter, born in Saronno, whose work was set to music by Ottorino Respighi.

ROCHLITZ, JOHANN (1769–1842): a German novelist, playwright, poet, and critic. In 1798 Rochlitz started the *Allgemeine musikalische Zeitung* in Leipzig. Carl Maria von Weber set his poems and, after he and Schubert met in Vienna (1822), Schubert set three of his poems, including "Alinde" and "An die Laute." (SOURCE: Reed, 1997)

RODRÍGUEZ MARÍN, FRANCISCO (1855–1943): Spanish poet, scholar, academician, and writer of fiction. The original works of Rodríguez Marín were poems and short stories that combined Andalusian wit with classicism. Director of the National Library, he is remembered as the editor of the annotated edition of *Don Quixote, 1964. The verses of Francisco Rodríguez Marín were set by Joaquín Rodrigo. PRINCIPAL WORKS: *Cantos populares españoles*, 5 vols., 1882–83; *Madrigales y sonetos*, 1909. (SOURCE: Steinberg, 3, 1973)

ROETHKE, THEODORE (1908–1963): American poet and essayist. Theodore Roethke was born in Saginaw, Michigan. His father, of Prussian heritage, owned a large greenhouse that figured as a central image in many of Roethke's best poems. He graduated from the University of Michigan, later took courses at Harvard, then taught English literature and creative writing before moving permanently to the University of Washington in Seattle in 1948, where he was named poet-in-residence. At the age of fifty-five he died of a heart attack while swimming. Roethke's first book, *Open House*, was composed of short, carefully rhymed poems. *The Lost Son* represented Roethke's breakthrough as a poetic stylist. This book contained lyric sequences in which flowers took on an almost spiritual life and became one of the great achievements of modern poetry. During the early 1950s Roethke experimented with subtly autobiographical poems that made use of nursery rhymes and Freudian psychology, gathered in *The Waking* (1953). In the mid-1950s he returned to formal poetry and exuberant love poems, many written for his young wife. Roethke was a *Transcendentalist, putting an *Emersonian emphasis on aspects of the natural world. Like many poets of his generation, Roethke suffered from periods of mental illness. He liked to identify himself with mad poets of the past like *William Blake. *Walt Whitman was the primary influence on Roethke's final work as he began to write long free verse sequences. The poetry of Theodore Roethke has been set by Douglas Moore, Samuel Barber, Celius Dougherty, Lee Hoiby, David Diamond, and Ned Rorem. PRINCIPAL WORKS: *The Lost Son*, 1948; *The Waking*, 1953; *The Far Field*, 1964; *On the Poet and His Craft: Selected Prose of Theodore Roethke*, ed. Ralph J. Mills, Jr., 1965; *Collected Poems*, 1966, 1968, and 1985. SELECTED READING:

Theodore Roethke: Essays on the Poetry, ed. Arnold Stein, 1965. (SOURCE: Hamilton, 1994)

ROISTER DOISTER: the title of the earliest English comedy, derived from the name of its leading character, Ralph Roister Doister, written by Nicholas Udall in the sixteenth century. Peter Warlock's song is from the second book of his collection of *Peterisms*.

SONG	COMPOSER	POET
"Roister Doister"	Peter Warlock	Nicholas Udall

ROLAND (Fr.), ORLANDO (It.): the most famous of Charlemagne's *Paladins, called the Christian *Theseus and the *Achilles of the west. Roland was the Count of Mans, Knight of Blaives, and the son of Duke Milo of Aiglant. Roland was Charlemagne's nephew; his mother was Bertha, the sister of Charlemagne. Fable says that he was eight feet tall, with an open expression that inspired respect. In literature Roland was the hero of *The Song of Roland*, of Boiardo's *Orlando Innamorato*, and of Ariosto's *Orlando Furioso*. *The Song of Roland*, an eleventh-century *chanson de geste*, tells the story of Roland's death together with all the Paladins at *Roncesvalles and of Charlemagne's vengeance. When Charlemagne had been six years in Spain, he sent Ganelon to Marsillus, the pagan king of Saragossa. Ganelon, smitten with jealousy, informed Marsillus of the route that the Christian army intended to take on its way home. The pagan king arrived at Roncesvalles in the Pyrenees just as Roland was leading the rearguard of twenty thousand men through the pass. They fought until one hundred thousand *Saracens lay dead and only fifty of Roland's own men survived (778). Another army of fifty thousand men charged off the mountain. Roland blew his enchanted horn. Charlemagne heard the sound, but Ganelon persuaded him that Roland was only hunting deer. So was Roland left to his fate. Legend has it that Roland escaped the general slaughter at Roncevalles and died of hunger and thirst attempting to cross the Pyrenees. Although he was buried elsewhere, his body was eventually removed to Roncesvalles. (SOURCE: Cooper, 1992)

SONG	COMPOSER	POET
"Le Cor"	Ange Flégier	Alfred de Vigny

"Rollicum Rorum": a drinking song in Thomas *Hardy's novel *The Trumpet Major*. The song was originally called "The Sergeant's Song," in which Napoleon is dared to march his men on London Town. (SOURCE: Kimball, 1996)

SONG	COMPOSER	POET
"Rollicum Rorum"	Gerald Finzi	Thomas Hardy

ROMANCE: *see* *MÉLODIE.

ROMANS: the Russian equivalent of "art song," derived from the French word *romance*, French having been the language of the Russian court during the eighteenth and nineteenth centuries.

ROMANTICISM: a movement in western literature and other arts, emerging in the first half of the nineteenth century, from about 1780 to about 1848. A definition of the basic principle of Romanticism is famously difficult partly because the Romantic temperament preferred the indefinite. "In the most abstract terms, Romanticism may be regarded as the triumph of the values of imaginative spontaneity, visionary originality, wonder, and emotional self-expression over the classical standards of balance, order, restraint, proportion, and objectivity" (Drabble, 2000). English language writers allied with Romanticism include William *Blake, Robert *Burns, William Wordsworth, Samuel Taylor *Coleridge, Lord *Byron, Percy Bysshe *Shelley, John *Keats, and Emily Brontë. SUGGESTED READING: A. Day, *Romanticism*, 1996.

RONCEVALLES: *see* *ROLAND.

RONDA: a town in Màlaga on the southern coast of Spain.

SONG	COMPOSER	POET
1. "De Ronda"	Joaquín Rodrigo	folk song
2. "El pan de ronda"	Manuel de Falla	María and Gregorio Martínez Sierra

RONDEL: a French verse form originally associated with dance rounds that were popular in the latter half of the nineteenth century. It consists of ten (in stricter compositions, thirteen) lines. Only two rhymes are used throughout the poem. The opening words are used twice as a refrain. This is a form of the rondeau, which had two rhymes and a refrain and usually consisted of five stanzas. (SOURCE: Drabble, 2000)

SONG	COMPOSER	POET
1. "Le Temps a laissé son manteau"	Claude Debussy	Charles d'Orléans
2. "Pour ce que plaisance est morte"	Claude Debussy	Charles d'Orléans
3. "Two Rondels"	Lee Hoiby	W. Crane, C. Scollard
4. "Rondele"	Frederick Jacobi	Geoffrey Chaucer

RONSARD, PIERRE DE (1524–1585): French poet. Ronsard's father was an official in the household of Francis I. After attending the College of Navarre, where he learned Latin and Greek as shown in his imitations of Greek and Latin poems, Ronsard was appointed a royal page, later spending three years in Great Britain on diplomatic missions. His long distinguished literary career began when he was appointed "master of poetry" to Charles IX. Although he first wrote poetry in imitation of the classics, he eventually developed into an original poet, writing *elegies, *odes on philosophical and religious subjects, and love *sonnets, which works made him the most famous of the *Pléiades group. For two centuries after his death Ronsard's reputation waned, but he was then rediscovered during the *Romantic era. His poetry was prized for the charm of its nature descriptions and the magnificence of his language and metrics. The poetry of Pierre de Ronsard was set by Lennox Berkeley, Francis Poulenc, Darius Milhaud, Albert Roussel, Frank Martin, Arthur Honegger, and André Caplet. WORKS in English: *Songs and Sonnets of Pierre de Ronsard*, trans. C. H. Page, 1903; *Selected Poems*, trans. C. Graves, 1924; *Sonnets pour*

Hélène, trans. H. Wolfe, 1934. SELECTED READING: K. R. W. Jones, *Pierre de Ronsard*, 1970. (SOURCE: Magill, 4, 1997)

ROOS, RICHARD, pseudonym: see *ENGELHARDT.

ROSEMONDE (Fr.), ROSAMOND (Eng.), ROSEMUNDE (Ger.): heroine in several legends: one, as the wife of a Lombard king (ca. 570 C.E.) whose story was told in *epic poems, including one by the English poet Swinburne; another, inspiring many romantic tales, as a mistress of the English King Henry II. A third sighting of Rosemonde occurs in a poem by *Apollinaire, set to music by Poulenc. Schubert composed incidental music for Wilhelmine von *Chézy's play *Rosamunde, Princess of Cyprus*, in which the song "Der Vollmond strahlt" is sung by Rosamunde's foster mother. Information from contemporary newspapers and articles sheds light on the basic story, which is based on a Spanish source. Its plot features a cursed, poverty-stricken princess and the usurper of her throne, who importunes her with his love but finally falls victim to his own plotting. In the improbable and complex plot, the princess is brought up by sailors; one of the characters is a prince who lives among shepherds; huntsmen and shepherd choruses abound. Another legend concerns Rosamond, wife of the Lombard King Albion. She was the daughter of King Kunimund of the Gepidae, a Germanic people. She is captured by Albion, who defeats and kills her father. When Albion forces her to drink from a cup made from her father's skull, she has him murdered by two of his own courtiers and takes refuge with the Byzantine prefect, Longinus. Although married to one of her fellow conspirators, Helmechis, she prefers the prefect. When Rosamond offers Helmechis a poisoned drink, he swallows half and forces her to drink the remainder. Yet another legend speaks of Rosamond, the fair, who was the daughter of Walter, Lord Clifford, and became the concubine of King Henry II. Henry had an extraordinary house built for her in such a manner that no one could come to visit her. The house was called Labyrinthus, constructed like a maze in a garden. But Queen Eleanor found her by a clue of thread and had her killed in 1177 C.E. Rosamond was buried at Godstow in a house of nuns. The legend of her murder by Queen Eleanor first appeared in the fourteenth century, and the story of her house and the labyrinth appeared even later. The unknown woman whom Apollinaire followed through the streets of Amsterdam in 1905 is the third woman who may be the Rosemonde of the Poulenc song. (SOURCES: Meister, 1980; Cooper, 1992)

SONG	COMPOSER	POET
1. "Le Manoir de Rosemonde"	Henri Duparc	Raymond de Bonnières
2. "Rosamunde"	Charles Ives	Wilhelmine von Chézy
3. "À Palais"	Francis Poulenc	Guillaume Apollinaire
4. "Der Vollmond strahlt"	Franz Schubert	Wilhelmine von Chézy
5. "Was Ever a Nymph like Rosamond"	Thomas Arne	Joseph Addison

ROSE OF SHARON: the popular name for two plants, a hibiscus and St. John's wort. The hibiscus is a shrub that grows to a height of five to fifteen feet. It produces broad, bell shaped single or double flowers of red, purple, violet, and white. It is the only member of its genus that is hardy in the northern United States. St. John's wort is a low evergreen shrub that makes good ground cover for sandy and shady spots. It bears a few two-inch-wide yellow flowers.

SONG	COMPOSER	POET
"The Rose of Sharon"	John La Montaine	Bible

ROSE OF THE NIGHT: an old Celtic legend affirms that, when a dead soul woos a living soul, in order that they both may be reborn as one soul, the sigh is a rose of flame in the midst of the dark night. (SOURCE: Kimball, 1996)

SONG	COMPOSER	POET
"The Rose of the Night"	Charles Griffes	Fiona MacLeod (William Sharp)

ROSSETTI, CHRISTINA (1830–1894): British poet and writer of religious prose. Christina Rossetti was born in a predominantly immigrant section of London, daughter of a political refugee from ★Naples who wrote works on the Masonic meaning of ★Dante. Rossetti was taught entirely at home by her mother, who was half English. Bilingual from infancy and precocious as a writer, she wrote her first volume at the age of twelve and her second at the age of seventeen; both were printed privately. When her father became blind, the family, never well off, was faced with true poverty. Rossetti's strong religious disposition narrowed her mental and emotional life and ruined her two love affairs. Soon, wracked with ill health, she evolved into a recluse, eventually becoming afflicted with Graves' disease and dying of cancer. Christina Rossetti's life was totally urban, but her poetry showed a strong feeling for nature. Outwardly she was a shy, humble woman. Her true personality showed only in her poems, mystical and visionary at the same time as realistic and sensuous. Her preoccupations in poetry were ever love, religion, children, nature, and death, which obsessed her. Rossetti had a special vocation for the ★sonnet and was, in fact, one of the foremost sonnetists of the English language. The verses of Christina Rossetti have been set by Ned Rorem, Richard Faith, Judith Zaimont, Miriam Gideon, John Musto, Henry Clough-Leighter, Charles Ives, Sidney Homer, and in German by Erich Korngold. WORKS: *Goblin Market and Other Poems*, 1862; *The Prince's Progress and Other Poems*, 1866; *A Pageant and Other Poems*, 1881; *Verses*, 1893; *New Poems*, ed. W. M. Rossetti, 1896. SELECTED READING: Ford Madox ★Ford, *Memories and Impressions*, 1911; M. F. Sandars, *The Life of Christina Rossetti*, 1930. (SOURCE: Kunitz, Haycraft, 1936)

ROSSETTI, DANTE GABRIEL (1828–1882): British poet and painter. Dante Gabriel Rossetti, called Gabriel by his family, was born in an immigrant section of London, the son of a father who was a political refugee from ★Naples and an author. Rossetti, brother to poet Christina ★Rossetti, was a precocious child, writing his first verses at five or six. At fourteen he left school and began to prepare for a career as a painter, to which his poetry took second place. He quit his lessons with Ford Madox Brown when ordered to paint still life. Rossetti was a part of the celebrated ★Pre-Raphaelite Brotherhood, who were in revolt against the stiffness of the official art of that day. Rossetti had always been moody and self-centered but when in remorse after the death of his wife, a slow decline began. Taking chloral and whiskey together soon reduced him to a kind of imbecility. Throughout all his difficulties, however, he painted and, after twenty years of silence as a poet, began to write again better than ever, although probably greater as a poet than as a painter. Rossetti's poetry is the writing of a painter, opulent colors and still forms. He was a superb poet in a very restricted sphere. The verses of Dante Gabriel Rossetti have been set by Claude Debussy (*La Demoiselle élue*), Elinor Remick Warren, Miriam Gideon, Charles Loeffler, Ralph Vaughan Williams, John Ireland, and Frederic Ayres. PRINCIPAL WORKS: *The House of Life*, in *Collected Works*, ed. W. M. Rossetti, 1969; *The Blessed Damozel*, in *Collected Works*, ed. W. M. Rossetti, 1969; *Ballads and Sonnets*, 1881. SELECTED READING: R. L. Mégroz, *Dante Gabriel Rossetti: Painter Poet of Heaven in Earth*, 1928; Evelyn Waugh, *Rossetti: His Life and Works*, 1931. (SOURCE: Kunitz, Haycraft, 1936)

ROSTAND, EDMOND (1868–1918): French playwright. Rostand was born in Marseilles to a Provençal family; his father was a renowned economist, poet, and scholar. Early on young Rostand displayed a strong leaning toward literature and debuted his first play at twenty with little success. In 1890 his first collection of poetry showed great promise despite much imitation of ★Hugo and ★Musset. In 1894–95 two of his plays had real success at the Comédie Française. As a poet Rostand exhibited a marked reaction against the gloom and seriousness of ★Naturalist drama. His plays, at best, have warmth, charm, wit, and poetic feeling, but they have at times been perceived as contrived and sentimental. Rostand's great success was *Cyrano de Bergerac* (1897), which was a romantic, swashbuckling drama, creative in its poetry and exciting and touching in its performance. Its success made him the youngest ever to be accepted by the Académie Française. *Chantecler* (1910) was his ambitious and experimental allegory, using masks of birds and beasts. The lyrics of Edmond Rostand were set by Emanuel Chabrier. WORKS in English translation: *Cyrano de Bergerac*, 1898; *The Romancer*, 1899; *The Princess Faraway*, 1899; *L'Aiglon*, 1900. READING: *A Critical Biography of French Literature*, 3, 1994. (SOURCE: France, 1995)

ROTHSCHILD: the name of a family of European bankers, financiers, and philanthropists. The Rothschild family was for many years one of the outstanding banking powers of Europe.

SONG	COMPOSER	POET
"1904"	Francis Poulenc	Guillaume Apollinaire

ROULOTTE: (Fr.), *a gypsy wagon*.

SONG	COMPOSER	POET
"Une roulotte couverte en tuiles"	Francis Poulenc	Paul Éluard

"Round Thy Coast": a duet and chorus composed by Henry Purcell, to text by John ★Dryden for their semi-opera *King Arthur*, produced in 1691. *See* ★*King Arthur* for plot details and song placements.

ROUSSEAU, JEAN-BAPTISTE (1670–1741): French poet and dramatist. Born in Paris, the son of a cobbler, Rousseau was disinterested in his studies. His talent appeared to lie in various types of verse writing. At the turn of the century Rousseau was popularly known as a Casanova due to his frequenting of cabaret society in Paris. In revenge for the failure of the plays he had begun to write, Rousseau composed scurrilous skits against his critics; they in turn escalated the battle by answering in kind. As a result, Rousseau was forced to flee into permanent exile in Switzerland. He later died in Brussels, in abject poverty, and his fate was lamented even by Voltaire, a former enemy. Rousseau's reputation as a poet was great even as it changed from a classical to a rationalist manner of writing. He was the last French poet to search for external purity of line and form. The verse of Jean-Baptiste Rousseau was set by Henri Desmarets and Johannes Brahms ("Der Frühling"). PRINCIPAL WORKS: *Cantate de Circé*, 1799; *Odes sacrées*, 1802; *Oeuvres diverses*, 1712; *Oeuvres choisies*, 1721; *Complete Works*, 1743, 1757. SELECTED READING: H. A. Grubbs, *Jean-Baptiste Rousseau*, 1941. (SOURCE: Kunitz, Colby, 1967)

ROZINANTE, ROSINANTE: the lame and halt riding horse belonging to ★Don Quixote. Although Rosinante was worn down to skin and bone, Don Quixote regarded it as a stalwart charger more priceless than Bucephalus, Alexander's horse, more wonderful than Babieca, El Cid's horse. The name, applied to similar scrawny animals, is from the Spanish word "rocin" (a jade), implying that once upon a time it had been a horse. It can be applied to any worn out and emaciated horse. (SOURCE: Cooper, 1992)

SONG	COMPOSER	POET
1. "Chansons de Don Quichotte"	Jacques Ibert	Pierre Ronsard; Alexandre Arnoux
2. "Don Quichotte à Dulcinée"	Maurice Ravel	Paul Morand

RÜCKERT, FRIEDRICH (1788–1866): German poet and Oriental scholar. Rückert taught Oriental languages at the University of Erlangen and later at Berlin. As interpretations of Oriental culture and literature, his translations from the Arabic and Sanskrit met with approval, notably from ★Goethe, who admired his work at widening Germans' interest in world literature. Rückert was skilled at imitating the patterns of Oriental poetry, also at writing patriotic verses during the War of Liberation from Napoleon. His large output is more notable for its neat workmanship in various verse forms than for vision or originality. The lyrics of *Kindertotenlieder*, set by Mahler, were written after the death of Rückert's two children. His poetry was also set by Smetana, Wolf, Brahms, Liszt, Robert and Clara Schumann, Max Reger, Robert Franz, Carl Loewe, and Fanny Mendelssohn Hensel. Schubert set six of his poems, including "Du bist die Ruh" and "Das sie hier gewesen." PRINCIPAL WORKS: *Barbarossa*, 1817; *Österlichen Rosen*, 1822; *Liebesfrühling*, 1823; *Kindertotenlieder*, 1872. (SOURCE: Mathieu, Stern, 1987)

RULE, BRITANNIA: an ★ode written in 1740 as part of a masque by James Thomson (1700–48) with music by Thomas Arne, which became Great Britain's national song. The ★masque deals with the struggles of King Alfred with the Danes and his final victory over them. Although it is an interesting work, the characters are life-less. "Rule, Britannia" marks the occasion when the king resolves to build a fleet to protect England's shores. The real King Alfred ruled Wessex from 871 to 900, fighting the Danes to make possible the unification of England. His other contribution to the nation was a great translation project that aimed to make available in English all the important books heretofore available only in Latin.

RUNE: *a secret, a mystery.*

SONG	COMPOSER	POET
"Elvershöh"	Carl Loewe	Johann Herder, trans. from Danish

RUNEBERG, JOHAN LUDVIG (1804–1877): a Swedish poet, born in Finland. Runeberg's father was a sea captain of Swedish descent, a man of means until the stroke that reduced his family to poverty. Family and friends enabled Johan to enter the University of Åbo (1822). After finishing school, Runeberg went to Helsinki where he became the center of a literary group (1830). Until 1857 he maintained himself and his family by teaching journalism at the University of Helsinki. At that time a national gift of money in recognition of his services to literature ended his financial worries. In the first collection of *Dikter*, a cycle of small poems combined classical, romantic, and realistic elements. Later, influenced by Greek tragedy and by ★Ossian, he placed his lyrics in a Viking setting, beginning in 1846 his two-volume celebrated work, *Fänrik Ståls Sägner* (Tales of Ensign Stål), which made him the national poet of Finland, and of Sweden to a degree, by painting battle scenes from Russia's 1808 war against Sweden and Finland. Runeberg's poetry, scholarly, patriotic, moral, and optimistic, has been set by Jean Sibelius, Selim Palmgren, and Wilhelm Stenhammar. PRINCIPAL WORKS in English: *The Songs of Ensign Stål*, trans. C. B. Shaw, 1925. (SOURCES: Steinberg, 3, 1973; Kunitz, Colby, 1967)

S ✺

SACCO AND VANZETTI: the two men, Nicola Sacco, a shoemaker, and Bartolomeo Vanzetti, a fish peddler, who were executed on August 23, 1927, in Massachusetts for holdup murders committed on April 15, 1920. The intense interest in the United States and abroad stemmed from the belief that the two men were accused by accident and convicted because of their unpopular political, social, and religious views. Italian-born Sacco and Vanzetti were members of an anarchist group, and the early 1920s was a time of great anti-alien and anti-radical hysteria. Before they were executed, many places in the world saw demonstrations against the procedure. It was generally agreed that there should have been a new trial in which all the evidence would be presented. (SOURCE: *Americana*, 2003)

SONG	COMPOSER	POET
"Sacco and Vanzetti"	Ruth Crawford Seeger	H. T. Tsiang

"Sad as Death at the Dead of Night": a song composed by Henry Purcell to a text written by Nathaniel ★Lee for his heroic play *Theodosius*, produced in 1680. For placement of songs and plot details, *see* ★*Theodosius*.

SAE MOOLIE: (Scot.) (pr. say mooly), *so moldy; so muley*.

SONG	COMPOSER	POET
"Supper"	Benjamin Britten	William Soutar

SAETA: an Andalusian religious song. A saeta (literally, *arrow*) is sung, unaccompanied, when the processions celebrating Holy Week pause.

SONG	COMPOSER	POET
"Saeta en forma de Salve a la Virgen de la Esperanza"	Joaquín Turina	Serafín and Joaquín Álvarez Quintero

SAGA: in Norse mythology believed to be a goddess who knows all things, hence a goddess of the poetic arts and history; now the name of a long historical epic composed by ★skalds, the poets and historiographers of the Teutons. (SOURCE: Kaster, 1964)

SAGARRA I CASTELLARNAU, JOSEP MARIA DE (1894–1964): Catalan poet and dramatist. José de Sagarra, as his Catalan name is stated in Spanish, was a prolific writer of short lyrics, long epic poems, two novels, and some plays. The facility with which he wrote made his efforts at times appear superficial, although fluent and vigorous. Sagarra translated all of ★Shakespeare into Catalan and ★Dante's *Divine Comedy* as well. Sagarra's verses were set by Eduardo Toldrà. PRINCIPAL WORKS: *El Mal Caçador*, 1916; *El Comte Arnau* (modern interpretations of Catalan legends), 1928; *Memòries*, 1954. (SOURCE: Steinberg, 3, 1973)

SAING GUY, DE: *see* ★ST. VITUS.

SAINT ELMO'S FIRE: a visible discharge of static electricity sometimes seen at the top of a mast of a ship or on the wing of an airplane during a storm. The name is taken from St. Elmo (Erasmus), the patron saint of sailors. (SOURCE: Nevins, 1964)

SONG	COMPOSER	POET
"La Petite Servante"	Francis Poulenc	Max Jacob

SAINT MARK'S SQUARE, PIAZZA SAN MARCO (It.): the most famous square in Venice. It is the only Venetian square called a *piazza*; others are called *campi*. Three sides of the square are pure Renaissance with arcades, columns, pilasters, and friezes. The two long sides look parallel, but are not. They slope inward so that eyes are drawn to the end, where stands the Basilica San Marco, in Byzantine style at its most oriental. The other short side of the square facing the Basilica is known as the Ala Napoleonica, the Napoleonic wing, built by order of Napoleon to enclose what he called "the most beautiful drawing room in all of Europe."

SALADIN (1138–1193): sultan of Egypt and Syria, founder of the Ayyubid dynasty. The Arabic form of this name is Salah al-Din Ysuf Ibn Ayyub. Saladin was of Kurdish parentage, born in Tikrit, Mesopotamia. While still an infant, he was taken to Baal-bek, and finally to Damascus. In 1164 the young Saladin (the name means "bounty of religion") interrupted his theological career to join his uncle in a military campaign against Egypt. After the uncle's death, Saladin was made commander of the Syrian troops in Egypt, then in 1169 took over the reins of government. He annexed Muslim Syria when the sultan of Damascus died (1174). Now that he was sultan of Egypt and Syria, his greatest ambition was to force the Crusaders to leave Palestine and Syria. Following a successful Muslim campaign, Saladin and ★Richard the Lion-Hearted made an armistice (1192), which left the Christians with a narrow ribbon of land along the coast, the Muslims retaining Jerusalem. Saladin brought unity to the divided Muslim area, treating the enemies more humanely than they had treated the Arabs. (SOURCE: *Americana*, 2003)

SALAMANCA (Sp.), SALAMANQUE (Fr.): a Spanish city located 107 miles northwest of Madrid. It occupies three hills on the north bank of the Tormes River. Sites of architectural interest are the Plaza Mayor (1729–33), one of the finest squares in Europe, the New Cathedral, begun in 1513, which adjoins the Old Cathedral of the twelfth century, and the main building of the university. Called Salamantica in ancient times, the city was taken by Hannibal in 222 B.C.E., then ruled by the Romans before being conquered by the Visigoths, ravished by the Moors, and finally retaken by the Christians later in the eleventh century.

SONG	COMPOSER	POET
"Le Bachelier de Salamanque"	Albert Roussel	René Chalupt

SALAMANDER: a kind of lizard, described in folklore as able to live in fire, which it quenched by the chill of its body. The Roman writer Pliny recounted that he tried the experiment once without success, for the creature was soon burnt to ashes.

SALIS-SEEWIS, JOHAN VON (1762–1834): a Swiss poet. Salis-Seewis was a nobleman who served in Paris as an officer of the Swiss Guard prior to the French Revolution. During the revolution he remained in Paris as a civilian. In 1789 he toured Germany, meeting ★Goethe, ★Schiller, and ★Herder, after which he returned to Switzerland to assume an administrative post. Thirteen Salis-Seewis poems, including "Der Jüngling an der Quelle," "Der Entfernten," and "Abschied von der Harfe," were set by Franz Schubert. (SOURCE: Reed, 1997)

SALL: (Scot.), *shall*.

SALLEY: a variety of willow tree.

SONG	COMPOSER	POET
1. "The Salley Gardens"	Benjamin Britten, John Ireland	William Butler Yeats
2. "Down by the Salley Gardens"	Ivor Gurney	William Butler Yeats

SALOME: a biblical character, said to have caused the beheading of ★John the Baptist. Salome was the daughter of Herodias and thus the stepdaughter of ★Herod

Antipas, the governor of Galilee. According to the Bible, Salome danced for Herod. He was so pleased that he offered to grant her any request. At her mother's suggestion, Salome asked for the head of John the Baptist. Herod ordered it done and sent the head to her on a platter. (SOURCE: *Americana*, 2003)

SALT WATER BALLADS: a 1902 ballad collection by John ★Masefield, one-time poet laureate of England, containing the familiar "Captain Stratton's Fancy" and "I Must Go Down to the Seas Again," inspired by his many sea voyages. Whereas the poet was concerned with outcasts, the despised and despairing, it was the publisher's idea to call the collection *Salt Water Ballads*. At the time of publication a parallel with ★Kipling's *Barrack Room Ballads* was implied, although Masefield vehemently denied it.

SAMAIN, ALBERT VICTOR (1858–1900): French poet. Albert Samain's parents were lower middle-class owners of a wine-shop in Lille. At fourteen, after the death of his father, Samain left school to help support his family. His only escape from his twelve-hour working days was to read Greek and English literature. Edgar Allen ★Poe was one of his favorites. In Paris (1880), he tried to place his journalistic articles but had no success. In 1881 he obtained a minor position in municipal government, which stabilized his income. Soon he had joined a literary circle, which published his first poems (1884–85). After he was persuaded by his friends to collect some of his poems as *Au jardin de l'infante* in 1893, the work became famous thanks to a laudatory review by François ★Coppée. Then a prize from the French Academy enabled him to travel to England, Holland, and Spain. Samain died one year after writing a two-act verse drama, *Polyphème,* which was added to the repertoire of the Comédie Française. Impractical and unambitious by nature, reticent and introverted, Samain identified with the second generation of ★Symbolists and had an ability to establish moods that were deliberately vague, composed of half-tones and disillusioned melancholy. His reputation in the United States was a result of his inclusion by Amy ★Lowell in *Six French Poets* (1915). The verse of Albert Samain has been set by Henry Hadley and Gabriel Fauré. PRINCIPAL WORKS: *Des lettres*, 1887–1900; *Correspondance inédite*, with Francis ★Jammes, 1945; *Carnets intimes*, 1939. SELECTED READING: E. H. Falk, *Renunciation as a Tragic Focus*, 1954; E. W. Gosse, *French Profiles*, 1913. (SOURCE: Kunitz, Colby, 1967)

SAMARKAND: the second largest city and former capital of the Uzbek Republic, lying in modern Turkestan, 140 miles east of Bukhara. Samarkand is an important educational center and renowned for its silk goods. It occupies the site of ancient Maracanda, destroyed by ★Alexander the Great in 329 B.C.E. During the 1300s Tamerlane, the Mongol conqueror, chose Samarkand as his capital. (SOURCE: *Americana*, 2003)

SONG	COMPOSER	POET
"Bruder Liederlich"	Richard Strauss	Detlev von Liliencron

SAMPOGNA: a rustic bagpipe.

SONG	COMPOSER	POET
"Deità silvane"	Ottorino Respighi	Antonio Rubino

SANCHO PANZA: the squire of ★Don Quixote in ★Cervantes's romance of the same name. Sancho Panza was a short, potbellied (in Spanish *panza* means *paunch*), rustic peasant, full of common sense but without any spirituality. He rode upon his ass, Dapple, and was famous for his proverbs. Panza is a rough, sharp, and humorous man, in contrast to the head-in-the-clouds Don Quixote. (SOURCE: Cooper, 1992)

SONG	COMPOSER	POET
"Chanson de la mort"	Jacques Ibert	Alexandre Arnoux

SANDBURG, CARL (1878–1967): American poet and biographer. Although born in Galesburg, Illinois, Sandburg lived in Chicago most of his life. These days he is probably best known for his admirable biography of Abraham Lincoln, but in the early 1920s there was a time when his fame was extensive in the United States and in England. The period called the "beat generation" brought a brief revival of Sandburg's popularity, after which he more or less dropped from sight. Because Sandburg was the first important American writer to spend his childhood speaking and writing English as a second language—Swedish, the first—the rhythm and diction of his work were unique. The rhythms of his written verse were refined by Sandburg's extensive public reading of his works. His verse expressed the power of modern industry and his Midwestern subjects' beliefs. His verse collection published in 1950 won the Pulitzer Prize. The poetry of Carl Sandburg was set by Roy Harris, Charles Naginski, Sam Raphling, Howard Swanson, Ernst Bacon, Ruth Crawford Seeger, Norman dello Joio, and Sergius Kagen. WORKS: *The Complete Poems of Carl Sandburg*, 1950. SELECTED READING: Mark Van Doren, *Sandburg*, 1969. (SOURCE: Drabble, 1985)

SAN GIMIGNANO (GEMINIANO), FOLGORE DA (1250?–?1317): Italian poet, real name Giacomo di Michele. This poet was a soldier and courtier in the walled city of San Gimignano. He wrote two cycles of ★sonnets on the months of the year and the days of the week, which gave a delightful account of the manners of his time. The verse of Folgore da San Gimignano was set by Charles Ives. (SOURCE: Wilkins, 1974)

SANTILLANA, IÑIGO LÓPEZ DE MENDOZA, MARQUÉS DE (1398–1458): Spanish poet and humanist. As the eventual heir of a leading nobleman of Castile, Santillana was educated by the best tutors. By 1413 he was a representative figure, militarily and politically as well as in literature, at the Castilian court of John II. During the complicated struggles of these years, Santillana's loyalty to the king at the Battle of Olmedo won him titles of Marquis of Santillana and Count of Manzanares. He retired to his great library at Guadalajara and died there at the age of fifty-nine. In his youth he wrote, mainly in the tradition of Provençal, powerful poems of courtly love, as well as rustic serranillas that told the story of traveling knights' encounters with mountain lasses, and more ambitious narrative ★canciones. In his final twenty years, Santillana wrote forty-two ★sonnets, the first to be written in any language but Italian. Influenced by ★Petrarch and anticipating the Renaissance, they speak of courtly love, politics, morality, and religion. The final category of Santillana's mature poetry treats moral, political, and religious themes in elegant and philosophical verses. The poems of the Marqués of Santillana were set by Joaquín Rodrigo. PRINCIPAL WORKS in ENGLISH: *Proverbs*, trans. Barnaby Googe, 1579. SELECTED READING: J. B. Trend, *Santillana: Prose and Verse*, 1940. (SOURCE: Kunitz, Colby, 1967)

SAPPHIC: referring to a poetic form consisting of quatrains that utilize a meter derived from the Greek poet, ★Sappho.

SAPPHO: the celebrated Greek poet of the Greek island of Lesbos, known as "the tenth Muse," who lived about 600 B.C.E. It appears that she left Lesbos because of political troubles, went to Sicily, and died there. In ancient times she, the most famous of Greek women poets, collected her works into nine books according to the type of poetry. The poems or fragments of poetry that have survived did so only because they were quoted by later critics and poets. ★Catullus translated one of her poems, borrowed some others, and used some of her meters; Ovid wrote about her and ★Horace used the Sapphic stanza, named for her. She preferred to write short lyrics to and about the girls she favored or informal hymns addressed to goddesses like Hera and ★Aphrodite, all written in the vernacular of Lesbos. Her principal subject was always love, expressed with great simplicity and beauty of phrase, and the poetry that survives consists mainly of love poems, many expressing passionate friendships with women, which explains her association with female homosexuality and the derivation of the words *lesbian* and *Sapphic*. (SOURCE: Cooper, 1992)

SONG	COMPOSER	POET
1. "Sapphische Ode"	Johannes Brahms	Hans Schmidt
2. "Lyrics of Sappho"	Mary Turner Salter	Sappho, trans. Bliss Carman
3. "Sappho"	Frederick Ayres	Sappho

SARACEN, SARACINA: a Muslim at the time of the Crusades.

SONG	COMPOSER	POET
1. "Melusina"	GianFrancesco Malipiero	Gabriele d'Annunzio
2. "Romance"	Joaquín Turina	Duque de Rivas
3. "Saracen Songs"	Harry T. Burleigh	Frederick G. Bowles

SARK: (Scot.), *a man's shirt; a woman's chemise.*

SONG	COMPOSER	POET
"Wee Willie"	Benjamin Britten	Robert Burns

SAROYAN, WILLIAM (1908–1981): American playwright and short-story writer. William Saroyan was born in Fresno, California, of Armenian parents. His father, a former Presbyterian minister, was a small grape-grower when he died. During junior high school, Saroyan read every book in the public library and wrote from the age of thirteen. His first short story was published in an Armenian magazine which was reprinted in *The Best Short Stories of 1934*. "The Daring Young Man on the Flying Trapeze" appeared as the title story of his first published volume. In 1939 Saroyan became a playwright with *My Heart's in the Highlands* and received the Pulitzer Prize for drama for *The Time of Your Life,* although he declined to accept it because "commerce has no right to patronize art." Saroyan went to Hollywood in 1942 to write and direct his own picture, *The Human Comedy,* but left when Hollywood did not allow him to direct. In New York he organized and directed The Saroyan Theater. Saroyan honestly preferred the company of the uncultured and wanted none of the social graces. The verses of William Saroyan have been set by Paul Bowles. PRINCIPAL WORKS: *The Daring Young Man on the Flying Trapeze,* 1934; *Three Times Three,* 1936, 1940; *The Trouble with Tigers,* 1938; *The Time of Your Life,* 1940; *My Name is Aram,* 1940; *The Human Comedy,* 1942. (SOURCE: Kunitz, Haycraft, 1942)

SASSOON, SIEGFRIED (1886–1967): English poet and prose writer. Sassoon was educated at Cambridge, and destined, believed his mother, to be a poet. Until World War I he lived in the countryside of Kent and Sussex and published his verse in private pamphlets. The poetry for which he became celebrated was written in the trenches of the war. However, the public found his cheerless realism, his abhorrence of war talk and the leaders of the conflict, and his compassion for his soldier colleagues too different from the revered works of Rupert Brooke. Sassoon organized a protest against the war and published his war poems in journals, neither of which were a success. Yet when volumes were published in the 1920s, he began to enjoy a high reputation and to think of himself as a real poet. In 1957 he converted to Catholicism, and later became a successful prose writer. The poetry of Siegfried Sassoon was set by Hugo Weisgall, John Alden Carpenter, Arthur Shepherd, and William Flanagan. PRINCIPAL WORKS: *Vigils,* 1935; *The Complete Memoirs of George Sherston,* 1937; *Sequences,* 1956. (SOURCE: Drabble, 2000)

SATURN: the ancient Roman corn god, his name derived from sowing (*satus,* sown). Saturn was identified with the Greek *Kronos, but had more in common with Demeter, the goddess of vegetation. Saturn and his wife Rhea were *Titans, the children of Earth and Heaven. Our Christmas festivities are a dim survival of his festival, the Saturnalia, that took place in December, during which presents were exchanged. The planet Saturn and the seventh day of the week, Saturday, are named for him. His reign was considered by the Roman poets to have been a golden age. Some Romans believed that Saturn was not a god but a former king, raised to deity by his greatness. (SOURCE: Graves (2), 1960)

SONG	COMPOSER	POET
1. "Gruppe aus dem Tartarus"	Franz Schubert, Ottmar Schoeck	Friedrich von Schiller
2. "Saturn"	Alan Hovhaness	Alan Hovhaness
3. "Who Is Silvia?"	Gerald Finzi	William Shakespeare
4. "Io mi levai"	Francesco Santoliquido	Omar Khayyam

SATYR: one of a group of forest gods or demons who were attendants of *Bacchus. Satyrs were akin to fauns, represented as having the legs and hind-quarters of a goat, bristly hair, small horns, and ears like goats, cloven feet, very lascivious, hence lustful men. (SOURCE: Cooper, 1992)

SONG	COMPOSER	POET
1. "Le Faune"	Claude Debussy	Paul Verlaine
2. "La Flûte de Pan"	Claude Debussy	Pierre Louÿs
3. "The Satyr"	Daren Hagen	Gwen Hagen
4. "Le Tombeau des Naïades"	Claude Debussy	Pierre Louÿs

SAUDADE (Port.): longing, melancholy, nostalgia; a supposed characteristic of Portuguese or Brazilian temperament; a vague and constant desire for something that does not and probably cannot exist, not an active discontent or poignant sadness, but an indolent, dreaming wistfulness. *Saudade* appears often in Brazilian and Portuguese popular music, but it will also be found in the art songs of such composers as Heitor Villa Lobos, Camargo Guarnieri, and Francisco Mignone. Peter Warlock composed a set of songs called *Saudades*. (SOURCE: *OED*, 1989)

SAUL, KING: a biblical figure, the first king of Israel, whose story is contained in the Old Testament, 1 Samuel 8–31. When the prophet Samuel passed on the rule of Israel to his sons, they corrupted the office. The elders of Israel asked Samuel to select a king with the objective of making Israel like other countries. This action was seen not as a rejection of Samuel, but of God. Saul, handsome and tallest of all Israeli men, was proclaimed king of Israel. Although Samuel had instructed him to wait, Saul performed the sacrifice that precedes the battle when he and his army were confronted by a large band of Philistines, Israel's traditional enemy. This action caused Samuel to put an end to Saul's rule as king of Israel, citing God's displeasure at Saul's many acts of disobedience. God selected ★David, the son of Jesse, to be the next king. Saul's torment at this rejection was so great that David was brought to the court with the hope that his harp playing would sooth King Saul. In Saul's court David gained favor with the people, which displeased Saul, who tried to have David killed. He offered David his daughter Michal as a wife if he would produce two hundred Philistine foreskins, which he hoped would be an impossible task that would lead to David's death. Instead, David triumphed and married Michal. David's fortunes rose as those of Saul fell. After Samuel's death, Saul could not get any messages from God about the large Philistine army facing him, so he traveled to Endor in disguise to consult the witch, who conjured Samuel up. The ghost of Samuel foretold that Saul and his sons would be killed in the battle and that victory would be to the Philistines. The results were as foretold. The bodies of Saul and his sons were found by the Philistines, and their armor was displayed in the temple of ★Astarte while their bodies were nailed to the wall. Later, when David fled Jerusalem, pursued by the army of his son ★Absalom, a veteran of Saul's army reminded David that this was his payment for usurping Saul's throne. (SOURCES: The Holy Bible; Comay, 2002)

SAUTER, SAMUEL (1766–1846): a German poet and schoolmaster from Baden. Both Beethoven and Schubert set his "Der Wachtelschlag." (SOURCE: Reed, 1997)

SAVISHNA: the prettiest girl in the village in a song by Mussorgsky, "Fair Savishna," sung by a *yurodivy. It is said that Mussorgsky had watched the scene he depicted from the window of a farmhouse in Minkino. The strange mingling of suppressed passion, shame, and bitterness in the yurodivy's words as he realized that the joys of love are not for him after all made an indelible impression on the composer.

SAVOIR FAIRE (Fr.): social tact, knowledge of how to behave in any situation that may arise.

SONG	COMPOSER	POET
"Avant le cinema"	Francis Poulenc	Guillaume Apollinaire

"Say, Cruel Amoret": a song composed by Henry Purcell set to words written by Thomas *Southerne for his play *The Wives Excuse*, produced in 1691. For plot details and placement of songs, *see* *Wives Excuse, The*.

SCARAMOUCHE (Fr.), SCARAMOUCH (Eng.), SCARAMUCCIA (It.): a stock character in old Italian *commedia dell'arte*. Scaramouche (lit., *little skirmisher*), a friend of *Pulcinella, was a braggart and a fool, very courageous with words but a coward, usually dressed in a black costume caricaturing the Spanish dons. (SOURCES: Cooper, 1992; Duchartre, 1966)

SONG	COMPOSER	POET
"Fantoches"	Claude Debussy	Paul Verlaine

SCENA (It.), SCÈNE (Fr.): a scene forming either part of an opera or composed separately as a concert piece, consisting largely of a recitative characterized by passion and drama, and often an aria section, for one or more voices with accompaniment. Examples: *La Dame de Monte Carlo*, Poulenc; *Infedele*, Mendelssohn; *Giovanna D'Arca*, Rossini; *Arianna à Naxos*, Haydn; *Cléopâtre*, Berlioz; *King Saul before the Battle*, Mussorgsky; *Der Wachtelgesang*, Beethoven; *L'Esule*, Verdi; *Andromache to her Son,* Barber. Some more extended ballads of Schubert and Loewe also qualify for entry in this category.

SCÈVE, MAURICE (?1501–1560?): French poet. Maurice Scève was born into a bourgeois family, his father a city magistrate. Scève's education was excellent, finishing with studies at an Italian university. When he returned to Lyons, he frequented circles of humanists and neo-Latin poets. He achieved literary renown when he won first place with his poem, "Eyebrow," in a competition of *blasons*, a poetic genre that sang the attributes of feminine beauty. *Délie* is a *canzoniere (song book) that expressed Scève's real sufferings and later liberation from a passionate affair with a beautiful girl. *Délie* is Scève's solitary masterpiece, a focal point of late medieval mysticism, imitated by all his disciples. When the public jeered at it for its obscurity, Scève retired to the country. Although his name was celebrated by all in 1548, by 1550 he was little known. One of his most important works was a gigantic epic, *Microcosme*

(1562), which covered the history of mankind since Adam. The poetry of Maurice Scève was set by Darius Milhaud. PRINCIPAL WORKS: *Délie, object de plus haute vertu*, 1544; *Le Saulsaye*, 1547; *Complete Poetic Works*, ed. P. Guégan, 1927. SELECTED READING: *Sixty Poems of Scève*, trans. Wallace Fowlie, 1949. (SOURCE: Kunitz, Colby, 1967)

SCHACK, ADOLF VON (1815–1894): German poet. A wealthy aristocrat, Schack was also a diplomat, linguist, traveler, and art collector. Born in Mecklenburg, he made his home in Munich after 1855. His poems were much admired by the naturalists, but it is his admirable translations from the Persian poets that are among his most outstanding contributions to literature. The poetry and translations of Adolf von Schack have been set by Johannes Brahms, Josef Marx, and Richard Strauss. (SOURCE: Garland, 1976)

SCHAFFY, MIRZA: *see* ★BODENSTEDT.

SCHEFFEL, JOSEPH VIKTOR VON (1826–1886): German poet and novelist. Scheffel's army father expected his son to enter government service, but his mother had sympathy for her son's artistic ambitions. At his father's insistence, Scheffel studied law at the universities of Munich, Berlin, and Heidelberg (1843–47). There he was inspired to write many drinking songs published as *Gaudeamus,* for which he was most famous. His law degree finished in 1849, Scheffel kept a position as a state auditor for two years, after which he traveled to Italy where he intended to paint. Soon he turned to literature. A verse epic, *Der Trompeter von Säkkingen*, completed in Capri, found an admiring public and became one of the most widely read books of the day, enjoying 250 printings since then. Having returned to Heidelberg, he wrote a successful historical novel, *Ekkehard* (1857). Scheffel never again completed a longer work due to his own poor health, but he received many honors before his death and was memorialized in statues. The verse of Joseph von Scheffel was set by Hugo Wolf. PRINCIPAL WORKS: *Gaudeamus*, 1868; *Der Trompeter von Säkkingen*, trans. J. Beck and L. Lorimer, 1893, as *The Trumpeter: A Romance of the Rhine*; *Poems of Places*, trans. H. W. Longfellow, 1876–79. SELECTED READING: M. Winkler, "The Life of Joseph Viktor von Scheffel," in *The German Classics*, Vol. 13, 1969 (SOURCE: Kunitz, Colby, 1967)

SCHENKENDORF, MAX VON (1783–1834): German poet. Schenkendorf shortened his first name to Max so as to express his admiration for ★Schiller's character in *Wallenstein*, Max Piccolomini. Schenkendorf's writings included patriotic poetry, folk-song-like stanzas that have a chivalrous and manly character but no ferocity or hatred, some historical poems, and a smaller amount of love poetry. His verse was set by Johannes Brahms. (SOURCE: Garland, 1976)

SCHILLER, FRIEDRICH VON (1759–1805): German poet, playwright, journalist, and editor. Schiller was educated locally in Württemberg, then studied law and finally medicine at a military academy. After leaving Württemberg he wrote for the Mannheim theater, then worked as a journalist and an editor. In Weimar, with ★Goethe's help, he obtained a history professorship at the University of Jena (1789–

91). Resigning because of illness, he lived in Weimar after 1799, where several of his plays were produced under Goethe's direction. Schiller became the principal writer (after Goethe) first of the *Sturm und Drang school, then of the classical movement in German literature. Goethe said, "The idea of freedom dominates all Schiller's work ... in his youth it was physical, in his later years it was ideal freedom that concerned him" (Vinson, Kirkpatrick, 1984). Schiller's best known poem on this subject, "Ode to Joy," was used by Beethoven in his Fifth Symphony. As a theorist, Schiller worked to define the nature and function of his own art, art in general, and the role of art and culture in human society. Schiller and Goethe worked together in joint authorship, wrote satirical *epigrams together on the state of German culture, and enjoyed a friendly rivalry producing *ballads. Schiller instinctively used the methods of the theater to invest his ballads with drama and, in contrast to ordinary folk ballads, with a philosophical, ethical, or moral idea, much admired by Dostoyevsky. The classical stage of Schiller's development marked a realization that true freedom cannot be achieved in a real world, but only in acceptance of moral responsibility. With his later plays he established historical drama as the major serious dramatic form in Germany. The poems of Friedrich von Schiller have been set to music by Schubert, Mendelssohn, Liszt, Schumann, Smetana, Carl Zelter, Johann Reichardt, Johann Zumsteeg, Ildebrando Pizzetti, Henri Sauguet, Ottmar Schoeck, and Václav Momášek. PRINCIPAL WORKS: Poetry: *Anthologie auf das Jahr 1782*; Gedichte, 2 vols., 1800–3. Plays: *Don Carlos*, prod. 1787; *Wallenstein*, trans. Coleridge, 1800; *Mary Stuart*, 1802; *The Maid of Orleans*, 1835; *William Tell*, 1825. SELECTED READING: John B. Simons, *Schiller*, 1981; Ilse Graham, *Schiller: A Master of the Tragic Form*, 1975. (SOURCES: Vinson, Kirkpatrick (1), 1984; Mathieu, Stern, 1987)

SCHLECHTA, FRANZ VON (1796–1875): an Austrian occasional poet. Son of an army officer, Franz Schlechta was successful as a government official and retired as head of a department in the Finance Ministry. Schubert, a fellow student with Schlechta at the Imperial College, set seven of his poems, four from manuscript, including "Fischerweise." (SOURCE: Reed, 1997)

SCHLEGEL, AUGUST VON (1767–1845): German poet, critic, and philosopher, brother to Friedrich. A member of a literary family in Hanover, Schlegel studied at Göttingen and became a private tutor. Later he turned to journalism and founded a literary journal with his brother. August gave a famous series of lectures in Berlin and Vienna that explained his *Romantic ideals. His marriage was dissolved (1804), after which he and Madame de Staël lived and traveled together until 1817. Spending his time in the study of Oriental languages, he performed his most important work not as a poet but as the translator of seventeen *Shakespeare plays into German verse (1797–1810). Zelter set Schlegel's verses and Schubert set nine of his poems, including the "Ständchen" of *Shakespeare, "Horch, horch, die Lerch" (SOURCE: Reed, 1997)

SCHLEGEL, FRIEDRICH VON (1772–1829): German poet, translator, critic, and orientalist. The descendant of a prominent literary family and brother to August, Schlegel was born in Hanover and trained for a career in business and law at the universities of Göttingen and Leipzig. After 1793 his major interests changed in the direction of philology and classical antiquity. Settled in Berlin in 1797, Schlegel formed the first romantic literary school and established a journal together with Ludwig ★Tieck and ★Novalis. His travels to Paris, where he lectured in philosophy, engaged him in a study of Oriental literature. Once married (to the aunt of Felix Mendelssohn), he and his wife moved to Vienna (1808), where he lectured on literature and philosophy, edited for journals, and was a member of a literary circle that included members of the Schubert circle. He was an original and creative thinker, and his intellect was perhaps greater than his poetic ability. The esoteric nature of his writings kept his works from being popular, but Franz Schubert set sixteen of his poems. PRINCIPAL WORKS: *Gedichte*, 1809; *The Aesthetic and Miscellaneous Works of Friedrich von Schlegel,* trans. E. J. Millington, 1849. SELECTED READING: R. Tymms, *German Romantic Literature*, 1955. (SOURCE: Kunitz, Colby, 1967)

SCHMIDT VON LÜBECK, GEORG (pseudonym of Georg Philipp Schmidt) (1766–1849): German poet, doctor, and civil servant. Born in Lübeck, the poet was the son of a successful merchant. He studied law and finance at the universities of Jena and Göttingen (1786–90), but changed his studies to medicine and qualified as a physician at Kiel University (1797). After practicing medicine for several years, Lübeck entered the Danish civil service. Acquainted with ★Goethe, ★Herder, and ★Schiller, Lübeck wrote his poetry in a nationalistic style called *Bardendichtung*. His *Gedichte*, first collected in 1821, included "Der Wanderer" (1816), set by Schubert. (SOURCE: Garland, 1976)

SCHNEEGLÖCKCHEN: (Ger.), *snow-drop*, a low-growing bulb plant with drooping white flowers that appear in early spring.

SONG	COMPOSER	POET
"Schneeglöckchen"	Robert Schumann	Friedrich Rückert

SCHOBER, FRANZ VON (1796–1882): a German poet born in Sweden, educated in Austria. Born into a wealthy family, Schober studied law in Vienna, later attempting careers as actor, author, and publisher. It pleased him to dabble in the arts as an amateur and to live romantically. While living in Hungary, he met Liszt and became his secretary for a few years. Schober and his family extended hospitality to Schubert for several years, and some members of the Schubert circle blamed Schober for Schubert's illness. Although he knew much about Schubert's private life, Schober never wrote down his memories. Twelve of his poems became Schubert songs, including "Am Bach im Frühling" and "An die Musik." Through Schober, Schubert's songs became known to the operatic baritone Michael Vogl, who became a great friend to Schubert and a champion of his art. (SOURCE: Reed, 1997)

"Schöne Fremde": *see* ★DICHTER UND IHRE GESELLEN.

SCHOPENHAUER, JOHANNA (1766–1838): a German author and novelist. Johanna Schopenhauer was the mother of Arthur Schopenhauer and a member of the ★Goethe circle in Weimar. She interpolated Friedrich von ★Gerstenberg's "Hippolits Lied" into her novel *Gabriele* (1821) where Schubert found it. (SOURCE: Reed, 1997)

SCHREIBER, ALOIS (1763–1841): a German poet, schoolmaster, and drama critic. Schreiber was a professor of literature at Heidelberg University and a prolific author. His poems were published in 1817. Loewe set Schreiber, and Schubert set four Schreiber poems, including "An den Mond in einer Herbstnacht," "Das Abendroth," and "Das Marienbild." (SOURCE: Reed, 1997)

SCHUBART, CHRISTIAN FRIEDRICH (1739–1791): a German poet and journalist. Born in Schwabia, Schubart was the son of a vicar. At school he showed poetic and musical talent, but when he moved on to university, he lived a disorderly life that brought with it illness and debts. Schubart worked as a tutor, then as a teacher and organist. He tried to escape the poverty that hung over his married life through his literary and musical activities and through drinking. Doors opened for him because of his wit, poetic and musical gifts, but his patrons were disturbed by his erratic behavior. When he indulged in an affair, his wife left him and he was banished. Schubart tried living in Mannheim, but he offended the elector; in Munich he converted to Catholicism, but that did not help; when he published a journal, his daring statements and satirical attacks brought a prison term of ten years. Released in 1787, he was a ruined man, dying at fifty-two. His irresponsible and impulsive personality was reflected in his poetry, whose themes were religious, patriotic, or political. Schubart's fame was actually due to the course of his life rather than his poetic output. English translations of Schubart's works are rare. Selections from his poems can be found in *The Poetry of Germany* by A. F. Baskerville, 1853. Franz Schubert set the verse of Christian Schubart, including "An den Tod," "An mein Clavier," and one of the most famous lieds, "Die Forelle." (SOURCE: Kunitz, Colby, 1967)

SCHWAGER: (Ger.) *brother-in-law*. Despite its literal meaning, it was also a familiar way of addressing an eighteenth-century *postilion* (a person who rides the left front horse of a team leading a carriage, or the left front horse of the only pair).

SONG	COMPOSER	POET
"An Schwager Kronos"	Franz Schubert	Johann Wolfgang von Goethe

SCHWANENGESANG: a collection of Schubert songs, seven poems by ★Rellstab and six by ★Heine, composed in August 1828, together with ★Seidl's "Die Taubenpost," composed in August of the same year, unquestionably Schubert's last song. Six months after Schubert's death, the songs were printed and given the title *Schwanengesang* by Haslinger, the publisher.

SCOTCH SNAP: a rhythmic device used in the arrangements of popular Scottish and Irish airs, usually a figure comprised of a sixteenth note followed by a dotted eighth note. In the eighteenth century no English composer failed to write his own "Scotch" song with a prominent use of the "snap." Sir Walter ★Scott and Robert ★Burns then wrote new verses to the old tunes. They were both associated with

George Thomson (1757–1851), a song collector who commissioned musical arrangements of Scottish airs by Beethoven and Haydn.

SCOTT, SIR WALTER (1771–1832): a Scottish poet, novelist, short-story writer, translator, editor, and playwright. Scott was born in Edinburgh, the son of a writer, and educated there, apprenticed to his father before being called to the bar (1792). Early on, his interest was focused on the old Border tales and ★ballads; it was further stimulated by his study of the old romantic poetry of France and Italy, and of the modern German poets. It resulted in his devoting much of his leisure to the exploration of the Border country. In 1797 he published translations of ★Goethe and ★Bürger. In 1802 there appeared three volumes of his *Minstrelsy of the Scottish Border*. After becoming a partner in a printing business, he published *Marmion*, *The Lady of the Lake*, *The Lord of the Isles*, and *Harold the Dauntless*, his last long poem. Somewhat eclipsed by ★Byron as a poet, Scott turned his attention to novel writing, some of which were *Rob Roy*, *The Bride of Lammermoor* (a Donizetti opera), *Ivanhoe*, *Kenilworth*, *Quentin Durward*, and *The Fair Maid of Perth* (an opera by Bizet). His venture into the book-selling business ended in bankruptcy, and Scott shortened his life by his efforts to pay off the creditors by himself. Although his dramatic works were not up to his other writing, he wrote or edited many important historical, literary, and antiquarian works. It was, however, as a novelist that Scott's influence was incalculable. He established the form of the historical novel and the form of the short story. He was read and imitated throughout the nineteenth century, and his incredible popularity all over Europe led to his works being set as operas, plays, and songs. Scott's reputation gradually declined until, in 1951, there was an upsurge of scholarly activity and reappraisal. His masterpieces are considered to be *The Antiquary*, *Old Mortality*, *The Heart of Midlothian*, known as the Waverley novels. The writing of Sir Walter Scott was set by Henry Bishop and by Franz Schubert, who set translations of seven passages from *The Lady of the Lake*, including the "Ave Maria" (1825). SELECTED READING: D. D. Devlin, ed., *Walter Scott: Modern Judgements*, 1968; T. Crawford, *Walter Scott*, 1982. (SOURCE: Drabble, 2000)

SCROGGIE: (Scot.) (pr. skruggee) *rough and horny; jaunty; bold*.

SONG	COMPOSER	POET
"My Hoggie"	Benjamin Britten	Robert Burns

SEA-MAW: (Scot.) *seagull*.

"See, Even Night Herself Is Here": a song composed by Henry Purcell to a text written by Elkanah ★Settle for his work *The Fairie-Queene*, produced in 1692 and 1693. For plot details and placement of songs, *see* ★*Fairie-Queene, The*.

"Seek Not to Know": a song from the tragic extravaganza *The Indian Queen*, written by John ★Dryden and Sir Robert Howard, first produced in 1677, then altered in 1695 to include music by Henry Purcell. *See* ★*Indian Queen, The* for plot details and placement of songs.

"See My Many Colored Fields": an aria composed by Henry Purcell to a text written by Elkanah ★Settle for his work *The Fairie-Queene*, produced in 1692 and 1693. For plot details and song placement, *see* ★*Fairie-Queene, The*.

"See Where Repenting Celia Lies": a song composed by Henry Purcell to words written by John Crowne for his play *The Married Beau*, produced in 1694. For plot details and placement of songs, *see* ★*Married Beau, The*.

SEGUIDILLA: a dance in triple time, faster than a bolero, often accompanied by castanets, usually in a major key; also a Spanish stanza form, lines of 7 and 5 syllables in stanzas of 4 or 7 lines. This form admits some metrical irregularities and assonance instead of rhyme. (SOURCE: Cockburn, Stokes, 1992; Steinberg, 1, 1973)

SONG	COMPOSER	POET
1. "Seguidilla murciana"	Manuel de Falla	Spanish folk song
2. "Seguidillas del Requiem eternam"	Fernando Sor	anonymous
3. "Sequidillas religiosas"	Manuel Plá	anonymous
4. "Seguidillas majas"	Blas de Laserna	anonymous
5. "Seguidilla dolorosa de una maja enamorada"	Luis Misón	anonymous

SEIDL, JOHANN (1804–1875): an Austrian poet, journalist, and schoolteacher. Seidl, a Viennese civil servant, was also a popular writer of both dialect and literary language poetry in Schubert's day. He was author of the Austrian national anthem. Seidl's works, from which both Carl Loewe and Franz Schubert set poems (Schubert set eleven, including "Die Taubenpost," "Bei dir," and "An den Mond"), were published posthumously in six volumes. (SOURCE: Reed, 1997)

SÉLÉNÉ (Fr.), SILENE: Goddess of the moon (*see* ★DIANA).

SENESCHAL: a steward in charge of the house of a medieval prince or dignitary.

SONG	COMPOSER	POET
"Archibald Douglas"	Carl Loewe	Theodore Fontane

SENN, JOHANN (1792–1857): Tyrolean poet and patriot. Senn was a fellow student of Schubert's at the Imperial College, but, as a liberal thinker who spoke in opposition to the imprisonment of fellow students, he was deprived of his scholarship. In March 1820 his rooms were raided by the secret police. Schubert, Franz von ★Bruchmann, Streinsberg, and he were all arrested. Senn was imprisoned for fourteen months and was then deported to the Tyrol. Although Senn was an officer in the 1831 Italian campaign, his future was ruined. He died penniless and alone. Schubert set two of Johann Senn's poems, "Schwanengesang" and "Selige Welt." (SOURCE: Reed, 1997)

SEPHESTIA: the heroine of *Menaphon*, a prose romance, with verse interludes written by Robert ★Greene, published in 1589, also known as "Greene's Arcadia." Princess Sephestia is shipwrecked on the coast of ★Arcadia. The shepherd Menaphon, walking on the seashore, sees pieces of floating wreckage and, on the shore, an old man and a woman with a child. He offers to help them. Sephestia explains that her husband may have drowned in the shipwreck and that the old man is their servant. Menaphon takes them to his home and falls in love with Sephestia. The complex story continues until Sephestia and her husband are reunited. Robert Greene wrote in the euphemistic style: an artificial style of late Elizabethan speech with many references to mythical birds and beasts and much alliteration. Among other lyrics in the romance is a cradle song that has been set by Benjamin Britten.

SONG	COMPOSER	POET
"Sephestia's Lullaby"	Benjamin Britten	Robert Greene

SERAPHIM: the highest order of angels in ancient Christian belief.

SONG	COMPOSER	POET
1. "The Choirmaster's Burial"	Benjamin Britten	Thomas Hardy
2. "Apparition"	Claude Debussy	Stéphane Mallarmé

SERRANAS: (Sp.), literally, *the girls from the sierras, the mountains.*

SETTLE, ELKANAH (1647/48–1673/74): English poet, pamphleteer, and dramatist. His reputation for heroic tragedy writing was equal to ★Dryden's, but, when the Earl of Rochester's patronage was withdrawn, Settle lost ground. Despite his bombast and enthusiastic style, Settle understood the theater, especially the use of stage machines and scenery. It is probable that Settle adapted ★Shakespeare's drama *A Midsummer Night's Dream* as The ★*Fairie-Queene,* for which Henry Purcell wrote the music (1692). SELECTED READING: F. C. Brown, *Elkanah Settle: His Life and Works,* 1910; R. E. Moore, *Henry Purcell and the Restoration Theatre,* 1961. (SOURCE: Drabble, 2000)

SEVEN SEALS: a reference in the Strauss song "Die sieben Siegel" to a vision had by ★St. John the Divine. At the time of the persecutions by Emperor Domitian, St. John wrote Revelation. It forms the final chapter of the New Testament, as a message of hope to those Christians who were suffering for their faith. John wrote that, in a vision, he saw a scroll sealed with seven seals held in the hand of the Almighty. When the seals were removed, there were seven visions, God's plan for Judgment Day. The larger part of the apocalyptic messages, trials, and tribulation that follow, appear in sevens. Thus the allusion in the Strauss song, where the seals are seven kisses placed in seven places upon the beloved to preserve her chastity, is presumed to be that the lady, if she remain faithful, will be saved from her lover's anger (a mildly irreverent pun).

SONG	COMPOSER	POET
"Die sieben Siegel"	Richard Strauss	Friedrich Rückert

SEVEN SPANISH POPULAR SONGS: a collection of songs by Manuel de Falla (1914) that utilizes traditional melodies of folk songs from various regions of Spain. There is some debate as to whether or not these are "pure" art songs in the strictest sense. The debate is pedantic, for they have established a model for contemporary songwriters throughout the Spanish-speaking world, presenting an interesting amalgam of popular and artistic elements. Spanish writer M. García Matos has listed the sources of the songs: the first and third songs are faithful copies of tunes and text; the second and sixth tunes have been slightly retouched; the seventh retouched and expanded; the fifth considerably retouched, while the fourth song is possibly a re-creation derived from various models. Falla's student Ernesto Halffter made one orchestration, and Luciano Berio made another in 1978.

SEVERN: a strongly tidal river in southwest England that runs from Craven Arms to Much Wenlock, passing through Gloucester, Worcester, and Shrewsbury.

SONG	COMPOSER	POET
"On Wenlock Edge"	Ralph Vaughan Williams	A. E. Housman

SHADWELL, THOMAS (1642–1692): British poet and dramatist. Thomas Shadwell attended Caius College, Cambridge in 1656, when his age was given as fourteen. In 1658 he left college to become a member of the Middle Temple and study law. He traveled on the Continent, and, at twenty-four, spent time in Ireland. Returning to England, only when his first play was a success, was he inspired to become a playwright. His most popular pieces were *Epsom Wells* (1672) and *The Squire of Alsatia* (1688). Shadwell crossed swords with *Dryden early on by saying that Dryden had underestimated the comic powers of Ben *Jonson. Dryden and his friends used their political influence to keep Shadwell's plays off stage for the end of the Charles II reign and all of James II's reign. When William II became king in 1689, however, Shadwell was made poet laureate in place of Dryden. In his old age, Shadwell suffered from gout for which he took opium, later dying of an overdose. He was basically an amiable, fat, lazy, drinking man who always wrote in a hurry. The verses of Thomas Shadwell were set by Henry Purcell. PRINCIPAL WORKS: *Epsom Wells*, 1673 (a comedy); *The *Tempest*, 1674 (a semi-opera); *The History of *Timon of Athens*, 1678 (a tragedy); *The Squire of Alsatia* (a comedy). SELECTED READING: A. S. Borgman, *Thomas Shadwell: His Life and Comedies*. (SOURCE: Kunitz, Haycraft, 1936)

SHAHRAZAD, SHÉHÉRAZADE (Fr.): the heroine of a collection of folk tales from three cultures: Indian, Persian, and Arab, called *Tales from the Thousand and One Nights*. Because of his wife's infidelity, King Sheriyar put her to death, together with her slaves and women attendants. Thenceforth, he made it his daily custom to marry a virgin, take her to bed that night, and kill her the next morning. He continued this activity for three years until the people protested and fled the country with their daughters. The king's *vizier had two daughters, Shahrazad and Dunyazad. Shahrazad was a very gifted girl, well acquainted with poetry and legends of ancient kings. When the vizier told her that he was unable to find virgins for the king, she said, "Give me to this king; either I shall die for the daughters of Muslims, or live as the cause of their deliverance." On the day of her wedding, Shahrazad said to her sister, "When I am received by the king, I shall send for you. Then, when the king has finished with me, you must ask me to tell some story to pass the night." In such a manner did the king and Dunyazad listen to countless tales of Shahrazad. During this time, Sharazad had borne the king three sons. On the thousand and first night, after she had ended her tale, she arose, kissed the ground before him and said, "O king, for many nights I have been telling you stories of the past. Now I ask a favor. For the sake of my three sons, I ask you to spare my life." The king arose, kissed his three sons, and said, "I swear by ★Allah. You were already spared before the coming of these children." Sharazad rejoiced and called down blessings upon the king.

SONG	COMPOSER	POET
"Shéhérazade"	Maurice Ravel	Théophile Gautier

SHAKESPEARE, WILLIAM (1564–1616): English poet and dramatist. Baptized in the Holy Trinity Church in Stratford-upon-Avon, William Shakespeare was the eldest son of a glover, who was also a bailiff and local justice of the peace. Not much is known of Shakespeare's beginnings as a writer or how he entered the theater. After the founding of the Lord Chamberlain's Men in 1594, Shakespeare worked with them and grew with them as they developed into London's leading company, occupying the Globe Theater from 1599 on. His 154 *Sonnets* appeared in 1609, he having turned to nondramatic writing between 1592 and 1594 when the plague, raging in London, had closed the theaters. The ★sonnets are very personal and show a wide range of variations within their basic form. "Some are lyrical, some express a lover's humility, some are meditations on eternal poetic themes, the transience of beauty and of love, some are on the power of art, the inevitability of death, some are intellectual, witty workings out of poetic conceits, some are tortured, introspective self-communings" (Scott-Kilvert, 2, 1997). The poetry of William Shakespeare has been set by composers of every nationality both in the original and in translation. Among these are: Schumann, Mendelssohn, Haydn, Strauss, Schubert, Mario Castelnuovo-Tedesco, Charles Ives, Benjamin Britten, Roger Quilter, Thomas Arne, Henry Purcell, Thomas Morley, Ralph Vaughan Williams, Ivor Gurney, Peter Warlock, Gerald Finzi, Mervyn Horder, Geoffrey Bush, Henry Bishop, Arthur Sullivan, William Schumann, Richard Hundley, Dominick Argento, Richard Cumming, David Diamond, Amy Beach, Marc Blitzstein, Theodor Chanler, Ernst Bacon, Douglas Moore, Virgil Thomson, John Edmunds, Ross Lee Finney, Dudley Buck, Richard Faith, Frederic Ayres, Thomas Pasatieri, Mary Howe, Hale Smith, John La Montaine, Wolfgang Fortner, Ernest Chausson, Jacques Leguerney, and Dimitri Kabalevsky. SELECTED READING: E. K. Chambers, *William Shakespeare: A Study of Facts and Problems*, 2 vols., 1930; S. Schoenbaum, *William Shakespeare: A Documentary Life*, 1975. These two works are the standard biographical studies. In addition, great critics who have written on Shakespeare are: John ★Dryden, Samuel ★Johnson, S. T. ★Coleridge, William Hazlitt, and G. B. Shaw. (SOURCES: Drabble, 1985; Scott-Kilvert, 2, 1997)

SHANGHAI: a song by Stephen Collins Foster, "Don't Bet Your Money on de Shanghai." *Shanghai* refers to the big Shanghai rooster, which has strange eating habits and is not a good fighter, so that the best money "rides." (SOURCE: Preminger, 1986)

SHANK'S MARE (Schusters Rappen): slang, *legs*; that is, using legs, walking instead of riding.

SONG	COMPOSER	POET
"Du sagst mir, dass ich keine Fürstin sei"	Hugo Wolf	Paul Heyse

SHAPIRO, HARVEY (b. 1924): American poet and editor. Although his parents came from a rural village outside Kiev in Russia, Shapiro was born in Chicago and later lived in Brooklyn. A graduate of Yale (1947) with a master's degree from Columbia, he was a gunner in a B17 bomber during World War II and given the Distinguished Flying Cross. From 1955 on Shapiro worked in magazines and newspapers: *Commentary, The New Yorker, The New York Times Magazine* (assistant editor), *The New York Times Book Review* (editor). Although his was a significant voice, Shapiro wrote only a small amount of poetry because he wrote only part time. His early verse was more formal than the later poetry, which showed sympathy and candor. He sought to draw meaning from his experiences in order to alleviate his lonely fight against depression and despair. Harvey Shapiro was mainly an urban poet, whose poetry was set by Clinton Scollard, Charles Griffes, and Henry Hadley. PRINCIPAL WORKS: *Battle Report*, 1966; *The Light Holds*, 1984; *National Cold Storage Co.*, 1988; *A Day's Portion*, 1994; *How Charlie Shavers Died*, 2001. (SOURCE: Kunitz, Haycraft, 1973)

SHAPIRO, KARL (1913–2000): American poet, critic, and editor. Shapiro was born in Baltimore, served in the army from 1941 to 1945, publishing while active in the Pacific theater, and attended the University of Virginia and Johns Hopkins University. He was appointed consultant in poetry at the Library of Congress (1946) and was a member of the faculty at Johns Hopkins (1947). From 1950 to 1956 Shapiro was the editor of *Poetry: A Magazine of Verse*. His teaching positions as professor of English were at the universities of Nebraska, Illinois, and California at Davis. His second volume of verse, *V-Letter and Other Poems*, brought him a Pulitzer Prize in 1945 and the Bollingen Prize in Poetry in 1969. Shapiro's poems were technically proficient and reveal a desire to confront the world as it is. His poetry written after the war is strikingly original, realistic, and detached. "He had an inkling that his destiny was to live as a free, quixotic, and iconoclastic spirit, a stormy presence in the house of letters" (Kunitz, Ignatow, 1998). With the publication of *Bourgeois* he experienced a change in direction, becoming fundamentally romantic. By 1964 Shapiro had dismissed meter and rhyme as nonessential and artificial impediments to the poetic process. He moved to a relaxed style, vernacular tone, and esprit. The verse of Karl Shapiro has been set by Hugo Weisgall and Judith Zaimont. PRINCIPAL WORKS: *Poems*, 1935; *Person, Place and Thing*, 1942; *V-Letter and Other Poems*, 1944; *Trial of a Poet*, 1947; *Poems 1940–53*, 1953; *Poems of a Jew*, 1958; *White-Haired Lover*, 1968; *The Poetry Wreck*, 1975; *Adult Bookstore*, 1978; *Wild Card*, 1998. SELECTED READING: Joseph Reino, *Karl Shapiro*, 1981. (SOURCE: Shapiro, 1988)

SHARP, WILLIAM (1855–1905): Scottish poet, novelist, biographer, and essayist. William Sharp was born in Paisley, spent most of his childhood in the Highlands, and was educated at Glasgow University. Under his own name he wrote essays, verse, minor novels, and biographies of ★Rossetti (1882), ★Shelley (1887), ★Heine (1888), and Robert ★Browning (1890). Sharp is chiefly remembered for mysterious Celtic tales and romances of peasant life, written in the manner of the "Celtic twilight" movement. The "Celtic twilight" collection of stories by ★Yeats, published in 1893, illustrated the mysticism of the Irish and their belief in fairies, ghosts, and spirits. "Celtic twilight" later became a generic phrase for the whole ★Irish Revival in literature. Sharp successfully concealed the identity of his pseudonym, Fiona McLeod, until his death, even going so far as to write a bogus entry to *Who's Who*. The poetry of "Fiona McLeod" and William Sharp has been set by Charles Griffes, Wintter Watts, Arnold Bax, and Alice Barnett. PRINCIPAL WORKS: Poetry: *Pharais*, 1893; *The Mountain Lovers*, 1895; *The Sin Eater*, 1895. Plays: *The House of Usna*, 1903; *The Immortal Hour*, 1900. (SOURCE: Drabble, 1985)

SHAULY: (Scot.), *surely*; also *a wooden scoop, shallow in size and character.*

SHAW: (Scot.), *wood.*

SHÉHÉRAZADE: *see* ★SHARAZAD.

SHELLEY, PERCY BYSSHE (1792–1822): British poet, essayist, pamphleteer, and dramatist. Since Shelley's grandfather was a peer of the realm, he was in line to inherit his grandfather's considerable estate in Sussex and to be a member of Parliament. During his six years at Eton, Shelley was already interested in science and had an appetite for trashy thrillers. At Eton he undertook a wide range of reading in philosophy and literature and began two pursuits that would continue all his life: writing and loving. When Shelley entered University College, Oxford in 1810 he was already a published and reviewed writer of a Gothic novel and a reader beyond the scope of the curriculum. In 1811, the publication of *The Necessity of Atheism* by Shelley and his friend Thomas Jefferson Hogg precipitated their expulsion from Oxford. The publication also sparked a break with Shelley's family and consequent money problems. After marrying in 1811, Shelley continued to write radical pamphlets on freedom of the press and the oppressiveness of religious dogma and superstition, using poetry like his *Queen ★Mab* to convey his radical political ideas such as free love and vegetarianism. When his grandfather died and he came into his inheritance, Shelley again found time to write poetry and develop his style. On the death of his wife, he married his long-time mistress. In 1818 they went to Italy, where Shelley and Lord ★Byron became friends. The life and the works of Shelley exemplify ★Romanticism: joyous ecstasy, brooding despair, restlessness, rebellion against authority, love of nature, the power of visionary imagination, and untamed spirit. Because Shelley always took the controversial side of an issue, his work evoked either the strongest vehemence or the warmest praise. Nevertheless, Shelley worship reached its zenith in 1886. Despite the fact that in the early twentieth century Shelley's reputation plunged to a nadir, his work has now come to symbolize the free and soaring spirit of humankind. The verses of Percy Bysshe Shelley have been set by Frederick Delius, Paul Hindemith, Benjamin Britten, Roger Quilter, Charles Ives, Edmund Rubbra, Mrs. H. H. A. Beach, Jean Berger, David Diamond, John Duke, Alice Barnett, Blair Fairchild, Alan Hovhaness, Richard Faith, and Giorgio Ghedini. PRINCIPAL

WORKS: *The Necessity of Atheism*, 1811; *Queen Mab, A Philosophical Poem: with Notes*, 1813, 1821; *Alastor; or, the Spirit of Solitude: and Other Poems*, 1816; *The Revolt of Islam; A Poem, in Twelve Cantos*, 1817; *Prometheus Unbound, A Lyrical Drama in Four Acts, with Other Poems*, 1820. SELECTED READING: Thomas Jefferson Hogg, *The Life of Percy Bysshe Shelley*, 1858; Jean Overton Fuller, *Shelley: A Biography*, 1968. (SOURCE: Greiner, 96, 1980)

SHE NEVER TOLD HER LOVE: an extract, not a "song," from act 2, scene 4 of Shakespeare's *Twelfth Night*. The lines are Viola's answer to the duke of Illyria's question regarding the existence of her alleged sister. The story of concealed love is really her own.

SONG	COMPOSER	POET
"She Never Told Her Love"	Franz Josef Haydn	William Shakespeare

"Shepherd, Shepherd, Leave Decoying": a duet composed by Henry Purcell to a text written by John *Dryden for their semi-opera *King Arthur*, produced in 1691. *See *King Arthur* for plot details and placement of songs.

SHILOH: a Tennessee town located northwest of Nashville, Shiloh Church being the site of a milestone battle of the Civil War that took place on April 6–7, 1862. Of the 77,000 men who took part on both sides, over 60,000 were raw recruits who had to be shown how to use their rifles. The inexperienced troops took heavy losses on Sunday, the first day, with one-third of Grant's command put out of action. Yet he did not retreat, but attacked at dawn of April 7, whipping the Confederates and breaking down the back door to the Confederacy. Almost 24,000 men died at Shiloh Church. (SOURCE: Wallechinsky, Wallace, 1975)

SONG	COMPOSER	POET
"Shiloh"	Hugo Weisgall	Herman Melville

SHINGLES: beaches covered with water-worn small stones and pebbles.

SONG	COMPOSER	POET
"Dover Beach"	Samuel Barber	Matthew Arnold

SHOVE, FREDEGOND (1889–1949): The poet daughter of British historian F. W. Maitland, who had married the sister of Vaughan William's first wife. Shove's husband, Gerald Shove, was renowned Cambridge University professor of economics. She is known primarily for Williams's "Four Poems of Fredegond Shove," which includes "The Water Mill." (Source: Vaughan Williams, 1964)

SHROPSHIRE LAD, A: a collection of sixty-three poems by A. E. Housman about Shropshire county in England, selections from which have been set to music by several British and American composers. His poems show the influence of traditional English *ballads and classical verse marked with youthful disillusionment and melancholia. When living in London, Housman felt exiled from the locale of his childhood. His intention was to write a cycle of poems in which there would be nostalgic references to Shropshire life and the main character a Shropshire lad in exile like himself. Among the many composers who have set these poems are George Butter-worth and Ralph Vaughan Williams.

SHYLOCK: the Jewish usurer in ★Shakespeare's *The Merchant of Venice,* an adaptation of which was written by Edmund Haraucourt. Fauré wrote incidental music for this project. Haraucourt made rather more of the "masques and revels" that allow Lorenzo to steal Jessica away. It is here that the two Fauré songs are found.

SONG	COMPOSER	POET
1. "Chanson (de Shylock)"	Gabriel Fauré	Edmond Haraucourt, trans.
2. "Madrigal (de Shylock)"	Gabriel Fauré	Edmond Haraucourt, trans.

SIBYL: any one of a number of prophetesses, whose special function was to intercede with the gods on behalf of human supplicants. The most famous sibyl is the Cumaean sibyl whom Aeneas consulted before descending to Avernus. (SOURCE: *Bulfinch,* 1978)

SONG	COMPOSER	POET
"Birthday Song"	Benjamin Britten	Robert Burns

SIC: (Scot.), *such.*

SIENA CATHEDRAL: the Gothic cathedral in the town of Siena, which is located in the Tuscan hills near Florence, Italy. The city has seventeen medieval neighborhoods, each with a church, museum, and a symbol of the *contrada* (neighborhood), whose colors are painted on the local street lights. The *contradas* compete in the Palio, a yearly horserace around the main square. One of the most famous in Italy, the medieval cathedral is made of black and white marble.

SONG	COMPOSER	POET
"Ihr seid die Allerschönste"	Hugo Wolf	Paul Heyse

SIL: the most important river in the province of Galicia, Spain.

SONG	COMPOSER	POET
"Aureana do Sil"	Frederic Mompou	Ramón Cabanillas

SILBERT, JOHANN (1772–1844): German poet and educator. Silbert studied at Mainz, later becoming professor of French language and literature at the Polytechnic Institute in Vienna. In 1819 his poetry was published, from which collection Franz Schubert took two settings, "Abendbilder" and "Himmelsfunken." (SOURCE: Reed, 1997)

SILENE: *see* ★SÉLÉNÉ

SILLER: (Scot.), *silver.*

SONG	COMPOSER	POET
"Bed-time"	Benjamin Britten	William Soutar

SILPELIT: a fantasy character of the fairy world from the imaginary island, ★Orplid, created by Eduard ★Mörike in his novel ★*Maler Nolten.*

SONG	COMPOSER	POET
"Elfenlied"	Hugo Wolf	Eduard Mörike

SILVANIRE, LA: a play by French dramatist Jean Mairet (1604–86). *La Silvanire* was performed in 1630 and published in 1631, accompanied by a preface in which Mairet recommends the adoption of unities of action, time, and place on the grounds of contemporary taste. *See also* ★SYLVIE, LA.

SILVESTRE, ARMAND (1838–1901): French poet, novelist, and playwright. Silvestre's works contain drama, art criticism, and Rabelaisian tales. His poetry shows a finished style and passages of ethereal beauty that impelled Fauré to set it to music. Despite this, it became common practice to criticize as inferior the poetry of Silvestre as well as other poets whom Gabriel Fauré chose for his songs. Yet clearly, Fauré drew meaningful inspiration from Silvestre's collection of words, his syllabic impulses, and his vague and mysterious suggestions. The verse of Armand Silvestre was also set by Henri Duparc, Jules Massenet, Léo Délibes, Louis Albert, and Cécile Chaminade. (SOURCE: Steinberg, 3, 1973)

SILVIA: a character in William ★Shakespeare's comedy *Two Gentlemen of Verona.* Silvia is the daughter of the duke of Milan and the beloved of Valentine, one of the two gentlemen, whose rival, Proteus, is the second gentleman. "Who Is Silvia?" occurs in act 4, scene 2. Proteus and a group of musicians have come to the courtyard of the Milanese palace to serenade Silvia. Also present during the serenade is Julia, a lady of Verona, formerly loved by Proteus, disguised as a boy. Schubert set Eduard von ★Bauernfeld's translation of the poem in July 1826. (SOURCE: Reed, 1997)

SONG	COMPOSER	POET
1. "An Silvia"	Franz Schubert	William Shakespeare
2. "Who Is Silvia?"	Gerald Finzi, Mervyn Horder	William Shakespeare

SIMON, SAINT: a saint usually linked with St. Jude. Both saints were apostles. In the gospels Simon was called the Zealous One, and Jude (also called Thaddeus) was brother to James the Less. Tradition says that St. Simon and St. Jude went to Persia to preach the gospel and were martyred there. (SOURCE: Nevins, 1964)

SONG	COMPOSER	POET
1. "Das Knäblein nach acht Tagen"	Peter Cornelius	Peter Cornelius
2. "La Ermita di San Simon"	Mario Castelnuoveo-Tedesco	romançero Español

SIMROCK, KARL (1802–1876): German translator of medieval German literature. Simrock wrote modern versions of the works of Walter von der Vogelweide, Wolfram von Eschenbach, and Gottfried von Strassburg, and of the *Niebelungenlied* (1827). Simrock's work was set by Johannes Brahms. (SOURCE: Magill, 4, 1984)

SINBAD, SINDBAD: hero of the story of this name in the Arabian Nights. Sinbad was a wealthy citizen of Baghdad, called "the Sailor" because of his seven voyages during which he had many strange adventures, including the discovery of the egg belonging to the giant bird Roc, and his encounter with the Old Man of the Sea. (SOURCE: Cooper, 1992)

SONG	COMPOSER	POET
"Asie"	Maurice Ravel	Tristan Klingsor

"Since from My Dear Astrea's Sight": a song from the 1690 semi-opera *Dioclesian* with music solely by Henry Purcell, written to the words of Massinger and ★Fletcher. *See* ★*Dioclesian* for plot and placement of songs.

"Since Times Are So Bad": a song composed by Henry Purcell to a text written by Thomas ★D'Urfey for Part II of his comedic semi-opera *Don Quixote*, produced in 1694–95. *See* ★*Don Quixote* for plot details and placement of songs.

"Sing, All Ye Muses": a duet composed by Henry Purcell to a text written by Thomas ★D'Urfey for Part I of his comedic semi-opera *Don Quixote*, produced in 1694–95. *See* ★*Don Quixote* for plot details and placement of songs.

SIR ANTHONY IN LOVE: Thomas ★Southerne's first comedy, produced in 1690, containing two songs composed by Henry Purcell. The "labyrinth of tangled plots" (Price, 1984) shows Southerne's inexperience. The main plot has to do with Lucia, who has robbed her keeper, Sir Gentle Golding, and fled to France. She disguises herself as Sir Anthony Love and, in order to take general revenge on the male sex, charms the local beauties to the confusion of their suitors. The climax occurs when Sir Anthony, disguised as Floriante, agrees to marry Sir Gentle, who does not even know yet that he has found his long-lost Lucia. Although three scenes require music, only one of them is important to the plot, act 4, scene 2. Sir Anthony appears for the first time in woman's clothing with her rakish companion Valentine, who never realized that she was a woman. In order to divert Valentine's attention from his beloved Floriante, Sir Anthony arranges for Valentine to meet a young English woman—herself—in a bedchamber. After the song, she uncovers her face, at which he is surprised to discover that his friend is now his lover. The song is Purcell's "Pursuing Beauty," in which women are warned to guard their innocence. In stanza 1, Valentine gazing on a mysterious woman is compared to an ocean explorer staring at a distant land. Stanza 2 issues from Sir Anthony's point of view, a sharp contrast reflecting the strong contradictions in his/her character. Many editions omit the instrumental ritornels, but the irregularities should not be ironed out to a simple format. In act 5, scene 2, Sir Anthony marries in a mock ceremony and, while waiting for her new husband to come to bed, listens to a song which was either "No More, Sir, No More" for soprano and baritone or "In Vain, Clemene," a passionate plea for free love. (SOURCE: Price, 1984)

SIR BARNABY WHIGG: a comedy written by ★Thomas D'Urfey with one song composed by Henry Purcell, produced in 1681. The main plot is romantic (in which Gratiana cleverly wins Wilding); the subplot is conventional (in which are featured foolish cuckolds, Captain Porpuss and Sir Walter Wiseacre, old sea stories, salty characters, and nautical talk). Purcell's song, "Blow, *Boreas, Blow," appears in an incidental entertainment of act 1. Captain Porpuss proclaims himself tired of goody-goody pastoral airs and demands some hearty masculine fare. He begins a sea story and then yields to an unspecified tenor who sings Purcell's song, in which a ship's captain curses the mountainous waves of the violent storm instead of praying for deliverance. The captain relives the storm, the moment of terror frozen by Purcell into two bars of recitative, and claims that he and his shipmates were unafraid. This song was a great favorite of the period. (SOURCE: Price, 1984)

SIRENS: sea *nymphs of Greek mythology, whose sweet voices lured mariners to their death from an island in the sea on which they lived. In certain ways they resembled birds, often winged. This has led to the theory that the sirens were originally unhappy souls of the dead.

SIR PATRICK SPENS: the Scottish hero of a medieval sea ballad. Although warned, Spens put to sea with his companions in the dead of winter and was shipwrecked.

SIRVENTES, SIRVENTE: lit., *to serve*; a form of poem or lay, usually satirical, employed by troubadours of the Middle Ages. The French and English form of this word arose by taking *sirventes* as a plural noun. (SOURCE: *OED*, 1989)

SITWELL, DAME EDITH (1887–1964): English poet. Sitwell began to write poetry at a very early age. With her two brothers Sacheverell and Osbert, also writers, she encouraged *Modernist artists and writers such as Wilfred *Owen. Upon publication of her first two volumes of verse she acquired a reputation as a controversial figure. Although she wrote prose works and a novel for money, they were not well received. During the war she enjoyed a period of great acclaim inspired by her poems of the blitz and the atomic bomb. After the war she did a triumphal lecture tour of America. Sitwell was well known in literary circles and elsewhere for her theatrical dress and manner. The standard set by her poetry is still a matter in dispute. She declared that her poems were abstract, "patterns in sound." The verse of Dame Edith Sitwell has been set by William Walton and Ned Rorem. PRINCIPAL WORKS: *Façade* (music by Walton), 1923; *Gold Coast Customs*, 1929; *Pope*, 1930; *English Eccentrics*, 1933; *Strange Songs*, 1942; *Green Song*, 1944; *The Song of the Cold*, 1945; *The Shadow of Cain*, 1947. SELECTED READING: V. Glendinning, *Edith Sitwell*, 1981. (SOURCE: Drabble, 2000)

SKALD, SCALD: an ancient Scandinavian poet; also, generally, in the northern countries, a poet. The term is usually applied to Norwegian and Icelandic poets of the Viking period who were attached to the courts up until ca.1250, although a clear idea of the function and character of their work was lacking. The oldest known skald whose work is known is Bragi Boddason the Old of the ninth century. (SOURCE: *OED*, 1989; Preminger, 1986)

SKALDIC POETRY: poems written under stricter metrical rules than the *Eddic poems by the Scandinavian *skalds (poets), some of whom were employed as official chroniclers at the courts. This poetry was published in English as *The Skalds*, 1945, 1968. (SOURCE: Jason, 8, 2003)

SKELLUM: (Scot.), *good for nothing.*

SKELP: (Scot.), v., *to bend; to strike or hit*; n. *a strip of metal for making a tube by bending and welding; also, a blow with the flat of the hand.*

SONG	COMPOSER	POET
"Black Day"	Benjamin Britten	William Soutar

SKIDDAW: the name of a mountain, one of two neighboring hills, in the English Lake District. The mountains were eroded from a thick group of slates, flags, and mudstones that outcropped in the north part of the Lake District. (SOURCE: *OED*, 1989)

SONG	COMPOSER	POET
"The Carol of Skiddaw Yowes"	Ivor Gurney	Ernest Casson

SKÖLDMÖ: a term used in the old northern countries, meaning *a shield maiden*, one who carries weapons and goes to battle. Often the term refers to warlike tribes at a certain barbarian level of culture, for example, Amazons. In Old Norse, such maidens were called *skjaldmeyjar*, in Old Danish, *skielmøer*. Written sources from the Viking Age tell that the maidens were known even in the tenth century, when they played a prominent role in poetry.

SKUGG: a grey squirrel sent by the visiting Benjamin Franklin (1706–1790) as a present for the children of Jonathan Shepley, the bishop of Asaph. Franklin was a frequent visitor at Twyford, the bishop's home. He had sent the squirrel from Philadelphia, but it had escaped from its cage and was killed by dogs. The children asked Franklin to write an epitaph for the animal.

SONG	COMPOSER	POET
"Here Lies Skugg"	Ross Lee Finney	Benjamin Franklin

SKULD: in Norse mythology, one of the three ★Fates. Veiled, she was believed to face the future, scroll in hand.

SLAVOPHILES: In the late 1830s the Slavophiles had become a distinct Russian group, some of whom had formerly been members of the Society of Wisdom Lovers. The literary journal *The Muscovite* (1841–56) was an outlet for Slavophile ideas. Slavophiles believed that philosophy, science, and faith should be ruled by the same principles and that it was incumbent upon philosophy and science to rise to faith. They believed in a national spirit and a concept of Russia's historical mission; that the individual should freely and spontaneously submit to the community, that moral and religious traditions ruled over formal legality, and that the integrity of the family was crucial. It was basically a rural outlook. They denigrated the west's leaning toward formal reasoning and a separation of faith from government, believing that western life had lost its spirituality and had devoted all its energies to material and legalistic values. Being for the most part landowners who took a vital interest in

Russia's economy, they promoted Russian folk ways and Russian folklore. A prominent Slavophile was the poet Aleksei ★Khomyakov. (SOURCE: Terras, 1991)

SLEEPING PRINCESS, THE: one of three early songs of Borodin that contain a secret program. "The Sleeping Princess," for example, specifically does not mention the princess waking up. Critics have made a parallel between the sleeping of the princess and the sleeping of Russia under a heavy yoke of bondage and the oppression of tsarist autocracy. Other Borodin songs with a hidden program are "Song of the Dark Forest," a veiled appeal to continue the struggle against the tyranny of the tsar, and "The Sea."

SLITHY: *writhing*, adapted by Lewis ★Carroll from the word *slither*.

SLOPIEWNIE: a set of five songs by Szymanowski to a text by Julian Tuwim (1894–1953). This title and the five songs themselves are untranslatable. Tuwim reverts to Old Slavonic words and word roots, creating new words and a Polish mood, instead of dealing with tangible texts. The title, *Slopiewnie* is based on the Polish word for "Slav," *Slowianin*. Both composer and poet were deeply interested in exploring their Polish heritage. *Slopiewnie* is a Polish mood word that is masterful and enticing; it is, however, so Polish that it is almost meaningless to anyone other than a Pole.

SMART, CHRISTOPHER (1722–1771): English poet, librettist, and translator. The cordials that were used to treat Smart's childhood frailty are believed to have led to his alcoholism, evinced in religious manias and attacks of delirium tremens. He began writing as a child, then attended Cambridge University, where he had a reputation as a poet but ran up so many debts that he had to leave the university. In London he wrote, composed music, published his own and others' work. Even after marriage he was unable to face the usual problems of domestic life, nor those of literary life or business. Most of his poetry shows a relative disengagement from reality and a search for psychological security. From 1757 to 1763 he was confined in an asylum. When he came out, he became friends with Dr. ★Johnson and Thomas Gray, but was not capable of leading a normal life, dying in debtors' prison. A sense of the mystical imbued his religious poetry, some of which appeared as librettos for oratorios. The poetry of Christopher Smart has been set by Conrad Susa. PRINCIPLE WORKS: *On the Eternity of the Supreme Being,* 1750; *On the Immensity of the Supreme Being,* 1751; *On the Omniscience of the Supreme Being,* 1752; *On the Power of the Supreme Being,* 1754; *On the Goodness of the Supreme Being,* 1755; *Hymns for the Amusement of Children,* 1772. SELECTED READING: Arthur Sherbo, *Christopher Smart: Scholar of the University,* 1967. (SOURCE: *Americana,* 2003)

SNELL: (Scot.), *bitter.*

SOCRATES (469?–399 B.C.E.): one of the greatest Greek philosophers. Socrates left no writings of his own, but his greatest student, ★Plato, has given us a brilliant account of his teachings. Socrates was only interested in philosophy of human problems. His guiding rule was "Know thyself." Socrates believed that goodness in man was based on wisdom, wickedness, or ignorance, that no wise man would deliberately choose what was bad for him in the long run, but that most men would choose evil, through ignorance, an evil that appeared to be good at the time. (SOURCE: Grant, 1980)

SONG	COMPOSER	POET
1. "Das Ende des Festes"	Ottmar Schoeck	Conrad Meyer
2. "Sokrates und Alcibiades"	Benjamin Britten	Friedrich Hölderlin

SODOM: a town in ancient Palestine, probably south of the Dead Sea. According to Genesis 19.24, both Sodom and ★Gomorrah were destroyed by fire and brimstone from heaven as a punishment for the depravity and wickedness of their inhabitants. Lot, the nephew of ★Abraham, was allowed to escape with his family from the destruction of Sodom, but, because his wife disobeyed God's order not to look back at the burning city, she was turned into a pillar of salt. (SOURCE: Delahunty et al., 2001)

SONG	COMPOSER	POET
"La Captive"	Hector Berlioz	Victor Hugo

SOLDIER, THE: a song set by both Edvard Grieg and Robert Schumann to a text by Hans Christian ★Andersen (the Schumann song in a translation done by ★Chamisso). The subject of the poem was derived from Andersen's dramatic and frightening childhood memory, the execution of a soldier who was stationed in Odense. The soldier had been the only friend of one of the members of the firing squad. Nine men take aim and fire. Eight miss, for their hands are trembling with compassion. Only the friend's bullet finds the mark.

SOLOGUB, FYODOR (pseudonym of Fyodor Teternikov) (1863–1927): Russian poet, novelist, dramatist, and short-story writer. Both of Sologub's parents were of peasant origin, the father a tailor, the mother a domestic servant. Educated at St. Petersburg Teachers Institute, Sologub was a high school teacher and inspector of schools for twenty-five years, teaching first in the provinces, then finally in St. Petersburg where he settled. In 1896 he gained recognition with *Stikhi*, a book of poems which made him a prominent representative of the first-generation Russian ★Symbolists. After his success with his novel, *A Petty Demon* (1907), his poetry grew stronger, nobler, and purer. Yet Romantic Satanism was a pervasive trait; evil forces, the dragon, and the snake were recurrent symbols. Death, suffering, and torture were favorite themes but balanced with gentle appreciation of nature. Sologub believed that the ugliness of the world is beyond human capacity to improve; therefore humans can only escape into the world of beauty and art, where peace will be found, created by the imagination. The verse of Fyodor Sologub was set by Tchaikovsky and Rachmaninoff. PRINCIPAL WORKS: *Stikhi* [Poems], 1896; *Teni: Rasshazy i stikhi* [Shadows: Stories and Poems]; *Plamenny krug* [Circle of Fire], 1908. SELECTED READING: E. Bristol, *Fyodor Sologub's Post-Revolutionary Poetry*, 1960. (SOURCE: Brown, 1985)

SOLOMON: biblical figure, the third king of Israel, son of ★David and ★Bathsheba. Solomon, renowned for his wisdom, is the purported Old Testament author of Proverbs, Ecclesiastes, and The Song of Solomon (a paean to physical love) as well as The Wisdom of Solomon, present in the ★Apocrypha, in the Septuagint and Roman Catholic Bibles, but omitted from the Jewish and Protestant Bibles. He is also the purported author of the pseudepigraphical *Odes of Solomon*, a book regarded by no group as canonical. The period of Solomon's reign over Israel was considered a golden age; he was renowned not only for his wisdom but also for his wealth. The building of the Temple of Jerusalem under his direction was the outstanding event in Solomon's life. When, in a dream, God offered Solomon anything he wanted, Solomon requested only wisdom. Thus did God promise to give him power and wealth as well as wisdom. One famous example of Solomon's wisdom was the story of the two prostitutes, each with one child. One night in the bed all four shared, one prostitute rolled over on her baby, killing him. When this woman substituted her dead child for the living child of her companion, there developed an argument over who was the mother of the living child. The argument was brought before the king. Solomon proclaimed that he would cut the living child in half with his sword and give one half to each woman. Thereupon, the true mother resigned her child to her rival, while the false one accepted the judgment. Thus did Solomon wisely discover who the real mother was. The rulers of Ethiopia have traditionally referred to themselves as "The Lion of ★Judah" because the queen of Sheba consulted Solomon and was given a son by him, supporting his reputation as a great lover. Solomon had 700 princesses as wives and 300 concubines, among them many foreigners, who turned him away from the God of Israel toward foreign gods like ★Astarte, Chemosh, and Molech for whom he built altars. God was displeased and promised to take the kingdom from Solomon upon his death. God's promise came to pass when Solomon's son Rehoboam was unable to maintain the kingdom and it split into northern and southern kingdoms. (SOURCE: Metzger, Murphy, 1994)

SONG	COMPOSER	POET
1. "Four Songs of Solomon"	George Rochberg	Solomon
2. "The Three Odes of Solomon"	Alan Hovhaness	Ancient Syriac
3. "Nimmersatte Liebe"	Hugo Wolf	Eduard Mörike

SOLVEIG: a character from Henrik ★Ibsen's ★*Peer Gynt*, which was set to music by Edvard Grieg. *See* ★*Peer Gynt* for the plot.

SONG	COMPOSER	POET
"Solveig's Song"	Edvard Grieg	Henrik Ibsen

SONGS AND DANCES OF DEATH: a cycle of four songs composed by Modest Mussorgsky on texts by his friend ★Golenishtchev-Kutúsov. The composer had originally planned to include the following characters in some form within his work: a monkish fanatic who dies in his cell as the monastery bell tolls heavily; a political exile who comes back, shipwrecked within sight of home, and perishes in the waves; a dying woman whose fevered mind calls up memories of love and visions of youth.

SONGS AND PROVERBS OF WILLIAM BLAKE: a collection of songs by Benjamin Britten, composed for the German baritone, Dietrich Fischer-Dieskau. The lyrical poetry of William ★Blake sets the misery and imprisonment of man's condition on earth against the possibility of joy and freedom sought by the symbolic sunflower. Each of the seven poems is prefaced by an introductory proverb, and each song is related to the proverb. The first six poems are drawn from Blake's *Proverbs of Hell* and *Songs of Experience*; the seventh is a conjunction of the beginning and end of his *Auguries of Innocence*.

SONGS OF INNOCENCE, SONGS OF EXPERIENCE: two separate books of poetry and engravings by William ★Blake, printer, poet, and artist (1757–1827). *Songs of Innocence*, containing thirty-one plates, was printed in 1789. The complete *Songs of Innocence and of Experience*, containing fifty-four plates, was published in 1794, although its full title was actually *Songs of Innocence and of Experience Shewing the Two Contrary States of the Human Soul*. "Innocence" represents mankind before its fall from Grace and "Experience," man's state after the fall. Blake stated that he received instructions on the technique of preparing these poems for publication in a vision, when he spoke with the spirit of his deceased younger brother. The contents are flavored by Blake's experience of ★Swedenborgian theology and his response to the secularism of the Church of England in his day. They also reflect his rebellion against the contemporary moral strictures, particularly with regard to human sexuality. At this time there were a variety of books in verse that commented on the ideal behavior of children. These works projected a particularly dull existence for children, one in which they would labor in silence, seen and not heard. In Blake's world it is the innocence of children that contains wisdom. In innocence, children romp, play, and laugh, the dirty chimney-sweep patiently awaits his heavenly reward, and "The Little Black Boy" knows that a time will come when Europeans will love him, and they will sit together and learn about God. *Songs of Innocence* originally contained twenty-two poems and the original *Songs of Experience* contained twenty-six poems. Singers who are preparing songs that are settings of the poems from these two books should consult an edition that has color reproductions of Blake's engravings, such as Erdman, 1974, because the whole work includes the poetry and the illustrations, even the design of the typeface. The Dover Editions of these two books are not only in color but also inexpensive. (SOURCES: Damon, 1965; Blake, 1971, 1984; Erdman, 1954, 1974)

SONG	COMPOSER	POET
1. "The Lamb"	E. Bacon, T. Chanler	William Blake
2. "Songs of Innocence, Songs of Experience"	William Bolcom	William Blake
3. "Songs and Proverbs of William Blake"	Benjamin Britten	William Blake
4. "Cradle Song"	Benjamin Britten	William Blake
5. "Little Fly"	John Alden Carpenter	William Blake
6. "A Cradle Song"	John Alden Carpenter	William Blake
7. "The Little Black Boy"	H. Cowell, R. Cumming	William Blake
8. "Infant Sorrow"	Sidney Homer	William Blake
9. "The Sick Rose"	Sidney Homer	William Blake
10. "The Angel"	Benjamin Lees	William Blake
11. "Divine Image"	Otto Luening	William Blake
12. "Songs of Innocence"	Paul Nordoff	William Blake
13. "5 Songs from Wm. Blake"	R. Thompson, V. Thomson	William Blake
14. "10 Songs of Wm. Blake"	R. Vaughan Williams	William Blake

SONGS OF TRAVEL: a cycle of nine songs by Ralph Vaughan Williams with texts by Robert Louis Stevenson. The set is a kind of English *Winterreise*, the wanderer philosophically accepting what life brings him. The vitality of the songs issues from a peculiarly English combination of sturdiness and melancholy lyricism. The song "I Have Trod the Upward and Downward Slope," found among Vaughan Williams's papers after his death, was designed as an epilogue. It quotes two other songs of the cycle, "The Vagabond," and "Bright Is the Ring of Words."

SONNET: a fixed poetic form of fourteen lines, used by French, Italian, and English poets. The traditional English sonnet is composed of three quatrains, each with new rhymes, finishing with a rhyming ★couplet. The French sonnet is composed of a pair of quatrains and a pair of tercets (three-line stanzas) separated typographically. (SOURCE: Drabble, 2000)

SOPHIE, SAINT, SAINT SOPHIA: a popular name for the Basilica of the Holy Wisdom (Greek, *Hagia Sophia*) in the Turkish city of Istanbul (formerly named Constantinople), originally a Christian church (563), then a mosque (1453), and since 1935 a museum. Hagia Sophia is the world's most famous Byzantine church. The construction began in 532, sponsored by Emperor Justinian, and is estimated to have cost what today would be seventy-five million dollars. Although it was dedicated in 537, an earthquake in 558 caused part of the structure to collapse. When it was rebuilt, the apex of the main dome was raised six meters. The building is a rectangle 260 by 240 feet, divided longitudinally, with nave and side aisles. The nave is covered by a dome 100 by 106 feet and 184 feet high. The aisles are vaulted in various designs, with women's galleries situated above. Gold leaf and a deep blue color appear on the upper parts of the walls and arches, and the vaults are covered with mosaics. When the Turks conquered Constantinople, they converted the church to a mosque and covered the mosaics that depicted human figures. In the twentieth century the government permitted the mosaics to be uncovered.

SONG	COMPOSER	POET
"Seule!"	Gabriel Fauré	Théophile Gautier

SOPHOCLES (?496–406 B.C.E.): Greek dramatist, second of the three great Athenian tragedians. Sophocles was younger than *Aeschylus and older than *Euripides. He was interested in the moral problems of human beings who were subject to the inscrutable laws of fate or necessity, before which even the gods must bow. Sophocles recognized that the fate that drags a victim to his doom is not wholly blind or unjust, that human error or wrongdoing also motivates the workings of destiny. Sophocles was the first playwright to make each play stand alone as an artistic whole. He was also the first to compose plays to suit the talents of individual actors. Poised, moderate, and urbane, qualities that Athenians admired, Sophocles loved Athens and lived there all his life, dying at the age of ninety. His writing was essentially classic, showing balance, wisdom, and power, but also sweetness. (SOURCE: *Americana*, 2003)

SONG	COMPOSER	POET
1. "Dover Beach"	Samuel Barber	Matthew Arnold
2. "Aeschylus and Sophocles"	Charles Ives	Walter Landor

SORIA: a Spanish province. Soria is located where the Duero River makes its turn to the north after flowing east from the Portuguese border. Although at one time it had been considered the epitome of Castilian beauty and austerity, the province had already been forgotten when Machado immortalized it with a poem at the beginning of the twentieth century. Machado's poetry stamped on the Spanish mind new images of the province's nobility, bright light, pure crisp air, and its subtle shades of brown, gold, and rust. (SOURCE: Casas, 1996)

SONG	COMPOSER	POET
"Abril galán"	Joaquín Rodrigo	Antonio Machado

"Sound, Fame, Thy Brazen Trumpet": a song from the 1690 semi-opera *Dioclesian* with music solely by Henry Purcell, to the words of Massinger and *Fletcher. *See *Dioclesian* for plot details and placement of songs.

SOUTAR, WILLIAM (1898–1943): Scottish poet and diarist. Born in Perth, Soutar was the son of a joiner, finishing his education at the University of Edinburgh after serving in the Royal Navy in World War I. By 1931 Soutar was bed-ridden following a failed operation to cure a disease contracted during the war. During the thirteen years before he died he continued to write, publishing eleven books of poetry in English and in Scots, but little prose, although that is more extensive than his verse. In order to encourage the use of the Scots language, he wrote much of his poetry for children, some of which was set to music by Benjamin Britten. One of his most popular works, *The Tryst*, was set by James MacMillan. PRINCIPAL WORKS: *Conflict*, 1931; *Seeds in the Wind: Poems in Scots*, 1933 (juvenile); *The Solitary Way*, 1934;

Poems in Scots, 1935; *Riddles in Scots*, 1937; *In the Time of Tyrants*, 1939; *The Expectant Silence*, 1944; *Collected Poems*, 1988. SELECTED READING: Alexander Scott, *Still Life* (biography), 1948; A. Scott, ed., *Diaries of a Dying Man*, 1954. (SOURCE: Mac-Dougall, Gifford, 2000)

SOUTHERNE, THOMAS (1660–1746): British dramatist. Thomas Southerne was born near Dublin, the son of a brewer. He was educated at Trinity College in Dublin. In 1680 he crossed the Irish Sea and was admitted to the Middle Temple for the study of law. Later becoming a playwright, Southerne had a success with *The Disappointment*, which was given a command performance in 1684, two weeks before the death of Charles II. He finished an uncompleted tragedy for ★Dryden and supported ★Congreve in his first dramatic attempt. Southerne wrote domesticated and sentimentalized tragedies. His most popular works were *The ★Fatal Marriage* in 1694 and ★*Oronooko* in 1696. Regarded as a political opportunist, he wrote ribald comedies between 1690 and 1693 as the times required and was a friend of ★Pope and Swift. Many verses of Thomas Southerne were set by Henry Purcell. PRINCI-PAL WORKS: *The ★ Wives' Excuse, or, Cuckolds Make Themselves*, 1692; *The Fatal Marriage*, 1694; *Oronooko*, 1696. SELECTED READING: J. W. Dodds, *Thomas Southerne, Dramatist*, 1933. (SOURCE: Kunitz, Haycraft, 1952)

SPANISH FRYAR, THE: a tragicomedy written by John ★Dryden, produced in 1680, containing two scenes with music and, in the 1695 revival, one song by Henry Purcell that replaced one by an anonymous composer. In act 1 a musical scene contains a choral procession of priests who escort the queen to the cathedral. In act 5 Torrismond, having married the queen, is falsely informed that she was responsible for the death of his father. The queen wonders why her new husband recoils from her. To ease her distress, she asks an attendant to sing "Farewell, Ungrateful Traytor," which was replaced in 1695 by Purcell's "Whilst I with Grief Did on You Look." (SOURCE: Price, 1984)

SPAUN, JOSEF VON (1788–1865): Austrian poet and civil servant. Spaun and Schubert attended the Imperial College at the same time, Spaun being two years Schubert's senior. They were also roommates for a few weeks, and Spaun's reminiscences of Schubert are of great interest. The first to realize Schubert's talents, Spaun introduced him to Josef Witteczek, Johann ★Mayrhofer, Franz ★Schober, and Johann Vogl. From 1821 to 1826 Spaun filled an official office in Linz, but retired in 1861 after a distinguished career in government. Schubert set one song to Spaun's text, "Der Jüngling und der Tod." (SOURCE: Reed, 1997)

SPENSER, EDMUND (ca.1552–1599): English poet. Spenser was the son of a cloth-maker, probably born in London, and educated at Cambridge. While still there, Spenser translated works of ★Petrarch and ★du Bellay. In 1579 he obtained a position in Leicester's household, where he wrote *Shepeardes Calendar* and began *The ★Faerie-Queene*. In 1580 Spenser went to Ireland as a lord deputy and acquired a castle in County Cork where he prepared the first three books of *The Faerie-Queene* for publication. The success of *The Faerie-Queene* prompted his publisher to put out Spenser's minor verse. He married in 1584 after wooing his wife with *Amoretti*, and he celebrated his marriage with *Epithalamium*. Books 4 to 6 of *The Faerie-Queene* were published in London (1596). Depressed in mind and in his health, Spenser returned to Ireland (1596 or 1597). A sudden insurrection was the cause of his castle being burned (1598), and some of his works were lost in the fire. Spenser died in London, almost destitute, and was buried near ★Chaucer in Westminster Abbey. Spenser's verse was set by Ned Rorem. PRINCIPAL WORKS: *Works*, 10 vols., ed. E. Greenlaw, C. G. Osgood, F. M. Padelford et al., 1932–57. (SOURCE: Drabble, 2000)

SPEYER: a German town where, in 1529, a special assembly, called the Diet at Speyer, was convened by the Catholic Church. It was decreed that the Bible should be taught only along lines authorized by the Roman Catholic Church and that the ★Mass should be restored in the German states where it had been discontinued. Following the Diet, fourteen imperial cities made formal protest against the decrees. Because they were called Protesters, the name Protestant became the description for the many sects of non-Catholics.

SONG	COMPOSER	POET
"Graf Eberstein"	Carl Loewe	Ludwig Uhland

SPLEEN: the perplexing title of a Paul ★Verlaine poem set as a song by Claude Debussy and Gabriel Fauré. At one time Verlaine was a teacher in a school located in the south of England. He chose the English word *spleen* for a poem of his own, the first lines of which were "Les roses étaient toutes rouges." This poem, along with another, "Green," are from a set of poems called *Aquarelles*. Debussy set both poems together with others, calling them *Ariettes oubliées* (Forgotten Songs), because they were published only fifteen years after their first appearance. When Fauré chose to set Verlaine's untitled poem, he chose to call it "Spleen." To further complicate matters, John Ireland's composed another song and called it "Spleen." This fascination with the English word "spleen" is easily explained. At one time, the body organ called the spleen (a ductless abdominal organ that plays a role in the maintenance of blood volume) was considered to be the seat of emotions and passions; the source of laughter and violent feelings. (SOURCE: Bédé, Edgerton, 1980)

SPRAGUE, CHARLES (1791–1875): American poet and banker. Charles Sprague was the son of Samuel Sprague, who participated in the Boston Tea Party. The entire Sprague family had been closely associated with the beginning of the United States. Young Sprague had a brief schooling in Boston. At the age of thirteen he was apprenticed to a firm of dry goods importers, and by his nineteenth year he had gone into partnership with a grocer. He became a bank teller, then a cashier, becoming respected first as a Boston business man, then as a banker. What leisure time he managed was devoted to reading and writing poetry, for which he won several minor poetry prizes in New York and Philadelphia. Sprague was a sincere poet, ably fitted to interpret the homely American scene. A collection of his poetry was published in 1841 and revised in 1850. The verses of Charles Sprague were set by Charles Ives. PRINCIPAL WORKS: *Prose and Poetical Writings*, 1841, 1850, 1870. SELECTED READING: E. Quincy, *Memoir of Charles Sprague*, 1875. (SOURCE: Kunitz, Haycraft, 1938)

SPRECHSTIMME, SPRECHGESANG: a vocal device created by Engelbert Humperdinck, wherein the singer is concerned only with the stated pitch, the rhythm, and the intervals but not with exactitude of pitch, perhaps touching the pitch but not sustaining it. In Arnold Schönberg's words, "The melody indicated for the speaking voice by notes (apart from a few specially indicated exceptions) is not meant to be sung. The reciter has the task of transforming this melody, always with a due regard to the prescribed intervals, into a speaking melody. This is accomplished in the following way: 1. The rhythm must be kept absolutely strict, as if the reciter were singing; that is to say, with no more freedom than he would allow himself if he were just singing the melody. 2. To emphasize fully the contrast between the sung note and the spoken note, whereas the sung note preserves the pitch, the spoken note gives it at first, but abandons it either by rising or by falling immediately after. The reciter must take the greatest care not to fall into a sing-song form of speaking voice; on the contrary, the difference between ordinary speech and a manner of speech that may be embodied in musical form is to be clearly maintained. But, again, it must not be reminiscent of song." Although Schönberg pioneered the use of sprechstimme in song literature, another example is found in Britten's "Serenade" for tenor. (SOURCE: Stevens, 1970)

STADLER, ALBERT (1794–1888): Austrian poet, local government official, and lawyer. Stadler attended the Imperial College from 1812 to 1813 at the same time as Schubert, later studying law in Vienna until 1817. During the time spent at the College, Stadler was a close friend of Schubert's and compiled a manuscript collection of Schubert's songs. On occasion he wrote poems and songs. Schubert set two of the poems, "Der Strom" and "Lieb Minne." (SOURCE: Reed, 1997)

STARNS: (Scot.), *stars*.

STEEPIES: (Scot.), *bread saturated with flavorful liquid as food for children; also steep, with precipitous sides.*

SONG	COMPOSER	POET
"Supper"	Benjamin Britten	William Soutar

STEER: (Scot.) (pr. steer), *to stir; harm.*

SONG	COMPOSER	POET
"Birthday Song"	Benjamin Britten	Robert Burns

STEID: (Scot.), *steed*.

STEIN, GERTRUDE (1874–1946): American avant-garde poet and novelist. Born in Pennsylvania, she spent her infancy in Vienna and Paris, her girlhood in Oakland, California. She was educated at Johns Hopkins and Radcliffe, where she was a student of William James. James's influence upon her was great, bringing her to a belief that art stems from the immediate understanding of experience untouched by prior conceptions. By 1902 she had settled in Paris where she was able to establish a salon for the literary, musical, and artistic avant-garde. (In 1969 her fine collection of art was sold for six million dollars.) At first she lived with her art critic brother Leo, and then with her lifelong companion, Alice B. Toklas. Her innovations had a stimulating effect on the younger generation of American novelists. It was Stein who gave the name "the lost generation" to the young men of the 1920s who came of age in the shadow of World War I. There is very little difference between the forms of Stein's poetry and prose. She used them both for experimental purposes. In prose she liked to avoid nouns, preferring verbs. With regard to poetry she wrote, "You can love a name and if you love a name then saying that name any number of times only makes you love it more" and "poetry is really the name of anything." That was, anything that did not involve "movement in space," that is, verbs. Stein did have literary influence, but mainly with her novels. Few poets were affected by her poetic procedures, and she, in turn, thought that poets were "drunk with nouns." Speaking of her renowned poem "A rose is a rose is a rose is a rose," she wrote, ". . . and what did I do I caressed completely caressed and addressed a noun" (Hamilton, 1994). The poetry of Gertrude Stein has been set by Paul Bowles, Gunther Schuller, David Diamond, William Flanagan, and Virgil Thomson. Thomson made two of her books into operas: *Four Saints in Three Acts* and *The Mother of Us All*. PRINCIPAL WORKS: *Three Lives*, 1909; *Tender Buttons*, 1914; *Stanzas in Meditation and Other Poems: 1929–1933*, 1956; *The Autobiography of Alice B. Toklas*, 1933; *Bewsie and Willie*, 1946; *Look at Me and Here I Am*, 1967. (SOURCE: Hamilton, 1994)

STÈLE (Fr.), STELA: an upright slab or pillar, usually with an inscription, especially one used as a gravestone.

SONG	COMPOSER	POET
"Deux stèles orientées"	Jacques Ibert	Victor Segalen

STEPPE: one of the vast tracts of land in southeastern Europe and Asia, generally level and without forests. The steppes are referred to nostalgically in many Russian poems.

STERNIE: (Scot.), adj. *starry*; n. *the rear part of something*.

SONG	COMPOSER	POET
"Bed-time"	Benjamin Britten	William Soutar

STEVENS, WALLACE (1879–1955): American poet and essayist. Wallace Stevens was born in Reading, Pennsylvania, and grew up in a comfortable upper middle-class family. From 1897 to 1900 he attended Harvard, where he was the editor of the literary magazine, *The Advocate*. Stevens planned to become a journalist and worked briefly at the *New York Herald Tribune*, but was not interested in the daily routines of journalism. On the advice of his father he entered the New York University Law School and was admitted to the bar (1904). He practiced law with middling success while reading and writing poetry. After 1908 his work for an insurance company's legal department led to an appointment with the Hartford Accident and Indemnity Company, of which he became a vice president in 1934. Thereafter Stevens divided his life sharply between his literary and business lives, living a middle-class life in Hartford, Connecticut, until his death. Stevens did not actually publish a book until he was forty-four years old. That book, *Harmonium*, is a landmark volume in modern American poetry. It has an almost baroque quality of language, in contrast to his later, barer style. Poems of the early period are marked by high spirits, a fascination with sensual experience, a fine sense of parody, and a strong emphasis on musicality of line. The interplay between reality and the imagination was the principal subject. Stevens believed in the ability of the imagination to transform reality. The works of the 1930s, 1940s, and early 1950s contain a strong religious strain. Stevens explained his concept of the poet's role: "What makes the poet the potent figure that he is . . . is that he creates the world to which we turn incessantly and without knowing it and that he gives to life the supreme fictions without which we are unable to conceive of it" (Hamilton, 1994). A hypersensitive and ingenious imagist, Stevens paints a world of half light and disembodied emotions in which his verbal mosaics contain syllables as pigments. The poetry of Wallace Stevens has been set by Vincent Persichetti, Peggy Glanville-Hicks, Louise Talma, Elie Siegmeister, and Lee Hoiby. PRINCIPAL WORKS: *Harmonium*, 1923; *The Auroras of Autumn*, 1954; *The Necessary Angel*, 1951, 1960; *The Collected Poems of Wallace Stevens*, 1954, 1955, and 1984. SELECTED READING: Frank Kermode, *Wallace Stevens*, 1969, 1989; Milton Bates, *Wallace Stevens: A Mythology of the Self*, 1985. (SOURCE: Hamilton, 1994)

STEVENSON, ROBERT LOUIS (LEWIS) (1850–1894): English writer of poetry, fiction, and travel books. Stevenson was born in Edinburgh, the son of an engineer. He originally intended to pursue his father's career, but ill-health made him study law. Although admitted to the bar in 1875, he had already determined to be a writer and was published in several periodicals. His chronic bronchial condition (perhaps tuberculosis) forced him to seek better health by traveling. By 1879, a year in which he traveled to California by an emigrant ship and returned to Europe, he was widely published. Stevenson, cultivating a Bohemian lifestyle, was fascinated by the Edinburgh low life and delighted in story-telling, swashbuckling romances. In 1883 *Treasure Island*, his first full-length work, was published and with it came fame. In 1888 he and his family went to the South Seas and visited the leper colony at Molokai. They settled in Samoa, where he temporarily regained his health, only to die suddenly from a brain hemorrhage. Critics found, under his light touch, a sense of apprehension, a preoccupation with sin and suffering, and an admiration for dubious or anti-heroes. Stevenson's works have remained constantly in print and filmed often, although his critical reputation has been somewhat overshadowed by the attention paid to his colorful personality and venturesome life. The verse of Robert Louis Stevenson has been set by Ralph Vaughan Williams, Seymour Barab, Sidney Homer, Alan Hovhaness, Richard Hundley, Charles Ives, and John Alden Carpenter. PRINCIPAL WORKS: Poetry: *A Child's Garden of Verses*, 1885; *Underwoods*, 1887; *Collected Poems*, 1950. Fiction: *New Arabian Nights*, 1882; *Treasure Island*, 1883; *The Strange Case of Dr. Jekyll and Mr. Hyde*, 1886; *Kidnapped,* 1886; *Island Nights' Entertainments*, 1894. SELECTED READING: *The Life of Robert L. Stevenson*, Graham Balfour, 1968. (SOURCES: Drabble, 1985; Furnas, 1952; I. Bell, 1993)

STIRLING CASTLE: a fortress and royal residence located in the town of Stirling in the Glasgow Lowlands of Scotland. The castle was built between the thirteenth and seventeenth centuries. It contains a Parliament Hall, a Chapel Royal with seventeenth-century wall paintings. The approach to the castle passes the Church of the Holy Rood in which Mary was crowned queen of Scots at the age of nine months.

SONG	COMPOSER	POET
"Archibald Douglas"	Carl Loewe	Theodore Fontane

STOCKBRIDGE: a Massachusetts city located 15 miles from Pittsfield in the Berkshire mountains. The city was originally established as a mission and became a center for teaching the Indian language Mahican. It is now primarily a summer resort. Ives's song is based on his experience of hearing church singing across the misty Housatonic River while on a Sunday morning walk near Stockbridge on one of the last days of his honeymoon.

SONG	COMPOSER	POET
"The Housatonic at Stockbridge"	Charles Ives	Robert Underwood Johnson

STOLBERG, FRIEDRICH, GRAF ZU (1750–1819): German poet, novelist, and translator. Stolberg was born in Schleswig-Holstein, one of two sons of the man who helped abolish serfdom in North Germany and Denmark. Stolberg had a happy childhood on country estates and in small towns, spent two years at the University of Halle, then continued his studies in Göttingen (1772), where he became a disciple of ★Klopstock and turned his attention from the law to literature (★Milton, Goldsmith, ★Shakespeare, ★Ossian, the Bible) and to the Greek language, which he studied intensively, translating Homer and ★Plato. On a trip to Switzerland (1775) he met ★Goethe and persuaded him to join him on a walking trip, where they met members of the ★Sturm und Drang movement, Voltaire, and ★Wieland. His first poem collection, written with his brother, was published in 1779. His love poetry was ★anacreontic; the other writing genres he tried resulted in five plays. Accepting several political positions in Denmark, Stolberg began to favor the political lyric over love lyrics. His many translations were admired even by ★Schiller. After converting to Catholicism in 1800, he was exploited by Catholics and Protestants alike, and the content of his writing turned to the religious. Nine of Graf Friedrich zu Stolberg's verses were set by Franz Schubert, including "Auf dem Wasser zu singen" and "Daphne am Bach." PRINCIPAL WORKS: *Jamben* [Iambs], 1784; *Die Insel* [The Island], 1788; *Reise in Deutschland, der Schweiz, Italien, und Sicilien in den Jahren 1791 und 1792* [Journey in Germany, Switzerland, Italy, and Sicily in 1791–92], 1794; *Geschichte der Religion Jesu Christi* [Stories of the Religion of Jesus Christ], 15 vols., 1806–18; *Die Gedichte von Ossian, dem Sohne Fingals* [Poems of Ossian, son of Fingal], trans. Stolberg, 1806. (SOURCE: Hardin, Schweitzer, 1990)

STOLL, JOSEF (1778–1815): Austrian poet, editor, and journalist. Stoll was the editor of the literary periodical *Prometheus*. In the year of Stoll's death, Schubert set four of his poems, including "Lambertine" and "Die Zeit," and his verses were also set by Carl Maria von Weber and Beethoven (two settings of "An die Geliebte"). (SOURCE: Reed, 1997)

STOONDIN: (Scot.), *thrilling*.

STORM, THEODOR (1817–1888): German poet and short-story writer. Storm, son of an attorney father, was born in Schleswig and studied law at Kiel and in Berlin. When Schleswig was incorporated into Denmark (1853), out of loyalty Storm moved to Potsdam where he became an assistant judge. There he began a literary career as a lyric poet. Storm ranks high in German literature because of his lyric poetry, where the stress is on mood, not action. Influenced greatly by *Eichendorff, *Mörike, and *Heine, he showed an unusually perceptive understanding of human nature. As often described, "a poet of the small scene," Storm devoted himself to the problems of family life, although he felt keenly the loneliness of the individual, which was a constant motive in his writing. His early poetry betrayed romantic influences of folk song, but later it became more realistic, manly, and restrained. The verses of Theodor Storm were set by Brahms, Hermann Reutter, and Alban Berg. PRINCIPAL WORKS: D. Broicher, *German Lyrics and Ballads Done into English Verses*, 1912; *The Penguin Book of German Verse*, 1957. SELECTED READING: E. O. Wooley, *Studies in Theodor Storm*, 1943. (SOURCE: Kunitz, Colby, 1967)

STORNELLATRICE (It.): a woman singer of stornellos, a poetry form similar to a madrigal.

SONG	COMPOSER	POET
"Stornellatrice"	Ottorino Respighi	Carlo Zangarini, Alberto Donini

STORNELLO: Italian term for an informal song, a "ditty."

SONG	COMPOSER	POET
"Stornello"	Giuseppe Verdi	anonymous

STOVIES: (Scot.), *a dish of potatoes, onions, sometimes with small pieces of meat; also hot houses.*

SONG	COMPOSER	POET
"Supper"	Benjamin Britten	William Soutar

STRAMBOTTO: an Italian folk lyric. A strambotto has six or eight lines, usually having to do with a satirical or amorous subject. Each line consists of eleven syllables. The strambotto and the *frottola were considered less elegant forms than the madrigal, which they preceded. The literal meaning of the word *strambo* is twisted, odd, or unusual. (SOURCE: Lakeway, White, 1989)

SONG	COMPOSER	POET
"Quattro strambotti di Giustiniani"	Giorgio Federico Ghedini	Justinian

STRASBOURG: a French trading center, a city of about 300,000 inhabitants on the German/French border, located on the Ill River, 250 miles east of Paris. Because of its canal link to the Rhine River, it is an ocean port of significance. The old city has many medieval buildings. Its famous Gothic cathedral, work on which started in the 1000s, has a huge clock, a splendid rose window, and a 465-foot spire. The university was founded in 1538. The city belonged to Germany until 1681, when it was united with France. After the Franco-Prussian War of 1870, France ceded the city to the Germans. It became French again after the Treaty of Versailles in 1919, was occupied by the Germans in 1940, but freed by the Allied troops in 1944. (SOURCE: *Americana*, 2003)

SONG	COMPOSER	POET
"Zu Strasbourg auf der Schanz"	Gustav Mahler	*Des Knaben Wunderhorn*

STREPHON: originally the shepherd; a character in Sidney's *Arcadia*, eventually adopted as a conventional name for a rustic lover. (SOURCE: Drabble, 2000)

SONG	COMPOSER	POET
"From Rosy Bow'rs"	Henry Purcell	Thomas D'Urfey

STRESA: an Italian city located 50 miles northwest of Milano on Lago Maggiore.

SONG	COMPOSER	POET
"Stresa"	Wintter Watts	Sara Teasdale

STUFF: the material out of which anything is or can be made; raw material; fabric.

SONG	COMPOSER	POET
"The Water Mill"	Ralph Vaughan Williams	Fredegond Shove

STURM UND DRANG: lit., *storm and stress*, a German literary movement. The phrase *Sturm und Drang* was taken from the title of a romantic drama based on the American War of Independence. In the latter part of the eighteenth century the German literary community was stirred up in a revolt against the current literary conventions, particularly the theory of "unities in drama." Led by the young Johann Wolfgang von ★Goethe, Johann Herder, and Friedrich von ★Schiller, the writers of this new movement called Sturm und Drang were galvanized and inspired by a return to nature. (SOURCE: Drabble, 2000)

STYX: the river of Hate that, according to classical mythology, flowed around the infernal regions nine times. The Styx was styled the "abhorred Styx, the flood of deadly hate" by ★Milton in his *Paradise Lost*. It was said by some to be a river in ★Arcadia, whose waters were so poisonous that they dissolved anything immersed in them, even ships. Whenever a god falsely swore by the Styx, he was forced to drink its water, which made him speechless for a year. The name *Styx* may have been taken from Styx, the eldest daughter of Oceanus and Tethys. She was the wife of Pallas. (SOURCE: Cooper, 1992)

SONG	COMPOSER	POET
"Dithyrambe"	Franz Schubert	Friedrich von Schiller

SUCKLING, SIR JOHN (1609–1642): English poet, playwright, and tract writer. From a Norfolk family, Sir John was educated at Trinity College, Cambridge, and inherited large estates. When he returned from travel on the Continent, he was knighted (1630). In 1631 he was in Germany as a member of the embassy staff. When he came back to England in 1632, he lived lavishly at court, where, supposedly, he invented the game of cribbage. As a leader of the Royalist Party, he was eventually forced to flee to France, where he is said to have committed suicide. His plays were admired chiefly for their lyrics, and Suckling was considered one of the most elegant and brilliant of the Cavalier poets. One of his most famous poems was "Ballad upon a Wedding," and his "Sessions of the Poets" is an opinion on the writers ★Jonson, Carew, and ★D'Avenant. His lyrics were set to music by Thomas Arne, Henry Lawes, Judith Zaimont, and Norman dello Joio. PRINCIPAL WORKS: *Fragmenta Aurea,* a collection of Suckling's chief works, 1646; *Works,* 2 vols., ed. T. Clayton and L. A. Beaurline, 1971. (SOURCE: Drabble, 2000)

SULEIKA: a character from ★Goethe's *West-östlicher Divan.* Schubert's "Suleika I" was addressed to the east wind and "Suleika II" to the west wind. Brahms thought that the first was "the loveliest song that has ever been written." In ★Hāfiz's ★*Divan,* Suleika is the beloved of Hatem. In his amorous pursuit of Marianne ★Willemer, Goethe pretended that he was Hatem and Marianne his Suleika.

SONG	COMPOSER	POET
1. "Suleika"	Felix Mendelssohn	Johann Wolfgang von Goethe
2. "Suleika I and II"	Franz Schubert	Johann Wolfgang von Goethe

SULLY PRUDHOMME, pseudonym of René François Prudhomme (1839–1907): French poet and essayist. Prudhomme's early scientific studies came to a close when they became impossible due to his developing eye trouble. Prudhomme eventually discovered his true poetic medium, although he first spent a short phase as a ★Parnassian. He learned that his predilection for positivism and simple, neat concepts pointed toward a medium of short, philosophical, and symbolic verses. Prudhomme's poetry was very popular during his lifetime and brought him the Nobel Prize in 1901. The verse of Sully Prudhomme has been set by Gabriel Fauré, Cécile Chaminade, Daniel Aubert, Ottorino Respighi, and Henri Duparc. PRINCIPAL WORKS: *Stances et poèmes,* 1865; *Les Épreuves,* 1866; *Les Solitudes,* 1869; *Les Destins,* 1872; *La France,* 1874; *La Justice,* 1878; *Le Prisme,* 1886; *Le Bonheur,* 1888; *Épaves,* 1908. (SOURCE: France, 1995)

SUNDA ISLANDS: two groups of islands, called Greater and Lesser Sunda Islands, south of the Malay peninsula in Indonesia, including Borneo, Sumatra, and Java, surrounding the Java Sea.

SONG	COMPOSER	POET
"Les Matelots"	Gabriel Fauré	Théophile Gautier

SUPERVIELLE, JULES (1884–1960): French poet, novelist, short-story writer, and dramatist. Supervielle was born of a French-Basque family living in Uruguay, soon orphaned, and raised by an uncle. His childhood on the pampas was happy as reflected in his fiction and poems. At the age of ten he was sent to Paris for schooling, later to attend the Sorbonne. Except for the years of World War II, which he spent in Uruguay, Supervielle remained in Paris for the rest of his life. His poetry, colored by a familiarity with the South American scene, showed an intimacy and lightness devoid of sentimentality. This was the basis for his fame. His themes are love, solitude, remembrance, nature, and death. Supervielle believed that man's unhappiness stems from insufficient knowledge of himself and his universe. His fiction has delicate language and his plots are imaginative and witty. The poetry of Jules Supervielle was set by Georges Auric. PRINCIPAL WORKS: *Le Voleur d'enfants*, 1926 [The Man who Stole Children], 1967; *Les Amis inconnus* [Unknown Friends], 1934; *Oublieuse mémoire* [Forgetful Memory], 1943; *Selected Writings*, 1967. SELECTED READING: T. Greene, *Jules Supervielle*, 1958; L. Jones, *Poetic Fantasy and Fiction: The Short Stories of Jules Supervielle*, 1973. (SOURCE: Serafin, 1999)

SURIKOV, IVAN ZAKHAROVICH (1840–1880): Russian playwright and poet. Born into a peasant family, Surikov worked in his father's store as a young man. After meeting Pleshcheyev, the poet and translator of foreign poets, Surikov produced his first play, soon becoming known as a dramatist and poet. Tchaikovsky set his poetry in his op. 47, no. 7, "Was I Not a Blade of Grass" [*Ya li v pole da ne travushka byla*]. (SOURCE: Miller, 1973)

SURREALISM: a movement founded in Paris in 1924, a revolutionary type of thought and action, concerned with literature and art as well as politics, philosophy, and psychology. The first Manifesto (1924) drew on Freud's theories about the unconscious and its relationship to dreams. It called for a resolution of the seeming contradictions between dreams and reality. Writers and painters first espoused the surrealist cause but then fostered the spontaneous joining of unrelated objects, thereby creating an extended conception of poetry. A great variety of surrealist poetry was published by Louis Aragon, Paul Éluard, and Robert Desnos. Surrealist artists in the 1920s did free ink drawings and field paintings. Then Salvador Dali joined the movement, using dream imagery that was influenced by Freud.

SUZANNE ET LE PACIFIQUE: a novel by Jean ★Giraudoux dealing with Suzanne, a girl who sails from St. Nazaire across the Atlantic Ocean through the Panama Canal to the South Seas. She is shipwrecked on an island but adapts easily to the lazy and happy life. For amusement she plays at games that revive her European memories. One of these games has to do with her former school and her teacher. The teacher in this brief cycle set to music by Arthur Honegger is addressing her girls—Jeanne, Adèle, Cécile, Irène, and Rosemonde—about a lesson in morality.

SWAWS: (Scot.), *waves, ripples.*

"Sweeter Than Roses": a song composed by Henry Purcell to text written by Richard Norton for his play *Pausanias*, produced in 1696. For plot details and placement of songs, *see* ★*Pausanias*.

SWEDENBORG, EMANUEL (1688–1772): a Swedish scientist, inventor, and mystical religious leader, also an authority on mathematics, metallurgy, astronomy, anatomy, and geology. Swedenborg was the son of a bishop and nobleman. In middle age he turned to religion, writing books that set forth what he called his "heavenly doctrines," which he claimed were based on Bible teachings that had been interpreted to him through direct communication with the spirit world. His followers, the Swedenborgians, organized churches in London, the United States, and Canada based on this doctrine. Swedenborg's teachings emphasized one God, ★Jesus Christ, in whom is the Trinity, and the belief that Jesus Christ will make his second coming in spirit, not in person. (SOURCE: Americana, 2000)

SYLVA: *see* ★SYLVIE, LA.

SYLVIE, LA: the title of a pastoral tragicomedy by Jean Mairet (1604–86), a French dramatist. *La Sylvie* was his second play performed in 1626, in which the heroine Sylvie was a shepherdess. Among Mairet's twelve plays was another pastoral tragicomedy titled *La ★Silvanire*, performed in 1630. In Albert Samain's poem titled "Arpège," set to music by Fauré, the use of the three words *Sylva, Sylvie*, and *Sylvanire* comprises an allusion to Mairet's works. (*See also* ★SILVIA.)

SONG	COMPOSER	POET
1. "Arpège"	Gabriel Fauré	Albert Samain
2. "Sylvie"	Gabriel Fauré	Paul de Choudens
3. "Invocation aux parques"	Francis Poulenc	anonymous

SYMBOLISM, SYMBOLISTS: a group of French writers of the nineteenth century who reacted against realist tendencies dominant in literature at the time. In poetry their rebellion was against the objectivity of the ★Parnassians, against direct description and for suggestion. ★Mallarmé explained, "It is not the thing but the effect that it produces" (Drabble, 2000). Symbolist poets explored the musical facets of language. Interested in all the arts, they admired Wagner's ability to combine the arts and were influenced by ★Baudelaire and by ★Poe's mystical writings. The Symbolists had a part in the Russian symbolist movement and also the Latin American modernista movement. Russian symbolism was split between those who stressed the spiritual mission of symbolism (★Bely and ★Ivanov) and those for whom symbolism was but an artistic orientation (★Bryusov). French Symbolists included Mallarmé, ★Verlaine, ★Rimbaud, ★Laforgue, and ★Maeterlinck. Their movement influenced painters, and also writers like ★Pound, ★Eliot, Wallace ★Stevens, ★Yeats, ★Joyce, ★Woolf, ★Claudel, ★Valéry, Stefan ★George, and ★Rilke. (SOURCES: Drabble, 2000; Terras, 1991)

SYMONS, ARTHUR (1865–1945): English poet, playwright, essayist, biographer, editor, translator, and critic. Arthur Symons was born in Pembrokeshire and educated in private schools abroad. While he was a journalist with the *Athenaeum*, *Saturday Review*, and *Academy*, his friends included ★Yeats and ★Wilde. Symons was one of those highly professional all round men of letters, whose significance is judged as part of a period rather than as an individual. He wrote copiously throughout a long working life. His better poems tend to be a few and erotic, concerned with his obsession with young dancers and singers. As editor of *The Savoy*, he had a flair for finding brilliant contributors—★Verlaine, Yeats, Conrad, Shaw, Beerbohm, Beardsley—whose reputations eventually exceeded his own. Probably his most important role was that in the ★Symbolist movement, which Yeats and ★Eliot said had influenced them profoundly. Symons brought the works of such French poets as ★Mallarmé, Verlaine, and ★Rimbaud to the attention of English and American writers. The verses of Arthur Symons have been set to music by Mario Castelnuovo-

Tedesco, Louis Campbell-Tipton, John Alden Carpenter, Henry Clough-Leightner, Harry Thacker Burleigh, John Ireland, and Norman dello Joio. PRINCIPAL WORKS: *Silhouettes,* 1892; *London Nights,* 1895; *The Symbolist Movement in Literature,* 1899, revised 1908. SELECTED READING: T. E. Welby, *Symons,* 1925; Roger Lhombreaud, *Symons: A Critical Biography,* 1963. (SOURCE: Vinson, 1979)

SYNE: immediately afterwards; next after that; at a later time; since then.

SYNGE, J. M. (1871–1909): Irish dramatist and poet. Synge was born in a Dublin suburb, the youngest of eight children of a well-educated Protestant family of the middle class. Synge took a degree from Trinity College in 1892. As a violin player, Synge then went to Germany with the idea of being a professional musician, but a literary interest took over. He ended up in Paris studying the new trends in French literature. Although he was not interested in politics, Synge joined a revolutionary Irish association. A lifelong Puritan and a celibate, Synge lived quietly and abstemiously. In 1898 he met with William B. ★Yeats, who advised him to go back to Ireland and start describing his own people. Thereafter, Synge's life was bounded by Ireland, his interest concentrated on observing of the speech, customs, and legends of the peasants. When the Irish National Theatre Society (later the Abbey Theatre) was founded, Synge had two plays ready, but the anti-theological implications of his work and his uncompromising view of human nature were unsuccessful. Then came *The Playboy of the Western World.* As late as 1912, there were riots whenever it was played. There were shouts from the audiences, pies hurled at the actors, and arrests. Synge did not mix actively in any disturbance. He was morbidly shy, a classic solitary. His magnificent language and lyric poetry touched the life-pulse of Ireland. The poetry of J. M. Synge was set by British composer Arnold Bax. PRINCIPAL WORKS: *Riders to the Sea,* 1904; *The Will of the Saints,* 1905; *The Playboy of the Western World,* 1907; *The Aran Islands,* 1907; *The Tinker's Wedding,* 1908; *In Wicklow,* 1908; *Poems and Translations,* 1909; *Deidre of the Sorrows,* 1910; *Collected Works,* 1910. SELECTED READING: P. P. Howe, *J. M. Synge: A Critical Study,* 1912. (SOURCE: Kunitz, Haycraft, 1942)

SYRINX: an ★Arcadian ★nymph of Greek legend. Being pursued by ★Pan, she took refuge in the River Ladon and prayed to be changed into a reed. Her prayer was answered. Pan made his pipes from the reed, hence the name *syrinx* for a pipe of Pan or a mouth organ. (SOURCE: Cooper, 1992)

SONG	COMPOSER	POET
"La Flûte de Pan"	Claude Debussy	Pierre Louÿs

SZÉCHÉNYI, LUDWIG COUNT VON (1781–1855): a Hungarian poet and musician. Széchényi was a high steward to the Archduchess Sophie and a prominent member of the Philharmonic Society. Schubert set two of his poems to music, one of which was "Der Flug der Zeit." (SOURCE: Reed, 1997)

T &

TABB, JOHN B. (1845–1909): American poet. Born in Virginia, his father a planter, Tabb had such poor eyesight that he had to be home-schooled. His strong desire was to be a musician. Although he was enthusiastic about the Confederacy when the Civil War began, Tabb's bad eyesight caused him to be rejected as a soldier. He became a blockade runner, making trips to London, Paris, and Bermuda before being captured. In prison he met Sidney ★Lanier, who befriended him and turned him toward poetry. After the war, Tabb went to Baltimore to study music, still a rebel at heart. He taught and prepared himself for the clergy, but changed his allegiance to Catholicism and was ordained in 1884. When in 1908 Father Tabb became totally blind, he gave up college teaching, but continued to write until he died of a stroke. A study of his poetry reveals that it has the same contradictions as does his character: vain and vindictive but humble and generous. Tabb was a lyricist because he believed that poetry should be song. Altogether Father Tabb was the American heir to the great metaphysical poets of the seventeenth century. The poetry of John Tabb was set by Charles Griffes. PRINCIPAL WORKS: *Poems*, 1883; *An Octave to Mary*, 1893; *Poems*, 1894; *Lyrics*, 1897; *Child Verses*, 1899; *Two Lyrics*, 1900; *Later Lyrics*, 1902; *The Rosary in Rhyme*, 1904; *Later Poems*, 1910. SELECTED READING: John B. Tabb, *John B. Tabb on Emily Dickinson*, 1950. (SOURCE: Kunitz, Haycraft, 1938)

TAGORE, RABINDRANATH (1861–1941): Indian poet, novelist, essayist, painter, composer, and educator. Western admirers of Tagore, believing him to be an eastern mystic, actually misinterpreted his writings, but the Indians knew and loved his lyrics on nature, love, and children. After 1913, when Tagore won the Nobel Prize for *Gitanjali* (Song Offerings), his influence declined in the west but not in India. In 1919 he resigned the Nobel Prize in protest against the British repressive measures in Jallianwala Bagh in the Punjab. Tagore took the part of the silent witness in act 2 of Philip Glass's work *Satyagraha*. Tagore's work influenced ★Pound and ★Yeats so much that Yeats wrote the introduction for Tagore's own prose translation of the 103 *Gitanjali* poems, written in Bengali. Tagore had done the translation while convalescing from illness aboard a ship bound for Great Britain. It explores the personal relationship between the poet and a divinity that Tagore called Jivandevata, which he translated as "Lord of my life." The most interesting of the *Gitanjali* are those dealing with death. Rabindranath Tagore's verse has been set by John Alden Carpenter, Paul Creston, Henry Hadley, Richard Hageman, Edward Horsman, Frank Bridge, Manuel Ponce, Alfredo Casella, and Ottorino Respighi in translation. (SOURCES: Kimball, 1996; Magill, 2, 1984)

"Take Not a Woman's Anger": a song composed by Henry Purcell to words written by Robert Gould for his play *The Rival Sisters*, produced in 1695. For plot details and placement of songs, *see* ★*Rival Sisters, The*.

TALIESIN: a Welsh bard of the sixth century, whose name signifies *radiant brow*. Probably not older than the thirteenth century is *The Book of Taliesin*, a collection of poems assigned by legend to him.

TAMARIND: a tall evergreen tree believed to be native to tropical Africa, possibly to southern Asia. It has been grown throughout the tropics, sometimes in southern Florida. Bearing a flower with yellow petals and red veins, the tamarind is cultivated for its attractive appearance and acidic pulpy fruit used for making chutney and curries. (SOURCE: *Americana*, 2003)

SONG	COMPOSER	POET
"Miel de Narbonne"	Francis Poulenc	Jean Cocteau

TANKA: *see* ★HAIKU.

TANTALUS: from Greek mythology, the son of ★Zeus and Hera (daughter of ★Cronos and Rhea), father of Pelops, grandfather of ★Atreus and great-grandfather of Agamemnon. Tantalus was the most favored mortal son of Zeus. Because he was privileged to dine on ★ambrosia and ★nectar with the gods on Mount ★Olympus, he found it easy to steal these foods to feed to mortal friends. This crime and the second to follow led to his terrible fate: he invited the gods to dine at his palace, where he served his son—slaughtered and cooked—to the assembled gods for dinner. This was intended as a cruel joke to show how easily the gods could be fooled. The gods, however, recognizing the horrific meal set before them, refused to eat and cursed Tantalus to an eternal punishment. Hanging from a tree branch over a lake, water reaching up to his waist and sometimes his neck, he was bound in Hell. Over his head were the heavy-laden branches of fruit trees. When he was thirsty and tried to sip the water at his neck, the pool drained, and when hunger caused him to reach out for fruit, a breeze pulled the tree branches just beyond his reach. It was said that Tantalus forgot his hunger and thirst when ★Orpheus sang in ★Hades for the return of ★Euridice. The words *tantilate, tantalize*—having something desirable kept out of reach—come from Tantalus. (SOURCES: Graves (2), 1960; Hamilton, 1969)

SONG	COMPOSER	POET
"Fahrt zum Hades"	Franz Schubert	Johann Mayrhofer

TAPSALTEERIE: (Scot.), *topsy turvy*.

TARA: located in Meath, Ireland, an ancient and noble assembly hall used for conferences, often referred to in Irish songs.

TARANTELLA: a rapid, whirling southern Italian dance popular with the peasantry since the fifteenth century. The name is popularly assumed to have been attributed to the bite of a tarantula, and the dance is a cure for the bite.

SONG	COMPOSER	POET
1. "Miranda"	Richard Hageman	Hilaire Belloc
2. "La Danza"	Gioacchino Rossini	Carlo Pepoli
3. "O sí che io sapevo sospirare"	Ermanno Wolf-Ferrari	anonymous

TARTAR: a name given the early Mongol races of Central Asia. Tartars lived in northeast Gobi during the 400s but were later driven southward by the Khitan tribes. During the 800s the Tartars founded the Mongolian Empire. In the 1200s the Mongols began a movement through Hungary, Romania, Poland, Turkey, Russia, and Bulgaria. Most of the present day Tartars are Muslims and speak some form of the Turkish language. *Tartar* comes from the Manchu word *tatar*, meaning archer or nomad. *Tatar* took the form of *Tartar* because the Mongols were associated with ★Tartarus, the word for mythical ★Hades. (SOURCE: *Americana*, 2003)

SONG	COMPOSER	POET
"La Captive"	Hector Berlioz	Victor Hugo

TARTARUS: the infernal regions. Tartarus was used as an equivalent to ★Hades by later writers, but Homer placed Tartarus as far beneath Hades as Hades is beneath the earth. It was here that ★Zeus confined the ★Titans. (SOURCE: Cooper, 1992)

SONG	COMPOSER	POET
1. "A Charm"	Benjamin Britten	Thomas Randolph
2. "Gruppe aus Tartarus"	Franz Schubert	Friedrich von Schiller

TARTARY, HAGS OF: the hags dwelling in the deeper of the two regions of the underworld. ★Tartarus was used by later writers as the infernal region equivalent to ★Hades, but Homer placed Tartarus as far beneath Hades as Hades is beneath the earth. ★Zeus confined the ★Titans to Tartarus. (SOURCE: *Bulfinch*, 1978)

SONG	COMPOSER	POET
"A Charm"	Benjamin Britten	Thomas Randolph

TATE, NAHUM (1652–1715): English playwright. Most of Tate's dramas were adaptations from earlier writers, such as his version of ★Shakespeare's *King Lear*, which was very popular with the public. With ★Dryden, Tate wrote part 2 of ★*Absalom and Architophel*, and for Henry Purcell he wrote the libretto of ★*Dido and Aeneas*. In 1690 Tate published, with Nicholas Brady, a well-known metrical version of the Psalms. Nahum Tate was appointed poet laureate of England in 1692. (SOURCE: Drabble, 2000)

TAURIS: *see* ★ORESTES.

TEASDALE, SARA (1884–1933): American poet. Sara Teasdale was born in St. Louis, Missouri, a child of overprotective parents. Delicate Teasdale was raised in an atmosphere of Victorian constraint. In 1914 she moved to New York and married a businessman from whom she was divorced in 1929. Her poetic output declined during the 1920s, and she became increasingly depressed and reclusive until she committed suicide in 1933. Teasdale was influenced by the work of ★Sappho, Christina ★Rossetti, Emily ★Dickinson, and ★Yeats, but she was unaffected by contemporary movements. She developed as a skilled lyricist, writing fragile, musical verse, usually in rhymed quatrains that originally dealt with idealized love and beauty, but later focused on death. *Love Songs*, published in 1917, brought her international recognition and a Columbia (now Pulitzer) Poetry Prize. Teasdale's artistic maturity and growing fascination with death are illustrated by *Flame and Shadow* (1920), *Dark of* *the Moon* (1926), and *Strange Victory* (published posthumously 1933). The poetry of Sara Teasdale has been set by Ernst Bacon, Judith Zaimont, A. Walter Kramer, Charles Naginski, Frederick Jacobi, Arthur Shepherd, Sergius Kagen, and John Duke. PRINCIPAL WORKS: *The Collected Poems of Sara Teasdale*, 1937; *Mirror of the Heart: Poems of Sara Teasdale*, 1984. SELECTED READING: William Drake, *Sara Teasdale: Woman and Poet*, 1979. (SOURCE: Hamilton, 1994)

"Tell Me No More I am Deceiv'd": a song composed by Henry Purcell to text written by William ★Congreve for the play *The Maid's Last Prayer*, produced in 1693. For plot details and placement of songs, *see* ★*Maid's Last Prayer, The.*

"Tell Me Why": a song from the 1690 semi-opera *Dioclesian* with music solely by Henry Purcell, written to the words of Massinger and ★Fletcher. *See* ★*Dioclesian* for plot and placement of songs.

TEME: an English river that runs close to the border with Wales.

SONG	COMPOSER	POET
"On Wenlock Edge"	Ralph Vaughan Williams	A. E. Housman

TEMPEST, THE: the play by William ★Shakespeare, probably written in 1611, performed before royalty in 1611 and 1613, printed in 1623, published in 1670, music added in 1674 to a ★Shadwell adaptation, revived by Charles ★D'Avenant and John ★Dryden in 1695, and produced that year, inspiring severely conflicting opinions as to whether the music was written by Henry Purcell. On this subject Curtis Price says, "But for those who have taken the trouble to learn something of English theatrical history, who are familiar with all of Purcell's dramatic works, and who are steeped in the style prevailing among the early eighteenth century epigones, the question has been answered beyond a reasonable doubt. No, Purcell did not set *The Tempest*, except for a song added to the fourth act in 1695" (Price, 1984). Consequently, this revival of *The Tempest*, although keeping Shakespeare's plot, lies somewhere between true opera and a play. It is, in fact, a semi-opera, following in the great traditions of lyrical spoken drama and including a ★masque. (Successful semi-operas contained either a character to connect spoken and sung parts or a masque that reflected and amplified the play itself.) In the 1695 adaptation, Prospero, duke of Milan, ousted from his throne by his brother Antonio and set adrift on the sea with the child Miranda, has been cast upon a lonely island. His knowledge of magic has enabled Prospero to release various spirits, including ★Ariel, formerly imprisoned by a witch. These characters now obey Prospero's orders. Shakespeare's main characters were kept, but there is a masque (a play within a play) in act 4 at the end of the work with characters such as Tethys, ★Neptune, Oceanus, and Amphitrite. "Dear Pretty Youth," the one piece generally believed to be by Purcell, is sung by Dorinda in A major, but a note says it can be sung by a tenor down one step. Some believe that it bowed to a vogue of the times to make maudlin stage effects involving children. Dorinda, who, freshly aware of her sexuality, asks Hippolito (a character of D'Avenant's, not Shakespeare's) how he can sleep in the presence of a woman as alluring as she. When she touches him, she sings, "Alas! My Dear, You're Cold as Stone." The recitative is made panicky by Purcell's chromatic recitative and followed by the aria of great pathos.

As to the other songs once ascribed to Purcell, they may have been written by John Weldon. Including a string of *da capo* arias, these are: "Arise, Ye Subterranean Winds," sung by a bass playing the part of a devil who rises up from a trap door to torment the three shipwrecked characters, two arias sung by Ariel, a soprano: "Come Unto These Yellow Sands" and "Dry Those Eyes," which she sings to Alonzo who mourns the supposed drowning of Ferdinand, "Fair and Serene," sung by Neptune, a bass, "Full Fathom Five," "Halcyon Days," sung in the masque by Amphitrite, a soprano, and "While These Pass o'er the Deep." (SOURCES: Price, 1984; Drabble, 2000)

TENNYSON, ALFRED, FIRST BARON (1809–1892): English poet and play-wright. Alfred, Lord Tennyson was born in Lincolnshire, the son of a rector, educated by his father and at Trinity College, Cambridge. Although Tennyson won the chancellor's medal for English verse in 1829, the first blank verse poem ever to win, his first poems were unfavorably reviewed by the critics. In 1832 he traveled on the Continent, visiting, in addition to other places, Cauteret, which countryside was to be a lasting inspiration to him. It is suggested that Tennyson was fearful of the family melancholic and unstable blood, and that he may have been an epileptic. In 1850 he was appointed poet laureate in succession to Wordsworth. With his "Ode on the Death of Wellington" (1852) and "The Charge of the Light Brigade" (1854) his fame was firmly established. Prince Albert visited Tennyson, but Queen Victoria made Tennyson come to see her. His drama *Becket* was produced in 1884, the same year that he was made a peer. Alfred, Lord Tennyson was buried in Westminster Abbey. In later years some described Tennyson's work as poetry of the drawing room. Auden thought that his genius was not for narrative, epic, and dramatic forms, but lyrical. T. S. ★Eliot called him a great master of metric as well as of melancholia, possessing the finest ear of any English poet since ★Milton. The verse of Tennyson was set by Liszt, Benjamin Britten, Frederick Delius, Charles Ives, Amy Beach, Lennox Berkeley, Gordon Binkerd, Sidney Homer, Horatio Parker, Ned Rorem, Roger Quilter, and Judith Zaimont. PRINCIPAL WORKS: Poetry: *Poems,* 1842 (this collection is taken from Tennyson's first two published poetry volumes and includes "Le Morte d'Arthur," the germ which became the "Idylls"); *The Princess,* 1847; *In Memoriam,* 1850; *Enoch Arden,* 1864; *The Holy Grail and Other Poems,* 1869; *Tiresias and Other Poems,* 1885. Plays: *Queen Mary,* 1875; *Harold,* 1876; *The Falcon,* 1884; *The Cup,* 1884; *Becket,* 1884. SELECTED READING: C. Ricks, *Tennyson,* 1972; R. B. Martin, *Tennyson: The Unquiet Heart,* 1980. (SOURCE: Drabble, 1985)

TEREBINTH: the turpentine tree.

TERESA, SAINT: a Carmelite nun from the age of eighteen. Saint Teresa was born into an affluent Spanish family of ★Ávila at a time when the Catholic Church in Spain was criticized for the laxity and softness of its monastic orders. In her forties she finally found her mission, reforming her religious order and personally founding seventeen convents.

SONG	COMPOSER	POET
"Let Nothing Disturb Thee"	David Diamond	St. Teresa of Ávila, trans. Longfellow

TESTAMENT: (Lat.), *testamentum*, a will, in religion a word extended to mean a covenant between God and man. The Old Testament contains the covenant made between God and Israel; the New Testament contains the covenant made by Christ in the name of his father with all of mankind. (SOURCE: Nevins, 1964)

SONG	COMPOSER	POET
"Testament"	Henri Duparc	Armand Silvestre

THAMES: a river of southeastern England that rises in the Cotswold Hills and flows through the heart of London before reaching the sea near Gravesend. From the source to the outskirts of London, the Thames, named the Tamesis during the Roman occupation of England, provides some of the finest Roman scenery in England. From prehistoric times the Thames Valley was the customary route into England for immigrant tribes, and archaeological fragments have been found from 200,000 B.C.E., such as bronze age canoes, Neolithic pottery, and Roman boats. Above Oxford the Thames is navigable only by rowboats and canoes. From Oxford to London the river is used by barges, small steamers, and pleasure boats. ★Spenser and other poets referred to it as the Themmes. (SOURCE: *OED*, 1989)

SONG	COMPOSER	POET
1. "London"	Benjamin Britten	William Blake
2. "Euphonium Dance"	Betty Roe	Jacqueline Froom
3. "Come, You Pretty False-Eyed Wanton"	Thomas Campion	Thomas Campion
4. "Impression du matin"	Charles Griffes	Oscar Wilde

THEBES: name of two cities, one in Egypt, one in Greece. Amenophis IV (1387–1366 B.C.E.), rejecting the priests of Amun, the ram-headed god of Thebes and the Theban sky-god, built a new city for the worship of Aton halfway between Thebes and Memphis. After Amenophis's death, Tutankhamen brought the court back to Thebes. In the Greek version Thebes was founded by ★Cadmus, and ★Oedipus became its king. (SOURCE: Cotterell, 1986)

SONG	COMPOSER	POET
1. "Misera, dove son?"	Wolfgang Amadeus Mozart	Pietro Metastasio
2. "Miniver Cheevy"	John Duke	Edwin Arlington Robinson

THEOCRITUS: a Greek pastoral poet of the third century B.C.E.

SONG	COMPOSER	POET
1. "Sonnets from the Portuguese"	Carlos Surinach	Elizabeth Barrett Browning
2. "I Thought Once How Theocritus had Sung"	Libby Larsen	Elizabeth Barrett Browning

THEODORA: the empress of the east, consort of the Emperor Justinian. In her youth an actress and courtesan in Constantinople, she had retired from the stage and reformed her conduct when she gained the affection of Justinian, who married her in 525 C.E. By 527 he had proclaimed her empress and his equal. Another Theodora, born circa 800, appears in history, but Empress Theodora, born ca. 500, is the one to whom song literature generally refers. (SOURCE: *Americana*, 2003)

THEODOSIUS: a heroic play written by Nathaniel ★Lee, produced in 1680, the first play for which Henry Purcell contributed music. The play opens in a temple of Constantinople during the early Christian era. Emperor Theodosius is obsessed with an unknown ★nymph whom he caught sight of as she bathed in the river. He takes holy orders and abdicates in favor of his sister Pulcheria. The priest Atticus sings an invocation, "Prepare, the Rites Begin." Atticus asks for silence as the emperor's cloistering ceremony begins. Theodosius hopes that the Christian faith will cool his desire for the river nymph. He invites Marina and Flavilia, royal maidens, to join him in his retreat, requesting that they join a convent. Atticus and two other priests ask Marina if she is willing to suffer in order to gain heaven, "Cans't Thou, Marina." Marina sings "The Gate to Bliss Does Open Stand," maintaining that she has no worldly pride. Flavilia, more complacent, sings "What Can Pomp or Glory Do?" The scene concludes act 1 with Atticus's bellicose solo, "Now the Fight's Done." In act 2, Prince Varanes, Theodosius's boyhood friend, loves Athenais, the daughter of a poor philosopher who refuses to allow them to marry, and sings "Sad as Death at the Dead of Night." The gloomy song tells the story of miserable Caelia, whose chastity has almost been taken. The second song, "Dream No More of Pleasures Past," alludes to betrayal: Varanes's surrender of Athenais to Theodosius, Theodosius's abandonment of Marina and Flavilla in act 1, Athenais's betrayal by the emperor, Varanes, and her father, and Varanes's betrayal by Athenais. In act 3, blameless Athenais decides to take vows that will help her escape the enticements of love. At her ceremony Theodosius realizes that his river nymph is Athenais and asks her to be his queen. Again her father insists that she is unworthy, but Theodosius praises her virtue in the song that follows in act 3, "Hail to the Myrtle Shade." In act 4, the emperor, deferring to his friend Varanes, allows Athenais to choose between them. At the end of scene 2, Athenais, after confessing her love for Varanes, agrees to her father's decree that she marry Theodosius at midnight. In act 5, she pretends to ready herself for the wedding, but asks her maid to bring the flute and sing to her. She drinks poison while her maid sings "Ah, Cruel Bloody Fate." As in other Purcell songs for serious plays, written to heighten the drama of a particular moment, this one does not excerpt well. (SOURCE: Price, 1984)

"There's Nothing So Fatal as a Woman": a song composed by Henry Purcell, set to the words of Thomas ★D'Urfey in his comedy *A Fool's Preferment*, produced in 1688. For plot details and placement of songs, *see* ★*Fool's Preferment, A*.

THESEUS: the most important hero of Attica, son of Aegeus and Aethra. Having no children, Aegeus consulted the Delphic oracle, who gave him a cryptic answer. On his return from Delphi, Aegeus stopped to visit a friend, who placed his daughter Aethra in Aegeus's bed that night. After hiding his sword and sandals, Aegeus ordered Aethra that, should she give birth to a son, she was to raise him in secret, to give him the sword and sandals when he was grown, and then send the child to him in

Athens. An unsuccessful war with Crete forced Athens to pay a penalty by sending seven young men and seven young women to Crete each year, to be sacrificed to the Minotaur. Aethra did give birth to Theseus. Once Aethra revealed his parentage to Theseus, he journeyed to Athens. Aegeus had brought *Medea and her son with him from Corinth, and Medea recognized Theseus to be a threat. She persuaded Aegeus to serve Theseus a cup of poisoned wine, but, just in time, Aegeus recognized the sword Theseus carried and realized that this was his son. Theseus helped his father secure the throne of Athens by dealing with a plotting uncle. When the time came to send the fourteen young people to Crete, Theseus volunteered to go and solve the problem. In Crete, Theseus was seen by *Ariadne, who fell in love with him. Theseus agreed with her proposal that they would marry if they could manage to kill the Minotaur with her help. Ariadne gave him a ball of magic thread with which he would mark the path and be able to find his way out of the maze where the Minotaur was kept. Theseus killed the Minotaur and successfully followed the thread out of the labyrinth. He and Ariadne fled to *Naxos where, after one night, he abandoned her and returned to Athens. He succeeded his father as king of Athens and began his series of legendary voyages. (SOURCES: Graves (2), 1960; Mayerson, 1971; *Bulfinch*, 1978)

SONG	COMPOSER	POET
1. "Arianna à Naxos"	Franz Josef Haydn	anonymous
2. "Lamento d'Arianna"	Goffredo Petrassi	Libero di Libero

THETIS: one of the *Nereids. *Zeus was pursuing Thetis unsuccessfully, when he was told about the prophecy of Themis: Thetis's son would become more powerful than his father. Zeus promptly married Thetis off to Peleus, by whom she became the mother of *Achilles. (SOURCE: Kaster, 1964)

SONG	COMPOSER	POET
"Zefiro torna"	Claudio Monteverdi	Francesco Petrarca

"They Tell Us That You Mighty Powers Above": a song composed by Henry Purcell for the tragic extravaganza *The Indian Queen*, written by John *Dryden and Sir Robert Howard, first produced in 1677, then altered in 1695 to include music by Purcell. *See *Indian Queen, The* for plot details and placement of songs.

THOMAS, DYLAN MARLAIS (1914–1953): Welsh poet, writer of prose and short stories. Born in Swansea, son of an English teacher, Thomas began to write poetry while still in school and worked as a journalist before moving to London in 1934. His career went on to include journalism, broadcasting, and film-making, during which time he acquired a reputation for wild living and extravagance both as a poet and as a personality. Thomas's style appealed to a broad audience. His style was widely imitated by his poet colleagues, and soon his popularity extended to radio and lecture engagements. His mature work was often a detailed reworking of early poetry. In 1950 he began to make yearly visits to the United States, doing lecture tours and readings, on the fourth of which he died. The verse of Dylan Thomas has been set by Peter Dickinson and Wallingford Riegger, and Igor Stravinsky wrote

"In Memoriam Dylan Thomas." PRINCIPAL WORKS: *Collected Poems 1934–1952*, 1952; *Deaths and Entrances*, 1946; *Under Milk Wood*, 1958, the work for which he is best known. SELECTED READING: *The Poems of Dylan Thomas*, ed. Daniel Jones, 1971. (SOURCE: Drabble, 2000)

THOMAS the APOSTLE, SAINT: the one who doubted the resurrection of Christ. Ancient tradition has him carrying the faith to India and being martyred near Mylapore. His feast is on December 21. (SOURCE: Nevins, 1964)

SONG	COMPOSER	POET
"Vom Tode Mariae"	Paul Hindemith	Rainer Maria Rilke

THOR: son of ★Odin, the Germanic version of the Indo-European thunder god, hot-tempered, red-headed. Thor's equals were ★Jupiter, ★Zeus, ★Indra, and the Hittite weather god. The arch-enemy of the frost giants, Thor was more like one of the them than the gods, in his strength, his size, his energy, and his huge appetite. His chariot was drawn across the sky by two goats. His three magic weapons were the hammer (a thunderbolt), iron gauntlets, and strength-increasing belt. Thor ruled over thunder and lightning, winds and rain, clear weather and fertility. (SOURCE: Kaster, 1964)

SONG	COMPOSER	POET
"Die betrogene Welt"	Wolfgang Mozart	anonymous

THOREAU, HENRY DAVID (1817–1862): American essayist and naturalist. Thoreau was born and died in Concord, Massachusetts, where his father ran a small pencil manufacturing company. Thoreau was a born naturalist, already collecting specimens at twelve. His earliest journals date from 1834, and the latest was finished just before his death. At sixteen he entered Harvard, where he was an indifferent scholar except for the classics. After the death of his brother and the demise of their private school venture, Thoreau lived with ★Emerson for two years as a disciple and man of all work. In 1845 he built himself a house on Walden Pond where he lived for two years in communion with the birds and animals, producing *A Week on the Concord and Merrimac Rivers*. In 1854, *Walden*, the second and last book to be published in his lifetime, came out. A cold that he caught turned into tuberculosis and he became bedridden, writing voluminously (without seeking publication) or dictating to his sister when he could no longer hold the pencil. Death came before his forty-fifth birthday. Thoreau was a New England countryman who universalized his narrow outlook. A natural rebel, an individualist, a Stoic, an ascetic, he had something fierce about him. His three writing styles were transcendentalist, ecstatic, or humorously reflective. His poetry was once described as "sound and scholarly doggerel with occasional lines of startling beauty" (Kunitz, Haycraft, 1938). Charles Ives set the poetry of Henry David Thoreau. PRINCIPAL WORKS: *A Week on the Concord and Merrimack Rivers*, 1849; *Walden, or, Life in the Woods*, 1854; *Excursions*, 1863; *The Maine Woods*, 1864; *Cape Cod*, 1865. SELECTED READING: Reginald Cook, *Concord Saunterer*, 1985; H. S. Salt, *The Life and Writings of Henry David Thoreau*, 1890. (SOURCE: Kunitz, Haycraft, 1938)

"Thou Doting Fool, Forbear": a song composed by Henry Purcell to a text by John ★Dryden from their semi-opera *King Arthur*, produced in 1691. *See* ★*King Arthur* for plot details and placement of songs.

"Though You Make No Return to My Passion": a song composed by Henry Purcell set to lyrics of Thomas ★Southerne for his play *The Maid's Last Supper*, produced in 1693. For plot details and placement of songs, *see* ★*Maid's Last Prayer, The*.

"Thousand, Thousand Ways, A": an air composed by Henry Purcell to a text written by Elkanah ★Settle for his work *The Fairie-Queene*, produced in 1692 and 1693. For plot details and song placements, *see* ★*Fairie-Queene, The*.

THOUSAND AND ONE NIGHTS, A: *see* ★SHARAZAD.

THRACE: a historic region of the Balkan peninsula, lying partly in Greece, partly in Turkey, and partly in Bulgaria. In antiquity it extended over the eastern part of the Balkan peninsula, bounded on the north by the ★Danube River and on the south by the Aegean Sea. Thracians spoke an Indo-European language. About 700 B.C.E. the Greeks began to colonize the coast of Thrace. The Thracians possessed few cultural refinements but much military prowess.

SONG	COMPOSER	POET
"Hark! Each Tree Its Silence Breaks"	Henry Purcell	Elkanah Settle

THRAE: (Scot.), *through*.

THRENODY: a song of lamentation, especially on a person's death.

"Thrice Happy Lovers": a song composed by Henry Purcell to a text written by Elkanah ★Settle for his work *The Fairie-Queene*, produced in 1692 and 1693. For plot details and placements of songs, *see* ★*Fairie-Queene, The*.

THULE, KING OF: the name given by ancients to an island, or point of land, six days sail from Britain. The location called King of Thule was considered to be the extreme northernmost limit of the world. This name is first found in Polybius's (ca. 150 B.C.E.) account of a voyage made by Pytheas in the late fourth century B.C.E. Pliny wrote, "It is an island in the Northern Ocean discovered by Pytheas, after sailing six days from the Orcades." Some consider it to be Shetland, agreeing with the descriptions of Ptolemy and Tacitus. Others insist that it was some part of the coast of Norway. The etymology of the word is unknown. (SOURCE: Cooper, 1992)

SONG	COMPOSER	POET
1. "Der König in Thule"	Franz Liszt, Johann Reichardt, Franz Schubert, Carl Zelter	Johann Wolfgang von Goethe
2. "Sanglots"	Francis Poulenc	Guillaume Apollinaire

THURINGIA: a 4,540-square-mile historical division of the former East Germany, now one of the sixteen states of Germany, located in the middle of the country, famous for the beautiful Thuringian Forest, a mountain range. The city of Erfurt has now replaced Weimar as the capital city. (SOURCE: *Americana*, 2000)

SONG	COMPOSER	POET
"Biterolf"	Hugo Wolf	Josef Scheffel

THURSDAY ANGELS: referring to French schoolchildren's half-day holiday on Thursday.

SONG	COMPOSER	POET
"Les Anges musiciens"	Francis Poulenc	Guillaume Apollinaire

"Thus the Ever Grateful Spring": an aria composed by Henry Purcell to a text written by Elkanah ★Settle for his work *The Fairie-Queene*, produced in 1692 and 1693. For plot details and song placements, *see* ★*Fairie-Queene, The.*

"Thus the Gloomy World": a song composed by Henry Purcell to a text written by Elkanah ★Settle for his work *The Fairie-Queene*, produced in 1692 and 1693. For plot details and placement of songs, *see* ★*Fairie-Queene, The.*

"Thus to a Ripe and Consenting Maid": a song by Henry Purcell, set to the words of William ★Congreve in his first comedy, *The Old Batchelour*, produced in 1693. For plot details and placement of songs, *see* ★*Old Batchelour, The.*

"Thy Genius, Lo!": a song composed by Henry Purcell to the lyrics of Nathaniel ★Lee written for his play, *The Massacre of Paris*, produced in 1689. For plot details and placement of songs, *see* ★*Massacre of Paris, The.*

THYRSIS: a standard name in pastoral poetry for any shepherd. Thyrsis is mentioned in ★Theocritus's *Idyll 1* (as a shepherd and poet from ★Etna who laments the death of ★Daphnis) and Virgil's *Seventh Bucolic*, in ★Milton's *L'Allegro*, 1638, as the pastoral singer who sings a lament for Daphnis. Thyrsis is acclaimed as having "brought to perfection the bucolic art." Thyrsis is also the name of the Attendant Spirit in ★Matthew Arnold's *Comus*, in ★Robert Herrick's *A Bucolic Betwixt Two: Lacon and Thyrsis,* in ★Tasso's *Aminta*, wherein Tasso portrayed himself as Thyrsis. (SOURCE: Benét, 1965)

SONG	COMPOSER	POET
1. "Die Spröde"	Hugo Wolf, Edmund Nick	Johann Wolfgang von Goethe
2. "Tell Me, Thyrsis"	Paul Nordoff	John Dryden
3. "An Thyrsis"	Franz Josef Haydn	Marianne von Ziegler

TICHBORNE, CHIDIOCK (1558–1586): English poet. Very little is known about Tichborne except that he wrote his poem "Lament" on the eve of his execution. Tichborne had been imprisoned in the Tower of London and sentenced to be executed after being implicated in a Catholic plot against Queen Elizabeth. Although only three of his poems were preserved in manuscripts, his verse has been set by Norman dello Joio and David Diamond. (SOURCE: Drabble, 2000)

TIECK, JOHANN LUDWIG (1773–1853): German poet, novelist, and critic. Johann Tieck, son of a rope maker, read voraciously by the age of five. His career as a writer began very early, when one of his teachers who wrote horror stories let Johann write the final chapters of his works. His brilliant talent as an actor was squelched by his father, who sent him to the universities of Halle, Göttingen, and Erlangen, where he acquired a knowledge of European literature and turned his attention to Elizabethan authors. On one of his journeys, he became acquainted with the scenery of southeast Germany, which he used later for his romantic tales. Upon his return to Berlin, a publisher hired Tieck as a hack writer for adaptations of French light novels to the taste of the German public. It was here that he developed his skills as a humorist. Being subject to visions and periods of depression and inclined toward the weird and horrifying led him to writing folk tales. The artist's life was glorified by Tieck as the only one worth living. Moving to Dresden, his life soon revolved around his dramatic readings of *Shakespeare. *Phantasus*, the work that brought him his greatest fame (1812–16), was a collection of poetry, dramas, tales, connected by long conversations. Tieck's work as a drama critic, editor, and translator was important, but when he died, he was forgotten. Some of Tieck's shorter tales have been translated into English. Mendelssohn, Weber, Schubert, Carl Zelter, Ildebrando Pizzetti, and Louise Reichardt set his poetry, and Brahms set his verse in the *Magelone Lieder* (*see Magelone Lieder* for the text of the narration). SELECTED READING: James Trainer, *Ludwig Tieck: From Gothic to Romantic*, 1964; E. H. Zeydel, *Ludwig Tieck, the German Romanticist*, 1935. (SOURCE: Kunitz, Colby, 1967)

TIEDGE, CHRISTOPH (1752–1841): German poet. Educated at Halle and Magdeburg, Tiedge made his living as a tutor and secretary until 1804, when he accompanied the Countess Elisa von der Recke, a poet herself, on a tour of Italy. He and the countess lived together from 1819 until her death. Tiedge's several philosophical poems enjoyed considerable success in his lifetime, but his writings have since fallen into oblivion. Beethoven, Clara Schumann, and Václav Momášek set his verses, and Schubert set his poem "An die Sonne." (SOURCE: Reed, 1997)

TIGRIS: the principal stream of the Shatt al-Arab river system in the Middle East. The Tigris is 1,270 miles long. Its drainage basin includes Turkey, Iran, and Iraq. In Iraq the flood plain of the Tigris forms part of the ancient region called Mesopotamia, the cradle of civilization in the Middle East and the site of the great Sumerian, Babylonian, and Assyrian states. The Tigris rises in east central Turkey and flows through the plain, joins the *Euphrates above Basra, and forms the Shatt al-Arab, which flows into the Persian Gulf.

SONG	COMPOSER	POET
"May the Tigris and Euphrates"	George Rochberg	Ancient Sumerian texts

TILBURY: a light, two-wheeled carriage intended for two people. It is this conveyance to which Georges Auric refers in his song, "Le Tilbury."

TIMON OF ATHENS: a drama by *Shakespeare, probably in collaboration with Middleton, thought to be written about 1607, and left unfinished. Adapted by Louis Grabon in 1678, it was later revived in an adaptation by Thomas *Shadwell and produced in 1693, which version had music by Henry Purcell. Its main purpose was to attack the late seventeenth-century moral code. Both Shakespeare and Shadwell endeavor to show good-natured Timon squandering his wealth on false friends. Shadwell supplies a new subplot in which Timon is anxious to marry beautiful, vain, and mercenary Melissa, but hesitates to cast aside his former lover, plain and faithful Evandra. Shadwell's act 2 *masque (a play within a play), for which Purcell wrote all the music, functions as a way to bring two themes together: hedonism versus stoicism and platonic love versus sex and passion. The Masque of *Cupid and *Bacchus occupies the center of the drama. It opens with the sound of twittering birds followed by a group of nymphs and shepherds praising the power of love. This pastoral scene is interrupted by revelers who come to ridicule and are answered aggressively by the nymphs. The debate is settled when Bacchus and Cupid enter to proclaim a truce. Price suggests that the allegory is clear: Bacchus represents Melissa and Timon's pleasure-loving side; Cupid is Evandra, kind and loving. Extolling the pleasures of the grove, two nymphs sing the opening duet, "Hark How the Songsters." (In the 1695 production Cupid sings as a solo the duet formerly sung by two nymphs.) "Love in Their Little Veins" is a treble solo aria and dissonance-free, unusual from Purcell at this time. Bacchus sings a boisterous love song set with obligato oboes and containing many sneering chromatics, "Hence! With Your Trifling Deity." Cupid sings two solos, "Come All, Come All to Me" and "The Cares of Lovers." A solo for an alto reveler and a duet for Cupid and Bacchus with chorus end the masque. (SOURCE: Price, 1984)

TIMOTHEUS: *see* *CHARON.

TINE: (Scot.), *lose, suffer loss*; *lost*.

TIPPET: an old-fashioned word for a woman's shoulder cape.

SONG	COMPOSER	POET
"Because I Could Not Stop for Death"	Sergius Kagen	Emily Dickinson

TIRANA: an Andalusian dance in 6/8 time usually accompanied by the guitar. The man dances while waving his hat or handkerchief and the woman waves her apron. Generally, the words took the form of four-line *coplas. (SOURCE: Cockburn, Stokes, 1992)

SONG	COMPOSER	POET
"El trípili"	Blas de Laserna	anonymous

TIRCIS: the French spelling of the stock character from the classical pastoral drama or poem. Tircis is a young handsome lover, probably the French version of the young lover in the *Commedia dell'Arte* mentioned in Lully's *Acis and *Galatea*, Molière's *The Imaginary Invalid*, and *La Fontaine's *Fables*, appearing in Watteau's paintings with his companions *Aminte, *Clitandre, and *Damis. (SOURCE: Bernac, 1970)

SONG	COMPOSER	POET
1. "Mandoline"	Claude Debussy, Gabriel Fauré	Paul Verlaine
2. "Clair de lune"	Gabriel Fauré	Paul Verlaine
3. "Canzonetta VI"	J. C. Bach	anonymous

TIRSIS: *see* ★TIRCIS.

TIRSO DE MOLINA (pseudonym for Gabriel Téllez) (1583–1648): Spanish poet and dramatist. As one of the three great Golden Age dramatists, together with Lope de ★Vega and ★Calderón de la Barca, Tirso de Molina wrote in a style more like Vega. Little is known about Tirso de Molina's early life, but the speculation is that he was of aristocratic but illegitimate birth. He studied at the University of Alacalá de Henares and entered the order of friars about 1600. While living in Toledo he met Lope de Vega and saw the opening of his own play there in 1615. Then he was sent to Hispaniola for two years, after which he returned to Madrid and entered that exciting life. His criticism of the nobility and government caused him to be banished in 1626 to the backwater of Trujillo. In 1632 he was named the historian of his Mercedarian order, during which period he wrote 400 plays. His greatest work, *The Trickster of Seville* (the first appearance of Don Juan), was published in 1630. Tirso's genius lay in his ability to put a real face upon the abstract concepts of free will and predestination. In 1633 he wrote *Prudence in Women*, which featured a strong woman and psychological realism. Tirso openly attacked corruption, political intrigue, and stupidity, but he was to be repaid for this by never being able to return to Madrid. His dramas had fewer performances, and he died in oblivion until reappraised as a writer at the beginning of the nineteenth century. The work of Tirso de Molina was set into music by Gustav Mahler. PRINCIPAL WORKS: *La Prudencia in mujer* [Prudence in Women], 1634; *El Burlador de Sevilla* [The Trickster of Seville], 1630; *Don Gil de las calzas verdes* [Don Juan of the Green Stockings], 1635. SELECTED READING: Barbara L. Mújica, Sharon D. Voros, and Matthew D. Stroud, eds., *Looking at the Comedia in the Year of the Quincentennial*, 1993. (SOURCE: Magill, 5, 1997)

TISIPHONE: the worst of the three ★Furies who punish those sent to ★Hades. In the infernal regions Aeneas saw Tisiphone apply her whip of scorpions to offenders whose guilt had not been revealed during their life on earth. (SOURCE: *Bulfinch*, 1978)

SONG	COMPOSER	POET
"A Charm"	Benjamin Britten	Thomas Randolph

TITANS: the six male and six female children of Heaven and Earth (Ouranos and Gaia). The Titans were eventually conquered by the Olympian gods led by ★Zeus, after which they were banished to ★Tartarus, where they were imprisoned at the bottom of a pit. The six male Titans were: Oceanus, Coesus, Crius, ★Hyperion, Iapetus, and ★Chronos (the father of Zeus). The six female Titans were: Theia, Rhea, Themis, Mnemosyne (the mother of the Graces), Phoebe, and Tethys. (SOURCES: Mayerson, 1971; *Bulfinch*, 1978)

SONG	COMPOSER	POET
1. "Prometheus"	Hugo Wolf, Franz Schubert, Johann Reichardt	Johann Wolfgang von Goethe
2. "Ihr, ihr Herrlichen!"	Max Reger	Friedrich Hölderlin
3. "Who Is Silvia?"	Gerald Finzi	William Shakespeare

TIT FOR TAT: an equivalent given in retaliation for an injury, from the Dutch *dit vor dat* (this for that), in French *tant pour tant*; also, the title of the last song and the song cycle by Benjamin Britten with texts by Walter ★de la Mare. The work is composed of five songs selected by Britten from his own early vocal compositions. In the preface to the musical score, Britten explains how he, as a middle-aged professional, came to the aid of himself as a boy when he found that his inexperienced compositorial fumbling needed repair. "I do feel [however] that the boy's vision has a simplicity and clarity which might have given a little pleasure to the great poet, with his unique insight into a child's mind." (SOURCE: Carpenter, 1992)

TOD: (Scot.) (pr. toad), *sly cunning person; fox; also cake or scone.*

SONG	COMPOSER	POET
"My Hoggie"	Benjamin Britten	Robert Burns

TOLEDO: a Spanish city located 41 miles southwest of Madrid. The Tagus River flows in a deep ravine at the base of the hill on which Toledo stands. A gloomy medieval city with architecture influenced by the Moors, it was El Greco's native city. Under King Alfonso, Toledo was the capital of Spain, but in 1561 Philip II made Madrid the capital. Toledo is renowned for the sabers and firearms made of its famous inlaid steel.

SONG	COMPOSER	POET
"Der Hidalgo"	Robert Schumann	Emanuel Geibel

TOLSTOI, COUNT LEV (1828–1910): Russian prose writer. Born in Central Russia, Tolstoi served in the army and took part in the Crimean War. The next decade was occupied with the creation of *War and Peace* (1865–69), an epic novel of the Napoleonic invasion. *Anna Karenina*, published in 1875, was next. Tolstoi's concern with moral questions led him to real changes in his life. His moral positions involved the lack of resistance to evil, renunciation of property, and abolition of government and churches. Yet he was not a disbeliever in God. As a result of his beliefs and his writing, he was excommunicated by the Church and his works were banned. His English reputation was furthered by the support of writers such as Matthew ★Arnold, George Bernard Shaw, John Galsworthy, E. M. Forster, and D. H. ★Lawrence. The work of Count Lev Tolstoi was set to music by Rimsky-Korsakov, Mussorgsky, Tchaikovsky, Rachmaninoff, Borodin, Hermann Reutter, Anton Arensky, César Cui, and Aleksandr Gretchaninov. PRINCIPAL WORKS: *Childhood*, 1852; *Boyhood*, 1854; *Youth*, 1857; *Sevastopol Sketches*, 1855–56; *The Cossacks*, 1863, Eng. trans. 1878, 1880; *War and Peace*, 1865–67; *Anna Karenina*, 1875–78; *The Death of Ivan Ilyich*, 1886; *The Kreutzer Sonata*, 1891; *Master and Man*, 1895; *Resurrection*, 1899; *Hadji Murad*, 1912; *Collected Works*, 1899–1902. (SOURCE: Drabble, 2000)

TOMMASEO, NICCOLÒ (1802–1874): Italian scholar and writer. Tommaseo was an important literary and political figure in his time. As a radical Catholic, he hoped for the spiritual regeneration of society. His life was characterized by a mix of sensuality and spirituality. The vast and varied output of his lyric and narrative poems was sometimes forced in style. Tommaseo was perhaps best known for his translations of Latin poets and the Bible, as well as of folk poetry. Some of the latter, especially translations from the Greek, were set by Ildebrando Pizzetti, for example, "San Basilio." PRINCIPAL WORKS: *Canti populari toscani, corsi, illirici, greci,* 1841–42. (SOURCE: Steinberg, 3, 1973)

TOM O'BEDLAM: a beggar who asks charity on a plea of insanity. In the sixteenth and seventeenth centuries many inmates of *Bedlam were dismissed due to over-crowded conditions. These half-crazed people, often dressed in fantastic costumes to excite pity, wandered about singing mad songs.

TOM THE RHYMER: a Scottish poet who flourished between 1250 and 1300, whose reputation was that of a prophet.

SONG	COMPOSER	POET
"Tom der Reimer"	Carl Loewe	Theodor Fontane

TONADILLA: one of the generic names for Spanish song that evolved as a diminutive of *tonada.* Tonadillas started to become popular in 1750 as entr'acte entertainments performed by two to four singing actors between the acts of a play. Songs, dialogue, and dancing were featured. Always satirical and topical, with a life span of two or three weeks, they brought on to the stage popular types—swashbucklers, ladies of ill repute, gypsies, muleteers, smugglers, and so on. Some 2,000 works of this type are preserved in the National Library of Madrid. Characteristic of the tonadilla are: the predominance of a short/long (iambic) foot in the concluding notes (a feminine cadence); a melodic structure with many disjunct intervals based on a chordal formation; a tendency to ornament some melodic notes by turning them into triplets. The vogue of the tonadilla, beginning to decline after 1790, disappeared with the Napoleonic invasion of Spain. During those years Manuel García arrived in Madrid and produced his *El Majo y la Maja,* which exploited Andalusian popular songs and dances. The operettas that he later wrote supplied Bizet with some of his principal themes for *Carmen.* (SOURCE: Chase, 1959)

TONNEAU: *See* *JEU DE TONNEAU.

TOPELIUS, ZACHARIAS (1818–1898): a Swedish poet, novelist, dramatist, and short-story writer. Topelius was born in Finland; his father was a district doctor. Topelius started his successful academic career with a Ph.D. from the University of Helsinki. This was followed by a professorship in Finnish history, ending with an appointment as president of the university from 1875 to 1878, when he retired and was given the title of state secretary. Topelius's early poems and prose were published in a semi-weekly newspaper of which he was the editor. Between 1845 and 1889 he published five collections of lyrics in book form, the first and best of which were the three titled *Ljungblommer* (Heath Blossoms). Topelius's lyrics were tuneful and sweet, their form simple and pure, inspired by Finnish folk poetry. His patriotic nationalism and naive piety made him a popular and fascinating storyteller. *Fältskärns Berättelser* (The Surgeon's Stories) was Topelius's best prose work, a charming account of the Swedish/Finnish history in the seventeenth and eighteenth centuries. In later years Topelius wrote primarily for children, including four volumes of fairy tales. His poetry was set by Agathe Backer-Gröndahl. WORKS: *Sagor* [Fairy Tales from Finland], 1847–52, trans. C. W. Foss, 1896; *Fältskärns Berättelser*, trans. Selma Borg, 1872. (SOURCE: Kunitz, Colby, 1967)

TOR: a craggy hill.

SONG	COMPOSER	POET
"Ariel"	Ned Rorem	Sylvia Plath

TOREADOR: a bullfighter.

SONG	COMPOSER	POET
"Toréador"	Francis Poulenc	Jean Cocteau

TORO: a city in the Zamora province of western Spain. In the northeastern corner Spain's border with Portugal is formed by the Duero River. As it flows from west to east it cuts Zamoro into two parts, the southern part being called Tierra de Vino (land of wine). Since the Middle Ages, the wines of Toro have been the most prestigious of the province—red, fruity, and robust. The city of Toro is no longer an important one, but was prominent in the eleventh century and later. Juana la Beltraneja challenged Isabel la Católica for the throne of Castile and, with her husband Alfonso V of Portugal, established her court here. The Battle of Toro then established Isabel as the legitimate heir. When in 1505 Fernando el Católico proclaimed his daughter Juana la Loca the queen of Castile, Toro became the seat of the royal court and remained so for some time. (SOURCE: Casas, 1996)

SONG	COMPOSER	POET
"Non vayas, Gil, al sotillo"	Amadeus Vives	Luís de Góngora

TRAFALGAR SQUARE: London's "living room," alive with people and roaring with traffic, commanding an open space that contains the National Gallery, street performers, and the 145-foot-high column that commemorates Admiral Lord Horatio Nelson.

SONG	COMPOSER	POET
"Euphonium Dance"	Betty Roe	Jacqueline Froom

TRAKL, GEORG (1887–1914): Austrian poet and playwright. In Salzburg, where he was born, Trakl took a degree in pharmacology (1910). His earliest poems were written late in the first decade of the twentieth century. Depressed while serving as pharmacist in the military, Trakl tried to find solace in drugs, to which he had easy access. His gruesome experiences as a lieutenant in the medical corps gave him a nervous breakdown. Sent to Krakow for psychiatric care, he died there from an overdose of cocaine. Together with Georg *Heym and Gottfried *Benn, Georg Trakl was one of the major poets of German literary *Expressionism and is today ranked as one of the outstanding poets of the early twentieth century. He developed his heritage of *Romanticism and French *Symbolism into a personal poetic style that was influenced by the significant stylistic and philosophic features of his fellow writers, among whom was *Rilke, an admirer. During the three periods of Trakl's writing, his poetic expression of the actual world changed into free rhythms, lack of rhyme, and a visionary style. The poetry of Georg Trakl was set by Paul Hindemith.

PRINCIPAL WORKS: *Aus goldenem Kelch*, 1939; *Gesammelte Werke*, 3 vols., 1949–51; *Decline: 12 Poems,* 1952; *20 Poems of Georg Trakl*, 1961; *Selected Poems*, 1969; *Dichtungen u. Briefe* [Poems and Letters], 1969; *Poems*, 1973. SELECTED READING: Francis Michael Sharp, *The Poet's Madness: A Reading of Georg Trakl*, 1981. (SOURCE: Magill, 4, 1984)

TRANSCENDENTALISM: a movement of thought—philosophical, religious, social, and economic—that grew up in New England between 1830 and 1850, inspired by the spirit of a revolutionary Europe. These philosophical views are represented in Emerson's short treatise, *Nature* (1836).

TREPAK: a Russian folk dance in duple time with heavy accents, originating among the Cossacks.

SONG	COMPOSER	POET
"Trepak"	Modest Mussorgsky	Arsenyi Golenishchev-Kutúzov

TRILLO Y FIGEROA, FRANCISCO DE (?1615–?1665): Spanish poet. Trillo y Figeroa, writing in light verse, was an imitator of ★Góngora. His verses were set by Amadeo Vives. PRINCIPAL WORKS: *Poesías varias, heróicas, satíricas y amorosas*, 1652. (SOURCE: Steinberg, 3, 1973)

TRINITY: a central doctrine of the Catholic Church, the three persons in one God: the Father, the Son, and the Holy Spirit. The doctrine of the Holy Trinity states that each of these persons is distinct from the others, yet each is the true God with all of the infinite perfections. (SOURCE: Nevins, 1964)

SONG	COMPOSER	POET
"Hymne"	Francis Poulenc	Jean Racine

TRÍPILI: an ancient Spanish song and dance.

SONG	COMPOSER	POET
"El Trípili"	Blas de Laserno	anonymous

TRISTAN L'HERMITE (ÉDOUARD LALO) (1601–1655): French poet and dramatist. Tristan L'Hermite, always correctly referred to by the entire name, was born in the province of La Marche. He was named after King Louis XI's adviser of that name and claimed him as a relation. While he was a page in the court of Henry IV, he was involved in a duel and was forced to flee to England. From his youth Tristan L'Hermite was a rake, addicted to gaming and women. He returned to France under the patronage of the Duke d'Orléans and became established as a writer. Elected to the Académie Française in 1649, he died seven years later in Paris, having become a close friend of the young Molière. He was best known for his plays, of which *Marianne* had its first performance in 1648, enjoying quite as much popularity as ★Corneille's *Le Cid*, the first performance of which took place the same year. Tristan L'Hermite's poetry, in the form of ★odes, madrigals, ★sonnets, ★epigrams, prayers, and ★hymns, showing a gift for picturesque, delicate images, was set by Claude Debussy, who appreciated his musicality of language and the combination of great sensuality with the utmost refinement. PRINCIPAL WORKS: Plays:

Penthée, 1637; *Marianne*, 1648; *Le Parasite*, 1653. Poetry: *Les Amours de Tristan*, 1638; *Les Vers heroïques*, 1648. Romance: *Le Page disgracié*, 1643. (SOURCE: Americana, 2003)

"Triumphant, Victorious Love": a song from the 1690 semi-opera *Dioclesian* with music solely by Henry Purcell, written to the words of Massinger and ★Fletcher. For plot details and placement of songs, *see* ★*Dioclesian.*

TROILUS AND CRESSIDA: Troilus, mentioned by Homer in *The Iliad*, was the son of ★Priam, who was killed before the epic begins. The name Cressida was created by the medieval storytellers, who fused the name of Chryseis (who was surrendered by ★Agamemnon to her father) with the name of Briseis (who was a slave girl taken from ★Achilles). There are many versions of the story written by ★Boccaccio, ★Chaucer, ★Dryden, Walter ★de la Mare, and ★Shakespeare (in which Troilus was infatuated and Cressida sensual as well as selfish). (SOURCE: Steinberg, 1, 1973)

TROUBADOURS: poet musicians of Provence in the eleventh, twelfth, and thirteenth centuries, who wrote short poems celebrating chivalry and the traditions of courtly love. Two of the leading troubadours, Bertran de Born and Bernard de Ventadorn, were received at the court of Eleanor of Aquitaine. It was through her influence that Provençal poetry was introduced at the courts of northern France, after which its emphasis on romantic love began to influence the verse epics written there.

TROUVÈRES: medieval poets of northern France in the late twelfth century, whose language was that of the Isle de France. They wrote principally narrative poems and shorter lyrics, somewhat influenced by the Provençal poetry of the ★troubadours.

TROY: in ★Homer's *Iliad*, a fortress city in the extreme northwest corner of Asia Minor, overlooking the strait of the Dardanelles; also the land of Troy with Ilium as the chief city. (SOURCE: Cooper, 1992)

SONG	COMPOSER	POET
"Andromache's Farewell"	Samuel Barber	Euripides

TRUEBA, ANTONIO DE (1819–1889): Basque poet, short-story writer, and novelist. Trueba was born in Biscay, and his works, written in Spanish, dealt often with his Basque countryside. In Biscay, once he had published *El libro de los cantares* (1851), he was titled "Antón el de los cantares." This book celebrated in simplest language the customs and life of his native Basque land. He is known primarily as a short-story writer, but the poetry of Antonio de Trueba was set by Manuel de Falla. (SOURCE: Cockburn, Stokes, 1992)

TSARSKOYE SELO: the village near St. Petersburg where the Tsar's summer palace was located.

SONG	COMPOSER	POET
"The Statue at Tsarskoye Selo"	César Cui	Alexandr Pushkin

"Turn Then Thy Eyes": a duet composed by Henry Purcell to a text written by Elkanah ★Settle for his work *The Fairie-Queene*, produced in 1692 and 1693. For plot details and placement of songs, *see* ★*Fairie-Queene, The.*

TWA CORBIES: (Scot.), *two ravens*, a famous Scottish poem.

SONG	COMPOSER	POET
"Twa Corbies"	Frederick Ayres	anonymous

"'Twas within a Furlong of Edinboro' Town": a song composed, probably, by Henry Purcell to a text written by Thomas Scott for his comedy *The Mock Marriage*, produced in 1695. For plot details and placement of songs, *see* ★*Mock Marriage, The.*

"Two Daughters of This Aged Stream Are We": a duet composed by Henry Purcell to a text by John ★Dryden, from their semi-opera *King Arthur*, produced in 1691. For plot details and placement of songs, *see* ★*King Arthur.*

TYNDAREUS: a legendary king of Sparta and the husband of Leda, who became the mother of ★Castor, ★Pollux, ★Helen, and Clytemnestra. According to one tradition, Leda, who was loved by ★Zeus in the form of a swan, laid an egg in which were all four children. Another tradition had it that Leda was embraced by both Zeus and Tyndareus during the same night and that Pollux and Helen were the children of Zeus and born from the egg, while Castor and Clytemnestra were the children of Tyndareus. (SOURCE: Kaster, 1964)

TYRANNICK LOVE; OR, THE ROYAL MARTYR: a heroic play by John ★Dryden, produced in 1669, containing music by Henry Purcell. The play is based primarily on the Roman emperor Maximian's cruelty to subjects and family alike in a mad resistance to rebellion, and secondarily on the legend of the martyrdom of St. Catherine by Maximian. It contains some of Dryden's most extravagant heroic verse, later ridiculed by ★Shadwell and by Dryden himself. The play had an elaborate production, featuring a showy destruction of a wheel of torture in act 5. The emperor is enamored of an unreceptive St. Catherine, attracted by her power to convert all nonbelievers, but fearful that he might fall under her influence.

TYUTCHEV, FYODOR (1803–1873): Russian lyric poet and essayist. The younger son in a noble family, Fyodor Tyutchev had an his overdeveloped imagination that was the basic element of his nervous, high-strung, creative personality. He was educated in the French language, spoke French all his life, and wrote letters and his prose in French. In 1818 Tyutchev entered Moscow University at the age of fourteen, in the same year that his translation from ★Horace was published by the Moscow Society of Lovers of Russian Literature. After his graduation at eighteen (1821), he took a position in the Foreign Office. During the next twenty years, he was given various diplomatic posts in Munich, where he cultivated German literati like ★Heine, whose works he then translated into Russian. Forty of his lyrics were published between 1836 and 1838 in ★Pushkin's periodical, *Contemporary*. About 1839 he was transferred to Turin in Italy. Homesick for Munich, he took an unauthorized leave, causing him to be discharged. In 1844 his article about Russia and Germany showed so much expertise that he was called back to St. Petersburg, where he spent the rest of his life in various high posts in government, was given many decorations, and frequented the best society of his day. In 1854, *Contemporary* published ninety-six of his poems. He was much admired by Turgenev. His poetry, 400 poems that range from perverse joy in destruction to a sublime desire to be "diffused in the slumbering universe," is notable for its delicacy and for its profound analysis of man's position in nature. The lyrics of Tyutchev, master of the Russian literary High Style, have been set to music by Rachmaninoff, Medtner, Rimsky-Korsakov, and Mayaskovsky. Two editions of his poetical works have appeared in Russia, and V. Nabokov translated some of his lyrics, to be found in *Three Russian Poets*, 1944. (SOURCE: Kunitz, Colby, 1967; Drabble, 2000)

U ✆

UGLY DUCKLING, THE: a fairy tale by Hans Christian ★Andersen about a swan hatched among ducklings and mocked as an ungainly member of the brood until it becomes apparent that he is a swan. Scholars believe that the story of the Ugly Duckling is intended to mirror the life of Danish writer Søren ★Kiekegaard, the father of existentialism. Kierkegaard, a short and extremely homely man—the ugly duckling—by his spiritual growth and philosophical writings was metamorphosed into a beautiful swan.

SONG	COMPOSER	POET
"The Ugly Duckling"	Sergei Prokofiev	Hans Christian Andersen

UHLAND, JOHANN LUDWIG (1787–1862): German poet, medievalist, philologist, and politician. Uhland was born in Tübingen and studied at the university there, where his grandfather was professor of theology and his father was the secretary. After receiving his doctorate in 1810, Uhland went to Paris to study French legal institutions, but he also did an original investigation of the Old French epic. As he started to practice law privately, having found a government post contrary to his liberal principles, his first book of poetry was published (1815). He wrote political poems that spoke of the constitutional struggle of the World Parliament and became a university lecturer in German language and literature (1829). Today he is best known as the chief representative of the Swabian school of poets, who sang of their native landscape. Uhland's forte was the ★ballad, often in the form of dialogue, with close connections to the Old German language, legends, and poetry. In a mix of strength and melancholy his poetry transformed everything personal into an experience that was shared by everyone. His *Wanderlieder* inspired Wilhelm ★Müller (Schubert's poet) to write his own. The poetry of Johann Uhland was set by Mendelssohn, Brahms, Fanny Mendelssohn Hensel, Max Reger, Edvard Grieg, and Carl Loewe, and Schubert set the well-known "Frühlingsglaube." PRINCIPAL WORKS: *The Poems of Uhland*, trans. William Collett Sandars, 1869. (SOURCE: Kunitz, Colby, 1967)

ULSTER: the name of the most northerly of Ireland's four provinces.

ULSTER CYCLE: a group of pagan sagas or romances from medieval manuscripts of Gaelic literature. Legendary heroes of ★Ulster are depicted, among them King Conchobar, Medb and Ailill, Fergus, ★Deidre, and Cu Chulainn. (SOURCE: *OED*, 1989)

ULYSSES, ULYSSE (Fr.): the Roman name for Odysseus, a mythical king of Ithaca. ★Homer's epic poem *The Odyssey* recounts the ten-year voyage of Odysseus during his years of wandering after the fall of ★Troy, his eventual return to Ithaca, a small rocky Greek island, and his killing of the suitors of his faithful wife Penelope. His adventures include encounters with the ★Cyclops, ★Circe, the Lotus Eaters, and the ★Sirens. He is represented as wise, eloquent, and full of artifice. Any long, adventurous journey can be described as an odyssey. (SOURCE: Cooper, 1992)

SONG	COMPOSER	POET
"Le Chant d'Euryclée"	Charles Gounod	François Ponsard

ULYSSES: a novel by James ★Joyce. By the time Joyce was writing *Ulysses* (1922), his style had become heavily weighted with symbolic and mythic content and the stream of consciousness technique. His characters are linked with various personages in Homeric mythology. In *Ulysses* Stephen Dedalus, a proud and sensitive Irishman, searches for the meaning of life. History is a nightmare from which he is trying to awake. He has known only poverty, and his religion is more a disturbance than a comfort. In a mythological parallel, Stephen is Telemachus, the son in search of a father. He finds a symbolic father in Leopold Bloom, an elderly Jewish advertising salesman (★Ulysses). Bloom takes Stephen into his home after the young man has been in a street fight with British soldiers. Bloom's wife, Molly, a sensual creature, is unfaithful to her patient husband and finds release in affairs with other men. In chapter 17 Stephen constructs the words of the Samuel Barber "Solitary Hotel," which suggests the clandestine affairs of Molly Bloom.

UNGARETTI, GIUSEPPE (1888–1970): Italian poet, journalist, editor, travel writer, and translator. Ungaretti was born in Alexandria, Egypt, and educated there and at the Sorbonne in Paris. He served in the Italian army infantry (1915–18) in both Italy and France, then worked as the Paris correspondent for an Italian paper before being named journalist for the Ministry of Foreign Affairs in Rome (1921–30). Ungaretti's teaching positions, as a professor of Italian literature, were in São Paulo, Brazil, the University of Rome, Columbia University, and Harvard University (1936–68); he won many poetry prizes and was decorated often. He and ★Montale were linked together as the most important modern Italian poets, although there was no fundamental affinity between the two, and Montale's influence was greater. Original in his verse was Ungaretti's epigrammatic and graphic imagery. Its subject was psychological innocence. He boldly discarded punctuation, traditional syntax, and meter; he introduced pauses, blank spaces, as he called them; his themes were mourning and love. The poetry of Giuseppe Ungaretti was set by Ildebrando Pizzetti and Alberto Peyretti. PRINCIPAL WORKS: *The Promised Land and Other Poems: An Anthology of Four Contemporary Poets*, ed. Sergio Pacifici, 1957; *Life of a Man*, ed.

and trans. Allen Mandelbaum, 1958, as *Selected Poems*, 1975; *Selected Poems*, ed. Patrick Creagh, 1971. SELECTED READING: Glauco Cambon, *Ungaretti*, 1967; Frederic J. Jones, *Ungaretti, Poet and Critic*, 1977. (SOURCE: Vinson, Kirkpatrick (2), 1984; Hainsworth, Robbey, 2002)

UNICORN: a mythological creature, probably based on descriptions of a rhinoceros, usually represented as having the body and head of a horse and a single horn in the center of its head. From the Latin: *unus* (one) and *cornu* (horn). A twelfth-century *bestiary describes the unicorn as a "very small animal like a kid, excessively swift, with one horn in the middle of his forehead; no hunter can catch him" (White, 1960). According to the Greek historian and physician Ctesias (400 B.C.E.), the unicorn is a type of wild ass from India. Its body is white, its head purple, with blue eyes. In the middle of its forehead is a pointed horn. The tip of this horn is red, the base is white, and the middle black. The *narwhal* horn, really a tooth, was considered a unicorn horn, thus lending credence to the stories of its existence. A narwhal horn was the accepted type of unicorn horn in England, because of its white color and its unyielding substance. Pliny describes the unicorn in this way: "The body resembles a horse, but in the head a stag, in the feet an elephant, and in the tail a boar, and has a deep bellow, and a single black horn three feet long projecting from the middle of the forehead. . . . His horn is as hard as iron and as rough as any file, twisted and curled like a flaming sword; very straight, sharp and everywhere black, excepting the point" (Graves, 1948). A famous series of French tapestries in the *Cloisters in New York City depicts the hunting and capture of a unicorn. According to White (1960), the unicorn can be caught when "a virgin girl is led to where he lurks, and there she is sent off by herself into the wood. He soon leaps into her lap when he sees her, and embraces her, and hence he gets caught." The fact that only a Virgin could lure the unicorn into her lap illustrates the virgin birth. The unicorn is said to be symbolic of *Christ. The single horn on its forehead, illustrates *Jesus' statement that he and God were one. Its swiftness reveals Christ's power over death and the devil, who could not capture him. The smallness of the creature represents the humbleness of Christ, while the similarities of its appearance to that of a kid symbolize Christ's sacrifice for mankind. The legend that appears in several passages of the King James version of the Bible, stating that the unicorn is extinct because it could not get to Noah's ship in time to be spared from the flood, should not be construed as an example of the credulity of biblical authors. It is, rather, a mistranslation of the Hebrew word *reem,* which probably should have been rendered buffalo or some such two-horned animal. (SOURCES: Hathaway, 1980; White, 1960; Graves, 1948; Borges, 1969)

SONG	COMPOSER	POET
"The Unicorn"	John Corigliano	William Hoffman

UNTERMEYER, LOUIS (1885–1978): American poet, novelist, anthologist, and translator. Untermeyer's father was a jewelry manufacturer in New York. Young Untermeyer's first passion was to be a concert pianist, but, recognizing his insufficient talent, he joined his father's business and devoted his evenings to art. From 1923 on Untermeyer spent all his time writing, editing, and lecturing. Although he wrote twenty-five original books of verse, this famous and one-time influential anthologist attracted most praise for collecting and publishing the best available anthologies of American poetry. For the general reader the anthologies are truly eclectic. They give useful selections from interesting poets who are otherwise difficult to access. Untermeyer's knowledge of modern poetry was extensive. The best of his own poetry consists of enjoyable and sharp *parodies. The rest of his poetic output is influenced most by *Heine, many of whose poems Untermeyer translated. His verse has been set by Charles Ives and A. Walter Kramer. PRINCIPLE WORKS: *Collected Parodies*, 1926; *Poetry—Its Appreciation and Enjoyment*, with H. Carter Davison, 1934; *From Another World*, 1935; *Heinrich Heine—Paradox and Poet*, 1937; *The Wonderful Adventures of Paul Bunyan; Now Retold*, 1945; *Long Feud: Selected Poems*, 1962. (SOURCE: Hamilton, 1994)

URANIA: the Greek muse of astronomy, usually represented with a globe.

SONG	COMPOSER	POET
"Uranians Flucht"	Franz Schubert	Johann Mayrhofer

URICON: the Roman town Uriconium on the site of the modern town Wroxeter in Shropshire, England. (SOURCE: *Norton,* 1996)

SONG	COMPOSER	POET
"On Wenlock Edge"	Ralph Vaughan Williams	A. E. Housman

USHAS: one of the selections in Gustav Holst's *Vedic Hymns*, meaning *Dawn*.

SONG	COMPOSER	POET
"Ushas"	Gustav Holst	*Rigveda*, trans. G. Holst

UZ, JOHANN PETER (1720–1796): German poet. The son of a goldsmith and jurist by profession, Uz studied at the University of Halle and then the University of Leipzig, where he attended *Gellert's lectures. He himself was active as a lecturer but his main energies were devoted to the law, although poetry was a serious avocation. As a neo-classicist, Uz was influenced by *Hagedorn, whose stylistic ideal he strove to emulate. In 1749 he published his first two books of *Lyrische Gedichte*, twenty-nine poems, and added thirty-one more poems to the 1755 edition. In 1768, he published two more books, in which there were six religious hymns. A perfectionist, he took infinite pains. Uz criticized *Klopstock for too much art, wanting noble simplicity, not rhetorical splendor, being the defender of the old-line conservative party in German literature. Mozart set Uz's verse ("An die Freude"), and five poems of his were set by Schubert, among them "Die Liebesgötter," "Die Nacht," and "Gott im Frühling." PRINCIPAL WORKS: *Sämtliche poetische Werke*, ed. August Sauer is the reliable critical edition, 1890. (SOURCE: Browning, 1978)

V

VAC: One of the songs from Gustav Holst's *Vedic Hymns*, meaning *speech*.

SONG	COMPOSER	POET
"Vac"	Gustav Holst	*Rigveda*, trans. G. Holst

VALDÈS, ILDEFONSO PEREDA: *see* ★PEREDA VALDÈS, LDEFONSO

VALÉRY, PAUL (1871–1945): French poet and essayist. Son of a French father and an Italian mother, Paul Valéry attended the School of Law at Montpellier University in 1889, but left, accepting that he was deplorable at the law. In this decision he was influenced by a fellow student, the poet Pierre ★Louÿs, and a visiting author, André ★Gide, who helped him discover contemporary French literature. Valéry worked at the War Department during the Dreyfus case and wrote little from 1900 to 1917. Then, encouraged by Gide to write, he published his first book of poetry, *La Jeune Parque* and became famous overnight at the age of forty-six. The verse was very dense and obscure, but gained him a large following. During the occupation of France he used his silence as a weapon against the Nazis. Although Valéry declared himself to be not a man of letters, for the last twenty-five years of his life he was the "official literary figure of France." Gide said: "Valéry plays life as you play a game of chess that must be won." Known as a philosophical poet, he was a master of metrical effects and language, capable of expressing abstract themes with a richness of sensuous imagery. Francis Poulenc and Spanish composer Federico Mompou set the verse of Paul Valéry. PRINCIPAL WORKS: *La Jeune Parque*, 1917; *The Serpent*, 1924; *An Evening with Mr. Teste*, 1925; *Variety*, 1927; *The Graveyard by the Sea*, 1932; *The Architect*, 1932. SELECTED READING: N. Suckling, *Paul Valéry and the Civilized Mind*, 1954. (SOURCE: Kunitz, Haycraft, 1942)

VAMBA (pseudonym of Luigi Bertelli) (1858–1920): Florentine journalist, illustrator, and children's author. In 1906 Vamba founded *Il giornalino della domenica*, a children's magazine that combined texts by renowned writers with avant-garde pictures. The pieces that became Vamba's best known book were in *Il giornalino di gian Burrasca* (1912). The work of Vamba was set by Mario Castelnuovo-Tedesco. (SOURCE: Hainsworth, Robbey, 2002)

VARUNA: two of the songs from Gustav Holst's *Vedic Hymns*, meaning *Sky* (no. 1) and *The Waters* (no. 2).

SONG	COMPOSER	POET
"Varuna I and II"	Gustav Holst	*Rigveda*, trans. G. Holst

VAUDEVILLE: one of the varieties of French song of the seventeenth and eighteenth centuries. The word is a corruption of *voix de ville*, meaning a popular tune heard in the street.

VEDAS: consisting of four branches of the Indian *Rigveda* (the Veda of the "rks," *verses*). The first and most important is the first, a collection in ten books of the

1,028 hymns of the *Rigveda*. Veda comes from the root "vid," *to know*. The chief deity addressed within is ★Indra, primarily a god of war often connected to storm and tempest. (SOURCE: Steinberg, 1, 1973)

SONG	COMPOSER	POET
"Vedic Hymns"	Gustav Holst	*The Rigveda*

VEDIC: derived from *vida* (knowledge), the ancient sacred literature of Hinduism, consisting of four collections of psalms, chants, sacred formulas, and so on, from which composer Gustav Holst set many pieces to music.

VEGA (CARPIO), LOPE DE (1562–1635): Spanish poet, novelist, and playwright. Born in Madrid, Vega Carpio was educated at a Jesuit school and then the Universidad Complutense. Leaving school in 1577, he went to Madrid to become a writer, fortunate to have the patronage of the Marqués de Las Navas (1583–87). A love affair gone wrong led to a judgment for libel, jail, and exile from Castille. Vega joined the Spanish Armada in its 1588 battle against England. Living in Valencia and Toledo, he worked as secretary to several royal personages. In 1608 Vega was a "familiar of the Inquisition," later prosecutor of the Apostolic Chamber. After 1610 he was allowed to live in Madrid, where he was ordained a priest in 1614. The *comedia*, a distinctive drama of the popular theaters of seventeenth-century Spain, was fashioned by Lope de Vega. From this his contemporaries and successors had their model for the new art of dramatic composition. The poetic works of Lope de Vega were varied and prolific; his prose work was substantial in a wide range of genres. He was a legend in his own time, cutting a fine social figure—a skilled dancer and equally skilled as a lover. His artistic interests included exploring the ways that passion can disrupt the social order and the way that what happens at a village level is part of great forces at work in the entire nation's evolution. Lope de Vega claimed to have written fifteen hundred plays (of which one-third survive), 1,600 ★sonnets, several volumes of miscellaneous verse. The works of Vega Carpio have been set by composers Joaquín Turina, Eduardo Toldrà, and Joaquín Rodrigo, and Brahms's two songs for contralto and viola, op. 91, no. 2, were set to verse of Lope de Vega, translated by Emanuel Geibel. PRINCIPAL WORKS: Poetry: *Poemas*, ed. L. Guarner, 1935; *Rimas humanas y divinas*, 1635; *La Gatomaquia*, 1607, ed. Agustin del Campo, 1948; *Sonetos*, ed. Manuel Arce, 1960. Plays: *La dama boba*, ed. E. R. Hesse, 1964, as *The Lady Nit-Wit*, 1958; *Fuenteovejuna*, ed. E. R. Hesse (with *La dama boba*), as *All Citizens are Soldiers*, 1969; *Peribáñez y el comendador de Ocañam*, ed. J. M. Ruano and J. E. Varey, 1980, trans. as *Peribáñez*, 1938, as *The Commander of Ocaña*, 1958; *El castigo sin vengenza*, ed. C. E. Kossoff, 1970, as *Justice Without Revenge*, in *Five Plays*, ed. R. D. F. Pring-Mill, 1961. SELECTED READING: Jack H. Parker and Arthur M. Fox, *Lope de Vega Studies: 1937–1962*, 1964. (SOURCE: Vinson, Kirkpatrick (2), 1984)

"Veilchen, Das": a song composed by Mozart to a text of ★Goethe, the first through-composed art song in music history. When Mozart found the poem in a volume of poetry, it was erroneously labeled as the creation of the poet ★Gleim. Goethe's verse had come from his libretto for a ★Singspiel, *Erwin und Elmira*, which tells an unhappy tale of love. Mozart himself added the text for the last measures of the song, "The poor violet. It was such a dear violet." There is conjecture that the composer was comparing his own ungainly appearance with that of the violet.

VELOTE: the Venetian equivalent (sometimes spelled *veluti)* of *rispetti.

VENISE, CINQ MÉLODIES DE: a set of songs composed by Gabriel Fauré, begun while he was on a trip to Venice, invited by a wealthy American patroness of the arts. The title indicates only the place where Fauré conceived the musical settings for five poems of Paul *Verlaine. There is very little "Venetian" about these songs ("Mandoline," the only one actually composed in Venice, "En Sourdine," "Green," "À Clymène," "C'est l'extase").

VENUS: Roman goddess of beauty and sensual love, corresponding to *Aphrodite in Greek mythology. Some accounts say that Venus sprang from the foam of the sea. Others say that she was the daughter of *Jupiter and Dione, a *nymph. Vulcan was her husband, but Venus had amours with Mars and many other gods and demigods. Venus was the mother of *Cupid (Eros) by Mercury and the mother of Aeneas by Anchises, being therefore regarded by the Romans as the founder of their race. (SOURCE: Cooper, 1992)

SONG	COMPOSER	POET
1. "Le Soir"	Charles Gounod	A. de Lamartine
2. "Bess o' Bedlam"	Henry Purcell	anonymous
3. "Fairest Isle"	Henry Purcell	John Dryden
4. "When Mars and Venus"	Ross Finney	Benjamin Franklin
5. "Mañanica era"	Enrique Granados	Fernando Periquet

VERBENA: a complex genus of 352 known plants, with 3,250 species and varieties, most of which are native to temperate and tropical America. Verbena hybrids are the most commonly seen these days. Their spears of large phloxlike flowers appear in various shades of red, blue, purple, yellow, and white. (SOURCE: *Americana*, 2003)

SONG	COMPOSER	POET
"La Belle au bois dormant"	Claude Debussy	Vincent Hyspa

"Vergebliches Ständchen": a song by Johannes Brahms. Brahms believed that the poem was a lower Rhine folk song and composed the music accordingly. Actually, it was written by A. W. Zuccalmaglio, who had assembled a collection of *Volkslieder* that became popular in the 1800s.

VERLAINE, PAUL (1844–1896): French poet. Among the most famous French mélodies are those using Verlaine's *Fêtes galantes* (1869), *Ariettes oubliées* from *Romances sans paroles* (1874), and *La Bonne Chanson* (1870). Born at Metz, Verlaine was the son of an infantry captain and spoiled by both parents. In 1851, Captain Verlaine moved his family to Paris. Paul studied at the Lycée Condorcet, where, at age fourteen he read *Baudelaire's *Les Fleurs du mal* and decided to become a poet. After receiving his bachelor's degree (1862) and while living in Paris, he frequented the cafes and became a member of Le *Parnasse contemporain, a literary group. His first works, *Poèmes saturniens* (1866) and *Fêtes galantes* (1869), were written under the influence of Le Parnasse and reflect their concern with form and objectivity. Nonetheless his distinctive voice emerges. By 1867 he had met and fallen in love with a beautiful sixteen-year-old girl, Mathilde Mauté. In 1870, the year they were married, he presented her with bouquets of flowers and a group of poems, *La Bonne Chanson*, but marital bliss was not to last for long. Madly infatuated with the boy poet ★Rimbaud, Verlaine deserted his wife, newborn son, home, and job to follow Rimbaud in his wanderings. While they traveled together, Verlaine produced his next significant work, *Romances sans paroles* (1874). In Brussels Verlaine shot Rimbaud in the arm during a quarrel. Later Verlaine was sentenced to two years in prison for another crime of passion. While in prison, he converted to the Roman Catholic faith. *Sagesse* (1881), a collection of prayer-like poems, is the result of this genuine religious conversion. After being released from prison, Verlaine taught French, Latin, and drawing in England. From 1878 to 1883 he tried farming, which ended in bankruptcy. Upon publication of his prose work, *Les Poètes maudits* (1884), he became one of the acknowledged leaders of the ★Symbolist movement. In 1885 he published a series of very personal poems in *Jadis et naguère*. From the year 1886, when he relocated permanently in Paris, his life became one of total debauchery, alternated with long recuperative stays in public hospitals. However, his discovery by the Symbolists led to his election as Prince of Poets upon the death of ★Léconte de L'Isle in 1894. Yet he died penniless in Paris. To Verlaine, verse was essentially musical and not confined by rhyme or regular patterns. The verse of Paul Verlaine has been set by Debussy, Fauré, Stravinsky, Max Reger, Darius Milhaud, Arthur Honegger, Ernest Chausson, Gustave Charpentier, Émile Paladilhe, Reynaldo Hahn, Frederick Delius, Benjamin Britten, Henry Hadley, John Alden Carpenter, Frank Martin, Charles Loeffler, and Ralph Vaughan Williams. The International editions of various composers setting poetry by Verlaine all contain serviceable English translations of his poetry. SELECTED READING: A. E. Carter, *Verlaine: A Study in Parallels*, 1969; Ruth L. White, *Verlaine et les musiciens*, 1992. (SOURCES: Bowman, 1971; Harvey, Heseltine, 1959; Bédé, Edgerton, 1980)

VESUVIUS, VESUVIO (It.): an Italian volcano located 10 miles east of ★Naples.

SONG	COMPOSER	POET
"Let the Dreadful Engines"	Henry Purcell	Thomas D'Urfey

VIDAME: a church officer who represents a bishop or abbot in secular affairs.

SONG	COMPOSER	POET
"Chanson du clair tamis"	Francis Poulenc	Maurice Fombeure

VIERECK, PETER (b. 1916): American poet. Viereck was born in New York and taught history at Mt. Holyoke College in Massachusetts. *Terror and Decorum: Poems 1940–1948* was his first collection, and it won the Pulitzer Prize. This collection and its successors contained poems that risked everything on rather trite or folksy humor. "Really serious themes were juxtaposed with absurd expositions of them so that the impression was either of banality or cleverness" (Hamilton, 1994). The poetry of Peter Viereck has been set by Jack Beeson. PRINCIPAL WORKS: *New and Selected Poems 1932–1967*, 1967; *Archer in the Marrow: The Applewood Cycles 1967–1987*, 1987. SELECTED READING: M. Henault, *Peter Viereck*, 1967. (SOURCE: Hamilton, 1994)

VILLAGE SCENES: a cycle of five songs by Béla Bartók with texts from Hungarian folk poetry. Bartók made use of a number of Slovak folk poems, arranging them in a sequence that presents the outline of a story telling of a girl's experience as she develops into a woman and becomes a mother. In "Haymaking," while gathering in the hay harvest, the girl breaks her rake, a veiled allusion to the loss of virginity. In "At the Bride's Home," the girl is filling white pillows with peacock feathers (the feathers symbolize the nest prepared by the bride). In "The Wedding," there are two different tunes. The slow sections refer to the dowry box and to the rose that is destined to fade. The box symbolizes the past happiness of youth that seems to be locked away in the box; the rose symbolizes the course of a woman's life after the high point of her marriage. In "Cradle Song," the young mother rocks her infant son's cot, sad in the knowledge that she will lose him when he marries. In "Youth's Dance," Bartók dispels all melancholy with this exuberant picture of children dancing.

VILLANCICO: a rustic song derived from *villano* (a villager or commoner), originally a species of dramatic interlude set in the vernacular, sung, not acted, with refrains and occasional short verses broken in. The villancico, in *epigrammatic form, belonging to the poetry of the fifteenth century, had two or more stanzas, each of seven lines. As the villancico form gradually became simplified during the fifteenth century, the final aspect was like a symmetrical ABBA, with each A section having a common coda or refrain. By the seventeenth or eighteenth centuries, it reappeared as a cantata for soli and chorus. In early times the favorite theme was love; later it acquired a more popular tone. With little counterpoint and less artifice, the musical idea was subordinate to the poetry. (SOURCE: *OED*, 1989; Stevens, 1970)

VILLANELLE: a poem in fixed form of lyric or pastoral nature, consisting usually of five three-line stanzas and a concluding *quatrain, with only two rhymes throughout. The first and third lines of the poem are repeated in alternate tercets and at the end of the final quatrain. The form was established in the sixteenth century and was very popular with *Banville and the *Parnassians. (SOURCE: *OED*, 1989)

VILLE DE MIRMONT, JEAN DE LA (1886–1914): French elegist. Ville de Mirmont, the son of a university professor, was killed in World War I, cutting short a very promising career. In *L'Horizon chimerique*, which was set by Fauré, Ville de Mirmont treated the subject of the sea unusually, primarily as the symbol of an undiscovered world, not as a source of human tragedy. (SOURCE: Magill, 4, 1984)

VILLIERS DE L'ISLE-ADAM, JEAN-MARIE-MATHIAS-PHILIPPE-AUGUSTE, COMTE DE (1838–1889): French poet, short-story writer, and dramatist. Villiers's family traced its noble ancestry to 1277, perhaps to 1065. His father was a marquis and a Knight of the Order of Malta, but the family was very poor when Auguste was born. He was an indifferent student but read a great deal, writing verse and a play in his teens. When the family moved to Paris (1857), Villiers met the *Parnassian poets. Through *Baudelaire, he began to read *Poe and made the acquaintance of Richard Wagner, whose music he interpreted superbly at the piano. His plays, although praised by Wagner and Dumas, were commercial disasters. Even though he lacked the bare necessities of life, Villiers visited Wagner at Triebschen and attended the Festival at Bayreuth. Barely kept alive by his low echelon jobs (sparring partner in a gym, ill-paid editorial positions, and so on), he placed art above any other consideration, even his life. Each word in his work had to be weighed delicately. He used satire to highlight the pretensions of his scientific age and to mock the customs of modern man. This blend of irony and lyricism made Villiers the icon of prose *symbolism. The verse of Auguste Villiers de L'Isle-Adam was set by Gabriel Fauré. PRINCIPAL WORKS: *Claire Lenoir*, trans. Arthur *Symons, 1925; *Axël*, trans. H. P. R. Fineberg, 1925, with preface by William Butler *Yeats; *Contes Cruels*, as *Sardonic Tales*, trans. H. Miles, 1927. SELECTED READING: Arthur *Symons, *The Symbolist Movement in Literature*, 1899. (SOURCE: Kunitz, Colby, 1967)

VILLON, FRANÇOIS (1431–?1463): French poet. Little is known of the youth of Villon except that he was born in Paris of poor parents, that his name was actually Montcorbier before he took the name of his patron, Guillaume de Villon, who was a priest and professor of canon law. Villon was sent to the University of Paris where he took a bachelor of arts degree (1449) and a master of arts (1452). In 1455 Villon began what was to be a life interrupted by banishment and prison terms caused by his involvement in street brawls, robberies, and so on. He knew that his troubles were of his own making. In 1462 his activities caused him to be thrown into Châtelet Prison, tortured, and sentenced to hang. This time Villon paid restitution and was sentenced to ten years' banishment from Paris. His movements are known for one more year, after which he may have lived in a monastery until his death. Villon's poetry is highly personal and lends itself to biographical interpretation. It gives a picture of France at the close of the medieval ages, making Villon the first great poet of Paris. His English translators include Algernon Charles Swinburne, Dante Gabriel *Rossetti, and Robert *Lowell. The poetry of François Villon was set by Frank Martin and Claude Debussy. PRINCIPAL WORKS: *Le Lais*, 1489, *The Legacy*, 1878; *Ballades en jargon*, 1489, *Poems in Slang*, 1878; *Les Oeuvres de Françoys Villon*, 1533, *The Poems of Master François Villon*, 1878; *Ballads Done into English from the French of F. Villon*, 1904; *The Testaments of François Villon*, 1924; *The Complete Works of François Villon*, 1928; *The Poems of François Villon*, 1954, 1977, 1982, trans. Galway Kinnell. SELECTED READING: John Fox, *The Poetry of Villon*, 1962. (SOURCE: Magill, 5, 1997)

VILLON, JACQUES (pseudonym for Gaston Duchamp) (1875–1963): French painter. Villon was the half-brother of the artist Duchamp. In 1911 he became a Cubist and, for a time, was the leader of a group that included Fernand Léger, Gabriel-Charles Gleyre, and Albert Gleizes. In 1919 he began to paint abstracts, after which his work passed through several phases, all marked by command of proportion and line. The poet Paul *Éluard was helped in his work on Villon's art by Villon's own words: "You must extract the rhythms and volume from the subject, the way you would extract a diamond from its matrix." (SOURCE: *Thames Hudson,* 1994; Kimball, 1987)

SONG	COMPOSER	POET
"Jacques Villon"	Francis Poulenc	Paul Éluard

VILMORIN, LOUISE DE (1902–1969): French poet and novelist. Louise de Vilmorin, a woman of great beauty, was a member of a family with broad scientific interests. ★Cocteau said that she was "a sort of prodigy, a woman who invents illustrious things . . . new, fresh, comic, poetic, ferocious, light, almost unbelievable." Her brief novels of love, death, and absence use fairy-tale elements, fantasy, ellipsis, and lyricism, while her wistful lyrics recall Nature, childhood, and lost love. She married twice, one husband an American and one a Slovakian count. In later years she was a close friend of the writer André Malraux, once minister of culture during the presidency of Charles de Gaulle. She was author of several novels and three major collections of poetry. Vilmorin's verse was set to music principally by Francis Poulenc, who was introduced to her work by Marie-Blanche de Polignac, a mentor to many gifted composers. Vilmorin and Poulenc became close friends, corresponding regularly for many years. Although Poulenc had previously favored the surrealist poetry of ★Éluard and ★Apollinaire, he was attracted by Vilmorin's unashamedly feminine and sentimental verse, wherein she often expressed her themes of love, death, and regret in phrases of both sadness and happiness. Poulenc prized her poetic audacity and exploited in his songs her use of text solely for its sonority. PRINCIPAL WORKS: *Fiançailles pour rire,* 1938; *Le Lit à colonne,* 1941; *Le Sable du sablier,* 1945; *La Retour d'Érika,* 1946; *Julietta,* 1951; *Madame de,* 1951 (filmed, 1952); *Histoire d'aimer,* 1955; *Le Violon,* 1960; *L'Heure maliciôse,* 1967; *Poèmes,* 1970. (SOURCE: France, 1995)

VINJE, AASMUND (1818–1870): a Norwegian poet, essayist, and journalist. Vinje was born on a farm in southern Norway, where his father worked as a farm hand. He grew up in a poor but happy house and studied at home. After graduating from normal school, he taught for two years. In 1848 he went to the capital and enrolled in a private school, where he met ★Ibsen and ★Bjørnson. Together, Vinje and Ibsen started a newspaper that prospered for only one year. After a time as a newspaper correspondent, Vinje started a weekly paper in which he wrote in standard Norwegian. Influenced by the nationalistic language movement, he shifted to a language based on the native dialect of Telemark, publishing his own works. The foundation of his work was always cultural or of social significance. Vinje's straightforward views on the union with Sweden cost him dearly, and he died in poverty, but not before he had strengthened and vitalized Norwegian literature in both poetry and prose. Vinje's poems were published in two collections: *Diktsamling* [Poems], 1863; *Blandkorn* [Mixed Grain], 1867. His verses were set by Edvard Grieg and Charles Ives. (SOURCE: Kunitz, Colby, 1967)

"Violon, Le": a song from the cycle *Fiançailles pour rire* composed by Francis Poulenc to poetry by Louise de ★Vilmorin. Poulenc says that he composed the song with a Hungarian restaurant in mind, also a tzigane orchestra, and a beautiful woman as the listener. "Couple amoureux" probably refers to the violinist and the violin, or to the more erotic aspects of the violin's shape. (SOURCE: Bernac, 1977)

VIRGIN MARY, THE: the mother of ★Jesus, not to be confused with ★Mary Magdalene or Mary, the sister of Martha and Lazareth. The Virgin Mary occupies a place in Catholic Christianity's theology second only to Jesus Christ, perhaps because of the Catholic Church's ambiguous attitude toward human sexuality, or perhaps because of the long tradition of pairs of male and female gods. The Catholic Church celebrates Mary as "the mother of God" and "the Queen of Heaven." In some instances the Church refers to Mary as co-redeemer, giving her credit, because of her seven sorrows, for suffering with Christ for the sins of humanity and the redemption of the world. The seven sorrows are:

1. The prophecy of Simeon. In Luke, Simeon, a devout Jew living in the Temple in Jerusalem, is told that he will not die until he sees the Messiah. When he sees Jesus, he utters the words "Now let your servant depart in peace" and so on, which come down to us as the Nunc Dimittus in the liturgy of the ★Mass. He prophesies Jesus' crucifixion. He also says that, as a spear will pierce Jesus' side, so will a sword pierce Mary's heart.
2. The flight into Egypt to protect the baby Jesus from the villainy of King Herod.
3. The three-day loss of Jesus when he disappears in the Temple as a young boy of twelve and is found expounding on the scriptures to the amazement of the scholars.
4. Meeting Jesus on the way to Calvary.
5. Mary at the foot of the Cross where Jesus gives Mary into the care of St. John.
6. Jesus taken down from the Cross. His corpse is laid in the arms of his mother. This has inspired many works of art entitled *Pietà*.
7. The burial of Jesus.

The most authentic details of Mary's life are to be found in the four Gospels of the New Testament and the book of Acts of the Apostles. From them we learn that Mary was a descendant of King ★David of Israel and a cousin of Elizabeth, the mother of ★John the Baptist. While she was engaged to ★Joseph, whom the Bible calls a "just man," an angel appeared to her and announced that she would give birth to the Messiah. Mary gave birth to Jesus in a barn in Bethlehem, where she and Joseph had gone to be registered for the census and to pay taxes under the reign of Caesar Augustus. This event, the miraculous accounts of angels singing in heaven, the star, the wise men from the east, the flight to Egypt, and the slaughter of the innocents are contained only in the later Gospels, attributed to ★Matthew and Luke. Some biblical scholars believe that these details were added much later in order to supply answers for those curious about the details of Jesus' life.

At a later time, Mary was involved in the public ministry of Jesus. It was she who caused him to perform his first miracle, that of changing water into wine at the wedding in ★Cana, details of which are given in the Gospel of John. Although

Mary is present during various events of Jesus' ministry, she plays no significant role in these accounts. On at least one occasion Jesus refuses to see her while he is busy teaching. Among later traditions, which accord Mary much greater significance than the events recorded in the New Testament, are many interesting details: Mary was the only child of an elderly, previously childless couple, Joachim and Anne. An angel had foretold her birth, thus putting Mary in the long tradition of miraculous births to elderly couples that began with ★Abraham and Sarah. Because she was to be the mother of God, Mary was conceived in a special state of grace known as the Immaculate Conception, so that she would be born without Original Sin. (SOURCES: The Holy Bible; Thurston, Attwater, 1963)

SONG	COMPOSER	POET
1. "The Blessed Virgin's Expostulation"	Henry Purcell	Nahum Tate
2. "Inno à Maria Nostra Donna"	G. F. Malipiero	Angelo Poliziano
3. "Ave Maria"	Franz Schubert	Sir Walter Scott
4. "Preghiera alla Madonna"	Franco Alfano	Luigi Orsini
5. "Das Marienleben" (cycle)	Paul Hindemith	Rainer Maria Rilke
6. "Nun wandre, Maria"	Hugo Wolf	*Spanisches Liederbuch*
7. "Mariä Wiegenlied"	Max Reger	Martin Boelitz
8. "Der heilige Josef singt"	Hugo Wolf	*Spanisches Liederbuch*
9. "Stirb', Lieb' und Freud'"	Robert Schumann	Justinus Kerner
10. "La Mer est plus belle"	Claude Debussy	Paul Verlaine
11. "Priez pour paix"	Francis Poulenc	Charles d'Orléans

VISTULA: the English transliteration of the River Wisla, located in the southeast quadrant of Poland.

SONG	COMPOSER	POET
"La Vistule"	Francis Poulenc	tr. Jacques Lerolle

VITERBO: a medieval Italian city in the interior of Italy, northwest of Rome. The old city nestles within twelfth-century walls. Its buildings, whose window boxes are bright with red geraniums, are made of peperino, the local stone that colors the center city a dark gray against the golden tufa rock of its walls and towers. The Fontana Grande in the piazza of the same name is the largest and most extravagant of Viterbo's authentic Gothic fountains.

SONG	COMPOSER	POET
1. "Ihr seid die Allerschönste"	Hugo Wolf	Paul Heyse, from the Italian
2. "Ich hab in Penna"	Hugo Wolf	Paul Heyse, from the Italian

VITO: a fiery Spanish dance performed by a woman standing on a table in a tavern to an audience composed of bullfighters.

SONG	COMPOSER	POET
"El vito"	Joaquín Nin	popular song

VITTORELLI, JACOPO (1749–1835): Italian poet. Vittorelli was from Venice, but little else is known about him. The texts of two songs once attributed to Metastasio are now recognized as the work of Vittorelli: "Non t'accostare all'urna" and "Guarda, che bianca luna." (SOURCE: Reed, 1997)

VITUS, SAINT: a Christian martyr said to have died during the reign of ★Diocletian. St. Vitus was the patron of those suffering from epilepsy and other disorders of the nerves, including St. Vitus's Dance (Sydenham's chorea). Allusions to St. Vitus are sometimes in the context of violent physical movement. (SOURCE: Delahunty et al., 2001)

SONG	COMPOSER	POET
"La Petite Servante"	Francis Poulenc	Max Jacob

VIZIER (Fr.), VISIR: a minister or councilor of state, from a high executive officer of the Ottoman Empire.

SONG	COMPOSER	POET
"Asie"	Maurice Ravel	Tristan Klingsor

VOCEÍSMO: a trend in Brazilian song writing. *Você* (you) is the Portuguese polite form of address, as *vous* in French. Composers of this genre include Francisco Mignone and Camargo Guarnieri.

VOGIE: (Scot.), *fond*; *proud*, *vain*; *elated*; (things) *ostentatious*.

SONG	COMPOSER	POET
"My Hoggie"	Benjamin Britten	Robert Burns

VOGL, JOHANN NEPOMUK (1802–1866): Austrian poet. Vogl wrote copiously in a belated ★Romantic manner. The three volumes of his *Balladen und Romanzen* appeared in 1835, and his once similarly popular *Bilder aus dem Soldatenleben*, in 1853. Vogl's verse was set by Carl Loewe.

VOLER: a French word with two meanings, *to fly* and *to steal*, the double meanings charmingly exploited by poet Louise de ★Vilmorin in her poem "Il vole," set to music by Francis Poulenc. There are also hints of a well-known fable by the seventeenth-century fable writer, ★La Fontaine, namely "The Crow and the Fox," in which the fox stole the cheese belonging to the crow. (SOURCE: Bernac, 1977)

"Von ewiger Liebe": a song by Johannes Brahms set to the poetry of Joseph Wenzig or Hoffman von ★Fallersleben. The poem has been universally ascribed to Wenzig, although it is nowhere to be found in the usual source books. It does, however, appear in the poems of Fallersleben, in a volume known to have been read by Robert Schumann, which was still in his library at Düsseldorf when Brahms visited there. Even the Brahms-detractor Hugo Wolf felt admiration for this song's intensity and breadth of line.

VOSS, JOHANN (1751–1826): German poet and translator. Voss's grandfather freed his serfs, and his father was the first in their family to escape from the farm and attend school. Johann studied Greek and Hebraic studies in Neubrandenburg, taking as his heroes the poets ★Hagedorn and ★Uz. University life was closed to him because of his family's poverty, but he became a teacher and obtained a position as tutor to the child of a noble family. Treated and paid badly, Voss acquired a life-long antagonism toward nobility. Having successfully submitted a poem to a literary magazine, Voss abandoned theology for poetry and for philology, which had not pre-viously been recognized as a branch of knowledge. Although Voss was accustomed to speaking Low German with the family, he began to read old works and translate them into High German, wanting to enrich the modern language. As editor of the periodical *Musealmanach,* he translated fifty-eight odes of ★Horace, completed Vir-gil, and parts of Ovid. His presence gave prestige to the University of Heidelberg from 1805 to 1826, and he waged war against ★Romanticism and Catholicism by his reviews. All those years Voss wrote poetry: odes, songs, poems, and idylls in the ★Theocritus tradition. The critic ★Schlegel divided Voss's poems into those that were philosophical or religious contemplation and those that were concerned with social intercourse. His works were best when he combined his poetic talent with his vast knowledge of philology. The poetry of Johann Voss was set by Mendelssohn, Weber, Johann Schulz, Josef Marx, and Václav Momášet. (SOURCE: Hardin, Schweitzer, 1989)

WABSTER: (Scot.), a variant of a webster, *a female weaver, a spider.*

SONG	COMPOSER	POET
"Bed-time"	Benjamin Britten	William Soutar

WAD: (Scot.) (pr. wayd), *wade through water; would.*

SONG	COMPOSER	POET
"Wee Willie"	Benjamin Britten	Robert Burns

WAG: (Scot.), n. *a mischievous boy or man, full of sport and humor;* v. *wave, brandish a weapon.*

SONG	COMPOSER	POET
"'Twas within a Furlong of Edinborough Town"	Henry Purcell	Robert Howard

WAGTAIL: a migrant bird that grooms its long tail incessantly. In Indian myth, the wagtail bears a holy cast mark and is the prophetic bird used in divination. Of great importance are the direction from which it appears and its proximity to other objects. Near the lotus, an elephant, horse, cow, or serpent it is good luck; close to bones, ashes, or refuse, it is bad luck. The wagtail is the ★Cupid of the Ainu myth; its feathers and bones are love charms. (SOURCE: Cooper, 1992)

SONG	COMPOSER	POET
"Wagtail and Baby"	Benjamin Britten	Thomas Hardy

WAIKIKI: a famous Hawaiian beach located a few miles south of Honolulu on the big island of Oahu.

SONG	COMPOSER	POET
"Waikiki"	Charles Griffes	Rupert Brooke

WALEY, ARTHUR (1899–1966): English poet and authority on and translator of Chinese and Japanese literature. Waley taught himself the languages when he worked in the Print Room at the British Museum. In 1918 he published *One Hundred and Seventy Chinese Poems* (which was given several editions), appealing to those who didn't usually read poetry. Waley's translations were unrhymed, elegant, and lucid. His idiosyncratic use of the stressed and unstressed syllables owed something to Gerard Manley ★Hopkins's "sprung rhythm." Waley published many works on oriental art, history, and culture but never visited any of those countries, despite many invitations. The verse of Arthur Waley was set to music by Aaron Copland. PRINCIPAL WORKS: *One Hundred Seventy Chinese Poems*, 1918; *The Tale of Genji*, 1925–33; *The Pillow Book of Sei Shonagon* (the diary of a tenth-century Japanese court lady), 1928; *Monkey* (translation of a sixteenth-century Chinese novel), 1942. SELECTED READING: Alison Waley, *A Half of Two Lives: A Personal Memoir*, 1982. (SOURCE: Drabble, 2000)

WALLER, EDMUND (1606–1687): British poet and playwright. Born in Buckinghamshire, Waller attended Eton and King's College, Cambridge, matriculating (perhaps without a degree) in 1620. As a wealthy landowner, he served in Parliament and was appointed a commissioner to treat with Charles I at Oxford in 1643. In that same year he was involved in an attempt to seize the City of London for Charles. As a result he was expelled from Parliament and imprisoned in the Tower of London for a year, then banished from the country, living in France from 1644 until 1651 when his banishment was revoked. Upon his return to England, he was elected a member of the House of Commons, where he sat until his death. Waller's verses made him an important influence on ★Dryden and later on ★Pope. He made the first extensive use of the balanced, end-stopped ★couplet. His language is abstract and elegant, his poetry civilized and controlled. He is now remembered mainly as the author of the beautiful lyric "Go, Lovely Rose." Edmund Waller's poetry has been set by Henry Lawes, Thomas Arne, John Blow, Ned Rorem, Seymour Barab, John Alden Carpenter, Samuel Adler, Howard Boatwright, Henry Clough-Leighter, and Richard Cumming. PRINCIPAL WORKS: *Poems*, ed. G. Thorn Drury, 2 vols., 1893. SELECTED READING: W. L. Cherniak, *The Poetry of Imitation: A Study of Waller*, 1968. (SOURCE: Vinson, 1979)

WALLONIE, WALLOON: a low-lying part of Belgium.

SONG	COMPOSER	POET
"Fagnes de Wallonie"	Francis Poulenc	Guillaume Apollinaire

WALPURGIS, SAINT: a Christian saint also known as Saint Walburga. A sister of Saints Willibald and Winnibald, St. Walpurgis was one of the missionary group of Anglo-Saxon monks and nuns who worked with St. Boniface in Germany. In 779 C.E. while abbess of Heidenheim she died. When, in 870, her body was moved to rest beside her brother Winnibald in Eichstatt, medicinal oils that were said to have miraculous powers flowed from the rock surrounding her tomb. In 893 her grave was opened and her relics distributed in Germany, France, and Flanders. St. Walpurgis was invoked as a protector of crops. One of her feast days is May 1, which is also the date of a pagan festival that marks the beginning of summer and witches' gatherings, but there is no connection between her and these Walpurgis nights. Her principal feast day is February 25. (SOURCE: Farmer, 1997)

"Wanderers Nachtleid II": a song by Schubert to a text by ★Goethe. In 1780 at the age of thirty-one, Goethe wrote the poem on the wall of a mountain hut on the Gickelhahn, near ★Ilmenau in ★Thuringia. When he returned at the age of sixty-four, he renewed the inscription, which was then preserved under glass for posterity.

WATTEAU, JEAN ANTOINE (1684–1721): French painter and originator of the style known as *Fêtes galantes* (elegant festivals, or gallant parties). Born in Valenciennes, Watteau was the son of a roof-tiler. He was originally apprenticed to the master of the Guild of St. Luke in Valenciennes, but was forced to leave his tutelage in 1700, because his father was unable to continue paying for his training. To further his studies, he journeyed to Paris, arriving in a penniless state. Eventually he joined the studio of Louis Metayer, where he was responsible for painting statues of St. Nicholas, for which efforts he was paid three livres a week plus his daily soup. In 1703 he entered the studio of the curator of the Luxembourg, where he was influenced by the works of Peter Paul Rubens, Titian, Paolo Veronese, and Jacopo Tintoretto. When he entered the Academy as a pupil in 1709, Watteau's genius was recognized, but he was not a full member until August 28, 1717, when a special distinction was given to him: the Academy allowed him to select the subject for his entry painting. The resulting work, *L'Embarquement pour l'Ile de* ★*Cythère*, was accepted and Watteau was admitted to the Academy as a painter of *Fêtes galantes*. This description is significant, because members were usually accepted as painters of specific traditional genres of paintings, such as "historical subjects" or "still lifes." Pictures in the *Fêtes galantes* genre continued to be produced by Watteau and his student Pater throughout Watteau's career. *Fêtes galantes* paintings are characterized by groups of fashionably dressed young men and women, obviously lovers, set in parklike settings. The couples are chatting, embracing, dancing, playing a guitar or some other instrument, and usually posed in symmetrical groupings organized throughout the park. Figures from *commedia dell'arte* also play a prominent part. The *Fêtes galantes* of Watteau and other members of his school are said to have inspired the *Fêtes galantes* of Paul ★Verlaine. (SOURCE: Camesasca, 1968)

WATTLES: interlaced rods and twigs spread with mud and used as building material.

SONG	COMPOSER	POET
"The Lake Isle of Innisfree"	Alan Hovhaness	William Butler Yeats

WATTS, ISAAC (1674–1748): English poet. Watts was the son of a nonconformist Southampton tradesman and keeper of a boarding school. He became a minister but was forced into retirement by ill-health. Although four collections of verse were published, Watts was chiefly remembered for his songs for children and his hymn writing, for example, "Oh God, Our Help in Ages Past" and "When I Survey the Wondrous Cross." These were so well known that Lewis ★Carroll parodied them in his "Alice" books. Watts was also the author of Pindaric odes, blank verse, and creative technical experiments in English Sapphics. The verse of Isaac Watts has been set by Jack Beeson and Virgil Thomson. PRINCIPAL WORKS: *Horae Lyricae*, 1706; *Hymns and Spiritual Songs*, 1707; *Divine Songs for the Use of Children*, 1715; *The Psalms of David Imitated*, 1719. (SOURCE: Drabble, 2000)

WEDDIT: (Scot.), *to pledge, wager, or engage with the prospect of marriage*; past tense of *wade*.

SONG	COMPOSER	POET
"A Riddle (The Child You Were)"	Benjamin Britten	William Soutar

WEISSE, CHRISTIAN (1642–1708): German dramatist and novelist. Son of a German teacher and preacher father who had been exiled from Bohemia for Protestant beliefs, Weisse attended the University of Leipzig where he wrote ten or more poems each day. He supported himself by lecturing and with positions as a private secretary and tutor. A job as rector of the Gymnasium was given him by his home town. He virtually never traveled but wrote importantly on pedagogical subjects. Weisse's principal fame came from a long series of dramas for the school stage, which at that time was the only outlet for dramatic talent. His most important goal was to educate businessmen for the service of the state, believing that training in eloquence was paramount. His language, containing remarkable realism, much dialect, and often crudities or violence, was in direct contrast to the courtly prose of his century. The works of Christian Weisse were set by Haydn, Beethoven, and Mozart. PRINCIPAL WORKS: *Der verfolgte Lateiner* (play), 1696. SELECTED READING: George C. Schoolfield, *The German Lyric of the Baroque*, Eng. tr., 1962. (SOURCE: Vinson, Kirkpatrick (1), 1984)

WELCOME SONG: a type of Purcellian song, usually written for a royal family celebration.

WELTSCHMERTZ: a romantic phenomenon or social-cultural phase, meaning literally *world grief*. Essentially, it meant the inability of many unstable and eccentric geniuses to adapt themselves to the hard realities of the world. Endless conflicts, gloom, and despair resulted from such difficulties. ★Goethe's ★Werther is one of the most celebrated characters to suffer such pessimism and disillusionment. Poets exhibiting *Weltschmertz* in German literature were notably Nicholaus ★Lenau and Heinrich ★Heine and, to some degree, Friedrich ★Hölderlin and Franz ★Grillparzer. In England there was Lord ★Byron and in America, Nathaniel Hawthorne, both similarly afflicted.

WENLOCK EDGE: a range of hills located in Shropshire, England, where pre-Cambrian rocks were prized up by earth forces until they stood on end. After a long period of time, another shove from below pushed them over until they stood upside down. Long Mynd is one of these rocks, the view from which includes Much Wenlock, a little country town with half-timbered houses and inns. (SOURCE: Hillaby, 1969)

SONG	COMPOSER	POET
"On Wenlock Edge"	Ralph Vaughan Williams	A. E. Housman

WERNER, FRIEDRICH (1768–1823): German poet and dramatist. Werner was a law school graduate and held several civil servant positions until 1807. At that time he resigned his post and devoted himself to travel and writing. His fame then rested on the historical dramas he wrote in the first decade of the nineteenth century. After three marriages, each of which was dissolved, Werner was ordained a priest (1813) and was named an honorary canon of St. Stephen's Cathedral in Vienna. Schubert set three of his poems. (SOURCE: Reed, 1997)

WESENDONCK, MATHILDE (1828–1902): wife of a Zürich silk merchant who, a supporter of Richard Wagner like his wife, rented a small house of his to the Wagners when they were in exile in Switzerland (1857). Wagner and Mathilde had a brief affair, and Wagner interrupted his work on the opera *Tristan und Isolde* to write five songs to Mathilde's poems.

WESTÖSTLICHE DIVAN, DER (The West-Easterly Divan): Johann Wolfgang von ★Goethe's major work dealing with oriental culture. His ★*Divan*, a collection of odes, was composed during the Napoleonic years when Goethe was preoccupied with oriental subjects and indifferent to politics. His aim was to familiarize German readers with the works of Arabian, Persian, and Indian poets. On June 18, 1815, he found a copy of the German translation of poems by Persian poet ★Hāfiz, which became his guide. Some dozen lines in Goethe's *Divan* are direct translations of Hāfiz—eastern in tone and color, western in thought. The *Divan* consists of several books, each preceded by short poems: *The Singer, Hāfiz, Love, Reflections, Ill-humored Sayings, Timur,* ★*Suleika, The Cup-bearer* ★*Parables, Parsee,* and *Paradise.* In Goethe's mind, Marianne Jung ★Willemer, his lover and his inspiration, was Suleika, and he himself was Hatem. The texts for Schubert's two Suleika songs were written by Marianne Willemer.

WEYLA: the protective deity of the imaginary island of ★Orplid, created by ★Eduard Mörike in his novel ★*Maler Nolten.* Mörike and his friend Ludwig Bauer spent many hours in the woods, peopling the island with gods, fairies, and heroes out of their fantasies. They imagined Weyla sitting on a reef in the moonlight, accompanying herself on the harp, the island rising out of the waters, the sea mist ascending from its shores.

SONG	COMPOSER	POET
"Gesang Weylas"	Hugo Wolf	Eduard Mörike

"What Can Pomp or Glory Do?": a song composed by Henry Purcell, set to words by Nathaniel ★Lee from his heroic play *Theodosius*, produced in 1680. For plot details and placement of songs, *see* ★*Theodosius*.

"What Ho! Thou Genius of This Isle": a song composed by Henry Purcell to a text by John ★Dryden from their semi-opera *King Arthur*, produced in 1691. For plot details and placement of songs, *see* ★*King Arthur*.

"What Power Art Thou": a song composed by Henry Purcell to a text written by John ★Dryden, from their semi-opera *King Arthur*, produced in 1691. For plot details and placement of songs, *see* ★*King Arthur*.

"When a Cruel Long Winter Has Frozen the Earth": a song composed by Henry Purcell to a text written by Elkanah ★Settle for his work *The Fairie-Queene*, produced in 1692 and 1693. For plot details and placement of songs, *see* ★*Fairie-Queene, The*.

"When First I Saw Bright Aurelia's Eyes": a song from the 1690 semi-opera *Dioclesian,* with music by Henry Purcell, written to the words of Massinger and ★Fletcher. For plot details and placement of the songs, *see* ★*Dioclesian*.

"When I Have Often Heard": an aria composed by Henry Purcell to a text written by Elkanah ★Settle for his work *The Fairie-Queene*, produced in 1692 and 1693. For plot details and song placements, *see* ★*Fairie-Queene, The*.

"When the World First Knew Creation": a song composed by Henry Purcell to a text written by Thomas ★D'Urfey for Part I of his comedic semi-opera *Don Quixote*, produced in 1694–95. For plot details and placement of songs, *see* ★*Don Quixote*.

"Whilst I with Grief Did on You Look": a song composed by Henry Purcell, set to the words of John ★Dryden, for the 1695 revival of his tragicomedy, *The Spanish Fryar*. For plot details and placement of songs, *see* ★*Spanish Fryar, The*.

WHIN: (Scot.), *of unknown origin, or a particularly hard igneous rock.*

SONG	COMPOSER	POET
"A Laddie's Sang"	Benjamin Britten	William Soutar

WHINNEY MUIR: a circle of ★purgatory, a moor covered with a prickly bush that stings the feet.

SONG	COMPOSER	POET
"Serenade"	Benjamin Britten	anonymous fifteenth-century verse

WHITMAN, WALT (1819–1892): American poet and journalist. Walter Whitman, who chose to be called Walt, was born on Long Island, son of a farmer/carpenter father, both parents Quakers with no intellectual interests. What little schooling Whitman had was in Brooklyn, where the family moved in 1823. Amiable, clumsy, and slovenly, Walt spent his summers in rural Long Island, which was good training for a future poet because he became aware of earth and marine nature without giving up his essential urban nature. From 1833 to 1841 he alternated between printing and country school teaching. The years 1841 to 1848 were a period of inner growth while he worked on the staffs of at least ten New York papers and magazines, *Brooklyn Eagle* and *Democratic Review* the most important of these. The year 1855 was a central date of Whitman's life: the first edition of *Leaves of Grass* was printed at his own expense, although eleven editions appeared in his lifetime, each one longer. He expected condemnation but silence was the result. Whitman addressed himself to the "plain man," but it was always the leaders of culture who hailed him. During the Civil War, admiring Lincoln, he was fired from the *Brooklyn Eagle* for an anti-slavery editorial. During the war Whitman tended both North and South soldiers at his own expense. In 1873, after a light stroke, he came to Camden, New Jersey, to live with his brother, becoming a permanent invalid. Visitors came from all over America, Europe, and England. Whitman wanted to be known as the prophet of democracy, but he was rejected by the common people. He called himself "a child, very old," and was. Whitman was accused of a lack of taste and sentimental egotism, but recognized as a genius. The poetry of Walt Whitman has been set by Paul Hindemith, Ernst Bacon, Ralph Vaughan Williams, Ned Rorem, Harry Burleigh, Charles Naginski, William Bolcom, Charles Ives, Frederick Delius, Lee Hoiby, Celius Dougherty, Louis Campbell-Tipton, Paul Creston, Otto Luening, and William Flanagan. PRINCIPAL WORKS: *Leaves of Grass*, 1855, 1856, 1860–61, and so on; *Drum Taps*, 1865; *Passage to India*, 1871; *As a Strong Bird on Pinions Free and Other Poems*, 1872; *Two Rivulets*, 1876; *November Boughs*, 1888; *Goodbye, My Fancy*, 1891. SELECTED READING: Gay Wilson Allen, *The Solitary Singer: A Critical Biography*, 1967; R. W. B. Lewis, *The Presence of Whitman*, 1962. (SOURCE: Kunitz, Haycraft, 1938)

WHITTIER, JOHN GREENLEAF (1807–1892): American poet. Son of a Quaker farmer, born in Massachusetts, Whittier was a tall, black-haired man with a swarthy skin typical of most New England farm boys, but, unlike others, he was color-blind and slightly deaf, and had a flair for rhyming. Whittier did his schooling in the district school. At the age of fourteen his introduction to the poetry of Robert *Burns intrigued him so much that he began to read everything he could find: poetry, history, and theology. In 1829 Whittier left home to become the editor of the *American Manufacturer* in Boston and contributed stories and sketches to many publications. In 1833 he declared himself an abolitionist, turned politician, helped found the Republican Party, and ran successfully for Congress, but remained a non-resistant Quaker. He led a parallel life as a writer and an editor, bringing out a volume of verse biennially. After the Civil War, Whittier's seventieth birthday was a cause for national celebration. He resented being regarded as a gentle saint because he had been a hero, a champion of difficult causes, had fought for the abolition of slavery, for temperance, for woman suffrage, and for peace. Whittier is now regarded as a third-rate poet, but a part of our national history, the poet of the country folk of Massachusetts before the triumph of industrialism. Whittier's best poems reflect the life of a New England farmer. He is the only poet set twice by Charles Ives. PRINCIPAL WORKS: *Legends of New England in Prose and Verse*, 1831; *Moll Pitcher*, 1832; *Voices of Freedom*, 1846; *Snow-Bound: A Winter Idyll*, 1866; *Poems of Nature*, 1886. SELECTED READING: Robert Penn Warren, *Whittier's Poetry: An Appraisal and a Selection*, 1971. (SOURCE: Kunitz, Haycraft, 1952)

WIDDIE: (Scot.)*, a noose, a rope*; *several twigs or wands of willow intertwined to make a rope*.

WIELAND, CHRISTOPH (1733–1813): a German poet and novelist who returned grace and beauty to German verse. His writings include ★*Oberon* (1780). Between 1762 and 1766 he published twenty-two translations of ★Shakespeare plays and introduced the English playwright to Germany. (SOURCE: Kunitz, Colby, 1967)

SONG	COMPOSER	POET
"Das Lied im Grünen"	Franz Schubert	Friedrich Reil

WILHELM MEISTER: the hero of ★Goethe's two-part work: *Wilhelm Meisters Lehrjahre* (apprenticeship) and *Wilhelm Meisters Wanderjahre* (travel years). The plot in brief: Wilhelm experiences an unfortunate love affair with the actress Mariane. Believing her to be unfaithful, he goes out into the world in search of happiness and knowledge of himself. Idealistic, sensitive, and highly romantic, he is directed by inclination toward the theater, acting, and writing. During his travels, he meets two actors, Laertes and Philine, a shallow girl, serious about nothing *(Singet nicht in Trauertönen)*. Melina, an addition to the group, suggests to Wilhelm that he use his money to buy costumes and props for their plays. Wilhelm agrees. He meets with a group of gypsies who have with them ★Mignon, a mysterious creature, a child of the streets, who dances for the crowd. She does not know her age or where she is from, but Wilhelm believes her to be twelve or thirteen. Interfering with her punishment at the hands of the head of the troop, Wilhelm buys her freedom and takes her with him on his travels, starting to educate her. She is unconsciously in love with him and suffers when Philine pays attention to him. An old man who carries a harp, *Der Sänger*, joins the group. Wilhelm hears him singing inside his room *(Wer sich der Einsamkeit)*. One day Wilhelm overhears Mignon singing "Kennst du das Land" *(Mignon, Mignon's Gesang, Mignon's Lied, Heiss mich nicht reden)* beginning each verse, says Goethe, with great solemnity. After a long absence Wilhelm hears the harper singing "An die Türen will ich schleichen." An emotionally complex character named Aurelie and her brother become members of the company. With her Aurelie has a little boy named Felix, who befriends Mignon, who, in turn, saves him from the harper's knife. When Aurelie dies, Wilhelm delivers the news of her death to her unfaithful lover, Lothario. While at Lothario's castle, he meets a charming woman named Therese. Wilhelm learns of Mariane's death and that Felix is his own son, to whom Aurelie was acting as a guardian. Wilhelm looks to Therese to be mother to Felix. In the neighborhood of the castle lives Natalia, who plans to have a little play performed in a birthday celebration. Mignon is to be the angel, but, when the play is over, she will not let them take off her angel's robe (*So lass mich scheinen, Mignon II, Mignon III*). Finding Wilhelm in Therese's arms, Mignon falls dead and is buried in her angel's dress. An old Italian marchese arrives and recognizes Mignon as his niece and explains the complex story of Mignon, who was the child of his brother Augustin, the old harper. She had been taken by a gypsy group, and Augustin had been afflicted with severe melancholia, as we found him at the beginning of the story. Schubert set three songs sung by the Harper: "Wer sich der Einsamkeit," "Wer nie sein Brot," and "An die Türen." Schumann, Liszt, and Wolf also set the Harper's songs. *See also* ★MIGNON. (SOURCE: Blackall, 1989)

WILHELM TELL: the legendary national hero of Switzerland, popular leader of the fifteenth-century uprising against Austrian rule, the subject of ★Schiller's play, *Wilhelm Tell* (1804). In act 3 of the play, "Des Buben Schützenlied," a song by Robert Schumann is sung by Tell's son Walter. The song is a simple telling of the boy's pride in archery. In act 1, scene 1, "Des Sennen Abschied," a farewell song is sung by the herdsman in the mountains, set by Liszt and Schumann. "Der Alpenjäger," sung by an Alpine hunter, was set by Liszt and Schubert in a Mayrhofer adaptation ("Auf hohes Bergesrücken"). Schubert's "Der Alpenjäger" is not found in *Wilhelm Tell*.

WILLEMER, MARIANNE VON (1784–1860): German actress. Willemer's true origins are unknown, but she was adopted by a Frankfurt family at age sixteen. Only a few weeks before her marriage to J. J. Willemer, a banker who was to marry for the third time, she met ★Goethe. An attraction between sixty-five-year-old Goethe and thirty-year-old Marianne was mutual and immediate when Goethe visited the couple (1814 and 1815). He and Marianne carried on an extensive correspondence, using the character names from the *West-östlicher Divan*, Hatem and Suleika. So engaging were her responses that she inspired his "Buch Suleika" in the *Divan*. Mendelssohn set Willemer, and Goethe used five of her poems in "Buch Suleika" without acknowledging her authorship. She is the true author of the Suleika poems, which Schubert set as the songs "Suleika I" and "Suleika II." (SOURCE: Reed, 1997)

WILLIAMS, (THOMAS LANIER) TENNESSEE (1914–1983): American playwright, novelist, and short-story writer. Tennessee Williams was born in Mississippi of pioneer Tennessee stock, also a descendent of early settlers of Nantucket Island. His grandfather, with whom he lived, was an Episcopal clergyman, and his mother's family were Quakers. When he was young he changed his first name, which he considered to be compromised by his lyric poetry, described by him as "a bad imitation of Edna Millay" (Kunitz, Colby, 1979). After the family moved to St. Louis during the Depression, he attended college but was forced to drop out for financial reasons. Working in a clerical job for two years, he wrote after work, sleeping so little that his health broke down. Eventually Williams finished his last two years of college and received as his first recognition a Rockefeller fellowship. Working in a series of menial jobs, he eventually found one with MGM. While in Hollywood, he wrote *The Glass Menagerie* after work. He then lived in New Orleans, where he wrote *A Streetcar Named Desire*. Most of his plays had long and successful runs on Broadway. Williams was awarded the New York Drama Critics Circle award twice, in 1945 and

1955, and won the Pulitzer Prize twice, in 1947 for *Streetcar* and in 1955 for *Cat on a Hot Tin Roof.* Tennessee Williams's writing has been set by Paul Bowles. PRINCIPAL WORKS: Plays: *The Glass Menagerie,* 1945; *A Streetcar Named Desire,* 1947; *Summer and Smoke,* 1948; *The Rose Tattoo,* 1951; *Camino Real,* 1953. Fiction: *The Roman Spring of Mrs. Stone,* 1950; *Where I Live,* 1978; *Vieux Carré,* 1979; *Short Stories,* 1986. SELECTED READING: L. B. Barnett, *Tennessee Williams: Writing on Life,* 1948; *The Collected Poems of Tennessee Williams,* ed. David Roessel and Nicholas Moschovakis, 2002. (SOURCE: Kunitz, Haycraft, 1973; Drabble, 2000)

WILLIAMS, WILLIAM CARLOS (1883–1963): American poet, novelist, and essayist. William Carlos Williams was born in Rutherford, New Jersey. As a medical student at the University of Pennsylvania he began a lifelong friendship with Ezra ★Pound, which continued during his serious medical career. After his internship, he studied advanced pediatrics in Germany, set up a private practice, and eventually became head pediatrician of the Paterson General Hospital. Both his poetry and his fiction drew upon his experience as a doctor who ministered to working-class patients. In the meantime, he was an active member of the avant-garde poetic movement centered in New York and never lost touch with the literary activities of Pound and his associates in Europe. In his poetry Williams offered realistic presentations of women, a distaste for fascism, and a desire to create particularly American poetics based on the rhythms and colorations of American speech, thought, and experience. His success with this goal saturated his poetry with more Americanisms than any poet since ★Whitman. Robert ★Frost's poems are true to the speech and thoughts of his New England people, but Williams expressed the speech and character of the whole nation. Poets Allen Ginsberg and Robert ★Lowell show his influence. One of the great forces in twentieth-century American verse, Williams published more than thirty-seven volumes of prose and poetry. His poetry has been set by Stephen Paulus and Milton Babbitt. PRINCIPAL WORKS: *In the American Grain,* 1925; *Paterson,* published serially in five books, 1946–61; *Autobiography,* 1951; *Pictures from Breugel,* 1962; *Selected Essays,* 1964. SELECTED READING: *Selected Poems,* ed. Charles Thomson, 1985, 1990; Paul Mariani, *William Carlos Williams: A New World Naked,* 1981. (SOURCE: Hamilton, 1994)

WINDHAM, DONALD (1920–1988): American writer of fiction, essays, memoirs, and stage adaptations. Windham was born in Atlanta. In 1945 he produced a play on Broadway with Tennessee ★Williams, *You Touched Me,* but in the 1950s had little success at home. His stories were published in European magazines, however, and Windham's first novel, *The Dog Star,* was praised by Thomas Mann and André ★Gide (1950). By 1960 his fortunes changed with *The New Yorker*'s publication of a suite of his stories, which later contributed to his memoir, *Emblems of Conduct,* and with the award of a Guggenheim fellowship (1960). He published five novels, a collection of short stories, two memoirs, and edited volumes of E. M. Forster's and Tennessee Williams's letters. Windham treated homosexuality both openly and as a subtext, but it never became his main topic. The writing of Donald Windham was set by Ned Rorem. (SOURCE: Kellner, 1991)

WINKLER, KARL (pseudonym, Theodor Hell) (1775–1856): German poet, journalist, translator, impresario, and librettist. Winkler was from Dresden, studied law at Wittenberg University, and worked in the civil service in Dresden as an archivist and public official. From 1814 Winkler served as secretary and then deputy director of the Dresden Court Theater. A publisher and editor of journals, Winkler also translated ★Camões and others into Italian, and was the librettist of *Die drei Pintos*. Schubert set his poem "Das Heimweh." (SOURCE: Reed, 1997)

WINTERREISE, DIE: a cycle of twenty-four songs by Franz Schubert to the poetry of Wilhelm ★Müller. *Die Winterreise* is a work set principally in the world of the psyche, thus "a true ★melodrama in the later ★Expressionist style. . . . we inhabit one person's thoughts, reflection, reactions to what he sees, his self-questioning and agonized wonderment. . . . [other people] are an amorphous mass of humanity who serve only to emphasize the wanderer's sense of isolation . . . from society." (SOURCE: Youens, 1991)

WINTHER, CHRISTIAN (1796–1876): a Danish poet, born in South Zealand. Upon the death of Winther's father, a vicar, his mother married a theologian. Matriculated at the University of Copenhagen to study theology, Winther took his degree in 1824. From 1825 to 1830 he tutored the children of a Copenhagen merchant, meanwhile writing love poems to the youngest daughter. Already enjoying a good reputation from poems that had been printed in various Copenhagen publications, he published in 1824 his first collection, *Digte* (Poems), which contained nature lyrics, romantic and realistic peasant idylls. A trip to Italy (1830) produced three collections of poems. The stress of an infatuation with the young wife of a clergyman resulted in his most memorable lyrics, *Digtninger* (Poetry), 1843 and *Lyriske Digte* (Lyrics), 1849. In 1855, after her divorce, he was able to marry the young woman. Their journey to Italy led to Winther's most admired work, an epic cycle, *Hjortene Flugt* (The Flight of the Stag), and to his reputation as the foremost Danish poet of love and nature. The verses of Christian Winther were set by Halfdan Kjerulf. SELECTED READING: A. S. Bushby, *The Danes Sketched by Themselves*, 1864; J. Volk, *Songs and Poems in Danish and English*, 1903. (SOURCE: Kunitz, Colby, 1967)

WIST: (Scot.), *knew*.

WITCH OF ENDOR, THE: a medium who resided in Endor. Having driven all the sorcerers and mediums from Israel, King ★Saul relied upon divine guidance in conducting his military campaigns. The instructions came to him in dreams or through messages from the prophet ★Samuel. God became displeased with Saul because he had often disobeyed and sent him no more instructions. In desperation before an important battle, he traveled in disguise to Endor to consult the medium. (This is the "Witch of Endor," a title never used in the Bible.) Saul asked the witch to call up a spirit for him. She demurred, reminding the king that he had made that act illegal, punishable by death. When Saul assured her that nothing would happen to her, she called up the spirit of Samuel as he had requested. Samuel was not pleased to be summoned and asked why he had been disturbed. Saul asked for help in his coming battle with the Philistines, but Samuel's answer was not comforting: God has abandoned Saul; *David will usurp Saul's throne; Saul and his sons will die in the battle the next day. At this news Saul fainted. The next day he and his sons died as predicted and, soon after, David became king of Israel. (SOURCE: 1 Samuel 28.1–25)

"With Dances and Songs": a song from the 1690 semi-opera *Dioclesian* with music solely by Henry Purcell, to the words of Massinger and *Fletcher's original play. For plot and placement of the songs, *see *Dioclesian*.

WITHOUTEN: the Middle English form of *without*. This form is used by Elinor Wylie in her poem "Little Elegy," which was set by several American composers, among them Ned Rorem and Mary Howe. Wylie chose to use *withouten* for two reasons: it fills out the poetic meter, and it establishes an atmosphere of antique and universal meaning.

"With This Sacred Charming Wand": a song composed by Henry Purcell to a text by *Thomas D'Urfey for Part I of his comedic semi-opera *Don Quixote*, produced in 1694–95. For plot details and placement of songs, *see *Don Quixote*.

WIVES EXCUSE, THE; OR, CUCKOLDS MAKE THEMSELVES: a play by Thomas *Southerne with some music by Henry Purcell, produced in 1691. In act 1, while waiting for their masters to leave a concert, several footmen are playing cards and complaining at being left outside. A curtain rises, revealing a concert room within, with people of quality listening to an unnamed song. One of them, Mr. Friendall, remarks that he could not understand the Italian words but that they were well sung in any case. Later in the scene, in answer to Mrs. Sightly's request for a song to be sung in English, Mr. Friendall suggests that musicians perform his very own lyric. The musicians protest that they are not set up to do that. After the argument, "Ingrateful Love! This Very Hour" is finally sung. The song hints at Mrs. Friendall's unfaithful conduct, but Friendall himself is oblivious. The song is very harsh for this humorous moment, and Purcell set the lyric in a serious style, combining it with a recitative containing long grace notes on key words. In acts 2 to 4, the plot concerns Friendall's philandering. At a dinner party in act 4, a song the music master refused to sing in act 1 is finally performed by Friendall. Purcell's setting of "Say, Cruel Amoret" reveals Friendall's vanity as well as his charm. In act 5, during a masquerade before the cast joins in a dance, we hear Purcell's Scotch air, "Corinna I Excuse Thy Face." Purcell's song "Hang This Whining Way of Wooing" was probably heard between the acts or during the masquerade. (SOURCE: Price, 1984)

WOLFE, HUMBERT (1885–1940): English poet and essayist, born in Italy and educated at Oxford. Saying he was "disturbed by metaphysics," Wolfe entered the Civil Service, serving during the 1930s as undersecretary at the London Ministry of Labor. By day he had been, in his words, "a most uncivil civil servant" and by night, a poet. Wolfe is considered to be not a genius, but a middle-brow poet, with some small lyric talent. He began writing romantic poetry and graduated to rude *epigrams, in poems that were almost always brief and to the point, well made in their way. Some of his sharpest work was concerned with the prejudice he encountered as a Jew. He even wrote an effective pamphlet attacking G. K. Chesterton for his anti-Semitism. Most critics agree that he was under praised for the fragility of his early verse and later over praised for a kind of pretentious allegorizing. The poetry of Humbert Wolfe has been set by John Duke and Hugo Weisgall. PRINCIPAL WORKS: *London Sonnets*, 1919; *Circular Saws*, 1922; *Kensington Gardens*, 1923; *Lampoons*, 1925; *Requiem*, 1927; *Dialogues and Monologues*, 1929; *Now a Stranger*, 1933; *The Upward Anguish*, 1938, *Kensington Gardens in War-Time*, 1940. (SOURCES: Kunitz, Haycraft, 1942; Hamilton, 1994)

WOOLF, (ADELINE) VIRGINIA, NÉE STEPHEN (1882–1941): English writer of novels, essays, and short stories. Their mother having died earlier, upon the death of their father, the Stephen children moved to Bloomsbury. There they formed the core of the Bloomsbury group, who were in revolt against the restrictions of Victorian society and were championing the development of English avant-garde art and literature. In 1912 Virginia married Leonard Woolf with whom she founded the Hogarth Press (1917), partly as a therapy for the attacks of mental illness she had suffered since childhood. Woolf wrote for *The Times Literary Supplement* from 1905 until her death. After she finished her highly experimental work *Between the Arts* (1941), another of her mental attacks led her to drown herself. A writer of classic feminist works, Virginia Woolf is now believed to be one of the most innovative writers of the twentieth century, one of her experimental techniques being the much-imitated stream of consciousness method. The work of Virginia Woolf has been set by composer Dominick Argento in his cycle "The Diary of Virginia Woolf." PRINCIPAL WORKS: *Mr. Bennett and Mrs. Brown*, 1923; *Orlando* (her biography), 1928; the feminist book, *A Room of One's Own*, 1929; *Between the Acts*, 1941. SELECTED READING: Quentin Bell's two-volume biography, *Virginia Woolf*, 1972. (SOURCE: Drabble, 2000)

WRECKIN: a prominent, isolated hilltop, one of the tallest mountains in Wenlock Edge.

SONG	COMPOSER	POET
"On Wenlock Edge"	Ralph Vaughan Williams	A. E. Housman

WYE: a tributary of the Severn River that rises at Plynlimmon, Wales, and winds through the limestone, ending at Chepstow and flowing into the Bristol Channel. The incoming tide deepens the river and makes it quiet, but as the tide ebbs, the river becomes voluble. (SOURCE: Hillaby, 1969)

SONG	COMPOSER	POET
"On Wenlock Edge"	Ralph Vaughan Williams	A. E. Housman

WYLIE, ELINOR (1885–1928): American poet and novelist. Elinor Wylie was born in New Jersey and grew up in Philadelphia and Washington, D.C. At the age of twenty she married a socialite; barely five years later she eloped with Horace Wylie, with whom she lived from 1911 to 1915, marrying him when her husband died. In 1923 she divorced Wylie and married William Rose Benét, man of letters and brother to the poet Stephen Vincent *Benét. She lived in Greenwich Village from 1922 until her death. Wylie's first book of poems was printed privately in London in 1912, followed in 1921 by *Nets to Catch the Wind*, and later, three more collections and four novels. Her striking beauty combined with her aristocratic and artistic self cast a spell upon many, author Edmund Wilson included. Wylie is now regarded as a minor poet, her period pieces scarcely read. Some poems from the earlier collections still have force and charm and a worldly voice, reminiscent of the intensities of Edna St. Vincent ★Millay. The poetry of Elinor Wylie has been set by Paul Nordoff, John Duke, and Randall Thompson. PRINCIPAL WORKS: *Collected Poems of Elinor Wylie*, 1932; *Collected Prose of Elinor Wylie*, 1933; *Last Poems*, 1943. SELECTED READINGS: Stanley Olson, *Elinor Wylie: A Life Apart*, 1979; Judith Farr, *The Life and Art of Elinor Wylie*, 1983. (SOURCE: Hamilton, 1994)

X ✍

XANADU: a city named in the poem "Kubla Khan" by Samuel Taylor ★Coleridge. "In Xanadu did Kubla Khan a stately pleasure dome decree, where Alph the sacred river ran through caverns measureless to man down to a sunless sea." So begins the poem, inspired by an opium-induced dream. Kubla Khan, or Kublai Khan, is a historical person. Born about 1215, he died in 1294. The grandson of Jenghiz Khan, he was the founder of the Yuan dynasty of China. He encouraged scholarship, the arts, and foreign trade, and he was visited by Marco Polo. *The Columbia Encyclopedia* suggests that, because Kubla Khan's capital city was Cambaluc, this is the city of Xanadu that Coleridge mentions. While the Alpheus was a sacred river running underground according to legend, it seems unlikely that the emperor of China "girdled round twice five miles of fertile ground" in Greece (Frazer, 1922). Furthermore, no one would refer to the Mediterranean as a "sunless sea." Xanadu was also the name of the mansion in Orson Welles's movie *Citizen Kane*. (SOURCE: Frazer, 1922)

XANGÒ: (pr. shan*go*) an fetish object or figure from the AmerIndian *macumba* rites, believed to have magical powers. According to Villa Lobos, Xangò has the power to confer fertility on a woman, thus his song is a fertility rite.

SONG	COMPOSER	POET
"Xangò"	Heitor Villa Lobos	traditional Brazilian Indian folk text

XIMBOMBA: a friction drum of Moorish origin.

SONG	COMPOSER	POET
"Ximbomba"	Roberto Gerhard	Pedrell song book

Y

YEATS, WILLIAM BUTLER (1865–1939): Irish poet and playwright, born Sandymount, Ireland; died Roquebrune, France. Yeats was the son of John Butler Yeats, a former lawyer and artist. The family relocated to England (1867–80). Yeats was devoted to the study of Irish lore and spent considerable time researching it at the British Museum. Greatly interested in mythology and mysticism, Yeats eschewed organized religion. His first major poem, *The Wanderings of Oisin*, was published in 1889 (*see* ★Ossian). He helped to found the Irish National Theatre Society, where he worked with J. M. ★Synge. In 1915 he was offered a knighthood, which he refused. In 1917 he married Georgie Hyde-Lees, who encouraged his interests in the occult. In 1923 he was elected to the senate of the Irish Free State, and he received the Nobel Prize for Literature the same year. The verse of William Butler Yeats has been set by Rebecca Clark, Thomas Dunhill, Ivor Gurney, Peter Warlock, Samuel Adler, Samuel Barber, John Alden Carpenter, Blair Fairchild, Richard Hageman, Sidney Homer, Vittorio Rieti, Ned Rorem, Charles Loeffler, and Yehudi Wyner. Extremely attractive to composers were Yeats's "The Fiddler of ★Dooney," "The ★Salley Gardens," and "When You Are Old." PRINCIPAL WORKS: *Fairy and Folk Tales of the Irish Peasantry*, 1888; *The Wanderings of Oisin and Other Poems*, 1889; *The Shadowy Waters*, 1900; *The Wild Swans at Coole*, 1917; *Collected Poems*, 1950. SELECTED READING: Edward Malins, *A Preface to Yeats*, 1974; *The World of W. B. Yeats*, ed. Robin Skelton and Ann Saddlemyer, 1965. (SOURCES: Drabble, 1985; Scott-Kilvert, 3, 1997)

"Ye Blustering Brethren of the Skies": a song composed by Henry Purcell to a text written by John ★Dryden, from their semi-opera *King Arthur*, produced in 1691. *See* ★*King Arthur* for plot details and placement of songs.

"Ye Gentle Spirits of the Air": an aria composed by Henry Purcell to a text written by Elkanah ★Settle for his work *The Fairie-Queene*, produced in 1692 and 1693. For plot details and song placements, *see* ★*Fairie-Queene, The*.

YEOMAN: in a royal or noble household, an attendant or officer who performs menial services.

SONG	COMPOSER	POET
"On Wenlock Edge"	Ralph Vaughan Williams	A. E. Housman

YESENIN: *see* ★ESENIN.

YESTREEN: (Scot.), *last night*.

"Ye Twice Ten Hundred Deities": a song from the tragic extravaganza, *The Indian Queen*, written by John ★Dryden and Sir Robert Howard, first produced in 1677, then altered in 1695 to include music by Henry Purcell. *See* ★*Indian Queen, The* for plot details and placement of songs.

YINCE: (Scot.), *once*.

YOUKALI: according to Kurt Weill, Youkali is "the land of our desires . . . where cares may be left behind . . . where love is shared . . . and promises are kept. Youkali is the hope in all human hearts, but only a dream. . . . There is no Youkali." The song "Youkali" is taken from the play *Marie Galante* by Jacques Deval. (SOURCE: Kimball, 1996)

SONG	COMPOSER	POET
"Youkali"	Kurt Weill	Roger Fernay

YOUNG, STARK (1881–1963): American poet, novelist, playwright, and drama critic. Born in Mississippi, Young attended the University of Mississippi at fourteen, then Columbia University (1902). After teaching English literature for a time, in 1921 he abandoned teaching for journalism, becoming an editor and for more than twenty years the drama essayist on the staff of the *New Republic*, assistant editor of *Theatre Arts Monthly*, and drama critic for *The New York Times*, all the while visiting Italy virtually annually. In 1938 he translated Chekhov's *The Sea Gull* for the Lunt-Fontanne production on Broadway. Subsequently he translated three of Chekhov's dramas, which Random House collected and published (1956). The verse of Stark Young was set by Norman dello Joio. PRINCIPAL WORKS: Poetry: *The Blind Man at the Window*, 1906. Fiction: *So Red the Rose*, 1934. Autobiography: *The Pavilion of People and Times Remembered*, 1951. Reviews: *Immortal Shadows*, 1948. (SOURCES: Kunitz, Haycraft, 1942; Lloyd, 1980)

"Your Hay is Mowed": a song composed by Henry Purcell to a text by John ★Dryden, from their semi-opera *King Arthur*, produced in 1691. *See* ★*King Arthur* for plot details and placement of songs.

"You Say, 'Tis Love": a song composed by Henry Purcell to a text by John ★Dryden, from their semi-opera *King Arthur*, produced in 1691. *See* ★*King Arthur* for plot details and placement of songs.

YOWE: a variation of the word *ewe*, or a flock of sheep.

SONG	COMPOSER	POET
"The Carol of Skiddaw Yowes"	Ivor Gurney	Ernest Casson

Z ✍

ZACATÍN (Sp.): a place or street where clothing is sold.

ZANGARINI, CARLO (1874–1943): Italian composer, librettist, and poet. Born in Bologna where he lived his entire life, Zangarini was celebrated for co-writing librettos for Puccini's *La Fanciulla del Oest*, Ermanno Wolf-Ferrari's *I Gioielli della Madonna*, and Riccardo Zandonai's *Conchita*. His poems set by Ottorino Respighi include "Invito alla danza," "Stornellatrice," and "Scherzo." Luigi Cherubini's opera *Médée* was translated into Italian by Zangarini.

ZAUM: a transrational language, pioneered by Aleksei Kruchonykh (1886–1968) and Velimir Klebnikov (1895–1922), in which words have no definite meaning, are intended to have direct evocative power without specific definable reference. Akin to abstractionism in art, zaum is one of the most avant-garde innovations in Russian poetry. (SOURCE: Jason, 8, 2003)

ZEPHYR, ZEPHIR, ZEPHYRUS: in classical mythology, the west wind, son of Astraeus and ★Aurora, lover of ★Flora, and identified with the Roman Favonius, thus, any soft, gentle wind. (SOURCE: Cooper, 1992)

SONG	COMPOSER	POET
1. "Crois mon conseil, chère Climène"	Claude Debussy	Tristan l'Hermite
2. "Attributs"	Francis Poulenc	Pierre de Ronsard
3. "Let the Dreadful Engines"	Henry Purcell	Thomas D'Urfey
4. "Mit einen gemalten Band"	Ludvig van Beethoven, Johann Reichardt, Othmar Schoeck	Johann Wolfgang v. Goethe
5. "Zephyr Returns"	Claudio Monteverdi	Francesco Petrarca
6. "I fauni"	Ottorino Respighi	Antonio Rubino

ZETTLER, ALOYS (1778–1828): Slovakian poet and civil servant. Zettler studied philosophy at the University of Prague. Although he was accepted to the order of the Holy Cross, he left at the end of his probationary period and moved to Vienna (1799). After eight years as an instructor at the Oriental Academy, Zettler entered the civil service and eventually became court secretary in the police and censorship department. He had been published in various Austrian periodicals from 1811 to 1816, but Zettler's collected poetry was published by his friend Christoph Kuffner in 1836. In 1815 Franz Schubert set Zettler's "Trinklied: Ihr Freunde und du gold'ner Wein." (SOURCE: Garland, 1976)

ZEUS: king of the gods on Mount ★Olympus, child of ★Kronos and Rhea, creator of the various races on the Earth. Those who are conversant with the subtleties of Christian dogma, or the righteous passions of the Jewish prophets, or the wisdom of the oriental sages will find the torrid, banal, petty, lewd, and lascivious activities of the Greek Pantheon bewildering. According to ★Hesiod, out of ★Chaos came Gaia, the earth. Gaia generated Ouranos, the heavens, to be her husband. They mated and produced many children, who in turn produced many offspring. One of these children was ★Kronos. Another child was a hideous monster, whom Ouranos hid away. Gaia, displeased with this treatment of her child, formed a scythe, which she gave to Kronos. Kronos, who was the only one of Gaia's children willing to confront his father, lay in wait with the scythe and "harvested his father's genitals" (Wender, 1985). He then threw them into the water; they floated off and generated ★Aphrodite. Having mated with Rhea and hearing a prophecy that he would be displaced by one of his own children, he swallowed whole every child that Rhea bore him. Rhea, about to bear another child, fled to Gaia and Ouranos and asked for help in protecting her unborn child. They sent her to Crete, where she delivered the child

Zeus, whom Gaia and Ouranos hid. Gaia then presented Kronos with his "son," a large stone wrapped up in swaddling clothes. Without even examining the bundle, Kronos swallowed him whole. Without his father's knowledge Zeus flourished. He gathered a group of gods on Mount Olympus to combat his father Kronos and his followers. Armed with thunder and lightning, Zeus and his comrades defeated the ★Titans, but not before he made Kronos regurgitate all the offspring of Rhea as well as the huge rock he had swallowed. Zeus was then proclaimed king of all the gods ruling from Olympus. As king of all the gods, Zeus had many amorous liaisons with goddesses, nymphs, and mortal women. He often disguised himself to accomplish his seductions, for example, encountering ★Danae in the form of a shower of gold, Leda as a swan, and Europa as a bull. His amorous attentions were not always heterosexual (*see* ★Ganymede). Zeus was also god of weather, his famous weapon, the thunderbolt, seen in most representations of him. (SOURCES: *Bulfinch*, 1978; Graves (1), 1960; Hamilton, 1969; Wender, 1985)

SONG	COMPOSER	POET
1. "Prometheus"	Franz Schubert, Johann Reichardt, Hugo Wolf	Johann Wolfgang von Goethe
2. "La Cigale"	Ernest Chausson	Charles Leconte de L'Isle

ZHUKOVSKY, VASILY (1783–1852): Russian poet, the natural son of a wealthy landowner father and a captive Turkish girl. Vasily Zhukovsky's name and patronymic were derived from his godfather. He was educated at the Boarding School for Nobility at the University of Moscow (1797–80), where he was initially influenced by pietism and interested in German and English literature. His first printed poem appeared in the university magazine, but he became well known with the publication of his "Gray's Elegy" translation. Zhukovsky's poetry was colored by motifs of grief and resignation resulting from an unrequited love affair. The publication of his thirty-nine ★ballads marked the beginning of Russian ★Romanticism. Having joined the militia (1812), he wrote a patriotic poem about the battle at Borodino personally witnessed by him. This made Zhukovsky the most famous poet in Russia. After 1815, however, the younger generation began to find his romanticism vague and western-oriented. When ★Pushkin's rising star eclipsed Zhukovsky's, his career at court suffered. He married a German woman and lived the rest of his life in Germany, a self-effacing, dreamy person with high-flown ideas about poetry. His translations of ★Byron, ★Goethe, ★Schiller, and ★Uhland created his reputation as Russia's greatest translator, but poets consider him to be a supreme craftsman because of the purity of his style, his rhythmic variety, and the beauty of his melody. As the first Russian poet to write of the inner life and its subtle shades of meaning, he was a great influence upon Pushkin, ★Lermontov, ★Tyutchev, and ★Fet. The poetry of Vasily Zhukovsky has been set by Rachmaninoff, Glinka, Aleksandr Alyabiev, Aleksandr Dargomizhsky, Alexis Verstovsky, Nikolai Titov, and A. P. Esaulov. Old translations of Zhukovsky's poetry can be found in John Bowring's *Specimens of the Russian Poets*, 1822. (SOURCE: Kunitz, Colby, 1967)

ZIGEUNERLIEDER, DIE: eight gypsy songs of Johannes Brahms for solo voice and piano. These are rearrangements of eight of his eleven vocal quartets, op. 103.

The German poet Hugo Conrat acquainted Brahms with the popular Budapest collection of Hungarian folk songs, twenty-five songs with simple piano accompaniment by Zoltan Nagy. Conrat made German translations and pressed Brahms to see them. Although the quartets were quickly written, the eight gypsy songs for solo voice and piano improved dissemination of the music, but, said the critics, impaired the original effect as quartets. Brahms himself called them "a sort of Hungarian Liebeslieder."

ZORONGO: a Spanish dance form from Andalusia.

SONG	COMPOSER	POET
"Zorongo"	Federico García Lorca	ancient Spanish song

ZWEIG, STEFAN (1881–1942): Austrian poet, novelist, dramatist, short-story writer, and translator. Zweig, the second son of a wealthy industrialist, published his first book in his teens. *Silberne Saiten* (1901), was well received by older poets Detlov von ★Lilencron, Richard ★Dehmel, and Rainer Maria ★Rilke. After receiving his doctorate from the University of Vienna (1904), where he became an outstanding member of a literary group called Jung Wien (Young Vienna), he traveled widely in Europe, India, and North America. By his mid-twenties Zweig was writing poetry only occasionally, having disowned his early work, perhaps recognizing that his work from 1906 on was still somewhat lacking in originality. In 1919 he moved to Salzburg and married. At an early age he had become aware of the crisis facing his era but maintained his apolitical stance, feeling that the tragedy of Jews was only a part of the larger tragedy of Europe. Yet, when Salzburg became dangerous, he moved to England (1934). Depressed by the fate of Europe, Zweig's fear that his humanist spirit would be crushed forever caused him to commit suicide (1942) together with his second wife. In life and in his work, Zweig had been a cultural mediator, attempting to inform, educate, inspire, and arouse literary appreciation across cultural and national boundaries. Two of his poems were set by Max Reger, others by Joseph Marx and Johannes Röntgen. PRINCIPAL POETRY: *Silberne Saiten*, 1901; *Die frühen Kränze*, 1906; *Die gesammelten Gedichte*, 1924; *Ausgewälte Gedichte*, 1932; *Silberne Seiten: Gedichte und Nachdictungen*, 1966. SELECTED READING: Hanns Arens, ed., *Stefan Zweig: A Tribute to His Life and Work*, trans. Christobel Fowler, 1951. (SOURCE: Jason, 7, 2003)

Abbreviations ⅋

AMERICANA, 2001, 2003
  Encyclopedia Americana. Danbury, Conn.: Grolier, 2001 and 2003.
AMERICAN POETRY, 1, 2
  American *Poetry: The Twentieth Century*, Vols. 1, 2. Ed. Kenneth Rexroth. New York: Harder and Harder, 1971.
ANDERSON, BUCKLER, 1966
  Anderson, George K., and William E. Buckler. *The Literature of England,* Vol. 1. Glenview, Ill.: Scott, Foresman, 1966.
ARBERRY, 1947
  Arberry, A. J. *Fifty Poems of Hafiz*. London: Cambridge University Press, 1947.
ARBERRY, 1958
  Arberry, A. J. *Classical Persian Literature*. London: Allen and Unwin, 1958.
ATKINS, 1969
  Atkins, Stuart. *The Age of Goethe*. New York: Houghton Mifflin, 1969.
AUSTER, 1984
  Auster, Paul, ed. *The Random House Book of Twentieth Century French Poetry*. New York: Random House, 1984.
BAGULEY, 1994
  Baguley, David, ed. *A Critical Biography of French Literature*, 6 vols. Syracuse, N.Y.: Syracuse University Press, 1994.
BANFIELD, 1985
  Banfield, Stephen. *Sensibility and English Song.* New York: Cambridge University Press, 1985.
BANFIELD, 1998
  Banfield, Stephen. *Gerald Finzi: An English Composer.* Boston: Faber and Faber, 1998.
BASHAM, 1959
  Basham, A. L. *The Wonder That Was India*. New York: Grove, 1959.
BÉDÉ, EDGERTON, 1980
  Bédé, Jean-Albert, and William B. Edgerton, eds. *Columbia Dictionary of Modern European Literature*, 2nd ed. New York: Columbia University, 1980.
BELL, 1993
  Bell, Ian. *Dreams of Exile: Robert Louis Stevenson, a Biography*. New York: H. Holt, 1993.
BENÉT, 1965
  Benét, William Rose. *The Reader's Encyclopedia*, Vol. 1, 2nd ed. New York: Crowell, 1965.
BERNAC, 1970
  Bernac, Pierre. *The Interpretation of French Song.* New York: Norton, 1970.
BERNAC, 1977
  Bernac, Pierre. *Francis Poulenc, The Man and His Songs*, trans. Winifred Radford. New York: Norton, 1977.
BEUM, 2000
  Beum, Robert, ed. *The Dictionary of Literary Biography,* Vol. 217. Detroit: Gale, 2000.

BLACKALL, 1989

>Blackall, Eric A., ed. and trans. *Goethe,* Vol. 9, *Wilhelm Meister's Apprenticeship.* New York: Suhrkamp, 1989.

BLAKE, 1971

>Blake, William. *Songs of Innocence.* New York: Dover, 1971.

BLAKE, 1984

>Blake, William. *Songs of Experience.* New York: Dover, 1984.

BOARDMAN, GRIFFIN, MURRAY, 1986

>Boardman, John, Jasper Griffin, and Oswyn Murray, eds. *The Oxford History of the Classical World.* Oxford: Oxford University Press, 1986.

BOERNER, JOHNSON, 1989

>Boerner, Peter, and Sidney Johnson, eds. *Faust through Four Centuries: Retrospect and Analysis.* Tübingen: Niemeyer, 1989.

BOREL, 1962

>Borel, Jacques, ed. *Oeuvres poétiques complètes de Paul Verlaine.* Paris: Pléiade, 1962.

BORGES, 1969

>Borges, Jorge Luis. *The Book of Imaginary Beings*, rev., enlarged, trans. Norman Thomas di Giovanni. New York: Dutton, 1969.

BOS, 1949

>Bos, Coenraad V. *The Well-Tempered Accompanist.* Bryn Mawr, Penn.: Theodore Presser, 1949.

BOWEN, 1974

>Bowen, Zack. *Musical Allusions in the Works of James Joyce.* Albany: State University of New York, 1974.

BOWMAN, 1971

>Bowman, Sylvia E., ed. *Twayne's World Authors Series, No. 158.* New York: Twayne, 1971.

BRERETON, 1967

>Brereton, Geoffrey, ed. *The Penguin Poets: French Verse,* Vol. 2. Baltimore: Penguin, 1967.

BRIDGWATER, KURTZ, 1968

>Bridgwater, William, and Seymour Kurtz, eds. *The Columbia Encyclopedia.* New York: Columbia University Press, 1968.

BRODY, FOWKS, 1971

>Brody, Elaine, and Robert A. Fowks, eds. *The German Lied and Its Poetry.* New York: New York University Press, 1971.

BROWN, 1985

>Brown, Clarence, ed. *The Portable Twentieth Century Russian Reader.* New York: Penguin, 1985.

BROWNE, 1928

>Browne, Edward G. *A Literary History of Persia,* Vol. 3. New York: Cambridge University Press, 1928.

BROWNING, 1978

>Browning, Robert M. *German Poetry in the Age of Enlightenment.* University Park: Penn State University, 1978.

BULFINCH, 1978

>Bulfinch, Thomas. *Bulfinch's Mythology.* New York: Avenel/Crown Publishing, 1978.

BULFINCH, 1979

Bulfinch, Thomas. *Myths of Greece and Rome*. New York: Penguin, 1979.

CAMESASCA, 1968

Camesasca, Ettore, notes and catalogue. *The Complete Paintings of Watteau*. New York: Abram, 1968.

CAPELL, 1957

Capell, Richard. *Schubert's Songs*, 2nd ed. New York: Macmillan, 1957.

CARPENTER, 1992

Carpenter, Humphrey. *Benjamin Britten*. New York: Scribner, 1992.

CASAS, 1996

Casas, Penelope. *Discovering Spain*. New York: Knopf, 1996.

CHANDLER, SCHWARTZ, 1991

Chandler, Richard E., and Kessel Schwartz, eds. *A New History of Spanish Literature*, rev. ed. Baton Rouge: Louisiana State University, 1991.

CHAPPELL, 1962

Chappell, William. *Old English Popular Music*. New York: Reprints of 1893 editions, 1962.

CHASE, 1959

Chase, Gilbert. *The Music of Spain*. New York: Dover, 1959.

CHRISTOPHER, 1972

Christopher, John B. *The Islamic Tradition*. New York: Harper and Row, 1972.

CLIVE, 1997

Clive, Peter. *Schubert and His World: A Biographical Dictionary*. New York: Oxford University Press, 1997.

CLOSS, 1962

Closs, August. *The Genius of the German Lyric*. London: Cresset, 1962.

COCKBURN, STOKES, 1992

Cockburn, Jacqueline, and Richard Stokes. *The Spanish Song Companion*. London: Victor Gollancz, 1992.

COLBY, 1985

Colby, Vineta, ed. *World Authors 1975–1980*. New York: Wilson, 1985.

COMAY, 2002

Comay, Joan. *Who's Who in Jewish History*, 3rd Ed. and rev. Lavinia Cohn-Sherbok. London, New York: Routledge, 2002.

COOPER, 1992

Cooper, J. C., ed. *Brewer's Book of Myth and Legend*. London, New York: Cassell, 1992.

COTTERELL, 1986

Cotterell, Arthur, ed. *Oxford Dictionary of World Mythology*. Oxford: Oxford University Press, 1986.

CRUDEN, 1953

Cruden, Alexander. *Cruden's Unabridged Concordance*. Grand Rapids, Mich.: Baker, 1953.

DAMON, 1965

Damon, S. Foster. *A Blake Dictionary*. Providence, R.I.: Brown University Press, 1965.

DELAHUNTY, et al., 2001

Delahunty, Andrew, Sheila Dignan, and Penny Stock. *The Oxford Dictionary of Allusions*. Oxford: Oxford University Press, 2001.

DELANEY, 1980

Delaney, John. *Dictionary of Saints*. Garden City, N.Y.: Doubleday, 1980.

DE LUCA, GIULIANO, 1966

De Luca, A. Michael, and William Giuliano, eds. *Selections from Italian Poetry*. Irvington on Hudson, N.Y.: Harvey, 1966.

DE LUCCHI, 1967

De Lucchi, Lorna, ed. and trans. *An Anthology of Italian Poems*. New York: Biblo and Tannen, 1967.

DEMETZ, JACKSON, 1968

Demetz, Peter, and W. T. H. Jackson. *An Anthology of German Literature 800–1750*. Englewood Cliffs, N.J.: Prentice Hall, 1968.

DEUTSCH, 1947

Deutsch, Otto Erich. *The Schubert Reader*. Trans. Eric Blom. New York: Norton, 1947.

DEUTSCH, 1950

Deutsch, Otto Erich. *Schubert Thematic Catalogue of all His Works in Chronological Order*. New York: Norton, 1950.

DE VORAGINE, 1993

De Voragine, Jacobus. *The Golden Legend*, Vol. 1. Trans. William Granger Ryan. Princeton: Princeton University Press, 1993.

DISHER, 1955

Disher, Maurice Willson. *Victorian Song: From Dive to Drawing Room*. London: Phoenix House Ltd., 1955.

DONADONI, 1969

Donadoni, Eugenio. *A History of Italian Literature*, 2 vols. New York: New York University Press, 1969.

DRABBLE, 1985, 2000

Drabble, Margaret, ed. *The Oxford Companion to English Literature*. Oxford: Oxford University Press, 1985, 2000.

DRINKER, 1949

Drinker, Henry S. *Texts of the Solo Songs of Hugo Wolf in English Translation*. Privately printed. New York: Association of American College Arts Program, 1949.

DUCHARTRE, 1966

Duchartre, Pierre Louis. *The Italian Comedy*. Trans. Randolph T. Weaver. New York: Dover, 1966.

DÜRER, 1928

Dürer, Albrecht. *Das Marienleben*. Leipzig: Insel-Verlag, 1928.

ELLMANN, O'CLAIR, 1973

Ellmann, Richard, and Robert O'Clair, eds. *The Norton Anthology of Modern Poetry*. New York: Norton, 1973.

EMERSON, 1997

Emerson, Ken. *Doo-dah! Stephen Foster and the Rise of American Popular Culture*. New York: Simon and Schuster, 1997.

EMMONS, SONNTAG, 2002

Emmons, Shirlee, and Stanley Sonntag. *The Art of the Song Recital*. 2nd ed. Prospect Heights, Ill.: Waveland, 2002.

ERDMAN, 1954

Erdman, David V. *Blake: Prophet Against Empire*. Princeton: Princeton University Press, 1954.

ERDMAN, 1974

Erdman, David V. *The Illuminated Blake*. New York: Anchor, 1974.

ERENSTEIN, 1989

Erenstein, Robert. "The Humour of the Commedia dell'Arte," in *The Commedia dell' Arte from the Renaissance to Dario Fo*, ed. Christopher Cairns. Lewiston, N.Y.: Mellon, 1989.

EWEN, 1972

Ewen, David. *Great Men of American Popular Song*. Englewood Cliffs, N.J.: Prentice Hall, 1972.

FARGNOLI, GILLESPIE, 1996

Fargnoli, A. Nicholas, and Michael P. Gillespie. *James Joyce A to Z*. New York: Oxford University Press, 1996.

FARMER, 1997

Farmer, David, ed. *The Oxford Dictionary of Saints*. New York: Oxford University Press, 1997.

FISCHER-DIESKAU, 1987

Fischer-Dieskau, Dietrich. *Schubert's Songs: A Biographical Study*. Trans. Kenneth S. Winton. New York: Knopf, 1987.

FLORES, 1965

Flores, Angel, ed. *Anthology of German Poetry from Hölderlin to Rilke*. Gloucester, Mass.: Peter Smith, 1965.

FLOWLIE, 1966

Flowlie, Wallace, trans. *Rimbaud Complete Works: Selected Letters*. Chicago: University of Chicago, 1966.

FRANCE, 1995

France, Peter, ed. *The New Oxford Companion to Literature in French*. Oxford: Clarendon Press, 1995.

FRAZER, 1922

Frazer, Sir James. *The Golden Bough*, abridged ed. New York: Macmillan, 1922.

FRIEDBERG, 1984

Friedberg, Ruth C. *American Art Song and American Poetry*, Vols. 1–3. Metuchen, N.J.: Scarecrow, 1984.

FURIA, 1990

Furia, Philip. *The Poets of Tin Pan Alley*. New York: Oxford University Press, 1990.

FURNAS, 1952

Furnas, J. C. *Voyage to Windward*. London: Faber and Faber, 1952.

GAER, 1951

Gaer, Joseph. *The Lore of the Old Testament*. Boston: Little, Brown, 1951.

GARLAND, 1976

Garland, Henry, and Mary Garland. *The Oxford Companion to German Literature*. Oxford: Oxford University Press, 1976.

GIBRAN, 1993

Gibran, George, ed. *The Portable Nineteenth Century Russian Reader*. New York: Penguin, 1993.

GIBSON, 1951

Gibson, Etienne. *Heloïse and Abélard*. Trans. L. K. Shook. Chicago: Regnery, 1951.

GINZBERT, 1913

Ginzbert, Louis. *The Legend of the Jews*. Philadelphia: Jewish Publishing, 1913.

GLAUERT, 1999

Glauert, Amanda. *Hugo Wolf and the Wagnerian Inheritance*. Cambridge: Cambridge University Press, 1999.

GLAZIER, HELLWIG, 1994

Glazier, Michael, and Monika K. Hellwig, eds. *The Modern Catholic Encyclopedia*. Collegeville, Minn.: Liturgical Press, 1994.

GOLDONI, 1883

Goldoni, Carlo. *Memoirs of Carlo Goldoni*. Trans. John Black. Boston: Houghton Mifflin, 1883.

GOLINO, 1977

Golino, Carlo L., ed. *Contemporary Italian Poetry*. Westport, Conn.: Greenwood, 1977.

GRABERT, MULOT, 1971

Grabert, W., and A. Mulot, eds. *Geschichte der Deutschen Literatur*. Munich: Schulbuch, 1971.

GRANT, 1980

Grant, Michael, ed. *Greek and Latin Authors*. New York: H. W. Wilson, 1980.

GRAVES, 1948

Graves, Robert. *The White Goddess*. New York: Farrar, Straus, and Giroux, 1948.

GRAVES, 1960 (1)

Graves, Robert. *Greek Gods and Heroes.* New York: Dell, 1960.

GRAVES, 1960 (2)

Graves, Robert, ed. *The Greek Myths*, 2 vols. New York: Pelican, 1997.

GRAVES, 1997

Graves, Robert, ed. *The Oxford Book of Saints*. Oxford: Oxford University Press, 1997.

GREEN, 1966

Green, Harry Plunkett. *Interpretation in Song*. London: Macmillan, 1966.

GREENFIELD, 1990

Greenfield, John R., ed. *Dictionary of Literary Biography*, Vol. 93. Detroit, Mich.: Gale, 1990.

GREINER, 5, 1980

Greiner, Donald J., ed. *Dictionary of Literary Biography*, Vol. 5. Detroit, Mich.: Gale, 1980.

GREINER, 96, 1980

Greiner, Donald J., ed. *Dictionary of Literary Biography*, Vol. 96. Detroit, Mich.: Gale, 1980.

GRIM, 1988, 1992

Grim, William E. *The Faust Legend in Music and Literature*, Vols. 1 and 2. Lewiston, N.Y.: Mellon, 1988, 1992.

GROVE, 2000

New Grove Dictionary of Music and Musicians, ed. Stanley Sadie. New York: Oxford University Press, 2000.

GUIRAND, 1963

    Guirand, Félix. *Greek Mythology*. London: Hamlyn, 1963.

GUIRAND, 1968

    Guirand, Félix, ed. *The New Larousse Encyclopedia of Mythology*, new ed. Trans. Richard Aldington and Delano Ames. London: Hamlyn, 1968.

HAINSWORTH, ROBBEY, 2002

    Hainsworth, Peter, and David Robbey, eds. *The Oxford Companion to Italian Literature*. Oxford: Oxford University Press, 2002.

HALL, 1953

    Hall, James Hurst. *The Art Song*. Norman: University of Oklahoma Press, 1953.

HAMILTON, 1969

    Hamilton, Edith. *Mythology*. New York: Mentor Books, 1969.

HAMILTON, 1973

    Hamilton, Ian, ed. *The Oxford Companion to Twentieth-century Poetry in English*. Oxford: Oxford University Press, 1973.

HAMILTON, 1994

    Hamilton, Ian, ed. *The Oxford Companion to Twentieth Century Poetry*. Oxford: Oxford University Press, 1994.

HARDIN, MEWS, 1993

    Hardin, James, and Siegfried Mews, eds. *Dictionary of Literary Biography*, Vols. 129, 133. Detroit, Mich.: Gale, 1993.

HARDIN, SCHWEITZER, 1989

    Hardin, James, and Christoph Schweitzer, eds. *Dictionary of Literary Biography*, Vol. 90. Detroit: Gale, 1989.

HARDIN, SCHWEITZER, 1990

    Hardin, James and Christoph Schweitzer, eds. *Dictionary of Literary Biography*, Vols. 94, 97. Detroit, Mich.: Gale, 1990.

HARDISON, 1958

    Hardison, O. B., Jr. *Poets of Today*. New York: Scribners, 1958.

HARRIS, 1986

    Harris, Trudier, ed. *Dictionary of Literary Biography*, Vol. 50. Detroit, Mich.: Gale, 1986.

HARVEY, HESELTINE, 1959

    Harvey, Paul, and J. E. Heseltine, eds. *The Oxford Companion to French Literature*. Oxford: Oxford University Press, 1959.

HATHAWAY, 1980

    Hathaway, Nancy. *The Unicorn*. New York: Viking, 1980.

HERBERT, 1929

    Herbert, Thomas. *Travels in Persia 1627–29*. New York: McBride, 1929.

HILLABY, 1969

    Hillaby, John. *A Walk Through Britain*. Boston: Houghton Mifflin, 1969.

HOWATSON, 1989

    Howatson, M. C., ed. *The Oxford Companion to Classical Literature*. Oxford: Oxford University Press, 1989.

HULLAH, 1866

    Hullah, John. *The Song Book*. London: Macmillan, 1866.

IONS, 1967

Ions, Veronica. *Indian Mythology*. London: Hamlyn, 1967.

JACKSON, 1906

Jackson, A. V. Williams. *Persia Past and Present: A Book of Travel and Research*. New York: Macmillan, 1906.

JASON, 2003

Jason, Philip K., ed. *Critical Survey of Poetry*, 2nd ed., 8 vols. Pasadena, Calif., Hackensack, N.J.: Salem, 2003.

JOHNS, 1973

Johns, Orrick. *Time of Our Lives: The Story of My Father and Myself*. New York: Octagon, 1973.

JOHNSON, MALONE, 1930–31

Johnson, Allen, and Duman Malone. *Dictionary of American Biography*, Vol. 3. New York: Scribner, 1930–31.

JONES, 1995

Jones, Allison, ed. *Larousse Dictionary of World Folklore*. New York: Larousse, 1995.

KASTER, 1964

Kaster, Joseph, ed. *Putnam's Concise Mythological Dictionary*. New York: Capricorn, 1964.

KAUFMAN, 1962

Kaufman, Walter, ed. *Twenty German Poets*. New York: Random House, 1962.

KELLNER, 1991

Kellner, Bruce. *Donald Windham: A Bio-Bibliography*. Westport, Conn.: Greenwood Press Group, 1991.

KENNARD, 1920

Kennard, Joseph Spencer. *Goldoni and the Venice of His Time*. New York: Macmillan, 1920.

KENNEDY, 1975

Kennedy, Ellen Conroy. *The Negritude Poets*. New York: Viking, 1975.

KERRIGAN, 1983

Kerrigan, William. *The Sacred Complex: On the Psychogenesis of Paradise Lost*. Cambridge, Mass.: Harvard University Press, 1983.

KIMBALL, 1987

Kimball, Carol. "Le Travail du Peintre: A Synthesis of the Arts," *The NATS Journal*, November/December, 1987, pp. 5-11, 24.

KIMBALL, 1996

Kimball, Carol. *Song: A Guide to Style and Literature*. Redmond, Wash.: Psst, 1996.

KUNITZ, COLBY, 1955

Kunitz, Stanley, and Vineta Colby, eds. *Twentieth Century Authors*, Supp. I. New York: Wilson, 1955.

KUNITZ, COLBY, 1967

Kunitz, Stanley, and Vineta Colby, eds. *European Authors, 1000–1900*. New York: Wilson, 1967.

KUNITZ, HAYCRAFT, 1936

Kunitz, Stanley, and Howard Haycraft, eds. *British Authors of the Nineteenth Century*. New York: Wilson, 1936.

KUNITZ, HAYCRAFT, 1938
> Kunitz, Stanley, and Howard Haycraft, eds. *American Authors: 1600–1800.* New York: Wilson, 1938.

KUNITZ, HAYCRAFT, 1942, 1973
> Kunitz, Stanley, and Howard Haycraft, eds. *Twentieth Century Authors.* New York: Wilson, 1942, 1973.

KUNITZ, HAYCRAFT, 1952
> Kunitz, Stanley, and Howard Haycraft, eds. *British Authors before 1800.* New York: Wilson, 1952.

KUNITZ, IGNATOW, 1998
> Kunitz, Stanley, and David Ignatow, eds. *Wild Card.* Urbana: University of Illinois Press, 1998.

LAKEWAY, WHITE, 1989
> Lakeway, Ruth C., and Robert C. White, Jr., eds. *Italian Art Song.* Bloomington, Ind.: Indiana University Press, 1989.

LEACH, 1984
> Leach, Maria, ed. *Funk and Wagnall's Standard Dictionary of Folklore, Myth, and Legend.* San Francisco: Harper, 1984.

LEVITT, 1995
> Levitt, Marcus C., ed. *Dictionary of Literary Biography*, Vol. 150. Detroit, Mich.: Gale, 1995.

LIDDELL, SCOTT, 1966
> Liddell, Henry George, and Robert Scott, eds. *A Lexicon*, abridged from Liddell and Scott's German–English Lexicon. London: Oxford University Press, 1966.

LIND, 1954
> Lind, L. R., ed. *Lyric Poetry of the Italian Renaissance.* New Haven: Yale University Press, 1954.

LITZ, 1966
> Litz, A. Walton. *James Joyce.* Boston: Twayne, 1966.

LLOYD, 1971
> Lloyd, Roger Bradshaigh. *The Stricken Lute: An Account of the Life of Peter Abelard.* Port Washington, N.Y.: Kennikat, 1971.

LLOYD, 1980
> Lloyd, James B., ed. *Lives of Mississippi Writers.* Jackson, Miss.: United, 1980.

LONSDALE, 1989
> Lonsdale, Roger, ed. *Eighteenth Century Women Poets.* New York: Oxford University Press, 1989.

MAC CLINTOCK, 1973
> MacClintock, Carol, ed. *The Solo Song, 1580–1730.* New York: Norton, 1973.

MACDOUGALL, GIFFORD, 2000
> MacDougall, Carl, and Douglas Gifford eds. and introduction, *Into a Room.* Glendaruel, Scotland: Argyll Publications, 2000.

MAGILL, 1984
> Magill, Frank N., ed. *Critical Survey of Poetry, Foreign Language Series*, Vols. 1–5. Englewood Cliffs, N.J.: Salem, 1984.

MAGILL, 1992

Magill, Frank N., ed. *Critical Survey of Poetry, English Language Series*, Vols. 1, 2, 3. Pasadena, Calif. and Englewood Cliffs, N.J.: Salem, 1992.

MAGILL, 1994

Magill, Frank N., ed. *Masterpieces of Latino Literature*. New York: HarperCollins, 1994.

MAGILL, 1997

Magill, Frank N., ed. *Cyclopedia of World Authors*, 5 vols. Pasadena, Calif. and Englewood Cliffs, N.J.: Salem, 1997.

MARINELLI, 1971

Marinelli, Peter V. *Pastoral*. London: Methuen, 1971.

MATHIEU, STERN, 1987

Mathieu, Gustave, and Guy Stern, eds. *Introduction to German Poetry*. New York: Dover, 1987.

MATTFELD, 1962

Mattfeld, Julius. *Variety Music Cavalcade, Musical-Historical Review 1620–1961*. Englewood Cliffs, N.J.: Prentice Hall, 1962.

MAY, METZGER, 1977

May, Herbert G., and Bruce M. Metzger, eds. *The New Oxford Annotated Bible with the Apocrypha*. New York: Oxford University Press, 1977.

MAYERSON, 1971

Mayerson, Philip. *Classical Mythology in Literature, Art, and Music*. Glenview, Ill.: Scott, Foresman, 1971.

MCINTRYRE, 1995

McIntyre, Ian. *Dirt and Deity: A Life of Robert Burns*. London: Harper Collins, 1995.

MEISTER, 1980

Meister, Barbara. *An Introduction to the Art Song*. New York: Taplinger, 1980.

METZGER, 1957

Metzger, Bruce. *An Introduction to the Apocrypha*. New York: Oxford University Press, 1957.

METZGER, MURPHY, 1994

Metzger, Bruce, and Roland E. Murphy, eds. *The New Oxford Annotated Bible with Apocrypha*. New York: Oxford University Press, 1994.

MILLER, 1973

Miller, Phillip L. *The Ring of Words*. Reprint of 1966 edition. New York: Norton, 1973.

MILTON, 1993

Milton, John. *Paradise Lost*, ed. Roy Flannagan. New York: Macmillan, 1993.

MIRSKY, 1958

Mirsky, Prince D. S. *A History of Russian Literature*. New York: Vintage, 1958.

MORIER, 1937

Morier, James. *The Adventures of Hajii Baba of Ispahan*. New York: Random House, 1937.

MURRAY, 1966

Murray, Gilbert. *A History of Ancient Greek Literature*. Reprint of the 1897 edition. New York: Ungar, 1966.

MURRAY, 1988

Murray, Alexander S. *Who's Who in Mythology*. New York: Wings, 1988.

NEVINS, 1964

Nevins, Albert J. (M.M.), ed. *The Maryknoll Catholic Dictionary*. New York: Grossett and Dunlap, 1964.

NEWMAN, 1969

Newman, Ernest. *Faust in Music, Musical Studies*. New York: Haskell, 1969.

NORTON, 1996

The Norton Anthology of Poetry, 4th ed. Marguerite Ferguson, Mary Jo Salter, Jon Stallworthy, eds. New York: Norton, 1996.

NOSKE, 1970

Noske, Frits. *French Song from Berlioz to Duparc*. Trans. Rita Benton. New York: Dover, 1970.

NOSS, 1974

Noss, John V. *The Religions of Mankind*. New York: Macmillan, 1974.

OED, 1989

Oxford English Dictionary, 2nd ed. John Simpson and Edmund Wiener, eds. London: Oxford University Press, 1989.

OLSON, SHEEHY, 2000

Olson, Dale A., and Daniel E. Sheehy. *The Garland Handbook of Latin American Music*. New York: Garland, 2000.

OSBORNE, 1974

Osborne, Charles. *The Concert Song Companion: A Guide to the Classical Repertoire*. London: Gollancz, 1974.

PALMER, MORE, 1936

Palmer, Philip Mason, and Robert Pattison More. *The Sources of the Faust Tradition from Simon Magus to Lessing*. New York: Oxford University Press, 1936.

PATRUDER, 1967

Patruder, C. A., ed. *Milton's Epic Poetry: Essays on Paradise Lost and Paradise Regained*. London: Harmondsworth, 1967.

PEARSALL, 1975 (1)

Pearsall, Ronald. *Victorian Popular Music*. Madison, N.J.: Fairleigh Dickinson University Press, 1975.

PEARSALL, 1975 (2)

Pearsall, Ronald. *Edwardian Popular Music*. Madison, N.J.: Fairleigh Dickinson University Press, 1975.

PHILLIPS, 1979

Phillips, Lois. *Lieder Line by Line and Word for Word*. New York: Scribner, 1979.

PILKINGTON, 1989 (1)

Pilkington, Michael. *Campion, Dowland, and the Lutenist Song Writers*. Bloomington: Indiana University Press, 1989.

PILKINGTON, 1989 (2)

Pilkington, Michael. *Gurney, Ireland, Quilter, and Warlock*. Bloomington: Indiana University Press, 1989

PREMINGER, 1986

Preminger, Alex, ed. *Princeton Encyclopedia of Poetry and Poetics*. Princeton: Princeton University Press, 1986.

PRICE, 1984

    Price, Curtis. *Henry Purcell and the London Stage*. Cambridge: Cambridge University Press, 1984.

QUARTERMAIN, 1986

    Quartermain, Peter, ed. *Dictionary of Literary Biography*, Vol. 48. Detroit, Mich.: Gale, 1986.

RANDALL, DAVIS, 2005

    Randall, Annie J., and Rosalind Gray Davis. *Puccini and the Girl: History and Reception of The Girl of the Golden West*. Chicago: University of Chicago Press, 2005.

REED, 1997

    Reed, John. *The Schubert Song Companion*. New York: Mandolin, 1997.

REES, 1992

    Rees, William, ed. *The Penguin Book of French Poetry: 1820–1980*. New York: Penguin, 1992.

REINHART, HARDIN, 1997

    Reinhart, Max, and James Hardin, eds. *The Dictionary of Literary Biography*, Vol. 179. Detroit, Mich.: Gale, 1997.

RIESEMANN, 1935

    Riesemann, Oskar von. *Mussorgsky*. Trans. Paul England. New York: Tudor, 1935.

RILKE, 1947

    Rilke, Rainer Maria. *The Life of the Virgin Mary*, German text, English trans. C. F. MacIntyre. Los Angeles: University of California Press, 1947.

RILKE, 1951

    Rilke, Rainer Maria. *The Life of the Virgin Mary*, German text, English trans. Stephen Spender. New York: Philosophical Library, 1951.

ROSSETTI, 1981

    Rossetti, Dante Gabriel. *The Early Italian Poets*, ed. Sally Purcell. Berkeley: University of California Press, 1981.

SALTER, 1968

    Salter, Frederick M. *Medieval Drama in Chester*. New York: Russell, 1968.

SAMBROOK, 1983

    Sambrook, James. *English Pastoral Poetry*. Boston: Twayne, 1983.

SCOTT-KILVERT, 1997

    Scott-Kilvert, Ian, ed. *The British Writers*, Vols. 1–3. New York: Scribner and The British Council, 1997.

SCHULBERG, 1971

    Schulberg, Lucille. *Historic India*. New York: Time-Life Books, 1971.

SERAFIN, 1999

    Serafin, Stephen R., ed. *Encyclopedia of World Literature in the Twentieth-century*, Vol. 3. Farmington Hills, Mich.: St. James, 1999.

SERAFIN, 2000

    Serafin, Stephen R., ed. *Dictionary of Literary Biography*, Vol. 220. Detroit, Mich.: Gale, 2000.

SHAPIRO, 1988

    Shapiro, Karl. *Poet: an Autobiography in Three Parts*. Chapel Hill, N.C.: Algonquin Books, 1988-90.

SHAW, 1963

    Shaw, George Bernard. *Complete Plays with Preface*, Vol. 2. New York: Dodd, Mead, 1963.

SHERRY, 1984

    Sherry, Vincent B., Jr., ed. *Dictionary of Literary Biography*, Vol. 27. Detroit, Mich.: Gale, 1984.

SHERRY, 1985

    Sherry, Vincent B., Jr. ed. *Dictionary of Literary Biography*, Vol. 40. Detroit, Mich.: Gale, 1985.

SIMPSON, 1910

    Simpson, Harold. *A Century of Ballads, 1810–1910.* London: Mills and Boon, 1910.

SMITH, 1974

    Smith, William J., ed. *Poems from Italy.* New York: Crowell, 1974.

SMITH, 1980

    Smith, Winifred. *The Commedia dell'Arte.* New York: Arno, 1980.

SPINK, 1974

    Spink, Ian. *English Song: Dowland to Purcell.* New York: Scribner, 1974.

STAFFORD, 1988

    Stafford, Fiona J. *The Sublime Savage: A Study of James MacPherson and the Poems of Ossian.* Edinburgh: Edinburgh University Press, 1988.

STANFORD, 1983

    Stanford, Donald E., ed. *Dictionary of Literary Biography*, Vols. 19, 20. Detroit, Mich.: Gale, 1983.

STANFORD, QUARTERMAIN, 1986

    Stanford, Donald E., and Peter Quartermain, eds. *Dictionary of Literary Biography*, Vol. 48. Detroit, Mich.: Gale, 1986.

STEINBERG, 1973

    Steinberg, S. H., ed. *Cassell's Encyclopaedia of World Literature*, Vols. 2, 3. New York: Morrow, 1973.

STEVENS, 1970

    Stevens, Denis. *A History of Song.* New York: Norton, 1970.

SWALES, 1987

    Swales, Martin, ed. *German Poetry: An Anthology from Klopstock to Ensenberger.* New York: Cambridge, 1987.

TEMPERLEY, 1989

    Temperley, Nicholas. *The Lost Chord: Essays on Victorian Music.* Bloomington: Indiana University Press, 1989.

TERRAS, 1985

    Terras, Victor, ed. *Handbook of Russian Literature.* New Haven: Yale University Press, 1985.

TERRAS, 1991

    Terras, Victor. *A History of Russian Literature.* New Haven: Yale University Press, 1991.

THAMES HUDSON, 1994

    Thames Hudson Dictionary of Art and Artists. New York: Thames and Hudson, 1994.

THOMPSON, 1992

    Thompson, Edward J. *Rabindranath Tagore: Poet and Dramatist*, Rev. Ed. New York: Oxford University Press, 1992.

THURSTON, ATTWATER, 1963

Thurston, Herbert, S. J., and Donald Attwater, eds. *Butler's Lives of the Saints*, 4 vols. New York: Kenedy, 1963.

TODD, HAYWARD, 1994

Todd, Albert, and Max Hayward, eds. *Twentieth Century Russian Poetry*. New York: Anchor, 1994.

TOWSEN, 1976

Towsen, John H. *Clowns*. New York: Hawthorne, 1976.

TURNER, 1979

Turner, Ronald A. "Johannes Brahms and *Die Schöne Magelone*." *NATS Journal*, 35 (May–June 1979), 37 ff.

UNGER, 1974

Unger, Leonard, ed. *American Writers*, Vols. 1–3. New York: Scribner, 1974.

UNGER, 1992

Unger, Leonard, ed. *American Writers*, Supplement 1. New York: Scribner, 1992.

UNTERMEYER, 1959

Untermeyer, Louis. *Lives of the Poets*. New York: Simon and Schuster, 1959.

UPTON, 1930

Upton, William Treat. *Art-Song in America*. New York: Ditson, 1930.

UPTON, 1938

Upton, William Treat. *A Supplement to Art-Song in America*. New York: Ditson, 1938.

VAUGHAN WILLIAMS, 1964

Vaughan Williams, Ursula. *Ralph Vaughan Williams*. London: Oxford University Press, 1964.

VILLAMIL, 1993

Villamil, Victoria. *A Singer's Guide to the American Art Song, 1870–1980*. Metuchen, N.J.: Scarecrow Press, 1993.

VINSON, 1979

Vinson, James, ed. *Great Writers of the English Language, Poets*. New York: St. Martin's Press, 1979.

VINSON, KIRKPATRICK, 1984 (1)

Vinson, James, and Daniel Kirkpatrick, eds. *Great Foreign Language Writers*. New York: St. Martin's Press, 1984.

VINSON, KIRKPATRICK, 1984 (2)

Vinson, James, and Daniel Kirkpatrick, eds. *Contemporary Foreign Language Writers*. New York: St. Martin's Press, 1984.

WAGGONER, 1984

Waggoner, Hyatt H. *American Poets from the Puritans to the Present*. Baton Rouge: Louisiana State University Press, 1984.

WAKEMAN, 1975

Wakeman, John, ed. *World Authors 1950–1970*. New York: Wilson, 1975.

WAKEMAN, 1980

Wakeman, John, ed. *World Authors 1970–75*. New York: Wilson, 1980.

WALLECHINSKY, WALLACE, 1975

Wallechinsky, David, and Irving Wallace. *The People's Almanach*. Garden City, N.Y.: Doubleday, 1975.

WALSH, 1991

  Walsh, Michael, ed. Butler's *Lives of the Saints*. New York: HarperCollins, 1991.

WATERMAN, 1966

  Waterman, John T. *A History of the German Language*. Seattle: University of Washington Press, 1966.

WEDEL et al., 1992

  Wedel, Giovanna, Glauco de Stasio, and Antonio Cambon, eds. *Dictionary of Literary Biography*, Vol. 114. Detroit, Mich.: Gale, 1992.

WELLS, 1988

  Wells, Robert, trans. *The Idylls of Theocritus*. New York: Carcanet, 1988.

WENDER, 1985

  Wender, Dorothea, trans. and ed. *Hesiod and Theogony*. New York: Penguin, 1985.

WHITE, 1960

  White, T. H. *The Bestiary: A Book of Beasts*. New York: Capricorn, 1960.

WHITINGER, 2005

  Whittinger, Raleigh, trans. and critical introduction. *Mörike: Nolten, The Painter*. Rochester, N.Y.: Camden House, 2005.

WIKIPEDIA, 2005

  Wikipedia, Desktop Publishing. http://en.wikipedia.org/wiki/Publishing.

WILDER, 1972

  Wilder, Alec. *American Popular Song: The Great Innovators 1900–1950*. New York: Oxford University Press, 1972.

WILKINS, 1974

  Wilkins, Ernest. *A History of Italian Literature*. Boston: Harvard University Press, 1974.

YOUENS, 1991

  Youens, Susan. *Retracing A Winter's Journey, Schubert's Winterreise*. Ithaca, N.Y.: Cornell University Press, 1991.

YOUENS, 1992 (1)

  Youens, Susan. *Hugo Wolf: The Vocal Music*. Princeton: Princeton University Press, 1992.

YOUENS, 1992 (2)

  Youens, Susan. *Schubert: Die schöne Müllerin*. New York: Cambridge, 1992.

YOUENS, 1996

  Youens, Susan. *Schubert's Poets and the Making of Lieder*. New York: Cambridge, 1996.

YOUNG, no date

  Young, Robert. *Analytical Concordance to the Bible*. New York: Funk and Wagnalls, no date.